ARMY HISTORICAL SERIES

AMERICAN MILITARY HISTORY

VOLUME 1

THE UNITED STATES ARMY

AND THE

FORGING OF A NATION, 1775–1917

Second Edition

Richard W. Stewart

General Editor

MILITARY INSTRVCTION

Center of Military History
United States Army
Washington, D.C., 2009

Library of Congress Cataloging-in-Publication Data

American military history / Richard W. Stewart, general editor. — 2nd ed.
    p. cm. — (Army historical series)
  Includes bibliographical references and index.
    1. United States—History, Military. 2. United States. Army—History. I. Stewart,
Richard W. (Richard Winship), 1951– II. Center of Military History. III. Title. IV.
Series.

E181.A44 2009
355'.00973—dc22   2009011595

Revised Edition—First Printed 2005—CMH Pub 30–21

For sale by the Superintendent of Documents, U.S. Government Printing Office
Internet: bookstore.gpo.gov   Phone: toll free (866) 512-1800;   DC area (202) 512-1800
Fax: (202) 512-2250 Mail: Stop SSOP, Washington, DC 20402-0001

ISBN 0-16-072362-0

Army Historical Series

CONTENTS

Maps

Illustrations

Illustrations courtesy of the following sources: cover illustration by Elzie R. Golden; 8, 79, 113, 132, 136, 142, 160, 161, 168, 173, 189, 193, 200, 216, 217, 230, 231 (*bottom*), 233, 254, 259, 263, 266, 276, 285, 293, 326, 336, 338, 352, 354, 358, 368, 375, 378, 385, Department of the Army; 20, 22, 237, 298, 308, 382, Corbis; 25, Fort Lewis Museum, Fort Lewis, Wash.; 24, 39, 40, 65, 88, 162, 184, 218, 278, 297, 318, West Point Museum Art Collection, U.S. Military Academy; 27, *A Treatise of Fortifications*, John Muller; 29, 162, 169, 225, 274, 286, 335, 343, 356, Library of Congress; 31, U.S. Army National Guard; 47, 56, PictureHistory.com; 71, 84, George Washington Bicentennial Commission; 77, 117, 118, 126, 139, Independence National Historical Park; 93, 232, National Park Service; 102, Yale University Art Gallery; 109, National Gallery of Art; 115, Metropolitan Museum of Art; 122, U.S. Senate Collection; 154; New Orleans Museum of Art; 174, Department of the Navy; 203, 204, 214, 224, 228, 231 (*top*), 239, 257, 261, 284, 287, 300, 301, 314, 321, 340, 341 (*top*), 348, 361, 366, National Archives; 373, David C. Cole. Other illustrations from public domain.

FOREWORD

American Military History provides the United States Army—in particular, its young officers, NCOs, and cadets—with a comprehensive but brief account of its past. The Center of Military History first published this work in 1956 as a textbook for senior ROTC courses. Since then it has gone through a number of updates and revisions, but the primary intent has remained the same. Support for military history education has always been a principal mission of the Center, and this new edition of an invaluable history furthers that purpose.

The history of an active organization tends to expand rapidly as the organization grows larger and more complex. The period since the Vietnam War, at which point the most recent edition ended, has been a significant one for the Army, a busy period of expanding roles and missions and of fundamental organizational changes. In particular, the explosion of missions and deployments since 11 September 2001 has necessitated the creation of additional, open-ended chapters in the story of the U.S. Army in action.

This first volume covers the Army's history from its birth in 1775 to the eve of World War I. By 1917, the United States was already a world power. The Army had sent large expeditionary forces beyond the American hemisphere, and at the beginning of the new century Secretary of War Elihu Root had proposed changes and reforms that within a generation would shape the Army of the future. But world war—global war—was still to come. The second volume of this new edition will take up that story and extend it into the twenty-first century and the early years of the war on terrorism.

The Center of Military History has continued to refine the new design for these volumes to reflect the highly visual nature of contemporary textbooks. This work's primary audience is still the young officer and NCO; but by adopting a more illustrated format, it also hopes to promote a greater awareness of the Army's history within the American public. In so doing, its authors remain mindful of the Center's responsibility to publish an accurate and objective account that reflects the highest professional historical standards. The Center owes no less to the soldier and the veteran, to the student and the teacher, and to those pursuing a personal interest in learning more about the Army's campaigns—and about its role in the larger history of the nation.

Washington, D.C.
24 September 2009

JEFFREY J. CLARKE
Chief of Military History

PREFACE

The story of the United States Army is always growing and changing. Historians constantly seek to reinterpret the past while accumulating new facts as America's Army continues to be challenged on new foreign battlefields. Nor does the Army, as an institution, ever stand still. It necessarily changes its organization, materiel, doctrine, and composition to cope with an ever-changing world of current conflict and potential danger. Thus, the Center of Military History is committed to preparing new editions of *American Military History* as we seek to correct past mistakes, reinterpret new facts, and bring the Army's story up to date. This new edition of that textbook, an important element in soldier and officer education since 1956, seeks to do just that.

This edition of *American Military History* builds on the previous edition, published in 2005, and expands its coverage to include an analysis of the wars in Afghanistan and Iraq up to January 2009. This expanded section is necessarily only an initial survey of the first eight years of the war on terrorism; it is far from the final word on the subject. It may take an additional decade or more to collect sufficient documents, interviews, memoirs, and other sources to know the details of military and political planning, the implementation of those plans on the global battlefield, and the impact on the Army as an institution and on the nation. The events of the past eight years are more like current events than they are history. History—the detailed telling of a story over time based upon all the extant evidence—requires more time to find and analyze the documents and facts and bring to bear on that evidence the insight that comes only from perspective. However, today's soldiers need their story told. The events in which they participate and in which they are such important elements need to be given some form and order, no matter how tentative. The Army continues to be the nation's servant, and the soldiers that make up that Army deserve their recognition. They continue to protect our freedom at great personal risk to themselves and incalculable cost to their loved ones. This is their continuing story.

Washington, D.C.
24 September 2009

RICHARD W. STEWART
Chief Historian

PREFACE TO THE 2005 EDITION

Despite the popular image of the solitary historian immured in the stacks of a library or archives, history is very much a collective enterprise. This is true not only in philosophical terms (all historians stand on the shoulders of previous generations of scholars) but also in the practical sense that historians rely heavily on the work of many others when they attempt to weave a narrative that covers centuries of history. *American Military History* is truly such a collaborative work.

Over the years numerous military historians have contributed to the earlier versions of this textbook published in 1956, 1969, and 1989. In this latest telling of the story of the U.S. Army, additional scholars inside and outside the Center of Military History have conducted research, written or revised chapters and inserts, or reviewed the texts of others. Other experts have edited text, proofed bibliographies, prepared maps, and located photographs to bring this book together.

It is important to highlight those historians and other professionals who have helped make this book a reality. Indeed, there were so many contributors that I hasten to beg forgiveness in advance if I have inadvertently left someone off this list. First, I wish to thank those many scholars outside the Center of Military History who voluntarily gave of their time to review chapters of this book and provide their expertise to ensure that the latest scholarship and sources were included. These scholars include: John Shy, Don Higginbotham, Robert Wright, John Mahon, William Skelton, Joseph Dawson, Joseph Glathaar, Gary Gallagher, Carol Reardon, Mark Grimsley, Perry Jamieson, Robert Wooster, Brian Linn, Timothy Nenninger, Edward Coffman, David Johnson, Stanley Falk, Mark Stoler, Gerhard Weinberg, Edward Drea, Steve Reardon, Allan R. Millett, Charles Kirkpatrick, and Eric Bergerud. Their careful reviews and suggested additions to the manuscript enriched the story immeasurably and saved me from numerous errors in interpretation and fact. Within the Center of Military History, of course, we have a number of outstanding historians of our own to draw upon. The Center is, I believe, as rich in talent in military history as anywhere else in the country; and I was able to take advantage of that fact. In particular, I would like to thank the following historians from the Histories Division for their writing and reviewing skills: Andrew J. Birtle, Jeffrey A. Charlston, David W. Hogan, Edgar F. Raines, Stephen A. Carney, William M. Donnelly, William M. Hammond, and Joel D. Meyerson. Within the division, every member participated in writing the short inserts that appear throughout the text. In addition to the names previously listed, I would be remiss if I did not also thank Stephen J. Lofgren, William J. Webb, Dale Andrade, Gary A. Trogdon, James L. Yarrison, William A. Dobak, Mark D. Sherry, Bianka J. Adams, W. Blair Haworth, Terrence J. Gough, William A. Stivers, Erik B. Villard, Charles E. White, Shane Story, and Mark J. Reardon. Whether they have been in the division for one year or twenty, their contributions to this work and to the history of the U.S. Army are deeply appreciated.

I particularly wish to thank the Chief of Military History, Brig. Gen. John Sloan Brown, for his patience and encouragement as he reviewed all of the text to provide his own insightful comments. He also found time, despite his busy schedule, to write the final two chapters of the second volume to bring the story of the U.S. Army nearly up to the present day. Also, I wish to thank Michael Bigelow, the Center's Executive Officer, for his contribution. In addition, I would like to note the support and guidance that I received from the Chief Historian of the Army, Jeffrey J. Clarke, and the Editor in Chief, John W. Elsberg. Their experience and wisdom is always valued. I wish to thank the outstanding editor of *American Military History*, Diane M. Donovan, who corrected my ramblings, tightened my prose, and brought consistency to the grammar and style. Her patience and skilled work made this a much finer book. I also wish to thank those who worked on the graphics, photographs, and maps that helped make this book so interesting and attractive. This book would not have been possible without the diligence and hard work of the Army Museum System Staff, as well as Beth MacKenzie, Keith Tidman, Sherry Dowdy, Teresa Jameson, Julia Simon, and Dennis McGrath. Their eye for detail and persistence in tracking down just the right piece of artwork or artifact or providing the highest quality map was of tremendous value.

Although countless historians have added to this text over the years, I know that any attempt to write a survey text on the history of the U.S. Army will undoubtedly make many errors of commission and omission. I take full responsibility for them and will endeavor, when informed, to correct them as best I can in future editions. In conclusion, I wish to dedicate this book to the finest soldiers in the world, to the men and women who have fought and died in service to the United States over two centuries and those who continue to serve to protect our freedom. They have built America into what it is today, and they continue to defend the principles upon which our great country was founded. This is their story.

Washington, D.C.   RICHARD W. STEWART
14 June 2004   Chief, Histories Division

INTRODUCTION

The history of the United States Army lies firmly in the mainstream of modern Western military development. Heir to European traditions, the American Army has both borrowed from and contributed to that main current. Molded by the New World environment, a product of democratic and industrial revolutions, it has at the same time evolved, along with the nation it serves, uniquely. To the present generation of Americans faced by continuing challenges to their national security, the role that force and military institutions have played in American history becomes of increasing interest and importance. This volume is an introduction to the story of the U.S. Army and the American military history of which the Army's story is an integral part.

What Is Military History?

Military history today has a much wider scope than previous generations of scholars granted it. More than simply the story of armed conflict, of campaigns and battles, it is the story of how societies form their institutions for their collective security and how those institutions operate in peace and war. It is the story of soldiers and the subculture of which they are a part. It includes the entire range of economic, social, legal, political, technological, and cultural issues that arise from the state's need to organize violence to preserve its existence and accomplish its national goals. Military history cannot be viewed as a separate, quaint, subset of the wider history of a society. It is an integral part of a society; and the essence of a military, the armed citizen, is a reflection of that society.

War is only one aspect of military history, though it remains the critical test for any military establishment and thus an essential aspect. The changes in warfare over time are thus a legitimate focus for the student of military history. The American Army has been both a recipient of and a contributor to the fruits of the changes in warfare pioneered by the Western world. The United States was born in the eighteenth century, during the great age of European dynastic wars involving, generally, armies of professional, uniformed soldiers whose maneuvers and battles left the civilian masses of a nation-state largely unaffected. Until the latter part of that century, wars were relatively simple and restricted in area, forces, and objectives. This changed with the advent of the "nation in arms" during the French Revolution and Napoleonic Wars. Warfare became conflicts of mass armies of conscripts, motivated by revolutionary ideology. With the spread of the industrial revolution in the following century, warfare grew even more complex and exerted an ever-increasing influence on more elements of society. This new era in warfare coincided with the evolution of the United States as an independent nation. In the first half of the twentieth century the effects of large-scale wars became so pervasive that they were felt not only by the combatant nations but throughout the entire world, now seemingly grown more compact due to the advent of faster transportation and communications means. The outcome in those wars was no longer measured in terms of the preservation of national honor or the conquest of territory, familiar in eighteenth century warfare, but in terms of national survival. Thus, as warfare in the past two centuries broadened to involve more and more people and more and more of the energies and resources of society to fight it—or during the Cold War, to deter it—the definition was extended to encompass more activities.

Broadly defined, military history lies on the frontier between general history and military art and science. It deals with the confluence and interaction of military affairs with diplomatic, political, social, economic, and intellectual trends in society. To understand it therefore requires some knowledge of both general history and military art. In its American context it represents many interrelated facets. Certainly it involves wars—all kinds of wars. It may surprise Americans, who traditionally have regarded themselves as a peaceable and unmilitary people, to learn that the range of warfare in their national experience has been quite wide, and the incidence quite frequent.

Born in a revolution, a violent struggle often considered a prelude to modern ideological struggles, the United States has since endured a bitter Civil War, participated in numerous international wars, and has recently been thrust into a global war on terrorism. In American national experience, war itself has undergone considerable change and oscillation from one mode to another. The American Revolution was a limited war of the eighteenth century variety, although one fought on the backdrop of a "people's war" between Tories and Patriots over the loyalty of each small village and town. The War of 1812, the Korean conflict of 1950–1953, and the Gulf War in 1991 were later models of limited conflict fought for specific, limited objectives short of the total destruction and occupation of the foes' homelands. The American Civil War introduced the age of total war to which World Wars I and II added their bloody chapters. The Cold War involved mobilizing and militarizing huge segments of society never before affected by warfare. The current war on terrorism, with its potential for direct attacks on the American homeland and the pervasive (and invasive) security requirements for defending against such attacks, affects all aspects of American society. Over the centuries, war has cut deeper and deeper into the life of the nation.

Broadly defined, military history lies on the frontier between general history and military art and science.

After World War II, under the shadow of nuclear weapons that threaten all civilization with annihilation, warfare returned to earlier forms. Guerrilla wars, foreshadowed in American experience by the long-continuing Indian Wars and the Philippine Insurrection of 1899–1902, returned as American forces became engaged in counterinsurgency warfare during the Vietnam War (1964–1973) and in support to various Central American nations, notably El Salvador, in the 1980s. Today, modern conflicts include operations that could be classified as "small wars" such as Operation JUST CAUSE in Panama in 1989 and humanitarian and peacekeeping operations in Haiti, Somalia, and the former Yugoslavia. The line between war and peace, already blurred by nation-building operations and "police actions," grew even more difficult to discern as the twentieth century drew to a close with the U.S. Army involved in dozens of small-scale operations around the world. The direct attack on America on September 11, 2001, featuring the use of terrorism to kill over 3,000 Americans at the World Trade Center towers and the Pentagon, further changed the equation in ways still not fully known.

Wars used to be regarded as clearly definable exercises in violence when diplomacy failed and statesmen handed over to soldiers the burden of achieving victory. They were usually marked by formal ceremonies: a declaration at the beginning and a surrender and peace treaty at the end. Since World War II these formalities are no longer the fashion. War and peace have become blurred. Neither in Korea nor in Vietnam was war officially declared. The debate in Congress before the initiation of hostilities in the Gulf War led only to a congressional resolution of support, not a declaration of war.

Endings of military operations also are not clearly marked. No peace treaty followed the surrender of Germany in World War II or the truce in Korea in 1953. The Vietnam War ended with a treaty, but one the North Vietnamese promptly violated. Despite a decisive tactical victory for the United States, the confused political and diplomatic situation after the Gulf War continued to simmer, with United Nations resolutions and arms inspection programs in shambles and economic embargoes rapidly disappearing. The renewal of the war with Iraq in March 2003 resolved many of the problems of a still-dangerous regime at the cost of creating a host of others. While changes in the nature of warfare have affected the conduct of war and the role of the military and society in it, participation in organized violence in all its forms is still a vital component of military history that must be studied. Not only must the causes, conduct, and consequences of a war be analyzed, but as the line between war and peace becomes more indistinct, the periods between the wars require renewed interest from students of military history.

Besides war in the broad sense, there is another major facet that military history must address and that military historians of this generation have found more and more integral to their subject. That is the study of the military as an institution and a manifestation of state power. The way in which a state organizes for violence and the multifaceted effects of that effort are critical to understanding war and its impact on the society of which the military is often but a reflection. To apply force, societies organize armies. Reflecting the national culture and varying in their impact on it, armies are institutions, social

Wars used to be regarded as clearly definable exercises in violence when diplomacy failed and statesmen handed over to soldiers the burden of achieving victory.

THE ARMY SEAL

The Army Seal was used originally during the American Revolution to authenticate documents. It displayed the designation "War Office," which was synonymous with Headquarters of the Army, and the Roman date MDCCLXXVIII (1778) the first time it was used. It remained unchanged until 1974, when the War Office banner was replaced with "Department of the Army" and the date was changed to 1775, the year in which the Army was established. The seal embodies the Army's ideals of loyalty, vigilance, perseverance, truth, courage, zeal, fortitude, remembrance, determination, constancy, achievement, dignity, and honor.

entities in themselves. Some armies have close relations with the societies from which they are drawn; others are a class apart. For example, during much of U.S. history the Army was scattered in frontier posts and physically isolated from the rest of society. But in the period since World War II, civil-military relations have been close. As institutions, armies take form and character. Their institutional outlines are manifested in a number of ways, some overt, some subtle: organization and administration, system of training, mode of supply, planning for mobilization and the conduct of war, methods of fighting on the battlefield, weaponry and utilization of technology, system of command and control, selection of manpower and leaders, and relations with the civilian population and authorities. The whole host of policies, doctrines, customs, traditions, values, and practices that have grown up about armies is an important part of the institutional story. The impact of the selective service system (the draft) on many aspects of American life in this century is in itself a significant story. Its ending, for all intents and purposes, in 1973 and the creation of the all-volunteer Army has equal and far-reaching significance. Many elements of that significance are still not yet fully revealed.

All the facets of change in the military as an institution thus represent histories in themselves and reflect other changes in the nature of warfare, technology, and a country's internal development and external responsibilities. A shift in one component will inevitably have an impact on the institutional structure. For example, a fundamental change in weaponry, equipment, or technology, be it the adoption of gunpowder, the rifled musket, the airplane, the tank, the atomic bomb, night-vision devices, or precision-guided munitions, will inevitably affect the traditional modes of fighting and reverberate throughout the institutional framework. The phenomenon of cultural lag evident in other human institutions also applies to military organizations, and some armies have been slower to adopt changes than others, often with fatal results in the test of battle.

While the U.S. Army as a social entity has evolved to meet its primary mission—to fight—in its American institutional context military history must also treat the Army as a social force in peace. From the beginning the Army has played a role in developing the country: in exploring, guarding the frontier, and constructing roads; in engineering, transportation, communication, sanitation, and medicine; and in flood control. At the same time the Army has served as a vehicle for social mobility of certain disadvantaged groups, for example, European immigrants in the nineteenth century, African Americans in the 1950s and 1960s, and Hispanic Americans today. The mixture of the European legacy, native environment, democratic ideals and values, and national experience in war and peace have combined to mold the Army into a distinct institution in American life, a unique blend of professional and civilian elements. Indeed, as Russell F. Weigley, a student of the Army's institutional history, has well expressed it, the story of the American Army is really a history of "two armies": "a Regular Army of professional soldiers and a citizen army of various components variously known as militia, National Guards, Organized Reserves, selectees."

It has been said that every generation rewrites its history. Its own needs and problems inevitably make it take fresh looks at its own past for light, understanding, guidance, and alternative courses of action. Nowhere is this necessity more evident than in the field of American military history today—broadly conceived. During most of the national existence of the United States the liberal democratic tradition and geographic isolation combined to subordinate in the public mind the role of force and military institutions in its history. Blessed by relatively weak neighbors on the north and south and safe behind its ocean barriers, the United States could define its security in terms of its own boundaries and frontiers. The military factor in its heritage, birth, and development tended to be discounted. But when scientists began to conquer space and time in the twentieth century and the European system that had maintained order in the nineteenth century began to crumble under the impact of two world wars, Americans began to find their security bound up with the fates of other countries. The nation that began the twentieth century with a strong sense of security by mid-century began to feel insecure. George F. Kennan, former director of the Policy Planning Staff of the Department of State, elaborates, "A country which in 1900 had no thought that its prosperity and way of life could in any way be threatened by the outside world had arrived by 1950 at a point where it seemed to be able to think of little else but this danger." The Cold War and then our involvement in the Global War on Terrorism put an end to America's lingering beliefs in isolation and safety. Not since the era of the founding fathers has survival in a dangerous world become such an urgent issue and the foundations of national security of such concern. An essential element of maintaining that national security must be the study of war in theory and practice. Both the theory and the practice of war must be analyzed together to gain the fullest perspective.

> Not since the era of the founding fathers has survival in a dangerous world become such an urgent issue.

Theory and Practice of War

One question that has long interested students of the theory and practice of military affairs is whether war is an art or a science. This is no small question in an age when the lure of technology seeks to reduce so much of human behavior to scientific principles or mechanistic templates. In the eighteenth century, the age of enlightenment, when the systematic study of war began, military theory regarded warfare as mathematical and scientific. A general who knew mathematics and topography, the theorists optimistically maintained, could conduct campaigns with geometrical precision and win wars without bloody battles. In Europe, the violent shock of Napoleonic warfare brought a rude end to the notion of war as a purely scientific or mathematical game. But insofar as the application of physical pressure upon the enemy involves the use of mechanical tools under certain predictable or calculable conditions, it is possible to speak in terms of military science. The systematic application of science to the development of weapons and to technology in general is a comparatively recent development. Since World War II, techniques of research and analysis have been enlisted from scientific fields to make calculations and choices among complex weapon systems and in the management of huge defense programs more exact. Over and above the techniques, the successful conduct of war at all levels of command requires assessing unpredictable variables and taking calculated risks under circumstances for which no precise precedent exists. Since the "fog of war" still holds and wars involve men as well as machines, warfare remains in many ways what it has always been essentially—an art.

Military theorists have long searched for the principles underlying the art of war. They have sought to distill from the great mass of military experience over the centuries simple but fundamental truths to guide commanders through the fog of war. They have evolved lists of principles from an analysis of the campaigns and the writings of the great captains of war, such as Julius Caesar, Frederick the Great, Napoleon Bonaparte, and Helmuth von Moltke. Occasionally the masters have provided their own set of precepts. Foremost among the analysts have been Henri de Jomini, Carl von Clausewitz, Ardant du Picq, Alfred Thayer Mahan, Ferdinand Foch, Giulio Douhet, Basil H. Liddell Hart, J. F. C. Fuller, and Sun Tzu. The axioms range from the Confederate Lt. Gen. Nathan B. Forrest's oft-misquoted advice, "Git thar fustest with the mostest men," to Napoleon's 115 maxims. The lists differ in emphasis as well as in number. Some theorists have stressed that the battle is all and the defeat of the enemy's armed forces the correct objective, others that the best path to victory is by indirect methods and approaches that avoid confrontations and rely upon maneuver and psychological pressure.

Today, all great nations recognize principles of war and incorporate them in one manner or another into military doctrine. The lists vary from nation to nation. In the modern dress of the Western world, the accepted principles are essentially a post-Napoleonic conception, advanced by Clausewitz, the great Prussian philosopher of war of the early nineteenth century, and his contemporary, Jomini, the well-known French general and theorist. Since the United States shares a common military heritage and a common body of military thought with Europe, American students of war have also sought to reduce the conduct of war to certain essential premises. The U.S. Army recognizes nine such principles: objective, offensive, maneuver, mass, economy of force, unity of command, security, surprise, and simplicity. The proper

American students of war have also sought to reduce the conduct of war to certain essential premises.

application of these principles is still essential to the exercise of effective military operations. First, let us define them.

Objective. Direct every military operation toward a clearly defined, decisive, and attainable objective. The ultimate military objective may be the complete destruction of an enemy's armed forces and his will to fight. The wider political objective may be the complete defeat and reconstruction of an enemy nation that will involve regime change and political, economic, and social reshaping. Each intermediate objective must have the precise mix of force applied to it to attain decisive results. Every commander must understand the overall military and political objectives of the application of force and how his element will contribute to attain those goals. The principle of objective, with a series of intermediate objectives, helps all elements of an operation focus on what must be done and by whom.

Offensive. Seize, retain, and exploit the initiative. In order to achieve victory, a commander must undertake offensive operations. Offensive operations make the enemy react to your moves and keep him on the defensive and off balance. Offensive permits the commander to retain the initiative. This does not mean that defensive operations have no place on the battlefield. Going onto the defensive can conserve forces, allow for a logistical pause, or force an enemy to attack to his distinct disadvantage. However, a defensive mindset ultimately surrenders the initiative to the enemy. Only offensive operations can, in the end, force your will on the enemy.

Maneuver. Place the enemy in a disadvantageous position through the flexible application of combat power. Maneuver is an essential ingredient of combat power. It contributes materially to exploiting successes and in preserving freedom of action and reducing vulnerability. The object of maneuver is to dispose a force in such a manner as to place the enemy at a relative disadvantage and thus achieve results that would otherwise be more costly in men and materiel. Successful maneuver requires flexibility in organization, administrative support, and especially command and control. It is the antithesis of permanence of location and implies avoidance of stereotyped patterns of operation.

Mass. Concentrate the effects of combat power at the decisive place and time. Mass is much more than mere numbers. Many armies through the years have had a greater number of soldiers on any given battlefield but still have failed to win. Mass is thus the concentration of military assets against a specific target. Mass focuses the right mix of combined arms (infantry, armor, artillery) and airpower to overcome even an otherwise superior enemy force. Proper application of mass can permit numerically inferior forces to achieve decisive combat results.

Economy of Force. Allocate minimum essential combat power to secondary efforts. Skillful and prudent use of combat power will enable the commander to accomplish the mission with minimum expenditure of resources. Combat power on the battlefield is a limited resource. If you use it in one place, it is not available in another. Commanders must choose carefully how to use the exact amount of necessary force in the primary and secondary attacks to ensure sufficient combat power at the right place and time. This will allow other assets to focus on other targets. At times, a commander may use his forces in one area to defend,

THE ARMY FLAG AND CAMPAIGN STREAMERS

Prior to 1956 the Army was the only armed service without a flag to represent the entire service. Prompted by the need for a flag to represent the Army in joint service ceremonies, in 1955 Secretary of the Army Wilber M. Brucker requested the creation of the Army Flag. The design was a simplified version of the Army Seal placed on a white background that included a scroll designation United States Army with the numerals 1775 displayed below and the Army's campaign streamers attached to the spearhead of the flagstaff.

The Army has defined an official campaign as a particular combat action or series of actions that has historical significance or military importance to the Army and the nation. The concept of campaign streamers began during the Civil War, when the War Department instructed regiments to inscribe the names of their meritorious battles on their national colors. In 1890 the War Department directed that regimental honors be engraved on silver rings placed on the staffs of regimental flags. In 1920 the War Department ordered that each regimental color would bear streamers, in the colors of the campaign medal ribbon, for each campaign in which the regiment had fought. The creation of the Army Flag provided a means to display all the Army's campaigns (175 in 2003).

Battle Streamers
Richard Hasenauer, 1976

deceive, or delay the enemy or even to conduct retrograde operations to free up the necessary forces for decisive operations in another area.

Unity of Command. For every objective, ensure unity of effort under one responsible commander. The decisive application of full combat power requires unity of command, which obtains unity of effort by the coordinated action of all forces toward a common goal. While coordination may be attained by cooperation, it is best achieved by vesting a single commander with the requisite authority to get the job done.

Security. Never permit the enemy to acquire an unexpected advantage. Security is essential to the preservation of combat power and is achieved by measures taken to prevent surprise, preserve freedom of action, and deny the enemy information of friendly forces. Since risk is inherent in war, application of the principle of security does not imply undue caution and the avoidance of all risk. Security frequently is enhanced by bold seizure and retention of the initiative, which denies the enemy the opportunity to interfere. The principle of security does require, however, that risks be calculated carefully and that no unnecessary chances are taken.

Surprise. Strike the enemy at a time or place or in a manner for which he is unprepared. Surprise can decisively shift the balance of combat power. Surprise may allow for success out of proportion to the effort expended. It is not essential that the enemy be taken completely unaware, but only that he becomes aware too late to react effectively. Factors contributing to surprise include speed, deception, application of unexpected combat power, effective intelligence and counterintelligence (including communications and electronic intelligence and security), and variations in tactics and methods of operation.

Simplicity. Prepare clear, uncomplicated plans and clear, concise orders to ensure thorough understanding and minimize confusion. Simplicity contributes to successful operations. If other factors are equal, the simplest plan is preferred. In multinational operations, differences in language, culture, and doctrine complicate the situation; simple plans and orders can help minimize the confusion inherent in such environments.

Many examples of the successful employment or violation of these principles can be cited in American military history, and illustrations will be given in appropriate places in subsequent chapters. Each case requires careful study in its own context. For example, we may note briefly that the proper objective has often eluded commanders in war. The British in the American Revolution, for example, were never clear as to their prime objective: whether to capture strategic positions, to destroy the Continental Army, or simply to try by an appropriate show of force to woo the Americans back to their allegiance to the Crown. As a result, their victories over Washington's army in the field seldom had much meaning. In another case, not until after many years of fighting the elusive Seminoles in the Florida swamps did Col. William J. Worth realize that the destruction of their villages and sources of supply would end the conflict. In the limited wars and expeditions since 1945, however, the United States has sought to achieve objectives short of the total destruction of the enemy or of his productive capacity. What was the objective in Vietnam? It was not the conquest of the North, but the establishment of a viable political entity in South Vietnam. That did not require so much military force as political. The objective is often even more elusive, and can change over time, in peacekeeping or humanitarian relief operations. In Somalia, the original mission in 1992 of providing food to a starving people changed over time into the objective of remaking a country and achieving political stability. A violent reaction by a number of factions resulted in an American retreat from that country. The traditional concept of "victory" and "winning" has taken on a different meaning in the new political context of warfare in the post–Cold War age. Overwhelming force has often been replaced with the necessity for restraint and only carefully applied military force. Fresh support has been given to Clausewitz's reminder that a successful war is one in which the political objectives for which it is waged are achieved by suitable means and at appropriate cost. Wars are fought to achieve political aims.

No principle has been more ingrained in American military thinking than the belief that only offensive action can achieve decisive results. Offensive action seizes and retains the initiative. One of many examples is

Many examples of the successful employment or violation of these principles can be cited in American military history.

Washington's brilliant attack at Trenton in 1776, when his small, tattered, and nearly starving force turned on their pursuers with a lightning attack against a Hessian outpost to revitalize the Revolution. There are some instances, however, when the defense has in certain cases more advantages than the offensive. Some of the most notable actions in American military history, such as Maj. Gen. Andrew Jackson's stand at New Orleans at the end of the War of 1812, have involved the defense. Yet it is offensive action that achieves the most decisive results and wins wars.

No one would deny the necessity of maneuver to success in military operations. Brilliant examples have occurred throughout American military history. During Operation DESERT STORM in 1991, the forces of General H. Norman Schwarzkopf's army moved hundreds of miles through the Saudi Arabian desert in a "great wheel" to attack the Iraqi flank. Attempts at direct assault, rather than maneuver, have often led to bloody and indecisive actions. In the Civil War, Maj. Gen. Ambrose E. Burnside of the Army of the Potomac conducted one of the bloodiest and most useless attacks of the war when he launched his army in a massive frontal assault against Confederate positions on Marye's Heights at Fredericksburg in 1862. Even a successful maneuver can be subject to criticism—witness the controversy over General of the Army Dwight D. Eisenhower's decision to advance across Europe along a continuous broad front rather than permit one of his major forces to thrust deep into Germany during World War II. Nevertheless, a well-organized and controlled force can often maneuver successfully to achieve victory over a larger, but more ponderous, enemy force.

The principle of mass, often called concentration, probably offers more examples of successful and unsuccessful application than any other. Eisenhower's invasion of the Normandy beaches in 1944 is a brilliant example of the massing of all elements of combat power at the decisive time and place. Conversely, those commanders who fail to mass enough forces or combat power often suffer defeat. On the second day at Gettysburg in 1863, General Robert E. Lee attacked the supposedly "undefended" high ground on the Union left at Little Round Top, but late in the day and with insufficient strength. However, earlier in 1863, Lee's division of his army at Chancellorsville into three separate elements is a classic success. He left one portion to engage the enemy in a holding battle at Fredericksburg while striking with the rest against the advancing Union Maj. Gen. Joseph Hooker. After halting Hooker in his tracks, Lee divided his army again and sent Lt. Gen. Thomas J. "Stonewall" Jackson around the Union right to launch a surprise attack on the enemy flank. The risk involved in this violation of the principle of mass was carefully calculated and brilliantly executed.

The successful application of economy of force has usually resulted in brilliant gains. MacArthur's "island hopping" strategy in World War II is an excellent example of economizing force by bypassing Japanese island strongholds and isolating them with air and naval power, while using the freed-up forces to strike elsewhere and keep the enemy off balance. No principle of war is probably more important today, in this era of limited war, than restraint in the use of force and the precise calculation of only the exact amount of force needed.

Unity of command was successfully achieved for the Union under Lt. Gen. Ulysses S. Grant, but only in 1864 after three years of confused leadership and divided objectives. In World War II, the interservice conflicts between General Douglas S. MacArthur and Admiral Chester W. Nimitz, each engaged in major offensive operations against Japan along two disparate axes of advance, indicate that this principle can in some respects be violated and military victory gained. But often lack of unity of command leads to misunderstandings, wasted resources, and confused objectives.

Security and surprise are obvious necessities and closely related. In the Civil War at Antietam, there were security violations on both sides. General Lee's orders for the concentrations of his forces were wrapped in some cigars and found by a Union soldier. Maj. Gen. George B. McClellan, the Union commander, failed to reconnoiter the approaches to the battlefield before the action took place. The success of the Chinese Communist intervention in Korea in November 1950 resulted both from a United Nations security failure and from a carefully planned surprise movement into Korea by massive Communist forces. Surprise can achieve startling results; security lapses can also achieve startling results—for the other side.

Of all the principles of war, none is now probably harder to follow above the battalion level than the principle of simplicity. Modern warfare, involving mechanization, electronic equipment, airborne and amphibious operations, joint or even combined operations with foreign forces, is inherently not simple. Even the ostensibly easy movement of a small tank-infantry-artillery team cannot be termed simple. In counterinsurgency operations or nation-building missions the integration of military with political, economic, sociological, and psychological factors often leads to an even higher degree of complexity. But a commander has to do all he can to make elements of the overall plan clear, concise, and direct. Even tactical operations can sometimes become too complex for the commanders to execute. Washington, fresh from a series of brilliant maneuvers at Trenton and Princeton, planned to use a complex attack against a British outpost at Germantown in 1777. His plan involved coordinating the movement and convergence of four columns of inexperienced troops moving over different roads at night. Columns got lost, delayed, and confused. Washington thus lost the advantage of surprise and failed to mass his forces; he was forced to retreat in defeat. The plan proved too complicated for successful execution.

The growing complexity and variety of modern warfare has led students of military affairs to take a fresh look at these principles. Since World War II a debate has been raging in military literature over the precise meaning and application of the principles, a debate fed by the new circumstances of nuclear and counterinsurgency warfare. The discussion revolves around four major questions: Are the present principles too exclusive? Are they too inclusive? Does modern insurgent and nuclear warfare make them obsolete? To what degree does technology change any of the principles? To some extent this is a debate over semantics. The defenders point out that the principles are as valid in modern as in ancient warfare; that each age must make its own applications of the "fundamental truths." Critics argue that they are not immutable scientific laws of universal applicability; that they require constant reexamination; that no two military situations are ever completely alike; that the

> A commander has to do all he can to make elements of the overall plan clear, concise, and direct.

principles are merely methods and common-sense procedures adopted by great captains in the past; and that changes in the conditions of war alter their relative importance. Moreover, some claim that new technology, computers and weapon systems, have destroyed whatever validity remained in the principles. The principles, these critics conclude, are no substitute for imaginative thinking, logical analysis, broad professional knowledge, and highly developed qualities of leadership.

Perhaps the key point to remember, whatever the outcome of the ongoing debate among the theorists, is that war remains fundamentally an art. Dennis Hart Mahan, famed West Point professor and teacher of the Civil War generals, put it well: "In war as in every other art based upon settled principles there are exceptions to all general rules. It is in discovering these cases that the talent of the general is shown." Even the defenders of the principles stress that the art of war lies in their interpretation and application. Within limits, the principles of war nevertheless remain a useful tool for analysis, a general frame of reference, and a checklist for examining past campaigns. Themselves an inheritance from the past, these adages offer no substitute for real historical inquiry or for thinking and action on the part of the officer. They represent generalizations and premises rather than fixed immutable rules. They provide general guides that on the whole have in the past led to military success. As in the past, the victorious captain will have to adapt concepts or improvise others most suitable to the particular circumstances facing him.

All theorists agree that in the final analysis the art of war is what men make it. To quote Mahan again, "No soldier who has made himself conversant with the resources of his art, will allow himself to be trammeled by an exclusive system." He must be flexible. He must learn to deal with men. Moreover, Napoleon stated that in war, "The moral is to the physical as three to one." The ability to penetrate the fog of war and make the correct decision is the heart of leadership, and leadership is at the heart of war. Indeed, flexibility and leadership might well be added as tenth and eleventh principles, basic concepts inherent to all the others. It is not surprising, therefore, that the qualities that make for good leadership have long interested the Army and that a whole body of literature has grown up about the theoretical and practical foundations of this phase of the military art.

The military like other professions has developed its own language to allow easy communication. Aside from the principles of war, it is useful for the student of military history to become familiar with other terms commonly encountered in the literature. In the theory of warfare, strategy and tactics have usually been put into separate categories. *Strategy* deals with both the preparation for and the waging of war and has often been defined as the art of projecting and directing campaigns. To *tactics*, its close partner, military jargon has reserved the art of executing plans and handling troops in battle. Strategy is usually regarded as the prelude to the battlefield, tactics as the action on the battlefield. As society and warfare have grown more complex, the term strategy has been gradually broadened from its eighteenth century connotation as the "art of the general," far beyond its original, narrow military meaning. In the nineteenth century, and even more in the twentieth, distinctions began to be blurred between strategy as a purely military phenomenon and national strategy of a broader variety involving a combination of political, economic, technological, and psychological factors, along with the military elements, in the management of national policy. As a result, the term *grand strategy* (or higher strategy) has come to connote the art of employing all the resources of a nation or coalition of nations to achieve the objects of war (and peace). The broad policy decisions governing the overall conduct of war or its deterrence are the prerogative of the chief of state and his principal advisers. The strategist, whether in the narrower or broader sense, deals in many uncertainties and his art is the calculated risk. At the opposite end of the scale are *minor tactics*, the term used to describe the maneuver of small units. Falling in between is the concept of *operational art* that involves the maneuver of large-scale units (divisions and corps) to achieve victory that often has strategic results.

Despite distinctions in theory, strategy, operational art, and tactics cannot always be easily separated in practice. The language of operational maneuver—putting one's army into the most favorable position to engage the enemy and depriving the enemy of freedom of movement—is also largely the language of tactics. Thus, *envelopment* is an attack on an enemy's flank and toward his rear, usually accompanied by an attack on his front. A *turning movement* is a wide enveloping maneuver, passing around the side of the enemy's main forces and attacking him from the rear. *Double envelopment* involves an attack on both flanks of the enemy while his center is held in check. A *penetration* is an attack on the enemy's front by driving a wedge into it or piercing it completely. It may be followed by an enveloping attack on one or both flanks. In connection with these four basic forms of attack, two terms are often used: *main effort*, concentrating on the critical point in the enemy's position, and *secondary effort*, pinning down the remainder of the enemy or moving against a secondary objective to obtain an important but less critical result.

Linking strategy, operational art, and tactics and attracting more and more attention is *logistics*, defined simply as the art of planning and carrying out the movement and maintenance of forces. This field also has been greatly broadened as warfare has expanded and grown more technological and complex. Logistics deals with the deployment of military forces and their equipment to the theater of operations, along with innumerable services, to feed, clothe, supply, transport, and house the troops. The connecting links—the network of railways, waterways, roads, and air routes by which an armed force in the field is reinforced and supplied from its base of operations in the home or friendly area— are the *lines of communications*. The *theater of operations* comprises the combat zone as well as the supply and administration area directly connected with military operations.

In modern warfare the major divisions of the military art (strategy, logistics, operational art, and tactics) are closely interdependent. One field merges into the others, and changes in one inevitably lead to changes in the others. Sometimes weapons have appeared on the battlefield before military theory and planning have fully absorbed them, and adjustments throughout the art have been slow to follow. In the Civil War, for example, the widespread use of the rifled musket upset the relation among the combat arms; the range and accuracy of these weapons in the hands of defending infantry shattered the effectiveness

> The strategist, whether in the narrower or broader sense, deals in many uncertainties and his art is the calculated risk.

of the concentrated attack in which Napoleonic strategy culminated. But, as often has been observed in the history of warfare, armaments and weapons are more readily changed than ideas. Napoleon's principles continued to be upheld, sometimes with disastrous consequences on the battlefield. An oft-cited case of the appalling repercussions of holding concepts too long or rigidly is the French offensive spirit in World War I that led to massed infantry attacks against entrenched German troops with machine guns.

It is clear that in modern warfare theory and practice have not always been the same. Wars, particularly in the great coalition conflicts of the twentieth century, are not run by rules or theories. Once joined, modern war has had a way of breeding its own strategy, tactics, and weapons. More than ever, for successful commanders, flexibility has become the only sure guide. World War I, beginning as a war of mass offensives, was a classic case of arrested strategy that required new tactics and weapons to dig the war out of the trenches. The Anglo-American strategy against Germany in World War II proved a compromise of the theory of mass and concentration upheld by the U.S. Army and Prime Minister Winston Churchill's attack on the periphery. Despite attention to principles, Allied strategy in World War II was a hybrid product hammered out largely on the "anvil of necessity." In war, moreover, military strategy varies with political direction and goals. In this vein, Clausewitz had argued that military strategy must respond to national policy and political aims. Perhaps he best summed up the political context of modern war in his assertion, "War is not merely a political act, but also a real political instrument, a continuation of policy carried out by other means." "War," he concluded, "admittedly has its own grammar, but not its own logic."

The American Military System

To organize for national security, each nation adopts the military system most suited to its culture, needs, and policies. Some nations have traditionally tended to concentrate significant segments of their economy on the maintenance of huge military forces and to determine national policies largely in terms of their military implications. While the United States shares with Europe a legacy of military thought and practice whose roots lie deep in the past, its military system has grown out of its own national experience.

The form of government, the traditions of the people, the nature of the country, and its geographical position in relation to other powers have had a profound influence upon American military institutions. In turn, those institutions reflect the American culture and way of life. Indeed, the Army is essentially an institutional form adapted by American society to meet military requirements. The American military system has been developed to place a minimum burden on the people and give the nation a reasonable defense without sacrificing its fundamental values. From the beginning, the United States has sought to reconcile individual liberty with national security without becoming a nation in arms. The balance is often difficult to achieve.

Chief characteristics of American culture that have a bearing on its military system include the value placed upon human beings as indi-

While the United States shares with Europe a legacy of military thought and practice whose roots lie deep in the past, its military system has grown out of its own national experience.

viduals; life, liberty, and the pursuit of happiness and peace; the desire to achieve decisive results quickly; a talent for the design and use of machinery; highly developed productive capacity and managerial skills; and great material wealth. These characteristics underline the American penchant for absolutes: the sharp distinction between war and peace; the insistence on complete victory; an abhorrence of casualties; and the desire for short, decisive, offensive action in warfare. They help account for the traditional American attitude toward war as an aberration in which the bully who disturbed the peace must be soundly and quickly thrashed so American society can return to normalcy. They also point to the importance of public opinion in a democracy in raising and supporting armed forces and to the reason why wars against disturbers of the peace are apt to take on the character of moral crusades. They help explain the traditional rhythm of sharp expansion of the armed forces in wartime and precipitate contraction after the end of hostilities.

In turn, these characteristics and attitudes have shaped the Army in its organizational relationships and in its philosophy of operations. They account also for such distinctive Army features as the development of great mechanical power, the stress on firepower rather than sheer manpower, and the concentration on quick victory by offensive operations.

Throughout its existence the United States has been compelled to provide for military security. The degree to which the provisions were made has varied with the nature and magnitude of the particular threat. Until technology reduced the distance separating the United States from the Old World, the forces in being could be, and were, small. At the same time the deep-seated American reluctance to devote a large proportion of the national wealth to the support of a standing military force played an important part in the development of a system based upon a small professional nucleus that could be expanded in time of need by the induction of citizen-soldiers. This initial system took advantage of the ocean barriers favoring the United States and the balance of power existing in Europe. In accord with Washington's injunction, it held forth the possibility of acquiring greater strength by temporary alliances during extraordinary emergencies but the avoidance of permanent, "entangling" alliances. Since World War II the rise of new foes and the destruction of the balance of power in Europe and the Far East caused a drastic change in the American military system. During the Cold War, the United States maintained relatively large standing air, land, and sea forces around the world, ready for immediate action and for cooperation with the forces of its many allies. Even with the collapse of the Soviet Union in 1991 and the end of the Cold War, American standing forces remained comparatively larger and more powerful than at any other time in our history. The challenge of worldwide terrorism will doubtless see new changes in our military system.

The American Army as it exists today has evolved through a historical process that parallels the social, economic, and political development of the United States. Its evolution may in general be divided into three periods: colonial, continental expansion, and global operations. During the colonial period (1607–1775), the militia of the various colonies defended the settlers while they were establishing themselves in

America and helped England eliminate the French from North America. This was the period of roots and origins, of the transplanting of military institutions from abroad, particularly from England, and of their modification in the New World. During the era of continental expansion (1775–1898), the militia and volunteers and the Continental Army and its successor, the Regular Army, played a significant role in bringing the United States into being, in winning important extensions of national territory, in saving the nation from internal destruction, and in exploring, policing, and governing the vast regions of the West. This was the period of national independence and consolidation. In the wars of this era, the Army's activities were concentrated on problems vital to the establishment, maintenance, and expansion of a nation based on new concepts of individual freedom and representative government. Only once in this period, during the Revolutionary War, did the Army fight with the help of allies and then only on a temporary basis.

The year 1898, which saw the outbreak of the Spanish-American War, the symbol of "looking outward," was an important turning point. It marked the emergence of the United States as a world power. In the third period (1898 to the present), the Army has carried the flag to the four corners of the earth. Its assigned role has been to serve as a principal instrument for promoting American policies and American interests overseas and protecting the nation against the menace of tyrannical power. In the two great world wars of the twentieth century, as well as in Korea and Vietnam, the United States fought alongside associated or allied nations. In the increasing complexity of modern war, its operations have become inseparably intertwined with those of the Navy and the Air Force. In the history of the nation and the Army of the twentieth century, World War II became an important dividing line whose full implications are still not entirely clear. Since World War II the revolution in the strategic position of the United States, its emergence as leader of the free world and of allies in military combination, the Cold War, the nuclear age, and the Global War on Terrorism have presented unprecedented challenges to traditional American concepts and institutions in national security.

Whatever the U.S. Army's future contribution, it is as an instrument of force, the primary mission of an army, that it has played its major role in American history. From desperate hand-to-hand engagements with the American Indian to vast battles with motorized and armored forces, from revolutionary war to world war, civil to foreign war, guerrilla to counterguerrilla war, from hot to cold war, and to the war on terrorism, the Army has figured prominently in the nation's conflicts while continuing to make important contributions to the general welfare and to the preservation of domestic order in peacetime.

One final point must be made about the essence of the American Army. We should always remember that it is the Army of the nation and as such responds to the nation's elected leaders. The leaders of the U.S. Army have consistently adhered to a principle basic to the American military system, that the Army is an instrument of civilian authority. This principle, which General Washington firmly established in practice during the Revolutionary War, was embodied in the Constitution of the United States as a fundamental safeguard of republican institutions.

The supremacy of civilian authority is the American solution to the problem of forestalling any possible danger from a standing army.

Until World War II, American military policy was centered on the maintenance of very small regular forces and reliance on citizen-soldiers in cases of national emergency. In the colonial period almost every able-bodied man was a member of the militia and could be called out in case of need; and this system continued in force at least theoretically during the first two centuries of national existence. It was usually, nonetheless, the citizen-volunteer who swelled the Army's ranks in earlier wars. This changed during the Cold War with the continuation of the idea of universal obligation for military duty under selective service in time of national emergency. The return to the earlier idea of a small professional regular army, backed up by an organized militia, the National Guard and Army Reserves, has changed the equation again. Yet this relatively small professional force undergoes other risks such as being separated physically, socially, and even culturally from society as a whole with all that entails for a nation that values civilian control of the military. It remains to be seen to what degree this return to a regular volunteer force, this time under the pressure of a worldwide struggle against terror, creates tensions between the military and society at large.

In an age when forces in being may determine the outcome of a war or an emergency action in peacetime, the principle of reliance on masses of citizen-soldiers has given way to the concept of small, efficient professional forces supported by a select body of trained reserves. The increasing complications of modern warfare, the great rapidity with which attacks can be launched with modern weapons, and the extensive overseas commitments of the United States have negated the traditional American habit of preparing for wars after they have begun. But whatever the future composition of the Army, it will still have to incorporate the historic principle, ingrained in the nation's military system, of being representative of the people and subject to civilian control.

To be truly progressive, a military system, like most evolving human institutions, must operate in two planes of time: the present and the future. In the field of national security, the choices in the twentieth century were never easy; those for the twenty-first promise to be even more challenging. The citizen and the soldier cannot know what path to follow unless they are aware of the breadth of alternatives that have been accepted or rejected in the past. Philosopher George Santayana's dictum that those who ignore the past are condemned to repeat its mistakes is nowhere more apt than in military history. At the same time the blend of the historical with the military art reinforces the caution that no two periods or operations are precisely alike, that the easy analogy and the false comparison must be avoided, and that the past must be interpreted in proper context and depth. For the fledgling officer, as well as for the citizen, American military history provides a laboratory of experience; an accumulation of continuities and disparities; a rich storehouse of courage, sacrifice, and knowledge; and a source of inspiration and wisdom. It is to the multifaceted story of the American Army, how it originated and developed and what it contributed to the nation in war and peace, that we now turn.

> In the field of national security, the choices in the twentieth century were never easy; those for the twenty-first promise to be even more challenging.

2

THE BEGINNINGS

The United States as a nation was in its origins a product of English expansion in the New World in the seventeenth and eighteenth centuries, a part of the general outward thrust of West European peoples in this epoch. British people and institutions, transplanted to a new continent and mixed with people of different origins, underwent changes that eventually produced a distinctive American culture. In no area was the interaction of the two influences—European heredity and American environment—more apparent than in the shaping of the military institutions of the new nation.

The European Heritage

The European military heritage reaches far back into antiquity. Organized armies under formal discipline and employing what we would recognize as definite systems of battlefield tactics first appeared in the empires of the Near East in the second millennium B.C. During that time, Mediterranean military establishments rivaled in numbers and in the scope of their conflicts anything that was to appear in the Western world before the eighteenth century. In the fourth century B.C., Alexander the Great of Macedonia brought all these empires and dominions, in fact most of civilization known to the Western world, under his suzerainty in a series of rapid military conquests. In so doing, he carried to the highest point of development the art of war as it was practiced in the Greek city-states. He used the phalanx—a solid mass infantry formation using pikes as its cutting edge—as the Greeks had long done. But he put far greater emphasis on heavy cavalry and contingents of archers and slingers to increase the maneuverability and capability of his armies.

The Romans eventually fell heir to most of Alexander's empire and extended their conquests westward and northward to include present-day Spain, France, Belgium, and England, bringing these areas within the pale of Roman civilization. The Romans built on the achievements of Alexander and brought the art of war to its zenith in the ancient world. They perfected, in the legion, a tactical military unit of great maneuverability comparable in some respects to the modern division; performed remarkable feats of military engineering; refined sophisticated war machines such as the ballista and the catapult; and developed elaborate systems for fortification and siege craft. With this system, they built a great empire that endured for hundreds of years.

As the *Pax Romana* ("Roman Peace") disintegrated in Western Europe, the Roman Empire in the West was succeeded first by a number of kingdoms of Germanic tribes and eventually by a highly decentralized political system known as feudalism, under which a multitude of warring nobles exercised authority over local areas of varying size. The art of war underwent profound change, with the armored knight on horseback succeeding to the battlefield supremacy that under the Greeks and Romans had belonged primarily to disciplined formations of infantry. Society in the Middle Ages was highly stratified, and a rigid division existed between the knightly or ruling noble class and the great mass of peasants who tilled the soil, most of them as serfs bound to the nobles' estates.

Warfare became for the most part a monopoly of the ruling classes, for only men of substance could afford horse and armor. Every knight owed a certain number of days of military service to his lord each year in a hierarchical, or pyramidal, arrangement, the king at the apex and the great mass of lesser knights forming the base. But lords who were strong enough could defy their superiors with relative impunity. Fortified castles with moat and drawbridge, built on commanding points of terrain, furnished sanctuaries where lesser lords with inferior forces could defy more powerful opponents. Nonetheless, wherever freemen were found, in town or countryside, they continued to bear arms on occasion as infantry, although often as mere adjuncts to armies composed of heavy cavalry. This yeoman class was stronger, for the most part, in England than on the Continent. Even after the Norman Conquest brought feudal institutions to England, the ancient Saxon tradition of the *fyrd*, or militia, which required every freeman between sixteen and sixty to bear arms in defense of his country, remained alive. In 1181 the English King Henry II declared in his Assize of Arms that every freeman should keep and "bear these arms in his [the king's] service according to his order and in allegiance to the lord King and his realm."

Vestiges of feudal institutions survived even into the twentieth century, nowhere more prominently than in European military organizations where the aristocracy, descendants of the old feudal nobility, long dominated the officer ranks and continued its traditions of service, honor, and chivalry. At the other end of the scale, the militia system, so prominent in British and American history, also owed much to medieval precedents, for the Saxon *fyrd* and Henry II's Assize of Arms underlay the militia tradition transplanted from England to America.

Between the fourteenth and sixteenth centuries, the feudal order as the basic political organization of European society gave way gradually to new national states under the hereditary rule of royal families. The growth of towns with their merchant and artisan classes and the consequent appearance of a money economy enabled ambitious kings to levy taxes and borrow money to raise and support military forces and to unify and rule their kingdoms. The Protestant Reformation of

Alexander the Great

the sixteenth century shattered the religious unity of Western Christendom. A long series of bloody wars ensued in which the bitter animosity of Protestant and Catholic was inextricably mixed with dynastic and national ambition in provoking conflict.

Changes in military organization, weapons, and tactics went hand in hand with political, social, and economic change. During the later Middle Ages, formations of disciplined infantry using longbow, crossbow, pike (a long spear), and halberd (a long-handled ax with a pike head at the end) reasserted their superiority on the battlefield. The introduction of gunpowder in the fourteenth century began a process of technological change in weapons that was to enhance that superiority; more immediately, gunpowder was used in crude artillery to batter down the high "curtain" walls of medieval castles. The age of the armored knight and the castle slowly gave way to an age of mercenary infantry and new types of fortifications.

The Military Revolution

During the sixteenth and seventeenth centuries in Western Europe, a profound change occurred in the military capabilities of that portion of the Continent, a change so profound that it can accurately be phrased a revolution in the military art. In a relatively short space of time, European armies transformed themselves into highly disciplined and powerful military machines that lay the foundations for the coming European dominance of the world.

There were a number of key elements to this revolution. Armies grew larger with more efficient means to supply their material wants with a corresponding increase in the scope of warfare. Advances in fortification techniques (especially the *Trace Italienne*, with its revolutionary use of bastions as artillery firing platforms) established powerful city-states able to protect an expanding middle class. Tactical innovations led to a more highly disciplined force in which infantry armed with muskets, cavalry, and artillery merged into a standing national army. More ambitious strategies resulted from these new, more capable forces. Finally, this new type of army and form of warfare had a tremendous social, economical, and political impact on society. This military revolution shaped Europe into a collection of warlike, even predatory, states where constant innovation and technological experimentation was necessary for survival.

When this energy and destructive power was forced outward from Europe as part of this competition, great empires formed to dominate the world until the middle of the twentieth century. The foundation of the empire building of the eighteenth and nineteenth centuries was laid in the sixteenth and seventeenth centuries, and its impact on the British Empire in America was profound.

In the religious and dynastic wars of the sixteenth and seventeenth centuries, as mercenary armies came more and more to be national armies, various weapons employing gunpowder gradually replaced pike and halberd as the standard infantry weapons, and armor gradually disappeared from the bodies of both infantry and cavalry soldiers. At first, musketeers were employed alongside pikemen in square formations, the pikemen protecting the musketeers while they reloaded. The army of

Gustavus Adolphus

Gustavus Adolphus in the Thirty Years' War in Germany (1618–1648) brought together these two weapons into a mixed, flexible formation that capitalized on their strengths and covered their weaknesses. When combined with dynamic leadership and artillery and cavalry support, the formations proved highly successful. As the wheel-lock musket succeeded the matchlock harquebus as a shoulder arm and the flintlock in turn supplanted the wheel lock, armies came to rely less and less on the pike, more and more on firepower delivered by muskets. By 1700, with the invention of a socket bayonet that could be fitted onto the end of the flintlock musket without plugging the barrel, the pike disappeared entirely and along with it the helmet and body armor that had been designed primarily for protection against pikes and swords. Meanwhile, commanders learned to maneuver large bodies of troops on the battlefield and to employ infantry, cavalry, and artillery in combination. The blending of such capabilities, today called combined-arms warfare, proved decisive on the early modern battlefield. National armies composed of professional soldiers came once again to resemble the imperial forces that had served Alexander the Great and the Roman emperors.

In the Thirty Years' War, religious passions combined with private armies led by rapacious military entrepreneurs to create a conflict of virtually unprecedented ferocity and destructiveness. In reaction to this descent into barbarism, European warfare turned away from "total" war and refocused on "limited" wars fought with professionals for dynastic and national rather than local or religious interests. After the chaos and destruction that had attended the religious wars, rulers and ruling classes in all countries seemed to seek some measure of stability and order. Beginning with the wars of Louis XIV of France in 1660, dynastic rivalries were to be fought out by professional armies within the framework of an established order. The eighteenth century European military system that resulted constituted a powerful environmental influence on the military origins of the United States.

Eighteenth Century European Warfare

In contrast to wars of the seventeenth century and the great world wars of the twentieth century, eighteenth century warfare was essentially limited in character. It was often fought by rival states for restricted territorial gains and not for the subjugation or total religious conversion of whole peoples or nations. Professional armies and navies, without the mass mobilization of men, economic resources, and public opinion that has characterized the more ideological conflicts of the seventeenth and twentieth centuries, generally conducted the war. Except in areas where military operations took place, the people in the warring nations carried on their everyday life as usual.

The professional armies employed in this "limited" warfare reflected the society from which they sprang. Although Europe's aristocratic class no longer exercised political power independent of its kings, it remained the dominant privileged class, producing the proprietors of the great estates and leaders of the national armies. The great masses of people remained for the most part without property or voice in the government, either tilling the soil on the nobles' estates or working in the shops and handicraft industries in the towns. Absolute monarchy was the prevailing form of government in every European country save England, the Netherlands, and certain smaller states on the Continent. In England, where the constitutional power of Parliament was successfully established over the king, Parliament was by no means a democratic institution but one controlled by the landed gentry and wealthy merchants.

The military distinction nobles had formerly found in leading their own knights in battle they now sought as officers in the armies of their respective kings. Aristocrats filled the higher commands, while "gentlemen" of lesser rank and means usually served as captains and lieutenants. Advancement to higher ranks depended as much on wealth and influence at the court of a monarch as on demonstrated merit on the battlefield. Eighteenth century officers were hardly professionals in the modern sense of the word, usually having entered the service as mere boys through inheritance or purchase of a commission. Except for technical specialists in artillery and engineering, they were not required to attend a military school to train for their duties.

As the officers came from the highest classes, so the men in the ranks came from the lowest. They were normally recruited for long terms of service, sometimes by force, from among the peasants and the urban unemployed; more than a sprinkling of paupers, ne'er-do-wells, convicts, and drifters were in the ranks. Since recruiting extended across international boundaries, foreign mercenaries formed part of every European army. Discipline, not patriotic motivation, was the main reliance for making these men fight. Penalties for even minor offenses ran as high as a thousand lashes, and executions by hanging or firing squad were frequent. The habit of obedience inculcated on the drill ground carried over into battle, where, it has often been said, the men advanced because they preferred the uncertainties of combat to the certainty of death if they disobeyed orders. The army of Frederick the Great of Prussia was built into a military machine of near clock-like precision by brutal discipline and unquestioning obedience throughout the officer corps and rank and file soldiers.

Most of the significant European wars of the period were fought over terrain that was open, relatively flat, and thickly populated. Generally, fighting took place only in favorable weather and during daylight hours; rain or darkness quickly called a halt to a battle. The large armies with their cumbersome formations were almost impossible to control under such conditions. By December opposing armies usually retired to winter quarters, where they awaited spring to resume hostilities. Road and river transportation systems were for the time highly developed, facilitating the movement of men and supplies. Food for men and forage for horses were usually available in the areas of military operations, but all supplies were customarily obtained by systematic and regular procedures, not by indiscriminate plunder. Each nation set up along the line of march of its army a series of fortresses or magazines in which replacement supplies, foodstuffs, "staples," and forage for the horses could be stored.

Eighteenth century armies were composed predominantly of infantry, with cavalry and artillery as supporting elements. Because battles were usually fought in open country, cavalry could be employed to full advantage. As for artillery, it was used in both attack and defense,

Eighteenth century officers were hardly professionals in the modern sense of the word, usually having entered the service as mere boys through inheritance or purchase of a commission.

either in campaigns of maneuver or in siege warfare. Some eighteenth century commanders used the three arms skillfully in combination, but the clash of infantry usually decided the issue. In the eighteenth century, infantry was truly the "Queen of Battle."

The standard infantry weapon of the time was the flintlock musket with bayonet, and probably the most famous model was the British Brown Bess. The Brown Bess had a smoothbore barrel three-feet-eight-inches long with a fourteen-inch socket bayonet and fired a smooth lead ball about three-quarters of an inch in diameter. The musket was highly inaccurate since the barrel had no rifling and the charge necessarily fit loosely, permitting the escape of gas and reducing the effect of the propelling charge. It misfired occasionally and was useless when the powder in the priming pan got wet. The rate of fire was at best about three rounds per minute. When the ball hit within its effective range, 150 to 200 yards, its impact was terrific, tearing ghastly holes in flesh and shattering bone; but the inherent inaccuracy of the weapon practically precluded its use, even for volley fire, at ranges greater than 100 yards. The ineffectiveness of the smoothbore musket as a firearm made its attached bayonet almost as important as its firepower, and infantry relied on the bayonet for shock action against an enemy softened by musketry fire, as well as in its continuing role as a final defense against cavalry attack.

Cavalrymen were armed variously with pistol and lance, carbine and sword, depending on the country and the time. Pistol and carbine were discharged at close range against the ranks of opposing infantry or cavalry, while lance and sword were used for close-in shock action. Cavalry was most effective when used in a reconnaissance or foraging role and as a pursuit force after an enemy infantry formation had been broken.

There were many different kinds of artillery with a wide variety of bore sizes. The larger pieces were mainly for siege warfare and were relatively immobile. Artillery used in the field was lighter and mounted on wheeled carriages pulled by men or horses. Whether siege or field, these artillery pieces were like the muskets smoothbore muzzle-loaders, very limited in range and highly inaccurate. Loading and firing were even slower than in the case of the musket, since the artillerymen had to swab out the cannon barrel with water after each round to prevent any residue of burning powder from causing a premature explosion. There was no traverse, and the whole carriage had to be moved to change the direction of fire. Cannon fired mainly solid iron balls or, at shorter ranges, grapeshot and canister. Grapeshot was a cluster of small iron balls attached to a central stem (thus resembling a bunch of grapes) and dispersed by the explosion of a propellant charge. Canister consisted of loose pellets placed in a can and when fired had even greater dispersion than grape. At close range against a tightly packed infantry formation, it was devastating.

The nature of the soldiers, their weapons, and the terrain go far to explain the tactics used. These tactics were usually designated *linear* tactics to distinguish them from earlier mass formations such as the Spanish *Tercio* or the column formations Napoleon later employed. Gustavus Adolphus, the Swedish king and military innovator, in the Thirty Years' War was among the first to use linear tactics. They came

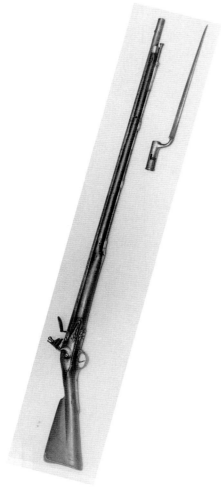

Brown Bess Musket, the British Infantryman's Basic Arm from About 1740 until the 1830s

American Artillery Crew in Action during the Revolutionary War, *Alan Archambault*

into general use in European armies during the later dynastic wars of Louis XIV of France, with the invention of the socket bayonet. Frederick the Great of Prussia carried them to their ultimate state of perfection, and his armies were the most methodically ordered in Europe. In the mid eighteenth century the Frederician system was the model that others tried to imitate.

In the employment of linear tactics, troops marched onto the battlefield in columns and then deployed into line. A line consisted of a number of battalions or regiments—the terms were then practically synonymous—formed three or more ranks deep. In the ranks the men stood shoulder to shoulder and delivered their fire. Loading, firing, and bayonet charge were all performed at command in a drill involving many separate motions. Firing, insofar as officers were able to maintain rigid discipline, was entirely by volley, the purpose being to achieve the greatest mass of firepower over a given area. The goal was always the "perfect volley." Individual, aimed fire, given the characteristics of the smoothbore flintlock musket, was deemed to be of little value.

Artillery was deployed in the line with the infantry, cavalry on the flanks or in the rear. Usually, commanders also kept an infantry force in reserve for use at a critical point in the battle. In the traditional eighteenth century battle, both forces would be drawn up in similar formation, and the battle would be opened by artillery fire from both sides. In the midst of this fire, the attacking infantry would move forward, maintaining the rigid linear formation in which it was trained and stopping as frequently as necessary to dress its lines and fill in the holes in the ranks made by enemy fire. At a range of 50 to 100 yards, the attacking line would halt on the command of its officers. At a second command, a volley would be fired and answered by the opposing line; or there might be a great deal of jockeying over who should fire first, for it was considered an advantage to take, not to give, the first volley and to deliver one's own answering volley at closer range. In any case, the exchange of volleys would continue until one side determined to try to carry the field by bayonet or cavalry charge, usually committing its reserves in this action. If either side was able to carry the field, the victorious commander then sought to execute a successful pursuit, destroying the enemy's army; the defeated commander attempted to withdraw his force in a semblance of order to a fortress or other defensive position, there to re-form and fight another day.

Despite the almost game-like movement of units on the battlefield like outsized chess pieces, eighteenth century battles were bloody affairs. At Zorndorf in 1758, for instance, the victorious army of Frederick lost 38 percent of its soldiers, the defeated Russians about half of theirs. Professional soldiers were difficult to replace, for there was no national reservoir of trained manpower to draw on and it took two years or more to train a recruit properly. Commanders, therefore, sparing of the blood of their soldiers, sought to avoid battle and to overcome the enemy by a successive series of maneuvers against his line of communications. They also tried to take advantage of terrain features and of fortified positions; to strike by surprise or against the flanks of the enemy, forcing him to realign his forces while fighting; and to employ artillery and cavalry to the greatest advantage in paving the way for infantry assault. Fortresses, normally constructed along the frontiers to impede the advance of an invading army, played a vital role in these maneuvers. It was considered axiomatic that no army could leave a fortress in its rear athwart its line of communications, that any major fortified point had to be reduced by siege. By 1700 the arts of both fortification and siege craft had been reduced to certain geometric principles by Marshal Sebastien Vauban, a distinguished soldier and engineer in the service of Louis XIV.

Vauban's fortresses were star-shaped and carried the style of the sixteenth century Trace Italienne (thick earthen walls with protruding bastions serving as artillery platforms) to its ultimate conclusion. Vauban designed thick stonewalls partially sunk into the earth and covered with earthen ramparts. Jutting forth from the walls were diamond-shaped bastions that allowed the mounted artillery to have mutually supporting fields of fire. Surrounding the fortress was a ditch or moat with a second, smaller wall in front of it with earth sloped against the wall to absorb the shock of cannon balls. These fortresses were expensive to build but nearly impregnable from direct assault.

Vauban's system for attacking this or any other type of fortified position was known as an approach by parallel lines. Once a fortress had been surrounded and outside aid cut off, batteries of siege artillery were brought up to within 600 yards of the fortress walls, the guns being so placed as to rake the lengths of the bastions with enfilade fire; behind these guns, the first parallel trench was dug to protect the gunners and assault troops. Zigzag approach trenches were then dug forward about 200 yards to the points from which a second parallel was constructed, then the same process was repeated with a third parallel. Infantry and siege artillery were moved forward as each parallel was completed until, in the third, they were beneath the outer wall of the fortress. From this vantage point the artillery could batter a breach in the main wall and the

Despite the almost game-like movement of units on the battlefield like outsized chess pieces, eighteenth century battles were bloody affairs.

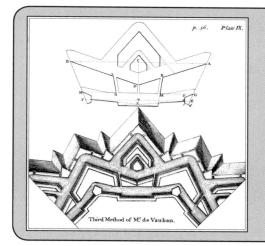

Third Method of M. de Vauban.

p. 56.   Plate IX.

VAUBAN

Sébastien Le Prestre de Vauban (1633–1707) was the foremost military engineer of his day. Born to a family of French nobility, Vauban entered the French Army at the age of seventeen, quickly showed a marked talent as an engineer, and captured the eye of King Louis XIV in the 1650s. For the next half century, he conducted nearly 50 sieges, fought in 140 engagements, fortified the French frontiers with 33 new fortresses, and remodeled 300 more. As well as revolutionizing siege craft and defensive fortifications, Vauban contributed to the growing professionalization of the military.

infantry could take the fortress by storm; but at that point in the battle the fortress commander usually surrendered to avoid further bloodshed. Under Vauban's system the capture of a fortress by a superior besieging force was usually only a matter of time; and the siege was conducted, often in leisurely fashion, along lines as rigidly fixed as those of the formal battle in the open field. But often time favored the defender, as sickness or supply problems forced the besieging force to withdraw. Logistics was often the key to successful defense or capture of a Vauban-type fortress.

Perhaps the most indelible picture of formal eighteenth century warfare that has survived is Voltaire's story of French and British officers at the Battle of Fontenoy in 1745 bowing politely to each other and each inviting the other side to fire the first volley, thus starting the carnage that was to follow. This picture has a certain ludicrous quality about it, but there was method in their madness as there was in eighteenth century warfare generally. The line that fired first was often at a disadvantage if a resolute enemy charged before they had a chance to reload.

The eighteenth century army was adapted to the European environment of the time, to the political and social climate as well as to the geography and terrain. Men knowledgeable in military matters at the time firmly believed that no body of poorly trained citizens, however numerous and inspired, could stand before the disciplined ranks of professionals. If today we can see many of the weaknesses in the eighteenth century military system that were not so obvious to contemporaries (its basic lack of flexibility, a paucity of true professional leadership, and its failure to effectively mobilize national resources for war), these perceptions result from a vastly different social and political environment.

The Colonial Scene

The environment in the British colonies of North America was different from that of Europe. America was a new continent, heavily forested and sparsely populated. The main enemy with whom the English colonists had first to contend was the American Indian, who neither

Colonial society from its very beginnings developed along more democratic and individualistic lines than society in England or continental Europe.

knew the rules of European warfare nor cared to learn them, but who had a military system of his own. Colonial society from its very beginnings developed along more democratic and individualistic lines than society in England or continental Europe. Military institutions and practices, though heavily influenced by English patterns, also evolved in the seventeenth and eighteenth centuries along different lines. It would be a mistake to call the society that took form in the thirteen English colonies in North America a new society, for in most respects it followed the English pattern of social, economic, and political organization. But England itself had stronger democratic traditions than existed on the Continent, and important differences in the environment gave these English traditions much stronger force in America. Here, there was no titled nobility exercising a monopoly on governmental office or holding a vested title to most of the land. While an aristocracy of wealth soon appeared, it was never able to exercise the same prerogatives as titled nobility. Besides, it was far easier to move from the poorer to the wealthier class, since acquisition of landed wealth was easier in a country where land was plentiful and labor to work it scarce. If older settled areas tended to develop something approaching the pattern of European class distinction, new frontiers were constantly opening up where dissatisfied individuals could move and find new opportunities. Life under these conditions bred a spirit of individualism and self-reliance.

In political life, this spirit found expression in the elected assemblies that played an increasingly important part in the government of each of the colonies. Each colony had a government modeled generally on England's. Though there were variations in the pattern, the prevailing form consisted of a royal governor appointed by the British Crown, a council appointed by the governor from the ranks of the colonial aristocracy, and a popular assembly elected by the landholders. Modeled on the British House of Commons, these popular assemblies in the colonies rested on a much broader democratic base, since property ownership—the main qualification for voting in Britain and America in this age—was far more widespread in the colonies. The colonial assemblies claimed the same prerogatives vis-à-vis the royal governor that the British Parliament exercised in its relations with the Crown, including control of the purse and regulation of the military establishment of the colony.

The growth of the colonies and resulting encroachment into Indian territories resulted in a dynamic that both enhanced and threatened the colonist's way of life. While the colonist based his growth on economics, the Indian's way of life—and way of warfare—grew out of social and cultural motivations.

The Indian method of warfare in the forest, perforce adopted by the colonists also, was the most significant influence in developing and preserving the spirit of individualism and self-reliance in the military sphere. Before the European came to America, the Indian had relied on bow and spear or tomahawk and knife; but he soon learned the value of muskets and was not long in obtaining them in trade for his valuable furs. With bow or musket, his method of fighting was the same. The Indian tribes with whom the colonists first came in contact had no organized system of war; warriors generally formed voluntary bands under war chiefs and took off on the warpath. In battle each Indian fought a separate opponent without regard for his fellows. Indians avoided pitched battle whenever possible, instead seeking victory by surprise and careful use of cover and concealment. Only when they had the advantage did they close in for hand-to-hand combat. In such combat the Indian brave lacked neither skill nor courage. Since he cared little about the rules of European warfare, he sometimes slaughtered men, women, and children indiscriminately or adopted prisoners permanently into his tribe. The favorite Indian tactic was a surprise raid on an isolated settlement. When the settlers organized a pursuit, the Indians lay in wait and ambushed them.

The European colonist soon adapted his tactics to the Indian's, quickly learning the value of surprise and stealth. To avoid ambush, he sent out scouts as the Indians did, frequently employing friendly Indians in the role. Instead of fighting in the closed formations of Europe, he too adopted the open formation and fought from behind trees, rocks, and fences. (If the Indians were accused of scalping dead and wounded, it should be noted that colonial soldiers occasionally did the same.) In such fighting more depended on individual initiative and courage than on strict discipline and control. Many of these tactics and techniques would serve the colonists well in their later war with Britain.

The European settlers also learned to benefit from some of the enemy's weaknesses. For all their cunning, the Indians never learned the lesson of proper security and often did not post guards at night. Nor did they like to fight in winter. Expeditions into the Indian country used as a favorite technique an attack on an Indian village at dawn and in the winter. This attack almost invariably came as a surprise; and the colonists, imitating the perceived savagery of their opponent, burned the Indian's villages and sometimes slaughtered all the inhabitants indiscriminately. Destruction of Indian villages and stocks of food proved to be the most effective colonial strategy, if also the most brutal.

The settlers tried to provide some permanent protection for their frontiers by erecting forts along the westernmost line of settlement in each colony, moving them forward as the line of settlement moved. These forts were not the elaborate earth and masonry structures of

KING PHILIP

Metacom, a Pokanoket chief from southern New England, was known to the English settlers of Plymouth, Massachusetts Bay, and Rhode Island as King Philip. The charismatic sachem forged a coalition of Wampanoag, Nipmuc, Pucumtuck, and Narragansett Indians to stem the flow of English settlers into their territories. Tensions ran high; after several settlers and Indians were killed in an intensifying spiral of violence, the conflict called King Philip's War began in 1675. Hostilities ended in 1676, when Metacom was captured and decapitated. His head remained on public display in Plymouth for nearly twenty-five years.

Europe but simple rectangular enclosures, their walls constructed of upright sharpened logs. Usually there were wooden blockhouses at each corner. These rude frontier forts served as points to which settlers and their families could retreat for protection in time of Indian trouble. Having no artillery, the Indians found the forts hard to take and could rely only on burning arrows to set them afire, on surprise attack, or on direct frontal assault. From the last alternative they almost invariably shrank. Their war chiefs possessed no power to order any group of braves to undertake an assault in which they would suffer heavy casualties for the sake of gaining an objective.

Colonial Militia

For fighting Indians, colonial governments were in no position to form professional armies, even had the nature of Indian warfare lent itself to such a practice. Instead they fell back on the ancient British tradition of the militia. This tradition took on new vitality in America at the same time it was declining in England, where, after Oliver Cromwell's time, most of the country's battles were fought on the sea and in foreign lands. The British government came to rely on its regular army and navy just as other European states did, despite a deep political tradition of opposition to a standing army. Each of the thirteen colonies (except for Pennsylvania, where Quaker influence was dominant) enacted laws providing for a compulsory militia organization generally based on the principle of the Saxon *fyrd* that required every able-bodied free male from sixteen to sixty to render military service. Each member of the militia was obligated to appear for training at his county or town seat a certain number of days each year, to provide himself with weapons, and to hold himself in readiness for call in case of Indian attack or other emergency.

Each colony maintained a separate militia establishment, and each concentrated on the problems of protecting or extending its own frontiers. Cooperation among the militias of the various colonies was confined to specific expeditions in which two or more colonies had an interest. The militia was by and large a local institution, administered in county and town or township under the general militia laws of each colony. It was closely integrated with the social and economic structure of colonial society. Though the royal governors or colonial assemblies appointed the general officers and the colonels who commanded militia districts, the companies in each locality usually elected their own officers. This practice seemingly put a premium on popularity rather than wealth or ability, but rank in the militia generally corresponded with social station in the community.

Each militiaman was expected to provide his own weapon—usually a smoothbore musket—and ammunition, clothing, and food for a short expedition, just as the British knight had been required to provide his own horse, armor, and suitable weapons for feudal warfare. Local authorities maintained reserve supplies of muskets to arm those too poor to buy them and collected stores of ammunition and sometimes small cannon that could be dragged along through the wilderness. For very long campaigns, the colonial government had to take charge, the assembly appropriating the money for supplies and designating the supply officers or contractors to handle purchasing and distribution.

> Each member of the militia was obligated to appear for training at his county or town seat a certain number of days each year, to provide himself with weapons, and to hold himself in readiness.

THE FIRST MUSTER

With no army from home to protect them, English settlers in America had to provide for their own defense. Initially, this was done at the local level; but on December 13, 1636, the Massachusetts Bay colony organized its disparate militia companies into three regionally based regiments. This date is considered the birthday of what would eventually become the U.S. National Guard. The picture depicts the first muster of the colony's East Regiment.

First Muster, *Don Troiani, 1985*

Although the militia was organized into units by county or township, it hardly ever fought that way. Instead the local unit served as a training and mobilization base from which individuals could be recruited for active operations. When a particular area of a colony was threatened, the colonial government would direct the local militia commander to call out his men and the commander would mobilize as many as he could or as he thought necessary, selecting the younger and more active men for service. For expeditions into the Indian country, usually individuals from many localities were chosen and formed into improvised units for the occasion. Selection was generally voluntary, but local commanders could be legally empowered to draft both men and property if necessary. Drafted men were permitted the option of hiring substitutes, a practice that favored the well-to-do. Volunteer, drafted man, and substitute, all paid while on active duty, alike insisted on the militiaman's prerogative to serve only a short period and return to home and fireside as quickly as possible.

As a part-time citizen army, the militia was naturally not a well-disciplined, cohesive force comparable to the professional army of the age. Criticism of the militia was frequent. Moreover, its efficiency, even for Indian fighting, varied from colony to colony and even from locality to locality within the same colony, depending on the ability and determination of commanders and the presence or absence of any threat. When engaged in eliminating an Indian threat to their own community, militiamen might be counted on to make up in enthusiasm what they lacked in discipline and formal training. When the Indian threat was pushed westward, people along the eastern seaboard tended to relax. Training days, one day a week in the early years of settlement, fell to one a month or even one a year. Festivities rather than military training increasingly became the main purpose of many of the gatherings, and the efficiency of the militia in these regions declined accordingly. In some towns and counties, however, the military tradition was kept alive by volunteers who formed their own units, purchased distinctive uniforms, and prepared themselves to respond in case of war or emergency. These units became known as the volunteer militia and were the predecessors of the National Guard of the United States. In Pennsylvania, which lacked a militia law until 1755 and then passed one that made militia service voluntary rather than compulsory, all units were composed of volunteers.

One of the more unpleasant manifestations of the militia system in America occurred in those colonies, most but by no means all in the south, with a large slave population. Fears of slave uprising and the rapidly growing imbalance between black and white populations in some areas of the colonies led to the establishment of militia units focused on detecting and defeating the smallest sign of trouble among the African slave population. In South Carolina in 1739, almost one hundred slaves organized themselves, seized weapons, and killed several white colonists before being suppressed by hastily raised militia soldiers. The resulting fear and legislative attempts to deal with the issue ensured that a primary focus of an organized militia in South Carolina, and later the rest of the southern colonies, was on internal security against the slaves.

On the frontier, where Indian raids were a constant threat, training days were frequent and militia had to be ready for instant action. Except on the frontier, where proficiency in this sort of warfare was a matter of survival, it is doubtful that colonial militia in general were really adept in forest fighting. Training days were devoted not to the techniques of fighting Indians but to learning the drill and motions required on a European battlefield. When raids were to be conducted against the Indians, often popularly elected officers selected individual volunteers from the militia to serve for the duration of the expedition. Thus the militia existed mostly as an internal defense force and a pool of trained manpower for ad hoc colonial expeditions against the Indians or other enemies, such as the nearby French Canadians.

The Colonies in the World Conflict, 1689–1783

While England was colonizing the eastern seaboard from Maine to Georgia, France was extending its control over Canada and Louisiana and asserting its claim to the Great Lakes region and the Mississippi Valley in the rear of the British colonies. (*Map 1*) Spain held Florida, an outpost of its vast colonial domains in Mexico, Central and South America, and the larger islands of the West Indies. England and France were invariably on opposite sides in the four great dynastic coalition wars fought in Europe between 1689 and 1763. Spain was allied with France in the last three of these conflicts.

Each of these European wars had its counterpart in struggles between British and French and Spanish colonists in America, intermingled with a quickening of Indian warfare all along the frontiers as the contestants tried to use the Indian tribes to their advantage. Americans and Europeans called these wars by different names. The War of the League of Augsburg (1689–1697) was known in America as King William's War, the War of Spanish Succession (1701–1713) as Queen Anne's War, the War of Austrian Succession (1744–1748) as King George's War, and the final and decisive conflict, the Seven Years' War (1756–1763) as the French and Indian War. All these wars involved control of the North American continent; in the last of them it became the principal point at issue in the eyes of the British government.

Map 1

The main centers of French strength were along the St. Lawrence River in Canada and at the cities of Quebec and Montreal. The strategic line along which much of the fighting took place in the colonies lay between New York and Quebec, either on the lake and river chain that connects the Hudson with the St. Lawrence in the interior or along the seaways leading from the Atlantic up the St. Lawrence. In the south, the arena of conflict lay in the area between South Carolina and Florida and Louisiana. In 1732 the British government established the colony of Georgia primarily as a military outpost in this region and as a dumping ground for their convicts.

In the struggle for control of North America, the contest between England and France was vital, the conflict with Spain, a declining power, important but secondary. This latter conflict reached its height in the

"War of Jenkins' Ear" (1739–1742), a prelude to the War of Austrian Succession, which pitted the British and their American colonists against the Spanish. In the colonies the war involved a seesaw struggle between the Spanish in Florida and the West Indies and the English colonists in South Carolina and Georgia. Its most notable episode, however, was a British expedition mounted in Jamaica against Cartagena, the main port of the Spanish colony in Colombia. The mainland colonies furnished a regiment to participate in the assault as British regulars under British command. The expedition ended in disaster, resulting from climate, disease, and the bungling of British commanders. Only about 600 of over 3,000 Americans who participated ever returned to their homes. The net result of the war itself was indecisive, and it did little to inspire the average American soldier with admiration for British military leadership.

The first three wars with the French were also indecisive. The nature of the fighting was much the same as that in the Indian Wars. Although the French maintained garrisons of regulars in Canada, they were never sufficient to bear the brunt of the fighting. The French Canadians also had their militia, a more centralized and all-embracing system than in the English colonies; but the population of the French colonies was sparse, scarcely a twentieth of that of the British colonies in 1754. The French relied heavily on Indian allies whom they equipped with firearms. They were far more successful than the British in influencing the Indians. Their sparse population posed little threat to Indian lands; and the French-controlled fur trade depended on Indian workers, while the British colonies saw Indians as an obstacle to settlement. The French could usually count on the support of the Indian tribes in the Great Lakes and Ohio Valley regions, though the British colonists did maintain greater influence with the powerful Iroquois Confederacy in New York. The French constructed forts at strategic points, like Niagara and Detroit, and garrisoned them with small numbers of regulars, a few of whom they usually sent along with militia and Indian raiding parties to supervise operations. Using guerrilla methods, the French gained many local successes and indeed kept the frontiers of the English colonies in a continual state of alarm, but they could achieve no decisive results because of the essential weakness of their position.

The British and their colonists usually took the offensive and sought to strike by land and sea at the citadels of French power in Canada. The British Navy's control of the sea made possible the mounting of sea expeditions against Canada and at the same time made it difficult for the French to reinforce their small regular garrisons. In 1710 a combined British and colonial expedition captured the French fort at Port Royal on Nova Scotia, and by the treaty of peace in 1713 Nova Scotia became an English possession. In 1745 an all-colonial expedition sponsored by Massachusetts captured Louisbourg on Cape Breton Island in what was perhaps the greatest of colonial military exploits, only to have the stronghold bargained away in 1748 for Madras, a post the French had captured from the British in India.

While militia units played an important part in the colonial wars, colonial governments resorted to a different device to recruit forces for expeditions outside their boundaries such as that against Louisbourg. This was the volunteer force, another institution that was to play an important part in all American wars through the end of the nineteenth century. Unlike the militia units, volunteer forces were built from the top down. One of the colonial governors or assemblies chose the commanding officer, who in turn enlisted his men. The choice of a commander was made with due regard for his popularity in the colony, since this was directly related to his ability to persuade officers and men to serve under him. While the militia was the main base for recruitment and the officers were almost invariably men whose previous experience was in the militia, indentured servants and drifters without military obligation were also enlisted. The enlistment period was only for the duration of a campaign, at best a year or so, not for long periods as in European armies. Colonial assemblies had to vote money for pay and supplies, and assemblies were usually parsimonious as well as unwilling to see volunteer forces assume any of the status of a standing army. With short enlistments, inexperienced officers, and poor discipline by European standards, even the best of these colonial volunteer units were, like the militia, often held in contempt by British officers.

The only positive British gain up to 1748 was Nova Scotia. The indecisive character of the first three colonial wars was evidence of the inability of the English colonies to unite and muster the necessary military forces for common action, of the inherent difficulty of mounting offensives in unsettled areas, and of a British preoccupation with conflicts in Europe and other areas. Until 1754 the British government contented itself with maintaining control of the seas and furnishing regulars for sea expeditions against French and Spanish strongholds. Until 1755 no British regulars took part in the war in the interior, though small "independent companies" of indifferent worth were stationed continuously in New York and occasionally in other colonies. No colony, meanwhile, was usually willing to make any significant contribution to the common cause unless it appeared to be in its own interest. Efforts to form some kind of union, the most notable of which was a plan that Benjamin Franklin promoted in a colonial congress held at Albany in 1754, all came to naught.

Between 1748 and 1754 the French expanded their system of forts around the Great Lakes and moved down into the Ohio Valley, establishing Fort Duquesne at the junction of the Allegheny and Monongahela Rivers in 1753 and staking a claim to the entire region. In so doing, they precipitated the final and decisive conflict that began in America two years before the outbreak of the Seven Years' War in Europe. In 1754 Governor Robert Dinwiddie of Virginia sent young George Washington at the head of a force of Virginia militia to compel the French to withdraw from Fort Duquesne. Washington was driven back and forced

THE CAPTURE OF LOUISBOURG

Guarding the mouth of the St. Lawrence River, the fortress of Louisbourg protected French settlements inland. The Massachusetts General Court voted in secret to attack the seemingly impregnable seaport 600 miles northeast of Boston. Colonial prisoners who had been held at the fort told of dispirited troops, masonry in disrepair, a shortage of gunpowder, and poorly mounted cannon. An eclectic American colonial force of 4,000 attacked after the drift ice left Gabarus Bay. A seven-week siege led to a spectacular victory in June 1745 for the colonists, who suffered minimal casualties.

to surrender, certainly an inauspicious beginning to his military career. The British government then sent over two understrength regiments of regulars under Maj. Gen. Edward Braddock, a soldier of forty-five years' experience on continental battlefields, to accomplish the task in which the militia had failed. Accustomed to the parade-ground tactics and the open terrain of Europe, Braddock placed all his faith in disciplined regulars and close-order formations. He filled his regiments with American recruits and early in June 1755 set out on the long march through the wilderness to Fort Duquesne with a total force of about 2,200, including a body of Virginia and North Carolina militiamen. (*Map 2*) Washington accompanied the expedition but had no command role.

Braddock's force proceeded westward through the wilderness in traditional column formation with 300 ax men in front to clear the road and a train of wagons in the rear. The heavy train so slowed his progress that about halfway he decided to let it follow as best it could and went ahead with about 1,300 selected men, a few cannon, wagons, and packhorses. As he approached Fort Duquesne, he crossed the Monongahela twice to avoid a dangerous and narrow passage along the east side where ambush might be expected. He sent Lt. Col. Thomas Gage (later to gain a measure of infamy as the general in charge of the raids on Lexington and Concord in 1775) with an advance guard to secure the site of the second crossing, deemed a likely spot for an ambush. Gage found no enemy, and the entire force crossed the Monongahela the second time on the morning of July 9, 1755, then confidently took up the march toward Fort Duquesne, only seven miles away.

About three-quarters of a mile past the Monongahela crossing, Gage's advance guard suddenly came under fire from a body of French and Indians concealed in the woods. Actually, it was a very inferior force of 70 French regulars, 150 Canadian militiamen (many mere boys), and 650 Indians who had just arrived on the scene after a hasty march from Fort Duquesne. Some authorities think Gage might have changed the whole course of the battle had he pushed forward and forced the enemy onto the open ground in their rear. Instead he fell back on the main body of Braddock's troops, causing considerable confusion. This confusion was compounded when the French and Indians slipped into the forests on the flanks of the British troops, pouring their fire into a surprised and terrified mass of men who wasted their return volleys on the air. "Scarce an officer or soldier," wrote one of the participants, "can say they ever saw at one time six of the Enemy and the greatest part never saw a single man."

None of the training or experience of the regulars had equipped them to cope with this sort of attack, and Braddock could only exhort them to rally in conventional formation. Two-thirds of his officers fell dead or wounded. The militia, following their natural instincts, scattered and took positions behind trees; but there is no evidence they delivered any effective fire, since French and Indian losses for the day totaled only twenty-three killed and sixteen wounded. The few British cannon appear to have been more telling. Braddock, mortally wounded himself, finally attempted to withdraw his force in some semblance of order; but the retreat soon became a disordered flight. The panic-stricken soldiers did not stop even when they reached the baggage wagons many miles to their rear.

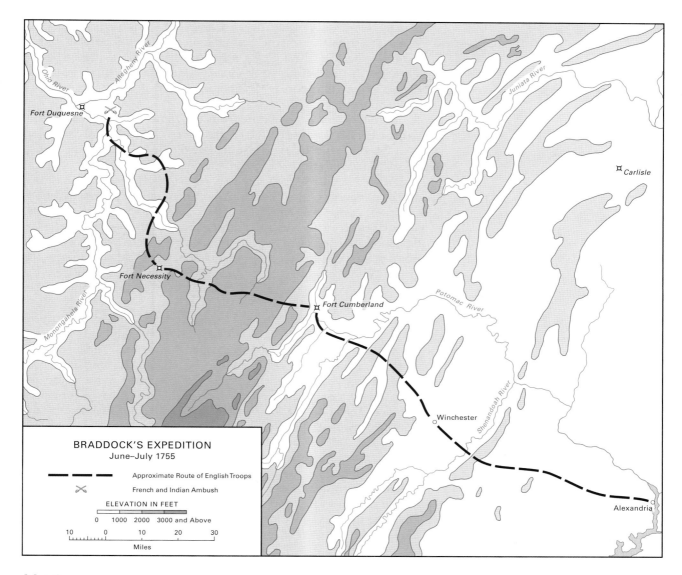

Map 2

Despite the completeness of the victory, the French and Indians made no attempt to pursue. The few French regulars had little control over the Indians, who preferred to loot the battlefield and scalp the wounded. The next day the Indians melted back into the forest, and the French commandant at Duquesne noted in his official report, "If the enemy should return with the 1,000 fresh troops that he has in reserve in the rear, at what distance we do not know, we should perhaps be badly embarrassed." The conduct of the battle was not so reprehensible as the precipitate retreat of the entire force to the safety of the settled frontiers when no enemy was pursuing it.

Although Braddock had been aware of the possibilities of ambush and had taken what he thought were necessary precautions, in the broader sense he violated the principles of security and maneuver: When the ambush came he had little idea how to cope with Indian tactics in the forest. As he lay dying on the wagon that transported him from the battlefield, the seemingly inflexible old British general is alleged to have murmured, "Another time we shall know better how to deal with them."

Braddock could not profit from his appreciation of the lesson, but the British Army did. "Over the bones of Braddock," writes Sir John Fortescue, the eminent historian of the British Army, "the British advanced again to the conquest of Canada."

After a series of early reverses of which Braddock's disastrous defeat was only one, the British government under the inspired leadership of Prime Minister William Pitt was able to achieve a combination of British and colonial arms that succeeded in overcoming the last French resistance in Canada and in finally removing the French threat from North America. In this combination, British regular troops, the British Navy, British direction, and British financial support were the keys to victory; the colonial effort, though considerable, continued to suffer from lack of unity.

As an immediate reaction to Braddock's defeat, the British Government sought to recruit regulars in America to fight the war, following the precedent set in the Cartagena expedition. Several American regiments were raised, the most famous among them Col. Henry Bouquet's Royal Americans. On the whole, however, the effort was a failure, for most Americans preferred short service in the militia or provincial volunteer forces to the long-term service and rigid discipline of the British Army. After 1757 the British government under Pitt, now convinced that America was the area in which the war would be won or lost, dispatched increasing numbers of regulars from England—a total of 20,000 during the war. The British regulars were used in conjunction with short-term militia and longer-term volunteer forces raised in the service of the various individual colonies. The most effective device to assure the sort of colonial cooperation the British desired was to shoulder the principal financial burden, reimbursing individual colonies for most of their expenses and providing the pay and supply of many of the colonial volunteer units to ensure their continued service. Massachusetts, Connecticut, and New York furnished about seven-tenths of the total colonial force employed.

Braddock's defeat was not repeated. In no other case during the French and Indian War was an inferior guerrilla force able to overcome any substantial body of regulars. The lessons of the debacle on the Monongahela, as the British properly understood, were not that regular forces or European methods were useless in America or that undisciplined American militia were superior to regular troops. They were rather that tactics and formations had to be adapted to terrain and the nature of the enemy and that regulars, when employed in the forest, would have to learn to travel faster and lighter and to take advantage of cover, concealment, and surprise as their enemies did. Or the British could employ colonial troops and Indian allies versed in this sort of warfare as auxiliaries, something the French had long since learned to do.

The British adopted both methods in the ensuing years of the French and Indian War. Light infantry, trained as scouts and skirmish-

"Another time we shall know better how to deal with them."

Braddock's Defeat, *Artist Unknown, ca. 1870*

ers, became a permanent part of the British Army organization. When engaged in operations in the forest, these troops were clad in green or brown clothes instead of the traditional red coat of the British soldier, with their heads shaved and their skins sometimes painted like the Indians'. Special companies, such as Maj. Robert Rogers' Rangers, were recruited among skilled woodsmen in the colonies and placed in the regular British establishment.

Despite this employment of light troops as auxiliaries, the British Army did not fundamentally change its tactics and organization in the course of the war in America. The reduction of the French fortress at Louisbourg in 1758 was conducted along the classic lines of European siege warfare. The most decisive single battle of the war was fought in the open field on the Plains of Abraham before the French citadel of Quebec. In a daring move, Maj. Gen. James Wolfe and his men scaled the cliffs leading up to the plain on the night of September 12, 1759, and appeared in traditional line of battle before the city the next morning. Maj. Gen. Louis Joseph, the Marquis de Montcalm, the able French commander, accepted the challenge; but his troops, composed partly of militia levies, proved unable to withstand the withering "perfect volleys" of Wolfe's exceptionally well-disciplined regiments.

The ultimate lesson of the colonial wars, then, was that European and American tactics each had a place; either could be decisive where conditions were best suited to its use. The colonial wars also proved that only troops possessing the organization and discipline of regulars, whatever their tactics, could actually move on, seize, and hold objectives and thus achieve decisive results.

Other important lessons lay in the realm of logistics, where American conditions presented difficulties to which European officers were unaccustomed. The impediments to supply and transport in a vast, undeveloped, and sparsely populated country limited both the size and variety of forces employed. The settled portions of the colonies produced enough food, but few manufactured goods. Muskets, cannon,

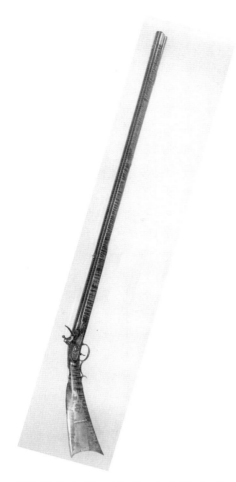

This flintlock rifle, originally intended for hunting, dates from 1800–1820. One of the few truly American art forms of early America, the rifle inspired the design of U.S. military rifles that emerged from U.S. armories beginning in 1803.

powder, ball, tents, camp kettles, salt, and a variety of other articles necessary for even the simple military operations of the period almost all had to come from Europe. Roads, even in the settled areas, were poor and inadequate; forces penetrating into the interior had to cut their roads as they went, as Braddock did. Movement by water, when possible, was by far more efficient. These logistical problems go far to explain why the fate of America was settled in battles involving hardly one-tenth the size of forces engaged in Europe in the Seven Years' War and why cavalry was almost never employed and artillery to no great extent except in fixed fortifications and in expeditions by sea when cannon could be transported on board ship. The limited mobility of large regular forces, whatever the superiority of their organization and tactics, put a premium both on small bodies of trained troops familiar with the terrain and on local forces, not so well trained, already in an area of operations. Commanders operating in America would ignore these logistical limitations at their peril.

The American Rifle

By the end of the French and Indian War, a new weapon had appeared on the frontier in Pennsylvania and to the south, one far better suited to guerrilla warfare than was the musket. This weapon would later become renowned as the Kentucky rifle. The effects of rifling a gun barrel, that is, of making spiral grooves that imparted a spinning effect to the bullet, giving it greater range and accuracy, had been known for some centuries in Germany and Switzerland. But the early rifles made there were too heavy and slow to load to be of military use. The Germans who settled in Pennsylvania developed, around 1750, a much lighter model, far easier and faster to load. They used a bullet smaller than the bore and a greased patch to keep the fit tight. This early American rifle could, in proper hands, hit a target the size of a man's head at 200 yards.

Despite its superior range and accuracy, the rifle was to undergo almost a hundred years of development before it would supplant the musket as the standard infantry weapon. At first, each individual piece was handmade and each required a custom-made bullet mold. The standard bayonet would fit none of them. The rifle was effective only in the hands of an expert trained in its use. The rate of fire was only

ROGERS' RANGERS

In 1755 Robert Rogers (1731–1795) recruited a company of woodsmen near his home in New Hampshire and was ordered by the British "to range the woods" and harass the French along the frontier. Rogers' Rangers, as his unit came to be known, was one of several ranger companies the British formed as a counter to the Indian allies of the French. Rogers and his men infiltrated into French-held areas of the northern colonies and Canada, using stealth and surprise to win several important engagements. After the French and Indian War, Rogers wrote down twenty-eight "Ranging Rules" learned during his encounters with an unconventional enemy; they are enshrined to this day in U.S. Army Ranger training.

GEORGE WASHINGTON
IN THE FRENCH AND INDIAN WAR

George Washington (1732–1799), as a 22-year-old lieutenant colonel in the Virginia militia, was a principal player at the opening of the French and Indian War. In 1754 he led a small force of Virginians to try to compel the French to relinquish control of Fort Duquesne, which was strategically placed to control the Ohio Valley. After a skirmish with a French reconnaissance party, he fell back to a hastily constructed stockade, Fort Necessity, where he resisted a larger French force before finally surrendering. A year later he served under Braddock and ultimately took part in Brig. Gen. John Forbes' successful campaign to capture what is now Pittsburgh.

about one-third that of the musket; and therefore, without bayonet, the rifle could hardly be used by troops in the line. For the guerrilla tactics of the frontier, however, where men did not fight in line but from behind trees, bushes, and rocks, it was clearly a superior weapon. Like the tactics of the American forest, it would have its place in any future war fought in America.

The Colonial Heritage

In the Indian Wars and the colonial wars with France, Americans gained considerable military experience, albeit much of it in guerrilla warfare that did not require the same degree of organized effort and professional competence as the European style. The British had, after all, directed the major effort against the French in Canada. Many colonials later to become famous in the Revolution had served their military apprenticeship as officers of middle rank in the French and Indian War: George Washington, Israel Putnam, Philip Schuyler, and John Stark, for instance, in provincial forces and Charles Lee, Horatio Gates, and Richard Montgomery in the British Army.

Certain traditions had been established that were to influence American military policy and practice right down to the two great world wars of the twentieth century. One of these was primary reliance on the militia for defense and on volunteer forces for special emergencies and expeditions. Another was that relatively permanent volunteer units should be formed within the militia. The fear of a standing army of professionals, an English heritage, had become an even stronger article of faith in America. The colonial experience also established a strong tradition of separatism among the colonies themselves, for each had for many years run its own military establishment. Within each colony, too, the civilian authority represented in the popular assembly had always kept a strict rein on the military, another tradition that was to have marked effect on American military development.

Some characteristics of the American soldier that were to be fairly constant throughout all future wars had also made their appearance. The American soldier was inclined to be highly individualistic and to resent discipline and the inevitable restrictions of military life; he sought to know why he should do things before he would put his heart into doing them. If in the end he accepted discipline and order as a stern necessity, he did so with the idea of winning victory as quickly as possible so he could return to his normal civilian pursuits.

These traditions and characteristics were the product of a society developing along democratic lines. The military strengths and weaknesses they engendered were to be amply demonstrated when the American soldier took up arms against his erstwhile comrade, the British regular, in the American Revolution.

DISCUSSION QUESTIONS

1. To what degree is the American Army a European Army?

2. How did our early colonial experience modify our European military inheritance?

3. What did the British learn about the nature of warfare in the Americas from their initial defeats in the French and Indian War? How could this have helped them in their later fight against the "colonists"?

4. Why did the British and American armies defeat the French and their French-Canadian allies?

5. What did the British learn about the military capabilities of their American "cousins"? What should they have learned?

6. Why didn't the rifle immediately replace the musket on the battlefield?

RECOMMENDED READINGS

Anderson, Fred. *Crucible of War: The Seven Years' War and the Fate of Empire in British North America, 1754–1766*. New York: Vintage Books, 2001.

Ferling, John E. *A Wilderness of Miseries: War and Warriors in Early America*. Westport, Conn.: Greenwood Press, 1980.

Leach, Douglas E. *Arms for Empire: A Military History of the British Colonies in North America*. New York: Macmillan, 1973.

Malone, Patrick M. *The Skulking Way of War: Technology and Tactics Among the New England Indians*. Baltimore: Johns Hopkins University Press, 1993.

Shy, John W. *Toward Lexington: The Role of the British Army in the Coming of the Revolution*. Princeton: Princeton University Press, 1965.

Other Readings

Anderson, Fred. *A People's Army: Massachusetts Soldiers and Society in the Seven Years' War*. Chapel Hill: University of North Carolina Press, 1984.

Fregault, Guy. *Canada: The War of Conquest,* trans. Margaret M. Cameron. Toronto: Oxford University Press, 1969.

Gipson, Lawrence H. *The British Empire Before the American Revolution,* 15 vols. New York: Alfred A. Knopf, 1963–1970, vols. 6–8.

Leach, Douglas E. *The Northern Colonial Frontier, 1607–1763.* New York: Holt, Rinehart, and Winston, 1966.

———. *Flintlock and Tomahawk: New England in King Philip's War.* New York: Macmillan, 1958.

Lepore, Jill. *The Name of War: King Philip's War and the Origins of American Identity.* New York: Alfred A. Knopf, 1998.

Melvoin, Richard I. *New England Outpost: War and Society in Colonial Deerfield.* New York: W. W. Norton, 1989.

Pargellis, Stanley. *Lord Loudon in North America.* Hamden, Conn.: Archon Books, 1968.

Parker, Geoffrey. *The Military Revolution: Military Innovation and the Rise of the West, 1500–1800,* 2d ed. New York: Cambridge University Press, 1996.

Peckham, Howard H. *The Colonial Wars, 1689–1762.* Chicago: University of Chicago Press, 1964.

Rawlyk, George A. *Yankees at Louisbourg.* Orono: University of Maine Press, 1967.

Richter, Daniel K. *The Ordeal of the Longhouse: The Peoples of the Iroquois League in the Era of European Colonization.* Chapel Hill: University of North Carolina Press, 1992.

Robinson, W. Stitt. *The Southern Colonial Frontier, 1607–1763.* Albuquerque: University of New Mexico Press, 1979.

Shea, William L. *The Virginia Militia in the Seventeenth Century.* Baton Rouge: Louisiana State University Press, 1983.

Stacey, Charles P. *Quebec 1759: The Siege and the Battle,* rev. ed. Toronto: Rubin Brass Studio, 2002.

White, Richard. *The Middle Ground: Indians, Empires, and Republics in the Great Lakes Region, 1650–1815.* New York: Cambridge University Press, 1991.

Wright, J. Leitch, Jr. *The Only Land They Knew: The American Indians in the Old South.* Lincoln: University of Nebraska Press, 1999.

3

The American Revolution, First Phase

The American Revolution came about fundamentally because by 1763 the English-speaking communities on the far side of the Atlantic had matured to the extent that their interests and goals were distinct from those of the ruling classes in the mother country. British statesmen failed to understand or adjust to the situation. Ironically enough, British victory in the Seven Years' War set the stage for the revolt, for it freed the colonists from the need for British protection against a French threat on their frontiers and gave free play to the forces working for separation.

In 1763 the British government, reasonably from its own point of view, moved to tighten the system of imperial control and to force the colonists to contribute to imperial defense. As part of an effort to make the costs of empire be borne by all British subjects, his majesty's government sought to create an "American Establishment," a force of 10,000 British regular soldiers in North America. The cost of this military force would be paid for by taxes the British Parliament levied on Americans. This imperial defense plan touched off the long controversy about Parliament's right to tax that started with the Stamp and Sugar Acts and led to a final provocative deed in December 1773 at the "Boston Tea Party." This party resulted in the destruction of a cargo of East India Company tea by a patriot mob in a protest against "taxation without representation."

The ten-year controversy over taxation escalated to violence in large measure because several successive British ministries failed to understand the differences that had grown between the American colonies and the metropolitan power. Although possessing a professional army and navy, the British government nevertheless failed to act decisively enough to enforce British regulations or work toward the more viable form of imperial union that the colonial leaders, at least until 1776, insisted they sought.

In response to the Boston Tea Party, the King and his ministers blindly pushed through Parliament a series of measures collectively known in America as the Intolerable Acts: closing the port of Boston, suspending civilian government in Massachusetts, and massing troops in Boston under the military rule of Maj. Gen. Sir Thomas Gage. Outraged by the heavy-handed response to one colony, the other American political leaders called for a continental congress, in effect an American parliament, to coordinate a political drive to defend what the colonists deemed to be their rights and interests as Englishmen.

Since 1763 the colonial leaders, in holding that only their own popular assemblies, not the British Parliament, had a right to levy taxes on Americans, had raised the specter of an arbitrary British government collecting taxes in America to support red-coated regulars who might be used not to protect the frontiers but to suppress American liberties. Placing Massachusetts under military rule gave that specter some substance and led directly to armed revolt.

The Outbreak

The First Continental Congress meeting at Philadelphia on September 5, 1774, addressed respectful petitions to Parliament and King but also adopted nonimportation and nonexportation agreements in an effort to coerce the British government into repealing the offending measures. To enforce these agreements, committees were formed in almost every county, town, and city throughout the colonies. In each colony, these committees soon became the effective local authorities, the base of a pyramid of revolutionary organizations with revolutionary assemblies, congresses, or conventions, and with committees of safety at the top.

This loosely knit combination of de facto governments superseded the constituted authorities and established firm control over the whole country before the British were in any position to oppose them. The de facto governments took over control of the militia and other colonial military resources such as armories and powder stores. They also identified which local militia officers could be trusted and which were known to be loyal to Britain. Where possible the various colonies reorganized the standing militia and formed rapid response units, including the famous Minutemen intended to turn out fully armed "in a minute's notice." In colonies where a British governor's official control over the militia could not be challenged, volunteer companies began training under the guidance of veterans of the French and Indian War. As winter turned into spring in 1775, patriot leaders were busily shaping the military forces that, if the necessity arose, might oppose the British Army in the field.

Massachusetts, the seat of the crisis, led the way in making military preparations. The Provincial Congress, eyeing Gage's unprecedented military force in Boston, directed town officials to formally enlist a third of their adult males as Minutemen. It began plans to combine local militia companies into regiments and started selecting generals to command the force. It also began to collect ammunition, artillery pieces, and other military stores at locations outside of Gage's immediate reach. One of the most important of these depots lay at Concord, about twenty miles inland from Boston.

THE MINUTEMAN

The Minuteman of 1775 did not represent an entirely new idea. The Massachusetts militia's tradition of readiness went back long before King Philip's War; a colonywide directive in 1645 ordered that 30 percent of the entire militia force be ready "at halfe an howers warning." The Minutemen were selected out of the wide pool of able-bodied militia—in essence the entire male population of the colony—to be ready at any time for emergency operations. They were organized into companies that usually consisted of neighbors. Most carried their own smoothbore flintlock muskets, though there was a fund to purchase weapons for militiamen too poor to buy their own. By the spring of 1775 some militia companies were drilling every week and practicing marksmanship. When word of a British advance on Concord spread through the country north of Boston in the early hours of that April Wednesday, the Minutemen were ready.

Minutemen Bid Their Families Farewell
Artist and Date Unknown

General Gage learned of the collection of military stores at Concord and determined to send a force of Redcoats to destroy them. His preparations were made with the utmost secrecy. Yet so alert and ubiquitous were the patriot eyes in Boston that when the picked British force of 700 men set out on the night of April 18, 1775, two messengers, Paul Revere and William Dawes, preceded them to spread the alarm throughout the countryside. At dawn on the next day, when the British arrived at Lexington, the halfway point to Concord, they found a body of militia drawn up on the village green. Some nervous finger—whether of a British regular or an American militiaman is unknown to this day—pressed a trigger. The impatient British regulars, apparently without any clear orders from their commanding officer, fired a volley then charged with the bayonet. The militiamen dispersed, leaving eight dead and ten wounded on the ground. The British column went on to Concord, engaged in another unanticipated skirmish, and destroyed such of the military stores as the Americans had been unable to remove. Their return journey to Boston took a civil disturbance issue and transformed it into open warfare.

By this time, the alarm had spread far and wide, and both ordinary militia and Minutemen had assembled along the British route. From behind walls, rocks, and trees, and from houses, they poured their fire into the columns of Redcoats, while the frustrated regulars found few targets for their accustomed volleys or bayonet charges. Only the arrival of reinforcements from Gage enabled the British column to get back to the safety of Boston. At day's end the British counted 273 casualties out of a total of 1,800 men engaged; American casualties numbered 95 men, including the toll at Lexington. What happened was hardly a tribute to the marksmanship of New England farmers—it has been estimated that 75,000 shots poured from their muskets that day—but it did testify to a stern determination of the people of Massachusetts to resist any attempt by the British to impose their will by armed force.

The spark lit in Massachusetts soon spread throughout the rest of the colonies. Whatever really may have happened in that misty dawn on Lexington Green, the news that speedy couriers riding horses to exhaustion carried through the colonies from New Hampshire to Georgia was of a savage, unprovoked British attack and of farmers rising in the night to protect their lives, their families, and their property. Lexington, like Fort Sumter, Pearl Harbor, and September 11 in subsequent years, furnished an emotional impulse that led all true patriots to gird themselves for battle. From the other New England colonies, militia poured in to join the Massachusetts men; together they soon formed a ring around Boston. Other forces mobilized under Ethan Allen of Vermont and Benedict Arnold of Connecticut seized the British forts at Ticonderoga and Crown Point, strategic positions on the route between New York and Canada. These posts yielded valuable artillery and other military stores. The Second Continental Congress, which assembled in Philadelphia on May 10, 1775, found itself forced to turn from embargoes and petitions to the problems of organizing, directing, and supplying a military effort.

Before Congress could assume effective control, the New England forces assembled near Boston fought another battle on their own. After Lexington and Concord, the New England colonies implemented their military plans and, as they had in the earlier wars with the French and Indians, moved to replace the militia gathered before Boston with volunteer forces, constituting what may be loosely called a New England army. Each of the four New England states raised and administered its own force under its own commander. As might be expected with such a loose organization, discipline was lax and there was no unified chain of command. Though Artemas Ward, the Massachusetts commander, exercised overall control by informal agreement, it was only because the other commanders chose to cooperate with him; all decisions were made in council. The volunteers in the Connecticut service had enlisted until December 10, 1775, those from the other New England states until the end of the year. The men were dressed for the most part in homespun clothes and armed with muskets of varied types; powder and ball were short, and only the barest few had bayonets.

Late in May Gage received limited reinforcements from England, bringing his total force to 6,500 rank and file. With the reinforcements came three major generals of reputation—Sir William Howe, Sir Henry Clinton, and Sir John Burgoyne—men destined to play major roles in England's loss of its American colonies. The newcomers all considered that Gage needed more elbow room and proposed to fortify Dorchester Heights, a dominant position south of Boston previously neglected by both sides. News of the intended move leaked to the Americans, who immediately countered by dispatching a force onto the Charlestown peninsula, where other heights, Bunker Hill and Breed's Hill, overlooked Boston from the north. (*Map 3*) The original intent was to fortify Bunker Hill, the eminence nearest the narrow neck of land connecting the peninsula with the mainland, but the working party sent out on the night of June 16, 1775 decided instead to move closer in and construct works on Breed's Hill—a tactical blunder, for these

As might be expected . . . discipline was lax and there was no unified chain of command.

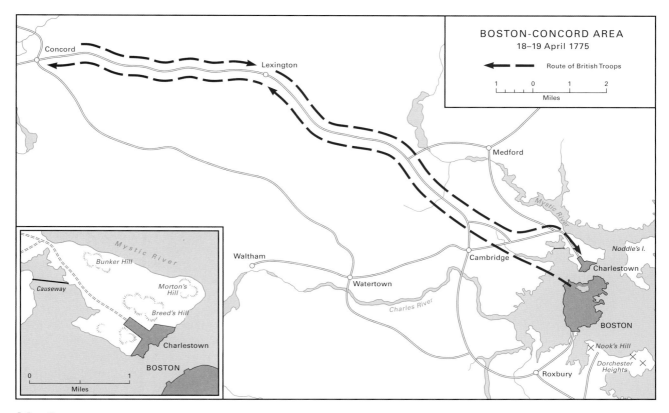

Map 3

exposed works could much more easily be cut off by a British landing on the neck in their rear.

The British scorned such a tactic, making a conscious decision to try and stop the conflict short with a psychologically crushing demonstration of brute force. However, the British generals committed a critical error, having assumed that the assembled "rabble in arms" would disintegrate in the face of an attack by disciplined British regulars. On the seventeenth Gage ferried some 2,200 of his men under Howe over to the tip of the Charlestown peninsula under the cover of Royal Navy warships. Howe then sent his troops directly against the American positions, by this time manned by perhaps an equal force. Twice the British advanced on the front and flanks of the redoubt on Breed's Hill; and twice the Americans, holding their fire until the compact British lines were at close range, decimated the ranks of the advancing regiments and forced them to fall back and re-form. With reinforcements Howe carried the hill on the third try, largely because the Americans had run short of ammunition and had no bayonets. The American retreat from Breed's Hill was, for inexperienced volunteers and militia, an orderly one; and Howe's depleted regiments were unable to prevent the escape. British casualties for the day totaled a staggering 1,054, almost half the force engaged, as opposed to American losses of about 440.

The Battle of Bunker Hill (Bunker gave its name to a battle actually fought on Breed's Hill) has been aptly characterized as a "tale of great blunders heroically redeemed." The American command structure violated the principle of unity of command from the start; in moving onto Breed's Hill, the patriots exposed an important part of their force in an indefensible position, violating the principles of security, mass, and maneuver. Gage and Howe, for their parts, sacrificed all the advantages the American blunders gave them, violating the principles of maneuver and surprise by undertaking a frontal attack on a fortified position. Their gamble to end the rebellion with a single stroke had failed.

Bunker Hill was a Pyrrhic victory, its strategic effect practically nil since the two armies remained in virtually the same position they had held previously. Its consequences, nevertheless, cannot be ignored. Although frequently depicted as a force of farmers and townsmen, fresh from their fields and shops, with hardly a semblance of orthodox military organization, the New Englanders used their militia training to field forces modeled on the British. Led by officers with, in some case, more direct combat experience than many of Gage's, the Americans had met and fought on equal terms with a professional British Army. On some of the more senior British commanders this astonishing feat had a sobering effect, for it taught them that American resistance was not to be easily overcome; never again would British commanders lightly attempt such an assault on Americans in fortified positions. Many Americans, on the other hand, misread the battle. Bunker Hill, along with Lexington and Concord, went far to create an American myth that the citizen-soldier when aroused by patriotic emotion is more than a match for the trained professional, a tradition that was to be reflected in American military policy for generations afterward.

Formation of the Continental Army

The response of George III and his ministers to the events at Lexington, Concord, and Bunker Hill was a determined effort to subdue the rebellious colonists by force. It took time to mount this effort, and after Bunker Hill the Americans enjoyed a respite lasting almost a year. During most of this period the Second Continental Congress reacted to the events in New England and New York by hesitantly assuming the mantle of leadership, but it continued to assert that these actions were defensive in nature. It charged that Americans had banded together to oppose the unconstitutional actions of Parliament but that they still hoped to find a formula for reconciliation by appealing directly to the King for justice. Military preparations were designed for a short struggle, to endure no longer than the end of the year 1776. Nevertheless, the Americans took advantage of the respite to create a national army, to consolidate their hold on the governmental machinery throughout the thirteen colonies, to invade Canada, and finally to force the British to evacuate Boston.

The creation of the Continental Army was in the long run perhaps their most significant achievement. Some time before Bunker Hill the Massachusetts Provincial Congress, aware of the necessity of enlisting the support of all the colonies in the struggle against the British, appealed to the Continental Congress to adopt the New England army. Because of the need to preserve secrecy, Congress made its decision as

The Americans had met and fought on equal terms with a professional British Army.

THE ARMY BIRTHDAY

The creation of a truly American Army on June 14, 1775, was highly significant to the history of our emerging nation. While the colonial militias and volunteer Minutemen were easily aroused in anger and invaluable in controlling population and resources in the countryside, they often melted away as fast as they were raised. In addition, those forces often identified with their own state or region. However, the first ten companies of Continental Army soldiers were a national force even before the nation was fully formed. The first continentals were recruited from several states and were sent from one end of the thirteen colonies and then states to another. In time a nation would grow out of the seeds planted by each continental soldier as he signed up not as a "summer soldier" or "sunshine patriot," to use the immortal words of Tom Paine, but as an American soldier in service to his nation whenever and wherever needed.

a committee of the whole. After determining the necessity of accepting national responsibility for the troops at Boston and in New York, Congress voted to create the Continental Army on June 14, 1775. On the same day it voted to raise ten companies of riflemen—the first soldiers to be enlisted directly in the Continental service—in Pennsylvania, Maryland, and Virginia to march north to join the army before Boston. The message was clear: This was no regional outbreak of violence but was instead the united response of all of the mainland North American colonies.

The next day, June 15, Congress chose George Washington, a Virginian, to be Commander in Chief. As was the case with the riflemen, Congress made the choice for geographical and political as much as for military reasons. The New Englanders felt a southerner should be chosen for the post to prove that this was not a New England–only conflict. Washington's military experience was perhaps greater than that of any other American, and he came from the largest and most important of the southern colonies. His impressive appearance, quiet and confident manner, and good work in the military committees of Congress had impressed all.

The choice proved fortunate. Washington himself recognized, when he accepted the command, that he lacked the requisite experience and knowledge in handling large bodies of men. His whole military experience had been in frontier warfare during the French and Indian War. But he had commanded a brigade of troops from several colonies during the capture of Fort Duquesne in the French and Indian War— he was the only native-born American up to that time to command a force of that size. Experience gained as a political leader in his native Virginia and in directing the business affairs of his large plantation at Mount Vernon also stood him in good stead. He brought to the task traits of character and abilities as a leader that in the end more than compensated for his lack of European military experience. Among these qualities were a determination and a steadfastness of purpose rooted in an unshakable conviction of the righteousness of the American cause, a scrupulous sense of honor and duty, and a dignity that inspired respect and confidence in those around him. Conscious of his own defects, he was always willing to profit by experience. From the trials and tribulations of eight years of war he was to learn the essentials of strategy, tactics, and military organization.

Congress also appointed four major generals and eight brigadiers to serve under Washington, set up a series of staff offices closely resembling those in the British Army, prescribed a pay scale and standard ration, and adopted Articles of War to govern the military establishment. The same mixture of geographical, political, and military considerations governed the choice of Washington's subordinates. Two-thirds of them came from New England, in recognition of the fact that the existing army was a New England army. Three others—Charles Lee, Horatio Gates, and Richard Montgomery—were chosen because of their experience in the British Army. Lee in particular, who had come from England to the colonies in 1773, was in 1775 deemed the foremost military expert in America, and he was for a time to be Washington's first assistant.

The army of which Washington formally took command on July 3, 1775, he described as "a mixed multitude of people ... under very little discipline, order or government." Out of this mixed multitude, Washington set out to create an army shaped in large part in the British image. Basing his observations on his experience with British regulars during the French and Indian War, he wrote: "Discipline is the soul of an army. It makes small numbers formidable; procures success to the weak and esteem to all." Employing Gates, his experienced Adjutant General, to prepare regulations and orders, the Commander in Chief set out to inculcate discipline. He and his staff made a strenuous effort to halt the random comings and goings of officers and men and to institute regular roll calls and strength returns. Suspicious of the "leveling" tendencies of the New Englanders, Washington made the distinction between officers and enlisted men more rigid. He introduced various punishments (lash, pillory, wooden horse, and drumming out of camp), and courts-martial sat almost constantly.

While establishing discipline in the existing army, Washington had at the same time to form a new one enlisted directly in the Continental service. Out of conferences with a congressional committee that visited camp in September 1775 emerged a plan for such an army, composed of 26 regiments of infantry of 728 men each, plus 1 regiment of riflemen and 1 of artillery, 20,372 men in all, to be uniformly paid, supplied, and administered by the Continental Congress and enlisted to the end of the year 1776. Except for the short term of enlistment, it was an excellent plan on paper; but Washington soon found he could not carry it out. Both officers and men resisted a reorganization that cut across the lines of the locally organized units in which they were accustomed to serve. The men saw as their first obligation their families and farms at home, and they were reluctant to reenlist for another year's service. On December 10, despite pressures and patriotic appeals, many of the Connecticut men went home and militia from New Hampshire and Massachusetts had to be brought in to fill their places in the line. Others, who had jeered and hooted when the Connecticut men left, also went home when their enlistment expired only three weeks later. On January 1, 1776, when the army became "Continental in every respect," Washington found that he had only slightly more than 8,000 troops in the lines around Boston instead of the 20,000 planned. Returns in early March showed only a thousand or so more. "I have often thought how

> "Discipline is the soul of an army. It makes small numbers formidable; procures success to the weak and esteem to all."

much happier I would have been," wrote a sorely tried commander, "if, instead of accepting a command under such circumstances, I had taken up musket on my shoulder and entered the ranks, or, if I could have justified the measure to posterity and my own conscience, had retired to the back country and lived in a Wigwam."

While waiting for the regiments to reach full strength, short-term militia continued to fill the gaps in the lines. A Continental Army had been formed, but it fell far short of the goals Washington and Congress had set for it. This army was enlisted for but a year, and the whole troublesome process would have to be repeated at the end of 1776. The short term of enlistment was, of course, a cardinal error; but in 1775 everyone, including Washington, had anticipated only a short campaign.

While organizing and disciplining his army, Washington had also to maintain the siege of Boston and overcome his deficiencies in supply. In these efforts he was more successful. Congress and the individual colonies sponsored voyages to the West Indies, where the French and Dutch had conveniently exported quantities of war materials. Washington put some of his troops on board ship and with an improvised navy succeeded in capturing numerous British supply ships. He sent Col. Henry Knox, later to be his Chief of Artillery, to Fort Ticonderoga; and Knox in the winter of 1775–1776 brought some fifty pieces of captured cannon to Cambridge over poor or nonexistent roads in icebound New York and New England. By March 1776, despite deficiencies in the number of continentals, Washington was ready to close in on Boston.

The Invasion of Canada and the Fall of Boston

The major military operations of 1775 and early 1776 were not around Boston but in faraway Canada, which the Americans considered the fourteenth colony needing only a little shove to join the others in rebellion against Britain. Canada seemed a tempting and vulnerable target. To take it would eliminate a British base at the head of the familiar invasion route along the lake and river chain connecting the St. Lawrence with the Hudson. Congress, while appealing to the Canadians to join in the cause, in late June 1775 instructed Maj. Gen. Philip Schuyler of New York to take possession of Canada if "practicable" and "not disagreeable to the Canadians."

Schuyler managed to get together a force of about 2,000 men from New York and Connecticut, thus forming the nucleus of what was to become known as the Northern Army. In September 1775 Brig. Gen. Richard Montgomery set out with this small army from Ticonderoga with the objective of taking Montreal. To form a second prong to the invasion, Washington detached a force of 1,100 under Col. Benedict Arnold, including a contingent of riflemen under Capt. Daniel Morgan of Virginia, to proceed up the Kennebec River, across the wilds of Maine, and down the Chaudière to join with Montgomery before Quebec. (*See Map 4.*) Montgomery, advancing along the route via Lake George, Lake Champlain, and the Richelieu River, was seriously delayed at the British fort at St. Johns but managed to capture Montreal on November 13. Arnold, meanwhile, had arrived opposite Quebec on November 8, after one of the most rugged marches in history. Part of

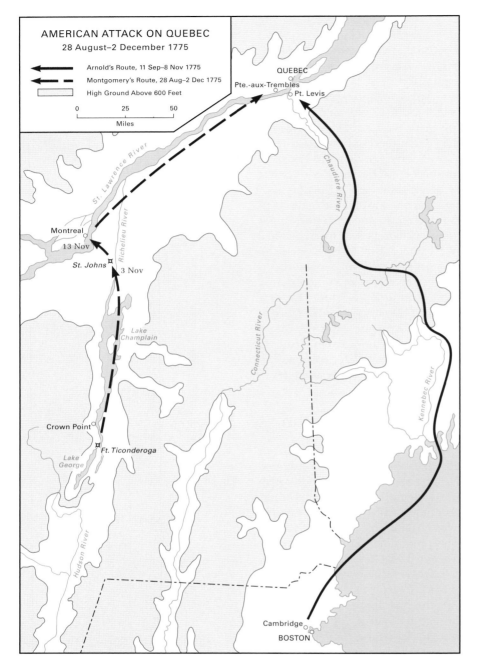

AMERICAN ATTACK ON QUEBEC
28 August–2 December 1775

← Arnold's Route, 11 Sep–8 Nov 1775

← ─ Montgomery's Route, 28 Aug–2 Dec 1775

High Ground Above 600 Feet

0   25   50
Miles

QUEBEC
Pte.-aux-Trembles
Pt. Levis

St. Lawrence River

Chaudière River

Montreal
13 Nov
St. Johns   3 Nov
Richelieu River

Lake Champlain

Connecticut River

Kennebec River

Crown Point

Lake George   Ft. Ticonderoga

Hudson River

Cambridge
BOSTON

Map 4

his force had turned back, and others were lost by starvation, sickness, drowning, and desertion. Only 600 men crossed the St. Lawrence on November 13, and in imitation of Wolfe scaled the cliffs and encamped on the Plains of Abraham. It was a magnificent feat, but the force was too small to prevail even against the scattered Canadian militia and British regulars who, unlike Montcalm, shut themselves up in the city and refused battle in the open.

Arnold's men were finally forced to withdraw to Point aux Trembles, where Montgomery joined them with all the men he could spare from the defense of Montreal—a total of 300. Although the Canadians did raise two regiments for the Continental Army, most did not rally to the American cause. With the enlistments of about half their men expiring by the new year, Arnold and Montgomery undertook a desperate assault on the city during the night of December 30 in the middle of a raging blizzard. The defenders outnumbered the Americans, and the attack was a failure. Montgomery was killed and Arnold wounded.

The wounded Arnold, undaunted, continued to keep up the appearance of a siege with the scattered remnants of his force while he waited for reinforcements. Continental regiments raised in New York, New Jersey, and Pennsylvania came in driblets. There were never enough to build a force capable of again taking the offensive, though a total of 8,000 men were eventually committed to the Canadian campaign. Smallpox and other diseases took their toll; and the supply line never brought in adequate food, clothing, or ammunition. Meanwhile, the British received reinforcements and in June 1776 struck back against a disintegrating American army that retreated before them almost without a fight. By mid-July the Americans were back at Ticonderoga, where they had started less than a year earlier. The initiative on the northern front passed to the British.

While the effort to conquer Canada was moving toward its dismal end, Washington finally took the initiative at Boston. On March 4, 1776, he moved onto Dorchester Heights and emplaced his newly acquired artillery in position to menace the city; a few days later he fortified Nook's Hill, standing still closer in. On March 17 the British moved out. It would be presumptuous to say that their exit was solely a consequence of American pressure. Sir William Howe, who succeeded Gage in command, had concluded long since that Boston was a poor strategic base and intended to stay only until the transports arrived to take his army to Halifax in Nova Scotia to regroup and await reinforcements. Nevertheless, Washington's maneuvers hastened his departure, and the reoccupation of Boston was an important psychological victory for the Americans, balancing the disappointments of the Canadian campaign. The stores of cannon and ammunition the British were forced to leave behind were a welcome addition indeed to the meager American arsenal.

The New Nation

The Declaration of Independence on July 4, 1776, established a new nation and transformed a limited uprising to secure rights within the British Empire into a far-reaching revolution aimed at complete independence from British control. Since the King and his ministers had determined to restore British rule, the Americans now faced a long, hard struggle for independence that required a sustained national effort such as they had not expected in 1775.

The new nation was still a weak confederation of thirteen independent states. Such national feeling as existed was a new phenomenon growing out of common opposition to British measures. Colonial tradition, divided loyalties, the nature of the economy, and the spirit of a revolt born in opposition to the use of military force to suppress popular liberties all worked against the creation of any new strong central authority capable of mobilizing resources effectively for the long struggle that lay ahead.

The thirteen states proclaiming their independence in 1776 possessed a total population of about 2.5 million people, but not all the males of military age were part of the military potential. About 20 percent were African American slaves who except under special circumstances were not eligible for service, though African Americans did serve in the Revolution in integrated units (a feature that Americans did not repeat until after World War II). A significant minority within the colonies remained loyal to the King, either reluctantly out of sense of obligation or passionately as armed supporters. As in any society, there were also the apathetic and indifferent who swayed with the tide. The genuine patriots still provided a far larger potential of military manpower than the British could possibly transport and supply across the Atlantic, but most of the men of military age were farmers with families. Whatever their patriotic sentiments, few were ready to undertake long terms of military service, fearing that their farms and families at home would suffer. Accustomed to the tradition of short-term militia

> The Americans now faced a long, hard struggle for independence that required a sustained national effort.

Presenting the Declaration of Independence, *John Trumbull, 1796*

service under local commanders, they infinitely preferred it to longer terms in the Continental Army.

The economy of the thirteen new states was neither self-sufficient nor truly national. The states were essentially a collection of separate agricultural communities accustomed to exchanging their agricultural surplus for British-manufactured goods and West Indian products. Manufacturing was still in its infancy, and America produced few of the essentials of military supply. Despite diligent efforts to promote domestic production during the war years, the Continental Army had to rely primarily on captures and imports from Europe and the West Indies, run through a British blockade, for much of its military hardware and even for clothing. While the country produced foodstuffs in ample quantity, transport from one area to another was difficult. The normal avenues of commerce ran up and down the rivers, not overland; roads running north and south were few and inadequate. There were always shortages of wagons, boats, and other means of transportation. Under these circumstances, it was far easier to support local militia for a few days or weeks than any sizable and continuously operating national army in the field.

The governmental machinery created after the Declaration was characterized by decentralization and executive weakness. The thirteen new "free and independent states" transformed their existing de facto revolutionary governments into legal state governments by adapting institutions. Almost invariably the new constitutions vested most of the powers of government in the state legislatures, successors to the popular assemblies of the colonial period, and severely restricted the executive authority of the governors. At the national level the same general distrust of strong authority was apparent; and the existing Continental Congress, essentially a gathering of delegates chosen by the state legislatures and without either express powers of its own or an executive to carry out its enactments, was continued as the only central governing body. Articles of Confederation stipulating the terms of union and granting Congress specific but limited powers were drawn up shortly after the Declaration, but jealousies among the states prevented ratification until 1781. In the interim, Congress exercised most of the powers granted it under the Articles; but the Articles did not include either the right to levy taxes or the power to raise military forces directly under its auspices. Congress could only determine the Confederation's need for troops and money to wage war and set quotas for the states to meet in proportion to their population and wealth. It had no means of ensuring that the states met their quotas; indeed, they seldom did.

One major weakness of this decentralized structure was that it provided no adequate means of financing the war. The state legislatures, possessing the power to tax that Congress lacked, hesitated to use it extensively in the face of popular opposition to taxation and was usually embarrassed to meet even its own expenses. Congress very early took unto itself the power to issue paper money and to negotiate domestic and foreign loans, but it shared these powers with the states, which also printed paper money in profusion and borrowed both at home and abroad to the extent they could. The paper money was a useful expedient in the early part of the war; indeed, the Revolution could not have been carried on without it. But successive issues by Congress and the states led to first gradual and then galloping inflation, leaving the phrase "not worth a Continental" as a permanent legacy in the American language. The process of depreciation and the exhaustion of credit gradually robbed both the states and Congress of the power to pay troops, buy supplies, and otherwise meet the multitudinous expenses of war.

Evolution of the Continental Army

It is not surprising that under these circumstances Washington never got the kind of army molded in the European image that he desired. The experience before Boston in 1775 was repeated many times, as local militia had to be called in frequently to give the American Army a numerical superiority in the field. The Continental Army nevertheless became the center of American resistance and its commander, Washington, the symbol of the patriot cause. The extent to which militia could be expected to rally to that cause was very largely determined by the Continental Army's success or failure in the field.

Though the militia belonged to the states, the Continental Army was a creation of the Continental Congress. Congress prescribed its size and composition, chose its generals, commissioned its officers, and governed the system for its administration and supply. Suspicious on principle of a standing army and acutely aware of historic examples of

> Articles of Confederation stipulating the terms of union and granting Congress specific but limited powers were drawn up shortly after the Declaration, but jealousies among the states prevented ratification until 1781. In the interim, Congress exercised most of the powers granted it under the Articles; but the Articles did not include . . . the power to raise military forces directly.

seizure of political power by military leaders, its members kept a watchful eye on the Army's commanders and insisted they defer to civilian authority. Washington countered these suspicions by constantly deferring to congressional wishes, and he was rewarded by the assiduity with which Congress usually adopted his recommendations.

Lacking an executive, Congress had to rely on committees and boards to carry out its policies—unwieldy devices at best and centers of conflicting interest and discord at worst. In June 1776 it set up a Board of War and Ordnance, consisting of five of its members, the lineal ancestor of the War Department. In 1777 Congress changed the composition of the board, directing that it henceforth be made up of persons outside Congress who could devote full time to their military duties. Neither of these devices really worked well, and Congress continually handled administrative matters by action of the entire membership or by appointment of special committees to go to camp. In 1781, with the implementation of the Articles of Confederation, the board was replaced by a single Secretary at War.

Under the Articles of Confederation, while the Continental Congress passed the authorizing legislation setting the terms, size, and configuration of the army, the states remained responsible for raising the troops. Therefore, recruiting and equipping efforts depended heavily on thirteen separate bodies, each acting in response to local conditions and concerns. State authorities called out militia sometimes at the request of Congress and sometimes on their own initiative. When they joined the Continental Army, the militia normally shared in its supplies and equipment. The states, however, maintained an interest in supplying and administering the troops of their own "lines" as well as their militia. As a result, the Continental agents continually went through delicate negotiations with state officials any time they tried to accomplish major tasks. Lines of authority crisscrossed at every turn.

It was an inefficient military system for an organized national effort. Washington could never depend on having enough trained men or supplies. He continually inveighed against sending militia to fight his battles and by early 1776 had concluded that he needed an army enlisted for the duration of the war. Congress did not, as has often been charged, ignore his wishes. In October it voted a new establishment, superseding the plan developed for the army before Boston in 1775 and haphazard arrangements made in the interim for raising Continental regiments in various states. This establishment was to contain eighty-eight infantry regiments, or about 60,000 men, enlisted to serve three years or "during the present war," with each state assigned a quota in proportion to its population. After the disastrous retreat across New Jersey in December 1776, Congress authorized additional regiments to be recruited by Washington's officers directly into the Continental service, including regiments of artillery and light cavalry. These regiments remained the authorized strength of the Continental Army until 1781, when Congress cut it to fifty-nine.

The large army fell short from the start. Many states found it impossible to sustain their quotas, especially as the war dragged on. By the winter of 1777–1778, the effort to enlist men for the duration of the war collapsed; the following spring, with the sanction of Washington, Congress reverted to a system of shorter enlistments and recommended to the states that they institute a system of drafting men from the militia for one year's service. This first American wartime draft was applied irregularly because it was not a national program. Each state followed its own policies and procedures, some effectively; but most states performed no better when trying to draft men than they had when trying to encourage volunteers. Bounties, instituted by both the states and the Congress very early in the war and progressively increased one step behind the pace of inflation, also produced only temporary and irregular results.

The coin did have another side. In reality the shortage of arms and ammunition and of facilities for producing them limited the number of men who could be kept continuously in the field as effectively as did the failure of enlistment drives. The militia system allowed many able-bodied males to perform part-time military service and still remain most of the time in the labor force that kept the economy going. It is doubtful whether the American economy could have sustained such an army as Washington and Congress had proposed in 1776, even had there been a central administration with adequate power. As it was, the small Continental Army that did remain in the field intermittently faced extreme hardship and even near starvation. On the other hand, the American ability to raise local armies in any threatened region helped to balance the strategic mobility that the British Fleet gave to the British Army. Although militia generally did not perform well in regular warfare, when highly motivated and ably led they could fight well on terrain suited to their capabilities. Washington and most of his generals recognized this and sought to use the mobilized militia for flank security or to perform envelopments of isolated British detachments and outposts. Given the conditions under which the Revolution was fought, the American military system was more effective than its critics have recognized, though it failed to provide adequately for a sustained military effort over a period of years.

Perhaps Washington's greatest achievement was simply in maintaining the Continental Army continuously in the field. Despite its many vicissitudes and defeats, that army remained constituted as an

EXTRACT FROM THE DRAFT ARTICLES OF CONFEDERATION, ARTICLE XVIII, JULY 12, 1776

The United States assembled shall have Authority for the Defence and Welfare of the United Colonies and every of them, to agree upon and fix the necessary Sums and Expences—To emit Bills, or to borrow Money on the Credit of the United Colonies—To raise Naval Forces—To agree upon the Number of Land Forces to be raised, and to make Requisitions from the Legislature of each Colony, or the Persons therein authoritized [sic] by the Legislature to execute such Requisitions, for the Quota of each Colony, which is to be in Proportion to the Number of white Inhabitants in the Colony, which Requisitions shall be binding, and thereupon the Legislature of each Colony or the Persons authorized as aforesaid, shall appoint the Regimental Officers, raise the Men, and arm and equip them in a soldier-like Manner; and the Officers and Men so armed and equipped, shall march to the Place appointed, and within the Time agreed on by the United States assembled.

ever-present threat to any British field force, while the American militia units solidified patriot control of all the areas not fully garrisoned by the British. The Army of the United States was thus shaped by the war into a distinctively American military organization, neither a replica of a professional European Army on which it was modeled nor yet the type of national army raised by conscription that was to appear in France after the Revolution of 1789.

The Continental Army operated in territorial divisions or departments, each containing one or more maneuver forces. Washington exercised direct command over the main area and defended the Middle States, operating most of the time in the area between New York City and Philadelphia. After the British retreat from Boston, the New England department operated mostly in the Rhode Island area. The Northern Department was located in northern New York, and the Southern Department controlled military operations in the Carolinas, Virginia, and Georgia. Two additional departments existed at times with limited independent roles: the Western Department centered on Pittsburgh, and the Canadian Department focused on Canada until the retreat from that region in the summer of 1776. A special territorial area, the Highlands Department, consisting of the mountains in the vicinity of West Point, was an area of such great strategic concern that it deserved its own department.

Although Washington was Commander in Chief of the Continental Army, the commanders of the other departmental armies still operated with a considerable measure of independence. Congress, rather than Washington, named their commanders and communicated directly with them. Of the two "separate armies," the Northern Army was by far the most important until 1777; the small Southern Army performed limited defensive missions in a relatively quiet sector of the country. By 1780 the situation was reversed as the British transferred their main effort to the southern states.

The Continental Army was composed mainly of infantry with limited cavalry and artillery. The basic unit of infantry organization was the regiment, composed of eight or more companies. Regiments were administrative formations; different terms were used when talking about tactical employment. A battalion served as the basic tactical unit. It contained eight platoons, the number needed in linear warfare to provide a constant wave of volley fire. Customarily in both the American and British armies of the Revolution, a regiment of eight companies would form a single battalion with each company serving as a single platoon. A brigade was usually formed of several regiments plus an attached direct support artillery company and was usually commanded by a brigadier general; a division consisted of several brigades commanded by a major general. In the northern areas, the artillery consisted of a brigade of four regiments and several separate companies under the Chief of Artillery, Henry Knox. Knox employed some of the separate companies in direct support of the infantry brigades but used others in garrison or general support assignments. The army's mounted arm consisted of four regiments of light dragoons, normally employed in reconnaissance and counterreconnaissance duties, plus several smaller units, including two deep-strike partisan corps (a mix of light dragoons and light infantry). Other regular forces included a corps of engineers; three companies of

Although Washington was Commander in Chief of the Continental Army, the commanders of the other departmental armies still operated with a considerable measure of independence.

sappers and miners; several military police elements; two regiments of artificers, who handled the servicing and repair of ordnance and vehicles; and a headquarters guard force.

Washington was provided with a staff generally corresponding to that of contemporary European armies. One of his critical staff officers was the Quartermaster General, responsible not only for transportation and delivery of supplies but also for arranging the camp, regulating marches, and employing the army's watercraft. There were also an Adjutant General (responsible for issuing orders for the commander and administrative paperwork), a Judge Advocate General, a Paymaster General, a Commissary General of Musters, several Commissary Generals of Provisions (procurement and issue of rations), a Clothier General, a Chief Surgeon, and a Chief Engineer. Each of the separate armies usually had staff officers in these positions, designated as deputies to those of the main army. Early in 1778 the Continental Army introduced a new innovation—the Inspector General. This officer provided a focal point for developing standard battle drills and written tactical texts and during the second half of the war emerged as Washington's de facto chief of staff.

All these staff officers had primarily administrative and supply functions. The modern concept of a general staff that acts as a sort of collective brain for the commander had no real counterpart in the eighteenth century. For advice on strategy and operations, Washington relied on a council of war made up of his principal subordinate commanders; and, conforming to his original instructions from Congress, he usually consulted the council before making major decisions.

Both organization and staff work suffered from the ills that afflicted the whole military system. Regiments were constantly under strength, were organized differently by the various states, and prior to Valley Forge used varying systems of drills and training. In the promotion of officers in the state lines, Continental commanders shared authority with the states; the confused system gave rise to all sorts of rivalries, jealousies, and resentment, leading to frequent resignations. Staff officers were generally inexperienced, and few had the patience and perseverance to overcome the obstacles posed by divided authority, inadequate means, and poor transportation and communication facilities. The supply and support services of the Continental Army never really functioned efficiently; and with the depreciation in the currency, they came close to collapse.

The British Problem

Whatever the American weaknesses, the British government faced no easy task when it undertook to subdue the revolt by military force. Even though England possessed the central administration, stable financial system, and well-organized army and navy that the Americans so sorely lacked, the whole establishment was ill prepared in 1775 for the struggle in America. A large burden of debt incurred in the wars of the preceding century had forced crippling economies on both Army and Navy. British administrative and supply systems, though far superior to anything the Americans could improvise, were also characterized by division and confusion of authority; and there was much corruption in high places.

Contrary to popular belief, American soldiers in the Revolutionary War generally carried cartridge boxes, rather than powder horns and shot pouches. The cartridge box held fixed cartridges of paper for faster loading, even in damp weather. This Pattern 1777 cartridge box represents one of the Army's first attempts at standardizing military equipment.

To suppress the revolt, Britain had first to raise the necessary forces, then transport and sustain them over 3,000 miles of ocean, and finally use them effectively to regain control of a vast and sparsely populated territory. Recruiting men for an eighteenth century army was most difficult. The British government had no power to compel service except in the militia in defense of the homeland, and service in the British Army overseas was immensely unpopular. To meet Howe's request for 50,000 men to conduct the campaign in 1776, the ministry resorted to an old practice of obtaining auxiliary troops, mercenaries, from many of the small German states, particularly Hesse-Cassell (hence Hessians). These German states were to contribute almost 30,000 men to the British service during the war—complete organizations with their own officers up to the rank of lieutenant general and schooled in the system of Frederick the Great. Howe did not get his 50,000 men; but by midsummer 1776 his force had grown to 30,000 British and Hessians, and additional reinforcements were sent to Canada during the year.

Maintaining a force of this size proved to be another problem. The attrition rate in America from battle losses, sickness, disease, and desertion was tremendously high. English jails and poorhouses were drained of able-bodied men; bounties were paid; patriotic appeals were launched throughout England, Scotland, and Ireland; and all the ancient methods of impressments were tried. But the British were never able to recruit enough men to meet the needs of their commanders in America and at the same time defend the home islands and provide garrisons in the Caribbean, the Mediterranean, Africa, and India.

Providing adequate support for this army over a long ocean supply line was equally difficult. Even for food and forage, the British Army had to rely primarily on sea lines of supply. Transports were in short supply, the hardships of the two-to-four-month voyage terrible, and the loss of men and supplies to natural causes heavy. Moreover, though the Americans could muster no navy capable of contesting British control of the seas, their privateers and the ships of their infant navy posed a constant threat to unprotected troop and supply transports. British commanders repeatedly had to delay their operations to await the arrival of men and supplies from England.

Once in America, British armies could find no strategic center or centers whose capture would bring victory. Flat, open country where warfare could be carried on in European style was not common. Woods, hills, and swamps suited to the operations of militia and irregulars were plentiful. A British Army that could win victories in the field over the continentals had great difficulty in making those victories meaningful. American armies seemed to possess miraculous powers of recuperation; a British force, once depleted or surrendered, took a tremendous effort to replace.

As long as the British controlled the seas, they could land and establish bases at nearly any point on the long American coastline. The many navigable rivers dotting the coast also provided water avenues of invasion well into the interior. But to crush the revolt, the British Army had to cut loose from coastal bases and rivers. When it did so, its logistical problems multiplied and its lines of communications became vulnerable to constant harassment. British armies almost inevitably came to grief every time they moved very far from the areas where they

British armies could find no strategic center or centers whose capture would bring victory.

could be nurtured by supply ships from the homeland. These difficulties, a British colonel asserted in 1777, had "absolutely prevented us this whole war from going fifteen miles from a navigable river."

The British could not, in any case, ever hope to muster enough strength to occupy with their own troops the vast territory they sought to restore to British rule. Their only real hope of meaningful victory was to use Americans loyal to the British cause to control the country, as one British general put it, to help "the good Americans to subdue the bad." However, there were many obstacles to making effective use of the Tories. Patriot organization, weak at the center, was strong at the grass roots, in the local communities throughout America; the Tories were neither well organized nor energetically led. The patriots seized the machinery of local government in most communities at the outset, held it until the British Army appeared in their midst, and then normally regained it after the British departed. Strong local control enabled the patriots to root out the more ardent Tories at the very outset, and by making an example of them to sway the apathetic and indifferent. British commanders were usually disappointed in the number of Tories who flocked to their standards and even more upset by the alacrity with which many of them switched their allegiance when the British Army departed. They found the Tories a demanding, discordant, and puzzling lot; they made no earnest effort to enlist them in British forces until late in the war. By 1781 they had with their armies some 8,000 "provincial rank and file"; perhaps 50,000 in all served the British in some military capacity during the war.

On the frontiers, the British could also expect support from the Indian tribes who almost inevitably drifted into the orbit of whatever power controlled Canada. But support from the Indians was a two-edged sword, for nothing could raise frontier enthusiasm for battle like the threat of an Indian attack. Ruthless Indian raids would often polarize a frontier community that otherwise might have remained sympathetic or at least neutral to the British cause.

Finally, the British had to fight the war with one eye on their ancient enemies in Europe. France, thirsting for revenge for its defeat in the Seven Years' War, stood ready to aid the American cause if for no other purpose than to weaken British power. By virtue of the Bourbon family connections, France could almost certainly carry Spain along in any war with England. France and Spain could at the very least provide badly needed money and supplies to sustain the American effort and force the British to divert their forces from the contest in America. At most, the combined Franco-Spanish fleet might well prove a match for the British Fleet and neutralize that essential control of the seas the British needed to carry on the American war. As the war dragged on, the British found themselves increasingly isolated from the international community.

Of Strategy

The story of the American Revolution can hardly be told in terms of long-term strategy and its success or failure. Neither side ever had any really consistent plan for the conduct of the war. The British, who retained the strategic initiative most of the time, failed to use it to great advantage. They were highly uncertain about their objective; they laid plans from year to year and seldom coordinated them even for a single year. Blame for this uncertain approach falls in almost equal part on the administration in England and the commanders in America. King George III; Lord North, his Principal Minister; and Lord George Germain, Secretary of State for the American Department, were the three British officials mainly responsible for the conduct of the war. If they never provided the timely guidance that might have been expected of them, their inability to do so came about in part because the commanders in the field never furnished accurate enough predictions of what to expect and differed so much among themselves as to the proper course to pursue. In assessing blame in this fashion, one must keep in mind the difficulties of logistics and communications under which the British labored, for these difficulties made it virtually impossible to coordinate plans over great distances or to assemble men and materials in time to pursue one logical and consistent plan.

The American strategy was primarily defensive and consequently had to be shaped largely in terms of countering British moves. Uncertainties as to the supply of both men and materials acted on the American side even more effectively to thwart the development of a consistent plan for winning the war. Yet Washington was never so baffled by the conditions of the war or uncertain of his objective as were the various British commanders. After some early blunders, he soon learned both his own and the enemy's strengths and weaknesses and did his best to exploit them. Though unable to develop a consistent plan, he did try to develop a consistent line of action. He sought to maintain his principal striking force in a central position to block any British advance into the interior; to be neither too bold nor too timid in seeking battle for limited objectives; to avoid the destruction of his army at all costs; and to find some means of concentrating a sufficient force to strike a decisive offensive blow whenever the British overreached themselves. He showed a better appreciation than did the British commanders of the advantages in mobility their Navy gave them. After 1778, when the French entered the war, he clearly saw that the decisive blow he desired could be struck only by a combined effort of the Continental Army and the French Fleet.

> The American strategy was primarily defensive and consequently had to be shaped largely in terms of countering British moves.

The British Offensive in 1776

If the British ever had a single strategic objective in the war, it was the Hudson River–Lake Champlain line. The British believed that by taking and holding this line they would separate New England, considered to be the principal center of the rebellion, from colonies they considered more malleable in the south. Howe proposed to make this the main objective of his campaign in 1776 by landing at New York, securing a base of operations there, and then pushing north. He wanted to concentrate the entire British force in America in New York, but the British government diverted part of it to Canada in early 1776 to repel the American invasion, laying the groundwork for the divided command that was so to plague British operations thereafter.

After the evacuation of Boston, Howe stayed at Halifax from March until June, awaiting the arrival of supplies and reinforcements. While he tarried, the British government ordered another diversion in the south,

George Washington at Princeton
Charles Peale Polk, 1777

GEORGE WASHINGTON AS MILITARY COMMANDER

Although George Washington is universally acknowledged as the "father of his country," it is only fitting to explain his position in history as a great military leader. If one merely scores him based on battlefield wins and losses, he might not be viewed in the first rank of commanders. However, his dynamic leadership qualities, strategic vision, and ability to make the most of tactical mobility make a mere tally of victories and defeats meaningless. Not for nothing did General Howe call him a "wily old fox."

Washington took the rawest of American raw material and made soldiers out of them. He then kept them together as an army in the field despite defeats and deprivations and often turned on the pursuing British forces like a fox and dealt them sharp blows before escaping again. He learned from his mistakes, maintained a force in being, bottled up the British in coastal enclaves, and finally isolated and forced the surrender of a large British Army. He was a great military commander.

aimed at encouraging the numerous loyalists who, according to the royal governors watching from their havens on board British warships, were waiting only for the appearance of a British force to rise and overthrow rebel rule. Unfortunately for the British, a naval squadron and army expedition sent from Ireland under Sir Peter Parker was delayed and did not arrive off the American coast until late in May. By this time all hopes of effective cooperation with the Tories had been dashed. Loyalist contingents had been completely defeated and dispersed in Virginia, North Carolina, and South Carolina.

Parker joined Lt. Gen. Henry Clinton, sent south by Howe, off the North Carolina coast. Undeterred by the local setbacks, they determined to attack Charleston, the largest city in the south. There, South Carolina militia and newly raised continentals from the Carolinas and Virginia had prepared and manned defenses under the guidance of Maj. Gen. Charles Lee, whom Washington had dispatched south to assist them. The South Carolinians, contrary to Lee's advice, centered their defenses in Fort Moultrie, a palmetto log fort constructed on Sullivan's Island, commanding the approach to the harbor. It was an unwise decision, somewhat comparable to that at Bunker Hill, but fortunately for the defenders the British had to mount an uncoordinated attack in haste. Clinton's troops landed on nearby Long Island, but on the day the Navy attacked, June 28, the water proved too deep for them to wade across to Sullivan's Island as expected. The British Army consequently sat idly by while the gunners in Fort Moultrie devastated the British warships. Sir Peter suffered the ultimate indignity when his pants were set afire.

The battered British Fleet hastily embarked the British soldiers and sailed north to join Howe at New York, for it was already behind schedule. For three years following the fiasco at Charleston the British were to leave the south unmolested. Overconfident Americans decided they did not need to send any large regular forces to the south, creating a weakness that would come back to haunt them. The latent loyalists in the south, whatever their potential strength in 1775, never recovered from the devastating blows they suffered while expecting British help. Loyalist refugees in London and New York, however, continued to insist that large numbers of loyal subjects of the King were still waiting for the British in the south, ready to rise again if only British troops returned.

Howe was meanwhile beset by other delays in the arrival of transports from England, and his attack did not get under way until late August, leaving insufficient time before the advent of winter to carry through the planned advance along the Hudson River–Lake Champlain line. He therefore started his invasion of New York with only the limited objective of gaining a foothold for the campaign the following year.

The British commander had, when his force was all assembled, an army of about 32,000 men, supported by a powerful fleet under the command of his brother, Admiral Richard Howe. To oppose him, Washington had brought most of his army down from Boston; Congress exerted its utmost efforts to reinforce him by raising Continental regiments in the surrounding states and issuing a general call for the militia. Few of Washington's roughly 19,000 troops could match Howe's forces in training, nor did his senior commanders have much in the way of experience in maneuvering large forces in the open.

Washington and Congress made the same decision the South Carolinians had made at Charleston and Maj. Gen. Sir Guy Carleton had made in Canada in 1775—to defend their territory in the most forward positions—and they paid the price for their mistake. The geography of the area gave the side possessing naval supremacy an almost insuperable advantage. The city of New York stood on Manhattan Island, surrounded by the Hudson, Harlem, and East Rivers. (*Map 5*) There was only one connecting link with the mainland, Kingsbridge across the Harlem River at the northern tip of Manhattan. Across the East River on Long Island, Brooklyn Heights stood in a position dominating the southern tip of Manhattan. With the naval forces at their disposal, the Howes could land troops on either Long Island or Manhattan proper and send warships a considerable distance up either the East or the Hudson River.

Washington decided he must defend Brooklyn Heights on Long Island if he was to defend Manhattan. He therefore divided his army between the two places—a violation of the principle of mass and the first step toward disaster. For all practical purposes, command on Long Island was also divided. Maj. Gen. Nathanael Greene, to whom Washington first entrusted the command, came down with malaria and was

Few of Washington's roughly 19,000 troops could match Howe's forces in training, nor did his senior commanders have much in the way of experience in maneuvering large forces in the open.

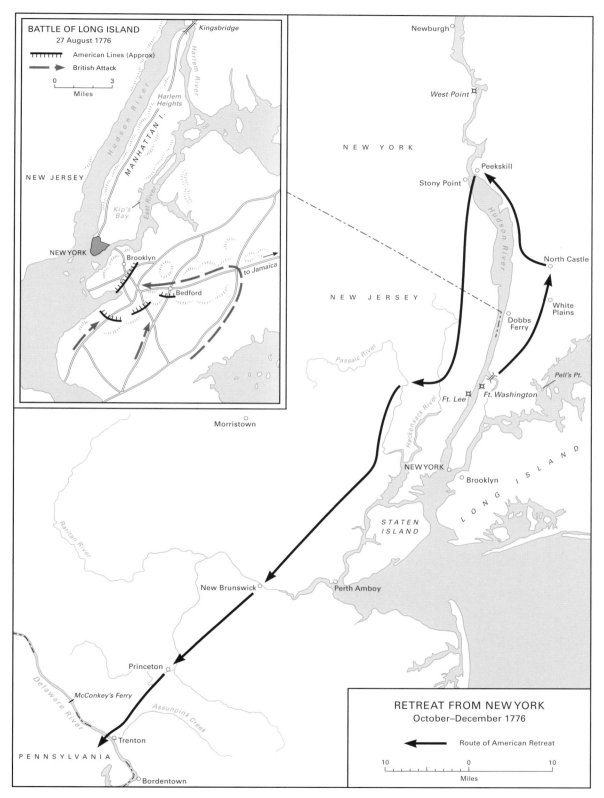

BATTLE OF LONG ISLAND
27 August 1776

⊥⊥⊥⊥⊥ American Lines (Approx)

➤ British Attack

0   3
Miles

Kingsbridge

Harlem River

Hudson River

Harlem Heights

MANHATTAN I.

East River

NEW JERSEY

Kip's Bay

NEW YORK

Brooklyn

Bedford

to Jamaica

Newburgh

West Point

NEW YORK

Peekskill

Stony Point

North Castle

Hudson River

White Plains

NEW JERSEY

Dobbs Ferry

Pell's Pt.

Ft. Lee

Ft. Washington

Passaic River

Hackensack River

Morristown

NEW YORK

Brooklyn

STATEN ISLAND

LONG ISLAND

Raritan River

New Brunswick

Perth Amboy

Princeton

McConkey's Ferry

Delaware River

Assunpink Creek

Trenton

PENNSYLVANIA

Bordentown

RETREAT FROM NEW YORK
October–December 1776

⟵ Route of American Retreat

10   0   10
Miles

Map 5

replaced by Maj. Gen. John Sullivan. Not completely satisfied with this arrangement, at the last moment Washington placed Maj. Gen. Israel Putnam over Sullivan; but Putnam hardly had time to become acquainted with the situation before the British struck. The forces on Long Island, numbering about 10,000, were disposed in fortifications on Brooklyn Heights and in forward positions in back of a line of thickly wooded hills that ran across the southern end of the island. Sullivan was in command on the left of the American forward line, Brig. Gen. William Alexander on the right. Four roads ran through the hills toward the American positions. (*See Inset, Map 5.*) Unfortunately Sullivan, in violation of the principle of security, left the Jamaica-Bedford road virtually unguarded.

Howe consequently was able to teach the Americans lessons in maneuver and surprise. On August 22 he landed a force of 20,000 on the southwestern tip of Long Island and, in a surprise attack up the Jamaica-Bedford road against the American left flank, crumpled the entire American position. Alexander's valiant fight on the right went for naught as some of the more inexperienced American units along the line fled in terror before the British and Hessian bayonets, falling back to the fortifications on Brooklyn Heights. Had Howe pushed his advantage immediately, he might have carried the heights and destroyed half of the American Army then and there. Instead, perhaps rendered cautious by his repulse the previous year at Bunker Hill, he halted at nightfall and began to dig trenches, signaling an intent to take the heights by "regular approaches" in traditional eighteenth century fashion. Washington managed to evacuate his forces across the East River on the night of August 29. According to one theory, wind and weather stopped the British warships from entering the river to prevent the escape; according to another, the Americans had placed impediments in the river that effectively barred their entry. In any case, it was a narrow escape, made possible in large measure by the skill, bravery, and perseverance of Col. John Glover's Marblehead Regiment, infantrymen who had been recruited from Massachusetts fishing villages, who manned the boats.

Washington had two weeks to prepare his defenses on Manhattan before Howe struck again, landing a force at Kip's Bay above the city of New York (now about 34th Street) on September 15 under the cover of a devastating naval bombardment. Raw Connecticut militia posted behind shallow trenches at this point broke and ran "as if the Devil was in them," defying even the efforts of a raging Washington to halt them. Howe once again had an opportunity to split the American Army in two and destroy half, but again he delayed midway across the island to wait until his entire force had landed. General Putnam was able to bring the troops stationed in the city up the west side of Manhattan to join their compatriots in new fortifications on Harlem Heights. There, the Americans held out for another month and even won a morale-enhancing skirmish; but this position was vulnerable to being outflanked.

In mid-October Howe landed again in Washington's rear at Pell's Point. The American commander then finally evacuated the Manhattan trap via Kingsbridge and took up a new position at White Plains. He left a garrison behind to hold Forts Washington and Lee, on opposite sides of the Hudson, in an attempt to block British ships from going up the river. Howe launched a probing attack on the American position at White Plains and was repulsed; but Washington, sensing his inability to meet the British in battle on equal terms, moved away to the north toward the Hudson highlands. Uncertain of Howe's next move, Washington divided his forces into three elements. Lee with one contingent remained on the east side of the Hudson to counter any advance into Connecticut. Washington crossed over to the west bank with a comparable force to counter any attempt by Howe to invade New Jersey. Maj. Gen. William Heath occupied the forts in the Highlands themselves to provide the lines of communication between the two maneuver forces and to prevent a British advance up the river. On November 16 Howe turned against Fort Washington and with the support of British warships on the Hudson stormed it successfully, capturing 3,000 American troops and large quantities of valuable munitions. Greene then hastily evacuated Fort Lee; by the end of November Washington, with mere remnants of his army, was in full retreat across New Jersey with Lord Charles Cornwallis, detached by Howe, in hot pursuit.

While Washington was suffering these disastrous defeats, the army that had been gathered was slowly melting away. Militia left by whole companies when their periods of service expired. Casualties and disease took their toll among the continentals. By early December Washington had crossed the Delaware River into Pennsylvania, where his small force began to regroup and draw supplies from Philadelphia's extensive network of depots. Other regiments, including forces released by the British retreat to Canada, slowly joined him while other regiments from Lee's force swung through the Highlands and started south toward Washington (without their general, who was captured in a tavern by a British cavalry raid). Washington's situation was precarious, but he determined to go on the offensive as soon as possible and began planning a lightning descent on West Jersey toward the end of December.

Neither the unreliability of the militia nor the short period of enlistment fully explained the debacle that had befallen the Continental Army. Washington's generalship also came under criticism. In contrast to the defeat of British invasion forces at Charleston and Lake Champlain, where militia seemed to be more effective than Continental regulars, the main defenses of the important city of New York crumpled at the first blow. Many faulted the Commander in Chief's decision to hold Fort Washington. General Lee, the ex–British colonel, ordered by Washington to bring his forces down from New York to join him behind the Delaware, delayed, believing that he might himself salvage the American cause by making incursions into New Jersey. He wrote Horatio Gates, "entre nous [between us], a certain great man is most damnably deficient."

There was only one bright spot in the picture in the autumn of 1776. While Howe was routing Washington around New York City, other British forces under Carleton were attempting to follow up the advantage they had gained in repulsing the attack on Canada earlier in the year. Carleton rather leisurely built a flotilla of boats to carry British forces down Lake Champlain and Lake George, intending at least to reduce the fort at Ticonderoga before winter. Benedict Arnold countered by throwing together a much weaker flotilla of American boats to contest the British passage. Arnold lost this naval action on

> While Washington was suffering these disastrous defeats, the army that had been gathered was slowly melting away.

the lakes, but he so delayed Carleton's advance that the British commander reached Ticonderoga too late in the year to consider undertaking a siege. He returned his army to winter quarters in Canada, leaving the British with no advance base from which to launch the next year's campaign. Once again Arnold had shown himself one of the most dynamic and courageous of the patriot commanders.

Although the consequences were to be far reaching, this limited victory did little to dispel the gloom that fell on the patriots after Washington's defeats in New York. The British, aware that Continental enlistments expired at the end of the year, had high hopes that the American Army would simply fade away and the rebellion would collapse. Howe halted Cornwallis' pursuit of Washington and sent Clinton with a detachment of troops under naval escort to seize Newport, Rhode Island. He then dispersed his troops into winter quarters, establishing a line of posts in New Jersey at Perth Amboy, New Brunswick, Princeton, Trenton, and Bordentown and retiring himself to New York. Howe had gained the object of the 1776 campaign, a strong foothold, and possibly, as he thought at the time, a great deal more.

Trenton and Princeton

While Howe rested comfortably in New York, he dispatched Clinton to capture Newport, Rhode Island, as a much-desired winter anchorage for the Royal Navy. Washington took advantage of this distraction. By the last week of December 1776, Washington had built up a small, but competent striking force of veteran regiments about 7,000 strong. If he was to use this force, he would have to do so before the enlistments expired on December 31. With great boldness, Washington formulated a plan to strike enemy garrisons along the Delaware River early on the twenty-sixth of December, when the troops might be expected to have relaxed their guard for holiday revelry. The plan was for American forces to cross the river simultaneously and conduct raids on the outposts at Trenton and Bordentown, each held by a reinforced brigade of Hessian soldiers. A Continental force of around 2,400 men under Washington's personal command was to cross the Delaware at McConkey's Ferry above Trenton and then proceed in two columns by different routes, converging on the opposite ends of the main street of Trenton in the early morning of December 26. (*See Map 6.*) A second force, mainly militia under Col. John Cadwalader, was to cross below near Bordentown to attack the Hessian garrison there. A third force, also militia, under Brig. Gen. James Ewing, was to cross directly opposite Trenton to block the Hessian route of escape across Assunpink Creek.

Christmas night was cold, windy, and snowy; and the Delaware River was filled with blocks of ice. These adverse conditions prevented Cadwalader and Ewing from fulfilling their parts of the plan. Driven on by Washington's indomitable will, the main force did cross as planned; the two columns, commanded respectively by Greene and Sullivan, converged on Trenton at eight o'clock in the morning of December 26, taking the Hessians completely by surprise. A New England private noted in his diary for that day: "This morning at 4 a clock we set off with our Field pieces and Marched 8 miles to Trenton where we ware

The British . . . had high hopes that the American Army would simply fade away and the rebellion would collapse.

Surrender of Hessian Troops to General Washington after the Battle of Trenton, December 1776, *Artist Unknown, 1850*

attacked by a Number of Hushing and we Toock 1000 of them besides killed some. Then we marched back and got to the River at Night and got over all the Hushing." This rather undramatic description of a very dramatic event was not far wrong, except in attributing the attack to the "Hushings." The Hessians surrendered after a fight lasting only an hour and a half. Forty were killed, and the prisoner count was 918. Only 400 escaped to Bordentown, only because Ewing was not in place to block their escape. The Americans lost only 2 dead and 2 wounded, among the wounded being future President James Monroe.

Encouraged by this success, Washington determined to make another foray. By an impassioned appeal to the patriotism of the men, supplemented by an offer of a $10 bounty in hard money, he persuaded at least part of his old army to remain for six more weeks. With a force of around 5,000 Washington again crossed the Delaware on the night of December 30–31. By this time Cornwallis had hastily gathered together the scattered British garrisons in New Jersey and took up a position confronting Washington at Trenton on January 2, 1777. Convinced that he had the Americans in a trap, he put off battle until the next day because of the exhausted state of his troops. In the night Washington slipped away, leaving campfires burning brightly to deceive

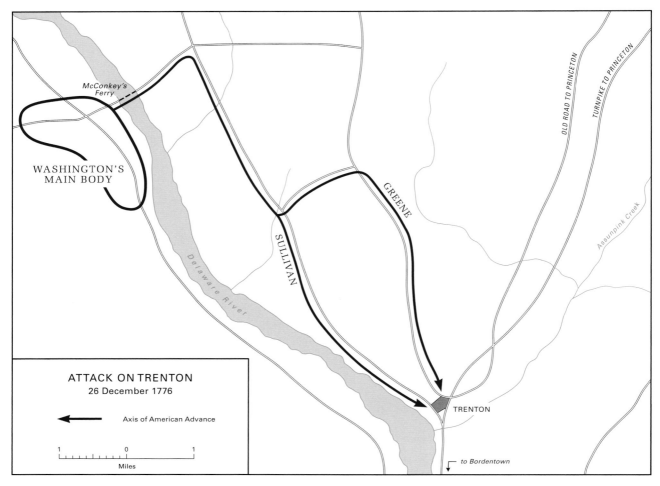

McConkey's
Ferry

WASHINGTON'S
MAIN BODY

OLD ROAD TO PRINCETON

TURNPIKE TO PRINCETON

GREENE

SULLIVAN

Delaware River

Assunpink Creek

TRENTON

to Bordentown

ATTACK ON TRENTON
26 December 1776

 Axis of American Advance

1   0   1
Miles

Map 6

the British. The next morning he struck another surprise blow at Princeton, inflicting heavy losses on three British regiments just leaving the town to join Cornwallis. Washington then went into winter quarters in the hills around Morristown, New Jersey. Cornwallis did not pursue. The British had had enough of winter warfare, and Howe drew in his outposts in New Jersey to New Brunswick and Perth Amboy.

Trenton and Princeton not only offset the worst effects of the disastrous defeats in New York but also restored Washington's prestige as a commander with friend and foe alike. In the execution of the two strokes east of the Delaware, Washington had applied the principles of offensive, surprise, and maneuver with great success and finally achieved stature as a military commander. If these victories did not assure him that he could recruit such an army as Congress had voted, they did at least guarantee that he would be able to field a force the following year. Sir William Howe found that, despite his smashing rout of the Americans in New York, he was left with little more than that city, a foothold in New Jersey, and the port of Newport in Rhode Island. The rebellion was far from being crushed.

DISCUSSION QUESTIONS

1. Discuss the various differences between the Massachusetts Minutemen and the British troops they fired on during the battles of Lexington and Concord.

2. What were the strengths and weaknesses of the British military system and the new American Army in the opening days of the Revolution? What challenges did each side face in its attempts to prosecute its military operations?

3. Given the state of the American Army in 1776, how do you think Washington should have conducted operations in the New York City area? What should Howe have done?

4. Discuss the element of surprise in Washington's attacks at Trenton and Princeton. Did he make good use of this principle? What were the dangers in relying on surprise?

5. What role did Congress play in setting military policy and determining military operations in the opening days of the Revolution? Why was this important?

6. Why was it important to create the Continental Army in 1775 rather than relying upon the existing state militias to prosecute the war?

RECOMMENDED READINGS

Flexner, James T. *George Washington in the American Revolution, 1775–1783.* Boston: Little, Brown, 1968.

Higginbotham, Don. *The War of American Independence: Military Attitudes, Policies, and Practices.* Boston: Northeastern University Press, 1983.

Mackesy, Piers. *The War for America, 1775–1783.* Lincoln: University of Nebraska Press, 1992.

Middlekauff, Robert. *The Glorious Cause: The American Revolution, 1763–1789.* New York: Oxford University Press, 1982.

Royster, Charles W. *A Revolutionary People at War: The Continental Army and American Character, 1775–1783.* New York: Norton, 1981.

Tourtellot, Arthur B. *William Diamond's Drum: The Beginning of the War of the American Revolution.* Garden City, N.Y.: Doubleday, 1959.

Ward, Christopher. *The War of the Revolution,* ed. John R. Alden, 2 vols. New York: Macmillan, 1952, vol. 1.

Other Readings

Alden, John R. *General Gage in America: Being Principally a History of His Role in the American Revolution.* New York: Greenwood Press, 1969.

Brown, Wallace. *The Good Americans: The Loyalists in the American Revolution.* New York: William Morrow, 1969.

Conway, Stephen. *The War of American Independence, 1775–1783.* New York: Edward Arnold, 1995.

Cress, Lawrence D. *Citizen in Arms: The Army and the Militia in American Society to the War of 1812.* Chapel Hill: University of North Carolina Press, 1982.

French, Allen. *The First Year of the American Revolution*. New York: Octagon Books, 1968.

Gross, Robert A. *The Minutemen and Their World*. New York: Hill & Wang, 1976.

Gruber, Ira D. *The Howe Brothers and the American Revolution*. New York: Atheneum, 1972.

Higginbotham, Don, ed. *Reconsiderations on the Revolutionary War: Selected Essays*. Westport, Conn.: Greenwood Press, 1978.

Hoffman, Ronald, and Peter J. Albert, eds. *Arms and Independence: The Military Character of the American Revolution*. Charlottesville: University Press of Virginia, 1984.

Palmer, Dave R. *The Way of the Fox: American Strategy in the War for America, 1775–1783*. Westport, Conn.: Greenwood Press, 1975.

Wright, Robert K., Jr. *The Continental Army*. Washington, D.C.: U.S. Army Center of Military History, 1983.

4

THE WINNING OF INDEPENDENCE, 1777–1783

he year 1777 was perhaps the most critical for the British. The issue, not necessarily understood clearly in London or America at the time, was whether the British could score such success in putting down the American revolt that the French would not dare enter the war openly to aid the American rebels. Yet it was in this critical year that British plans were most confused and British operations most disjointed. The British campaign of 1777 therefore provides one of the most striking object lessons in American military history of the dangers of divided command.

The Campaign of 1777

With secure bases at New York and Newport, Sir William Howe had a chance to get the early start in 1777 that had been denied him the previous year. His first plan, advanced on November 30, 1776, was probably the most comprehensive put forward by any British commander during the war. He proposed to maintain a small force of about 8,000 to contain Washington in New Jersey and 7,000 to garrison New York, while sending one column of 10,000 from Newport into New England and another column of 10,000 from New York up the Hudson to form a junction with a British force moving down from Canada. On the assumption that these moves would be successful by autumn, he would next capture Philadelphia, the rebel capital, then make the southern provinces the "objects of the winter." For this plan, Howe requested 35,000 men, 15,000 more effective troops than he had remaining at the end of the 1776 campaign. Lord George Germain, the Secretary of State responsible for strategic planning for the American theater, could promise Howe only 8,000 replacements. Even before receiving this news, but evidently influenced by Trenton and Princeton, Howe refined his plan and proposed to devote his main effort in 1777 to taking Philadelphia. On March 3, 1777, Germain informed Howe that the Philadelphia plan was approved but that there might be only 5,500 reinforcements. At the same time Germain and the king urged a "warm diversion" against New England.

Meanwhile, Sir John Burgoyne, who had succeeded in obtaining the separate military command in Canada, submitted his plan for an advance south to "a junction with Howe." Germain and the king also approved this plan on March 29, though they had earlier approved of Howe's intention to go to Philadelphia. Because of the lag in communicating across the Atlantic, Germain and other senior planners in London viewed themselves merely as coordinators and providers of resources, not as operational commanders. Operational decisions, they felt, should be made by the commanders on the scene. They seem to have expected that Burgoyne and Howe would work together without direction from London. Specifically, they believed that Howe would be able to form his junction with Burgoyne by the warm diversion or that he would take Philadelphia quickly and then turn north to aid Burgoyne. In any case, they felt sure that Howe's drive south would draw Washington and most American troops away from Burgoyne. Once Germain approved the two separate plans, difficulties in communicating in a timely manner left Howe and Burgoyne to go their separate ways.

Howe's Philadelphia plan left only enough force in New York under General Sir Henry Clinton for what the latter would call "a damn'd starved offensive," but Clinton's orders called upon him only to assist Burgoyne's drive. His first priority remained the safety and security of New York City and its outposts. There is no question that Burgoyne knew before he left England for Canada that Howe was going to Philadelphia, but ambitious "Gentleman Johnny" was determined to make a reputation in the American war. Never one to doubt his own abilities and having enjoyed swift victory by driving the Americans from the Ticonderoga complex with minimal effort, Burgoyne quickly convinced himself that he could succeed alone. Even when he learned certainly on August 3, 1777, that he could not expect Howe's cooperation, he persisted in his design. As Howe thought Pennsylvania was filled with loyalists, Burgoyne cherished the illusion that legions of Tories in upstate New York and western New England were simply awaiting the appearance of the king's troops to rally to the colors.

Again in 1777 the late arrival of Howe's reinforcements and supply ships gave General George Washington time that he sorely needed. Men to form the new Continental Army came in slowly, and not until June did the Americans have a force of 8,000. On the northern line, the defenses were even more thinly manned. Supplies for troops in the field were also short, but the arrival of the first three ships bearing secret aid from France vastly improved the situation. They were evidence of the covert support of the French government; a mission Congress sent to France was meanwhile working diligently to enlist open aid and to embroil France in a war with England. The French Foreign Minister, Charles Gravier, the Comte de Vergennes, had already decided to take that risk when and if the American rebels demonstrated their serious purpose and ability to fulfill it by some signal victory in the field.

With the first foreign material aid in 1777, the influx of foreign officers into the American Army began. These officers were a mixed

Again in 1777 the late arrival of Howe's reinforcements and supply ships gave General George Washington time that he sorely needed.

blessing. Most were adventurers in search of fortune or of reputation with little aptitude for adjusting themselves to American conditions. Few were willing to accept any but the highest ranks. Nevertheless, many brought with them professional military knowledge and competence the Continental Army sorely lacked. When the misfits were culled out, the knowledge and competence were used to considerable advantage. Louis DuPortail, a Frenchman, and Thaddeus Kosciuszko, a Pole, did much to advance the art of engineering in the Continental Army. Casimir Pulaski, another Pole, organized its first genuine cavalry contingent. Johann de Kalb and Friedrich Wilhelm von Steuben, both Germans, and Maj. Gen. Gilbert du Montier, the Marquis de Lafayette, an influential French nobleman who financed his own way, were all to make valuable contributions as trainers and leaders. But as the 1777 campaign began, these foreign volunteers had not yet had time to make much of an impact on the Continental Army.

Friedrich Wilhelm von Steuben
Charles Willson Peale, 1782

In the spring of 1777 Washington's army occupied high ground at Middlebrook, New Jersey, in a position either to bar Howe's overland route to Philadelphia or to move rapidly up the Hudson to oppose any northward advance. Washington confidently expected Howe to move north to form a junction with Burgoyne but decided he himself must stay in front of the main British Army wherever it went. Following the principle of economy of force, he disposed a small part of his army under Maj. Gen. Israel Putnam in fortifications guarding the approaches up the Hudson, and at a critical moment detached a small force to aid Maj. Gen. Philip Schuyler against Burgoyne. The bulk of his army he kept in front of Howe in an effort to defend Philadelphia. Forts were built along the Delaware River, and other steps were taken to block the approach to the Continental capital by sea.

In the effort to defend Philadelphia, Washington again failed but hardly so ignominiously as he had the year before in New York. With American forts and a galley squadron blocking a direct advance up the Delaware River, in August Howe put most of his army on board ship and sailed down the coast and up the Chesapeake Bay to Head of Elk (now Elkton) in Maryland, putting himself even farther away from Burgoyne. (*See Map 7.*) Surprised by Howe's movement, Washington did not oppose the landing but rapidly shifted his own force south and took up a position at Chad's Ford on Brandywine Creek, blocking the approach to Philadelphia.

There, on September 11, 1777, Howe executed a flanking movement reminiscent of his tactics on Long Island the previous year. He sent Lt. Gen. Wilhelm van Knyphausen's largely Hessian column directly against the American position at Chad's Ford to fix the American attention on that part of the battlefield. During the predawn darkness Howe and Lord Charles Cornwallis took the larger part of the British army north by back roads and crossed the Brandywine at unguarded lesser fords miles upstream, hoping to take Washington from the flank and rear.

Confusing reports caused by inadequate reconnaissance befuddled Maj. Gen. John Sullivan, who commanded the American forces on that flank. Washington himself realized what was happening only at the eleventh hour. He immediately ordered Sullivan to lay a trap, set up a reverse slope ambush on high ground, and shifted reinforcements

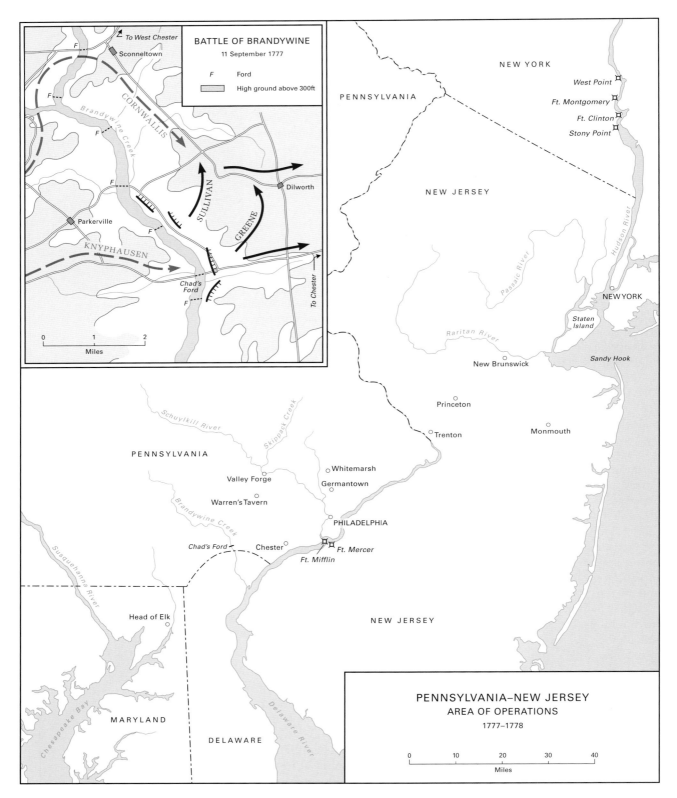

BATTLE OF BRANDYWINE
11 September 1777

F   Ford

High ground above 300ft

To West Chester

Sconneltown

CORNWALLIS

Brandywine Creek

Parkerville

KNYPHAUSEN

SULLIVAN

GREENE

Dilworth

Chad's Ford

To Chester

0   1   2
Miles

NEW YORK

PENNSYLVANIA

West Point
Ft. Montgomery
Ft. Clinton
Stony Point

NEW JERSEY

Hudson River

Passaic River

NEW YORK

Staten Island

Raritan River

Sandy Hook

New Brunswick

Princeton

Monmouth

Trenton

Schuylkill River

Skippack Creek

PENNSYLVANIA

Whitemarsh

Valley Forge

Germantown

Warren's Tavern

Brandywine Creek

PHILADELPHIA

Chad's Ford

Chester

Ft. Mercer

Ft. Mifflin

Susquehanna River

Head of Elk

NEW JERSEY

Chesapeake Bay

Delaware River

MARYLAND

DELAWARE

PENNSYLVANIA–NEW JERSEY
AREA OF OPERATIONS
1777–1778

0   10   20   30   40
Miles

Map 7

NATHANAEL GREENE (1742–1786)

A Quaker with no prior military experience, Nathanael Greene rose through the ranks of the Continental Army and became one of George Washington's most trusted generals. In 1777 Greene became the Continental Army's Quartermaster, though he longed for a battlefield command. That opportunity came in August 1780, when General Gates, the hero of Saratoga, was resoundingly defeated by the British at Camden in South Carolina. As commander of the southern campaign of 1780–1782, Greene brilliantly combined conventional and unconventional fighting. His strategy forced the decisive battle of Yorktown, which broke the back of British control in the southern colonies.

Nathanael Greene
Charles Willson Peale, 1783

under Maj. Gen. Nathanael Greene from positions facing Knyphausen to extend Sullivan's line. Cornwallis and Howe moved slowly, preventing the British plan from working as intended; ironically, that very slowness worked to their advantage. Because the Americans lacked iron discipline, they kept creeping up to the crest of their ridge to look for the British. Alert scouts, mostly Hessian jaegers (woodsmen armed with rifles), noted the movement; and Howe avoided walking into the trap.

What followed was one of the most intense battles of the war. In a series of five separate attacks, the British drove Sullivan off the high ground in some confusion. General Greene with two brigades of Virginians allowed Sullivan's men to fall back through their lines and then carried out a valiant rear-guard action lasting until dark. Once he could hear the sounds of the fighting, Knyphausen drove across the ford and struck Brig. Gen. Anthony Wayne's defenses that had been weakened by the transfers, forcing the Americans to fall back. Darkness and the heavy, bloody fighting left Howe's men too exhausted to pursue, and the Continental Army retired in good order to Chester. However, the way to Philadelphia was now left open to Howe.

Howe followed his victory at the Brandywine with a series of maneuvers comparable to those he had executed in New York and entered Philadelphia with a minimum of fighting on September 26. A combined attack of British Army and Navy forces shortly afterward reduced the forts on the Delaware and opened the river as a British supply line.

On entering Philadelphia, Howe dispersed his forces, stationing 9,000 men at Germantown, north of the city; 3,000 in New Jersey; and the rest in Philadelphia. As Howe had repeated his performance in New York, Washington sought to repeat Trenton by a surprise attack on Germantown. The plan was much like that he used at Trenton but involved far more complicated movements by much larger bodies of troops. Four columns (two assault forces of continentals under Sullivan and Greene and two flank security forces of militia), moving at night over different roads, were to converge simultaneously on Germantown at dawn on October 4. (*See Map 8.*) The plan violated the principle of simplicity, for such a maneuver would have been difficult even for well-trained

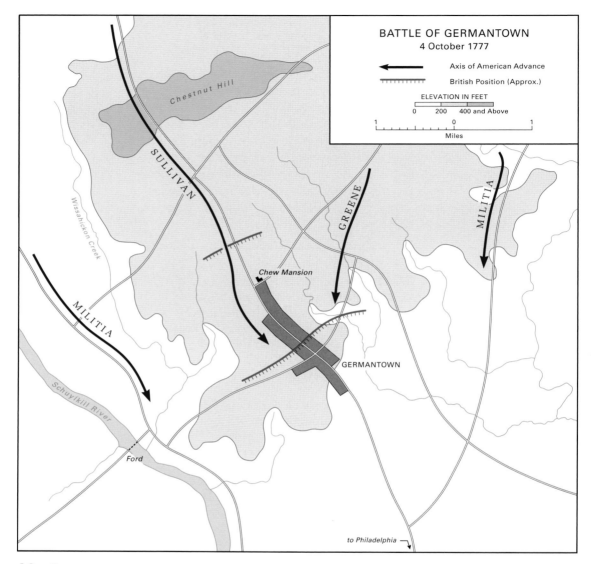

BATTLE OF GERMANTOWN
4 October 1777

Axis of American Advance

British Position (Approx.)

ELEVATION IN FEET

0   200   400 and Above

1   0   1
Miles

Map 8

professionals to execute. The two columns of continentals arrived at different times and fired on each other in an early morning fog. Despite losing the element of surprise, the Americans drove forward and smashed two elite battalions of British light infantry.

Initial success rapidly turned to disappointment. Part of a British regiment took cover in Cliveden, the Chew family mansion, and opened a galling fire on Americans attempting to move up or join the advance. Instead of isolating and bypassing this annoyance, the inexperienced American generals held up a large portion of the Maryland Division while they argued whether they could leave a "fortress" in their rear. The British, though surprised, had better discipline and cohesion and were able to re-form and send fresh troops into the fray. Once Washington realized that he had lost the chance for a decisive victory, he wisely chose to avoid risking his army and broke contact. The Americans retreated about 8:00 a.m., leaving Howe's troops in command of the field.

After Germantown Howe once again concentrated his army and moved to confront Washington at Whitemarsh, hoping to lure the Virginian into a rash attack. The ploy failed, so he withdrew to winter quarters in Philadelphia without giving battle. Washington chose the site for his own winter quarters at a place called Valley Forge, twenty miles northwest of the city. Howe had gained his objective, but it proved of no lasting value to him. Congress fled west to York, Pennsylvania. No swarms of loyalists rallied to the British standards. And Howe had left Burgoyne to lose a whole British army in the north.

Burgoyne set out from Canada in June, his object to reach Albany by fall. (*See Map 9.*) His force was divided into two parts. The first and largest part (7,200 British and Hessian regulars and 650 Tories, Canadians, and Indians under his personal command) was to take the route down Lake Champlain to Ticonderoga and thence via Lake George to the Hudson. The second (700 regulars and 1,000 Tories and Indians under Col. Barry St. Leger) was to move via Lake Ontario to Oswego and thence down the Mohawk Valley to join Burgoyne before Albany. In his preparations, Burgoyne evidently forgot the lesson the British had learned in the French and Indian War: In the wilderness, troops had to be prepared to travel light and fight like Indians. He carried 138 pieces of artillery and a heavy load of officers' personal baggage. Numerous ladies of high and low estate accompanied the expedition. When he started down the lakes, Burgoyne did not have enough horses and wagons to transport his artillery and baggage once he had to leave the water and move overland.

At first Burgoyne's American opposition was very weak: only about 2,500 continentals at Ticonderoga and about 450 at old Fort Stanwix, the sole American bulwark in the Mohawk Valley. Dissension among the Americans was rife; the New Englanders refused to support Schuyler, the aristocratic New Yorker who commanded the Northern Army, and openly intrigued to replace him with their own favorite, Maj. Gen. Horatio Gates. Ticonderoga fell to Burgoyne on June 27 all too easily. The American forces dispersed, and Burgoyne pursued the remnants down to Skenesborough. Once that far along, he decided to continue overland to the Hudson instead of returning to Ticonderoga to float his force down Lake George, though much of his impedimenta still had to be carried by boat down the lake.

The overland line of advance was already a nightmare, running along wilderness trails, through marshes, and across wide ravines and creeks swollen by abnormally heavy rains. Schuyler, who had wrestled with supply problems during the French and Indian Wars on this very ground, adopted the tactic of making it even worse by destroying bridges, felling trees into Burgoyne's path, and digging trenches to let the waters of swamps onto drier ground. The British were able to move at a rate of little more than a mile a day and took until July 29 to reach Fort Edward on the Hudson. By that time Burgoyne was desperately short of horses, wagons, and oxen. Yet Schuyler, with an unstable force of 4,500 men discouraged by continual retreats, was in no position to give battle.

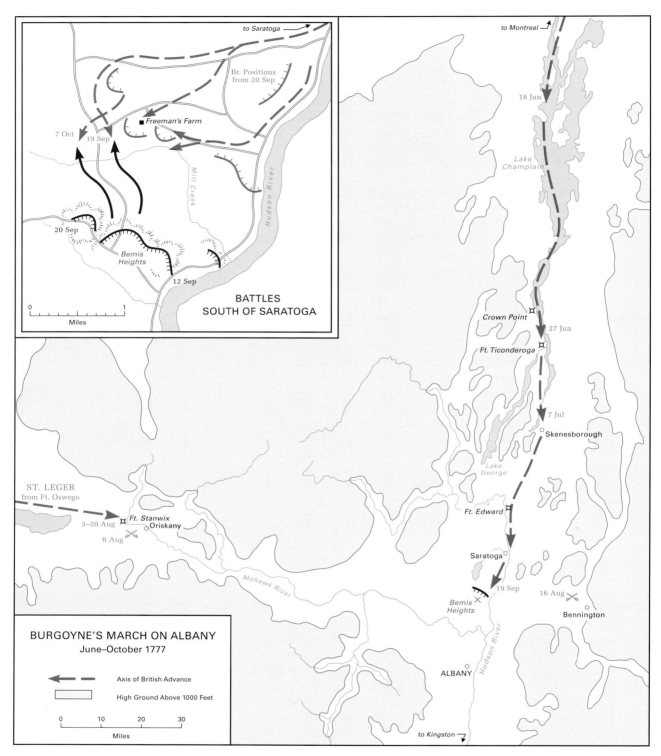

BATTLES
SOUTH OF SARATOGA

to Saratoga

Br. Positions
from 20 Sep

Freeman's Farm

7 Oct   19 Sep

20 Sep

12 Sep

Bemis
Heights

Mill Creek

Hudson River

0   1
Miles

to Montreal

18 Jun

Lake
Champlain

Crown Point

27 Jun

Ft. Ticonderoga

7 Jul

Skenesborough

Lake
George

Ft. Edward

Saratoga

19 Sep

16 Aug

Bemis
Heights

Bennington

ST. LEGER
from Ft. Oswego

3–20 Aug   Ft. Stanwix
Oriskany
6 Aug

Mohawk River

ALBANY

Hudson River

to Kingston

BURGOYNE'S MARCH ON ALBANY
June–October 1777

    Axis of British Advance

High Ground Above 1000 Feet

0   10   20   30
Miles

Map 9

Washington did what he could to strengthen the Northern Army at this juncture. He first dispatched Maj. Gen. Benedict Arnold, his most aggressive field commander, and Maj. Gen. Benjamin Lincoln, a Massachusetts man noted for his influence with the New England militia. On August 16 he detached Col. Daniel Morgan with 500 riflemen from the main army in Pennsylvania and ordered them along with 750 men from Putnam's force in the New York highlands to join Schuyler. The riflemen were calculated to furnish an antidote for Burgoyne's Indians who despite his efforts to restrain them were terrorizing the countryside.

It was the rising militia, rather than Washington, that was to provide the Northern Army with the most numerous reinforcements. Nothing worked more to produce this result than Burgoyne's employment of Indians. The murder and scalping of a white woman, Jane McCrea, dramatized the Indian threat as nothing else probably could have. New England militiamen now began to rally to the cause, though they still refused to cooperate with Schuyler. New Hampshire commissioned John Stark, a colonel in the Continental Army and a veteran of Bunker Hill and Trenton, as a brigadier general in the state service (a rank Congress had denied him), and Stark quickly assembled 2,000 men. Refusing Schuyler's request that he join the main army, Stark took up a position at Bennington in southern Vermont to guard the New England frontier. On August 11 Burgoyne detached a force of 650 men under Hessian Col. Friedrich Baum to forage for cattle, horses, and transport in the very area Stark was occupying. At Bennington on August 16, Stark annihilated Baum's force and nearly did the same to a second column of reinforcements Burgoyne sent to rescue Baum. Burgoyne not only failed to secure his much-needed supplies and transport but also lost about a tenth of his command.

Meanwhile, St. Leger with his Tories and Indians had appeared before Fort Stanwix on August 2. The garrison, fearing massacre by the Indians, was determined to hold out to the bitter end. On August 4, the Tryon County militia under Brig. Gen. Nicholas Herkimer set out to relieve the fort but was ambushed by the Indians in a wooded ravine near Oriskany. The militia, under the direction of a mortally wounded Herkimer, took cover in the woods and fought a bloody, ferocious, close-quarters battle all afternoon in a summer thunderstorm. Both sides suffered heavy losses; and though the militia was unable to relieve Stanwix, the losses discouraged St. Leger's Indians, who were already restless in the static siege operation at Stanwix. More significantly, the Continental garrison of the fort sallied out during the Oriskany fight and destroyed most of St. Leger's camp and siege supplies.

Despite Shuyler's own weak position, when he learned of the plight of the Stanwix garrison he courageously detached Benedict Arnold with 950 continentals to march to its relief. Arnold devised a ruse that took full advantage of the dissatisfaction and natural superstition of the Indians. Employing a half-wit Dutchman, his clothes shot full of holes, and a friendly Oneida Indian as his messengers, Arnold spread the rumor that the continentals were approaching "as numerous as the leaves on the trees." The Indians, who had special respect for any madman, departed in haste; and St. Leger was forced to abandon the siege and retreat to Canada.

BENEDICT ARNOLD (1741–1801)

Benedict Arnold was one of the most talented American generals of the Revolutionary War, a man whose energy was matched only by his ego. He was instrumental in defeating the British at Saratoga, a victory that gained the fledgling United States the open support of France. In 1780 Arnold commanded West Point, a fort situated on a bluff overlooking a tricky double bend in the Hudson River. All vessels had to pass the guns of West Point, and its possession would have assured the British easy communication between their forces in Canada and those occupying New York City. Smarting at Congress' lack of appreciation for his role at Saratoga three years earlier, Arnold plotted with Maj. John André of the British Army to deliver West Point to the enemy. André, wearing civilian clothes, was captured after one of their meetings and subsequently hanged as a spy; Arnold escaped to command British coastal expeditions during the closing years of the war. He died in London in 1801.

Benedict Arnold
Copy of Engraving by H. B. Hal
After John Trumbull

Bennington and Stanwix were serious blows to Burgoyne. By early September he knew he could expect help from neither Howe nor St. Leger. Disillusioned about the Tories, he wrote Germain: "The great bulk of the country is undoubtedly with Congress in principle and zeal; and their measures are executed with a secrecy and dispatch that are not to be equaled. Wherever the King's forces point, militia in the amount of three or four thousand assemble in twenty-four hours; they bring with them their subsistence, etc., and the alarm over, they return to their farms." Nevertheless, gambler that he was, Burgoyne crossed the Hudson to the west side on September 13 and 14. A victim of his own preconceptions and already seeking to protect himself politically, Burgoyne now stated that his orders required him to get to Albany at all costs. While his supply problem daily became worse, his Indians, sensing approaching disaster, drifted off into the forests, leaving him with little means of gaining intelligence of the American dispositions.

The American forces were meanwhile gathering strength. Congress finally deferred to New England sentiment on August 19 and replaced Schuyler with Gates. Gates was more the beneficiary than the cause of the improved situation, but his appointment helped morale and encouraged the New England militia. (Washington's emissary, General Lincoln, also did his part.) Gates did not change Schuyler's tactics and continued to take full advantage of Burgoyne's plight. He advanced his forces four miles north and took up a position, surveyed and prepared by the Polish engineer Kosciuszko on Bemis Heights, a few miles below Saratoga. Against this position, Burgoyne launched his attack on September 19 and was repulsed with heavy losses. In the battle, usually known as the First Battle of Freeman's Farm, Arnold persuaded Gates to let him go forward to counter the British attack. Colonel Morgan's riflemen, in a wooded terrain well suited to the use of their specialized weapon, took a heavy toll of British officers and men.

After Freeman's Farm, the lines remained stable for three weeks. Burgoyne had heard that Clinton, with the force Howe had left in New York, had started north to relieve him. Clinton in fact had finally received reinforcements from Europe and launched a lightning strike against Putnam's weakened Highlands Department. The British stormed Forts Clinton and Montgomery on the Hudson on October 6 and forced a path through the mountains. Clinton could not do more because he received explicit orders from Howe to send the reinforcements on to Philadelphia. He took a chance and sent out a small diversion to Kingston but returned to New York when that probe indicated it could do nothing of value.

Burgoyne was left to his fate. Gates strengthened his entrenchments and calmly awaited the attack he was sure Burgoyne would have to make. Militia reinforcements increased his forces to around 10,000 by October 7. Meanwhile, Burgoyne's position grew more desperate. Unable to hold his supply line open, Burgoyne faced a choice. He could cut his losses and fall back toward Canada and safety, or he could stay and fight. He chose to stay and fight in hopes of defeating the army in front of him and pushing on to Albany. Food was running out; the animals had grazed the meadows bare; and every day more men slipped into the forest, deserting the lost cause. With little intelligence of American strength or dispositions, on October 7 Burgoyne sent out a reconnaissance in force to feel out the American positions. On learning that the British were approaching, Gates sent out a contingent including Morgan's riflemen to meet them; a second battle developed, usually known as Bemis Heights or the Second Battle of Freeman's Farm. Although Gates intended to fight a cautious, defensive battle, he lost control of his own men. Arnold, an open supporter of Schuyler and critic of the cautious Gates, had been placed under house arrest for insubordination. When Arnold learned of Burgoyne's probe, he impetuously broke arrest and rushed into the fray, distinguishing himself before he was wounded in leading an attack on Breymann's Redoubt. The British suffered severe losses, five times those of the Americans, and were driven back to their fortified positions.

Two days after the battle, Burgoyne withdrew to a position in the vicinity of Saratoga. Militia soon worked around to his rear and hemmed him in from the north as well. His position hopeless, Burgoyne finally capitulated on October 17 at Saratoga. The total prisoner count was nearly 6,000, and great quantities of military stores fell into American hands. The victory at Saratoga brought the Americans out well ahead in the campaign of 1777 despite the loss of Philadelphia. What had been at stake soon became obvious. In February 1778 France negotiated a treaty of alliance with the American states, tantamount to a declaration of war against England.

> The British suffered severe losses, five times those of the Americans, and were driven back to their fortified positions.

Valley Forge

The name of Valley Forge has come to stand, and rightly so, as a patriotic symbol of suffering, courage, and perseverance. The hard core of continentals who stayed with Washington during that bitter winter of 1777–1778 suffered much indeed. Supply problems caused some men to go without shoes, pants, and blankets. Weeks passed when there

VALLEY FORGE

After a disappointing fall campaign that ended with a British army occupying Philadelphia, George Washington cast about for winter quarters for his troops. He found a site among the thickly wooded hills around Valley Forge. The American camp lay somewhat to the north, but within easy striking distance, of the main road from Philadelphia to York, where the Continental Congress had taken refuge. This allowed his army to provide protection for the revolution's governing body. Valley Forge lay in a rich agricultural region that the contending armies had picked over extensively during the previous year. Dependent almost entirely on a wretchedly mismanaged supply system, the Americans were chronically short of food and clothing through much of the winter until Nathanael Greene, one of America's ablest commanders, took over as Quartermaster General. Steuben's drill instruction has received wide credit for bolstering American morale, but Greene's efficiency proved equally important. When in June 1778 the Continental Army finally marched out of Valley Forge to face the British again, it was well prepared in mind and body for what would follow.

was no meat, and men were reduced to boiling and eating their shoes. It was no place for "summer soldiers and sunshine patriots."

The symbolism of Valley Forge should not be allowed to obscure the fact that the suffering was largely unnecessary. While the soldiers shivered and went hungry, food rotted and clothing lay unused in depots throughout the country. True, access to Valley Forge was difficult, but little determined effort was made to get supplies into the area. The supply and transport system had broken down. In mid-1777 both the Quartermaster and Commissary Generals resigned along with numerous subordinate officials in both departments, mostly merchants who found private trade more lucrative. Congress, in refuge at York, Pennsylvania, and split into factions, found it difficult to find replacements. If there was not, as most historians now believe, an organized cabal seeking to replace Washington with Gates, there were many, both in and out of the Army, who were dissatisfied with the Commander in Chief; and much intrigue went on. Gates was made President of the new Board of War set up that winter, and at least two of its members were Washington's enemies. In the administrative chaos at the height of the Valley Forge crisis, there was no functioning Quartermaster General at all.

Washington weathered the storm, and the Continental Army would emerge from Valley Forge a more effective force than before. With his advice, Congress instituted reforms in the Quartermaster and Commissary Departments that temporarily restored the effectiveness of both agencies. Washington's ablest subordinate, General Greene, reluctantly accepted the post of Quartermaster General. The Continental Army itself gained a new professional competence from the training given by Steuben.

Steuben appeared at Valley Forge in February 1778. He represented himself as a baron, a title of dubious validity, and as a former lieutenant general on the staff of Frederick the Great. (In reality he had been only a captain. The fraud was harmless, for Steuben had a broad knowledge of military affairs and had the ability to communicate with the American soldiers and teach them the basics of their new craft.) Appointed by Washington as Inspector General in charge of a training program, Steuben vigorously drilled the troops that remained under arms during the winter of 1777–1778 at Valley Forge. He taught the Continental Army a simplified but effective version of the drill formations and movements of European armies and the proper care of equipment and supplemented American marksmanship with instruction on the use of the bayonet, a weapon in which British superiority had previously been marked. All through the training, Steuben never lost sight of a major difference between the American citizen-soldier and the European professional. He early noted that American soldiers had to be told why they did things before they would do them well, and he applied this philosophy in his training program. His trenchant good humor and vigorous profanity delighted the Continental soldiers and made the rigorous drill more palatable. After Valley Forge, continentals would fight on equal terms with British regulars in the open field.

First Fruits of the French Alliance

While the Continental Army was undergoing its ordeal and transformation at Valley Forge, Howe dallied in Philadelphia, forfeiting whatever remaining chance he had to win a decisive victory before the effects of the French alliance were felt. He had had his fill of the American war; and the king accepted his resignation from command, appointing General Clinton as his successor. As Washington prepared to sally forth from Valley Forge, the British Army and the Philadelphia Tories said goodbye to Howe in a series of lavish parties. However, Clinton already had orders to evacuate the American capital. With the French in the war, the strategic situation had changed dramatically. England now had to ensure the safety of the long ocean supply line to America, as well as its valuable commercial possessions in other parts of the world, in particular the rich sugar plantations of the Caribbean. Clinton's orders were to detach 5,000 men to the West Indies and 3,000 to Florida and to return the rest of his army to New York by sea. He was then to give thought to recovering the southern states, where once again ever-hopeful refugees insisted the majority of the population would rally to the royal standard.

As Clinton prepared to depart Philadelphia, Washington had high hopes that the war might be won in 1778 by a cooperative effort between his army and the French Fleet. Charles Hector, the Comte d'Estaing, with a French naval squadron of eleven ships of the line and transports carrying 4,000 troops left France in May to sail for the American coast. D'Estaing's fleet was considerably more powerful than any Admiral Howe could immediately concentrate in American waters. For a brief period in 1778, the strategic initiative passed from British hands; Washington hoped to make full use of it.

Clinton had already decided, before he learned of the threat from d'Estaing, to move his army overland to New York prior to making any detachments, largely because he lacked sufficient transports to make the voyage by sea. On June 18, 1778, he set out with about 10,000 men. Washington, having gathered by that time about 12,000, immediately occupied Philadelphia and then took up the pursuit of Clinton. His council of war was divided, though none of his generals advised a

> With the French in the war, the strategic situation had changed dramatically.

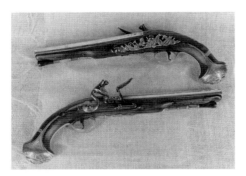

A fellow Virginian presented these English-made pistols (manufactured about 1749) to General Washington as a token of esteem in March 1778.

"general action." The boldest, General Wayne, and the young General Lafayette urged a "partial attack" to strike at a portion of the British Army while it was strung out on the road. The most cautious, Maj. Gen. Charles Lee, who had been exchanged and had rejoined the army at Valley Forge, advised only guerrilla action to harass the British columns. On June 26 Washington decided to take a bold approach, though he issued no orders indicating an intention to bring on a general action. He sent forward an advance guard composed of almost half his army to strike at the British rear when Clinton moved out of Monmouth Court House on the morning of June 27. Lee, the cautious, claimed the command from Lafayette, the bold, when he learned the detachment would be so large.

In the early morning Lee advanced over rough ground that had not been reconnoitered and made contact with the British rear, but Clinton reacted quickly and maneuvered to envelop the American right flank. Lee, feeling that his force was in an untenable position and underestimating the training transformation of the American Army during the encampment at Valley Forge, fell back in confusion. Washington rode up and, exceedingly irate to find the advance guard in retreat, exchanged harsh words with Lee. He then assumed direction of what had to be a defense against a British counterattack. The battle that followed, involving the bulk of both armies, lasted until nightfall on a sultry day with both sides holding their own. For the first time the Americans fought well with the bayonet as well as with the musket and rifle, and their battlefield behavior generally reflected the Valley Forge training. Nevertheless, Washington failed to strike a telling blow at the British Army, for Clinton slipped away in the night and in a few days completed the retreat to New York. Lee demanded and got a court-martial at which he was judged, perhaps unjustly, guilty of disobedience of orders, poor conduct of the retreat, and disrespect for the Commander in Chief. As a consequence he retired from the Army, though the controversy over his actions at Monmouth was to go on for years.

Washington meanwhile sought his victory in cooperation with the French Fleet. D'Estaing arrived off the coast on July 8, and the two commanders at first agreed on a combined land and sea attack on New York; but d'Estaing feared he would be unable to get his deep-draft ships across the bar that extended from Staten Island to Sandy Hook to get at Howe's inferior fleet. They decided to transfer the attack to the other and weaker British stronghold at Newport, Rhode Island, a city standing on an island with difficult approaches. They agreed that the French Fleet would force the passage on the west side of the island and an American force under General Sullivan would cross over and mount an assault from the east. The whole scheme soon went awry. The French Fleet arrived off Newport on July 29 and successfully forced the passage; Sullivan began crossing on the east on August 8, and d'Estaing began to disembark his troops. Unfortunately, at this juncture Admiral Howe appeared with a reinforced British Fleet, forcing d'Estaing to reembark his troops and put out to sea to meet him. As the two fleets maneuvered for advantage, a great gale scattered both on August 12. The British returned to New York to refit and the French Fleet to Boston; d'Estaing decided to move on to tasks he considered more pressing in the West Indies. Sullivan was left to extricate his forces from an untenable position as best he could, and the first experiment in Franco-American cooperation came to a disappointing end with recriminations on both sides.

The fiasco at Newport ended any hopes for an early victory over the British as a result of the French alliance. By the next year, as the French were forced to devote their major attention to the West Indies, the British regained the initiative on the mainland; the war entered a new phase.

The New Conditions of the War

After France entered the war in 1778, it rapidly took on the dimensions of a major European as well as an American conflict. In 1779 Spain declared war against England, and in the following year Holland followed suit. The necessity of fighting European enemies in the West Indies and other areas and of standing guard at home against invasion weakened the British effort against the American rebels. Yet the Americans were unable to take full advantage of Britain's embarrassments, for their own effort suffered more and more from war weariness, lack of strong direction, and inadequate finance. Moreover, the interests of the European states fighting Britain did not necessarily coincide with American interests. Spain and Holland did not ally themselves with the American states at all, and even France found it expedient to devote its major effort to the West Indies. Finally, the entry of ancient enemies into the fray spurred the British to intensify their effort and evoked some, if not enough, of that characteristic tenacity that has produced victory for England in so many wars. Despite the many new commitments the British were able to maintain in America an army that was usually superior in numbers to the dwindling Continental Army, though it was never strong enough to undertake offensives again on the scale of those of 1776 and 1777.

Monmouth was the last major engagement in the north between Washington's and Clinton's armies. In 1779 the situation there became a stalemate and remained so until the end of the war. The defense system Washington set up around New York with its center at West Point was too strong for Clinton to attack. The British commander did, in late spring 1779, attempt to draw Washington into the open by descending in force on unfinished American outpost fortifications at Verplanck's Point and Stony Point, but Washington refused to take the bait. When Clinton withdrew his main force to New York, the American commander retaliated on July 15, 1779, by sending General Wayne with an elite corps of light infantry on a stealthy night attack on Stony Point, a successful action more notable for demonstrating the proficiency with which the Americans now used the bayonet than for any important strategic gains. Thereafter the war around New York became largely an affair of raids, skirmishes, and constant vigilance on both sides. Twice in 1780 large British forces pushed into northern New Jersey in foraging operations intended to lure Washington into the open, but both times the flexible American defensive belt repulsed them easily.

Clinton's inaction allowed Washington to attempt to deal with British-inspired Indian attacks. Although Burgoyne's defeat ended the threat of invasion from Canada, the British continued to incite the Indians all along the frontier to bloody raids on American settlements. From Fort Niagara and Detroit, they sent out their bands, usually led by Tories, to pillage and burn in the Mohawk Valley of New York, the Wyoming Valley of Pennsylvania, and the new American settlements in Kentucky. Although local defense was primarily the responsibility of state governments and the militia, the pressure on the Mohawk frontier soon prompted a Continental response. In August 1779 Washington detached General Sullivan with a force to deal with the Iroquois in Pennsylvania and New York. Sullivan laid waste the Indians' villages and defeated a force of Tories and Indians at Newtown on August 29. Although Sullivan's mission did not end Indian frontier raids, it essentially broke the back of Iroquois power and ensured the flow of supplies to the army from these fertile areas.

In the winter of 1778–1779, the colony of Virginia had sponsored an expedition that struck a severe blow at the British and Indians in the northwest. Young Lt. Col. George Rogers Clark, with a force of only 175 men ostensibly recruited for the defense of Kentucky, overran all the British posts in what is today Illinois and Indiana. Neither he nor Sullivan, however, was able to strike at the sources of the trouble—Niagara and Detroit. Indian raids along the frontiers continued, though they were somewhat less frequent and less severe.

British Successes in the South

Late in 1778 the British began to turn their main effort to the south. The king's ministers hoped to bring the southern states into the fold one by one. From bases there, they would strangle the recalcitrant north. A small British force operating from Florida cooperated with the first reinforcements sent by Clinton and quickly overran thinly populated Georgia in the winter of 1778–1779. Alarmed by this development, Congress sent General Lincoln south to Charleston in December 1778 to command the Southern Army and organize the southern effort. It hoped that he could repeat his performance during the Saratoga campaign as a leader who could mix Continental regulars and militiamen. Lincoln gathered 3,500 continentals and militiamen; but in May 1779, while he maneuvered along the Georgia border, the British commander, Maj. Gen. Augustine Prevost, slipped around him to raid Charleston. The city barely managed to hold out until Lincoln returned to relieve it. (*Map 10*)

In September 1779 Admiral d'Estaing arrived off the coast of Georgia with a strong French Fleet and 6,000 troops. Lincoln hurried south with 1,350 Americans to join him in a siege of the main British base at Savannah. Unfortunately, the Franco-American force had to hurry its attack because d'Estaing was unwilling to risk his fleet in a position dangerously exposed to autumn storms. The French and Americans mounted a direct assault on Savannah on October 9, abandoning their plan to make a systematic approach by regular parallels. The British in strongly entrenched positions repulsed the attack in what was essentially a Bunker Hill in reverse, with the French and Americans suffering staggering losses. D'Estaing then sailed away to the West Indies, Lincoln returned to Charleston, and the second attempt at Franco-American

Although Burgoyne's defeat ended the threat of invasion from Canada, the British continued to incite the Indians all along the frontier to bloody raids on American settlements.

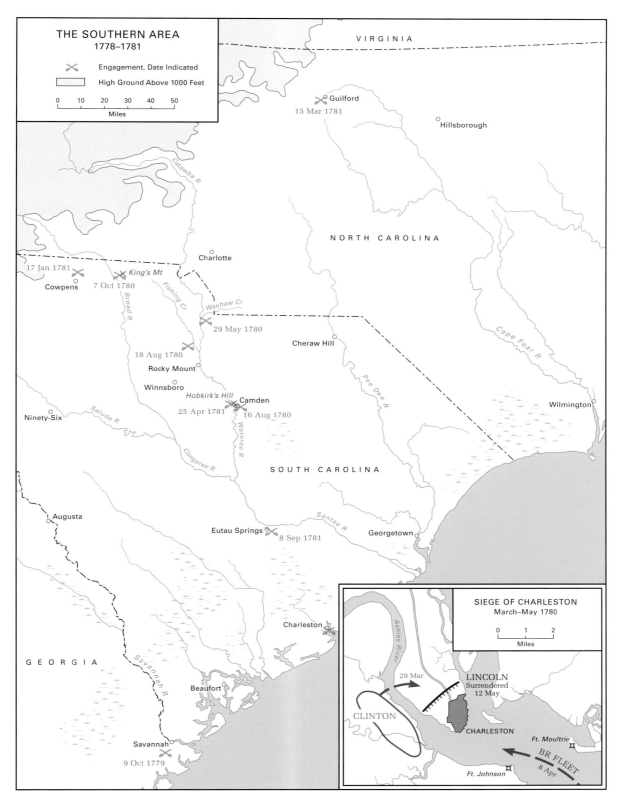

THE SOUTHERN AREA
1778–1781

✗ Engagement, Date Indicated

▨ High Ground Above 1000 Feet

0 10 20 30 40 50
Miles

VIRGINIA

✗ Guilford
15 Mar 1781

○ Hillsborough

Catawba R

NORTH CAROLINA

○ Charlotte

17 Jan 1781 ✗
Cowpens

✗ King's Mt
7 Oct 1780

Broad R

Fishing Cr

Waxhaw Cr
✗
29 May 1780

○ Cheraw Hill

Cape Fear R

18 Aug 1780 ✗

Rocky Mount

Winnsboro

Hobkirk's Hill
25 Apr 1781 ✗

Pee Dee R

Camden ○
✗
16 Aug 1780

○ Wilmington

Ninety-Six ○

Saluda R

Congaree R

Wateree R

SOUTH CAROLINA

Santee R

Augusta ○

Eutau Springs ✗
8 Sep 1781

Georgetown ○

Charleston ○ ✗

GEORGIA

Savannah R

Beaufort ○

Savannah ✗
9 Oct 1779

SIEGE OF CHARLESTON
March–May 1780

0   1   2
Miles

Ashley River

29 Mar

LINCOLN
Surrendered
12 May

CLINTON

CHARLESTON

Ft. Moultrie

BR FLEET
8 Apr

Ft. Johnson

Map 10

cooperation ended in much the same atmosphere of bitterness and disillusion as the first.

Meanwhile Clinton, urged on by the British government, determined to push the southern campaign in earnest. In October 1779 he withdrew the British garrison from Newport, pulled in his troops from outposts around New York, and prepared to move south against Charleston with a large part of his force. With d'Estaing's withdrawal, the British regained control of the sea along the American coast, giving Clinton a mobility that Washington could not match. While Clinton drew from New York and Savannah to achieve a decisive concentration of force (14,000 men) at Charleston, Congress had sent only piecemeal reinforcements to Lincoln over difficult overland routes.

Applying the lessons of his experience in 1776, Clinton this time carefully planned a coordinated Army-Navy attack. First, he landed his force on John's Island to the south, then moved up to the Ashley River, investing Charleston from the land side. (*See Inset, Map 10.*) Lincoln, under strong pressure from the South Carolina civilian authorities, concentrated his forces in a citadel defense on the neck of land between the Ashley and Cooper Rivers, leaving Fort Moultrie and other harbor defenses lightly manned. On April 8 British warships successfully forced the passage past Moultrie, investing Charleston from the sea. The siege then proceeded in traditional eighteenth century fashion, and on May 12, 1780, despite a masterful delaying defense that humiliated Clinton, Lincoln had to surrender his entire force of 5,466 men in the greatest disaster to befall the American cause during the war. Meanwhile, Col. Abraham Buford with 350 Virginians was moving south to reinforce the garrison. When he learned of the garrison's fate, Buford tried to withdraw; but Lt. Col. Banastre Tarleton with a force of British light cavalry and infantry took Buford by surprise at the Waxhaws, a district near the North Carolina border, and slaughtered most of Buford's men after they attempted to surrender. This brutality shocked most Americans and, as had happened with the Jenny McCrea incident, motivated the militia forces to take to the field in ever-increasing numbers.

After the capture of Charleston, Clinton returned to New York with about a third of his force, leaving General Cornwallis with 8,000 men to follow up the victory. Cornwallis established his main seaboard bases at Savannah, Beaufort, Charleston, and Georgetown. In the interior, he extended his line of control along the Savannah River westward to Ninety-Six and northward to Camden and Rocky Mount. Cornwallis' force, however, was too small to police so large an area, even with the aid of the Tories who took to the field. Though no organized Continental force remained in the Carolinas and Georgia, American guerrillas, led by Brig. Gens. Thomas Sumter and Andrew Pickens and Lt. Col. Francis Marion, began to harry British posts and lines of communications and to battle the bands of Tories. A bloody, ruthless, and confused civil war ensued, its character determined in no small degree by Tarleton's action at the Waxhaws. In this way, as in the Saratoga campaign, the American grass roots strength began once again to assert itself and to deny the British the fruits of military victory.

On June 22, 1780, the Maryland Division (two understrength brigades) from Washington's army arrived at Hillsborough, North Carolina, to form the nucleus of a new Southern Army around which militia could

FRANCIS MARION (1732–1795)

When Charleston, South Carolina, fell to the British in 1780, organized American resistance broke down, initially leaving the defense of the southern colonies in the hands of guerrilla bands. One of the most famous guerrilla leaders was Francis Marion, who became known as the Swamp Fox for his tactic of hiding in back-country marshes before sallying forth to harass the British with lightning raids. Marion and other guerrillas played a key role in General Greene's Southern Campaign, pinning down British units while Continental Army regulars prepared for the decisive battles to come in 1780–1781.

"The Swamp Fox" Brigadier General Francis Marion with SC Militia
Robert Wilson oil painting, 1980

rally and which could serve as the nerve center of guerrilla resistance. In July Congress, without consulting Washington, provided a commander for this army in the person of General Gates, the hero of Saratoga. Gates soon lost his northern laurels. Gathering a force of about 4,000 men, over half of them militia, and ignoring the advice of his subordinates who were more familiar with the terrain, he set out to attack the British post at Camden, South Carolina. Instead of taking a more circuitous route that could be supported logistically, Gates marched through a district already denuded of food. Cornwallis hurried north from Charleston with reinforcements, and his army of 2,200 British regulars made contact with Gates outside Camden on the night of August 15.

In the battle that ensued the following morning, Gates deployed his militia on the left and the continentals under Maj. Gen. Johann de Kalb on the right. Morning fog, compounded by the smoke muskets, prevented each of the two parts of the American force from seeing what was happening to the other. The militia was still forming when Cornwallis struck, and they fled in panic before the British onslaught. On the other side of the field, de Kalb's continentals drove back the British forces opposing them. At this point the British who had driven the militia from the field wheeled on the continentals and brought an end to the valiant but hopeless fight. Tarleton's cavalry pursued the fleeing Americans for thirty miles, killing or making prisoner those who lagged. Gates himself fled too fast for Tarleton, reaching Hillsborough, 160 miles away, in three days and leaving his men to fend for themselves. To add to the disaster, Tarleton caught up with General Sumter, whom Gates had sent with a detachment to raid a British wagon train, and virtually destroyed his force in a surprise attack at Fishing Creek on August 18. Once more South Carolina seemed safely in British hands.

Nadir of the American Cause

In the summer of 1780 the American cause seemed to be at as low an ebb as it had been after the New York campaign in 1776 or after the defeats at Ticonderoga and Brandywine in 1777. Defeat in the south was not the only discouraging aspect of patriot affairs. In the north, a creeping paralysis had set in as the patriotic enthusiasm of the early war years waned. The Continental currency had depreciated virtually out of existence, and Congress was impotent to pay the soldiers or purchase supplies. At Morristown, New Jersey, in the winter of 1779–1780, the army suffered worse hardships than at Valley Forge. Congress could do little but attempt to shift its responsibilities onto the states, giving each the task of providing clothing for its own troops and furnishing certain quotas of "specific supplies" for the entire Army. The system of specific supplies worked not at all. Not only were the states laggard in furnishing supplies, but when they did it was seldom at the time or place they were needed. This breakdown in the supply system was more than even General Greene as Quartermaster General could withstand; in early 1780, under heavy criticism in Congress, he resigned his position.

Under such difficulties, Washington had to struggle to hold even a small Army together. Recruiting of continentals, difficult to begin with, became almost impossible when the troops could neither be paid nor supplied adequately and had to suffer such winters as those at Morristown. Enlistments and drafts from the militia in 1780 produced not quite half as many men for one year's service as had enlisted in 1775 for three years or the duration. While recruiting lagged, morale among those men who had enlisted for the longer terms naturally fell. Mutinies in 1780 and 1781 were suppressed only by measures of great severity.

Germain could write confidently to Clinton: "so very contemptible is the rebel force now ... that no resistance ... is to be apprehended that can materially obstruct ... the speedy suppression of the rebellion ... the American levies in the King's service are more in number than the whole of the enlisted troops in the service of the Congress." The French were unhappy. In the summer of 1780 they occupied the vacated British base at Newport and moved in a naval squadron and 4,000 troops under the command of Lt. Gen. Jean Baptiste Donatien de Vimeur, the Comte de Rochambeau. Rochambeau immediately warned his government: "Send us troops, ships and money, but do not count on these people nor on their resources, they have neither money nor credit, their forces exist only momentarily, and when they are about to be attacked in their own homes they assemble ... to defend themselves." Another French commander thought only one highly placed American traitor was needed to decide the campaign.

Clinton had in fact already found his highly placed traitor in Benedict Arnold, the hero of the march to Quebec, the naval battle on the lakes, Fort Stanwix, and Saratoga. "Money is this man's God," one of his enemies had said of Arnold earlier; evidently, he was correct. Lucrative rewards promised by the British led to Arnold's treason, though he evidently resented the slights Congress had dealt him; and he justified his act by claiming that the Americans were now fighting for the interests of Catholic France and not their own. Arnold wangled an appointment as commander at West Point and then entered into a plot to deliver this key post to the British. Washington discovered the plot on September 21, 1780, just in time to foil it, though Arnold himself escaped to become a British brigadier.

Arnold's treason in September 1780 marked the nadir of the patriot cause. Yet in the closing months of 1780, the Americans somehow put

Arnold's treason in September 1780 marked the nadir of the patriot cause.

together the ingredients for a final and decisive burst of energy in 1781. Congress persuaded Robert Morris, a wealthy Philadelphia merchant, to accept a post as Superintendent of Finance; Col. Timothy Pickering, an able administrator, would replace Greene as Quartermaster General. Greene, as Washington's choice, was then named to succeed Gates in command of the Southern Army. General Lincoln, exchanged after Charleston, was appointed Secretary at War; and the old board was abolished. Morris took over many of the functions previously performed by unwieldy committees. Working closely with Pickering, he abandoned the old paper money entirely and introduced a new policy of supplying the army by private contracts, using his personal credit as eventual guarantee for payment in gold or silver. It was an expedient but, for a time at least, it worked.

Greene's Southern Campaign

It was the frontier militia assembling "when they were about to be attacked in their own homes" who struck the blow that actually marked the turning point in the south. Late in 1780, with Clinton's reluctant consent, Cornwallis set out on the invasion of North Carolina. He sent Maj. Patrick Ferguson, who had successfully organized the Tories in the upcountry of South Carolina, to move north simultaneously with his "American Volunteers," spread the Tory gospel in the North Carolina back country, and join the main army at Charlotte with a maximum number of recruits. Ferguson's advance northward alarmed the independent-minded "over-mountain men" in western North Carolina, southwest Virginia, and what is now east Tennessee. A picked force of mounted militia riflemen gathered on the Catawba River in western North Carolina, set out to find Ferguson, and brought him to bay at King's Mountain near the border of the two Carolinas on October 7. In a battle of patriot against Tory (Ferguson was one of only a handful of British soldiers present), the patriots' triumph was complete. Ferguson himself was killed, and few of his command escaped death or capture. Some got the same "quarter" Tarleton had given Buford's men at the Waxhaws.

King's Mountain was as fatal to Cornwallis' plans as Bennington had been to those of Burgoyne. The North Carolina Tories, cowed by the fate of their compatriots, gave him lame support. The British commander on October 14, 1780, began a wretched retreat in the rain back to Winnsboro, South Carolina, with militia harassing his progress. Meanwhile,

KING'S MOUNTAIN

Sir Henry Clinton remembered King's Mountain as "the first ... of a Chain of Evils that ... at last ended in the total loss of America." On October 7, 1780, when only a few continentals and isolated guerrillas blocked the restoration of British rule in the south, 1,400 "over-mountain men" and militia surrounded and overran the wooded hilltop position of 1,100 Tories and killed their leader, Major Ferguson. The victory not only gave the patriots time to regroup for the campaign that eventually led to Yorktown but also proved a major patriot victory in the vicious struggle for political allegiances in the south.

Clinton, acting on guidance from London, launched an expedition of 2,500 men under Benedict Arnold to establish a base in Virginia to reinforce Cornwallis.

The frontier militia had turned the tide; but having done so, they returned to their homes. To keep the tide moving against the British was the task of the new commander, General Greene. When Greene arrived at Charlotte early in December 1780, he found 1,500 men fit for duty, only 949 of them continentals. The army lacked clothing and provisions and had little systematic means of procuring them. Greene decided not to engage Cornwallis' army in battle until he had built up his strength, instead to pursue delaying tactics to wear down his stronger opponent. To accomplish this goal, he built on Gates' earlier dispositions. Gates had created a mobile screening force from his best troops. Greene first took the unorthodox step of dividing his army in the face of a superior force, moving part under his personal command to Cheraw Hill and the augmented light screening forces under Brig. Gen. Daniel Morgan west across the Catawba over 100 miles away. It was an intentional violation of the principle of mass. Greene wrote:

I am well satisfied with the movement.... It makes the most of my inferior force, for it compels my adversary to divide his, and holds him in doubt as to his own line of conduct. He cannot leave Morgan behind him to come at me, or his posts at Ninety-Six and Augusta would be exposed. And he cannot chase Morgan far, or prosecute his views upon Virginia, while I am here with the whole country open before me. I am as near to Charleston as he is, and as near Hillsborough as I was at Charlotte; so that I am in no danger of being cut off from my reinforcements.

Left unsaid was the fact that divided forces could live off the land much easier than one large force and would constitute two rallying points for local militia instead of one. Greene was in effect sacrificing mass to enhance maneuver.

Cornwallis, at this point in his career an aggressive commander often prone to act before thinking, had determined to gamble everything on a renewed invasion of North Carolina. Ignoring Clinton's warnings, he depleted his Charleston base by bringing almost all his supplies forward. In the face of Greene's dispositions, Cornwallis divided his army into not two but three parts. He sent a holding force to Camden to contain Greene, directed Tarleton with a fast-moving contingent of 1,100 infantry and cavalry to find and crush Morgan, and moved cautiously with the remainder of his army up into North Carolina to cut off any of Morgan's force that escaped Tarleton.

On January 17, 1781, Tarleton caught up with Morgan west of King's Mountain at a place called the Cowpens, an area of open forest near the Broad River. (*Map 11*) Morgan chose this site to make his stand less by design than by necessity, for he had intended to get across the Broad. Nevertheless, on ground seemingly better suited to the action of regulars, he achieved a little tactical masterpiece, making the most effective use of his heterogeneous force, numerically equal to that of Tarleton but composed of three-fourths militia. Selecting a low hill as the center of his position, he placed his Continental infantry on it, deliberately leaving his flanks open. In front of the main line he posted militia infantry in two lines, instructing the first line to fire two volleys

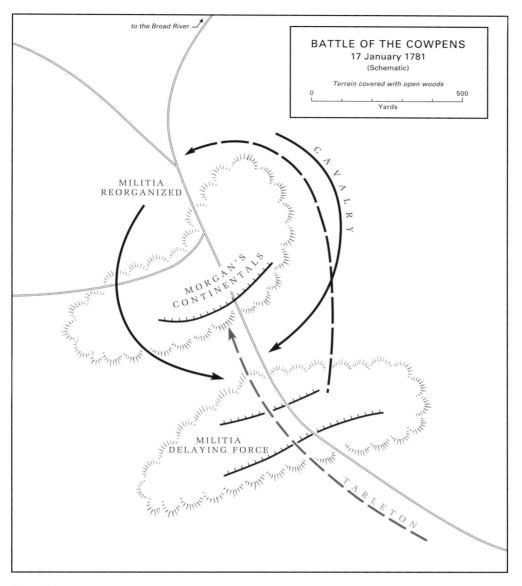

Map 11

and then fall back on the second, the combined line to fire until the British pressed them, then to fall back to the rear of the continentals and re-form as a reserve. He placed Lt. Col. William Washington's cavalry detachment behind the hill, ready to charge the attacking enemy at the critical moment. Every man in the ranks was informed of the plan of battle and the part he was expected to play in it.

On finding Morgan, Tarleton ordered an immediate attack. His men moved forward in regular formation and were momentarily checked by the militia rifles; but, taking the retreat of the first two lines to be the beginning of a rout, Tarleton's men rushed headlong into the steady fire of the continentals on the hill. When the British were well advanced, the American cavalry struck them on the right flank, broke

Caught in a classic double envelopment, the British surrendered after suffering heavy losses.

the British cavalry, and then wheeled on the infantry. The militia, having re-formed, charged out from behind the hill to hit the British left. Caught in a classic double envelopment, the British surrendered after suffering heavy losses. Tarleton managed to escape with only a small force of cavalry he had held in reserve. It was on a small scale and with certain significant differences a repetition of the classic double envelopment of the Romans by a Carthaginian army under Hannibal at Cannae in 216 b.c., an event of which Morgan, no reader of books, probably had not the foggiest notion. But it was a clever use of the terrain and troops by one of the American Army's most intuitive and inspirational commanders.

Having struck this fatal blow against Tarleton, Morgan still had to move fast to escape Cornwallis. Covering 100 miles and crossing two rivers in five days, he rejoined Greene early in February. Cornwallis by now was too heavily committed to the campaign in North Carolina to withdraw. Hoping to match the swift movement of the Americans, he destroyed all his superfluous supplies, baggage, and wagons and set forth in pursuit of Greene's army. The American general retreated through North Carolina into southern Virginia and crossed to safety behind the Dan River. Cornwallis' exhausted forces began to retreat into North Carolina to reach their depot and replenish their supplies. As the British started south, Greene recrossed the Dan and followed, keeping just out of reach of his adversary to avoid any battle he did not wish. Finally, on March 15, 1781, at Guilford Court House in North Carolina, on ground he had chosen himself, Greene gave battle. By this time he had collected 1,500 continentals and 3,000 militia to oppose the 1,900 regulars the British could muster. The British nominally won this contest because they managed to hold the field after a hard-fought battle, but they suffered disproportionate casualties of about one-fourth of the force engaged. It was like Bunker Hill a Pyrrhic victory. His ranks depleted and his supplies exhausted, Cornwallis withdrew to Wilmington on the coast to once again rebuild his army. Then he decided to move north to join the British forces General Clinton had sent to Virginia.

Greene, his army in better condition than six months earlier, pushed quickly into South Carolina to reduce the British posts in the interior. He fought two battles—at Hobkirk's Hill on April 25 and at Eutaw Springs on September 8—losing both but with approximately the same results as at Guilford Court House. One by one the British interior posts fell to Greene's army or to militia and partisans. By October 1781 the majority of the British had been forced to withdraw to their two strongholds along the coast, Charleston and Savannah. Greene had lost battles but won a campaign. In so doing, he paved the way for the greater victory to follow at Yorktown.

Yorktown: The Final Act

As Howe and Burgoyne went their separate ways in 1777, each seemingly determined to satisfy only personal ambitions, so Clinton and Cornwallis in 1781 paved the road to Yorktown with their disagreements and lack of coordination. Clinton was Cornwallis' superior in this case, but the latter enjoyed the confidence of Germain to an extent that Clinton did not. Clinton, believing that without substantial reinforcements the British could not operate far from coastal bases, had opposed Cornwallis' ventures in the interior of the Carolinas. When Cornwallis came to Virginia, he did so without even informing his superior of his intention.

Since 1779 Clinton had sought to paralyze the state of Virginia by conducting raids up its great rivers, arousing the Tories, and establishing a base in the Chesapeake Bay region. (*See Map 12.*) He thought this base might eventually be used as a starting point for one arm of a pincers movement against Pennsylvania for which his own idle force in New York would provide the other. A raid conducted in the Hampton Roads area in 1779 was highly successful; but when Clinton sought to follow it up in 1780, the force sent for the purpose had to be diverted to Charleston to bail out Cornwallis after King's Mountain. Finally, in 1781 he got an expedition into Virginia, a contingent of 1,600 under the American traitor, Benedict Arnold. In January Arnold conducted a destructive raid up the James River all the way to Richmond. His presence soon proved to be a magnet that drew forces of both sides to Virginia.

In an effort to trap Arnold, Washington dispatched Lafayette to Virginia with 1,200 of his scarce continentals and persuaded the French to send a naval squadron from Newport to block Arnold's escape by sea. The plan went awry when a British fleet drove the French squadron back to Newport and Clinton sent another 600 men to Virginia along with a new commander, Maj. Gen. William Phillips. Phillips and Arnold continued their raids, which Lafayette was too weak to prevent. Then on May 20 Cornwallis arrived from Wilmington and relieved Phillips. With additional temporary reinforcements sent by Clinton, he was able to field a force of about 7,000 men, about a quarter of the British strength in America. Washington sent down an additional reinforcement of 800 continentals under General Wayne; but even with Virginia militia, Lafayette's force remained greatly outnumbered.

Cornwallis and Clinton were soon working at cross-purposes. Cornwallis proposed to carry out major operations in the interior of Virginia, but Clinton saw as little practical value in this tactic as Cornwallis did in Clinton's plan to establish a base in Virginia to launch amphibious raids along the Chesapeake Bay. Cornwallis had no respect for his superior's military skills and saw no reason to give up his independent command. Instead, he did his level best to ignore Clinton's orders. Cornwallis at first turned to the interior and engaged in a fruitless pursuit of Lafayette north of Richmond. Then, on receiving Clinton's positive order to return to the coast and return part of his force to New York, Cornwallis moved back down the Virginia peninsula to take up station at Yorktown, a small tobacco port on the York River just off the Chesapeake Bay. In the face of Cornwallis' insistence that he must keep all his troops with him, Clinton vacillated, reversing his own orders several times and in the end granting Cornwallis' request. Lafayette and Wayne followed Cornwallis cautiously down the peninsula, lost a skirmish with him at Green Spring near Williamsburg on July 6, and finally took up a position at Williamsburg to keep an eye on Yorktown.

Meanwhile, Washington had been trying to persuade the French to cooperate in a combined land and naval assault on New York in the

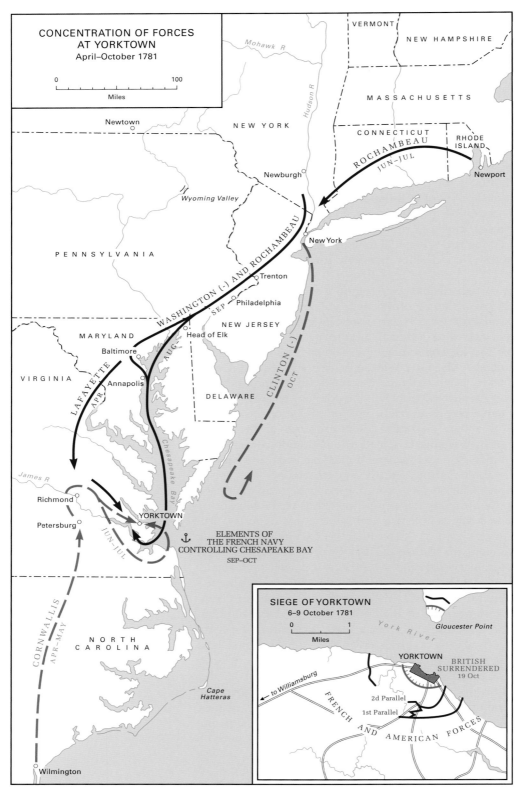

CONCENTRATION OF FORCES
AT YORKTOWN
April–October 1781

0   100
Miles

VERMONT

NEW HAMPSHIRE

MASSACHUSETTS

Mohawk R

Hudson R

NEW YORK

CONNECTICUT

RHODE
ISLAND

Newtown

Newburgh

ROCHAMBEAU
JUN–JUL

Newport

Wyoming Valley

New York

PENNSYLVANIA

WASHINGTON (-) AND ROCHAMBEAU

Trenton

SEP

Philadelphia

CLINTON (-)

OCT

MARYLAND

Head of Elk

NEW JERSEY

AUG

Baltimore

DELAWARE

VIRGINIA

Annapolis

LAFAYETTE
APR

Chesapeake Bay

James R

Richmond

Petersburg

JUN–JUL

YORKTOWN

ELEMENTS OF
THE FRENCH NAVY
CONTROLLING CHESAPEAKE BAY
SEP–OCT

CORNWALLIS
APR–MAY

NORTH
CAROLINA

Cape
Hatteras

SIEGE OF YORKTOWN
6–9 October 1781

0   1
Miles

York River

Gloucester Point

YORKTOWN

BRITISH
SURRENDERED
19 Oct

to Williamsburg

2d Parallel

1st Parallel

FRENCH AND AMERICAN FORCES

Wilmington

Map 12

summer of 1781. Rochambeau brought his 4,000 troops down from Newport and placed them under Washington's command. The prospects were still bleak, since the combined Franco-American regular force numbered but 10,000 and would still be outnumbered by Clinton's 17,000 in well-fortified positions. Then on August 14 Washington learned that the French Fleet in the West Indies, commanded by Admiral Francois de Grasse, would not come to New York but would arrive in the Chesapeake later in the month and remain there until October 15. He saw immediately that if he could achieve a superior concentration of force on the land side while de Grasse still held the bay, he could destroy the British army at Yorktown before Clinton had a chance to relieve it.

The movements that followed illustrate most effectively a successful application of the principles of the offensive, surprise, objective, mass, and maneuver. Even without unified command of Army and Navy forces, Franco-American cooperation this time was excellent. Admiral Louis, the Comte de Barras, immediately put out to sea from Newport to join de Grasse. Washington sent orders to Lafayette to contain Cornwallis at Yorktown. Employing an elaborate deception to convince Clinton that the Americans were about to attack New York, on August 21 Washington started the major portion of the Franco-American army on a rapid secret movement to Virginia via the Chesapeake Bay, leaving only 2,000 Americans under General Heath behind to watch Clinton.

On August 30, while Washington was on the move south, de Grasse arrived in the Chesapeake with his entire fleet of twenty-four ships of the line and a few days later debarked 3,000 French troops to join Lafayette. Admiral Thomas Graves, the British naval commander in New York, meanwhile had put out to sea in late August with nineteen ships of the line, hoping either to intercept Barras' squadron or to block de Grasse's entry into the Chesapeake. He failed to find Barras; and when he arrived off Hampton Roads on September 5, he found de Grasse already in the bay. The French admiral sallied forth to meet Graves, and the two fleets fought an indecisive action off the Virginia capes. Yet for all practical purposes the victory lay with the French, for while the fleets maneuvered at sea for days following the battle, Barras' squadron slipped into the Chesapeake and landed heavy artillery for the siege. Then de Grasse got back into the bay and joined Barras, confronting Graves with so superior a naval force that he decided to return to New York to refit.

Surrender of Cornwallis

When Washington's army arrived at Williamsburg on September 26, the French Fleet was in firm control of the bay, blocking Cornwallis' sea route of escape. A decisive concentration had been achieved. Counting 3,000 Virginia militiamen, Washington had a force of over 9,000 Americans and 6,000 French troops with which to conduct the siege. It proceeded in the best traditions of Marshal Sebastien Vauban under the direction of French engineers. Cornwallis obligingly abandoned his forward position on September 30, and on October 6 the first parallel was begun 600 yards from the main British position. Artillery placed along the trench began its destructive work on October 9. By October 11 the zigzag connecting trench had been dug 300 yards forward and

Surrender of Lord Cornwallis at Yorktown, Virginia, October 19th, 1781
John Trumbull, 1820

work on the second parallel had begun. Two British redoubts needed to be reduced to extend the line to the York River. Washington brilliantly carried out that action by using a surprise attack at bayonet point just after dark: Americans under Lafayette took Redoubt 10; and Frenchmen under Lafayette's brother-in-law, the Viscount Louis-Marie Noailles, secured Redoubt 9. This accomplished, Cornwallis' only recourse was a desperate attempt to escape across the river to Gloucester Point, where the allied line was thinly held. A storm on the night of October 16 frustrated his attempt to do so, leaving him with no hope except relief from New York. Clinton had been considering such relief for days, but he acted too late. On the very day, October 17, that Admiral Graves set sail from New York with a reinforced fleet and 7,000 troops for the relief of Yorktown, Cornwallis began negotiations on terms of surrender. On October 19 his entire army marched out to lay down its arms with the British band playing an old tune, "The World Turned Upside Down."

So far as active campaigning was concerned Yorktown ended the war, though neither side realized it at the time. Both Greene and Washington maintained their armies in positions near New York and Charleston for nearly two years more, but with only some minor skirmishing in the south. Cornwallis' defeat led to the resignation of the British Cabinet and the formation of a new government that decided the war in America was lost. With some success, Britain devoted its energies to trying to salvage what it could in the West Indies and in India. The independence for which Americans had fought thus virtually became a reality when Cornwallis' command marched out of its breached defenses at Yorktown.

The Summing Up: Reasons, Lessons, and Meaning

The American victory in the War of the Revolution was a product of many factors, no one of which can be positively assigned first importance. Washington, looking back on the vicissitudes of eight years, could only explain it as the intervention of "Divine Providence." American historians in the nineteenth century saw that divine providence as having been manifested primarily in the character and genius of the modest Commander in Chief himself. Washington's leadership was clearly one of the principal factors in American success; it seems fair to say that the Revolution could hardly have succeeded without him. Yet in many of the events that led to victory—Bennington, Saratoga, King's Mountain, and Cowpens, to name but a few—his personal influence was remote.

Today many scholars stress not the astonishment that Washington felt at the victory of a weak and divided confederation of American states over the greatest power of the age but the practical difficulties the British faced in suppressing the revolt. These were indeed great, but they do not appear to have been insuperable if one considers military victory alone and not its political consequences. The British forfeited several chances for military victory in 1776–1777, and again in 1780 they might have won had they been able to throw 10,000 fresh troops into the American war. American military leaders were more resourceful and imaginative than their British counterparts, and they proved quite capable of profiting from British blunders. In addition to George Washington, Nathanael Greene, Henry Knox, Daniel Morgan, and Benedict Arnold showed remarkable military abilities; of the foreign volunteers, Steuben and the young Lafayette were outstanding. The resourcefulness of this extraordinary group of leaders was matched by the dedication to the cause of the Continental rank and file. Only men so dedicated could have endured the hardships of the march to Quebec, the crossing of the Delaware, Valley Forge, Morristown, and Greene's forced marches in the southern campaign. British and Hessian professionals never showed the same spirit; their virtues were exhibited principally in situations where discipline and training counted most.

The militia, the men who fought battles and then went home, also exhibited this spirit on many occasions. The militiamen have been generally maligned as useless by one school of thought and glorified by another as the true victors in the war. Any balanced view must recognize that their contributions were great, though they would have counted for little without the Continental Army to give the American cause that continued sustenance that only a permanent force in being could give it. It was the ubiquity of the militia that made British victories over the continentals in the field so meaningless. And the success with which the militia did operate derived from the firm political control the patriots had established over the countryside long before the British were in any position to challenge it—the situation that made the British task so difficult in the first place.

For all these American virtues and British difficulties and mistakes, the Americans still required French aid—money, supplies, and in the last phase military force—to win a decisive and clear-cut military victory. Most of the muskets, bayonets, and cannon used by the Continental Army came from France. The French contested the control of the seas that was so vital to the British and compelled them to divert forces from the American mainland to other areas. The final stroke at Yorktown, though a product of Washington's strategic conception, was possible only because of the temporary predominance of French naval power off the American coast and the presence of a French army. The French entered the war for reasons of their own national interest, but they were no less instrumental in the winning of American independence.

French aid was doubly necessary because the American war effort lacked strong national direction. The Revolution showed conclusively the need for a central government with power to harness the nation's resources for war. It is not surprising that in 1787 nearly all those who had struggled so long and hard as leaders in the Continental Army or in administrative positions under the Congress were to be found in the ranks of the supporters of a new constitution that created such a central government with a strong executive and the power to "raise armies and navies," call out the militia, and directly levy taxes to support itself.

The strictly military lessons of the Revolution were more equivocal. Tactical innovations were not radical; but they did represent a culmination of the trend, which started during the French and Indian War, toward employment of light troops as skirmishers in conjunction with traditional linear formations. By the end of the war both armies were fighting in this fashion. The Americans strove to develop the same proficiency as the British in regular line-of-battle tactics, while the British adapted to the American terrain and tactics by employing skirmishers and fighting when possible from behind cover. Washington was himself a military conservative, and Steuben's training program was designed to equip American troops to fight in European fashion with modifications to provide for the increased use of light infantry. The guerrilla tactics that characterized many actions, principally those of the militia, were no product of the design of Washington or his leading subordinates but of circumstances over which they had little control. The American rifle, most useful in guerrilla actions or in the hands of skirmishers, played no decisive role in the Revolution. It was of great value in wooded areas, as at Saratoga and King's Mountain; but for open-field fighting, its slow rate of fire and lack of a bayonet made it inferior to the musket.

Since both militiamen and continentals played roles in winning the war, the Revolutionary experience provided ammunition for two diametrically opposed schools of thought on American military policy: the one advocating a large Regular Army, the other reliance on the mili-

BADGE OF MILITARY MERIT

In 1782, near the end of the Revolutionary War, General Washington created the Badge of Military Merit, an individual award for enlisted men. Exceptional gallantry or extraordinary fidelity and essential service, documented by local commanders and approved by General Washington, qualified a soldier for a heart-shaped, purple-cloth badge with the word "MERIT" embroidered in the heart's center that the recipient wore over the left breast. Only three men, all from Connecticut units, received the Badge of Military Merit: Sgts. Daniel Bissell, Jr., William Brown, and Elijah Churchill in 1783. The award fell into disuse after the Continental Army disbanded. Despite assertions that the Purple Heart created in 1932 was a revived Badge of Military Merit, the only connection between the two awards was some similarity in design and color.

tia as the bulwark of national defense. The real issue, as Washington fully recognized, was less militia versus regulars—for he never believed the infant republic needed a large standing army—than the extent to which militia could be trained and organized to form a reliable national reserve. The lesson Washington drew from the Revolution was that the militia should be "well regulated," that is, trained and organized under a uniform national system in all the states and subject to call into national service in war or emergency.

The lesson had far greater implications for the future than any of the tactical changes wrought by the American Revolution. It balanced the rights of freedom and equality proclaimed in the Declaration of Independence with a corresponding obligation of all citizens for military service to the nation. This concept, which was to find explicit expression in the "nation in arms" during the French Revolution, was also implicit in the American; and it portended the end of eighteenth century limited war fought by professional armies officered by an aristocratic class. As Steuben so well recognized, American continentals were not professional soldiers in the European sense and militia even less so. They were instead a people's army fighting for a cause. In this sense then, the American Revolution began the "democratization of war," a process that eventually lead to the new concept of a nation in arms.

DISCUSSION QUESTIONS

1. What were the flaws in the British plan of 1777? Would the offensive have been successful if it were implemented as planned?

2. List the reasons behind Burgoyne's defeat at Saratoga. How could he have done things differently? Could he have been successful?

3. Why were the British not more successful in rallying Tory support to the Crown?

4. Discuss the strengths and weaknesses of a guerrilla army such as that formed in the south by Sumter, Pickens, and Marion? Can guerrilla forces alone defeat regular troops?

5. What were the critical elements of the American victory at Yorktown?

6. How crucial was foreign support in the American victory in the Revolution?

RECOMMENDED READINGS

Billias, George A., ed. *George Washington's Generals*. Westport, Conn.: Greenwood Press, 1967.

Higginbotham, Don, ed. *Reconsiderations on the Revolutionary War: Selected Essays*. Westport, Conn.: Greenwood Press, 1978.

Hoffman, Ronald, and Peter J. Albert, eds. *Arms and Independence: The Military Character of the American Revolution*. Charlottesville: University of Virginia Press, 1984.

Middlekauf, Robert. *The Glorious Cause*. New York: Oxford University Press, 1986.

Morgan, John S., and Daniel J. Boorstein. *The Birth of the Republic, 1763–1789*. Chicago: University of Chicago Press, 1993.

Shy, John. *A People Numerous and Armed: Reflections on the Military Struggle for American Independence*. Ann Arbor: University of Michigan Press, 1990.

Wright, Robert K., Jr. *The Continental Army*. Washington, D.C.: U.S. Army Center of Military History, 1983.

Other Readings

Billias, George A., ed. *George Washington's Opponents: British Generals and Admirals of the American Revolution*. New York: William Morrow, 1969.

Bowler, R. Arthur. *Logistics and the Failure of the British Army in America, 1775–1783*. Princeton: Princeton University Press, 1975.

Buchanan, John. *The Road to Guilford Courthouse: The American Revolution in the Carolinas*. Hoboken, N.J.: John Wiley and Sons, 1999.

Buel, Richard, Jr. *Dear Liberty: Connecticut's Mobilization for the Revolutionary War*. Middletown, Conn.: Wesleyan University Press, 1980.

Calloway, Colin G. *The American Revolution in Indian Country: Crisis and Diversity in Native American Communities*. New York: Cambridge University Press, 1995.

Carp, E. Wayne. *To Starve the Army at Pleasure: Continental Army Administration and American Political Culture, 1775–1783*. Chapel Hill: University of North Carolina Press, 1984.

Cress, Lawrence D. *Citizens in Arms: The Army and Militia in American Society to the War of 1812*. Chapel Hill: University of North Carolina Press, 1982.

Dann, John C., ed. *The Revolution Remembered: Eyewitness Accounts of the War for Independence*. Chicago: University of Chicago Press, 1983.

Larrabee, Harold A. *Decision at the Chesapeake*. New York: C. N. Potter, 1964.

Rossie, Jonathan G. *The Politics of Command in the American Revolution*. Syracuse: Syracuse University Press, 1975.

Royster, Charles. *A Revolutionary People at War: The Continental Army and American Character, 1775–1783*. New York: Norton, 1981.

5

THE FORMATIVE YEARS
1783–1812

On September 24, 1783, three weeks after the signing of the Treaty of Paris formally ended the war, Congress directed General George Washington to discharge "such parts of the Federal Army now in Service as he shall deem proper and expedient." For the time being, Washington retained the force facing the British at New York and discharged the rest of the continentals. After the British quit New York, he kept only one infantry regiment and a battalion of artillery, 600 men in all, to guard the military supplies at West Point and other posts.

The period leading up to this demobilization was a stormy one for the Congress. During the winter of 1782 the Army had grown impatient, and rumors that it would take matters into its own hands gained credence when several anonymous addresses were circulated among the officers at Newburgh, urging them not to fight if the war continued or not to lay down their arms if peace were declared and their pay accounts left unsettled. In an emotional speech to his old comrades, Washington disarmed this threat. He promised to intercede for them; in the end, Congress gave in to the officers' demands, agreeing to award the men their back pay and to grant the officers full pay for five years instead of half pay for life. Demobilization then proceeded peacefully, but it was against the background of these demands and threats that Congress wrestled with a major postwar problem, the size and character of the peacetime military establishment. In the way of most governments, Congress turned the problem over to a committee, this one under Alexander Hamilton, to study the facts and make recommendations for a military establishment.

The Question of a Peacetime Army

Congress subscribed to the prevailing view that the first line of national defense should be a "well-regulated and disciplined militia sufficiently armed and accoutered." Its reluctance to create a standing army was understandable; a permanent army would be a heavy expense, and it would complicate the struggle between those who wanted a strong national government and those who preferred the existing loose federation of states. Further, the recent threats of the Continental officers strengthened the popular fear that a standing army might be used to coerce the states or become an instrument of despotism. The English experience with General Oliver Cromwell and his military dictatorship in the mid-seventeenth century still exerted a powerful influence over the political ideas of the mother country and the former colonies.

General Washington, to whom Hamilton's committee turned first for advice, echoed some of these fears. He pointed out that a large standing army in time of peace had always been considered "dangerous to the liberties of a country" and that the nation was "too poor to maintain a standing army adequate to our defense." The question might also be considered, he continued, whether any surplus funds that became available should not better be applied to "building and equipping a Navy without which, in case of War we could neither protect our Commerce, nor yield that assistance to each other which, on such an extent of seacoast, our mutual safety would require." He believed that America should rely ultimately on an improved version of the historic citizens' militia, a force enrolling all males between eighteen and fifty liable for service to the nation in emergencies. He also recommended a volunteer militia, recruited in units, periodically trained, and subject to national rather than state control. At the same time Washington did suggest the creation of a small Regular Army "to awe the Indians, protect our Trade, prevent the encroachment of our Neighbors of Canada and the Floridas, and guard us at least from surprises; also for security of our magazines." He recommended a force of four regiments of infantry and one of artillery, totaling 2,630 officers and men.

Hamilton's committee also listened to suggestions made by General Friedrich von Steuben; Maj. Gen. Louis le Bèque du Portail, Chief Engineer of the Army; and Benjamin Lincoln, Secretary at War. On June 18, 1783, the committee submitted a plan to Congress similar to Washington's but with a more ambitious militia program. Congress, however, rejected the proposal. Sectional rivalries, constitutional ques-

THE NEWBURGH "CONSPIRACY"

Mutiny was in the air on March 15, 1783. Having suffered through years of deprivation, many soldiers were angry that the Continental Congress seemed unwilling to pay them their salaries or to fulfill pledges for postwar pensions. When Washington learned that the Army's officers planned to meet to threaten the Congress, he decided to crash the party. Just as the meeting was about to begin, Washington entered the room and made a speech urging the officers to remain loyal. Seeing that many remained unswayed, he took out a letter, hesitated, and then reached into his pocket to produce a pair of glasses, explaining, "Gentlemen, you will permit me to put on my spectacles, for I have not only grown gray but almost blind in the service of my country." This simple act accomplished what his oratory had not. Ashamed and teary eyed, the assembled officers immediately pledged their loyalty to Congress. Mutiny had been avoided.

tions, and, above all, economic objections were too strong to be overcome. The new republic lacked even a rudimentary administrative and revenue base.

The committee thereupon revised its plan, recommending an even larger army that it hoped to provide at less expense by decreasing the pay of the regimental staff officers and subalterns. When asked, Washington admitted that detached service along the frontiers and coasts would probably require more men than he had proposed, but he disagreed that a larger establishment could be provided more economically than the one he had recommended. A considerable number of the delegates to Congress had similar misgivings; and when the committee presented its revised report on October 23, Congress refused to accept it. During the winter of 1783 the matter rested. Under the Articles of Confederation an affirmative vote of the representatives of nine states was required for the exercise of certain important powers, including military matters, and on few occasions during this winter were enough states represented for Congress to renew the debate.

In the spring of 1784 the question of a permanent peacetime army became involved in the politics of state claims to western lands. The majority of men in the remaining infantry regiment and artillery battalion were from Massachusetts and New Hampshire, and those states wanted to be rid of the financial burden of providing the extra pay they had promised the men on enlistment. Congress refused to assume the responsibility unless the New England states would vote for a permanent military establishment. The New England representatives, led by Elbridge Gerry of Massachusetts, insisted that Congress had no authority to maintain a standing army, but at the same time they wanted the existing troops to occupy the western forts situated in land claimed by the New England states. New York vigorously contested the New England claims to western lands, particularly in the region around Oswego and Niagara, and refused to vote for any permanent military establishment unless Congress gave it permission to garrison the western forts with its own forces.

The posts that had been the object of most concern and discussion dominated the Great Lakes and the St. Lawrence River. (*See Map 13.*) Located on American territory south of the boundary established by the peace treaty of 1783, the posts were in the hands of British troops when the war ended; but by the terms of the treaty they were to be turned over to the United States as speedily as possible. Congress agreed that a force should be retained to occupy the posts as soon as the British left. The problem was how and by whom the troops were to be raised. A decision was all the more urgent because the government was in the midst of negotiating a treaty with the Indians of the Northwest. As Washington had suggested, a sizable force "to awe the Indians" would facilitate the negotiations. But the deadlock between the New England states and New York continued until early June 1784.

Finally, on the last two days of the session, Congress rushed through a compromise. It ordered the existing infantry regiment and battalion of artillery disbanded, except for eighty artillerymen retained to guard military stores at West Point and Fort Pitt. It tied this discharge to a measure providing for the immediate recruitment of a new force of 700 men, a regiment of eight infantry and two artillery companies,

Alexander Hamilton
John Trumbull, 1792

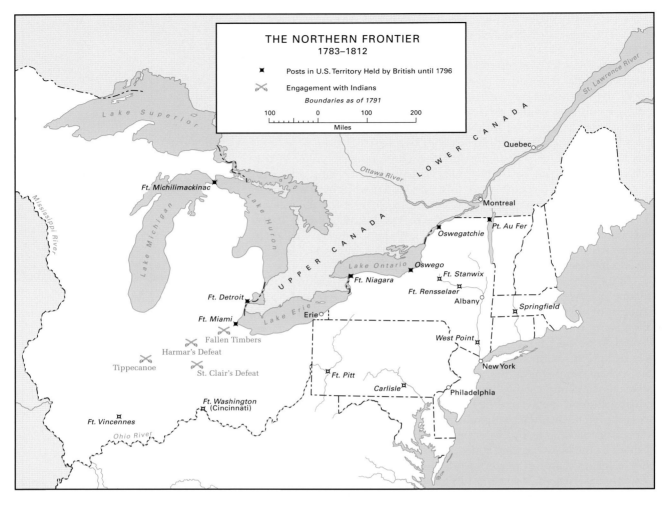

THE NORTHERN FRONTIER
1783–1812

✠ Posts in U.S. Territory Held by British until 1796

⚔ Engagement with Indians
Boundaries as of 1791

100 0 100 200
Miles

Map 13

which was to become the nucleus of a new Regular Army. By not making requisitions on the states for troops, but merely recommending that the states provide them from their militia, Congress got rid of most of the New England opposition on this score; not assigning a quota for Massachusetts and New Hampshire, Congress satisfied the objections of most of the other states.

Four states were called upon to furnish troops: Pennsylvania (260), Connecticut (165), New York (165), and New Jersey (110). Lt. Col. Josiah Harmar of Pennsylvania was appointed commanding officer. By the end of September 1784 only New Jersey and Pennsylvania had filled their quotas by enlisting volunteers from their militia.

Congress had meanwhile learned that there was little immediate prospect that the British would evacuate the frontier posts. Canadian fur traders and the settlers in Upper Canada had objected so violently to this provision of the peace treaty that the British government secretly directed the Governor-General of Canada not to evacuate the posts without further orders. The failure of the United States to comply with a stipulation in the treaty regarding the recovery of debts owed to loyalists provided the British an excuse to postpone the evacuation of the posts for twelve more years. So the New Jersey contingent of Colonel Harmar's force was sent to Fort Stanwix, in upstate New York, to assist in persuading the Iroquois to part with their lands. The remainder of the force moved to Fort MacIntosh, thirty miles down the Ohio River from Fort Pitt, where similar negotiations were carried on with the Indians of the upper Ohio.

Toward a More Perfect Union

Postwar problems revealed a number of serious defects in the Articles of Confederation. The federal government lacked a separate executive branch and a judiciary. Although Congress exercised a certain amount of executive as well as legislative power, it lacked the power to tax. To some of the delegates the conflicts and dissension between the states over the western lands seemed to carry the seeds of civil war. Rioting and disturbances in Massachusetts throughout the fall and winter of 1786 strengthened the pessimism of those who feared the collapse of the new nation. A severe commercial depression following on the heels of an immediate postwar boom was causing particular distress among the back-country farmers. Angry mobs gathered in the Massachusetts hills, broke up the meetings of the courts, harried lawyers and magistrates out of the villages, and began to threaten the government arsenal in Springfield.

On October 20, 1786, Congress responded to the threat by calling on several states to raise a 1,340-man force to serve for three years. This time the New England states did not object to congressional action; but before any of the soldiers voted by Congress could reach the scene, local militiamen repulsed an attack on the Springfield Arsenal led by Daniel Shays in late January 1787. A few days later a large reinforcement from the eastern part of the state arrived at Springfield and put an end to the disorders. Recruiting for the force authorized by Congress continued until the following April. By then about 550 men had been enlisted, and the question of expense was becoming bothersome. Congress therefore directed the states to stop recruiting and to discharge the

CONGRESS AND CIVILIAN CONTROL

The framers of the Constitution were deeply concerned over the potential danger of military power. Hence, they carefully crafted a separation of the powers concerning national security issues between the executive and legislative branches. The framers designated the President as "Commander in Chief of the Army and Navy of the United States, and of the Militia of the several States, when called into the actual service of the United States." To balance this executive authority, they stipulated that Congress would "raise and support Armies ... provide and maintain a Navy ... make Rules for the Government and Regulation of the land and naval Forces," and "provide for calling forth the Militia." Consequently, the founding fathers effectively precluded either the executive or the legislature from having sole power over the military while ensuring that civilian control over the military was a basic principle of the new United States.

troops already raised, except those in two artillery companies retained to guard West Point and the Springfield Arsenal. Shays' Rebellion was thus responsible for the first augmentation of the federal Army. More important, it was one of the incidents that helped persuade Americans that they needed a stronger government.

Rising concern over the ineffectiveness of the federal government, particularly in matters of finance and commercial regulation, finally led to the convening of a Constitutional Convention in the spring of 1787. To strengthen the military powers of the government was one of the principal tasks of the convention, a task no less important than establishing its financial and commercial authority. The general problem facing the convention, that of power and the control of power, came into sharp focus in the debates on military matters, since the widespread suspicion of a strong central government and the equally widespread fear of a standing army were merged in the issue of the government's military powers. Those who mistrusted a powerful government argued against a broad grant of authority not only in the fields of taxation and commercial regulation, but, and with especial force, in military matters as well. Even those like Hamilton who wanted to give the central government wide latitude in handling both purse and sword were also somewhat wary of standing armies. They too were concerned over the possible usurpation of political power by a military force or its use by officeholders as an instrument for perpetuating their personal power. Hamilton and his supporters nevertheless were willing to have the country run the risk of sacrificing some freedom for safety's sake. In the final compromise the problem of the military powers of the central government was resolved through the system of checks and balances built into the new Constitution.

Central to the system of checks and balances was the idea of specified and reserved powers. The states were to have all the powers not specifically granted to the central government. The Constitution clothed the central government with adequate authority to raise and maintain an army without calling on the states. By giving Congress power to levy taxes, the Constitution provided the central government with the necessary financial means; by creating a separate executive branch, the Constitution made it possible for the government to conduct its daily business without constant reference to the states. The Constitution gave Congress the exclusive power to declare war, raise armies, and provide for a navy. It also empowered Congress to call forth the militia "to execute the Laws of the Union, suppress Insurrections and repel Invasions." But authority over the militia was a shared power. Congress could provide for organizing, arming, and disciplining the militia and governing "such Part of them as may be employed in the Service of the United States," but the Constitution specifically reserved to the states the authority to appoint militia officers and to train the militia "according to the discipline prescribed by Congress."

The militia issue was also central to the shaping of the Second Amendment to the Constitution: the right to keep and bear arms. If the founding fathers recognized the centrality of freedom of speech, the press, and assembly, they also made clear those freedoms would only remain secure if the people could keep and bear arms as an ultimate check on the power of the government. The Second Amendment has

In the final compromise the problem of the military powers of the central government was resolved through the system of checks and balances built into the new Constitution.

been much politicized since its adoption as part of the Bill of Rights, but there is no question that the architects of our government believed that the people in arms—the militia—were the final guarantors of our freedom. Any subsequent reinterpretations of that amendment must start with the fact that our leaders, fresh from their experiences in the Revolutionary War, relied on the militia as the centerpiece of our national military establishment. The concept of the militia and the right to bear arms are inextricably joined.

The new Constitution introduced an important innovation by assigning all executive power to the President. The Secretary of War, therefore, became directly responsible to the President and not to Congress. The Constitution specifically provided that the President should be Commander in Chief of the Army and Navy. As such, his powers were exclusive, limited only "by their nature and by the principles of our institutions." The President had the right to assume personal command of forces in the field, but he could also delegate that right. As Commander in Chief, he was responsible for the employment and disposition of the armed forces in time of peace and for the general direction of military and naval operations in time of war.

In April 1789 Washington became the first President under the new Constitution; on August 7 Congress created the Department of War. There was no change, however, in either the policy or the personnel of the department. General Henry Knox, who had succeeded Washington as commander of the Army and had been handling military affairs under the old form of government, remained in charge. Since there was no navy, a separate department was unnecessary; at first the War Department included naval affairs under its jurisdiction. Harmar, who had been given the rank of brigadier general during the Confederation period, was confirmed in his appointment, as were his officers; and the existing miniscule Army was taken over intact by the new government. In August 1789 this force amounted to about 800 officers and men. All the troops, except the two artillery companies retained after Shays' Rebellion, were stationed along the Ohio River in a series of forts built after 1785.

So small an Army required no extensive field organization to supply its needs. In keeping with the accepted military theory that the Quartermaster was a staff officer necessary only in time of war, the Confederation Congress had included the Quartermaster General and his assistants among the others discharged in 1783 and had placed the military supply system under civilian control. It had made the civilian Secretary responsible for the transport, safekeeping, and distribution of military supplies and the Board of Treasury responsible for procuring and purchasing all military stores, including food and clothing. Except during a brief period in which the Secretary of War was allowed to execute contracts for Army clothing and subsistence, the new federal government retained the supply system established under the Confederation, adding in 1792 the civilian Office of the Quartermaster General to transport supplies to the frontier posts during the Indian expeditions. In 1794 Congress established the Office of the Purveyor of Public Supplies in the Treasury and the Office of Superintendent of Military Stores in the War Department to continue the same broad supply functions established in the Confederation period.

Henry Knox
James Harvey Young, 1873

This organization of military supply remained in effect with only slight modification until 1812.

The contract system the Office of the Purveyor of Public Supplies used to procure food and equipment operated much as it had in colonial times. Contracts were awarded to the lowest bidder, who agreed to deliver and issue authorized subsistence at a fixed price to troops at a given post. The contractor was obliged to have on hand at all times sufficient rations to feed the troops, providing subsistence for at least six months in advance at the more distant posts. The procurement, storage, and distribution of all other supplies for the Army were centralized in Philadelphia, where the Purveyor contracted for all clothing, camp utensils, military stores, medicines, and hospital stores and the Superintendent of Military Stores collected and issued them when needed by the troops. The contract system was supposed to be more economical and efficient than direct purchase, but its weaknesses were soon apparent. The quality of the supplies and the promptness of their delivery were dictated by the contractor's profit interest and relative degree of corruptness.

The method of arms procurement was a variation of the contract purchase system. Convinced that the development of a domestic arms industry was essential to independence, Hamilton had urged as early as 1783 "the public manufacture of arms, powder, etc." A decade later Secretary Knox reported to Congress that although arms could be purchased more cheaply in Europe, the bargain price was of little significance "compared with the solid advantages which would result from extending and perfecting the means upon which our safety may ultimately depend." Congress responded by expanding the number of U.S. arsenals and magazines for the stockpiling of weapons and by establishing national armories for the manufacture of weapons. The first national armory was established at Springfield, Massachusetts, in 1794 and a second the same year at Harpers Ferry, Virginia. Despite these developments the government still purchased most of its armament abroad, and many years would pass before domestic industry could supply the government's needs.

The Militia

Time and again Washington pointed out that the only alternative to a large standing army was an effective militia, yet his efforts and those of Knox and Hamilton to make the militia more effective by applying federal regulation failed. Congress passed the basic militia law in May 1792. It called for the enrollment of "every able-bodied white male citizen" between eighteen and forty-five and the organization of the militia into divisions, brigades, regiments, battalions, and companies by the individual states, each militiaman providing his own "arms, munitions, and other accouterments." The law that survived the legislative process bore little resemblance to the one Washington and Knox had proposed. It left compliance with its provisions up to the states and in the end did little more than give federal recognition to the colonial militia organization that had plagued Washington during the Revolution. Despite these limitations, the act did preserve the idea of a citizen soldiery, a concept of profound importance to the future of the country; and it also provided for the creation of special volunteer units to supplement the

Time and again Washington pointed out that the only alternative to a large standing army was an effective militia.

Washington Reviewing the West Army at Fort Cumberland, Maryland
Frederick Kemmelmeyer, ca. 1794

obligatory mass system. The volunteers, organized into companies, met regularly for military training under elected officers. With antecedents in the organized military associations of the colonial era, this volunteer force later became the National Guard.

Training and discipline were the keys to an effective militia, but despite the act of 1792 the militia was to be neither disciplined nor well trained. When permitted to fight in less standardized fashion, either from behind fortifications or as irregulars, militiamen could give a good account of themselves. But only highly trained troops could be expected to successfully employ the complicated, formal linear tactics of the day. Strictly interpreting the constitutional provision that reserved to the states the authority to train the militia, Congress left the extent and thoroughness of training completely to the states and merely prescribed Steuben's system of discipline and field exercises as the rules to be followed.

The limitations placed on the length of tours of duty and the circumstances for which the militia might be called into federal service further impaired its usefulness. No militiamen could be compelled to serve more than three months in any one year, nor could the President order the militia to duty outside the United States. The effect of these limitations would be readily apparent during the War of 1812.

The President first exercised his authority to employ militia for suppressing insurrection and executing the laws of Congress in 1794, when he sent a large force of militia under Maj. Gen. Henry Lee into western Pennsylvania during the Whiskey Rebellion. Lee encountered no resistance. As a show of force, the demonstration was impressive; as an indication of the military value of the militia in an emergency, it was inconclusive.

Military Realities in the Federalist Period

The military policies of the new nation evolved realistically in response to foreign and domestic developments. First, there was little actual military threat to the United States from a foreign nation. Britain had no desire or design to reconquer its lost colonies, although both Britain and Spain sought to curb the United States from expanding beyond the borders established by the treaty of 1783. The military alliance that bound the United States to England's archrival, France, was a potential source of danger, but England and France were at peace until 1793. When the U.S. and France fought an undeclared war from 1798 to 1800, it was almost entirely a naval confrontation. Second, the jealousy of the individual states toward one another and toward the federal government made it difficult to establish a federal army at all and defeated efforts to institute federal regulation of the militia beyond the minimum permitted by the Constitution. Third, the federal government, plagued by financial problems, had to pare expenditures to the bone. Fourth, Americans were extremely reluctant to serve in the Army, either as regulars or as volunteers, for more than a brief period. At no time could the government recruit enough men to bring the Regular Army up to authorized strength. In view of these drawbacks, a large regular military establishment was not feasible. Even a well-trained militia that could augment the regular force was lacking.

The Indian Expeditions

Free of the threat of foreign invasion, the young republic nevertheless faced a serious security problem in the West, where the new settlers demanded protection against the Indians as well as an equitable administration of the vast new territories won in the peace of 1783. The Indian problem was an old one. Under the relentless pressure of the pioneers and because of the grants made to Continental soldiers, the frontier was rapidly receding. The Confederation Congress had tried to cope with the situation by concluding a series of treaties with the various Indian groups, but the treaties failed to keep pace with the expansion of the frontier boundaries. The Indians, supported by British arms and the British presence in the Northwest, ferociously resisted the incursions of the settlers. In the years of the Confederation, they killed or captured over 1,500 settlers in the Kentucky Territory alone.

The Indians fought the settlers all along the frontier, but several factors militated against federal intervention in the Southwest during the first years of Washington's administration. In 1790 the United States concluded a treaty with the Creeks, the most powerful of the Southwest tribes, a treaty that the Spanish in Louisiana, eager to maintain their

Free of the threat of foreign invasion, the young republic nevertheless faced a serious security problem in the West.

ARTHUR ST. CLAIR
(1736?–1818)

A Scotsman by birth, Arthur St. Clair came to America as a young officer in the British Army during the French and Indian War. In 1762 he resigned his commission and settled outside of Pittsburgh, Pennsylvania. When the Revolution began, he joined the Continental Army and served ably throughout the conflict. After the war, he returned to civil life, serving in the Continental Congress before becoming governor of the Northwest Territory. Stubborn and unimaginative, St. Clair was never popular with his troops. He was, however, a true patriot, a brave and generally competent soldier, and a thoroughly honest man.

Arthur St. Clair
Charles Willson Peale, 1782

profitable trade with the Indians, would be likely to support. Georgia and South Carolina introduced a further argument against intervention when they objected to the presence of federal forces within their borders.

The situation was entirely different in the Northwest. There, federal troops had been occupied chiefly in driving squatters out of the public domain and protecting the Indians' treaty rights, a duty that neither endeared them to the settlers nor trained them in the art of war. Since the enactment of the Northwest Ordinance in 1787, settlers had been pouring into the Ohio country and were demanding federal protection. Their demands carried a veiled threat: If the government ignored their plight, they would turn to Spain and England for succor. The federal union could be destroyed in its infancy, or at the very least its future expansion could be forestalled by resurgent European influence in the region.

Tardily and somewhat inadequately, the new government groped for a response to the West's challenge. In President Washington's first annual message to Congress, he called for the defense of the frontier against the Indians. Congress responded by raising the authorized strength of regulars to 1,283. Aware that this force was inadequate to protect the entire frontier, Secretary Knox planned to call on the militia to join the regulars in an offensive to chastise the Miami Indian group as a show of force. In June 1790 he ordered General Harmar, in consultation with Arthur St. Clair, Governor of the Northwest Territory, to lead the expedition. Under an authorization given him the preceding fall, St. Clair called on Pennsylvania and Kentucky to send 1,500 militiamen to Harmar at Fort Washington, now Cincinnati. (*See Map 13.*)

The untrained and undisciplined militia was a weak reed on which to lean in a sustained campaign against the Indians, but Knox knew the militia's strengths as well as its weaknesses. Depending on the fast-striking, mounted militiamen to support the regulars, Knox wanted Harmar to conduct a "rapid and decisive" maneuver, taking advantage of the element of surprise, to find and destroy the Indian forces and their food supplies. But the two-phased operation Harmar and St. Clair

"MAD" ANTHONY WAYNE (1745–1796)

Anthony Wayne achieved fame during the Revolution as an aggressive commander with a fiery temper. After the war, he fell hopelessly in debt. Seeking immunity from prosecution, he ran for Congress and was elected, only to be unseated a few months later due to election irregularities. Down and out, Wayne eagerly grasped at the opportunity to take command of the Army after St. Clair's defeat. The government made the offer with some trepidation, as Washington believed Wayne was "addicted to the bottle." Thomas Jefferson considered him to be the type of person who would "run his head against a wall where success was both impossible and useless." He proved, however, to be the right man for the job.

Anthony Wayne
James Shaples, Sr., 1795

concocted bore little resemblance to Knox's proposed tactics. Harmar planned a long march northward from Fort Washington to the Miami villages concentrated at the headwaters of the Wabash River. A second column under Maj. John Hamtramck would ascend the Wabash from Fort Vincennes, Indiana, destroying villages along the way and finally joining with Harmar's column after a 150-mile march.

The expedition was a complete failure. Hamtramck left Vincennes with 330 regulars and Virginia militia on September 30; but after an eleven-day march, during which a few Indian villages were burned, the militia refused to advance farther. Harmar also set out on September 30. After struggling through the wilderness for more than two weeks with a force of 1,453 men, including 320 regulars, he reached the neighborhood of the principal Indian village near what is now Fort Wayne, Indiana. Instead of pushing on with his entire strength, Harmar on three successive occasions sent forward unsupported detachments of about 200 to 500 militiamen plus fifty or sixty regulars. The undisciplined militia could not be restrained from scattering in search of Indians and plunder. After two of the detachments suffered heavily in brushes with the Indians, Harmar took the rest of his army back to Fort Washington. His conduct was severely criticized; but a court of inquiry, noting the untrained troops with which Harmar had been provided and the lateness of the season, exonerated him.

Secretary Knox's injunctions for a rapid and decisive maneuver were again ignored when the government decided to send another expedition against the Northwest Indians in 1791. Congress raised the size of the invasion force, adding a second infantry regiment to the Regular Army and authorizing the President to raise a corps of 2,000 men for a term of six months, either by calling for militia or by enlisting volunteers into the service of the United States. The President commissioned Governor St. Clair a major general and placed him in command of the expedition. So slowly did recruiting and the procuring of supplies proceed that St. Clair was unable to set out before September 17; only by calling on the neighboring states for militia was he able to bring his force up to strength. When St. Clair's force finally marched out of Fort Washington, it consisted of about 600 regulars, almost all the actual infantry strength of the U.S. Army, in addition to about 800 enlisted "levies" and 600 militiamen.

By November 3, St. Clair had advanced about one hundred miles northward from Cincinnati. Most of his force, now numbering about 1,400 effectives, encamped for the night near the headwaters of the Wabash. Neglecting the principle of security, St. Clair had not sent out scouts; just before dawn a horde of about 1,000 Indians fell upon the unsuspecting troops. Untrained, low in morale as a result of inadequate supplies, and led by a general who was suffering from rheumatism, asthma, and "colic," the army was thrown into confusion by the sudden assault. St. Clair and less than half his force survived unscathed: there were 637 killed and 263 wounded.

The United States was alarmed and outraged over St. Clair's defeat. Some urged that the government abandon the Indian Wars and accept the British proposal for an Indian buffer state in the Northwest, but Washington well understood the strategic implications of such a scheme and decided instead to mount a third expedition. He appointed Maj. Gen. "Mad" Anthony Wayne, the dashing commander of the Pennsylvania Line during the Revolution, to succeed St. Clair. Congress doubled the authorized strength of the Army by providing for three additional regiments, two of which were to be infantry and the other a composite regiment of infantry and light dragoons. It tried to avoid the bad effects of short-term enlistment by adding the new regiments to the Regular Army as a temporary augmentation to be "discharged as soon as the United States shall be at peace with the Indian tribes." Congress also agreed to Secretary of War Knox's proposed reorganization of the Army into a "Legion," a term widely used during the eighteenth century that had come to mean a composite organization of all combat arms under one command. Instead of regiments, the Army was composed of four "sublegions," each commanded by a brigadier general and consisting of 2 battalions of infantry, 1 battalion of riflemen, 1 troop of dragoons (cavalrymen trained to fight either mounted or dismounted), and 1 company of artillery.

Egotistical, blustery, and cordially disliked by many of his contemporaries, General Wayne nevertheless displayed little of his celebrated madness during the expedition. His operation was skillfully planned. Correcting previous mistakes, he insisted on rigid discipline and strict training; conscious of the welfare of his men, he saw to it that supplies were adequate and equipment satisfactory. These military virtues finally won for the United States its elusive victory.

In the spring of 1793 General Wayne took the Legion down the river to Cincinnati, where he tried to persuade the Indians to submit peacefully. When negotiations broke down, the Legion followed the route that Harmar and St. Clair had taken. Wayne was in even poorer health than St. Clair but more determined. Like St. Clair, he moved slowly and methodically, building a series of forts and blockhouses along his line of march. Despite his efforts to improve morale, he found desertion as serious a problem as had his predecessors.

> Some urged that the government abandon the Indian Wars and accept the British proposal for an Indian buffer state in the Northwest, but Washington well understood the strategic implications of such a scheme.

Battle of Fallen Timbers

Reinforced by mounted militia in July 1794, Wayne led about 3,000 men to within a few miles of Fort Miami, a post the British had recently established on the site of what is now Toledo. There, on August 20, 1794, almost within sight of the British guns, the Indians attacked. The Americans held their ground and then with a furious bayonet charge drove the enemy out of the cover of fallen trees that gave the Battle of Fallen Timbers its name. In the open prairie, the Indians were at the mercy of Wayne's mounted volunteers; in less than an hour the rout was complete.

Ignoring the protest of the British commander at Fort Miami, Wayne remained for several days, burning the Indian villages and destroying crops before leading the Legion back to Cincinnati. The western tribes, their resistance broken, finally agreed on August 3, 1795, in the Treaty of Greenville to make peace and cede their lands in Ohio to the United States. Their submission had been hastened by news that England was about to evacuate the frontier posts.

In the years following the Battle of Fallen Timbers, settlers pushed rapidly into Ohio and beyond into lands still claimed by the Indians. To resist these encroachments, Tecumseh, chief of the Shawnees, and his brother, the Prophet, organized a tribal confederacy aimed at keeping the settlers out. Urged on by the settlers, Governor William Henry Harrison of the Indiana Territory decided in the summer of 1811 to strike at the Indians before they could descend on the settlements. Secretary of War William Eustis approved Harrison's scheme and placed 300 regulars under his command in addition to his 650 militia including mounted riflemen. Moving north from Vincennes at the end of September, Harrison built a fort on the edge of the Indian country and then continued to the neighborhood of Tecumseh's principal village on Tippecanoe Creek. (*See Map 13.*) On November 6 he halted about a mile west of the village, encamping his force in the form of a trapezoid around the wagons and baggage on a piece of high-wooded ground that rose above the marshy prairies.

The Indians struck just before dawn. Harrison's situation was very similar to that of St. Clair, and for a time his force seemed about to suffer the same fate. Furious hand-to-hand combat followed the Indians' wild charge that carried them into the camp itself. Although taken by surprise, the soldiers rallied and then counterattacked. The end came when the mounted riflemen charged in on the Indians and drove them from the field. Harrison lost 39 men killed and missing and had 151 wounded, of whom 29 died. The engagement by no means solved the frontier problem in the Northwest, but this problem was soon overshadowed by the outbreak of war with England. Its most permanent legacy was a tradition of battlefield courage that helped Harrison win the Presidency in 1841.

The Perils of Neutrality

While the United States was launching a new government and defending the frontier, France had undergone a revolution that within a few years led to a general European war. Britain joined the coalition against France in 1793 and in the first year of the war instituted a blockade, seizing at least three hundred American merchant vessels. In 1794 Chief Justice of the U.S. Supreme Court John Jay negotiated a treaty with Britain to settle a number of border and trade issues unresolved after the War of Independence. The treaty eased the mounting crisis in Anglo-American relations. Through acquiescing in the British doctrine of contraband, the United States settled some long-standing questions, including evacuation of the frontier posts, but only at the expense of domestic unity and peaceful relations with the French. Regarding Jay's treaty as evidence of a pro-British policy on the part of the United States, France retaliated by seizing American vessels that were trading with the British, by sending secret agents to stir up the Creek Indians along the southern frontier, and by meddling in American politics in an attempt to bring about the defeat of the "pro-British" administration. These were the new and serious problems that President Washington bequeathed to his successor, John Adams, in 1797.

Adams inherited a military establishment with an authorized strength of about 3,300 officers and men. In 1797 Congress dropped the Legion that had served well in the frontier fighting, and the Army returned to a regimental type of organization with four regiments of infantry, a Corps of Artillerists and Engineers, and two companies of light dragoons more appropriate to the duties of border defense. During 1796 and early 1797 there had been some redeployment into the Southwest; by 1797 nine companies of infantry, about two companies of artillery, and the entire force of dragoons were stationed along the southwestern frontier. Up in the old Northwest, there were five infantry companies at Detroit and smaller detachments at a dozen scattered forts elsewhere in the territory. Fort Washington was the major installation. There were also small garrisons at the important seaports that had been fortified after 1794 by French technicians, émigrés of the recent revolution. The rest of the Army was stationed along the Canadian border from the lakes eastward and at the older posts, like West Point, Carlisle, and Fort Pitt.

The Quasi War with France

When the French continued to attack American vessels and refused to receive the newly appointed American Minister, President Adams called Congress into special session to consider national defense. He particularly urged that immediate steps be taken to provide a navy. He also recommended that harbor defenses be improved, that additional cavalry be raised, that the Militia Act of 1792 be revised to provide for better organization and training, and that the President be authorized to call an emergency force, although he saw no immediate need for the last. Congress approved the naval recommendations; but except for a modest appropriation for harbor defenses and an act authorizing the President to call out 80,000 militiamen for a maximum term of three months, it voted down the military recommendations.

By the spring of 1798 France's actions had thoroughly upset the country. President Adams again recommended an expanded defense program, which this time fared somewhat better in Congress. Congress passed the recommended naval increases and created the separate Navy

When the French continued to attack American vessels and refused to receive the newly appointed American Minister, President Adams called Congress into special session to consider national defense.

THE FOUNDING OF WEST POINT

In October 1776 the Continental Congress authorized a committee to begin planning for a military academy, but political support for the idea remained uncertain until the need for domestically trained engineers and artillerists overcame the fear inspired by the European experience with professional military officers and totalitarianism. Despite the 1794 creation of the rank of cadet in the Corps of Artillerists and Engineers manning the fortifications at West Point, New York, formal instruction of those cadets did not begin until September 21, 1801. By ordering that instruction, President Jefferson reversed his early opposition to a military academy, seeing it as a way of promoting the study of engineering and science in the growing nation. On March 16, 1802, Congress approved the

West Point, New York
Seth Eastman, 1875

President's action and authorized the creation of the Corps of Engineers and a military academy under its control at West Point. That date marks the official birth of the U.S. Military Academy, but the institution's organization and funding remained uncertain for more than a decade.

Department. Of the three regiments the administration recommended adding to the Regular Army, Congress authorized the additional artillery but not the cavalry. With respect to the infantry regiment, the Secretary of War proposed to Congress that it might also create a marine infantry unit. Instead, Congress voted the U.S. Marine Corps into existence, making it part of the Army or Navy, according to whether the marines served on land or on shipboard. Congress also increased the number of companies in each of the four regular infantry regiments from eight to ten; voted a sizable sum for harbor defenses and ordnance; and authorized a Provisional Army, the emergency force that Adams had suggested the year before.

Again Congress tried to avoid the defects of short-term enlistments by setting the duration of the "existing differences between the United States and the French Republic" as the term of enlistment for the Provisional Army. Reluctant to abandon its traditional reliance on short-term militia volunteers, Congress turned down another presidential request for an increase in the Regular Army, instead giving him the authority to accept privately armed and equipped volunteer units for short-term service. Adams never made use of this authority but went ahead with the plans to raise the twelve infantry regiments and one cavalry regiment that made up the Provisional Army. He persuaded Washington to come out of retirement to accept command as a lieutenant general and at Washington's request appointed Alexander Hamilton as the senior major general. By the beginning of 1799 the officers had been appointed, and in May 1799 recruiting began. By the time the Provisional Army was disbanded in June 1800, around 4,100 men had been mobilized, assembled in camps, and given from six to twelve months' training. Hamilton directed the preparation of new drill regulations to replace Steuben's, but before the task was finished the French crisis had ended and the Provisional Army was discharged.

The possibility that the United States might ally itself with Britain helped persuade the French to agree to negotiations. Furthermore, the French had been pressing Spain to return Louisiana as a step toward restoring their colonial empire in America, and for this venture peace with the United States was necessary. On September 30, 1800, the United States and France signed a treaty in which France agreed to recognize American neutrality, thus formally ending the alliance of 1778, and to refrain from seizing American vessels that were not carrying contraband. On the very next day, October 1, 1800, France and Spain signed a secret treaty that turned Louisiana over to France. A few months later England and her allies made peace with France.

Defense under Jefferson

President Thomas Jefferson took office in 1801 committed to a policy of peace and economy. With Europe at peace and American relations with France and England better than they had been for ten years past, Congress proceeded to economize. It sold the Navy that had acquitted itself so well in the quasi war with France, retaining only the frigates and a few of the other larger ships. Instead of ships for the defense of U.S. harbors and coastline, Jefferson touted the idea of building a number of small, armed gunboats as a less expensive alternative. The Army did not feel the effect of the economy drive until March 1802. Until then the military establishment was much as Adams had left it after the Provisional Army troops had been discharged, with an authorized strength of 5,438 officers and men and an actual strength of about 4,000. In the reduction of March 1802 Congress cut back the total strength of the Army to 3,220 men, approximately what it had been in 1797 when Adams took office. It was more than 50 percent stronger in artillery, but the more expensive cavalry was eliminated.

When Congress reduced the size of the Army it also abolished the Office of the Quartermaster General and in its place instituted a system of contract agents. It divided the country into three military departments, each with a military agent. Each agent, with his assistants, was responsible for the movement of supplies and troops within his department. Since the assistant agents were also appointed by the President, the three military agents had no way to enforce accountability on their subordinates. This system soon led to large property losses.

Since the Revolution, the Army had suffered from a lack of trained technicians, particularly in engineering science, and had depended largely upon foreign experts. As a remedy Washington, Knox, Hamilton, and others had recommended the establishment of a military school. During Washington's administration, Congress had added the rank of cadet in the Corps of Artillerists and Engineers with two cadets assigned to each company for instruction. But not until the Army reorganization of 1802 did Congress create the separate Corps of Engineers, consisting of ten cadets and seven officers, assigned to West Point to serve as the staff of a military academy. Within a few years the U.S. Military

With Europe at peace and American relations with France and England better than they had been for ten years past, Congress proceeded to economize.

Academy became a center of study in military science and a source of trained officers. By 1812 it listed eighty-nine graduates, sixty-five of them still serving in the Army and playing an important role in operations and the construction of fortifications.

The Army and Westward Expansion

Not long after Thomas Jefferson became President, rumors reached America that France had acquired Louisiana from Spain. The news was upsetting. Many Americans, including Jefferson, had believed that when Spain lost its weak hold on the colonies the United States would automatically fall heir to them. But, with a strong power like France in possession, it was useless to wait for the colonies to fall into the lap of the United States like ripe fruit. The continued presence of France in North America also raised a new security problem. Up to this time the problem of frontier defense had been chiefly pacifying the Indians, keeping the western territories from breaking away, and preventing American settlers from molesting the Spanish. Now, with a strong, aggressive France as backdoor neighbor, the frontier problem became tied up with the question of security against possible foreign threats. The transfer of Louisiana to France also marked the beginning of restraints on American trade down the Mississippi. In the past, Spain had permitted American settlers to send their goods down the river and to deposit them at New Orleans. Just before transferring the colony, however, Spain revoked the American right of deposit, an action that made it almost impossible for Americans to send goods out by this route.

These considerations persuaded Jefferson in 1803 to inquire about the possibility of purchasing New Orleans from France. When Napoleon, anticipating the renewal of the war in Europe, offered to sell the whole of Louisiana for $15 million, Jefferson quickly accepted and suddenly doubled the size of the United States. The Army, after taking formal possession of Louisiana on December 20, 1803, established small garrisons at New Orleans and the other former Spanish posts on the lower Mississippi. Jefferson later appointed Brig. Gen. James Wilkinson, who had survived the various reorganizations of the Army to become senior officer, as first Governor of the new territory. (*Map 14*)

Six months before the Louisiana Purchase, President Jefferson had persuaded Congress to support an exploration of the unknown territory west of the Mississippi River. The acquisition of the Louisiana Territory now made such an exploration even more desirable. It was no accident that the new nation and its president turned to the Army for this most important mission. Soldiers possessed the toughness, teamwork, discipline, and training appropriate to the rigors they would face. The Army also had a nationwide organization, even in 1803, and thus the potential to provide requisite operational and logistical support. It was perhaps the only truly national institution in America other than the Congress itself.

To lead the expedition, Jefferson chose Capt. Meriwether Lewis, a 28-year-old infantry officer who combined the necessary leadership ability and woodland skills with the potential to be an observer of natural phenomena. Lewis in turn received the President's permission to select William Clark as his cocaptain. A former infantry company

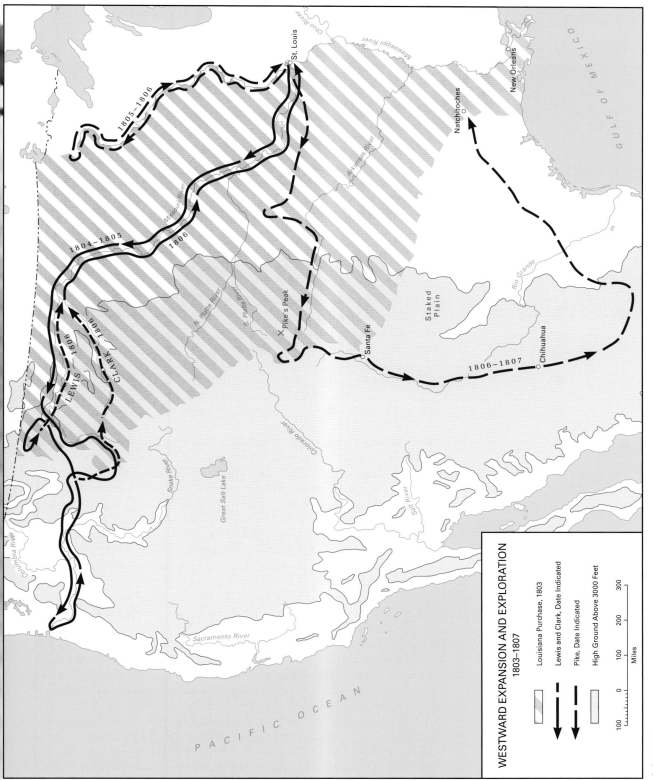

New Orleans

GULF OF MEXICO

St. Louis

Ohio River

Mississippi River

1805–1806

Natchitoches

Missouri River

Arkansas River

1804–1805

1806

Rio Grande

1806

LEWIS

CLARK

1806

Pike's Peak

Santa Fe

Staked Plain

1806–1807

Chihuahua

N. Platte River

S. Platte River

Snake River

Great Salt Lake

Colorado River

Salt River

Columbia River

Sacramento River

PACIFIC OCEAN

WESTWARD EXPANSION AND EXPLORATION
1803–1807

Louisiana Purchase, 1803

Lewis and Clark, Date Indicated

Pike, Date Indicated

High Ground Above 3000 Feet

Miles

100   0   100   200   300

Map 14

THE LEWIS AND CLARK EXPEDITION

The Lewis and Clark Expedition (1803–1806) was a military mission from start to finish. The U.S. Army furnished the organization and much of the manpower, equipment, and supplies. Over the course of two years, four months, and ten days, the soldiers traveled 7,689 miles and brought back invaluable geographic and scientific data, including the first detailed map of the region. The Lewis and Clark Expedition has become an enduring symbol of the American spirit, selfless service, and human achievement. It succeeded in large measure because it tapped the spirit of the American soldier and the organization, leadership, and courage of the U.S. Army.

William Clark
Charles Willson Peale, ca. 1810

Meriwether Lewis
Charles Willson Peale, ca. 1807

commander, Clark was a superb leader of men and an expert woodsman. Both men had served under General Wayne along the western frontier. Of the 48 men who accompanied Lewis and Clark up the Missouri River to the Mandan villages in 1804, 34 were soldiers and 12 were contract boatmen. The two other men were York, Clark's manservant, and George Drouillard, the contract interpreter. Of the 31 individuals who made the trip with Lewis and Clark to the Pacific coast in 1805 and back in 1806, 26 were soldiers. The other five were York, Drouillard, and the Charbonneau family (Toussaint, Sacagawea, and their newborn son, Jean Baptiste).

From the summer of 1803 to the fall of 1806, the expedition was an Army endeavor, officially the "Corps of Volunteers for North Western Discovery." It led Americans across the breadth of the vast continent for the first time. Its scientific agenda brought back invaluable information about flora, fauna, hydrology, and geography. Its benign intent resulted in peaceful commerce with Indians encountered en route. The expedition was, all things considered, a significant example of America's potential for progress and creative good.

While Lewis and Clark were exploring beyond the Missouri, General Wilkinson sent out Capt. Zebulon M. Pike on a similar expedition to the headwaters of the Mississippi. In 1807 Wilkinson organized another expedition. This time he sent twenty men under Captain Pike westward into what is now Colorado. After exploring the region around the peak that bears his name, Pike encountered some Spaniards who, resentful of the incursion, placed his party under armed guard and escorted it to Santa Fe. From there, the Spanish took the Americans into Mexico and then back across Texas to Natchitoches, once more in American territory. Despite the adversity, the Lewis and Clark Expedition and those of Captain Pike contributed much to the geographic and scientific knowledge of the country and today remain as great epics of the West.

To march across the continent might seem the manifest destiny of the republic, but it met with an understandable reaction from the Spanish. The dispute over the boundary between Louisiana and Spain's frontier provinces became a burning issue during Jefferson's second administration. Tension mounted in 1806, as rumors reached Washington of the dispatch of thousands of Spanish regulars to reinforce the mounted Mexican militiamen in east Texas. Jefferson reacted to the rumors by calling up the Orleans and Mississippi Territories' militia and sending about 1,000 regulars to General Wilkinson to counter the Spanish move. The rumors proved unfounded; at no time did the Spanish outnumber the American forces in the area. A series of cavalry skirmishes occurred along the Sabine River, but the opposing commanders prudently avoided war by agreeing to establish a neutral zone between the Arroyo Hondo and the Sabine River. The two armies remained along this line throughout 1806, and the neutral zone served as a de facto boundary until 1812.

American Reaction to the Napoleonic Wars

The second round of the great conflict between England and France began in 1803, shortly after the purchase of Louisiana. It was a much more serious affair than the earlier conflict. Both Britain and France adopted policies under which American merchant shipping, whether carrying contraband or not, was subject to search and seizure. The Napoleonic Wars and the consequent depredations on American commerce were less a threat to national security than a blow to national pride. Jefferson responded to the challenge by withdrawing American shipping from the seas. His successor in 1809, James Madison, adopted the even riskier policy of economic coercion. A series of trade and embargo acts from 1807 to 1810 attempted to force England and France to limit their trade restrictions in their dealings with the United States.

Legislation failed to keep the United States from becoming embroiled in the war and was unsuccessful in forcing England or France to respect neutral trade. Neither Jefferson nor Madison recognized that under the new scheme of economic warfare being waged by both England and France the American measures were in effect provocative acts likely to bring the United States into the war on one side or the other. The resultant crippling of American trade so thoroughly disunited the American people that the government could not count on the loyalty and support of a sizable part of the population when conflict did break out.

International tension was so great in the months after the Embargo Act of 1807 that Congress, while rejecting Jefferson's proposal for recruiting a 24,000-man volunteer force, authorized the recruitment of 6,000 men as a temporary addition to the Army. In the last month of his administration President Jefferson sent more than 2,000 of these

> Legislation failed to keep the United States from becoming embroiled in the war and was unsuccessful in forcing England or France to respect neutral trade.

127

men to General Wilkinson to defend "New Orleans and its dependencies" against an expected English invasion. The invasion never materialized, but poor leadership and bureaucratic mismanagement bordering on criminal combined with the tropical heat to accomplish what no British invasion could have done. More than 1,000 men, half of Wilkinson's army, died in Louisiana.

By January 1810 relations with Britain had so deteriorated that President Madison recommended the recruitment of a volunteer force of 20,000. Congress, apparently satisfied with the existing militia system, again refused to vote for a volunteer force. Not until January 1812 did it increase the Army's strength, when it added thirteen additional regiments, totaling about 25,700 men, and authorized the President to call 50,000 militiamen into service.

The additional men would soon be needed. On June 18, 1812, Congress declared war against England. At the same time a Senate proposal to declare war against France failed by only two votes.

DISCUSSION QUESTIONS

1. To what extent was George Washington the "indispensable man" in the formation of the United States of America and in ensuring the practice of civilian control of the military?

2. How has the concept of the militia changed since the early days of the republic?

3. How would you characterize the U.S. Army under the Articles of Confederation? What effect did Shays' Rebellion have upon the military needs of the new republic?

4. Discuss the tangible benefits to the United States resulting from the Lewis and Clark Expedition. Why did President Jefferson choose the U.S. Army to perform this mission?

5. Which tactics worked and which did not in fighting the Indians on the early frontier? Which force was more suited to fighting these campaigns: regulars or militia? Why?

6. Of what value was the newly established U.S. Military Academy at West Point to the Army and to the country as a whole?

RECOMMENDED READINGS

Ambrose, Stephen E. *Undaunted Courage: Meriwether Lewis, Thomas Jefferson, and the Opening of the American West*. New York: Simon & Schuster, 1996.

Bird, Harrison. *War for the West, 1790–1813*. New York: Oxford University Press, 1997.

Coakley, Robert W. *The Role of Federal Military Forces in Domestic Disorders, 1789–1878*. Washington, D.C.: U.S. Army Center of Military History, 1989.

Coffman, Edward M. *The Old Army: A Portrait of the American Army in Peacetime, 1789–1898*. New York: Oxford University Press, 1985.

Crackel, Theodore J. *Mr. Jefferson's Army: Political and Social Reform of the Military Establishment, 1801–1809*. New York: New York University Press, 1987.

Guthman, William H. *March to Massacre: A History of the First Seven Years of the United States Army, 1784–1791*. New York: McGraw-Hill, 1975.

Kohn, Richard H. *Eagle and Sword: The Federalists and the Creation of the Military Establishment in America, 1783–1802*. New York: Free Press, 1975.

Prucha, Francis P. *The Sword of the Republic: The United States Army on the Frontier, 1783–1846*. Bloomington: Indiana University Press, 1977.

Stagg, J. C. A. *Mr. Madison's War: Politics, Diplomacy, and Warfare in the Early American Republic, 1783–1830*. Princeton: Princeton University Press, 1983.

Sword, Wiley. *President Washington's Indian War: The Struggle for the Old Northwest, 1790–1795*. Norman: University of Oklahoma Press, 1985.

Other Readings

Adams, Henry. *The Formative Years: A History of the United States During the Administrations of Jefferson and Madison,* ed. Herbert Agar. Westport, Conn.: Greenwood Press, 1974.

Brookhiser, Richard. *Alexander Hamilton, American*. New York: Free Press, 1999.

Callahan, North. *Henry Knox: General Washington's General*. New York: Rinehart, 1958.

Cleaves, Freeman. *Old Tippecanoe: William Henry Harrison and His Time*. New Town, Conn.: American Political Biography Press, 1990.

DeVoto, Bernard, ed. *The Journals of Lewis and Clark*. Boston: Houghton Mifflin, 1997.

Jacobs, James R. *The Beginnings of the U.S. Army, 1783–1812*. Port Washington, N.Y.: Kennikat Press, 1972.

Perkins, Bradford. *Prologue to War: England and the United States*. Berkeley: University of California Press, 1961.

Slaughter, Thomas P. *The Whiskey Rebellion: Frontier Epilogue to the American Revolution*. New York: Oxford University Press, 1986.

6

THE WAR OF 1812

To Great Britain the War of 1812 was simply a burdensome adjunct of its greater struggle against Napoleonic France. To the Canadians it was clearly a case of naked American aggression. But to the Americans it was neither simple nor clear. The United States entered the war with confused objectives and divided loyalties and made peace without settling any of the issues that had induced the nation to go to war.

Origins of the War

The immediate causes of the war were seizure of American ships, insults and injuries to American seamen by the British Navy, and rapid expansion of the American frontier. The British outrages at sea took two distinct forms. One was the seizure and forced sale of merchant ships and their cargoes for allegedly violating the British blockade of Europe. Although France had declared a counterblockade of the British Isles and had seized American ships, England was the chief offender because its Navy had greater command of the seas. The British further outraged the United States by capturing men from American vessels for forced service in the Royal Navy. The pretext for impressment was the search for deserters, who, the British claimed, had taken employment on American vessels.

The reaction in the United States to impressments differed from that aroused by the seizure of ships and cargoes. In the latter case the maritime interests of the eastern seaboard protested vigorously and demanded naval protection, but rather than risk having their highly profitable trade cut off by war with England, they were willing to take an occasional loss of cargo. Impressments, on the other hand, presented no such financial hardship to the ship owners, whatever the consequences for the unfortunate seamen, and the maritime interests tended to minimize it.

To the country at large the seizure of American seamen was much more serious than the loss of a few hogsheads of flour or molasses.

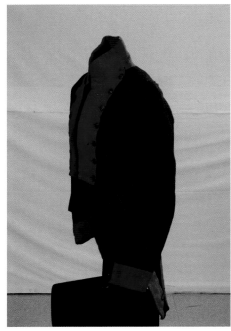

Uniform Coat Worn by a Private of Connecticut Artillery, ca. 1808

When a British naval vessel in June 1807 attacked and disabled the USS *Chesapeake* and impressed several members of the crew, a general wave of indignation rose in which even the maritime interests joined. This was an insult to the flag; and had President Thomas Jefferson chosen to go to war with England, he would have had considerable support. Instead he decided to clamp an embargo on American trade. In New England, scores of prosperous ship owners were ruined and a number of thriving little seaports suffered an economic depression from which few recovered. While the rest of the country remembered the *Chesapeake* affair and stored up resentment against Britain, maritime New England directed its anger at Jefferson and his party.

The seat of anti-British fever was in the Northwest and the lower Ohio Valley, where the land-hungry frontiersmen had no doubt that their troubles with the Indians were the result of British intrigue. Stories circulated after every Indian raid of British Army muskets and equipment found on the field. By 1812 the westerners were convinced their problems could best be solved by forcing the British out of Canada and annexing it to the United States.

While the western "war hawks" urged war in the hope of conquering Canada, the people of Georgia, Tennessee, and the Mississippi Territory entertained similar designs against Florida, a Spanish possession. The fact that Spain and England were allies against Napoleon presented the southern war hawks with an excuse for invading Florida. By this time, also, the balance of political power had shifted south and west; ambitious party leaders had no choice but to align themselves with the war hawks, and 1812 was a presidential election year.

President James Madison's use of economic pressure to force England to repeal its blockade almost succeeded. The revival of the Non-Intercourse Act against Britain, prohibiting all trade with England and its colonies, coincided with a poor grain harvest in England and with a growing need for American provisions to supply the British troops fighting the French in Spain. As a result, on June 16, 1812, the British Foreign Minister announced that the blockade on American shipping would be relaxed. Had there been fast trans-Atlantic communications of any kind, war might well have been averted. However, before the news of the British concessions reached him, Madison had sent a message to Congress on June 1 listing all the complaints against England and asking for a declaration of war. Dividing along sectional lines, the House had voted for war on June 4; but the Senate approved only on June 18 and then by only six votes.

The Opposing Forces

At the outbreak of the war, the United States had a total population of about 7.7 million people and was very unprepared for war. A series of border forts garrisoned by very small Regular Army detachments stretched along the Canadian boundary: Fort Mackinac, on the straits between Lake Michigan and Lake Huron; Fort Dearborn, on the site of what is now Chicago; Fort Detroit; and Fort Niagara, at the mouth of the Niagara River on Lake Ontario. (*Map 15*) The actual strength of the Regular Army in June 1812 totaled 11,744 officers and men, including an estimated 5,000 recruits enlisted for the additional

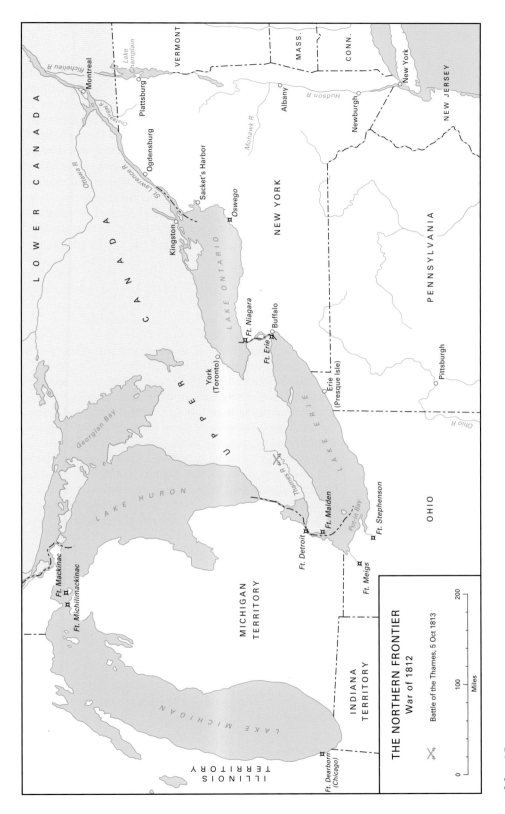

THE NORTHERN FRONTIER
War of 1812

✕ Battle of the Thames, 5 Oct 1813

0   100   200
Miles

LOWER CANADA

UPPER CANADA

VERMONT

MASS.

CONN.

NEW YORK

NEW JERSEY

PENNSYLVANIA

OHIO

MICHIGAN TERRITORY

INDIANA TERRITORY

ILLINOIS TERRITORY

Montreal
Plattsburg
Lake Champlain
Richelieu R
Chateaugay R
Ottawa R
St. Lawrence R
Ogdensburg
Sacket's Harbor
Kingston
Oswego
Lake Ontario
York (Toronto)
Ft. Niagara
Ft. Erie
Buffalo
Erie (Presque Isle)
Pittsburgh
Ohio R
Lake Erie
Thames R
Ft. Malden
Put-in Bay
Ft. Stephenson
Ft. Detroit
Ft. Meigs
Lake Huron
Georgian Bay
Ft. Mackinac
Ft. Michilimackinac
Lake Michigan
Ft. Dearborn (Chicago)
New York
Albany
Newburgh
Hudson R
Mohawk R

Map 15

force authorized the preceding January, in contrast to an overall authorized strength of 35,600. The U.S. Navy consisted of 20 vessels: the 3 large 44-gun frigates, 3 smaller frigates of the *Constellation* class rated at 38 guns, and 14 others.

Congress did not lack the will to prepare for war. In March 1812 it had tried to place the Army's supply system on a more adequate footing by establishing a Quartermaster Department on the military staff in place of the inefficient and costly military agent system. At the same time Congress created the Office of the Commissary General of Purchases in the War Department, and for the first time since the Revolution the Army's supply system was placed under the exclusive control of the Secretary of War. In May Congress had made provision for an Ordnance Department responsible for the inspection and testing of all ordnance, cannon balls, shells, and shot; the construction of gun carriages and ammunition wagons; and the preparation and inspection of the "public powder." It enlarged the Corps of Engineers by adding a company of bombardiers, sappers, and miners and expanded and reorganized the Military Academy at West Point. In addition to increasing the Regular Army, Congress had authorized the President to accept volunteer forces and to call upon the states for militia. The difficulty was not planning for an army, but raising one.

One of the world's major powers was ranged against the United States; but on the basis of available resources, the two belligerents were rather evenly matched. Most of Britain's forces were tied up in the war against Napoleon, and for the time being very little military and naval assistance could be spared for the defense of Canada. At the outbreak of the war, there were about 7,000 British and Canadian regulars in Upper and Lower Canada (now the provinces of Ontario and Quebec). With a total white population of only half a million, Canada itself had only a small reservoir of militia to draw upon. When the war began, Maj. Gen. Isaac Brock, the military commander and civil governor of Upper Canada, had 800 militiamen available in addition to his 1,600 regulars. In the course of the war, the two provinces put a total of about 10,000 militiamen in the field; whereas in the United States, probably 450,000 of the militiamen saw active service, though not more than half of them ever got near the front.

UNCLE SAM

One of the enduring symbols of America is that of Uncle Sam. His origins are somewhat obscure, but the most convincing story is that he was originally a Troy, New York, meatpacker named Sam Wilson. Sam Wilson was given a contract in 1812 to supply meat for the troops in New York and New Jersey. His firm put the preserved meat in wooden barrels and stamped them "U.S." When the barrels reached the troops, some of whom were apparently from the Troy area, the troops supposedly remarked that the "U.S." must stand for Uncle Sam! Ostensibly from these humble beginnings grew a character in nineteenth century political cartoons of a tall, bearded man dressed in striped pants and wearing a vest and star-spangled hat. James Montgomery Flagg would render this American symbol most powerfully in his 1916–1917 recruiting poster of a stern Uncle Sam pointing a finger at the viewer and stating, "I want you for U.S. Army."

TECUMSEH

After Tecumseh's death in battle while leading warriors of his own Shawnee and other tribes during the War of 1812, he became a revered symbol of the noble warrior dying in battle for a cause. Tecumseh had watched Indian lands in the Northwest Territory whittled away by a series of treaties with individual tribes and urged intertribal cooperation to halt the advance of white settlement. Yet his idea of a united Indian front against white expansion never came to pass. Instead, clan and local loyalties prevailed. Tecumseh did not enjoy unanimous backing even from his own tribe, the Shawnees. His program of unity and organization was attractive to the very white people he opposed, for it was just what they would have done; but it ran counter to the customs and traditions of the Indian people he meant to defend and failed to attract them in sufficient numbers.

The support of Indian tribes gave Canada one source of manpower that the United States lacked. After the Battle of Tippecanoe, Tecumseh, the Shawnee chief, had led his warriors across the border into Canada. There, along with the Canadian Indians, they joined the forces opposing the Americans. Perhaps 3,500 Indians were serving in the Canadian forces during the Thames River campaign in the fall of 1813, probably the largest number that took the field at any one time during the war.

The bulk of the British Navy was also fighting in the war against Napoleon. In September 1812, three months after the outbreak of war with the United States, Britain had no more than eleven ships of the line, thirty-four frigates, and about an equal number of smaller naval vessels in the western Atlantic. These were all that could be spared for operations in American waters, which involved the tremendous tasks of escorting British merchant shipping, protecting the St. Lawrence River, blockading American ports, and at the same time hunting down American frigates.

A significant weakness in the American position was the disunity of the country. In the New England states, public opinion ranged from mere apathy to actively expressed opposition to the war. A good many Massachusetts and Connecticut ship owners outfitted privateers (privately owned and armed vessels that were commissioned to take enemy ships), but how much of this was a result of patriotism and how much was hope for profit remains a matter of conjecture. Many New Englanders went so far as to sell grain and provisions to the British. Throughout the war, there were serious problems in raising and sustaining the militia from New England. Nevertheless, several of those states spent hundreds of thousands of dollars on local defense even if they contributed little directly to the federal effort. And despite the regional disaffection with the war, New England was second only to the Mid-Atlantic States in providing regular units: New England raised thirteen regiments of soldiers, whereas New York, New Jersey, and Pennsylvania combined provided fifteen.

Canada was not faced with the same degree of public opinion challenges. Nevertheless, many inhabitants of Upper Canada were recent immigrants from the United States who had no great desire to take up arms against their former homeland. Other Canadians thought that the superiority of the United States in men and material made any defense hopeless. That General Brock was able to overcome this spirit of defeatism and obtain the degree of support he needed to defend Canada is a lasting tribute to the quality of his leadership.

The Strategic Pattern

The fundamental military strategy of the United States was simple enough. The primary undertaking would be the conquest of Canada. The United States also planned an immediate naval offensive, whereby a swarm of privateers and the small Navy would be set loose on the high seas to destroy British commerce. The old invasion route into Canada by way of Lake Champlain and the Richelieu River led directly to the most populous and most important part of the enemy's territory. The capture of Montreal would cut the line of communications upon which the British defense of Upper Canada depended, making the fall of that province inevitable. But this invasion route was near the center of disaffection in the United States from which little local support could be expected. The places where enthusiasm for the war ran high and where the Canadian forces were weak offered a safer theater of operations, though one with fewer strategic opportunities. Thus, in violation of the principles of objective and economy of force, the first assaults were delivered across the Detroit River and across the Niagara River between Lake Erie and Lake Ontario rather than along the Hudson–Lake Champlain–Montreal line of advance.

The war progressed through three distinct stages. In the first, lasting until the spring of 1813, England was so hard pressed in Europe that it could spare neither men nor ships in any great number for the conflict in North America. The United States was free to take the initiative, to invade Canada, and to send out cruisers and privateers against enemy shipping. During the second stage, lasting from early 1813 to the beginning of 1814, Britain was able to establish a tight blockade but still could not materially reinforce the troops in Canada. During this stage the American Army, having gained experience, won its first successes. The third stage, in 1814, was marked by the constant arrival in North America of British regulars and naval reinforcements, which enabled the enemy to raid the North American coast almost at will and to take the offensive in several quarters. At the same time, in this final stage of the war American forces fought their best fights and won their most brilliant victories.

The First Campaigns

The first blows of the war were struck in the Detroit area and at Fort Mackinac. President Madison gave Brig. Gen. William Hull, Governor of the Michigan Territory, command of operations in that area. Hull arrived at Fort Detroit on July 5, 1812, with a force of about 1,500 Ohio militiamen and 300 regulars, which he led across the river into Canada a week later. (*See Map 15.*) At that time the whole enemy force on the Detroit frontier amounted to about 150 British regulars, 300 Canadian militiamen, and some 250 Indians led by Tecumseh. Most of the enemy forces were at Fort Malden, about twenty miles south of Detroit, on

This wooden, barrel-type canteen was the Regular Army's most popular model from the Revolutionary War through the early republic.

"REGULARS BY GOD"

On July 5, 1814, the 22d U.S. Infantry demonstrated at Chippewa, Canada, that the American republic had fielded a professional army capable of standing up to the British Army on a conventional battlefield. That spring Brig. Gen. Winfield Scott formed the 1st Brigade of regulars, consisting of the 9th, 11th, 22d, and 25th Infantries, near Buffalo, New York. An ardent student of European military training, Scott quickly shaped his brigade into a disciplined force that took the British by surprise when deployed to block a British advance into New York. Deceived by the gray uniforms American militia units usually wore, the British only belatedly realized they had encountered regular troops. The U.S. soldiers steadily advanced toward their opponents, seemingly unperturbed by musket volleys that tore through their ranks, causing the British commanding general to exclaim, "Those are Regulars, by God!" Today the memory of the victory at Chippewa lives on in the tradition of gray uniforms worn by cadets of the Military Academy at West Point and in the unofficial motto, "Regulars by God," of the 6th and 22d Infantries.

the Canadian side of the river. General Hull had been a dashing young officer in the Revolution, but by this time age and its infirmities had made him cautious and timid. Instead of moving directly against Fort Malden, Hull issued a bombastic proclamation to the people of Canada announcing their imminent liberation from "tyranny and oppression"; but he stayed at the river landing almost opposite Detroit. He sent out several small raiding detachments along the Thames and Detroit Rivers, one of which returned after skirmishing with the British outposts near Fort Malden.

In the meantime General Brock, who was both energetic and daring, sent a small party of British regulars, Canadians, and Indians across the river from Malden to cut General Hull's communications with Ohio. By that time Hull was discouraged by the loss of Fort Mackinac, whose sixty defenders had quietly surrendered on July 17 to a small group of British regulars supported by a motley force of fur traders and Indians who at Brock's suggestion had swiftly marched from St. Joseph Island, forty miles to the north. Hull also knew that the enemy in Fort Malden had received reinforcements (which he overestimated tenfold) and feared that Detroit would be completely cut off from its base of supplies. Taking counsel of his fears, on August 7 he began to withdraw his force across the river into Fort Detroit. The last American had scarcely returned before the first men of Brock's force appeared and began setting up artillery opposite Detroit. By August 15 five guns were in position and opened fire on the fort, and the next morning Brock led his troops across the river. Before Brock could launch his assault, the Americans surrendered. Militiamen were released under parole; Hull and the regulars were sent as prisoners to Montreal. Later paroled, Hull returned to face a court-martial for his poor conduct during the campaign, was sentenced to be shot, and was immediately pardoned.

On August 15, the day before the surrender, the small garrison at distant Fort Dearborn, acting on orders from Hull, had evacuated the post and started out for Detroit. The column was almost instantly attacked by a band of Indians who massacred the Americans before returning to destroy the fort.

With the fall of Mackinac, Detroit, and Dearborn, the entire territory north and west of Ohio fell under enemy control. The settlements in Indiana lay open to attack, the neighboring Indian tribes hastened to join the winning side, and the Canadians in the upper province lost some of the spirit of defeatism with which they had entered the war.

Immediately after taking Detroit, Brock transferred most of his troops to the Niagara frontier, where he faced an American invasion force of 6,500 men. Maj. Gen. Stephen van Rensselaer, the senior American commander and a New York militiaman, was camped at Lewiston with a force of 900 regulars and about 2,300 militiamen. Van Rensselaer owed his appointment not to any active military experience, for he had none, but to his family's position in New York. Inexperienced as he was in military art, van Rensselaer at least fought the enemy, which was more than could be said of the Regular Army commander in the theater, Brig. Gen. Alexander Smyth. Smyth and his 1,650 regulars and nearly 400 militiamen were located at Buffalo. The rest of the American force, about 1,300 regulars, was stationed at Fort Niagara.

Van Rensselaer planned to cross the narrow Niagara River and capture Queenston and its heights, a towering escarpment that ran perpendicular to the river south of the town. From this vantage point, he hoped to command the area and eventually drive the British out of the Niagara peninsula. Smyth, on the other hand, wanted to attack above the falls, where the banks were low and the current less swift; and he refused to cooperate with the militia general. With a force ten times that of the British opposite him, van Rensselaer decided to attack alone. After one attempt had been called off for lack of oars for the boats, van Rensselaer finally ordered an attack for the morning of October 13. The assault force numbered 600 men, roughly half of them New York militiamen. The attack did not go well. Several boats drifted beyond the landing area; and the first echelon of troops to land, numbering far fewer than 500, was pinned down for a time on the riverbank below the heights. The men eventually found an unguarded path, clambered to the summit, and, surprising the enemy, overwhelmed his fortified battery and drove him down into Queenston.

Later in the morning the Americans repelled a hastily formed counterattack, during which General Brock was killed. This, however, was the high point of van Rensselaer's fortunes. Although 1,300 men were successfully ferried across the river under persistent British fire from a fortified battery north of town, less than half of them ever reached the American line on the heights. Most of the militiamen refused to cross the river, insisting on their legal right to remain on American soil; and General Smyth ignored van Rensselaer's request for regulars. Meanwhile, British and Canadian reinforcements arrived in Queenston, and Maj. Gen. Roger Sheave, General Brock's successor, began to advance on the American position with a force of 800 troops and 300 Indian skirmishers. Van Rensselaer's men, tired and outnumbered, put up a stiff resistance on the heights but in the end were defeated, with 300 Americans killed or wounded and nearly 1,000 captured.

After the defeat at Queenston, van Rensselaer resigned and was succeeded by the unreliable Smyth, who spent his time composing windy proclamations. Disgusted at being marched down to the river on several occasions only to be marched back to camp again, the new army

With a force ten times that of the British opposite him, van Rensselaer decided to attack alone. . . . The attack did not go well.

that had assembled after the battle of Queenston gradually melted away. The men who remained lost all sense of discipline, and finally at the end of November the volunteers were ordered home and the regulars were sent into winter quarters. General Smyth's request for leave was hastily granted, and three months later his name was quietly dropped from the Army rolls.

Except for minor raids across the frozen St. Lawrence, there was no further fighting along the New York frontier until the following spring. During the Niagara campaign the largest force then under arms, commanded by Maj. Gen. Henry Dearborn, had been held in the neighborhood of Albany, more than two hundred and fifty miles from the scene of operations. Dearborn had a good record in the Revolutionary War and had served as President Jefferson's Secretary of War. Persuaded to accept the command of the northern theater, except for Hull's forces, he was in doubt for some time about the extent of his authority over the Niagara front. When it was clarified, he was reluctant to exercise it. Proposing to move his army, which included seven regiments of regulars with artillery and dragoons, against Montreal in conjunction with a simultaneous operation across the Niagara River, Dearborn was content to wait for his subordinates to make the first move. When van Rensselaer made his attempt against Queenston, Dearborn, still in the vicinity of Albany, showed no sign of marching toward Canada. At the beginning of November he sent a large force north to Plattsburg and announced that he would personally lead the army into Montreal, but most of his force got no farther than the border. When his advance guard was driven back to the village of Champlain by Canadian militiamen and Indians and his Vermont and New York volunteers flatly refused to cross the border, Dearborn quietly turned around and marched back to Plattsburg, where he went into winter quarters.

Henry Dearborn
Charles Willson Peale, 1796

If the land campaigns of 1812 reflected little credit on the Army, the war at sea brought lasting glory to the infant Navy. Until the end of the year the American frigates, brigs of war, and privateers were able to slip in and out of harbors and cruise almost at will; and in this period they won their most brilliant victories. At the same time, American privateers were picking off English merchant vessels by the hundreds. Having need of American foodstuffs, Britain was at first willing to take advantage of New England's opposition to the war by not extending the blockade to the New England coast; but by the beginning of 1814 it was effectively blockading the whole coast and had driven most American naval vessels and privateers off the high seas.

The Second Year, 1813

On land, the objects of the American plan of campaign for 1813 were the recapture of Detroit and an attack on Canada across Lake Ontario. (*See Map 15.*) For the Detroit campaign, Madison picked Brig. Gen. William Henry Harrison, governor of the Indian Territory and hero of Tippecanoe. The difficulties of a winter campaign were tremendous, but the country demanded action. Harrison therefore started north toward Lake Erie at the end of October 1812 with about 6,500 men. In January 1813 a sizable detachment of around 1,000 men pushed on to Frenchtown, a small Canadian outpost on the

Raisin River, twenty-six miles south of Detroit. There, the American commander, Brig. Gen. James Winchester, positioned his men, their backs to the river with scant natural protection and their movements severely hampered by deep snow. A slightly larger force of British regulars, militiamen, and Indians under Col. Henry Proctor soundly defeated the Americans, killing over 100 Kentucky riflemen and capturing about 500. The brutal massacre of wounded American prisoners by their Indian guards made "Remember the Raisin" the rallying cry of the Northwestern Army, but any plans for revenge had to be postponed, for Harrison had decided to suspend operations for the winter. He built Forts Meigs and Stephenson and posted his army near the Michigan border at the western end of Lake Erie.

The Ontario campaign was entrusted to General Dearborn, who was ordered to move his army from Plattsburg to Sacket's Harbor, where Commodore Isaac Chauncey had been assembling a fleet. Dearborn was to move across the lake to capture Kingston and destroy the British flotilla there, then proceed to York (now Toronto), the capital of Upper Canada, to capture military stores. Finally, he was to cooperate with a force from Buffalo in seizing the forts on the Canadian side of the Niagara River.

The American strategy was basically sound. The capture of Kingston, the only tenable site for a naval station on the Canadian side of Lake Ontario, would give the United States control of the lake and, by cutting the British lines of communications, frustrate enemy plans for operations in the west. After the fall of Kingston, the operations against York and the Niagara forts would be simple mopping-up exercises. When the time came to move, however, Dearborn and Chauncey, hearing a rumor that the British forces in Kingston had been reinforced, decided to bypass that objective and attack York first. About 1,700 men sailed up Lake Ontario without incident, arriving off York before daybreak on April 27. Dearborn, who was in poor health, turned over the command of the assault to Brig. Gen. Zebulon Pike, the explorer of the Southwest. The landing, about four miles west of the town, was virtually unopposed. The British garrison of 600 men, occupying a fortification about halfway between the town and the landing, was overwhelmed after sharp resistance; but just as the Americans were pushing through the fort toward the town, a powder magazine exploded, killing or disabling many Americans and a number of British soldiers. Among those killed was General Pike. Remnants of the garrison fled toward Kingston, 150 miles to the east. The losses were heavy on both sides—almost 20 percent of Dearborn's forces had been killed or wounded. With General Dearborn incapacitated and General Pike dead, the troops apparently got out of hand. They looted and burned the public buildings and destroyed the provincial records. After holding the town for about a week, they recrossed the lake to Niagara to join an attack against the forts on the Canadian side of the Niagara River.

Meanwhile, Sacket's Harbor had been almost stripped of troops for the raid on York and for reinforcing the army at Fort Niagara. At Kingston, across the lake, Sir George Prevost, the Governor General of Canada, had assembled a force of 800 British regulars in addition to militia. Taking advantage of the absence of Chauncey's fleet, which was at the other end of the lake, Prevost launched an attack on Sacket's Har-

The troops apparently got out of hand. They looted and burned the public buildings and destroyed the provincial records.

THE BURNING OF YORK

American strategy in 1813 focused on cutting Canada in half. An assault force under the direct command of Zebulon Pike landed at York, present-day Toronto, then the capital of Upper Canada. The Americans also hoped to capture two British warships to shift the balance of naval power on Lake Ontario but failed. After occupying the town for three days and carrying away military supplies, the Americans torched many of the town's public buildings. Burning public places was an acceptable form of warfare at the time, and later the British burned Washington, D.C.

bor with his entire force of regulars on the night of May 26. The town was defended by about 400 regulars and approximately 750 militiamen under the command of Brig. Gen. Jacob Brown of the New York militia. Brown posted his men in two lines in front of a fortified battery to cover a possible landing. Coming ashore under heavy fire, the British nevertheless pressed rapidly forward, routed the first line, and pushed the second back into the prepared defenses. There, the Americans held. The British then tried two frontal assaults but were repulsed with heavy losses. While they were re-forming for a third attack, General Brown rallied the militia and sent it toward the rear of the enemy's right flank. This was the turning point. Having suffered serious losses and in danger of being cut off, the British hurriedly withdrew to their ships.

On the same day Prevost sailed against Sacket's Harbor, General Dearborn at the western end of Lake Ontario was invading Canada with an army of 4,000 men. The operation began with a well-executed and stubbornly resisted amphibious assault led by Col. Winfield Scott and Comdr. Oliver Hazard Perry, U.S. Navy, with Chauncey's fleet providing fire support. Outnumbered by more than two to one, the British retreated, abandoning Fort George and Queenston to the Americans. (*See Map 16.*) An immediate pursuit might have sealed the victory; but Dearborn, after occupying Fort George, waited several days and then sent about 2,000 men after the enemy. The detachment advanced to within ten miles of the British and camped for the night with slight regard for security and even less for the enemy's audacity. During the night a force of about 700 British soldiers attacked the camp and thoroughly routed the Americans. Dearborn withdrew his entire army to Fort George. About two weeks later, a 500-man detachment ventured fifteen miles outside the fort and, when attacked, surrendered to a force of British and Indians that was half as large. After these reverses there was no further action of consequence on the Niagara front for the remainder of the year. Dearborn, again incapacitated by illness, resigned his commission in early July. Both armies were hard hit by disease, and the American forces were further reduced by the renewal of the war in the west and by an attempt against Montreal.

Hull's disaster at Detroit in 1812 and Harrison's unsuccessful winter campaign had clearly shown that any offensive action in that quarter depended upon first gaining control of Lake Erie. Commander Perry had been assigned the task of building a fleet and seizing control of the lake. Throughout the spring and summer of 1813, except for the time

WINFIELD SCOTT (1786–1866)

Born to a southern aristocratic family near Petersburg, Virginia, the six-foot-five-inch Scott was commonly referred to as Old Fuss and Feathers because of his attention to detail and elaborate uniforms. Many disliked him personally because of his arrogant demeanor and overt political ambition. While he never received a formal military education, Scott was a voracious reader who studied the great works on military science. He was a dynamic and brave battlefield commander during the War of 1812 and devised a useful drill for his men that trained them well for the fight. Most scholars recognize that Scott was the most gifted and influential military thinker in America from the War of 1812 through the early years of the American Civil War.

he had joined Dearborn's force, the 27-year-old Perry had been busy at Presque Isle assembling his fleet, guns, and crews. By the beginning of August his force was superior to that of the British in every respect except long-range armament. Sailing up the lake, he anchored in Put-in-Bay, near the line still held by General Harrison in the vicinity of Forts Meigs and Stephenson. There, on September 10 Perry met the British Fleet, defeated it, and gained control of Lake Erie.

As soon as the damage to Perry's ships and the captured British vessels had been repaired, Harrison embarked his army and sailed against Fort Malden. A regiment of mounted Kentucky riflemen under Col. Richard M. Johnson moved along the shore of the lake toward Detroit. Vastly outnumbered on land and now open to attack from the water, the British abandoned both Forts Malden and Detroit and retreated eastward. Leaving a detachment to garrison the forts, Harrison set out after the enemy with the Kentucky cavalry regiments, five brigades of Kentucky volunteers, and a part of the 27th Infantry, a force of about 3,500 men. On October 5 he made contact with the British on the banks of the Thames River about eighty-five miles from Malden. (*See Map 15.*) The enemy numbered about 2,900, of whom about 900 were British regulars and the remainder Indians under Tecumseh. Instead of attacking with infantry in the traditional line-against-line fashion, Harrison ordered a mounted attack. The maneuver succeeded completely. Unable to withstand the charging Kentuckians, the British surrendered in droves. The Indians were routed; Tecumseh, who had brought so much trouble to the western frontier, was killed. Among those who distinguished themselves that day was Commander Perry, who rode in the front rank of Johnson's charge.

As a result of the victory, which illustrated successful employment of the principles of offensive and mass and highlighted the importance of combined land-sea operations, Lake Erie became an American lake. The Indian confederacy was shattered. The American position on the Detroit frontier was reestablished, a portion of Canadian territory was brought under American control, and the enemy threat in that sector

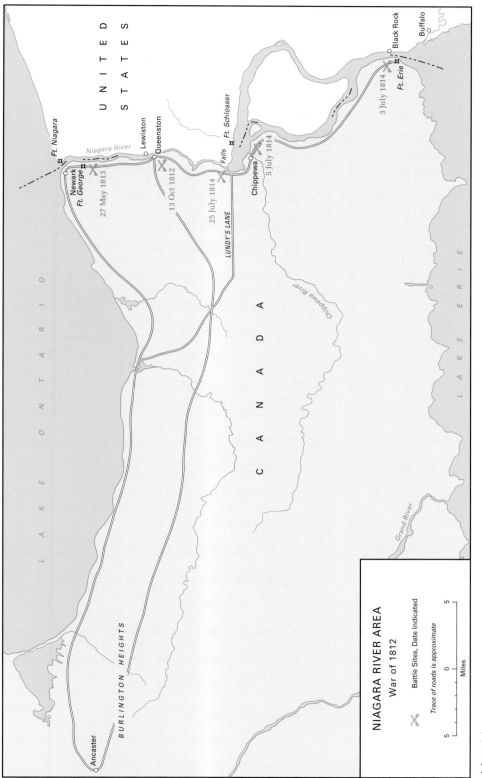

NIAGARA RIVER AREA
War of 1812

⚔ Battle Sites, Date Indicated

Trace of roads is approximate

5   0   5
|_____|_____|
Miles

Map 16

UNITED STATES

CANADA

LAKE ONTARIO

LAKE ERIE

Niagara River

Chippewa River

Grand River

BURLINGTON HEIGHTS

Ancaster

Ft. Niagara

Newark
Ft. George

27 May 1813

Lewiston

Queenston

13 Oct 1812

25 July 1814

LUNDY'S LANE

Falls

Ft. Schlosser

Chippewa

5 July 1814

3 July 1814

Ft. Erie

Black Rock

Buffalo

was eliminated. There was no further fighting here for the rest of the war. It was a decisive victory.

The small remnant of the British force that had escaped capture at the Thames—no more than 250 soldiers and a few Indians—made its way overland to the head of Lake Ontario. Harrison, after discharging his Kentucky volunteers and arranging for the defenses of the Michigan Territory, sailed after it with the remainder of his army. He arrived at the Niagara frontier at an opportune time, since the American forces in that theater were being called upon to support a two-pronged drive against Montreal.

The expedition against Montreal in the fall of 1813 was one of the worst fiascoes of the war.

The expedition against Montreal in the fall of 1813 was one of the worst fiascoes of the war. It involved a simultaneous drive by two forces: one, an army of about 4,000 men assembled at Plattsburg on Lake Champlain under the command of Brig. Gen. Wade Hampton, and another of about 6,000 men under the command of Maj. Gen. James Wilkinson, which was to attack down the St. Lawrence River from Sacket's Harbor. Hampton and Wilkinson were scarcely on speaking terms, and there was no one on the spot to command the two of them. Neither had sufficient strength to capture Montreal without the other's aid; each lacked confidence in the other, and both suspected that the War Department was leaving them in the lurch. At first contact with the British, about halfway down the Chateaugay River, Hampton retreated and, after falling back all the way to Plattsburg, resigned from the Army. Wilkinson, after a detachment of about 2,000 men was severely mauled in an engagement just north of Ogdensburg, also abandoned his part of the operation and followed Hampton into Plattsburg.

In the meantime, during December 1813 the British took advantage of the weakened state of American forces on the Niagara frontier. They recaptured Fort George and crossed the river to take Fort Niagara, which remained in British hands until the end of the war. Before evacuating Fort George, the Americans had burned the town of Newark and part of Queenston. In retaliation the British, after assaulting Fort Niagara with unusual ferocity, loosed their Indian allies on the surrounding countryside and burned the town of Buffalo and the nearby village of Black Rock.

During 1813 a new theater of operations opened in the south. Maj. Gen. (of the Tennessee militia) Andrew Jackson, an ardent expansionist, wrote the Secretary of War that he would "rejoice at the opportunity of placing the American eagle on the ramparts of Mobile, Pensacola, and Fort St. Augustine." (*Map 17*) For this purpose Tennessee had raised a force of 2,000 men to be under Jackson's command. Congress, after much debate, approved only an expedition into that part of the gulf coast in dispute between the United States and Spain and refused to entrust the venture to the Tennesseans. Just before he went north to take part in the Montreal expedition, General Wilkinson led his regulars into the disputed part of West Florida and without meeting any resistance occupied Mobile, while the Tennessee army was left cooling its heels in Natchez.

An Indian uprising in that part of the Mississippi Territory soon to become Alabama saved General Jackson's military career. Inspired by Tecumseh's earlier successes, the Creek Indians took to the warpath in the summer of 1813 with a series of outrages culminating in the mas-

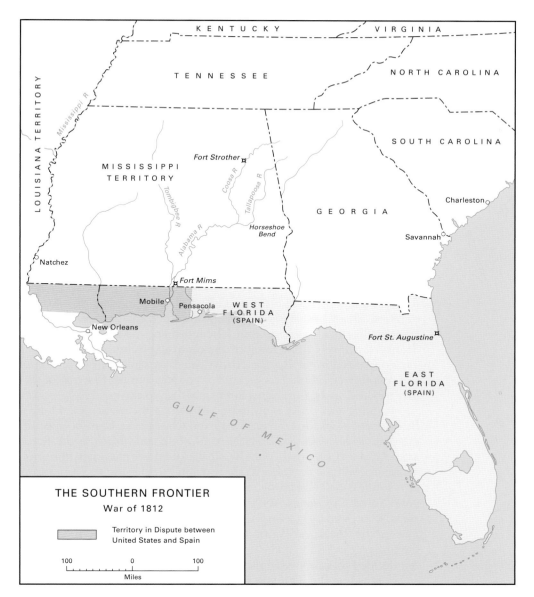

Map 17

sacre of more than 500 men, women, and children at Fort Mims. Jackson, with characteristic energy, reassembled his army, which had been
dismissed after Congress rejected its services for an attack on Florida,
and moved into the Mississippi Territory. His own energy added to his
problems, for he completely outran his primitive supply system and dangerously extended his line of communications. The hardships of the
campaign and one near defeat at the hands of the Indians destroyed any
enthusiasm the militia might have had for continuing in service. Jackson
was compelled to entrench at Fort Strother on the Coosa River and
remain there for several months until the arrival of a regiment of the
Regular Army gave him the means to deal with the mutinous militia.

"OLD HICKORY"

Known as Old Hickory, Andrew Jackson (1767–1845) was said to be as tough as a hickory tree. During his duel with Charles Dickinson in 1806, he broke two of his ribs and a bullet lodged so near his heart that he suffered for his remaining thirty-nine years. A militia general who until 1813 had never led troops in combat, he is best known for his efforts in the Creek War, 1813–1814, and during the War of 1812 in the four battles at New Orleans. Jackson became the seventh U.S. President.

At the end of March 1814 Jackson decided he had sufficient strength for a decisive blow against the Indians, who had gathered a force of about 900 warriors and many women and children in a fortified camp at the Horseshoe Bend of the Tallapoosa River. Jackson had about 2,000 militia and volunteers, nearly 600 regulars, several hundred friendly Indians, and a few pieces of artillery. The attack was completely successful. A bayonet charge led by the regulars routed the Indians, whom Jackson's forces ruthlessly hunted down and killed all but a hundred or so of the warriors. "I lament that two or three women and children were killed by accident," Jackson later reported. The remaining hostile tribes fled into Spanish territory. As one result of the campaign Jackson was appointed a major general in the Regular Army. The campaign against the Creeks had no other effect on the outcome of the war, but for that matter neither had any of the campaigns in the north up to this point.

Fighting also broke out during 1813 along the east coast, where a British fleet blockaded the Delaware and Chesapeake Bays, bottling up the American frigates *Constellation* at Norfolk and *Adams* in the Potomac. (*Map 18*) Opposed only by small American gunboats, the British under Admiral Sir John Warren sought "to chastise the Americans into submission" and at the same time to relieve the pressure on Prevost's forces in Canada. With a flotilla that at times numbered fifteen ships, Rear Adm. Sir George Cockburn, Warren's second in command, roamed the Chesapeake during the spring of 1813, burning and looting the prosperous countryside. Reinforced in June by 2,600 regulars, Warren decided to attack Norfolk, its navy yard and the anchored *Constellation* providing the tempting targets. Norfolk's defenses rested chiefly on Craney Island, which guarded the narrow channel of the Elizabeth River. The island had a seven-gun fortification and was manned by 580 regulars and militia in addition to 150 sailors and marines from the *Constellation*. The British planned to land an 800-man force on the mainland and, when low tide permitted, to march onto the island in a flanking movement. As the tide rose, another 500 men would row across the shoals for a frontal assault. On June 22 the landing party debarked four miles northwest of the island, but the flanking move was countered by the highly accurate marksmanship of the *Constellation's* gunners and was forced to pull back. The frontal assault also suffered from well-directed American fire, which sank three barges and threw the rest into confusion. After taking eighty-one casualties, the British sailed off in disorder. The defenders counted no casualties.

Frustrated at Norfolk, Warren crossed the Roads to Hampton, where he overwhelmed the 450 militia defenders and pillaged the town.

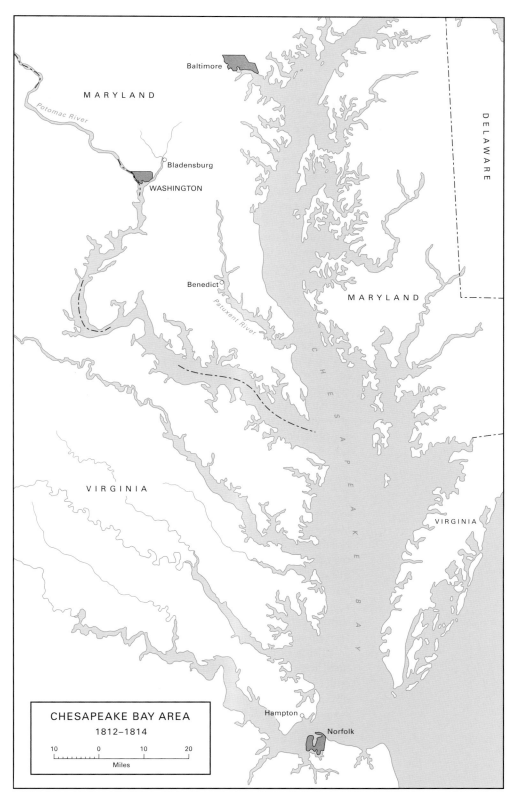

MARYLAND

Baltimore

Potomac River

Bladensburg

WASHINGTON

Benedict

Patuxent River

MARYLAND

DELAWARE

VIRGINIA

C H E S A P E A K E   B A Y

VIRGINIA

Hampton

Norfolk

CHESAPEAKE BAY AREA

1812–1814

10   0   10   20

Miles

Map 18

The conduct of the war in 1812 and 1813 revealed deficiencies . . . that would plague the American cause to the end.

A portion of the fleet remained in the bay for the rest of the year, blockading and marauding; but the operation was not an unalloyed success. It failed to cause a diversion of American troops from the northern border and, by strengthening popular resentment (Cockburn was vilified throughout the country), helped unite Americans behind the war effort.

The conduct of the war in 1812 and 1813 revealed deficiencies in the administration of the War Department that would plague the American cause to the end. In early 1813 Madison replaced his incompetent Secretary of War William Eustis with John Armstrong, who instituted a reorganization that eventually resulted in the substitution of younger, more aggressive field commanders for the aged veterans of the Revolution. Congress then authorized an expansion of the Army staff to help the Secretary manage the war. In March it re-created the Offices of the Adjutant General, Inspector General, Surgeon, and Apothecary General and assigned eight topographical engineers to the staff.

Competent leadership meant little, however, without sufficient logistical support; and logistics, more than any other factor, determined the nature of the military campaigns of the war. Lack of transportation was a major problem. The United States was fighting a war on widely separated fronts that required moving supplies through a wilderness where roads had to be built for wagons and packhorses. For this reason, ammunition and clothing supplies proved inadequate. General Harrison had to depend on homemade cartridges and clothing from Ohio townsmen for his northwestern campaign, and Brig. Gen. Winfield Scott's regulars would fight at Chippewa in the gray uniforms of the New York militia. Winter found the troops without blankets, inadequately housed, and without forage for their horses. Most important, the subsistence supply failed so completely that field commanders found it necessary to take local food procurement virtually into their own hands.

Transportation difficulties accounted for only part of the problem. The supply system devised in 1812 proved a resounding failure. Congressional intent notwithstanding, the Quartermaster General had never assumed accountability for the money and property administered by his subordinates or administrative control over his deputies in the south and northwest. Moreover, the functions of his office, never clearly defined, overlapped those of the Commissary General. In a vain attempt to unravel the administrative tangle, Congress created the Office of Superintendent General of Military Supplies to keep account of all military stores and reformed the Quartermaster Department, giving the Quartermaster General stricter control over his deputies. In practice, however, the deputies continued to act independently in their own districts.

Both Congress and the War Department overlooked the greatest need for reform as the Army continued to rely on contractors for the collection and delivery of rations for the troops. With no centralized direction for subsistence supply, the inefficient, fraud-racked contract system proved to be one of the gravest hindrances to military operations throughout the war.

The Last Year of the War, 1814

After the setbacks at the end of 1813, a lull descended on the northern frontier. In March 1814 Wilkinson made a foray from Plattsburg with about 4,000 men and managed to penetrate about eight miles into Canada before 200 British and Canadian troops stopped his advance. It was an even more miserable failure than his attempt of the preceding fall.

In early 1814 Congress increased the Army to 45 infantry regiments, 4 regiments of riflemen, 3 of artillery, 2 of light dragoons, and 1 of light artillery. The number of general officers was fixed at 6 major generals and 16 brigadier generals in addition to the generals created by brevet. Secretary of War Armstrong promoted Jacob Brown, who had been commissioned a brigadier general in the Regular Army after his heroic defense of Sacket's Harbor, to the rank of major general and placed him in command of the Niagara–Lake Ontario theater. He also promoted the youthful George Izard to major general and gave him command of the Lake Champlain frontier. He appointed six new brigadier generals from the most able, but not necessarily most senior, colonels in the Regular Army, among them Winfield Scott, who had distinguished himself at the battle of Queenston Heights and was now placed in command at Buffalo.

British control of Lake Ontario, won by dint of feverish naval construction during the previous winter, obliged the Secretary of War to recommend operations from Buffalo, but disagreement within the President's Cabinet delayed adoption of a plan until June. Expecting Commodore Chauncey's naval force at Sacket's Harbor to be strong enough to challenge the British Fleet, Washington decided upon a coordinated attack on the Niagara peninsula. (*See Map 16.*) Secretary Armstrong instructed General Brown to cross the Niagara River in the vicinity of Fort Erie and, after assaulting the fort, either to move against Fort George and Newark or to seize and hold a bridge over the Chippewa River, as he saw fit.

Brown accordingly crossed the Niagara River on July 3 with his force of 3,500 men, took Fort Erie, and then advanced toward the Chippewa River, sixteen miles away. There, a smaller British force, including 1,500 regulars, had gathered to oppose the Americans. General Brown posted his army in a strong position behind a creek with his right flank resting on the Niagara River and his left protected by a swamp. In front of the American position was an open plain, beyond which flowed the Chippewa River; on the other side of the river were the British.

BREVET RANK

A brevet was a commission or promotion giving an officer in either the regulars or the volunteers a nominal rank higher than the one for which he received a salary. The Continental Congress adopted it during the American Revolution to recognize heroism in combat and long-term meritorious service. Thus, a particular brave captain could be "promoted" to brevet major during a war but would revert to his permanent rank at the end of the war. After 1812 a brevetted officer could receive additional pay only if the President had assigned him a position that required the higher rank. The wholesale dispensation of brevets during the Civil War discredited the system, and Congress abolished it altogether following the War with Spain.

JACOB J. BROWN (1775–1828)

After trying his hand at teaching, writing, surveying, and working as a secretary to Alexander Hamilton, Jacob Brown became a prosperous landowner in western New York in the early 1800s. His stature in the community led to his appointment as the local militia commander. When war broke out, Brown made up for his lack of military knowledge with enthusiasm and combativeness. Dubbed the Fighting Quaker because of his religious background, Brown was one of the most successful American commanders of the war. After the war he rose to become the Commanding General of the Army.

Jacob J. Brown
John Wesley Jarvis, 1815

In celebration of Independence Day, General Scott had promised his brigade a grand parade on the plain the next day. On July 5 he formed his troops, numbering about 1,300; but on moving forward discovered British regulars had crossed the river undetected and had lined up on the opposite edge of the plain. Scott ordered his men to charge, and the British advanced to meet them. The two lines approached each other, alternately stopping to fire and then moving forward, closing the gaps torn by musketry and artillery fire. They came together first at the flanks, about sixty or eighty yards apart at the center. At this point the British line crumbled and broke. By the time a second brigade sent forward by General Brown reached the battlefield, the British had withdrawn across the Chippewa River and were retreating toward Ancaster on Lake Ontario. Scott's casualties amounted to 48 killed and 227 wounded; British losses were 137 killed and 304 wounded.

Brown followed the retreating British as far as Queenston, where he halted to await Commodore Chauncey's fleet. After waiting two weeks for Chauncey, who failed to cooperate in the campaign, Brown withdrew to Chippewa. He proposed to strike out to Ancaster by way of a crossroad known as Lundy's Lane, from which he could reach the Burlington Heights at the head of Lake Ontario and at the rear of the British.

Meanwhile, the British had drawn reinforcements from York and Kingston and more troops were on the way from Lower Canada. Sixteen thousand British veterans, fresh from Arthur Wellesley, the Duke of Wellington's victories over the French in Europe, had just arrived in Canada, too late to participate in the Niagara campaign but in good time to permit the redeployment of the troops that had been defending the upper St. Lawrence. By the time General Brown decided to pull back from Queenston, the British force at Ancaster amounted to about 2,200 men under General Phineas Riall; another 1,500 British troops were gathered at Fort George and Fort Niagara at the mouth of the Niagara River.

As soon as Brown began his withdrawal, Riall sent forward about 1,000 men along Lundy's Lane, the very route by which General Brown intended to advance against Burlington Heights; another force of more than 600 British troops moved out from Fort George and followed Brown along the Queenston road; while a third enemy force of about 400 men moved along the American side of the Niagara River from Fort Niagara. Riall's advance force reached the junction of Lundy's Lane and the Queenston road on the night of July 24, the same night Brown reached Chippewa, about three miles distant. Concerned lest the British force on the opposite side of the Niagara cut his line of communications and entirely unaware of Riall's force at Lundy's Lane, General Brown on July 25 ordered Scott to take his brigade back along the road toward Queenston in the hope of drawing back the British force on the other side of the Niagara. In the meantime, that force had crossed the river and joined Riall's men at Lundy's Lane. Scott had not gone far when much to his surprise he discovered himself face-to-face with a strong enemy element.

The ensuing battle, most of which took place after nightfall, was the hardest fought, most stubbornly contested engagement of the war. For two hours Scott attacked and repulsed the counterattacks of the numerically superior British force, which, moreover, had the advantage of position. Then both sides were reinforced. With Brown's whole contingent engaged, the Americans now had a force equal to that of the British, about 2,900. They were able to force back the enemy from his position and capture his artillery. The battle then continued without material advantage to either side until just before midnight, when General Brown ordered the exhausted Americans to fall back to their camp across the Chippewa River. The equally exhausted enemy was unable to follow. Losses on both sides had been heavy, each side incurring about 850 casualties. On the American side, both General Brown and General Scott were severely wounded, Scott so badly that he saw no further service during the war. On the British side, General Riall and his superior, General Drummond, who had arrived with the reinforcements, were wounded. Riall was taken prisoner.

Both sides claimed Lundy's Lane as a victory, with some justification, but Brown's invasion of Canada was halted. Commodore Chauncey, who failed to prevent the British from using Lake Ontario for supply and reinforcements, contributed to the ambiguous outcome. In contrast to the splendid cooperation between Harrison and Perry on Lake Erie, relations between Brown and Chauncey were far from satisfactory. A few days after the Battle of Lundy's Lane the American army withdrew to Fort Erie and held this outpost on Canadian soil until early in November.

Reinforced after Lundy's Lane, the British laid siege to Fort Erie at the beginning of August but were forced to abandon the effort on September 21 after heavy losses. Shortly thereafter General Izard arrived with reinforcements from Plattsburg and pushed forward as far as Chippewa, where the British were strongly entrenched. After a few minor skirmishes, he ceased operations for the winter. The works at Fort Erie were destroyed, and the army withdrew to American soil on November 5.

During the summer of 1814 the British had been able to reinforce Canada and to stage several raids on the American coast. Eastport, Maine, on Passamaquoddy Bay, and Castine, at the mouth of the Penobscot River, were occupied without resistance. This operation was

BATTLE OF BLADENSBURG, AUGUST 24, 1814

Derisively known as the Bladensburg Races due to the unseemly manner in which U.S. troops left the field, the defeat owed more to poor command arrangements than the inexperience of the militia that formed the bulk of American forces. The U.S. commander, Brig. Gen. William H. Winder, was indecisive and exhausted from having to organize the defense of the capital without a staff. His subordinates were often uncooperative, while on the day of the battle he received the unwelcome "help" of Secretary of State James Monroe. Without consulting anyone, Monroe redeployed the army in a most unfortunate manner. Even President Madison wandered onto the field, almost getting himself captured in the process. In the end, the troops could not overcome the disarray of their superiors.

something more than a raid since Eastport lay in disputed territory, and it was no secret that Britain wanted a rectification of the boundary. No such political object was attached to British forays in the region of Chesapeake Bay. (*See Map 18.*)

On August 19 a force of some 4,000 British troops under Maj. Gen. Robert Ross landed on the Patuxent River and marched on Washington. At the Battle of Bladensburg, five days later, under the eyes of President Madison, who had arrived on the scene with a number of civilian officials just before the battle, Ross easily dispersed the 5,000 militia, naval gunners, and regulars hastily gathered together to defend the capital. The British then entered Washington, burned the Capitol Building, the White House, and other public buildings and returned to their ships.

Baltimore was next on the schedule, but that city had been given time to prepare its defenses. A rather formidable line of redoubts covered the land approach; the harbor was guarded by Fort McHenry and blocked by a line of sunken gunboats. On September 13 a spirited engagement fought by Maryland militia, many of whom had run at Bladensburg just two weeks before, delayed the invaders and caused considerable loss, including General Ross, who was killed. When the fleet failed to reduce Fort McHenry, the assault on the city was called off.

The British attacks in the Chesapeake Bay region were both high and low points for the American cause. The destruction of Washington after a humiliating defeat was certainly demoralizing. However, the successful defense of Baltimore, and in particular the stirring events around the defense of Fort McHenry that would be enshrined forever in Francis Scott Key's poem, "The Star-Spangled Banner," had a far-reaching impact on the war and on later American history.

Two days before the attack on Baltimore, the British suffered a much more serious repulse on Lake Champlain. After the departure of General Izard for the Niagara front, Brig. Gen. Alexander Macomb had remained at Plattsburg with a force of about 3,300 men. Supporting this force was a small fleet under Commodore Thomas Macdonough. Across the border in Canada was an army of British veterans of the Napoleonic Wars whom Prevost was to lead down the route Burgoyne had taken thirty-seven years before. Moving slowly up the Richelieu River toward Lake Champlain, Prevost crossed the border and on

September 6 arrived before Plattsburg with about 11,000 men. There, he waited for almost a week until his naval support was ready to join the attack. With militia reinforcements, Macomb now had about 4,500 men manning a strong line of redoubts and blockhouses that faced a small river. Macdonough had anchored his vessels in Plattsburg Bay, out of range of British guns but in a position to resist an assault on the American line. On September 11 the British flotilla appeared and Prevost ordered a joint attack. There was no numerical disparity between the naval forces but an important one in the quality of the seamen. Macdonough's ships were manned by well-trained seamen and gunners, the British ships by hastily recruited French-Canadian militia and soldiers with only a sprinkling of regular seamen. As the enemy vessels came into the bay the wind died; and the British were exposed to heavy raking fire from Macdonough's long guns. The British worked their way in and came to anchor; and the two fleets began slugging at each other, broadside by broadside. At the end the British commander was dead and his ships battered into submission. Prevost immediately called off the land attack and withdrew to Canada the next day.

Macdonough's victory ended the gravest threat that had arisen so far. More important, it gave impetus to peace negotiations then under way. News of the two setbacks, Baltimore and Plattsburg, reached England simultaneously, aggravating the war weariness of the British and bolstering the efforts of the American peace commissioners to obtain satisfactory terms.

New Orleans: The Final Battle

The progress of the peace negotiations influenced the British to continue an operation that General Ross, before his repulse and death at Baltimore, had been instructed to carry out: a descent upon the gulf coast to capture New Orleans and possibly sever Louisiana from the United States. (*See Map 17.*) Maj. Gen. Sir Edward Pakenham, one of the Duke of Wellington's distinguished subordinates, was sent to America to take command of the expedition. On Christmas Day, 1814, Pakenham arrived at the mouth of the Mississippi to find his troops disposed on a narrow isthmus below New Orleans between the Mississippi River and a cypress swamp. They had landed two weeks earlier at a shallow lagoon some ten miles east of New Orleans and had already fought one engagement. In this encounter, on December 23, General Jackson, who had taken command of the defenses on December 1, almost succeeded in cutting off a British advance detachment of 2,000, but after a three-hour fight in which casualties on both sides were heavy, he was compelled to retire behind fortifications covering New Orleans.

Opposite the British and behind a ditch stretching from the river to the swamp, Jackson had raised earthworks high enough to require scaling ladders for an assault. About 3,500 men with another 1,000 in reserve manned the defenses. It was a varied group, composed of the 7th and 44th Infantry Regiments, Major Beale's New Orleans Sharpshooters, LaCoste and Daquin's battalions of free African Americans, the Louisiana militia under General David Morgan, a band of Choctaw Indians, the Baratarian pirates, and a motley battalion of fashionably dressed sons and brothers of the New Orleans aristocracy. To support

Battle of New Orleans, *Jean Hyacinthe de Laclotte, 1815*

his defenses, Jackson had assembled more than twenty pieces of artillery, including a battery of nine heavy guns on the opposite bank of the Mississippi.

After losing an artillery duel to the Americans on January 1, Pakenham decided on a frontal assault in combination with an attack against the American troops on the west bank. The main assault was to be delivered by about 5,300 men, while about 600 men under Lt. Col. William Thornton were to cross the river and clear the west bank. As the British columns appeared out of the early morning mist on January 8, they were met with murderous fire, first from the artillery, then from the muskets and rifles of Jackson's infantry. Achieving mass through firepower, the Americans mowed the British down by the hundreds. Pakenham and one other general were killed and a third badly wounded. More than 2,000 of the British were casualties; the American losses were trifling.

Suddenly, the battle on the west bank became critical. Jackson did not make adequate preparations to meet the advance there until the

British began their movement, and by then it was too late. The heavy guns of a battery posted on the west bank were not placed to command an attack along that side of the river; and only about 800 militia, divided in two groups a mile apart, were in position to oppose Thornton. The Americans resisted stubbornly, inflicting greater losses than they suffered, but the British pressed on, routed them, and overran the battery. Had the British continued their advance, Jackson's position would have been critical; but Pakenham's successor in command, appalled by the repulse of the main assault, ordered Thornton to withdraw from the west bank and rejoin the main force. For ten days the shattered remnant of Pakenham's army remained in camp unmolested by the Americans, then reembarked and sailed away.

The British appeared off Mobile on February 8, confirming Jackson's fear that they planned an attack in that quarter. They overwhelmed Fort Bowyer, a garrison manned by 360 regulars at the entrance to Mobile Harbor. Before they could attack the city itself, however, word arrived that a treaty had been signed at Ghent on Christmas Eve, two weeks before the Battle of New Orleans. The most lopsided victory of the war, which helped propel Andrew Jackson to the Presidency, had been fought after the war was officially over.

The news of the peace settlement followed so closely on Jackson's triumph in New Orleans that the war as a whole was popularly regarded in the United States as a great victory. Yet, at best, it was a draw. American strategy had centered on the conquest of Canada and the harassment of British shipping. The land campaign had failed miserably, and during most of the war the Navy was bottled up behind a tight British blockade of the North American coast. The initial success of the privateering effort had enriched a few individuals but was no substitute for a robust navy and did little to achieve the war aims. Ironically, the greatest losers in the war were probably the Indians. The Battles of the Thames in the north and Horseshoe Bend in the south dealt them blows from which they never recovered and in the south set the stage for the forcible removal of most members of the tribes of the "Five Civilized Nations" to the west.

If it favored neither belligerent, the war at least taught the Americans several important lessons. Although the Americans were proud of their reputation as the world's most expert riflemen, the rifle played only a minor role in the war. On the other hand, the American soldier displayed unexpected superiority in gunnery and engineering. Artillery contributed to American successes at Chippewa, Sacket's Harbor, Norfolk, the siege of Fort Erie, and New Orleans. The war also boosted the reputation of the Corps of Engineers, a branch that owed its efficiency chiefly to the Military Academy. Academy graduates completed the fortifications at Fort Erie, built Fort Meigs, planned the harbor defenses of Norfolk and New York, and directed the fortifications at Plattsburg. If larger numbers of infantrymen had been as well trained as the artillerymen and engineers, the course of the war might have been entirely different.

Sea power played a fundamental role in the war; and when combined sea-land operations went well, the resulting campaign was generally successful. In the west, both opponents were handicapped in overland communication, but the British were far more dependent on the

The news of the peace settlement followed so closely on Jackson's triumph in New Orleans that the war as a whole was popularly regarded in the United States as a great victory.

Great Lakes for the movement of troops and supplies for the defense of Upper Canada. In the east, Lake Champlain was strategically important as an invasion corridor to the populous areas of both countries. Just as Perry's victory on Lake Erie decided the outcome of the war in the far west, Macdonough's success on Lake Champlain decided the fate of the British invasion in 1814 and helped influence the peace negotiations.

The much-maligned militia performed, on the whole, as well and as poorly as the Regular Army. The defeats and humiliations of the regular forces during the first years of the war matched those of the militia, just as in a later period the Kentucky volunteers at the Thames and the Maryland militia before Baltimore proved that the state citizen-soldier could perform well. The keys to the militiamen's performance, of course, were training and leadership, the two areas over which the national government had little control. The militia, occasionally competent, was never dependable; though in relationship to the regulars its record was comparable. However, in the nationalistic period that followed the war, when the exploits of the regulars were justly celebrated, an ardent young Secretary of War, John Calhoun, would be able to convince Congress and the nation that the first line of American defense should be a standing army.

DISCUSSION QUESTIONS

1. What advantages did the United States have in the War of 1812 that it did not have during the American Revolution? What disadvantages?

2. Discuss why the contractor system of supply failed so miserably.

3. How did the effectiveness of the militiamen and regulars compare in this war?

4. Give some positive and negative examples of leadership during the war of 1812. Did either side adhere to the principle of unity of command? If so, when?

5. What was the tactical significance of the Battles of Lundy's Lane and Chippewa? What effect did the battles have on American and British morale?

6. What were the American strategic objectives of the war? Were they achieved?

RECOMMENDED READINGS

Gilpin, Alec R. *The War of 1812 in the Old Northwest*. East Lansing: Michigan State University Press, 1958, especially chs. 3–7, 10–11.

Hickey, Donald R. *The War of 1812: A Forgotten Conflict*. Urbana: University of Illinois Press, 1989.

Horsman, Reginald. *The Causes of the War of 1812: National Honor or National Interest?*, 2d ed., ed. Bradford Perkins. Huntington, N.Y.: R. E. Krieger Pub. Co., 1976.

James, Marquis. *Andrew Jackson: The Border Captain*. Norwalk, Conn.: Easton Books, 1960, chs. 9–20.

Lord, Walter. *The Dawn's Early Light*. Baltimore: Johns Hopkins University Press, 1994.

Mahon, John K. *The War of 1812, 2d ed.* New York: Da Capo Press, 1991.

Malcolmson, Robert. *Lords of the Lake: The Naval War on Lake Ontario*. Annapolis, Md.: Naval Institute Press, 1999.

May, Ernest, ed. *The Ultimate Decision: The President as Commander in Chief*. New York: George Braziller, 1960, ch. 2.

Owsley, Frank L., Jr. *Struggle for the Gulf Borderlines: The Creek War and the Battle of New Orleans, 1812–1815*, 2d ed. Tuscaloosa: University of Alabama Press, 2000.

Remini, Robert V. *Andrew Jackson and the Course of American Empire, 1767–1821*. New York: Harper & Row, 1977.

Whitehorne, Joseph A., Carlton Jones, and Joseph W. A. Whitehorne. *The Battle of Baltimore, 1814*. Mount Pleasant, S.C.: The Nautical and Aviation Publishing Company of America, 1997.

Other Readings

Adams, Henry. *The War of 1812,* ed. H. A. DeWeerd. New York: Cooper Square Press, 1999.

Brooks, Charles B. *The Siege of New Orleans*. Seattle: University of Washington Press, 1961.

Coles, Harry L. *The War of 1812*. Chicago: University of Chicago Press, 1965.

Graves, Donald E. *When Right and Glory Lead! The Battle of Lundy's Lane, 1814,* 2d ed. Toronto: Robin Brass Studio, 1997.

Mahan, Alfred T. *Sea Power in Its Relation to the War of 1812*. New York: Scribner, 1903.

Mason, Philip, ed. *After Tippecanoe: Some Aspects of the War of 1812*. East Lansing: Michigan State University Press, 1963.

Muller, Charles. *The Darkest Day: The Washington-Baltimore Campaign During the War of 1812*. Philadelphia: University of Pennsylvania Press, 2003.

Stagg, J. C. A. *Mr. Madison's War: Politics, Diplomacy, and Warfare in the Early American Republic, 1783–1830*. Princeton: Princeton University Press, 1983.

7

TOWARD A PROFESSIONAL ARMY

The War of 1812 sent the Army of the young republic a decidedly mixed message of valor and glory interspersed with cowardice and blunders. The performance of both regulars and militia had been very uneven, although each improved as the conflict drew to a close. In a sort of role reversal, what glory did appear from the victories on the Niagara frontier in 1814 had gone not to the fabled citizen-soldier but to the oft-despised professional. Admittedly, the militia, when properly led as during the Battle of New Orleans, had on occasion done well; but after the war many military realists questioned the ability of the Army to employ him effectively. There were several reasons for this. It was extremely hard to obtain from state governments accurate figures on how many militiamen were available. Another critical limitation on their effectiveness was that since militiamen by their very nature were citizen-soldiers, they did not necessarily live close to where fighting would occur, especially if that were on the frontier. Moreover, the states jealously kept control of arming, disciplining, and training their militia and resisted having the men serve out of state. Though training was crucial, the War Department was limited to making recommendations and supplying training manuals. The Army could not enforce the type of rigorous training that had enabled Bvt. Maj. Gen. Winfield Scott to convert regular soldiers, some of them as raw as militiamen, into the professionals who had excited the admiration of even the British at Chippewa and Lundy's Lane.

For the thirty years after the War of 1812 to the beginning of the Mexican War, the Army of the United States would slowly and painfully evolve into a professional force with generally recognized standards of training, discipline, and doctrine. The first branch schools would open their doors. The U.S. Military Academy would turn out highly motivated professional officers, many of whom were trained engineers, to lead the Army. The new officer corps, including many experienced veterans of the War of 1812 who had supplanted the superannuated veterans of the Revolutionary War, would gain an increased sense of identification as a corporate body of professionals. These officers, tested in countless postings on the expanding frontier and bloodied in the Creek and Seminole Wars, would serve as a skilled cadre, ready when called upon in 1846 to lead a "lightning war" of conquest against Mexico that would vastly increase the size of the United States.

Organizing an Army

As soon as President James Madison proclaimed the peace in February 1815, the Congress, forced to meet at Blodgett's Hotel because the Capitol lay in blackened ruins, acted promptly to create a small but efficient professional army that was thought adequate, with the addition of the militia, to guard against a repetition of the disasters of the War of 1812. Congress voted a peacetime army of 10,000 men (in addition to the Corps of Engineers), about a third of the actual wartime strength, a figure in marked contrast to the 3,220-man regular peacetime establishment under President Thomas Jefferson. Organization and leadership were also improved. The nine wartime military districts, headed generally by superannuated holdovers from the Revolution, were converted into two divisions, a northern with four territorial departments and a southern with five, commanded by officers who had made their reputations in the War of 1812: Maj. Gen. Jacob Brown, Division of the North, and Maj. Gen. Andrew Jackson, Division of the South.

By midsummer 1815, for the first time in nearly a year, President Madison had a full-time Secretary of War. After the forced resignation of Secretary of War John Armstrong at the end of August 1814, mainly as a result of the burning of Washington, Secretary of State James Monroe served as Secretary of War until March 1815, when illness induced him to turn over the office to Secretary of the Treasury Alexander J. Dallas as an additional duty. In the spring of 1815 Madison appointed William H. Crawford, Minister to France, as Secretary of War. By August 1815 he had returned from Paris and was able to take up his duties.

Crawford had a record of distinguished service in the U.S. Senate. He had declined the appointment as Secretary of War later offered to Armstrong; but he had maintained a deep interest in the War Department, especially in the General Staff that Congress created in the spring of 1813. Because its purpose was mainly to conduct the housekeeping functions of the Army, it was not a general staff as the term was used a hundred years later but resembled rather the modern special staff. Under it had been placed the Quartermaster, Topographical, Adjutant General, Inspector General, Ordnance, Hospital, Purchasing, and Pay Departments; the Judge Advocates; the Chaplains; the Military Academy; and the commanding generals of the nine military districts and their logistical staffs. Furthermore, by stationing in Washington at the War Department certain officers of the General Staff—the Adjutant and Inspector General (a dual function performed by one officer) with two assistants, the Commissary General of Ordnance with three assistants, the Paymaster of the Army, and the Assistant Topographical Engineer—Congress had provided a management staff for the Secretary of War, who hitherto had only a few clerks to assist him.

Rare Pattern 1812 Bell Crown Shako Manufactured ca. 1830

Watching events from Paris in the fall of 1813, Secretary Crawford begged Albert Gallatin "For God's sake" to "endeavor to rid the army of old women and blockheads, at least on the general staff." The reorganization of the Army in the spring of 1815 weeded out most of the incompetents. When Crawford took office he recommended to Congress the retention of the General Staff, because the history of the early campaigns in the late war had convinced him of "the necessity of giving to the military establishment, in time of peace, the organization which it must have to render it efficient in a state of war."

The only major change he recommended was the addition of the Quartermaster General to the management staff in Washington. He also recommended an increase in the Corps of Engineers. Crawford's proposals went into effect by Act of Congress on April 24, 1816; and a few days later Congress authorized the President to employ a "skilful assistant" in the Corps of Engineers, thus securing the services of a brilliant military engineer, Brig. Gen. Simon Bernard, who had served under Napoleon. Congress also voted $838,000, by today's standards nearly $8 million, for a major program of coastal fortification, an effort to prevent a repetition of the humiliations suffered in the War of 1812.

At the same time Congress appropriated $115,800 for new buildings at the U.S. Military Academy at West Point and $22,171 for books, maps, and instruments. Given the small size of the federal government in the early republic, these were substantial sums to devote to the fledgling institution. With Secretary Crawford's sponsorship, facilities and staff of the academy were expanded, the curriculum broadened, regulations for admission tightened, and provision made for a Board of Visitors. In September 1816 the cadets first received gray uniforms, honoring (according to tradition) the regulars of Chippewa and Lundy's Lane, who wore the rough gray kersey of the New York militia because they lacked jackets of regulation federal blue.

Having fostered a peacetime professional army, Crawford might have used his considerable influence with Congress to strengthen it if he had been left in office longer, as he wished. But in the fall of 1816 President Madison asked him to resign and become Secretary of the Treasury in order to bring Henry Clay into the cabinet as Secretary of War. Clay and several others declined the appointment. For more than a year George Graham, the War Department's chief clerk, was Acting Secretary of War. During that period, as the threat from Europe lessened, Congress began to lose interest in the peacetime army. The actual strength had fallen to about 8,200 men at the time John C. Calhoun took the oath as Secretary of War on December 8, 1817. The new Secretary was faced with proposals to cut the Army's authorized strength, abolish the General Staff, and discontinue the Military Academy. But before Calhoun could devote his talents to staving off such proposals, he was faced with an outbreak of Indian warfare on the border between Georgia and the Spanish province of Florida.

William Harris Crawford
Daniel Huntington, 1875

The War Hatchet Raised in Florida

The Indians threatening the Georgia frontier were the Lower Creeks, a faction of the Creek Nation that had fled to Florida after being defeated in 1814. Called the Red Sticks because of their red war

Major General Andrew Jackson,
President of the United States
*Thomas Sully, ca. 1820, from engraving
by James B. Longacre*

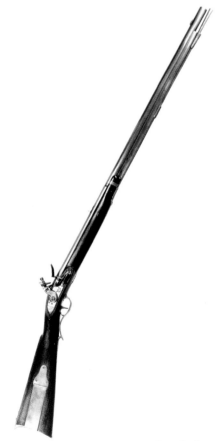

U.S. Model 1803 Harpers Ferry Rifle

clubs, they settled in the swamps and palmetto forests along with Seminole Indians. The Seminoles were an amalgam of Indian bands mixed with fugitive African American slaves who had migrated from the river valleys of Georgia and Alabama to the protective swamps and pine barrens of Florida. These Indians went unrestrained by weak Spanish officials, shut up in their enclaves at St. Augustine on the east coast, St. Marks in central northern Florida, and Pensacola on the west coast.

Poorly treated by settlers and U.S. government agents, these Indians were ripe for open resistance. The spark came from an unexpected source. The Lower Creeks and Seminoles, already suspicious and disgruntled, were encouraged to attack American settlers in Georgia by two British adventurers from the Bahamas. Lt. Col. Edward Nicholls had employed the Indians in his abortive expedition against Mobile in the summer of 1814 and had left them well armed when he sailed away to England in 1815. Another instigator was a trader, Alexander Arbuthnot. Both incited the Indians by telling them the false story that the southern part of Georgia, which the Creeks had surrendered in the treaty of 1814, had been returned to them by the Treaty of Ghent and thus Americans were settling on lands that belonged to the Indians.

By the fall of 1817 the U.S. Army was attempting to protect the settlers by reinforcing Fort Scott, a log fort built at the southwestern tip of Georgia where the Chattahoochee and Flint Rivers combine to form the Apalachicola. Flowing through Florida to the Gulf, the Apalachicola provided a supply route from Mobile or New Orleans to the fort. At the end of November 1817 an Army keelboat ascending the Apalachicola in advance of supply transports was attacked from the bank by a party of Indians who killed or captured thirty-four of the forty persons aboard: soldiers and wives of soldiers.

The news of the attack, reaching Washington on December 26, 1817, brought on the conflict known as the First Seminole War. Calhoun ordered General Jackson to proceed immediately from Nashville to Fort Scott and take command and authorized him to request additional militia in case he thought the force on the scene (800 regulars and about 1,000 Georgia militia) insufficient. Jackson, who had already reported to the War Department that he was expecting trouble in Florida, "the war hatchet having been raised," acted promptly. Calculating that the three-month Georgia militia might have gone home before he could arrive at Fort Scott, he sent out a call for 1,000 six-month volunteers from West Tennessee. Dispatching to Fort Hawkins in central Georgia an officer with $2,000 to buy provisions and ordering further stores to come forward by ship from New Orleans, Jackson, escorted by two mounted companies, set off in advance of the troops.

Riding into Fort Hawkins on the evening of February 9, Jackson was enraged to discover that the contractor who had agreed to supply him with rations had failed to do so. For more than a thousand men, he reported to Calhoun, there was not "a barrel of flour or a bushel of corn." Procuring locally some pigs, corn, and peanuts, he kept going, arriving at Fort Scott on March 9. There, he learned that ships loaded with provisions from Mobile had come into the mouth of the Apalachicola. To Jackson it was all important to protect these boats from Indians who might attack them from the riverbank. He set off next morning with his Georgia militiamen and 400 regulars from Fort Scott on a protective march down the east bank of the Apalachicola. Six days later he was at the river mouth. He halted his force and ordered Lt. James Gadsden of the Corps of Engineers to build a fort, named Fort Gadsden, for storing the supplies he was expecting from New Orleans.

Jackson's supply flotilla, delayed by a gale, did not arrive until March 25. The following day he began his campaign. His objective was a large Indian settlement on the Suwannee River, 150 miles to the east, where a force of several thousand Indians and slaves under a Seminole chief, Billy Bowlegs, was said to be preparing for battle. Because he needed a supply base nearer than Fort Gadsden, he decided to take the Spanish fort of St. Marks on the way and arranged for the supplies to be brought by ship to the bay of St. Marks.

Stopping at the Ochlockonee River to make canoes for the crossing and farther along to clean out some Indian villages, on April 7 Jackson took St. Marks, in the process capturing Arbuthnot, whom he imprisoned. In the meantime a brigade of friendly Upper Creek Indians had ridden up along with the first detachment of the Tennessee volunteers. Because of the failure in supply, the main body of Tennesseeans did not catch up with Jackson until April 11, when he was well on the swampy trail to Bowlegs' Town.

The campaign was something of an anticlimax. From Bowlegs' Town the Indians and slaves had fled, having been warned by Arbuthnot. The only gains were corn and cattle to feed Jackson's troops and the capture of a third adventurer from the Bahamas, Robert C. Ambrister, who had been arming and drilling Bowlegs' men. Ambrister was taken back to St. Marks and along with Arbuthnot was tried by a military court and executed. Dismissing the Georgia militia and the Indian brigade, Jackson proceeded west with his regulars and Tennesseeans. At Fort Gadsden, early in May, he learned that Indians were assembling in Pensacola. He seized Pensacola, ran up the American flag, and left a garrison there as well as at St. Marks when he returned to Nashville late in May.

Jackson's highhanded actions in the First Seminole War—his invasion of Spanish territory, capture of Spanish forts, and execution of British subjects—might have had serious diplomatic repercussions if Spain or Great Britain had chosen to make an issue of them; but neither nation did. Negotiations with Spain for the purchase of Florida were already under way, and shortly after the return of the forts to Spain, the Adams-Onís Treaty ceded Florida to the United States in February 1819.

For the Army the most significant aspect of the war had been the near total breakdown in the supply system. From the time Jackson rode out of Nashville in late January 1818 until his first encounter with the Indians early in April, he had had to devote all his energies to feeding his troops. The principal reason for this was the failure of civilian contractors. The folly of depending on civilians for so essential an item as rations had been amply demonstrated in the War of 1812, and Jackson's experience in the First Seminole War only underscored it. At Calhoun's suggestion the Congress in April 1818 required contractors to deliver rations in bulk at depots and provided a better system of Army-controlled transportation and supply methods. For the first time since the Revolutionary War, the Army had a Subsistence Department, headed by the Commissary General of Subsistence.

John C. Calhoun and the War Department

Calhoun was convinced that the American frontier ought to be protected by regulars rather than by the militia. Calling the militia into active service, he wrote Brig. Gen. Edmund P. Gaines, was "harassing to them and exhausting to the treasury. Protection is the first object, and the second is protection by the regular force." But providing a regular force capable of protecting the frontiers north, south, and west, as well as the seacoast, was another matter. In 1820 the Congress called upon the Secretary of War to report on a plan for the reduction of the Army to 6,000 men. Calhoun suggested that the reduction, if it had to come, could be effected by cutting the enlisted personnel of each company to half strength. In time of war the Army could be quickly expanded to a force of 19,000 officers and men. This was the start of the "expansible army" concept.

On March 2, 1821, Congress passed the Reduction Act that cut the enlisted strength of the Army by half (from 11,709 to 5,586) but cut the size of the officer corps by only a fifth (from 680 to 540). Thus, even though the Congress had cut the end strength of the Army overall, its limited reduction of the officer corps confirmed that the idea of an expansible army was beginning to achieve a measure of acceptance. Calhoun, although concerned with the drastic nature of the cuts, pronounced himself reasonably satisfied. The retention of a proportionally larger officer cadre would allow the Army to expand more rapidly upon the approach of war. This was a key milestone on the road to recognizing that the Regular Army and its officer corps was the first line of our nation's defense rather than relying totally upon the militia or hastily raised, equipped, and trained volunteer units.

The Reduction Act also provided for 7 regiments of infantry and 4 regiments of artillery instead of the existing 8 regiments of infantry, a rifle regiment, a regiment of light artillery, and a corps of artillery comprising 8 battalions. The Ordnance Department was staffed by artillery officers; no ordnance officers were commissioned until 1832. The Northern and Southern Divisions were abolished and replaced by an Eastern and a Western Department, under the respective commands of Generals Scott and Gaines. Only one major general was provided. Because General Jackson had resigned from the Army to become Governor of Florida, the commission remained with General Brown, the hero of Sacket's Harbor in the War of 1812.

To provide a senior line officer in the chain of command, lack of which had been a serious deficiency during the War of 1812, Calhoun brought Brown to Washington in a position that later became known as Commanding General of the Army. Brown held it until his death in 1828, when he was succeeded by Maj. Gen. Alexander Macomb. When Macomb died in 1841, Maj. Gen. Winfield Scott was appointed. Made a brevet lieutenant general in 1847 (the first three-star general since George Washington), Scott served as Commanding General of the Army until his retirement in 1861.

Secretary Calhoun's administration accomplished many other important innovations in Army management. Beginning in mid-1822, recruiting depots were opened in major cities, east and west, to enlist men for the Army at large, not for specific units. Though regimental

> The retention of a proportionally larger officer cadre . . . was a key milestone on the road to recognizing that the Regular Army and its officer corps was the first line of our nation's defense.

recruiting continued, the General Recruiting Service in its first three years of operation enlisted about 68 percent more men than did the regiments. General Scott prepared a new manual of infantry tactics for regulars and militia and, on the basis of his research in Paris in 1815, prepared the Army regulations of 1821, going minutely into every detail of the soldier's life, including the ingredients of his soup. The first commissioned Surgeon General, Joseph Lovell, whom Calhoun appointed, further improved the soldier's diet. Also, by requiring daily weather reports from all medical officers, in an attempt to find some correlation between weather and army diseases, Lovell provided basic data for the first study of weather in the United States and the most complete data of the sort in the world.

Under Calhoun, the work of seacoast fortification went steadily forward. By 1826 eighteen harbors and ports from the Penobscot River to the mouth of the Mississippi had been fortified with a total of thirty-one works, generally consisting of sloping earthworks covered with grass and backed by stone or brick walls. By 1843 the harbor defense program had been extended to thirty-five or forty coastal areas with sixty-nine fortifications either in place or under construction. By then the War Department was placing greater emphasis on heavy artillery (24- and 32-lb. guns and 8-inch howitzers) to keep pace with increasingly heavy naval armaments.

Calhoun early turned his attention to the Military Academy, where Crawford's attempts at rehabilitation had been impeded by controversy stirred up by the arbitrary actions of Superintendent Capt. Alden Partridge. After Partridge was removed and Bvt. Maj. Sylvanus Thayer was appointed Superintendent in July 1817, the academy became a vital force in maintaining a corps of professionally trained officers. The War Department had sent Thayer to Europe in 1815 as one of the first of a succession of Army officers sent abroad in the early nineteenth century to study, among other things, foreign military schools. With Calhoun's support, Thayer organized the West Point cadets into tactical units, created the Commandant of Cadets, improved the curriculum, and introduced new methods of instruction. Under his administration, West Point became the premier school for engineers in the United States. For his achievements during his sixteen-year superintendence, Thayer became known as the father of the U.S. Military Academy.

Military education was further advanced in 1824, when, as a result of Calhoun's proposal for a "school of practice" for men in service,

SYLVANUS THAYER (1785–1872)

Sylvanus Thayer, "father of the Military Academy," became Superintendent of that struggling institution just nine years after graduating from it. Thayer assumed command in 1817 and instituted sweeping reforms that reflected lessons from his recent tour of European military academies. He introduced a strict code of discipline, emphasized honor and integrity, formalized and expanded the curriculum, ranked cadets within each class, improved the faculty, and confirmed West Point as the foremost engineering school in the nation. When Thayer left in 1833, the U.S. Military Academy was fully comparable to its European counterparts.

the Artillery School at Fortress Monroe was established. It was the first of the Army's specialist schools; but unlike most modern schools, it instructed not individuals but an entire unit, which was assigned there for a year's tour of duty. It was closed in 1835, when all the students were sent to Florida to meet the threat of the Second Seminole War, and it was not reopened until 1858. In 1826, the Infantry School of Practice was established at Jefferson Barracks, Missouri. Both schools were major milestones in the development of a standard doctrine and common training regimen for the new professional army.

In 1818 Calhoun formed the first official and complete artillery system for the three categories of artillery (field, siege and garrison, and seacoast), following recommendations by a board of artillery and ordnance officers he had appointed to study the issue. The system was based largely on that of field carriages developed by the famous French artillerist, General Jean Baptiste de Gribeauval. During the next twenty years growing doubts about the Gribeauval system led succeeding Boards of Ordnance to recommend a newer French system, based on that of the British, called the stock-trail because the carriage used a single trail of a solid block of wood rather than the old twin trail. It was simpler than the previous system and introduced interchangeability in carriages and parts. Approved by Secretary of War Joel R. Poinsett and adopted in 1839, the stock-trail was used in the Mexican War. The same board that recommended it also endorsed the introduction of rockets and rocket units into the U.S. Army. The rocket contemplated was patterned after the famous Congreve the British used in the War of 1812.

Pioneering in the West

In the three decades after 1815, the Army pushed westward ahead of the settlers, surveying, fortifying, and building roads. (*Map 19*) Stockades and forts built and garrisoned in Iowa, Nebraska, and Kansas became the footholds of settlement in the wild frontier; just outside the walls could be found gristmills, sawmills, and blacksmith shops, all of them erected by the troops. Fort Leavenworth, established in 1827 as the first permanent fort on the western bank of the Missouri River, was the main base for Army expeditions sent out along the Santa Fe and Oregon Trails. An important Army explorer in the 1830s, Capt. Benjamin L. E. Bonneville of the 7th Infantry, took a four-year leave of absence and made valuable observations concerning the Pacific coast. These early expeditions were made by infantrymen using steamboats, wagons, and oxcarts. The expert horsemanship and tactical mobility of the Indians on the Great Plains also prompted the Army in 1832 to organize its first battalion of mounted rangers. The battalion was expanded the following year into a regiment of dragoons, essentially horse-mounted infantry, the first cavalry-type units to appear in the Regular Army since 1815.

A western man became Secretary of War in 1831. Lewis Cass, former Governor of Michigan, was to be the first long-term Secretary since Calhoun. Like Calhoun, he had hardly assumed office when an Indian war broke out. By 1831 American emigrants pouring westward after the opening of the Erie Canal in 1824 were settling on Indian

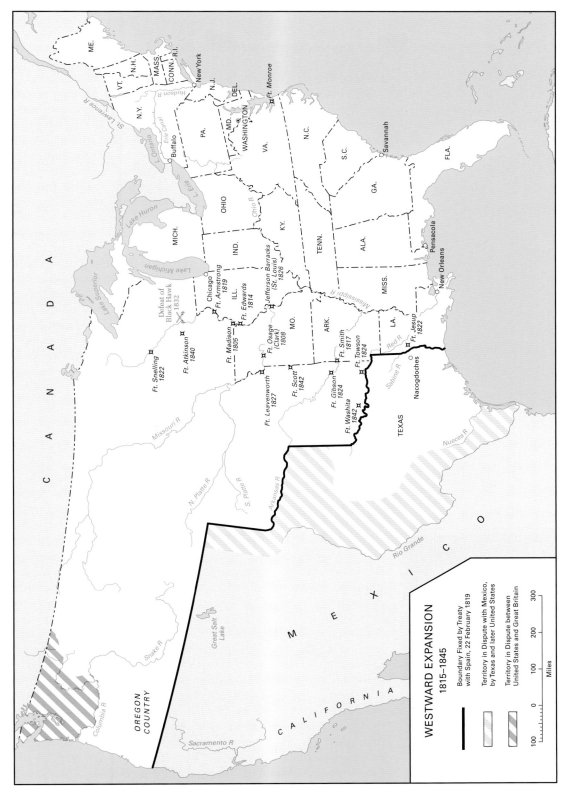

WESTWARD EXPANSION
1815–1845

Boundary Fixed by Treaty
with Spain, 22 February 1819

Territory in Dispute with Mexico,
by Texas and later United States

Territory in Dispute between
United States and Great Britain

Miles

100   0   100   200   300

Map 19

CANADA

MEXICO

CALIFORNIA

OREGON COUNTRY

TEXAS

ME.
N.H.
VT.
MASS.
CONN. R.I.
N.Y.
PA.
N.J.
DEL.
MD.
WASHINGTON
VA.
N.C.
S.C.
GA.
FLA.
OHIO
IND.
ILL.
MICH.
KY.
TENN.
ALA.
MISS.
LA.
ARK.
MO.

New York
Ft. Monroe
Buffalo
Savannah
Pensacola
New Orleans
Nacogdoches
Chicago

St. Lawrence R
L. Ontario
Erie Canal
L. Erie
Lake Huron
Lake Michigan
Lake Superior
Hudson R
Ohio R
Mississippi R
Missouri R
N. Platte R
S. Platte R
Arkansas R
Red R
Sabine R
Nueces R
Rio Grande
Columbia R
Snake R
Sacramento R
Great Salt Lake

Ft. Snelling
1822
Ft. Atkinson
1840
Defeat of
Black Hawk
1832
Ft. Armstrong
1819
Ft. Madison
1805
Ft. Edwards
1814
Jefferson Barracks
(St. Louis)
1826
Ft. Osage
(Clark)
1808
Ft. Leavenworth
1827
Ft. Scott
1842
Ft. Gibson
1824
Ft. Smith
1817
Ft. Towson
1824
Ft. Washita
1842
Ft. Jesup
1822

lands in western Illinois from which the Sac and Fox Indians had been pushed out to the prairies west of the Mississippi River. A band of Sac warriors under Chief Black Hawk, called the British Band because they had served with the British during the War of 1812, crossed the Mississippi in the spring of 1831 and began burning settlers' houses. General Gaines, commanding the Western Department, moved in with a large body of regulars and volunteers; and Black Hawk retired across the river. But the chief returned a year later with 500 warriors and 1,500 women and children with the intention of reestablishing his people on the east bank of the river.

Cass, who knew the importance of impressing the Indians with a show of force, ordered Col. Henry Atkinson, commanding at Jefferson Barracks, to take the field with regulars of the 6th Infantry and told General Scott to bring about 1,000 infantry and artillery from the East Coast. The Governor of Illinois called out a large force of militia. (Among them was the young Abraham Lincoln, elected captain of his company, who later became the sixteenth President of the United States.) After an inconclusive brush with the Indians, most of the Illinois volunteers returned home. On August 2, 1832, Atkinson with 500 regulars and as many volunteers as he had been able to collect caught up with the Indians in southern Wisconsin at the confluence of the Bad Axe River and the Mississippi and defeated them decisively, with the help of an Army steamboat carrying a 6-lb. gun firing canister. Five days after the battle General Scott arrived, but he had with him only a remnant of his forces. Cholera had broken out aboard his crowded transports on the Great Lakes, killing or disabling one third of the force. Many others had deserted or could not be brought forward for fear of contagion. Nevertheless, by that time Scott's men were no longer needed.

The Second Seminole War, 1835–1842

Early in 1832, at the direction of Secretary Cass, the U.S. Indian commissioner in Florida negotiated a treaty with the Seminoles, ratified in 1834, by which the Indians would relinquish their lands in Florida and move to Arkansas. The deadline was eventually set at January 1, 1836. However, many of the Indians were determined to resist what they viewed as the theft of their lands. Long before the deadline, the Seminoles, led by a charismatic half-Indian named Osceola, demonstrated that they would not go peaceably. Numerous sugar plantations in north and central Florida were raided and burned. These outbreaks of violence led the Army to reinforce Fort Brooke on Tampa Bay and Fort King, near present-day Ocala in central Florida, about a hundred miles to the northeast. By December 1835, nine companies of artillery and two of infantry—five hundred thirty-six officers and men—were in Florida under the command of Bvt. Brig. Gen. Duncan L. Clinch.

On the afternoon of December 28, 1835, Osceola with sixty warriors hidden near Fort King killed Wiley Thompson, the agent appointed to superintend the removal, as he was taking a walk outside the fort. Also killed was his dinner companion, Lt. Constantine Smith, and several nearby settlers. The same day another party of 180 warriors attacked a slow-moving column of 110 regulars led by Bvt. Maj. Francis L. Dade, about halfway between Fort Brooke and Fort King. The strung-out col-

Knapsack for Volunteer Militia, ca. 1830

OSCEOLA

Osceola was born to a Red Stick Creek mother and a father of Scots descent. He immigrated to Florida after General Jackson's defeat of the Red Sticks in the Creek War (1813–1814). In Florida, Osceola joined a Seminole Indian band and rose to prominence despite his non-Seminole origins. Having refused to sign the treaty forcing the Seminoles and other Florida Indians to emigrate to reservations in Arkansas, he became a leader of those who fought emigration. From 1835 to 1837, he resisted Army efforts to capture or kill him and his followers. He was legendary for his ability to use the swampy terrain, guerrilla tactics, and the fighting abilities of his followers to repel or damage larger forces. Osceola was seized in October 1837 while negotiating under a flag of truce. Suffering from several illnesses, he was transported to Fort Moultrie, South Carolina, where he died on January 30, 1838.

Osceola of Florida
George Catlin, 1838

umn, which included a 6-lb. cannon, was ambushed by carefully concealed Seminoles under war leaders Micanopy, Alligator, and Jumper. The first volley cut down Major Dade and almost half his force. The remnant retreated under fire and hastily erected a triangular log breastwork some two hundred yards from the ambush site. The defenders kept shooting as long as the ammunition held out, but gradually their fire slackened. By late in the afternoon, the defenders were helpless and the Indians rushed the breastworks, wielding their tomahawks and clubs. Only two men from the column escaped back to Fort Brooke, both severely wounded; and one died of his wounds within the next few months. The Second Seminole War had begun. (*See Map 20.*)

Although the Dade Massacre took place west of a line dividing the Eastern and Western Departments and was therefore in General Gaines' department, President Andrew Jackson and Secretary Cass preferred to give the command to General Scott. Gaines, who was then on an inspection trip in New Orleans, was ordered to the western frontier of Louisiana to take command of all U.S. troops in the region adjoining the boundary with Texas.

General Scott left Washington on January 21, 1836. Stopping in South Carolina and Georgia to arrange for militia and supplies and to set up a depot in Savannah, he did not arrive at his headquarters in Florida near St. Augustine until February 22. Because of logistical troubles and the difficulty of moving troops over primitive, unexplored terrain to Tampa Bay (where he had planned a three-pronged offensive to bottle up the Seminoles in a swamp nearby), it was April 5 before he could begin his campaign there. By that time the Seminoles had melted away into the Everglades. Since hot weather had set in, the militiamen, whose three-month terms of service had expired, were ready to go home. As a South Carolina militia officer summed up the campaign,

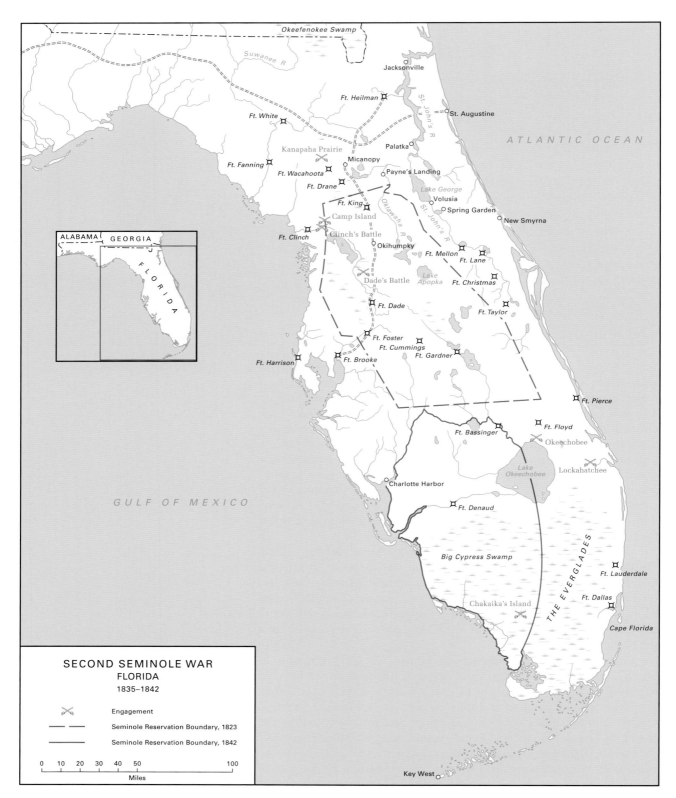

Okeefenokee Swamp

Suwanee R.

Jacksonville

Ft. Heilman

St. Augustine

Ft. White

St. John's R.

Palatka

ATLANTIC OCEAN

Kanapaha Prairie

Ft. Fanning

Micanopy

Payne's Landing

Ft. Wacahoota

Lake George

Ft. Drane

Volusia

Spring Garden

New Smyrna

Ft. King

Camp Island

Clinch's Battle

Okihumpky

Ft. Mellon

Ft. Lane

Ft. Clinch

Oklawaha R.

St. John's R.

Dade's Battle

Lake Apopka

Ft. Christmas

Ft. Dade

Ft. Taylor

Ft. Foster

Ft. Cummings

Ft. Harrison

Ft. Brooke

Ft. Gardner

Ft. Pierce

Ft. Bassinger

Ft. Floyd

Okeechobee

GULF OF MEXICO

Lake Okeechobee

Lockahatchee

Charlotte Harbor

Ft. Denaud

Big Cypress Swamp

THE EVERGLADES

Ft. Lauderdale

Chakaika's Island

Ft. Dallas

Cape Florida

ALABAMA   GEORGIA

FLORIDA

SECOND SEMINOLE WAR
FLORIDA
1835–1842

 Engagement

— — — Seminole Reservation Boundary, 1823

——— Seminole Reservation Boundary, 1842

0 10 20 30 40 50 100

Miles

Key West

Map 20

"Two months were consumed in preparations and effecting nothing, and the third in marching to Tampa and back again."

Though Scott's experiences in the Second Seminole War resembled in some respects those of Jackson in the First Seminole War eighteen years before, there were two important differences. First, the logistical failure was a failure in transportation, not in supply. The depots had been adequately stocked; but wagons, roads, and Army maps were lacking. Second, General Scott had to contend with the intrusion of a subordinate commander, General Gaines, who disregarded orders and brought a large force of Louisiana militiamen from New Orleans by ship to Tampa Bay in February. Supplying this force with rations intended for Scott's troops, Gaines fought an inconclusive battle with the Indians and returned to New Orleans in March.

During May General Scott at his headquarters near St. Augustine managed to antagonize many of the Florida settlers by accusing them of cowardice. He further alienated the volunteers by officially requesting the War Department in Washington that he be sent 3,000 "good troops (not volunteers)." Floridians burned him in effigy and cheered when he was transferred to Georgia at the end of May to put down an uprising of the Creek Nation, which was threatening to spill over from eastern Alabama into Georgia and Florida. There, the general got into trouble again with Bvt. Maj. Gen. Thomas S. Jesup, in command of operations in Alabama. Jesup had the temerity to win a battle with the Indians before Scott could put his own elaborate plans into effect, to the latter's great displeasure. In a letter to one of the President's advisers, Jesup charged Scott with unnecessary delay: "the Florida scenes enacted all over again."

The upshot of the controversy with Jesup was Scott's recall to Washington to face a court of inquiry. The court absolved him of all blame for the Florida fiasco, but he did not return to the Seminole War. Instead, he was given diplomatic missions for which he had demonstrated his ability during the South Carolina Nullification Crisis in 1833, when he managed to strengthen the federal forts around Charleston without provoking hostilities. He was also successful in resolving several conflicts that broke out between American and Canadian settlers on the northern frontier and in persuading 15,000 Cherokee Indians in Georgia to move west peaceably.

The war in Florida continued for six years. General Jesup, commanding from late 1836 to May 1838, was not able either to persuade the Indians to leave Florida or to drive them out. He did, however, manage to drive a wedge between the Seminoles and their escaped slave allies and, in a major coup, to capture the Seminole leader Osceola by luring him into a conference under a flag of truce. Despite this treachery, however, the war dragged on. Jesup assembled a large force of over 4,500 regulars and 4,000 volunteers. He divided this force into separate columns and launched them into Seminole strongholds in central and southern Florida. Colonel Zachary Taylor, in command of one of the columns, collided with a strong and dug-in Seminole force of 500 warriors near Lake Okeechobee. Attacking on Christmas Day 1837, Taylor and his column of around 1,000 men charged the Seminole positions. After several hours of intense fighting, one wing of the Seminoles broke and retreated into the safety of the swamps. The rest

The war in Florida continued for six years. General Jesup . . . was not able either to persuade the Indians to leave Florida or to drive them out.

were then routed in one of the largest and hardest fought battles of the Second Seminole War. It cost Taylor 26 killed and 112 wounded, while the Seminoles lost fewer than 14; but it was still a victory for the army. It also earned Taylor his brevet as brigadier general.

Bvt. Brig. Gen. Zachary Taylor succeeded Jesup as overall commander in Florida in May 1839. He adopted a policy of dividing the disaffected region into small districts and searching out the Indians with a pack of bloodhounds—a brief and unsuccessful experiment that aroused a furor in the United States. Taylor's search-and-destroy methods might have produced results, given time, but the War Department insisted on another attempt at negotiation and suspended hostilities. The raids were resumed. Taylor asked to be relieved and was followed by Bvt. Brig. Gen. Walker K. Armistead, who again tried negotiation and failed. In May 1841 Armistead was succeeded by Col. William J. Worth, who brought about a radical change. Hitherto the campaign in Florida had been suspended during the summer season when fever and dysentery were prevalent. Worth campaigned throughout the summer of 1841, preventing the Indians from raising and harvesting crops. By waging a ruthless war of extermination and by destroying food supplies and dwellings, he routed the Indians out of their swamps and hammocks and permitted the war to be officially ended in August 1842; though scattered bands held out in the Everglades for years to come.

The Second Seminole War had been guerrilla warfare of a kind the Army was not equipped to fight. The effort depleted the Regular Army so seriously that in July 1838 its authorized strength had to be increased from 7,000 to 12,500 men. About 10,000 regulars and as many as 30,000 short-term volunteers had been engaged from 1835 to 1842 in one of the longest sustained campaigns fought against the American Indian. Almost 1,600 men had lost their lives in battle or from disease, and about $30 million had been spent to ship 3,800 half-starved Seminoles west. Many of the regular units that had fought in the war went on to Georgia and Alabama to aide in the forced removal of the Cherokees from their ancestral lands along the "Trail of Tears" to their new western reservation. This was not the last time that the Army was forced to be the instrument of a ruthless policy of dispossession directed against the American Indian.

With money and effort, the Army had bought experience, especially in transportation—the most pressing problem of the war. For example, the Quartermaster General had developed a light pontoon wagon, lined with India rubber cloth, for crossing rivers. At General Jesup's request, the Secretary of War revived the corps of artificers that had been authorized for the War of 1812. It provided mechanics and laborers to keep wagons and boats in repair. The war also taught a great deal about water transportation. Before it was over, the Army was turning away from dependence on steamboats hired from private contractors to Army-owned steamboats, more reliable and cheaper in the end. (Contractors once again had proved unreliable partners in the military effort.) The problem of navigating shallow rivers was solved by building flat-bottomed bateaux. These lessons in transportation were to be put to good use in the Mexican War; but the lesson that contractors were on the whole unreliable and corrupt had to learned and relearned at the Army's expense on a regular basis.

Westward Expansion and the Texas Issue

Army pioneering expeditions from Fort Leavenworth in the 1820s and 1830s had been undertaken mainly for making treaties with the Great Plains Indians and for protecting trading caravans. Beginning in the early 1840s the prime consideration was to help the American settlers pouring westward. In 1842, 2d Lt. John C. Fremont of the Corps of Topographical Engineers led an expedition to explore and map the Platte River country for the benefit of emigrants moving over the Oregon Trail; his second expedition in 1843 reached Sacramento in Upper California.

In 1842 Fremont reported seeing emigrant parties of 64 men with 16 or 17 families. Three years later, when Col. Stephen W. Kearny marched five companies of the 1st Dragoons over the Oregon Trail primarily for the protection of the emigrants, he saw on the trail 850 men and about 475 families in long caravans followed by thousands of cattle. The trickle had begun to turn into a flood.

Some of the pioneers on the Oregon Trail settled in Upper California; but the main stream of American migration into Mexican territory flowed to Texas. Between 1825 and 1830, approximately 15,000 immigrants with several thousand African American slaves poured into Texas. In March of 1836 they proclaimed their independence from Mexico. The Mexicans, under General Antonio Lopez de Santa Ana, moved against the rebels and destroyed the garrison in the Alamo after a siege that lasted thirteen days. American volunteers rushed across the Sabine River to help the Texans. General Gaines, stationed on the western frontier of Louisiana to defend Louisiana and maintain American neutrality, was authorized to cross the Sabine River (generally regarded as the boundary line) but not to go beyond Nacogdoches, fifty miles west of the Sabine, which marked the extreme limit of American claims. He was at the Sabine when Maj. Gen. Sam Houston won his victory over Santa Ana at San Jacinto on April 21, 1836. Fired by wild rumors of Mexican reinforcements, Gaines crossed the Sabine with a force of regulars and in July occupied Nacogdoches, remaining there until recalled in December 1836.

For nearly ten years Texas existed as an independent nation, desiring annexation to the United States but frustrated because annexation had become tied up with the slavery controversy. Northerners saw annexation as an attempt by the South to extend slavery. During this decade Mexico, refusing to recognize Texan independence, made sporadic attempts to recover its lost province. Raids marked by the extreme ruthlessness and ferocity of both Texans and Mexicans kept the country along the border in constant turmoil.

On Stone, *A. Koellner. This lithograph shows the full dress of an officer in the Dragoon Corps, ca. 1841.*

173

Stephen Watts Kearny (1794–1848)

Kearny served in the Army from the War of 1812 through his death in 1848. He served with the 1st Dragoons from its formation in 1833 through the Mexican War. Well-liked and respected by his men, Kearny is known to some as the father of U.S. Cavalry. He protected pioneers traveling on the Santa Fe, Mormon, and Oregon Trails and gained fame for his western explorations and his heroic service during the War with Mexico.

The Professional Officer

The exploration of the West and the Seminole and Creek Wars severely tested the fledgling U.S. Army. The Army's organization fluctuated according to the political winds of the time with only a slowly evolving sense by the nation's leaders that a standing professional Army was essential for national security. Problems in supply, training, equipment, and pay were only painfully sorted out under the press of circumstances. Central to solving these problems was the slow but steady evolution of a professional officer corps. This growth can in no small measure be attributed to the quality of new officers emerging from the U.S. Military Academy. Year after year young cadets were tested and trained to increasingly rigorous standards and commissioned to take their places as professional officers. Their training as professional engineers as well marked them as valuable commodities in civilian life; and whether they remained in the Army for a career or fulfilled their obligation and left the service, they contributed to the Army and to the society as a whole.

Tested in combat in the Seminole Wars, placed in charge of a small team of explorers, charged with building a road or dredging a harbor, Army officers developed a strong sense of corporate identity that bound them closer and closer together as a distinct entity within society. They developed professional codes of standards, behavior and ethics that provided a self-policing mechanism essential to any profession. As they moved, often with their families, from post to post on the expanding frontiers of the country, they turned inward to their own community to build a support structure of obedience, duty, and honor. Common opportunities for training, starting at West Point and continuing at the various branch schools, when coupled with shared experience in combat or at isolated military posts, bred an increasing identification with an officer class. The officer corps was beginning to view itself as a distinct entity within the Army and the nation. These officers soon found themselves thrown together and tested again in the fire of battle upon the outbreak of war with Mexico. The war would see West Point–trained officers clearing the path into Mexico City as the nation again called upon the Army to lead the way into new lands.

Discussion Questions

1. Discuss the importance of the U.S. Military Academy at West Point to the Army of the early nineteenth century. In what sense did the U.S. Army become more professional during this period? What reforms contributed to this result?

2. The wars against the Seminoles lasted for years and took thousands of troops to subdue and remove a relative handful of Indians. Why did this take so long? Which tactics worked and which did not?

3. What were the major roles and missions of the Army in the early settlement of the West from 1815 to 1845? How effective was the Army in performing these missions?

4. What was the "expansible army" policy proposed by Secretary of War Calhoun? To what degree do we have an expansible army today? What were some alternatives to this idea in the nineteenth and twentieth centuries?

5. What were the advantages and disadvantages of using contractors to provide military support such as rations, clothing, transportation, and other services during this period? Why was the Army so slow to develop its own internal logistics capability?

6. Compare and contrast the Army on the eve of the War of 1812 to the Army on the eve of the war with Mexico. What were the similarities and differences? What factors accounted for the changes?

Recommended Readings

Coffman, Edward. *The Old Army: A Portrait of the American Army in Peacetime, 1784–1898*. New York: Oxford University Press, 1986.

Johnson, Timothy. *Winfield Scott: The Quest for Military Glory*. Lawrence: University Press of Kansas, 1998.

Mahon, John K. *History of the Second Seminole War, 1839–1842*. Gainesville: University of Florida Press, 1985.

Morrison, James L., Jr. *"The Best School in the World": West Point, The Pre–Civil War Years, 1833–1866*. Kent, Ohio: Kent State University Press, 1986.

Prucha, Francis P. *The Sword of the Republic: The United States Army on the Frontier, 1783–1846*. New York: Macmillan, 1969.

Remini, Robert V. *Andrew Jackson and the Course of American Empire, 1761–1821*. New York: Harper & Row, 1977.

Skelton, William B. *An American Profession of Arms: The Army Officer Corps, 1784–1861*. Lawrence: University Press of Kansas, 1992.

Other Readings

Browning, Robert S. *Two If By Sea: The Development of American Coastal Defense Policy*. Westport, Conn.: Greenwood Press, 1983.

Goetzmann, William H. *Army Exploration in the American West 1803–1863*. Austin: Texas State Historical Association, 1991.

Sprague, John T. *The Origin, Progress, and Conclusion of the Florida War.* Tampa, Fla.: University of Tampa Press, 2000.

Walton, George H. *Sentinel of the Plains: Fort Leavenworth and the American West.* Englewood Cliffs, N.J.: Prentice-Hall, 1973.

8

THE MEXICAN WAR AND AFTER

Receiving by the new telegraph the news that James K. Polk had been elected to the Presidency in November 1844, President John Tyler interpreted the verdict as a mandate from the people for the annexation of Texas, since Polk had come out strongly in favor of annexation. On March 1, 1845, Congress jointly resolved to admit Texas into the Union and the Mexican Government promptly broke off diplomatic relations. President Polk continued to hope that he could settle by negotiation Mexico's claim to Texas and acquire Upper California by purchase as well. In mid-June, nevertheless, anticipating Texas' Fourth of July acceptance of annexation, he ordered Bvt. Brig. Gen. Zachary Taylor to move his forces from Fort Jesup on the Louisiana border to a point "on or near" the Rio Grande to repel any invasion from Mexico.

The Period of Watchful Waiting

General Taylor selected a wide sandy plain at the mouth of the Nueces River near the hamlet of Corpus Christi and beginning July 23 sent most of his 1,500-man force by steamboat from New Orleans. Only his dragoons moved overland, via San Antonio. By mid-October, as shipments of regulars continued to come in from all over the country, his forces had swollen to nearly 4,000, including some volunteers from New Orleans. This force constituted nearly 50 percent of the 7,365-strong Regular Army. A company of Texas Rangers served as the eyes and ears of the Army. For the next six months tactical drilling, horse breaking, and parades, interspersed with boredom and dissipation, went on at the big camp on the Nueces. Then in February Taylor received orders from Washington to advance into disputed territory to the Rio Grande. Negotiations with the Mexican government had broken down.

Bragg, Lee, Grant, and Davis in the Mexican War

For the first time in the Mexican War, graduates of the U.S. Military Academy held a majority of field and staff officer positions. General Scott later commented that without these officers the war would have lasted longer and been much more costly. The West Pointers vindicated themselves and the academy in the eyes of many average Americans. The Mexican War also proved to be a training ground for men like Braxton Bragg, Robert E. Lee, Ulysses S. Grant, and Jefferson Davis, who thirteen years after the conflict in Mexico led large armies during the American Civil War.

The march of more than a hundred miles down the coast to the Rio Grande was led by Bvt. Maj. Samuel Ringgold's battery of "flying artillery," organized in late 1838 on orders from Secretary of War Joel R. Poinsett. It was the last word in mobility, for the cannoneers rode on horseback rather than on limbers and caissons. Taylor's supply train of 300 ox-drawn wagons brought up the rear. On March 23 the columns came to a road that forked left to Point Isabel, ten miles away on the coast, where Taylor's supply ships were waiting, and led on the right to his destination on the Rio Grande, eighteen miles southwest, opposite the Mexican town of Matamoros. Sending the bulk of his army ahead, Taylor went to Point Isabel to set up his supply base, fill his wagons, and bring forward four 18-lb. siege guns from his ships.

At the boiling brown waters of the Rio Grande opposite Matamoros, Taylor built a strong fort, which he called Fort Texas, and mounted his siege guns. At the same time he sent messages of peace to the Mexican commander on the opposite bank. These were countered by threats and warnings and on April 25, the day after the arrival at Matamoros of General Mariano Arista with two or three thousand additional troops, by open hostilities. The Mexicans crossed the river in some force and attacked a reconnoitering detachment of sixty dragoons under Capt. Seth B. Thornton. They killed eleven men and captured Thornton and the rest, many of whom were wounded.

Taylor reported to President Polk that hostilities had commenced and called on Texas and Louisiana for about 5,000 militiamen. His immediate concern was that his supply base might be captured. Leaving an infantry regiment and a small detachment of artillery at Fort Texas under Maj. Jacob Brown, he set off May 1 with the bulk of his forces for Point Isabel, where he stayed nearly a week strengthening his fortifications. After loading two hundred supply wagons and acquiring two more ox-drawn 18-pounders, he began the return march to Fort Texas with his army of about 2,300 men on the afternoon of May 7. About noon the next day, near a clump of tall trees at a spot called Palo Alto, he saw across the open prairie a long dark line with bayonets and lances glistening in the sun. It was the Mexican Army.

Battles of Palo Alto and Resaca de la Palma

Containing some of the best regular units in the Mexican Army, General Arista's forces barring the road to Fort Texas stretched out on a front a mile long and were about 4,000 strong. Taylor, who had placed part of his force in the rear to guard the supply wagons, was outnumbered at least two to one; and in terrain that favored cavalry, Arista's cavalry overwhelmingly outnumbered Taylor's dragoons. On the plus side for the Americans, their artillery was superior. Also, among Taylor's junior officers were a number of capable West Point graduates, notably 2d Lt. George C. Meade and 2d Lt. Ulysses S. Grant, who were to become famous in the Civil War.

On the advice of the young West Pointers on his staff, Taylor emplaced his two 18-lb. iron siege guns in the center of his line and blasted the advancing Mexicans with canister. His field artillery—bronze 6-lb. guns firing solid shot and 12-lb. howitzers firing shell, in quick-moving attacks threw back Arista's flanks. The Mexicans were using old-fashioned bronze 4-pounders and 8-pounders that fired solid shot and had such short ranges that their fire did little damage. During the battle Lieutenant Grant saw their cannon balls striking the ground before they reached the American troops and ricocheting so slowly that the men could dodge them.

During the afternoon a gun wad set the dry grass afire, causing the battle to be suspended for nearly an hour. After it resumed, the Mexicans fell back rapidly. By nightfall, when both armies went into bivouac, Mexican casualties, caused mostly by cannon fire, numbered 320 killed and 380 wounded. Taylor lost only 9 men killed and 47 wounded. One of the mortally wounded was his brilliant artilleryman, Major Ringgold.

At daybreak the Americans saw the Mexicans in full retreat. Taylor decided to pursue but did not begin his advance until afternoon, spending the morning erecting defenses around his wagon train, which he intended to leave behind. About two o'clock he reached Resaca de la Palma, a dry riverbed about five miles from Palo Alto. There, his scouts reported that the Mexicans had taken advantage of his delay to entrench themselves strongly a short distance down the road in a similar shallow ravine known as Resaca de la Guerra, whose banks formed a natural breastwork. Narrow ponds and thick chaparral protected their flanks.

Taylor sent forward his flying artillery, now commanded by Lt. Randolph Ridgely. Stopped by a Mexican battery, Ridgely sent back for help; Taylor ordered in a detachment of dragoons under Capt. Charles A. May. The dragoons overran the Mexican guns but on their return were caught in infantry crossfire from the thickets and could not prevent the enemy from recapturing the guns. American infantrymen later captured the pieces. Dense chaparral prevented Taylor from making full use of his artillery. The battle of Resaca de la Palma was an infantry battle of small-unit actions and close-in, hand-to-hand fighting.

The Mexicans, still demoralized by their defeat at Palo Alto and lacking effective leadership, gave up the fight and fled toward Matamoros. Their losses at Resaca de la Palma were later officially reported as 547 but may have been greater. The Americans lost 33 killed and 89 wounded. In the meantime, Fort Texas had been attacked by the Mexicans on May 3 and had withstood a two-day siege with the loss of only two men, one of them its commander for whom the fort was later renamed Fort Brown.

> Lieutenant Grant saw their cannon balls striking the ground before they reached the American troops and ricocheting so slowly that the men could dodge them.

The panic-stricken Mexicans fleeing to Matamoros crossed the Rio Grande as best they could, some by boats, some by swimming. Many drowned; others were killed by the guns of Fort Texas. If Taylor's regulars, flush with victory and yelling as they pursued the enemy, had been able to catch up with Arista, they could probably have taken his demoralized army, complete with guns and ammunition. But Taylor had failed to make any provision for crossing the Rio Grande. He blamed the War Department's failure to provide him with pontoon equipment (developed during the Second Seminole War), which he had requested while he was still at Corpus Christi. Since that time, however, he had done nothing to acquire bridge materials or boats, although the West Pointers had urged him to do so. Lieutenant Meade reported that "the old gentleman would never listen or give it a moment's attention." Not until May 18, after Taylor had brought up some boats from Point Isabel, was he able to cross into Matamoros. By that time Arista's army had pulled back into the interior to rest, recoup, and fight another day.

War Is Declared

On the evening of May 9, the day of the battle of Resaca de la Palma, President Polk received a message from the War Department that informed him of the attack on Captain Thornton's detachment on April 25. Polk, already convinced by the breakdown in negotiations with Mexico that war was justified, immediately drafted a message declaring that a state of war existed between the United States and Mexico. Congress passed the declaration, and Polk signed it on May 13. Congress then appropriated $10 million and substantially increased the strength of the Army. (After the Second Seminole War the authorized strength had been cut from 12,500 to 8,500. This had been done by reducing the rank and file strength of the regiments, instead of eliminating units, thus firmly establishing the principle of an expansible Army.) Congress raised the authorized enlisted strength of a company from 64 to 100 men, bringing the rank and file up to 15,540, and added a regiment of mounted riflemen and a company of sappers, miners, and pontoniers (engineers for pontoon bridges). Also, the President was authorized to call for 50,000 volunteers for a term of one year or the duration of the war.

The President went into the war with one object clearly in view—to seize all of Mexico north of the Rio Grande and the Gila River and westward to the Pacific.

The President went into the war with one object clearly in view—to seize all of Mexico north of the Rio Grande and the Gila River and westward to the Pacific. After his discussions with Maj. Gen. Winfield Scott, the outlines of a three-pronged thrust emerged. (*Map 21*) General Taylor was to advance westward from Matamoros to the city of Monterrey, the key to further progress in northern Mexico. A second expedition under Brig. Gen. John E. Wool was to move from San Antonio to the remote city of Chihuahua in the west, an expedition later directed southward to Saltillo near Monterrey. A third prong under Col. Stephen W. Kearny was to start at Fort Leavenworth, capture Santa Fe and ultimately continue to San Diego on the coast of California. Part of Kearny's forces under volunteer Col. Alexander W. Doniphan later marched south through El Paso to Chihuahua. Although small in numbers, only 1,600 strong, Kearny's and Doniphan's forces posed strategic threats to Mexico's northern states.

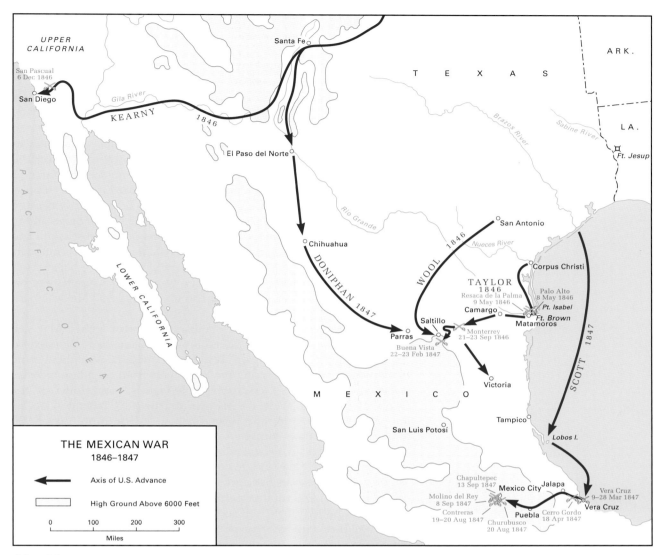

Map 21

Polk was counting on "a brisk and a short war"; not until July did he and his Secretary of War, William L. Marcy, even begin to consider the possibility of an advance on Mexico City by landing a force on the Gulf of Mexico near Vera Cruz. General Scott was not so optimistic. He was more aware of the problems of supply, transportation, communications, and mobilization involved in operations against Mexico, a country with a population of 7 million and an army of about 30,000, many with experience gained by twenty years of intermittent revolution. Scott's preparations seemed too slow to Polk. Ostensibly for that reason, but also because success in the field might make the politically motivated Scott a powerful contender for the Presidency, Polk decided not to give him command of the forces in the field. When news came of the victories at Palo Alto and Resaca de la Palma, Polk promoted Zachary Taylor to the brevet rank of major general and gave him command of the army in Mexico, risking the possibility that Taylor might also use a victory to vault into high political office.

Monterrey Campaign

Taylor's plan was to move on Monterrey with about 6,000 men via Camargo, a small town on the San Juan River, a tributary of the Rio Grande about 130 miles upriver. From Camargo, where he intended to set up a supply base, a road led southwest about 125 miles to Monterrey in the foothills of the Sierra Madres. His troops were to march overland to Camargo, his supplies to come by steamboat up the Rio Grande. But he could not move immediately because he lacked transportation—partly because of his failure to requisition in time and partly because of the effort required to build more wagons in the United States and to collect shallow-draft steamboats at river towns on the Mississippi and the Ohio and send them across the Gulf of Mexico. Ten steamboats were in operation at the end of July, but wagons did not begin arriving until November, after the campaign was over. To supplement his wagon train, reduced to 175, Taylor had to rely on 1,500 Mexican pack mules and a few native oxcarts.

In manpower Taylor had an embarrassment of riches. May saw the arrival of the first of the three-month militia he had requested on April 26 from the governors of Texas and Louisiana. With them came thousands of additional six-month volunteers from neighboring states recruited by Bvt. Maj. Gen. Edmund P. Gaines, commander of the Department of the West, on his own initiative—a repetition of his impulsive actions during the Second Seminole War. More than 8,000 of these short-term volunteers were sent before Gaines was censured by a court-martial for his unauthorized and illegal recruiting practices and transferred to New York to command the Department of the East. Very few of his recruits had agreed to serve for twelve months. All the rest were sent home without performing any service; in the meantime they had to be fed, sheltered, and transported. In June the volunteers authorized by Congress began pouring into Point Isabel and were quartered in a string of camps along the Rio Grande as far as Matamoros.

By August Taylor had a force of about 15,000 men at Camargo, an unhealthy town deep in mud from recent heavy rains and sweltering under heat that rose as high as 112 degrees. Many of the volunteers became ill, and more than half were left behind when Taylor advanced toward Monterrey at the end of August with 3,080 regulars and 3,150 volunteers. The regulars with a few volunteers were organized into the First and Second Divisions, the volunteers mainly into a Field Division, though two regiments of mounted Texans were thought of as the Texas Division. More than a fourth of the troops were mounted, among them the First Mississippi Rifle Regiment under a West Point graduate recently elected to Congress, Col. Jefferson Davis. The mounted riflemen had percussion rifles; the infantrymen were armed with flintlock smoothbore muskets. Taylor placed great reliance on the bayonet. He had a low opinion of artillery, and though warned that field pieces were not effective against the stone houses of Mexican towns, he had in addition to his four field batteries only two 24-lb. howitzers and one 10-inch mortar, the latter his only real siege piece.

By September 19 Taylor's army reached Monterrey, a well-fortified city in a pass of the Sierra Madres leading to the city of Saltillo. Monterrey was strongly defended by more than 7,000 Mexicans with better artillery than the Mexicans had had at Palo Alto—new British 9- and 12-lb. guns. Taylor, encamped on the outskirts of Monterrey, sent out reconnoitering parties accompanied by engineers and on September 20 began his attack. On the north the city was protected by a formidable citadel, on the south by a river; and it was ringed with forts. Taylor sent one of his regular divisions, with 400 Texas Rangers in advance, around to the west to cut off the road to Saltillo; and after a miserable night of drenching rain it accomplished its mission the next day, September 21, though at a cost of 394 dead or wounded, a high proportion of them officers. Taylor placed his heavy howitzers and one mortar in position to fire on the citadel and sent the remainder of his forces to close in from the eastern outskirts of the town. By the third day both attacks were driving into the city proper, the men battering down doors of the stone and adobe houses with planks, tossing lighted shells through apertures, and advancing from house to house rather than from street to street—tactics that were to be used a century later by American troops in Italian and German towns.

The climax came when the 10-inch mortar was brought up to lob shells on the great plaza into which the Mexican troops had been driven. On September 24 the Mexican commander offered to surrender on condition that his troops be allowed to withdraw unimpeded and that an eight-week armistice go into effect. Taylor agreed to the proposal. He had lost some 800 men to battle casualties and sickness, besides quantities of arms and ammunition, and he was about 125 miles from his base. Moreover, he believed that magnanimity would advance the negotiations for peace that had begun when President Polk allowed General Antonio Lopez de Santa Anna to return to Mexico from exile in Havana to exert his influence in favor of a treaty.

When Polk received the news from Monterrey by courier October 11, he condemned Taylor for allowing the Mexican Army to escape and ordered the armistice terminated. On November 13 Taylor sent a thousand men 68 miles southwest to occupy Saltillo, an important road center commanding the only road to Mexico City from the north that was practicable for wagons and guns. Saltillo also commanded the road west to Chihuahua and east to Victoria, capital of Tamaulipas, the province that contained Tampico, the second largest Mexican port on the gulf. The U.S. Navy captured Tampico November 15. On the road to Chihuahua was the town of Parras, where General Wool's expedition of about 2,500 men arrived early in December after a remarkable march from San Antonio. On the way Wool had learned that the Mexican troops holding Chihuahua had abandoned it; accordingly, he joined Taylor's main army. Taylor thus acquired a valuable West Point–trained engineer officer who had been scouting with Wool, Capt. Robert E. Lee.

Taylor was planning to establish a strong defensive line, Parras-Saltillo-Monterrey-Victoria, when he learned that most of his troops would have to be dispatched to join General Scott's invasion of Mexico at Vera Cruz, an operation that had been decided upon in Washington in mid-November. Scott arrived in Mexico in late December. He

Both attacks were driving into the city proper, the men . . . advancing from house to house rather than from street to street—tactics that were to be used a century later by American troops in Italian and German towns.

Gen' Scott's Entrance into Mexico, *C. Nebel, ca. 1855*

proceeded to Camargo and detached almost all of Taylor's regulars, about 4,000, and an equal number of volunteers, ordering them to rendezvous at Tampico and at the mouth of the Brazos River in Texas. Taylor, left with fewer than 7,000 men, all volunteers except two squadrons of dragoons and a small force of artillery, was ordered to evacuate Saltillo and go on the defensive at Monterrey.

Enraged, Taylor attributed Scott's motive to politics. Hurrying back to Monterrey from Victoria, he decided to interpret Scott's orders as "advice" rather than as an order. Instead of retiring his forces to Monterrey, he moved 4,650 of his troops (leaving garrisons at Monterrey and Saltillo) to a point eighteen miles south of Saltillo, near the hacienda of Agua Nueva. This move brought him almost eleven miles closer to San Luis Potosi, 200 miles to the south, where General Santa Anna was assembling an army of 20,000. Most of the 200 miles were desert, which Taylor considered impassable by any army; moreover, both he and Scott believed that Santa Anna would make his main effort against Scott's landing at Vera Cruz, the news of which had leaked to the newspapers. On February 8, 1847, Taylor wrote a friend, "I have no fears."

At the time he wrote, Santa Anna was already on the march north toward Saltillo. Stung by newspaper reports that he had sold out to the Americans, Santa Anna risked a daring strategic move. He was determined to win a quick victory, and he thought he saw his opportunity when his troops brought him a copy of Scott's order depleting Taylor's forces, found on the body of a messenger they had ambushed and killed. Leading his army across barren country through heat, snow, and rain, by February 19 Santa Anna had 15,000 men at a hacienda at the edge of the desert, only thirty-five miles from Agua Nueva. One of the hardest fought battles of the Mexican War was about to begin.

Battle of Buena Vista

On the morning of February 21 scouts brought word to General Taylor that a great Mexican army was advancing, preceded by a large body of cavalry swinging east to block the road between Agua Nueva and Saltillo. That afternoon Taylor withdrew his forces up the Saltillo road about 15 miles to a better defensive position near the hacienda Buena Vista, a few miles south of Saltillo. There, a mile south of the clay-roofed ranch buildings, mountain spurs came down to the road on the east, the longest and highest known as La Angostura; between them was a wide plateau cut by two deep ravines. West of the road was a network of gullies backed by a line of high hills. Leaving General Wool to deploy the troops, Taylor rode off to Saltillo to look after his defenses there.

By next morning, Washington's Birthday (the password was "Honor to Washington"), the little American army of fewer than 5,000 troops, most of them green volunteers, was in position to meet a Mexican army more than three times its size. The American main body was east of the road near La Angostura, where artillery had been emplaced, commanding the road. West of the road, the gullies were thought to be sufficient protection.

Santa Anna arrived with his vanguard around eleven o'clock. Disliking the terrain, which by no means favored cavalry (the best units in his army), he sent a demand for surrender to Taylor, who had returned from Saltillo. Taylor refused. Then Santa Anna planted artillery on the road and the high ground east of it and sent a force of light infantry around the foot of the mountains south of the plateau. About three o'clock a shell from a Mexican howitzer on the road gave the signal for combat; but the rest of the day was consumed mainly in jockeying for position on the mountain spurs, a competition in which the Mexicans came off best, and the placing of American infantry and artillery well forward on the plateau. After a threatening movement on the Mexican left, Taylor sent a Kentucky regiment with two guns of Maj. Braxton Bragg's Regular Army battery to the high hills west of the road, but no attack occurred there. Toward evening Taylor returned to Saltillo, accompanied by the First Mississippi Rifles and a detachment of dragoons. At nightfall his soldiers, shaken by the size and splendid appearance of the Mexican army, got what sleep they could.

The next day, February 23, the battle opened in earnest at dawn. Santa Anna sent a division up the road toward La Angostura, at the head of the defile; but American artillery and infantrymen quickly broke it, and no further action occurred in that sector. The strongest assault took place on the plateau, well to the east, where Santa Anna launched two divisions, backed by a strong battery at the head of the southernmost ravine. The Americans farthest forward, part of an Indiana regiment supported by three cannons, held off the assault for half an hour; then their commander gave them an order to retreat. They broke and ran and were joined in their flight by adjoining regiments. Some of the men ran all the way back to Buena Vista, where they fired at pursuing Mexican cavalrymen from behind the hacienda walls.

About nine o'clock that morning, when the battle had become almost a rout, General Taylor arrived from Saltillo with his dragoons, Colonel Davis' Mississippi Rifles, and some men of the Indiana regiment whom he had rallied on the way. They fell upon the Mexican cavalry that had been trying to outflank the Americans north of the plateau. In the meantime Bragg's artillery had come over from the hills west of the road, and the Kentucky regiment also crossed the road to join in the fight. A deafening thunderstorm of rain and hail broke early in the afternoon, but the Americans in the north field continued to force the Mexicans back.

Just when victory for the Americans seemed in sight, Santa Anna threw an entire division of fresh troops, his reserves, against the plateau. Rising from the broad ravine where they had been hidden, the Mexicans of the left column fell upon three regiments—two Illinois and one Kentucky—and forced them back to the road with withering fire, while the right stormed the weak American center. They seemed about to turn the tide of battle when down from the north field galloped two batteries, followed by the Mississippians and Indianans led by Jefferson Davis, wounded but still in the saddle. They fell upon the Mexicans' right and rear and forced them back into the ravine. The Mexicans' left, pursuing the Illinois and Kentucky regiments up the road, was cut to pieces by the American battery at La Angostura.

That night Santa Anna, having lost 1,500 to 2,000 men killed and wounded, retreated toward San Luis Potosi. The Americans, with 264 men killed, 450 wounded, and 26 missing, had won the battle. A great share of the credit belonged to the artillery; without it, as General Wool said in his report, the army could not have stood "for a single hour." Moving with almost the speed of cavalry, the batteries served as rallying points for the infantry. The fighting spirit of the volunteers and the able and courageous leadership of the officers were beyond praise. Perhaps the greatest contribution to the victory had been Zachary Taylor himself. Stationed all day conspicuously in the center of the battle, hunched on his horse "Old Whitey" with one leg hooked over the pommel of his saddle, disregarding two Mexican bullets that ripped through his coat, and occasionally rising in his stirrups to shout encouragement, he was an inspiration to his men, who swore by him. Under such a leader they felt that defeat was impossible.

Taylor knew little of the art of war. He was careless in preparing for battle and neglected intelligence; he often misunderstood the intention of the enemy and underestimated the enemy's strength. But he possessed a high degree of physical and moral courage, which according to Jomini are the most essential qualities for a general. He constantly sought to regain the initiative by attacking the enemy. He and his subordinates used the principle of the offensive to turn the tide of the battle several times by the end of the long day.

Buena Vista ended any further Mexican threat against the lower Rio Grande. On the Pacific coast, Colonel Kearny led one of the most extraordinary marches in American history, across deserts and rugged mountains. His force left Fort Leavenworth, Kansas, on June 2, 1846, and headed for California via the Santa Fe Trail. After capturing Santa Fe without firing a shot on August 18, he continued his march to the west. Convinced through an erroneous intelligence report from "Kit" Carson that California had already fallen to U.S. forces, Kearny left most of his forces in Santa Fe and continued on to California with a single dragoon company. He marched his men nearly 1,000 miles over snow-capped mountains and through desolate, snake-infested deserts. After finally reaching California on December 4, the exhausted dragoons were reinforced by thirty-five marines. Learning that the Californios, or

A high degree of physical and moral courage . . . according to Jomini are the most essential qualities for a general.

native Mexican population, were in revolt, Kearny attacked a force of seventy-five Californios at San Pascual two days later to assist the beleaguered American garrison at San Diego. Kearny's dragoons took heavy losses against the skilled Californio lancers, but they withdrew before crushing Kearny's force. After relieving the garrison at San Diego, Kearny joined other U.S. forces in the region to recapture Los Angeles. On January 8, 1847, a joint force of sailors, marines, and dragoons under Kearny engaged 350 Californios at the San Gabriel River, south of Los Angeles. After a brief but hard-fought battle, the Californios withdrew and formally capitulated on January 13.

Early in February 1847 a force of Missouri volunteers detached from Kearny's command and led by Colonel Doniphan had set out from Santa Fe to pacify the region of the upper Rio Grande. Crossing the river at El Paso, they defeated a large force of Mexicans, mostly militia, at Chihuahua, less than a week after Taylor's victory at Buena Vista. Thus by March 1847, America's hold on Mexico's northern provinces was secure. All that remained to complete the victory was the capture of Mexico City.

The Landing at Vera Cruz

From a rendezvous at Lobos Island almost fifty miles south of Tampico, General Scott's force of 13,660 men, of whom 5,741 were regulars, set sail on March 2, 1847, for the landing near Vera Cruz—the first major amphibious landing in the history of the U.S. Army. On March 5 the transports were off the coast of their target, where they met a U.S. naval squadron blockading the city. In a small boat, Scott, his commanders, and a party of officers including Lee, Meade, Joseph E. Johnston, and Pierre G. T. Beauregard ran close inshore to reconnoiter and were almost hit by a shell fired from the island fortress of San Juan de Ulua opposite Vera Cruz. That shell might have changed the course of the Mexican War and the Civil War as well.

Scott chose for the landing a beach nearly three miles south of the city, beyond the range of the Mexican guns. On the evening of March 9, in four hours more than 10,000 men went ashore in landing craft, sixty-five heavy surf boats that had been towed to the spot by steamers. The troops proceeded inland over the sand hills with little opposition from the Mexican force of 4,300 behind the city's walls. The landing of artillery, stores, and horses, the last thrown overboard and forced to swim for shore, was slowed by a norther that sprang up on March 12 and blew violently for four days, but by March 22 seven 10-inch mortars had been dragged inland and emplaced about half a mile south of Vera Cruz. That afternoon the bombardment began.

Town and fort replied, and it was soon apparent that the mortars were ineffective. Scott found himself compelled to ask for naval guns from the commander of the naval force, Commodore Matthew C. Perry. The six naval guns—three 32-pounders firing shot and three 8-inch shell guns—soon breached the walls and demoralized the defenders. On March 27, 1847, Vera Cruz capitulated.

Scott's next objective was Jalapa, a city in the highlands about seventy-four miles from Vera Cruz on the national highway leading to Mexico City. Because on the coast the yellow fever season was approaching,

Scott was anxious to move forward to the uplands at once, but not until April 8 was he able to collect enough pack mules and wagons for the advance. The first elements, under Bvt. Maj. Gen. David E. Twiggs, set out with two batteries. One was equipped with 24-lb. guns, 8-inch howitzers, and 10-inch mortars. The other was a new type of battery equipped with mountain howitzers and rockets, officered and manned by the Ordnance Corps. The rocket section, mainly armed with the Congreve, carried for service tests a new rocket, the Hale, which depended for stability not on a stick but on vents in the rear, which also gave it a spin like that of an artillery projectile. The rockets were fired from troughs mounted on portable stands. In addition to his two batteries, General Twiggs had a squadron of dragoons, in all about 2,600 men. He advanced confidently, though Scott had warned him that a substantial army commanded by Santa Anna lay somewhere ahead. On April 11, after Twiggs had gone about thirty miles, his scouts brought word that Mexican guns commanded a pass near the hamlet of Cerro Gordo.

Battle of Cerro Gordo

Near Cerro Gordo, the national highway ran through a rocky defile. On the left of the approaching Americans, Santa Anna with about 12,000 men had emplaced batteries on mountain spurs; and on the right of the Americans, farther down the road, his guns were emplaced on a high hill, El Telegrafo. He thus had firm command of the national highway, the only means he thought Scott had of bringing up his artillery.

Fortunately for Twiggs, advancing on the morning of April 12, the Mexican gunners opened fire before he was within range and he was able to pull his forces back. Two days later Scott arrived with reinforcements, bringing his army up to 8,500. A reconnaissance by Captain Lee showed that the rough country to the right of El Telegrafo, which Santa Anna had considered impassable, could be traversed to enable the Americans to cut in on the Mexican rear. The troops hewed a path through forest and brush; when they came to ravines, they lowered the heavy siege artillery by ropes to the bottom then hoisted it up the other side. By April 17 they were able to occupy a hill to the right of El Telegrafo, where they sited the rocket battery. Early on the morning of April 18 the battle began.

Though Santa Anna, by then forewarned, had been able to plant guns to protect his flank, he could not withstand the American onslaught. The Mexicans broke and fled into the mountains. By noon Scott's army had won a smashing victory at a cost of only 417 casualties, including 64 dead. Santa Anna's losses were estimated at more than a thousand.

Scott moved next morning to Jalapa. The way seemed open to Mexico City, only 170 miles away. But now he faced a serious loss in manpower. The term of enlistment of seven of his volunteer regiments was about to expire, and only a handful agreed to reenlist. The men had to be sent home at once to minimize the danger of yellow fever when they passed through Vera Cruz. The departure of the volunteers, along with wounds and sickness among the men remaining, reduced the army to 5,820 effectives.

In May Scott pushed forward cautiously to Puebla, then the second largest city in Mexico. Its citizens were hostile to Santa Anna and had lost hope of winning the war. It capitulated without resistance on May 15 to an advance party under General Worth. Scott stayed there until the beginning of August, awaiting reinforcements from Vera Cruz (which by mid-July more than doubled his forces) and awaiting the outcome of peace negotiations then under way. A State Department emissary, Nicholas P. Trist, had arrived on the scene and made contact with Santa Anna through a British agent in Mexico City. Trist learned that Santa Anna, elected President of Mexico for the second time, would discuss peace terms for $10,000 down and $1 million to be paid when a treaty was ratified. After receiving the down payment through the intermediary, however, Santa Anna made it known that he could not prevail upon the Mexican Congress to repeal a law it had passed after the battle of Cerro Gordo that made it high treason for any official to treat with the Americans. It was clear that Scott would have to move closer to the capital of Mexico before Santa Anna would seriously consider peace terms.

Contreras, Churubusco, Chapultepec

For the advance on Mexico City, Scott had about 10,000 men. He had none to spare to protect the road from Vera Cruz to Puebla; therefore, his decision to move forward was daring. It meant that he had

Pillow's Attack Advancing through the Woods of Chapultepec, *James Walker, 1848*

CHAPULTEPEC AND "LOS NIÑOS"

Chapultepec, an imposing castle nearly 200 feet above the Valley of Mexico, housed a military academy for young men. Nearly fifty cadets stayed to oppose an American advance. U.S. troops used scaling ladders to assault the castle and captured the garrison of 1,000 after a sharp fight. During the battle, five cadets were killed and a sixth wrapped himself in the Mexican flag and jumped to his death in the valley below. Simply known as "los niños" (the children), the cadets' heroic actions proved a powerful image of Mexican resistance, pride, and nationalistic spirit.

abandoned his line of communications or, as he phrased it, "thrown away the scabbard." On August 7 Scott moved off with the lead division, followed at a day's march by three divisions with a three-mile-long train of white-topped supply wagons bringing up the rear. Meeting no opposition—a sign that Santa Anna had withdrawn to defend Mexico City—Scott by August 10 was at Ayolta on a high plateau fourteen miles from the city.

The direct road ahead, entering the capital on the east, was barred by strongly fortified positions. Scott therefore decided to take the city from the west by a wide flanking movement to the south, using a narrow muddy road that passed between the southern shores of two lakes and the mountains and skirted a fifteen-mile-wide lava bed, the Pedregal, before it turned north and went over a bridge at Churubusco to the western gates of Mexico City.

The Pedregal, like the terrain around El Telegrafo, had been considered impassable; but Captain Lee again made a way through. He found a mule path across its southwestern tip that came out at the village of Contreras. Scott sent a force under Bvt. Maj. Gen. Gideon J. Pillow to work on the road, supported by Twiggs' division and some light artillery. They came under heavy fire from a Mexican force under General Gabriel Valencia. Pillow, manhandling his guns to a high position, attacked on August 19; but his light artillery was no match for Valencia's 68-lb. howitzer, nor his men for the reinforcements Santa Anna brought to the scene. American reinforcements made a night march in pouring rain through a gully the engineers had found through the Pedregal to fall upon the Mexicans' rear on the morning of August 20 simultaneously with an attack from the front. In seventeen minutes the battle of Contreras was won, with a loss to Scott of only 60 killed or wounded; the Mexicans lost 700 dead and 800 captured, including 4 generals.

Scott ordered an immediate pursuit, but Santa Anna was able to gather his forces for a stand at Churubusco, where he placed a strong fortification before the town at the bridge and converted a thick-walled stone church and a massive stone convent into fortresses. When the first American troops rode up around noon, they were met by heavy musket and cannon fire. The Mexicans fought as never before; not until midafternoon could Scott's troops make any progress. At last the fire of the Mexicans slackened, partly because they were running out of ammunition; and the Americans won the day, a day that Santa Anna admitted had cost him one third of his forces. About 4,000 Mexicans had been killed or wounded, not counting the many missing and captured. The battle had also been costly for Scott, who had 155 men killed and 876 wounded, approximately 12 percent of his effective force.

The victory at Churubusco brought an offer from Santa Anna to reopen negotiations. Scott proposed a short armistice, and Santa Anna quickly agreed. For two weeks Trist and representatives of the Mexican government discussed terms until it became clear that the Mexicans would not accept what Trist had to offer and were merely using the armistice as a breathing spell. On September 6 Scott halted the discussions and prepared to assault Mexico City.

Though refreshed by two weeks of rest, his forces now numbered only about 8,000. Santa Anna was reputed to have more than 15,000 and had taken advantage of the respite to strengthen the defenses of the city. And ahead on a high hill above the plain was the Castle of Chapultepec guarding the western approaches.

Scott's first objective, about half a mile west of Chapultepec, was a range of low stone buildings, containing a cannon foundry, known as El Molino del Rey. It was seized on September 8, though at heavy cost from unexpected resistance. At eight o'clock on the morning of September 13, after a barrage from the 24-lb. guns, Scott launched a three-pronged attack over the causeways leading to Chapultepec and up the rugged slopes. Against a hail of Mexican projectiles from above, his determined troops rapidly gained the summit, though they were delayed at the moat waiting for scaling ladders to come up. By half past nine o'clock the Americans were overrunning the castle despite a valiant but doomed defense by brave young Mexican cadets. Scarcely pausing, they pressed on to Mexico City by the two routes available and by nightfall held two gates to the city. Exhausted and depleted by the 800 casualties suffered that day, the troops still had to face house-to-house fighting; but at dawn the next day, September 14, the city surrendered.

Throughout the campaign from Vera Cruz to Mexico City, General Scott had displayed not only dauntless personal courage and fine qualities of leadership but great skill in applying the principles of war. In preparing for battle he would order his engineers to make a thorough reconnaissance of the enemy's position and the surrounding terrain. He was thus able to execute brilliant flanking movements over terrain that the enemy had considered impassable, notably at Cerro Gordo and the Pedregal, the latter a fine illustration of the principle of surprise. Scott also knew when to violate the principles of warfare, as he had done at Puebla when he deliberately severed his line of communications. Able to think beyond mere tactical maneuver, Scott was perhaps the finest strategic thinker in the American Army in the first half of the nineteenth century.

"He sees everything and counts the cost of every measure," said Captain Lee. Scott for his part ascribed his quick victory over Mexico, won without the loss of any battle, to the West Pointers in his army, Lee, Grant, and many others. As for the troops, the trained and disciplined regulars had come off somewhat better than the volunteers; but all the army on the whole had fought well. Scott had seen to it that the men fought at the right time and place. Grant summed it up: "Credit is due to the troops engaged, it is true, but the plans and strategy were the general's."

Occupation and Negotiation in Mexico City

The collection of revenues, suppression of disorder, administration of justice, all the details of governing the country were in the hands of the Army.

For two months the only responsible administration in Mexico was the American military government under Scott. The collection of revenues, suppression of disorder, administration of justice, all the details of governing the country were in the hands of the Army. It has been said that some Mexicans believed that Scott's administration of their city was more efficient and respectful of Mexican property than their own government's. It was an instructive lesson in the value of a careful and relatively enlightened occupation policy. When the Mexicans finally organized a government with which Commissioner Trist could negotiate a peace treaty, dispatches arrived from Washington instructing Trist to return to the United States and ordering Scott to resume the war. Knowing that the Mexicans were now sincerely desirous of ending the war and realizing that the government in Washington was unaware of the situation, both Trist and Scott decided to continue the negotiations.

On February 2, 1848, the Treaty of Guadalupe Hidalgo was signed. The U.S. Senate ratified it on March 10, but powerful opposition developed in Mexico. Not until May 30 were ratifications exchanged by the two governments. Preparations began immediately to evacuate American troops from Mexico. On June 12 the occupation troops marched out of Mexico City; on August 1, 1848, the last American soldiers stepped aboard their transports at Vera Cruz and quitted Mexican soil.

By the Treaty of Guadalupe Hidalgo the United States agreed to pay Mexico $15 million and to assume the unpaid claims by Americans against Mexico. In return, Mexico recognized the Rio Grande as the boundary of Texas and ceded New Mexico (including the present states of Arizona, New Mexico, Utah, and Nevada, a small corner of present-day Wyoming, and the western and southern portions of Colorado) and Upper California (the present state of California) to the United States. Mexico lost almost half of its land area to the United States by the terms of the treaty.

The Army on the New Frontier

The victory over Mexico, as well as the settlement of the Oregon boundary frontier in June 1846, added to the United States a vast territory that was to occupy the Army almost exclusively in the postwar years. For generations, the Army was to be the only force for law and order throughout thousands of square miles. First, the Army needed to explore this vast new conquest. In this task the Corps of Topographical Engineers played the leading role. Some knowledge of the new region had been gained by expeditions such as those of Capt. Benjamin L. E. Bonneville, Kearny, and 2d Lt. John C. Fremont; more had been gained during the Mexican War by "topogs" attached to Kearny's march to California and Wool's to Saltillo and after the war by Maj. William H. Emory's work with the Mexican Boundary Commission. But much still remained to be done.

The most significant and far-reaching explorations were those to locate routes for transcontinental railroads. The first effort was directed toward the southwest, seeking an "ice-free, mountain-free" route. In

Topographical Engineers Exploring the Colorado River near Chimney Peak

that area, the necessity for defense against Comanches, Apaches, and Navahos meant that most of the Army had to be stationed between San Antonio and Fort Yuma. Forts had to be constructed, roads built, rivers sought as avenues of supply, and Indian trails mapped. In 1853 Congress authorized similar explorations on a northern route to the Pacific from Chicago and a central route from St. Louis.

Railroad construction did not begin until after the Civil War. Emigrants setting out for the West, in increasing numbers after the discovery of gold in California in 1849, used wagon trains across plains populated by warlike Indian tribes. The Army guarded the several transcontinental wagon routes and managed to keep the tribes in check. During the decade of the fifties there were no fewer than twenty-two distinct Indian "wars," as well as the unusual task of controlling some particularly troublesome settlers.

In 1857 reports filtered back to the east from Utah that the settlement of Mormons there had deliberately massacred a party of Arkansas pioneers at a place called Mountain Meadow. The settlers, having been attacked by a party of Indians, surrendered to a Mormon militia contingent posing as rescuers and allowed themselves to be disarmed. On September 11, 1857, the Mormons summarily executed 120 of the survivors: men, women, and all children over the age of ten. Seventeen children were "adopted" by the Mormons but were later returned east to their relatives. This and other instances of defiance of federal authority prompted the dispatch of two sizable military expeditions from Fort Leavenworth. However, despite some tensions, a full-scale "Mormon War" never became a reality.

Army expeditions such as those from Fort Leavenworth, marching through primitive country where no local procurement was possible, had to carry all requirements, from horseshoe nails to artillery. Supplying the frontier posts, some as far as a thousand miles from inland waterways, entailed great effort. All goods had to be hauled in wagons or carried by pack train. The difficulty of supplying posts in the arid regions of the Southwest led in 1855 to an interesting experiment, strongly backed by Secretary of War Jefferson Davis, in the use

JEFFERSON DAVIS AND THE CAMELS

As Secretary of War, Jefferson Davis (1808–1889) believed that the deserts of the American southwest were ideally suited for the use of camels. At his urging, Congress in 1855 authorized money to purchase camels from North Africa and ship them to Texas. Despite the hardiness of the animals and their ability to carry heavy loads over difficult terrain, the camel experiment was not a success. The beasts smelled horrible, frightened mules and horses, and were apparently even more ornery than mules. Despite several successful uses, most were eventually sold at public auction or released into the wild to slowly die out.

of camels as pack animals. Seventy-five were imported from the Middle East and sent to Texas. They showed that they could carry heavy loads, walk sure-footedly over ground no wagon could traverse, and subsist by grazing and on little water; but their appearance on the roads stampeded wagon and pack trains, and teamsters hated and feared them. The public and the Army turned against them, and the camel experiment ended in failure.

Increasing the Peacetime Army

By the end of 1848 the Army had reverted to a peacetime strength somewhat smaller than the 10,000 authorized in 1815. It was stretched very thin by its manifold duties on the vast new frontier. On the recommendations of General Scott and Secretary of War George W. Crawford, Congress in June 1850 approved enlarging the companies serving on the frontier to 74 privates, a considerable increase over the 50 in the dragoons, 64 in the mounted rifles, and 42 in the artillery and infantry authorized at the end of 1848. Thereafter 90 of the 158 companies were enlarged; by the end of 1850 the Army was authorized 12,927 officers and men.

When Jefferson Davis became Secretary of War in 1853, he strongly urged a larger Army, one that could expand to 27,818 men in time of war by enlarging the company to 128 men. Davis desired new mounted regiments for frontier service, because only highly mobile units could hope to handle the Indians. In March 1855 Congress added 4 new regiments to the existing 15 (2 of dragoons, 1 of mounted rifles, 4 of artillery, and 8 of infantry). They were the 1st and 2d Cavalry Regiments and the 9th and 10th Infantry Regiments. The mounted arm thus consisted of dragoons, mounted rifles, and cavalry until the Civil War, when all mounted regiments were called cavalry.

Weapons and Tactics on the Eve of the Civil War

At Davis' insistence the new infantry units were armed with percussion-cap, single shot, muzzleloading rifled muskets instead of smoothbore muskets. Nineteenth century technological developments had made possible an accurate, dependable muzzleloading rifle with at least as fast a rate of fire as the smoothbore musket. This was partly due to the application of the percussion-cap principle to the rifle and partly to the adoption in 1855 of the Minié ball or bullet, a lead projectile tapering forward from its hollow base. To load and fire, the soldier bit open the paper cartridge, poured the powder down the barrel, rammed in the paper to seat the charge, and then rammed the bullet home. He then put the cap in place, full-cocked the piece, aimed, and fired. Sparks from the cap fired the powder. The force of the explosion expanded the hollow base of the bullet to fit the rifling, and the bullet left the barrel spinning and thus with considerable accuracy. Its effective range was 400 to 600 yards as compared with only around 100 yards for smoothbore muskets. The rate of fire was a theoretical three rounds per minute, though this was seldom attained in practice.

In 1855 the national armories began making only rifles and started converting smoothbores into rifles, but the work took time. By the end of 1858 the Springfield and Harpers Ferry Armories had manufactured only 4,000 of the new type of rifle, the Springfield .58, a muzzleloader. Breechloading, permitting a much more rapid rate of fire, had to await the development of a tight-fitting, but easy-moving bolt and a cartridge that would effectively seal the breech. Many breechloaders were on the market in the 1850s; and the Army began testing all available models but did not complete its tests before 1861. Effective breechloading rifles required metallic rather than paper cartridges to prevent escape of gases at the breech. Metallic cartridges were invented in 1856 but were not produced in large numbers until after 1861.

The introduction of rifling into field and coast artillery increased the accuracy and more than doubled the effective range; but rifled guns, which had to await the development of advanced manufacturing techniques, did not immediately supplant the smoothbores. During this period an important smoothbore piece was introduced for the light batteries, the 12-lb. bronze cannon called the Napoleon for Napoleon III. Capt. Robert P. Parrott's rifled cannon was developed in 1851 but did not come into use on an appreciable scale until the Civil War. The application of the Minié principle to artillery did much to further the use of rifled artillery; though grape and canister, shell (high explosive

BREECHLOADERS VERSUS MUZZLELOADERS

By the nineteenth century the theoretical advantages of breechloading firearms—faster firing and easier loading while concealed or mounted—had long been known. The U.S. Army adopted breechloaders, in the form of the Hall rifles and carbines, during much of the first half of the nineteenth century; but practical difficulties, in the form of a complicated mechanism and an inadequate gas seal at the breech, outweighed the benefits. By the Civil War technical advances would make breechloading more feasible, but the enormous industrial problem of equipping the armies with new weapons and ammunition would make existing muzzleloaders the mainstay of both Union and Confederate forces. Private purchase and political influence within the Union Army, however, allowed the successful fielding of some breechloading rifles and carbines, notably the Sharps, Spencer, and Henry designs. Just after the Civil War the Army, faced simultaneously with the need to acquire a modern rifle and a peacetime budget, adopted the Allin "trap-door" action as a means to convert its enormous wartime stock of rifled muskets.

DENNIS HART MAHAN (1802–1871)

After graduating at the top of West Point's Class of 1824, under the leadership of Sylvanus Thayer, Dennis Hart Mahan remained at the Academy as a professor of engineering, mathematics, and military science, 1824–1871. Mahan's 1847 Elementary Treatise on Advance-Guard, Out-Post, and Detachment Service of Troops became the first major American work on strategy and tactics. Derived from Antoine-Henri de Jomini's analysis of Napoleonic warfare, Mahan's emphasis on rules and principles and failure to address technological change or innovation would play a significant role in the Civil War. Most of the academy graduates on both sides of the conflict had studied under Mahan, and many other officers used his book as a field manual. Mahan's thought had an enduring impact on U.S. Army doctrine, just as his oldest son, Alfred Thayer Mahan, would later shape naval strategy.

and shrapnel), and solid shot, all used in the Mexican War, were still standard.

Rockets declined in favor. The brief experience with them in the Mexican War had not been impressive. After the war, continued experimentation failed to remove faults of eccentricity in flight and instability. The rockets often exploded prematurely, so troops were reluctant to use them; moreover, they tended to deteriorate in storage. More important than any of these considerations was the fact that the new rifled artillery was decidedly superior to rockets in range, accuracy, and reliability.

Tactical doctrine did not entirely keep pace with the development of weapons. In an effort in that direction, Secretary Davis prescribed light infantry tactics for all infantry units. In general, this meant reducing the line of the infantry from three to two ranks and placing increased emphasis on skirmishers. Formations, however, were still rigid: Men stood shoulder to shoulder (it was almost impossible to load a muzzleloader lying down), and intervals between units were small. These relatively dense formations would in the early days of the Civil War offer inviting targets, but it was perhaps the most effective way to mass small-arms fire until the early twentieth century development of the machine gun.

At the U.S. Military Academy during this period, such great names as Robert E. Lee and Dennis Mahan, author of many works on engineering and fortification, appeared on the roster of staff and faculty. The Artillery School of Practice was reopened; and, with the appearance in 1849 of Bvt. Maj. Alfred Mordecai's *Artillery for the United States Land Service*, the Army had for the first time a full, accurate description of its system of artillery. Secretary Davis sent Mordecai, along with Maj. Richard Delafield and Capt. George B. McClellan, to Europe to study all aspects of the Crimean War in particular and European military institutions and development in general. The study of American military theory was stimulated by the publication in 1846 of Henry Wager Halleck's Elements of Military Art and Science. Such volumes as Scott's Instructions for Field Artillery, the General Regulations for the Army of the United States, Hardee's Tactics, and the new volume on infantry tactics sponsored by Davis were made available to Army officers and a few others; though not enough were obtained to furnish copies to the militia. A number of military schools had been founded throughout the country, with the South having a slight edge, an advantage that was to provide numerous capable officers to the Confederacy when the Civil War broke out.

DISCUSSION QUESTIONS

1. How risky was the strategy of a three-pronged attack on Mexico? What could have gone wrong?

2. What were President Polk's diplomatic and political objectives during the Mexican War? What methods did he use to obtain them?

3. Why did the mix of volunteer and Regular Army units work well in the Mexican War? What could have gone wrong?

4. Discuss the strengths and weaknesses of Generals Scott and Taylor. Under whom would you rather have served, and why?

5. How would you characterize the occupation of Mexico City? What lessons could be drawn from this experience?

6. Discuss the role of technological advances in weaponry on the verge of the Civil War. What tactical options changed for commanders on the battlefield as a result of those advances?

RECOMMENDED READINGS

Bauer, K. Jack. *The Mexican War, 1846–1848*. New York: Macmillan, 1974.

———. *Zachary Taylor: Soldier, Planter, Statesman of the Old Southwest*. Newtown, Conn.: American Political Biography Press, 1994.

Chance, Joseph E. *Jefferson Davis's Mexican War Regiment*. Jackson: University Press of Mississippi, 1991.

Eisenhower, John. *So Far from God: The U.S. War with Mexico*. New York: Anchor Books, 1990.

Johnson, Timothy D. *Winfield Scott: The Quest for Military Glory*. Lawrence: University Press of Kansas, 1998.

McCaffrey, James. *Army of Manifest Destiny: The American Soldier in the Mexican War*. New York: New York University Press, 1992.

Risch, Erna. *Quartermaster Support of the Army: A History of the Corps, 1775–1939*. Washington, D.C.: U.S. Army Center of Military History, 1962, chs. 6–8.

Utley, Robert M. *Frontiersmen in Blue: The United States Army and the Indian, 1848–1865*. Lincoln: University of Nebraska Press, 1981.

Winders, Richard B. *Mr. Polk's Army: The American Military Experience in the Mexican War*. College Station: Texas A&M University Press, 1997.

Other Readings

Bill, Alfred Hoyt. *Rehearsal for Conflict: The War With Mexico, 1846–1848*, 2d ed. New York: Cooper Square, 1969.

Connor, Seymour A., and Odie B. Faulk. *North America Divided: The Mexican War, 1846–1848*. New York: Oxford University Press, 1971.

Dawson, Joseph G. III. *Doniphan's Epic March: The 1st Missouri Volunteers in the Mexican War.* Lawrence: University Press of Kansas, 1999.

Frazier, Donald, ed. *The United States and Mexico at War: Nineteenth Century Expansion and Conflict.* New York: Macmillan, 1998.

Goetzmann, William H. *Army Exploration in the American West, 1803–1863.* Austin: Texas State Historical Association, 1991.

Johannsen, Robert W. *To the Halls of the Montezumas: The Mexican War in the American Imagination.* New York: Oxford University Press, 1985.

Lavender, David. *Climax at Buena Vista: The American Campaigns in Northeastern Mexico.* Philadelphia: Lippincott, 1966.

Singletary, Otis A. *The Mexican War.* Chicago: University of Chicago Press, 1960.

Smith, George W., and Charles Judah. *Chronicles of the Gringos: The U.S. Army in the Mexican War, 1846–1848: Accounts of Eyewitnesses and Combatants.* Albuquerque: University of New Mexico Press, 1968.

9

THE CIVIL WAR, 1861

During the administration of President James Buchanan, 1857–1861, tensions over the issue of extending slavery into the western territories mounted alarmingly and the nation ran its seemingly inexorable course toward disunion. Along with slavery, the shifting social, economic, political, and constitutional problems of the fast-growing country fragmented its citizenry. After open warfare broke out in Kansas Territory among slaveholders, abolitionists, and opportunists, the battle lines of opinion hardened rapidly. Buchanan quieted Kansas by calling in the Regular Army, but it was too small and too scattered to suppress the struggles that were almost certain to break out in the border states.

In 1859 John Brown, who had won notoriety in "Bleeding Kansas," seized the Federal arsenal at Harpers Ferry, Virginia, in a mad attempt to foment a slave uprising within that slaveholding state. Again Federal troops were called on to suppress the new outbreak, and pressures and emotions rose on the eve of the 1860 elections. Republican Abraham Lincoln was elected to succeed Buchanan; although he had failed to win a majority of the popular vote, he received 180 of the 303 electoral votes. The inauguration that was to vest in him the powers of the presidency would take place March 4, 1861. During this lame-duck period, Mr. Buchanan was unable to control events and the country continued to lose its cohesion.

Secession, Sumter, and Standing to Arms

Abraham Lincoln's election to the Presidency on November 6, 1860, triggered the long-simmering political crisis. Lincoln's party was opposed to the expansion of slavery into the new western territories. This threatened both the economic and political interests of the South, since the Southern states depended on slavery to maintain their way of life and their power in Congress. South Carolina on December 20 enacted an ordinance declaring that "the union now subsisting between South Carolina and other States, under the name of the 'United States

Above: *Noncommissioned Officer Frock Coat, ca. 1861;* Below: *Artillery Fuse or Primer Pouch Made by Watervliet Arsenal, ca. 1861*

of America,' is hereby dissolved." Within six weeks, six other deep-South states seceded from the Union and seized Federal property inside their borders, including military installations, save Fort Pickens outside Pensacola and Fort Sumter in Charleston Harbor. (*Map 22*) To the seven states that formed the Confederate States of America on February 18, 1861, at Montgomery, Alabama, the U.S. government's retention of the forts was equivalent to a warlike act. To provide his fledgling government with a military force, on March 6 the new Confederate Executive, Jefferson Davis, called for a 100,000-man volunteer force to serve for twelve months.

The creation of a rival War Department south of the 35th Parallel on February 21 shattered the composition of the Regular Army and disrupted its activities, particularly in Texas, where Maj. Gen. David E. Twiggs surrendered his entire command. With an actual strength of 1,080 officers and 14,926 enlisted men on June 30, 1860, the Regular Army was based on five-year enlistments. Recruited heavily from men of foreign birth, the U.S. Army consisted of 10 regiments of infantry, 4 of artillery, 2 of cavalry, 2 of dragoons, and 1 of mounted riflemen. It was not a unified striking force. The Regular Army was deployed within seven departments, six of them west of the Mississippi. Of 198 line companies, 183 were scattered in 79 isolated posts in the territories. The remaining 15 were in garrisons along the Canadian border and on the Atlantic coast. They were patently unprepared for the mission of forcibly returning the Southern states to the union.

Created by Secretary of War John C. Calhoun and expanded by Secretary of War Davis in 1853, the departments of the U.S. Army had become powerful institutions by the eve of the Civil War. Within each of the trans-Mississippi departments, a senior colonel or general officer by brevet commanded 2,000 officers and men. All the states east of the Mississippi constituted the Department of the East, where Bvt. Maj. Gen. John E. Wool controlled 929 regulars.

A department commander was responsible for mobilizing and training militia and volunteer forces called into Federal service and for coordinating his resources with any expeditionary force commander who operated inside his territory or crossed through his department. A department commander often doubled in command, having responsibility for the administration of his department as well as for conduct of operations in the field. He often had a dual staff arrangement, one for the department and another for the campaign. For strategic guidance and major decisions he looked to the President and General in Chief; for administrative support he channeled his requirements through the Secretary of War to the appropriate bureau chief. In the modern sense he had no corps of staff experts who could assist him in equating his strategic goals with his logistical needs. In many respects the departmental system was a major reason why the Union armies during the Civil War operated like a team of balky horses. A system well suited to the demands of maintaining a small peacetime force could not effectively organize and manage combat forces consisting of hundreds of thousands of soldiers.

The 1,676 numbered paragraphs of the U.S. Army Regulations governed the actions of a department commander. The provisions concerning Army organization and tactics were archaic in most cases

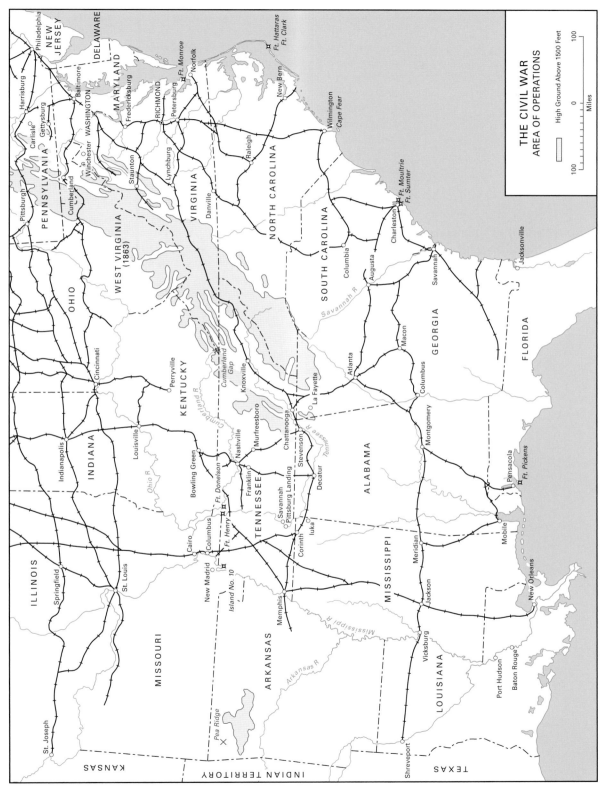

THE CIVIL WAR
AREA OF OPERATIONS

High Ground Above 1500 Feet

Map 22

despite Davis' efforts in 1857 to update the regulations to reflect the experience of the Mexican War. During the Civil War the Regulations would be slightly modified to incorporate the military laws passed by two wartime Congresses. In the South, these same regulations would govern the policy and procedures of the Confederate forces.

The roster of the Regular Army was altered considerably by Davis' action in creating the Confederate Army. Of the 1,080 in the active officer corps, 286 resigned or were dismissed and entered the Confederate service. (Conversely, only 26 enlisted men are known to have violated their oaths.) West Point graduates on the active list numbered 824; of these, 184 were among the officers who turned their backs on the United States and offered their swords to the Confederacy. Of the 900 graduates then in civil life, 114 returned to the Union Army and 99 others sought Southern commissions. General in Chief Winfield Scott and Col. George H. Thomas of Virginia were among the few prominent Southerners who fought for the Union. More serious than their numbers, however, was the high caliber of the officers who joined the Confederacy; many were regimental commanders, and three had commanded at departmental level.

With military preparations under way, Davis dispatched commissioners to Washington a few days after Lincoln's inauguration on March 4, 1861, to treat for the speedy takeover of Forts Sumter and Pickens. Informally reassured that the forts would not be provisioned without proper notice, the envoys returned to Montgomery expecting an uneventful evacuation of Sumter. President Lincoln had to move cautiously, for he knew Sumter's supplies were giving out. As each March day passed, Sumter aggravated the harshness of Lincoln's dilemma. In case of war, the fort had no strategic value. And if Lincoln reinforced it, Davis would have his act of provocation and Lincoln might drive eight more slaveholding states out of the Union. Yet if Sumter was not succored, the North might cool its enthusiasm for the Union concept and become accustomed to having a confederation south of the Mason-Dixon Line. There were no easy choices for the new President.

President Lincoln spent two weeks listening to the conflicting counsel of his constitutional advisers and made up his own mind on March 29 to resupply Fort Sumter with provisions only. No effort would be made to increase its military power. By sea he soon dispatched a token expedition and on April 8 notified South Carolina's governor of his decision. The next move was up to the local Confederate commander, Brig. Gen. Pierre G. T. Beauregard. On the eleventh, Maj. Robert Anderson, Sumter's commander, politely but firmly rejected a formal surrender demand. At 4:30 the next morning Confederate batteries began a 34-hour bombardment. Anderson's ninety-man garrison returned it in earnest, but Sumter's guns were no match for the concentric fire from Confederate artillery. Offered honorable terms on April 14, Anderson surrendered the Federal fort, saluted his U.S. flag with fifty guns, and, with his command, was conveyed to the fleet outside the harbor to be taken to New York City.

Unquestionably, the Confederates fired the first shot of the war and with that rash act removed many difficulties from Lincoln's path in his efforts to preserve the Union. On the fifteenth Lincoln personally penned a proclamation declaring the seven Southern states in insurrec-

> More serious than their numbers, however, was the high caliber of the officers who joined the Confederacy.

THE BALLOON EXPERIMENT

On June 19, 1861, Thaddeus Lowe (1832–1913) ascended from the lawn of the White House in a tethered, hydrogen-filled spherical balloon and telegraphed his observations of the Confederate lines across the Potomac to the ground. It was a stunt—an effective one. Lowe, one of the country's leading balloonists before the war and passionately convinced that aerial reconnaissance would greatly aid military operations, needed high-level support to force balloons upon a skeptical Army hierarchy.

View of Balloon Ascension, ca. 1862

With the backing of President Lincoln, he achieved a trial. The Army rarely used balloons to their best advantage, and the experiment lapsed after Chancellorsville.

tion against the laws of the United States. To strangle the Confederacy, on the nineteenth Lincoln declared the entire coast from South Carolina to Texas under naval blockade. To augment the reduced Regular Army, Lincoln asked the governors of the loyal states for 75,000 militiamen to serve for three months, the maximum time permissible under existing laws. With a unanimity that astonished most people, the Northern states responded with 100,000 men. Within the eight slave states still in the Union, the call for militia to suppress the rebellion was angrily and promptly rejected; and the President's decision to coerce the Confederacy moved Virginia, North Carolina, Tennessee, and Arkansas to join it. The border states of Missouri, Kentucky, Maryland, and Delaware were still undecided; and each side moved cautiously to avoid pushing them into the other's camp.

As spring changed into summer the magnitude of the job that the Union had proclaimed for itself—the conquest of an area the size of western Europe, save Scandinavia and Italy, defended by a plucky and proud people and favored by military geography—was imperfectly understood. Although Lincoln later emerged as a diligent student of warfare, he was as yet unversed in the art. His only service in the military had been as a junior officer of volunteers during the Black Hawk war, and he had seen no combat action. His rival, Davis, from the outset knew his military men quite well and thoroughly understood the mechanics of building a fighting force. He had commanded a volunteer regiment in the Mexican War and was experienced at the national policy level due to his service as Secretary of War. Yet, as time passed, Davis would mismanage his government and its military affairs more and more.

Union Volunteers in Camp

Virginia's secession caused Col. Robert E. Lee, Scott's choice to be the Union's field leader, to resign his commission and offer his services to his state. The Confederates moved their capital to Richmond, Virginia, site of the largest iron works in the South and 100 miles south of the Union capital, Washington. On May 23 Union forces crossed into northern Virginia and occupied Arlington Heights and Alexandria. With Virginia and North Carolina in rebellion, Lincoln extended the naval blockade and called for a large volunteer army backed by an increased regular force.

Correctly anticipating that Congress in its session to open on July 4 would approve his actions, Lincoln, on his own authority, established 40 regiments of U.S. Volunteers (42,034 men) to serve three years or for the duration of the war. He ordered the Regular Army increased by 1 regiment of artillery, 1 of cavalry, and 8 of infantry (actually, 9 regiments were added), or 22,714 men, and the Navy by 18,000 sailors. The new regular infantry regiments were each to have 3 battalions of about 800 men, in contrast to the 1-battalion structure in the existing regular and volunteer regiments. However, because the recruits preferred the larger bonuses, laxer discipline, and easygoing atmosphere of the volunteers, most of the newly constituted regiments were never able to fill their additional battalions to authorized strength. The volunteer units were state units, not Federal or regular units.

The enthusiastic response to Lincoln's various calls forced him to ask the governors to scale down the induction of men. The overtaxed camps could not handle the increasing manpower. In raising the Army, Lincoln used methods that dated back to Washington's day. The combat efficiency and state of training of the new units varied from good to very poor. Some militia regiments were well trained and equipped, others were regiments in name only. The soldiers often elected their own company officers, and the governors commissioned majors and colonels. The President appointed generals. Although many of the newly commissioned officers proved to be enthusiastic, devoted to duty, and eager to learn, incompetents were also appointed. Before the end of 1861, however, officers were being required to prove their qualifications before examining boards of regular officers; those found unfit were allowed to resign.

Frequently advised by governors and congressmen, Mr. Lincoln selected generals from among leading politicians to give himself a broader base of political support. Some political generals, such as John A. Logan and Francis P. Blair, Jr., distinguished themselves, whereas many others proved military hindrances. Lincoln gave a majority of the commissions in the first forty volunteer units to regulars on active duty, to former West Pointers like George B. McClellan (who had resigned to pursue a business career) or to those who had held volunteer commissions during the Mexican War. On the other hand, Davis never gave higher than a brigade command to a Confederate volunteer officer until he had proved himself in battle.

Both North and South failed to develop a good system to replace individuals in volunteer units. The Confederacy, though hamstrung by its insistence that Texans be commanded by Texans and Georgians by Georgians and by governors' insistent demands for retaining home guards, did devise a regimental system that stood up well until the closing days of the war. Except for Wisconsin, Illinois, and Vermont, the Union armies never had an efficient volunteer replacement system. As battle losses mounted and the ranks of veteran regiments thinned, commanders were forced to send men back to their home states on recruiting duty or face the disbandment of their regiments. Northern governors with patronage in mind preferred to raise new regiments, allowing battle-tested ones to decline to company proportions.

The enlisted Regular Army was kept intact for the duration of the war. Many critics believed that the Union should have used regulars to cadre the volunteer units. But this practice was initially impossible during the summer of 1861 for at least two reasons. Lincoln did not foresee a long war, and the majority of regulars were needed on the frontier until trained men could replace them. In addition, Lincoln's critics overlooked the breakdown in morale that would have accompanied the breakup of old line regiments, many of which had histories and honors dating back to the War of 1812. An officer holding a regular commission in 1861 had to resign to accept a commission in the volunteers

THE BALTIMORE RIOTS

As a slave state with economic and cultural ties to both sections, Maryland required careful handling from Abraham Lincoln's government, which faced isolation if the state seceded. On April 19, 1861, while marching through Baltimore to catch the Washington train, four companies of the 6th Massachusetts Regiment traded shots with a mob. Four soldiers and twelve civilians died. Initially, President Lincoln agreed to route units away from Baltimore. When more units arrived in Washington, however, the government imposed military rule on Baltimore, imprisoning secessionists without trial and suppressing newspapers. The state legislature rejected secession, saving Maryland for the Union.

unless the War Department specifically released him. Most regulars were loath to resign, uncertain that they would be recalled to active duty after the war. Thus, during 1861 and part of 1862, promotion in the Regular Army was slow. All regulars could accept commissions in the volunteers by 1862, and in many cases the year they had spent in small-unit command seasoning had its reward in advancing them to higher commands. Ulysses S. Grant and William T. Sherman, both U.S. Military Academy graduates returning from civilian life, asked specifically for volunteer regimental commands at first and soon advanced rapidly to general officer posts.

The Opponents

As North and South lined up for battle, the preponderance of productive capacity, manpower, and agricultural potential clearly lay on the side of the North. Its crops were worth more annually than those of the South, which had concentrated on growing cotton, tobacco, and rice. Between February and May 1861 the Confederate authorities missed the opportunity to ship baled cotton to England and draw bills against it for the purchase of arms. In sea power, railroads, material wealth, and industrial capacity to produce iron and munitions, the North was vastly superior to the South. This disparity became even more pronounced as the ever-tightening blockade gradually cut off the Confederacy from foreign imports. The North had more mules and horses, a logistical advantage of great importance since supplies had to be carried to the troops from rail and riverheads.

The difference in manpower was also critical. According to the census of 1860, the population of the United States numbered 31,443,321. About 23 million of them were in the twenty-two Northern states and 9 million in the eleven states that later seceded. Of the latter total, 3.5 million were slaves. The size of the opposing armies would reflect this disparity. At one time or another about 2.1 million men would serve in the Northern armies, while 800,000–900,000 men would serve the South. Peak strength of the two forces would be about 1 million and 600,000, respectively.

Yet not all the advantages lay with the North. The South possessed good interior lines of communications; and its 3,550-mile coastline, embracing 189 harbors and navigable river mouths, was difficult to blockade effectively. Possessors of a rich military tradition in wars against the British, Spanish, Mexicans, and Indians, the Southerners initially managed to form redoubtable cavalry units more easily than the North and used them with considerable skill against the invading infantry. As the war moved along, the armies on both sides demonstrated high degrees of military skill and bravery. Man for man they became almost evenly matched, and their battles were among the bloodiest in modern history.

Jefferson Davis hoped that the sympathy or even the intervention of European powers might more than compensate for the Confederacy's lack of material resources. This hope, largely illusory from the start, became less and less likely of realization with the emancipation of the slaves, with every Union victory, and with the increasing effectiveness of the blockade.

Militarily, the South's greatest advantage over the North was simply the fact that if not attacked it could win by doing nothing. To restore the Union the Federal forces would have to conquer the Confederacy. Thus the arena of action lay below the strategic line of the Potomac and Ohio Rivers. Here, geography divided the theater of war into three interrelated theaters of operations. The Eastern Theater lay between the Atlantic Ocean and the Appalachian Mountains; the Western Theater embraced the area from the Appalachians to the Mississippi; and the Trans-Mississippi Theater ran westward to the Pacific Ocean.

In the east, the triangular shape of northern Virginia made it a difficult target to attack and provided it some advantage. The northern apex of the state aimed like an arrow at the Federal capital. The Potomac River and the lower Chesapeake Bay formed the right leg of the triangle; its left bounded on the Blue Ridge and the adjacent Shenandoah Valley. The base of the triangle followed the basin of the James and Appomattox Rivers, whereon stood Richmond, halfway between the bay and the valley. For three-and-a-half years Federal commanders would be defeated on the legs and in the center of this triangle as they tried to take Richmond and defeat the Army of Northern Virginia. Operating on these interior lines, General Lee would strike any Union force attempting to invade and follow up with lightning invasions of the North to keep it off balance. In the three neighboring counties of Virginia within this triangle, more than half a million men would clash in mortal combat over the course of four years. More soldiers—Union and Confederate—would die in these three counties than in the Revolutionary War, the War of 1812, the War with Mexico, and all the Indian Wars combined. (*See Map 23.*)

The hammer for swinging against the anvil of Union forces in Virginia came from the line of the Ohio River as Union forces moved along the invasion routes of the Green, Cumberland, Tennessee, and Mississippi Rivers. To breach the lower reaches of the Appalachians, the Federals needed the railroad centers at Nashville, Chattanooga, and Atlanta; with them they could strike north through the Carolinas toward the line of the James. But in the spring of 1861, the anvil and hammer concept had not yet occurred to the military leaders in Washington. Only the General in Chief, Scott, had a concrete strategic proposal for waging total war. He recommended that Lincoln take the time to train

ANACONDA PLAN

General in Chief Winfield Scott devised his plan for the blockading and slow crushing of the rebellion, likened to a snake slowly strangling its prey, because he wanted to avoid a bloody and destructive war that would for generations estrange the South from the rest of the nation. He reckoned that the Confederacy would have no choice but to sue for peace and readmission to the Union once economic hardship spread throughout the South and Europe refused to grant diplomatic recognition to the rebellious southern states. Critics said such a plan might take years to work, if it ever did; thus the best strategy was a quick, decisive military campaign against Richmond. After four bloody years, the implementation of something very like the Anaconda Plan drove the South to its knees.

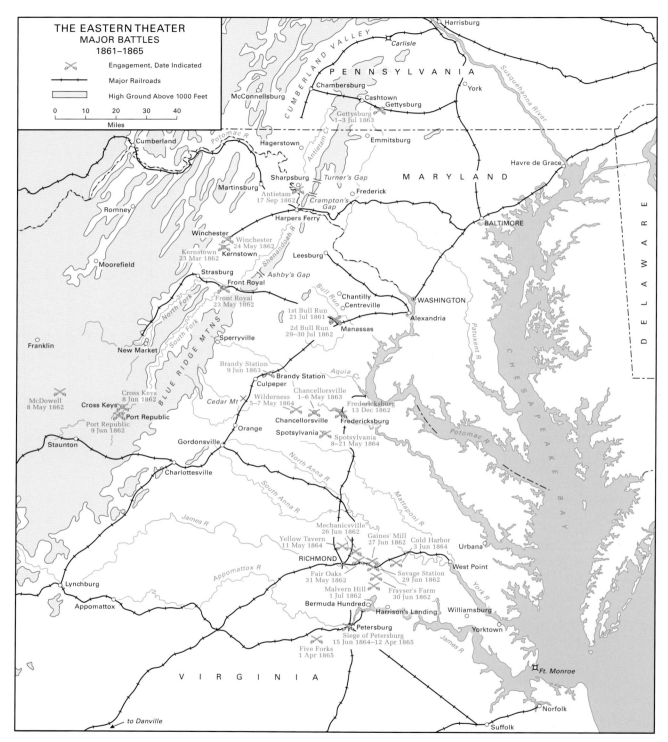

THE EASTERN THEATER
MAJOR BATTLES
1861–1865

 Engagement, Date Indicated

━━━━ Major Railroads

▨▨▨ High Ground Above 1000 Feet

0   10   20   30   40
Miles

Harrisburg

CUMBERLAND VALLEY

Carlisle

P E N N S Y L V A N I A

McConnellsburg

Chambersburg

Cashtown
Gettysburg

York

Gettysburg
1–3 Jul 1863

Cumberland

Hagerstown

Emmitsburg

Havre de Grace

Antietam Cr

Sharpsburg   *Turner's Gap*

M A R Y L A N D

Martinsburg

Frederick

Antietam
17 Sep 1862   *Crampton's Gap*

Romney

BALTIMORE

Harpers Ferry

Winchester

Winchester
24 May 1862

Shenandoah R

Leesburg

DELAWARE

Kernstown
23 Mar 1862   Kernstown

Moorefield

Strasburg

Ashby's Gap

North Fork   Front Royal

Bull Run   Chantilly
Centreville

WASHINGTON

Front Royal
23 May 1862

South Fork   Sperryville

1st Bull Run
21 Jul 1861   Manassas

Alexandria

Franklin

New Market

B L U E   R I D G E   M T N S

2d Bull Run
29–30 Jul 1862

CHESAPEAKE

Brandy Station
9 Jun 1863

Aquia Cr

McDowell
8 May 1862

Cross Keys
8 Jun 1862   Cross Keys

Brandy Station
Culpeper

Cedar Mt   Wilderness
5–7 May 1864

Chancellorsville
1–6 May 1863

Fredericksburg
13 Dec 1862

Potomac R

Patuxent R

Port Republic   Port Republic
9 Jun 1862

Chancellorsville   Fredericksburg

Staunton

Orange   Spotsylvania

Spotsylvania
8–21 May 1864

Gordonsville

B A Y

Charlottesville

North Anna R

South Anna R

James R

Matapony R

Mechanicsville
26 Jun 1862

Gaines' Mill
27 Jun 1862   Cold Harbor
3 Jun 1864

Urbana

Yellow Tavern
11 May 1864

Lynchburg

RICHMOND

West Point

Appomattox R

Fair Oaks
31 May 1862   Savage Station
29 Jun 1862

York R

Appomattox

Malvern Hill
1 Jul 1862   Frayser's Farm
30 Jun 1862

Williamsburg

Bermuda Hundred   Harrison's Landing

Yorktown

Petersburg

James R

Siege of Petersburg
15 Jun 1864–12 Apr 1865

Five Forks
1 Apr 1865

Ft. Monroe

V I R G I N I A

Norfolk

to Danville

Suffolk

Map 23

an army of 85,000 men and that he enforce the naval blockade of the Confederacy. Then the Army was to advance down the Mississippi to divide and conquer the South. The press ridiculed the strategy, calling it the Anaconda Plan, analogous to an anaconda snake's slowly squeezing its prey to death. But few leaders examined the South in terms of its military geography or concentrated on a strategy to prevail over it. Instead, most thought in terms of political boundaries and a short war, perhaps even just one major battle, which would end with the capture of Richmond.

First Bull Run (First Manassas)

In the early summer of 1861 the partly trained ninety-day militia, the almost untrained volunteers, and one newly organized battalion of regulars—a total force of 50,000 Federals commanded by Brig. Gen. Irvin McDowell—defended the nation's capital. Thirty miles to the southwest, covering the rail and road hub at Manassas, Virginia, General Beauregard posted 20,000 Confederates, to be joined by 2,000 more within a few days. To the left, on their defensive line along the Potomac, the Confederates stationed another 11,000 men under Brig. Gen. Joseph E. Johnston in the Shenandoah Valley town of Winchester. Opposing Johnston around Martinsburg, with the mission of keeping the Confederates in place, was Maj. Gen. Robert Patterson with 18,000 Federals. On the extreme right of the Confederate northern Virginia defense line was Col. John B. Magruder's force, which had recently repulsed Maj. Gen. Benjamin F. Butler's Union troops at Big Bethel, Virginia, on 10 June and forced them back into their sanctuary at Fort Monroe.

Big Bethel, the first large-scale engagement of the Civil War, demonstrated that neither opponent was as yet well trained. The Confederates had started preparations earlier to protect northern Virginia and therefore might have had a slight edge on their opponents. General McDowell, only recently a major of regulars, had less than three months to weld his three types of units (militia, volunteer, and regular) into a single fighting force. He attempted to do too much himself, and there were few competent staff officers in the vicinity to help him. McDowell's largest tactical unit was a regiment until just before he marched out of Alexandria. Two to four brigades, plus a battery of regular artillery—the best arm against raw infantry—formed a division. In all, thirteen brigades were organized into five divisions. McDowell parceled out his forty-nine guns among his brigade commanders, who in turn attached them to their regiments. His total force for the advance was 35,732 men, but of these one division of 5,752 men dropped off to guard roads to the rear.

McDowell's advance against Beauregard on four parallel routes was hastened by Northern opinion, expressed in editorials and Congressional speeches, which demanded immediate action. Scott warned Lincoln against undertaking the "On to Richmond" campaign until McDowell's troops had become disciplined units. But Lincoln, eager to use the ninety-day militia before they departed, demanded an advance, fully aware that the Confederates were also unseasoned and cherishing the belief that one defeat would force the South to quit. Scott, influenced by false intelligence that Beauregard would move immediately on

Lincoln, eager to use the ninety-day militia before they departed, demanded an advance, fully aware that the Confederates were also unseasoned and cherishing the belief that one defeat would force the South to quit.

Washington, acceded. McDowell's battle plan and preparations acceler-ated accordingly. The plan, accepted in late June, called for Butler and Patterson to prevent the Confederates facing them from reinforcing Beauregard while McDowell advanced against Manassas to outflank the Southern position. Scott called it a good plan on paper but knew Johnston was capable of frustrating it if given the chance. McDowell's success against the Confederate center depended upon a rapid thirty-mile march, if 35,000 Federals were to keep 22,000 Confederates from being reinforced.

On July 16, 1861, the largest army ever assembled on the North American continent up to that time advanced slowly on both sides of the Warrenton pike toward Bull Run. McDowell's marching orders were good, but the effect was ruined by one unwise caution to the brigade commanders: "It will not be pardonable in any commander … to come upon a battery or breastwork without a knowledge of its position." The caution recalled to McDowell's subordinates the currently sensa-tionalized bugbear of the press of the Federal forces' being fooled by "masked batteries." (The term originated at Sumter, where a certain battery was constructed, masked by a house that was demolished just before the guns opened fire.) Accordingly, 35,000 men moved with extreme caution just five miles on the seventeenth. The next day the Federals occupied Centreville, four miles east of Stone Bridge, which carried the Warrenton pike over Bull Run creek. (*Map 24*)

Beauregard's advance guards made no effort to delay the Federals but fell back across the battle line, now extending three miles along the west bank of Bull Run, which meandered from Stone Bridge southeast until it joined the Occoquan stream. The country was fairly rough, cut by streams and thickly wooded. It presented formidable obstacles to attack-ing raw troops, but a fair shelter for equally raw troops on the defensive. On the eighteenth, while McDowell's main body waited at Centreville for the trains to close up, the leading division demonstrated against Beauregard's right around Mitchell's Ford. The Federal infantry retired after a sharp musketry fight, and a 45-minute artillery duel ensued. It was the first exchange of four standard types of artillery ammunition for all muzzleloading guns, whether rifled or smoothbore. Solid shot, shell, spherical case or shrapnel, and canister from eight Federal guns firing 415 rounds were answered by seven Confederate pieces returning 310 rounds. Steadily withdrawing its guns, the oldest and best-drilled unit of the South, the Washington Light Artillery of New Orleans, broke off the fight against well-trained U.S. regular artillery. Both sides had used rifled artillery, which greatly increased the accuracy and gave a range more than double that of the smoothbores. Yet throughout the war rifled guns never supplanted the new, easily loaded Napoleons. In the fight, defective Confederate ammunition fired from three new 3-inch iron rifles would not fly point foremost but tumbled and lost range against McDowell's gunners. That the error went undetected for days reveals the haste in which Davis had procured his ordnance.

Sure that his green troops could not flank the Confederate right, McDowell tarried two more fateful days before he attacked in force. Engineers reconnoitered for an undefended ford north of Stone Bridge. Finding no vedettes at the ford near Sudley Springs, McDowell decided to envelop the Confederate left on July 21 and destroy the Manassas

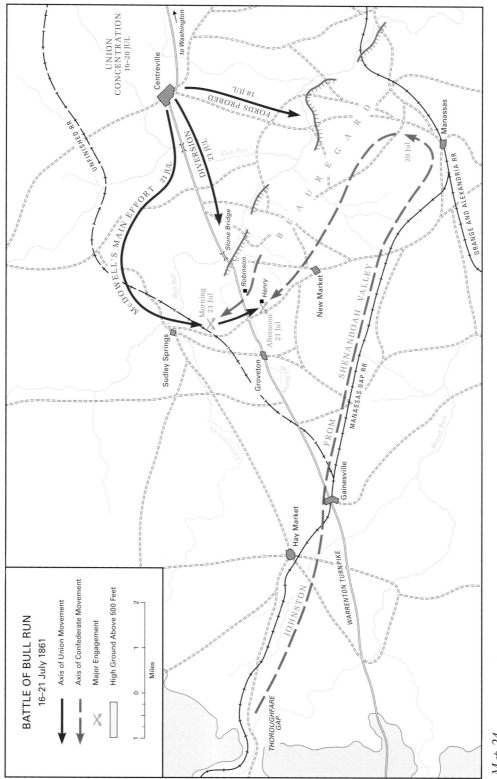

BATTLE OF BULL RUN

16–21 July 1861

Axis of Union Movement

Axis of Confederate Movement

Major Engagement

High Ground Above 500 Feet

Miles

1   0   1   2

to Washington

UNION CONCENTRATION
16–20 JUL

Centreville

Manassas

FORDS PROBED   18 JUL

UNFINISHED RR

DIVERSION   21 JUL

Cub Run

BEAUREGARD

20 Jul

ORANGE AND ALEXANDRIA RR

McDOWELL'S MAIN EFFORT   21 JUL

Stone Bridge

Robinson

Henry

New Market

Morning   21 Jul

Afternoon   21 Jul

SHENANDOAH VALLEY

MANASSAS GAP RR

Bull Run

Sudley Springs

Groveton

Young's Br

Catharpin Cr

FROM

Gainesville

Broad Run

Hay Market

WARRENTON TURNPIKE

JOHNSTON

THOROUGHFARE GAP

Map 24

Gap Railroad to keep Johnston from reinforcing the outnumbered Beauregard. The idea was excellent, but the timing was slow.

While McDowell frittered away four-and-a-half days before he was ready to envelop in force, new tools of warfare swung the advantages of mobility, surprise, and mass at critical points toward Beauregard. On July 17 spies in Washington told of McDowell's departure from Alexandria. By electric telegraph Beauregard in turn alerted Richmond. Davis, also telegraphing, ordered commanders around Richmond, at Aquia Creek, and at Winchester to concentrate their available strength at Manassas. Johnston lost no time in deceiving Patterson by using Col. J. E. B. Stuart's cavalry as a screen and adroitly maneuvering his infantry away from the valley. Johnston selected the best overland routes for his artillery and cavalry marches and arranged for railroad officials to move his four infantry brigades. Brig. Gen. Thomas Jackson's lead brigade, accompanied by Johnston himself, covered fifty-seven miles in twenty-five hours by road and rail to reach Beauregard on the twentieth.

At daylight on the twenty-first McDowell unmasked the first phase of his attack plan. Three brigades of Brig. Gen. Daniel Tyler's division appeared before Stone Bridge; and a huge, 30-lb. Parrott rifle dragged into place by ten horses commenced a slow fire directed by six cannoneers of the 2d U.S. Artillery. Five brigades in two divisions directly under McDowell's command meanwhile marched on an eight-mile circuitous route toward the undefended ford at Sudley Springs. McDowell's goal was the Confederate left rear and a chance to cut the railroad. The movement was not unobserved, however. At 9:00 A.M. a signal flag wigwag from the Henry house announced the point of the enveloping columns at Sudley's crossing, and the intelligence was immediately relayed to Beauregard and Johnston, three miles away on the Confederate right.

The first weight of the Federal attack fell against eleven Confederate companies and two guns. For an hour McDowell's regiments, firing one by one and moving forward cautiously in piecemeal fashion, tried to overrun Beauregard's left flank. The timid tactics gave Beauregard time to redeploy ten regiments across a three-mile front to form a second defensive line across the north face of the hill behind the Henry house. At 10:30 A.M., as the summer sun grew hotter, a portentous dust cloud ten miles northwest of Manassas heralded the arrival of Kirby Smith's brigade, the tail of Johnston's reinforcements from the Shenandoah Valley.

For two hours the roar of the battle swelled in volume. Federal musketry crashes and the thunder from the heavier pieces indicated that McDowell was now committing whole brigades supported by four batteries of artillery. North of the Warrenton turnpike, the Confederate infantry began to lose its brigade cohesion and fall back in disorder. As Beauregard and Johnston rode to the sound of battle, 10,000 Federals were punishing 7,000 Confederates in the vicinity of the Henry and Robinson houses. Johnston, though senior in command, turned the battle over to Beauregard and galloped off toward Manassas to direct the arrival of reinforcements. Brig. Gen. Barnard E. Bee's brigade was pushed back from its advanced position toward the flat-crested hill behind the Henry house, where Jackson's newly arrived brigade had formed. In rallying his routed troops, Bee shouted: "Look at Jackson's Brigade; it stands like a stone wall! Rally behind the Virginians!" (Out

In rallying his routed troops, Bee shouted: "Look at Jackson's Brigade; it stands like a stone wall! Rally behind the Virginians!"

212

of these words came a nickname that Jackson would carry to his grave, and after his death in 1863 the Confederate War Department officially designated his unit the Stonewall Brigade.) Screened by a wooded area, three brigades regrouped behind Jackson's lines; and the rally became a great equalizer as McDowell's strength dissipated to 9,000 men with no immediate infantry reserves in sight.

The cloud of dust moved closer to Manassas Junction, but McDowell ignored it and allowed a lull to settle over his front for almost two hours. At 2:00 P.M., having deployed two batteries of regular artillery directly to his front around the Henry house with insufficient infantry protection, McDowell renewed the battle. By midafternoon the dust had blended sweaty uniforms into a common hue, and more and more cases of mistaken identity were confusing both sides in the smoke of the battle. Then, as part of the confusion, came a fateful episode. To the right front of McDowell's exposed artillery, a line of advancing blue-clad infantry, the 33d Regiment, Virginia Volunteers, suddenly appeared through the smoke. The Federal artillery commander ordered canister, but the chief artillery officer on McDowell's staff overruled the order, claiming that the oncoming blue uniforms belonged to friendly infantry arriving in support. The Virginians advanced to within seventy yards of the Federal guns, leveled their muskets, and let loose. The shock of their volley cut the artillery to shreds; and for the remainder of the day nine Federal guns stood silent, unserved, and helpless between the armies.

About 4:00 P.M., Beauregard, with two additional fresh brigades, advanced his entire line. Shorn of their artillery, the faltering Federal lines soon lost cohesion and began to pull back along the routes they knew; there was more and more confusion as they retired. East of Bull Run, Federal artillery, using Napoleon smoothbores in this initial pull-back from the field, proved to the unsuspecting Confederate cavalry, using classic saber-charging tactics, that a determined line of artillery-men could reduce cavalry to dead and sprawling infantry in minutes.

As in so many battles of the Civil War yet to come, there was no organized pursuit in strength to cut the enemy to ribbons while he fled from the immediate area of the battlefield. At Bull Run, the Federal withdrawal turned into a panic-stricken flight about 6:30 P.M., when Cub Run Bridge, about a mile west of Centreville, was blocked by over-turned wagons. President Davis, just arrived from Richmond, had two daylight hours to arrive at a decision for pursuit. In council with John-ston and Beauregard, Davis instructed the whole Confederate right to advance against the Centreville road, but apparently his orders were never delivered or Beauregard neglected to follow them. Davis thus lost a splendid opportunity for seeing in person whether the unused infan-try and artillery on the right of his line could have made a concerted effort to destroy McDowell's fleeing forces. Logistically, Federal booty taken over the next two days by the Confederates would have sustained them for days in an advance against Washington.

Strategically, Bull Run was important to the Confederates only because the center of their Virginia defenses had held. Tactically, the action highlights many of the problems and deficiencies that were typi-cal of the first year of the war. Bull Run was a clash between large, ill-trained bodies of recruits who were slow in joining battle. The rumor of

SHIELD OF THE CAPITAL: THE WASHINGTON FORTS

In 1861, after the secession of the southern states, the city of Washington stood as a symbol of the Union. In the midst of hostile Virginia and unfriendly Maryland, northern leadership worried over the safety of their capital. After the disaster at Bull Run, General McClellan appointed Maj. John G. Barnard to supervise the construction of a fortification system for Washington. By the end of the year, Barnard had overcome manpower and terrain problems to construct forty-eight forts around the city. With the fighting in northern Virginia from 1862–1864, the threat to the capital remained and its defenses were continually improved. By the end of the war, Washington had become the world's most heavily fortified city, surrounded by sixty-eight enclosed forts and batteries with over 900 guns, supported by another ninety-three batteries for field guns and twenty miles of trenches.

Officers of 55th Infantry at Fort Gaines, near Tenley, D.C.

masked batteries frightened commanders; plans called for maneuvering the enemy out of position, but attacks were frontal; security principles were disregarded; tactical intelligence was nil; and reconnaissance was poorly executed. Soldiers were overloaded for battle. Neither commander was able to employ his whole force effectively. Of McDowell's 35,000 men, only 18,000 crossed Bull Run and casualties among these, including the missing, numbered about 2,708. Beauregard, with 32,000 men, ordered only 18,000 into action and lost 1,982.

Both commanders rode along the front, often interfering in small-unit actions. McDowell led his enveloping column instead of directing all his forces from the rear. Wisely, Johnston left the battlefield and went to the rear to hasten his Shenandoah Valley reserves. Regiments were committed piecemeal. Infantry failed to protect exposed artillery. Artillery was parceled out under infantry command; only on the retreat was the Union senior artillery officer on the scene allowed to manage his guns. He saved twenty-one guns of the forty-nine that McDowell had. Beauregard's orders were oral, vague, and confusing. Some were delivered, others were never followed.

The Second Uprising in 1861

The Southern victory near Manassas had an immediate and long-range effect on the efforts of both the Northern and the Southern states. First, it compelled Northern leaders to face up to the nature and scope of the struggle and to begin the task of putting the Union on a full war footing. Second, it made them more willing to heed the advice of professional soldiers directing military operations along a vast continental land front from Point Lookout, Maryland, to Fort Craig in central New Mexico. Third, Confederate leaders, after their feeling of invincibility quickly wore off, called for 400,000 volunteers, sought critical military items in Europe, and turned to planning operations that might swing the remaining slaveholding states and territories into the Confederacy. Finally, the most potent immediate influence of Bull Run was upon the European powers, which eyed the Confederacy as a belligerent with much potential for political intervention and as a source of revenue. Unless the U.S. Navy could make it unprofitable for private merchant ships to deliver arms to Southern ports and depart with agricultural goods, speculative capital would flow increasingly into the contraband trade.

Strategically, in 1861 the Navy made the most important contribution toward an ultimate Union victory. At considerable expense and in haste to make the blockade effective, the Navy by the end of the year had assembled 200 ships of every description, armed them after a fashion, and placed them on station. With new congressional acts regarding piracy, revenue, confiscation, and enforcement in hand, commanders of this motley fleet intercepted more and more swift blockade runners steaming out of Nassau, Bermuda, and Havana on their three-day run to Wilmington, North Carolina; Charleston, South Carolina; or Savannah, Georgia. In two round trips a blockade runner, even if lost on its third voyage, still produced a considerable profit to its owner. By the end of 1861 such profit was no longer easy, because the Navy had many new fast ships specially fitted for blockade duty in service.

After 1861 the naval character of the war changed. There was no Civil War on the high seas except for the exciting exploits of three or four Confederate cruisers that raided commercial shipping. As the war progressed, both opponents perfected the nature and construction of ships and naval ordnance for a war that would be fought in coastal waters or inside defensible harbors. The three main weapons, the rifled naval gun, the armored ram, and the torpedo mine, were developed and used in novel ways. To offset the defensive use of these weapons by the South, the U.S. Navy beginning in August 1861 landed more and more Army expeditionary forces and gradually gained footholds in the vicinity of Mobile, Savannah, Charleston, and Wilmington. By the end of the war, joint Navy-Army expeditions would convert the sea blockade into a military occupation and would seal off all major ports in the South. Even more important were the river fleets of the U.S. Navy on the Ohio, Missouri, and Mississippi Rivers. These fleets, operating closely with the local Army commanders, provided essential elements in the evolving Union strategy of splitting the Confederacy along the natural invasion routes of the river valleys.

The defeat at Bull Run was followed by "a second uprising" in the North that greatly surpassed the effort after Sumter's surrender. President Lincoln and Congress set to with a will to raise and train the large Federal armies that would be required to defeat the South, to select competent Army field commanders, and to reorganize and strengthen the War Department. On July 22, 1861, Lincoln called for a 500,000-man force of three-year volunteers and during the rest of July

Army Camp #6, *Amos G. Chapman, n.d.*

quickly disbanded the ninety-day militia. The more experienced men entered the newly authorized volunteer force. Meanwhile, the volunteer quota and the increase of regulars, mobilized after Sumter, had so far progressed that camps and garrisons, established at strategic points along the 1,950-mile boundary with the border states and territories, were bustling with activity. As July ended, Congress authorized the volunteers to serve for the duration of the war and perfected their regimental organization. Four regiments were grouped into a brigade, and three brigades formed a division. The infantry corps structure would be fixed when the President directed. In effect, the Lincoln administration was building a Federal force, as opposed to one based on joint state-Federal control and support. State governors, given a quota according to a state's population, raised 1,000-man volunteer regiments, bought locally whatever the units needed, shipped them to federal training centers, and presented all bills to the U.S. government. Accordingly, Congress floated a national loan of $250 million.

Pending the transformation of volunteer forces, both opponents necessarily suspended major military operations in the east for the remainder of 1861. President Lincoln conferred frequently with General Scott and his military advisers about steps already taken to strengthen Union forces along the continental front. Regular Army units were consolidating their position at Fort Craig and Fort Union to protect the upper Rio Grande valley against any Confederate columns coming from Texas. To protect communication lines to the Pacific and the southwest and to guard Federal supplies at Fort Leavenworth, Kansas, and St. Louis, Missouri, Union troops were deployed in eastern Kansas and across central Missouri.

In terms of territorial gain and long-term strategic value, the Western Theater of Operations was more active in 1861 than was the Eastern. Both Union and Confederacy coveted Kentucky and Missouri. The confluence of the Tennessee, Cumberland, and Ohio Rivers lay within Kentucky; while the vast Mississippi-Missouri river network flowed through Missouri. Whoever controlled these two states and these rivers had a great strategic advantage. At the onset of hostilities, Kentucky adopted a policy of neutrality. The loss of Kentucky, in Lincoln's judgment, would be "nearly the same as to lose the whole game," so he carefully respected Kentucky's decision in May to remain neutral. But a Confederate force occupied the strategically important town of Columbus, Kentucky, overlooking the Mississippi River, on fears that Brig. Gen. Ulysses S. Grant, poised across the Ohio River at Cairo, Illinois, would do so first. The rebel move into Kentucky violated that state's neutrality stance, and Kentucky's legislature responded by requesting that Union forces remove the Confederate invaders. On September 6 Grant launched a joint Army-Navy operation into Kentucky and occupied the towns of Paducah and Southland at the mouth of the Tennessee and Cumberland Rivers. This move prevented further Confederate advances in Kentucky and positioned Grant's forces for campaigns in 1862.

In Missouri, pro-Southern and Unionist sympathizers fought a violent campaign for control. A 6,000-man Federal force under Brig. Gen. Nathaniel Lyon defeated Southern militia to occupy the state capital at Jefferson City. A Confederate army of nearly 13,000 moved from Arkansas to destroy the smaller Union force. At Wilson's Creek, Lyon launched a preemptive strike against the rebel camp in the early morning of 10 August, dividing his numerically inferior troops and assaulting from the north and south. The Southern army quickly recovered and regrouped. Outgunned, the Union force fought off three Confederate counterattacks against Bloody Hill before it was able to break contact and withdraw. Based on the number of troops engaged, Wilson's Creek was the most costly Civil War battle in 1861, with the Confederates losing 1,222 killed and wounded. Union casualties were 1,317, including Lyon, the first general officer to be killed in the conflict. The victory at Wilson's Creek buoyed Confederate morale. But Union forces under Charles C. Fremont and later Henry W. Halleck occupied central Missouri and contained rebel forces in the southwestern corner of the state for the remainder of 1861.

A battle with equally long-term consequences was fought for western Virginia. Forty counties elected to secede from Virginia and asked for Federal troops to assist them in repelling any punitive expeditions emerging from the Shenandoah Valley. Between May and early July 1861, Ohio volunteers, under the command of Maj. Gen. George B. McClellan, occupied the Grafton area of western Virginia, hoping to protect the railroad that linked the Ohio Valley with Baltimore. In a series of clashes at Philippi, Beverly, and along the Cheat River, McClellan's forces checked the invading Confederates, paving the way for West Virginia's entrance into the Union. Even the arrival of Jefferson Davis' principal military adviser and Commander of the Confederate forces in Virginia, not yet the Commander of the Army of Northern Virginia, General Robert E. Lee, failed to reverse Union gains. Lee attempted to coordinate several overly ambitious offensives in the Tygart and Kanawha River valleys; but poor roads, dispirited troops, miserable weather, and shortages of supply led to a series of failures. He returned to Richmond after this failure of his first major campaign by the end of

General McClellan's Field Glasses, ca. 1861

October 1861. His reputation as a military commander suffered, while that of his principal foe, General McClellan, soared; some saw McClellan as the "hope of the North."

Although the border strife intensified in the west, Scott attended to the more important front facing Virginia. The nation's capital was imperiled, the Potomac was directly under Confederate guns, and Maryland and Delaware were being used as recruiting areas for the Southern cause. On July 22, Lincoln, following Scott's advice, summoned McClellan, who was thirty-five years old at the time, to Washington, and assigned him command, under Scott, of all the troops in the Washington area. McClellan's reputation was unrivaled, and the public had acclaimed him for his victories in western Virginia. On August 21 McClellan named his force the Army of the Potomac and commenced molding it, with considerable skill, into a formidable machine.

McClellan organized the Army of the Potomac into eleven 10,000-man divisions, each with three brigades of infantry, a cavalry regiment, and four six-gun batteries. In general the other Union armies adopted this structure, and the Confederates deviated from the model only in their cavalry organization. In the Army of Northern Virginia, for example, General Lee treated his cavalry as a tactical arm, grouped first as a division and later as a cavalry corps. Union cavalry consisted of little more than mounted infantry, carrying out a multitude of duties, such as serving as pickets, wagon train escorts, and couriers for the division commander. McClellan planned, once Lincoln activated the corps, to withdraw one-half of the artillery pieces from each infantry division and center them at corps level as a reserve to be deployed under army command. He insisted that the .58-caliber single-shot, muzzleloading Springfield rifle be the standard weapon of the infantry, and most of the Army of the Potomac possessed it when corps were organized on March 8, 1862.

McClellan completely transformed the military atmosphere around Washington before the end of 1861. He was an able administrator, but his critics doubted his abilities as a top field commander. And from the day McClellan activated the Army of the Potomac, he was politically active in trying to oust Winfield Scott. Finally, on November 1, the aged and harassed General in Chief, taking advantage of a new law, retired from the Army. That same day, acting on assurances that McClellan could handle two tasks concurrently, Lincoln made McClellan the General in Chief and retained him in command of the Army of the Potomac. By the ninth, basing his action on Scott's earlier groundwork, McClellan carved out five new departments in the west, all commanded by Regular Army officers. In addition, he continued the work of the new Department of New England, where General Butler was already forming volunteer regiments for scheduled amphibious operations off the Carolina coast and in the Gulf of Mexico.

For the Union cause in Kentucky, the new General in Chief's move came none too soon. After Kentucky declared for the Union on September 20, both sides rapidly concentrated forces in western Kentucky. Maj. Gen. Albert S. Johnston, recently appointed to command Confederate forces in the west, fortified Bowling Green and extended his defensive line to Columbus. Union troops immediately occupied Louisville and planned advances down the railroad to Nashville, Tennessee,

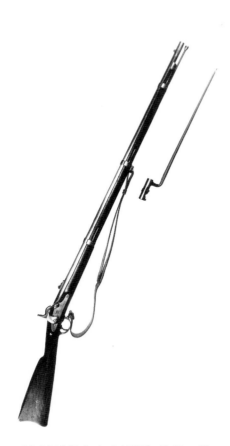

Model 1861 Springfield Rifle, Caliber .58

and eastward into the Appalachians. By November 15, the commanders of the Departments of the Ohio and the Missouri, dividing their operational boundaries in Kentucky along the Cumberland River, were exchanging strategic plans with McClellan in anticipation of a grand offensive in the spring of 1862.

The outpouring of troops and their preparations for battle disrupted the leisurely pace of the War Department. In haste to supply, equip, and deploy the second quota of volunteers, a score or more of states competed not only against one another but also against the Federal government. Profiteers demanded exorbitant prices for scarce items, which frequently turned out to be worthless. Unbridled graft and extravagance were reflected in the bills that the states presented to the War Department for payment. After Bull Run a concerted, widespread movement emerged for the dismissal of Secretary of War Simon Cameron, who had failed to manage his office efficiently. Cameron selected Edwin M. Stanton, former Attorney General in President Buchanan's Cabinet, as his special counsel to handle all legal arguments justifying the War Department's purchasing policies. Knowing that the cabinet post had considerable potential, Stanton worked hard to restore the War Department's prestige. Behind the scenes Stanton aided his fellow Democrat, McClellan, in outfitting the Army of the Potomac. As the summer faded, Stanton, having once scoffed at Lincoln early in the war, ingratiated himself with the President and his key Cabinet members by urging his pro-Union views. In January 1862 Lincoln replaced Cameron with Stanton, who immediately set out to make his cabinet position the most powerful in Lincoln's administration.

Self-confident, arrogant, abrupt, and contemptuous of incompetent military leaders, Stanton was also fiercely energetic, incorruptible, and efficient. Respecting few men and fearing none, he did his best to eliminate favoritism and see to it that war contracts were honestly negotiated and faithfully filled. Few men liked Stanton, but almost all high officials respected him. Stanton insisted that the Army receive whatever it needed, and the best available, so no campaign by any Union army would ever fail for want of supplies.

From the day that Stanton took office, the structure of the War Department was centralized to handle the growing volume of business. Each bureau chief reported directly to Stanton, but the responsibility became so heavy that he delegated procurement and distribution matters to three assistant secretaries. Because the Quartermaster General's Department transported men and materiel, operated the depot system, constructed camps, and handled the largest number of contracts, it soon became the most important agency of the General Staff. Hardworking, efficient, and loyal, Montgomery C. Meigs as Quartermaster General was an organizing genius and one of the few career officers to whom Stanton would listen. To complete his department, Stanton added three major bureaus during the war: the Judge Advocate General's Office in 1862; the Signal Department in 1863; and the Provost Marshal General's Bureau in 1863 to administer the draft (enrollment) act. In the same year the Corps of Topographical Engineers merged with the Corps of Engineers.

Stanton faced mobilization problems and home front crises of unprecedented magnitude. Loyal states were bringing half a million

> Stanton insisted that the Army receive whatever it needed, and the best available, so no campaign by any Union army would ever fail for want of supplies.

men under arms. Grain, wool, leather, lumber, metals, and fuel were being turned into food, clothing, vehicles, and guns, and thousands of draft animals were being purchased and shipped from every part of the North. A well-managed Federal authority was needed to assume the states' obligations, to train volunteer units in the use of their tools of war, and then to deploy them along a vast continental front. By exploiting the railroad, steamship, and telegraph, the War Department provided field commanders a novel type of mobility in their operations. Stanton's major task was to control all aspects of this outpouring of the nation's resources. If war contracts were tainted, the Union soldiers might despair. Moral as well as financial bankruptcy could easily wreck Union hopes of victory. In addition, Stanton had the job of suppressing subversion, of timing the delicate matter of enrolling African Americans in the Army, and of cooperating with a radical-dominated Congress, a strong-willed Cabinet, and a conservative-minded Army. With a lawyer's training, Stanton, like Lincoln, knew little about military affairs, and there was little time for him to learn. Anticipating that President Lincoln would soon call for War Department plans for the spring 1862 offensives, Stanton researched every document he could find on Army administration, consulted his bureau chiefs about readiness, and prepared himself to work with the General in Chief on strategic matters.

When he took office, Stanton found that the War Department had a rival in the form of the Joint Congressional Committee on the Conduct of the War. The committee originated in an investigation of a badly executed reconnaissance at Ball's Bluff on the Potomac on October 21, 1861, in which volunteer officer and popular former Senator Col. Edward D. Baker, was killed. By subsequently searching out graft and inefficiency, the committee did valuable service, but it also vexed the President, Stanton, and most of the generals during the war. Composed of extreme antislavery men without military knowledge and experience, the committee probed the battles, tried to force all its views regarding statecraft and strategy on the President, and put forward its own candidates for high command. Suspicious of proslavery men and men of moderate views, it considered that the only generals fit for office were those who had been abolitionists before 1861.

As the year ended both North and South were earnestly preparing for a hard war. Both opponents were raising and training huge armies totaling nearly a million men. Fort Sumter and bloody Bull Run were over, and each side was gathering its resources for the even bloodier struggles to come.

DISCUSSION QUESTIONS

1. How was the War Department organized in 1861? Discuss the administrative and tactical organization of the U.S. Army units at the onset of the Civil War.

2. What military and political challenges did Lincoln as Commander in Chief face after the secession of the Southern states? How did Fort Sumter change the situation?

3. What advantages and disadvantages did each side have at the beginning of the war? Discuss their relative importance to the ultimate outcome.

4. Discuss the campaign of First Bull Run. What were the goals of the two armies, and how did they seek to achieve them? Why did the Confederates win? Why did the Union lose?

5. How did McClellan reorganize the Union Army? Was the reorganization effective? What were its principal strengths and weaknesses?

6. Assess the relative strengths and weaknesses of the Union and Confederate war efforts at the end of 1861. Which side do you think was in the best overall position?

RECOMMENDED READINGS

Catton, Bruce. *The Coming Fury: The Centennial History of the Civil War,* 3 vols. Garden City: Doubleday, 1963, vol. 1.

Davis, William C. *Look Away: A History of the Confederate States of America.* New York: Free Press, 2002.

Foote, Shelby. *The Civil War: A Narrative,* 3 vols. New York: Random House, 1958, vol. 1.

Hagerman, Edward. *The American Civil War and the Origins of Modern Warfare: Ideas, Organization and Field Command.* Bloomington: Indiana University Press, 1988.

Josephy, Alvin M., Jr. *The Civil War in the American West.* New York: Vintage Books, 1993.

Linderman, Gerald E. *Embattled Courage: The Experience of Combat in the American Civil War.* New York: Free Press, 1987.

Newell, Clayton R. *Lee vs. McClellan: The First Campaign.* Washington, D.C.: Regnery, 1996.

Rafuse, Ethan S. *A Single Grand Victory: The First Campaign and Battle of Manassas.* Wilmington, Del.: Scholarly Resources, Inc., 2002.

Other Readings

Brooksher, William R., *Bloody Hill: The Civil War Battle of Wilson's Creek.* Washington, D.C.: Brassey's Inc., 1995.

Davis, William C. *Battle of Bull Run: A History of the First Major Campaign of the Civil War.* Garden City: Doubleday, 1977.

Freeman, Douglas Southall. *Lee's Lieutenants: A Study in Command,* 3 vols. New York: Scribner Classics, 1997, vol. 1.

McPherson, James M. *Battle Cry of Freedom.* New York: Oxford University Press, 1988.

Mitchell, Joseph B. *Military Leaders of the Civil War,* 2d ed. McLean, Va.: EPM Publications, 1988.

Piston, William G., and Richard W. Hatcher III. *Wilson's Creek: The Second Battle of the Civil War and the Men Who Fought It.* Chapel Hill: University of North Carolina Press, 2000.

Sears, Stephen W. *George B. McClellan: The Young Napoleon.* New York: Da Capo Press, 1999.

10

THE CIVIL WAR, 1862

In 1862 the armed forces of the United States undertook the first massive campaigns to defeat the Southern Confederacy. Better organization, training, and leadership would be displayed on both sides as the combat became more intense. Young American citizen-soldiers would find that war was not a romantic adventure, and their leaders would learn that every victory had its price. It was to be a year of bitter lessons for both sides.

As the winter of 1861–1862 wore on, General in Chief George B. McClellan, who more often than not took counsel of his fears, exaggerated his difficulties and the enemy's strength while discounting the Confederacy's problems. He organized, drilled, and trained the Army of the Potomac while western forces under his general command accomplished little. President Abraham Lincoln and the Union waited impatiently for a conclusive engagement. But neither the Union nor the Confederate Army showed much inclination to move, each side seemingly intent on perfecting itself before attempting to strike what each hoped would be a decisive blow.

The President was particularly eager to support Unionist sentiment in east Tennessee by moving forces in that direction. Above all he wanted a concerted movement to crush the rebellion quickly. In an effort to push matters, Lincoln issued General War Order No. 1 on January 27, 1862. This order, besides superfluously telling the armies to obey existing orders, directed that a general movement of land and sea forces against the Confederacy be launched on February 22, 1862. Lincoln's issuance of an order for an offensive several weeks in advance, without considering what the weather and the roads might be like, has been scoffed at frequently. But apparently he issued it with the primary purpose of getting McClellan to agree to move.

The War in the East: The Army of the Potomac Moves South

As the year 1862 began, in the Eastern Theater plans prepared in Washington were aimed at the capture of Richmond rather than

Naval Engagement in Hampton Roads, *J. Davis after C. Parsons, 1863*

destruction of the army commanded by Joseph E. Johnston, now a full general. Precise methods for reaching the Confederate capital differed. President Lincoln favored an overland advance that would always keep an army between the Confederates and Washington. McClellan agreed at first and then changed his views in favor of a waterborne move by the Army of the Potomac to Urbana on the Rappahannock. From there, he could drive to Richmond before Johnston could retire from the Manassas area to intercept him. He felt that the Washington fortifications, an elaborate system of earthen forts and battery emplacements then in advanced stages of construction, would adequately protect the capital while the field army was away. Johnston, however, rendered this plan obsolete; he withdrew from Manassas to Fredericksburg, halfway between the two capitals and astride McClellan's prospective route of advance. Early in March McClellan moved his army out to the deserted Confederate camps around Manassas to give his troops some field experience. While he was in the field, Lincoln relieved him as General in Chief, doubtless on the ground that he could not command one army in the field and at the same time supervise the operations of all the armies of the United States. Lincoln did not appoint a successor. For a time he and Secretary of War Edwin M. Stanton took over personal direction of the Army with the advice of a newly constituted Army board consisting of the elderly Maj. Gen. Ethan A. Hitchcock and the chiefs of the War Department bureaus.

When events overtook the Urbana scheme, McClellan began to advocate a seaborne move to Fort Monroe, Virginia (at the tip of the peninsula formed by the York and James Rivers), to be followed by an overland advance up the peninsula. If the troops moved fast, he maintained, they could cover the seventy-five miles to Richmond before Johnston could concentrate his forces to stop them. This plan had promise, for it took advantage of Federal control of the seas and a useful base of operations at Fort Monroe and there were fewer rivers to cross than by the overland route. Successful neutralization of the Confederate ironclad *Virginia* (formerly the U.S.S. *Merrimac*) by the Union's revolutionary ironclad Monitor on March 9 had eliminated any naval threat to supply and communications lines, but the absence of good roads and the difficult terrain of the peninsula offered drawbacks to the plan. Lincoln approved it, providing McClellan would leave behind the number of men that his corps commanders considered adequate to ensure the safety of Washington. McClellan gave the President his assurances but failed to take Lincoln into his confidence by pointing out that he considered the Federal troops in the Shenandoah Valley to be covering Washington. In listing the forces he had left behind, he counted some men twice and included several units in Pennsylvania not under his command.

Embarkation began in mid-March, and by April 4 advance elements had moved out of Fort Monroe against Yorktown. The day before, however, the commander of the Washington defenses reported that he had insufficient forces to protect the city. In addition, Lt. Gen. Thomas J. "Stonewall" Jackson had become active in the Shenandoah Valley. Lincoln thereupon told Stanton to detain one of the two corps that were awaiting embarkation at Alexandria. Stanton held back Brig. Gen. Irvin McDowell's corps of 30,000 men, seriously affecting McClellan's plans.

General George B. McClellan
Matthew Brady, 1861

Jackson's Valley Campaign

While a small Confederate garrison at Yorktown made ready to delay McClellan, Johnston hurried his army to the peninsula. In Richmond, Confederate authorities had determined on a spectacularly bold diversion. Robert E. Lee, who had moved rapidly to the rank of full general, had assumed the position of military adviser to Confederate President Jefferson Davis on March 13. Charged with the conduct of operations of the Confederate armies under Davis' direction, Lee saw that any threat to Washington would cause progressive weakening of McClellan's advance against Richmond. He therefore ordered Jackson to begin a rapid campaign in the Shenandoah Valley close to the Northern capital. (*See Map 25.*) The equivalent of three Federal divisions was sent to the valley to destroy Jackson. Lincoln and Stanton, using the telegraph and what military knowledge they had acquired, devised plans to bottle up Jackson and destroy him. But Federal forces in the valley were not under a locally unified command. They moved too slowly; one force did not obey orders strictly; and directives from Washington often neglected to take time, distance, or logistics into account. Also, in Stonewall Jackson, the Union troops were contending against one of the most outstanding field commanders America has ever produced. Jackson's philosophy of war was: "Always mystify,

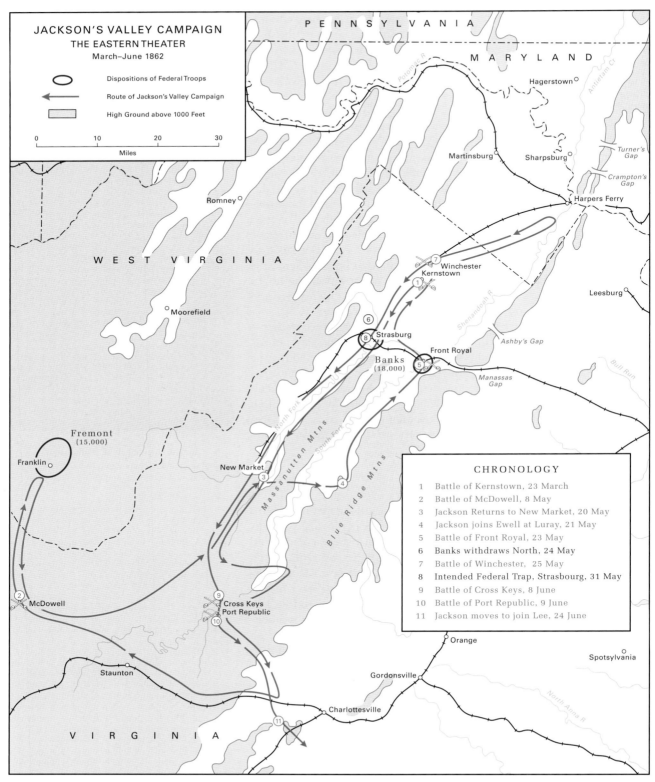

JACKSON'S VALLEY CAMPAIGN
THE EASTERN THEATER
March–June 1862

⬭ Dispositions of Federal Troops

← Route of Jackson's Valley Campaign

▨ High Ground above 1000 Feet

0   10   20   30
Miles

P E N N S Y L V A N I A

M A R Y L A N D

W E S T   V I R G I N I A

V I R G I N I A

Hagerstown

Martinsburg

Sharpsburg

Antietam Cr

Turner's Gap

Crampton's Gap

Harpers Ferry

Leesburg

Romney

Moorefield

Winchester
Kernstown

Shenandoah R.

Ashby's Gap

Strasburg

Front Royal

Banks
(18,000)

Manassas Gap

Bull Run

Fremont
(15,000)

Franklin

North Fork

South Fork

New Market

Massanutten Mtns

Blue Ridge Mtns

McDowell

Cross Keys
Port Republic

Staunton

Orange

Spotsylvania

Gordonsville

Charlottesville

North Anna R.

CHRONOLOGY

1 Battle of Kernstown, 23 March
2 Battle of McDowell, 8 May
3 Jackson Returns to New Market, 20 May
4 Jackson joins Ewell at Luray, 21 May
5 Battle of Front Royal, 23 May
6 Banks withdraws North, 24 May
7 Battle of Winchester, 25 May
8 Intended Federal Trap, Strasbourg, 31 May
9 Battle of Cross Keys, 8 June
10 Battle of Port Republic, 9 June
11 Jackson moves to join Lee, 24 June

Map 25

mislead, and surprise the enemy, if possible; and when you strike and overcome him, never give up the pursuit as long as your men have strength to follow; for an army routed, if hotly pursued, becomes panic-stricken and can then be destroyed by half their number."

The Shenandoah Valley was essential to both sides. It provided the rebels with critical agricultural provisions and was crucial in the Union's defense of Washington, D.C. As a result, the Union Army attempted to hold it with 23,000 troops while General Jackson and his force of 10,000 maneuvered rapidly throughout the region. The valley took on additional importance when General McClellan began his advance on Richmond during the Peninsula Campaign, because McClellan pulled troops out of the valley to reinforce his move against the Confederate capital. Jackson responded quickly, using the mountains as shields to his operations and crisscrossing through various gaps and passes to appear unexpectedly near the surprised Union forces. He began by making a long forced march to strike the Union position at Kernstown on March 23, 1862. The tactical victory that resulted not only threw the Federals off balance, but it also prevented troops from being transferred to the Union invasion and thus kept a full Union corps of 40,000 men under General McDowell from joining the Peninsula Campaign. This movement along with several other forced marches during the campaign earned Jackson's men the epithet "foot cavalry" for their ability to cover great distances to strike the Union at its weakest points.

Jackson went on to defeat Union forces at McDowell, Virginia, on May 8; at Front Royal on May 23; and at Winchester on May 25. The Union command subsequently committed nearly 50,000 troops in multiple converging columns to trap Jackson. Instead of retreating, Jackson audaciously attacked and defeated elements of that force at Cross Keys and Port Republic on June 8 and 9. After that, Federal troops withdrew from the valley, allowing Jackson, again in a forced march, to join Lee in time for the Seven Days' Battles. Jackson's Valley Campaign was one of the most brilliant military operations of the Civil War, and military historians continue to study it for its effective use of the principles of maneuver, offensive, and surprise.

Peninsula Campaign

When McClellan reached the peninsula in early April he found a force of ten to fifteen thousand Confederates under Maj. Gen. John B. Magruder barring his path to Richmond. Magruder, a student of drama and master of deception, so dazzled McClellan that instead of brushing the Confederates aside he spent a month in a siege of Yorktown. But Johnston, who wanted to fight the decisive action closer to Richmond, decided to withdraw slowly up the peninsula. At Williamsburg, on May 5, McClellan's advance elements made contact with the Confederate rear guard under Maj. Gen. James Longstreet, who successfully delayed the Federal advance. McClellan again pursued in leisurely fashion, always believing that he was outnumbered and about to be attacked in overwhelming force by Johnston. By May 25 two corps of the Army of the Potomac had turned southwest toward Richmond and crossed the sluggish Chickahominy River. The remaining three corps were on the north side of the stream with the expectation of making contact with

McDowell, who would come down from Fredericksburg. Men of the two corps south of the river could see the spires of the Confederate capital, but Johnston's army was in front of them. (*Map 26*)

Drenching rains on May 30 raised the Chickahominy to flood stage and seriously divided McClellan's army. Johnston decided to grasp this chance to defeat the Federals in detail. He struck on May 31 near Fair Oaks. His plans called for his whole force to concentrate against the isolated corps south of the river, but his staff and subordinate commanders were not up to the task of executing them. Assaulting columns became confused, and attacks were delivered piecemeal. The Federals, after some initial reverses, held their ground and bloodily repulsed the Confederates.

When Johnston suffered a severe wound at Fair Oaks, President Davis replaced him with General Lee. Lee for his part had no intention of defending Richmond passively. The city's fortifications would enable him to protect Richmond with a relatively small force while he used the main body of his army offensively in an attempt to cut off and destroy the Army of the Potomac. He ordered Jackson back from the Shenandoah Valley with all possible speed.

The Seven Days' Battles

McClellan had planned to use his superior artillery to break through the Richmond defenses, but Lee struck the Union Army before it could resume the advance. Lee's dispositions for the Battle of Mechanicsville on June 26 present a good illustration of the principles of mass and economy of force. On the north side of the Chickahominy, he concentrated 65,000 men to oppose Brig. Gen. Fitz-John Porter's V Corps of 30,000. Only 25,000 were left before Richmond to contain the remainder of the Union Army. When Lee attacked, his timing and coordination were not yet refined. Jackson of all people seemed lethargic and moved slowly; and the V Corps defended stoutly during the day. McClellan thereupon withdrew the V Corps southeast to a stronger position at Gaines' Mill. Porter's men constructed light barricades and made ready. Lee massed 57,000 men and assaulted 34,000 Federals on June 27. The fighting was severe, but numbers told and the Federal line broke. Darkness fell before Lee could exploit his advantage, and McClellan took the opportunity to regroup Porter's men with the main army south of the Chickahominy.

At this point McClellan yielded the initiative to Lee. With his line of communications to White House, his supply base on the York River, cut and with the James River open to the U.S. Navy, the Union commander decided to shift his base to Harrison's Landing on the south side of the peninsula. His rear areas had been particularly shaky since Confederate cavalry under Brig. Gen. J. E. B. Stuart had ridden completely around the Union Army in a daring raid in early June. The intricate retreat to the James, which involved 90,000 men, the artillery train, 3,100 wagons, and 2,500 head of cattle, began on the night of June 27 and was accomplished by using two roads. Lee tried to hinder the movement but was held off by Federal rear guards at Savage Station on June 29 and at Frayser's Farm (Glendale) on the last day of the month.

General "Jeb" Stuart, C.S.A., 1863
George S. Cook

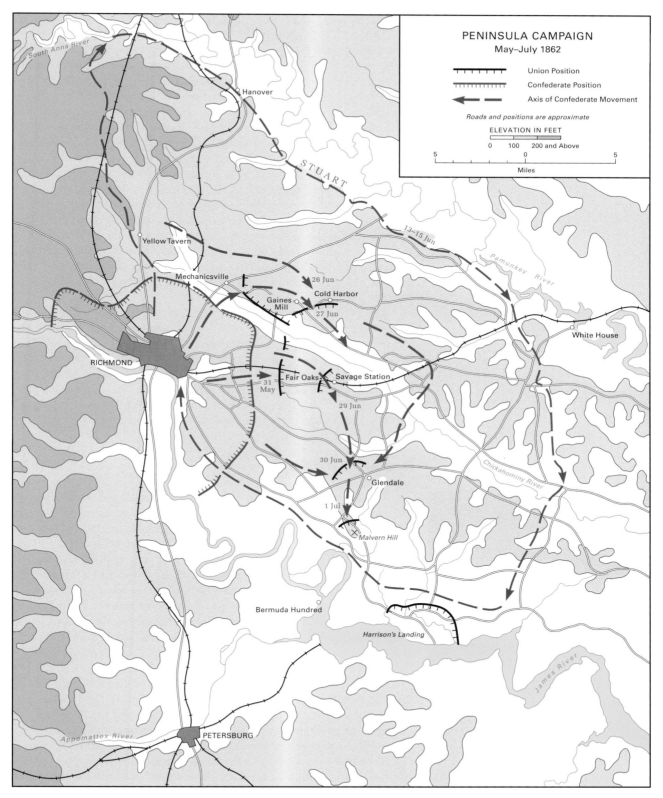

PENINSULA CAMPAIGN
May–July 1862

▬▬▬	Union Position
╥╥╥╥╥	Confederate Position
◀━ ━ ━	Axis of Confederate Movement

Roads and positions are approximate

ELEVATION IN FEET

0   100   200 and Above

5 ___ 0 ___ 5
Miles

South Anna River

Hanover

STUART

13–15 Jun

Pamunkey River

Yellow Tavern

Mechanicsville   26 Jun

Gaines   Cold Harbor
Mill
27 Jun

White House

RICHMOND

31
May   Fair Oaks   Savage Station

29 Jun

Chickahominy River

30 Jun

Glendale

1 Jul

✕ Malvern Hill

Bermuda Hundred

Harrison's Landing

James River

Appomattox River   PETERSBURG

Map 26

By the first day of July McClellan had concentrated the Army of the Potomac on a commanding plateau at Malvern Hill, northwest of Harrison's Landing. The location was strong, with clear fields of fire to the front and the flanks secured by streams. Massed artillery could sweep all approaches, and gunboats on the river were ready to provide fire support. The Confederates would have to attack by passing through broken and wooded terrain, traversing swampy ground, and ascending the hill. At first Lee felt McClellan's position was too strong to assault. Then, at 3:00 P.M. on July 1, when a shifting of Federal troops deceived him into thinking there was a general withdrawal, he changed his mind and attacked. Again staff work and control were poor. The assaults, all frontal, were delivered piecemeal by only part of the army against Union artillery, massed hub to hub, and supporting infantry. The Confederate formations were shattered, costing Lee some 5,500 men. On the following day the Army of the Potomac fell back to Harrison's Landing and dug in. After reconnoitering McClellan's position, Lee ordered his exhausted men back to the Richmond lines for rest and reorganization. His attacks, while costly, had saved Richmond for the Confederacy.

The Peninsula Campaign cost the Union Army 15,849 men killed, wounded, and missing. The Confederates, who had done most of the attacking, lost more: 20,614. Improvement in the training and discipline of both armies since the disorganized fight at Bull Run was notable. But just as significant was the fact that higher commanders had not yet thoroughly mastered their jobs. Except in McClellan's defensive action at Malvern Hill, which was largely conducted by his corps commanders, neither side's higher command had been able to bring an entire army into coordinated action.

Second Bull Run

H. W. Halleck
Alonzo Chappel, 1862

The failure of the Union forces to take Richmond quickly forced President Lincoln to abandon the idea of exercising command over the Union armies in person. On July 11, 1862, he selected as new General in Chief Maj. Gen. Henry W. Halleck, who had won acclaim for the victories in the west. The President did not at once appoint a successor in the west, which was to suffer from divided command for a time. Lincoln wanted Halleck to direct the various Federal armies in close concert to take advantage of the North's superior strength. If all Federal armies coordinated their efforts, Lincoln reasoned, they could strike where the Confederacy was weak or force it to strengthen one army at the expense of another; eventually they could wear the Confederacy down, destroy the various armies, and win the war.

Halleck turned out to be a disappointment. He never attempted to exercise field command or assume responsibility for strategic direction of the armies. But, acting more as military adviser to the President, he nevertheless performed a valuable function by serving as a channel of communication between the Chief Executive and the field commanders. He adeptly translated the President's ideas into terms the generals could comprehend and expressed the soldiers' views in language that Mr. Lincoln could understand. However, he did not solve the strategic coordination problem of the Union.

Orange and Alexandria Railroad Military Bridge

Shortly before Halleck's appointment, Lincoln decided to consolidate the various Union forces in the Shenandoah Valley and other parts of western Virginia—45,000 men—under the victor of a small battle in the west at Island No.10, Maj. Gen. John Pope. Pope was brought East with high expectations, but he immediately disenchanted his new command by announcing that in the West the Federal armies were used to seeing the backs of their enemies. Pope's so-called Army of Virginia was ordered to divert pressure from McClellan on the peninsula. But Jackson had left the valley, and Federal forces were scattered. On August 3 Halleck ordered McClellan to withdraw by water from the peninsula to Aquia Creek on the Potomac and to affect a speedy junction at Fredericksburg with Pope. Meanwhile, Pope began posting the Army of Virginia along the Orange and Alexandria Railroads to the west of Fredericksburg.

Lee knew that his Army of Northern Virginia was in a dangerous position between Pope and McClellan, especially if the two were to unite. On July 13 he sent Jackson with forces eventually totaling 24,000 men to watch Pope. After an initial sparring action at Cedar Mountain on August 9, Jackson and Pope stood watching each other for nearly a week. Lee, knowing that McClellan was leaving Harrison's Landing, departed Richmond with the remainder of the Army of Northern Virginia and joined Jackson at Gordonsville. The combined Confederate forces outnumbered Pope's, and Lee resolved to outflank and cut off the Army of Virginia before the whole of McClellan's force could be brought to bear.

A succession of captured orders enabled both Lee and Pope to learn the intentions of the other. Pope ascertained Lee's plan to trap him against the Rappahannock and withdrew to the north bank astride the railroad. Lee, learning that two corps from the Army of the Potomac would join Pope within days, acted quickly and boldly. He sent

General Halleck's Hardee Hat
Manufactured ca. 1859

General Longstreet

Lee, by great daring and rapid movement, had successfully defeated one formidable Union army in the presence of another even larger one.

Jackson off on a wide turning movement through Thoroughfare Gap in the Bull Run Mountains around the northern flank of Pope's army and subsequently followed the same route with the divisions commanded by General Longstreet.

Pope took note of Jackson's move but first assumed that it was pointed toward the Shenandoah Valley. Then Jackson, covering nearly sixty miles in two days, came in behind Pope at Manassas on August 26, destroyed his supply base there, and slipped away unmolested. Pope marched and countermarched his forces for two days trying to find the elusive Confederates. At the same time the Union commander failed to take Lee's other forces into account. As a result he walked into Lee's trap on the site of the old battlefield at Bull Run. Pope attacked Jackson, posted behind an abandoned railroad embankment, but again the attack consisted of a series of piecemeal frontal assaults that were repulsed with heavy casualties. By then Porter's V Corps from the Army of the Potomac had reached the field and was ordered to attack Jackson's right (south) flank. By this time also, Longstreet's column had burst through Thoroughfare Gap; and deploying on Jackson's right, it blocked Porter's move.

The next day, August 30, Pope renewed his attacks against Jackson, who he thought was retreating. Seizing the opportunity to catch the Federal columns in an exposed position, Lee sent Longstreet slashing along the Warrenton turnpike to catch Pope's flank in the air. The Federal army soon retired from the field; and Pope led it back to Washington, fighting an enveloping Confederate force at Chantilly on the way.

Lee, by great daring and rapid movement, and by virtue of having the Confederate forces unified under his command, had successfully defeated one formidable Union army in the presence of another even larger one. Halleck, as General in Chief, had not taken the field to coordinate Pope and McClellan, and Pope lost the campaign despite the advantage of interior lines.

President Lincoln, desiring to use McClellan's admitted talents for training and reorganizing the battered eastern armies, had become convinced that bitter personal feelings between McClellan and Pope prevented them from working effectively in the same theater. On September 5 Halleck, upon the President's order, dissolved the Army of Virginia and assigned its units to the Army of the Potomac. He sent Pope to a command in Minnesota. The Union authorities expected that McClellan would be able to devote several months to training and reorganization, but Lee dashed these hopes.

Lee Invades Maryland

Up to this point the Confederates in the east had been following an inherently defensive strategy, though tactically they frequently assumed the offensive. But Davis and Lee, for a complicated set of political and military reasons, determined to take the offensive and invade the North in coordination with Maj. Gen. Braxton Bragg's drive into Kentucky. Militarily, in the east, an invasion of Maryland would give Lee a chance to defeat or destroy the Army of the Potomac, uncovering such cities as Washington, Baltimore, and Philadelphia, and to cut Federal communications with the states to the west. Lee also retained hopes that he could bring Maryland into the Confederacy.

The Army of Northern Virginia, organized into two corps (Longstreet's consisting of five divisions and Jackson's of four divisions) plus Stuart's three brigades of cavalry and the reserve artillery, numbered 55,000 effectives. Lee did not rest after the second battle of Bull Run but quickly crossed the Potomac and encamped near Frederick, Maryland, from which he sent Jackson to capture an isolated Federal garrison at Harpers Ferry. The remainder of Lee's army then crossed South Mountain and headed for Hagerstown, about twenty-five miles northwest of Frederick, with Stuart's cavalry screening the right flank. In the meantime McClellan's Army of the Potomac, 85,000 men organized into six corps, marched northwest from Washington and reached Frederick on September 12. Of the 85,000, however, 20,000 were green troops that had only joined the Army in the summer of 1862.

At this time McClellan had a stroke of luck. Lee, in assigning missions to his command, had detached Maj. Gen. D. H. Hill's division from Jackson and attached it to Longstreet and had sent copies of his orders, which prescribed routes, objectives, and times of arrival, to Jackson, Longstreet, and Hill. But Jackson was not sure that Hill had received the order. He therefore made an additional copy of Lee's order and sent it to Hill. One of Hill's orders, wrapped around some cigars, was somehow left behind in an abandoned camp, where it was picked up on September 13 by Union soldiers and rushed to McClellan. Waving the captured orders, McClellan is supposed to have stated, "Here is a paper with which, if I cannot whip Bobbie Lee, I will be willing to go home." This windfall gave the Federal commander an unmatched opportunity to defeat Lee's scattered forces in detail if he pushed quickly through the gaps. However, McClellan vacillated for sixteen hours. Lee,

The Bloody Lane, Battle of Antietam, *James Hope, 1889*

informed of the lost order, sent all available forces to hold the mountain gaps, so it was nightfall on the fourteenth before McClellan fought his way across South Mountain.

Lee retreated to Sharpsburg on Antietam Creek, where he turned to fight. Pinned between Antietam Creek and the Potomac with no room for maneuver and still outnumbered since Jackson's force had yet to return to the main body after capturing Harpers Ferry, Lee relied on the advantage of interior lines and the boldness and the fighting ability of his men. It was a dangerous move, however, and could have resulted in the total destruction of his army.

McClellan delayed his attack until September 17, when he launched an uncoordinated series of assaults that drove back the Confederates in places but failed to break their line. Heavy fighting swelled across ripe fields and up through rocky glens that became known to history as the West Wood, the Cornfield, the East Wood, Bloody Lane, and Burnside's Bridge. (*Map 27*) One Southerner remembered the attacking Union columns: "With flags flying and the long unfaltering lines rising and falling as they crossed the rolling fields, it looked as though nothing could stop them." But when the massed fire of field guns and small arms struck such human waves, a Union survivor recalled, it "was like a scythe running through our line."

McClellan, like too many leaders during the Civil War, could not bring himself to commit his reserve (the V Corps under Porter) at the strategic moment. Although adored by his men, as one of the veterans wrote after the war, he "never realized the metal that was in his grand Army of the Potomac." Jackson's last division arrived just in time to head off the final assaults by Maj. Gen. Ambrose E. Burnside's corps, and at the end of the day Lee still held most of his line. Casualties were heavy. Of 70,000 Federal troops nearly 13,000 were killed, wounded, or missing; and of the 40,000 or more Confederates engaged, almost 10,000 were casualties. It was the bloodiest single day of the war, and the bloodiest day in American history. Although Lee audaciously awaited new attacks on September 18, McClellan left him unmolested; and that night the Army of Northern Virginia withdrew across the Potomac.

Lincoln's Emancipation Proclamation

Antietam was tactically a draw, but the fact that Lee was turned back from his invasion of the North made it a strategic victory and gave President Lincoln an opportunity to strike at the Confederacy psychologically and economically by issuing his preliminary Emancipation Proclamation on September 22, 1862. Lincoln, while opposed to slavery and its extension to the western territories, was not an abolitionist. He had stated publicly that the war was being fought over union or secession, with the slavery question only incidental, and had earlier overruled several generals who were premature emancipators. But he wanted to strike at the economy and military sustainment power of the Confederate states and to appeal to antislavery opinion in Europe. He had awaited the opportune moment that a Union victory would give him and decided that Antietam was suitable. Acting on his authority as Commander in Chief, he issued the proclamation that all slaves in states or districts in rebellion against the United States on January 1, 1863, would be thenceforward

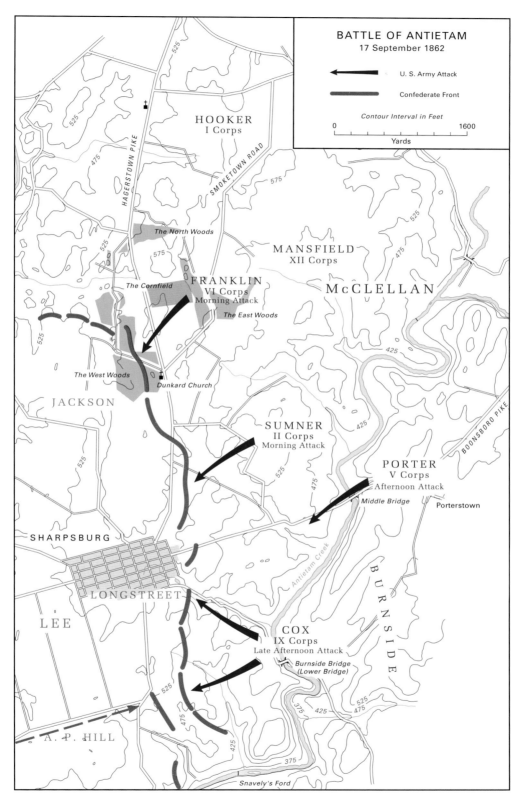

BATTLE OF ANTIETAM
17 September 1862

U. S. Army Attack

Confederate Front

Contour Interval in Feet

0   1600

Yards

HOOKER
I Corps

HAGERSTOWN PIKE

SMOKETOWN ROAD

The North Woods

MANSFIELD
XII Corps

McCLELLAN

FRANKLIN
VI Corps
Morning Attack

The Cornfield

The East Woods

The West Woods

Dunkard Church

JACKSON

SUMNER
II Corps
Morning Attack

PORTER
V Corps
Afternoon Attack

Middle Bridge

Porterstown

SHARPSBURG

Antietam Creek

BOONSBORO PIKE

LONGSTREET

LEE

COX
IX Corps
Late Afternoon Attack

BURNSIDE

Burnside Bridge
(Lower Bridge)

A. P. HILL

Snavely's Ford

Map 27

THE EMANCIPATION PROCLAMATION

Throughout the Civil War, four slave states—Delaware, Maryland, Kentucky, and Missouri—had not seceded. Union strategy depended on retaining these states and the loyalty of their influential slaveholding residents. Therefore, the Lincoln administration overrode early efforts by some northern generals (Fremont in Missouri in 1861 and Hunter in coastal enclaves of South Carolina early in 1862) to end slavery within their commands. Only when Union forces held several of the Confederacy's leading cities (Memphis, Nashville, and New Orleans) and had defeated a southern offensive at the battle of Antietam in September 1862 was Lincoln able to issue a proclamation that freed Confederate slaves, but not those in the border states or in Union-occupied territory. Union armies continued to advance, though, and more than 100,000 former slaves from the liberated regions were able to join the ranks of the U.S. colored troops during the last two years of the war.

and forever free. The proclamation had no effect initially: only the states in rebellion were affected, and those states had no intention of implementing the proclamation. Slaves in the slaveholding border states that remained loyal to the Union were not touched, nor were the slaves in those Confederate areas that had been subjugated by Union bayonets. Thus the Emancipation Proclamation had no immediate effect behind the Confederate lines, except to cause a good deal of excitement. But thereafter, as Union forces penetrated the South, the newly freed people deserted the farms and plantations and flocked to the colors.

African Americans had served in the Revolution, the War of 1812, and other early wars; but they had been barred from the Regular Army and, under the Militia Act of 1792, from the state militia. The Civil War marks their official debut in American military forces. Recruiting of African Americans began under the local auspices of Maj. Gen. David Hunter in the Department of the South as early as April 1862. There was a certain appeal to the idea that blacks might assure the freedom of their enslaved brethren in the South by joining in the battle for it, even if they served for lower pay in segregated units under white officers. On July 17, 1862, Congress authorized recruitment of Afri-

107th Infantry Guards in Front of the Guard House

can Americans while passing the antislavery Second Confiscation Act. The Emancipation Proclamation put the matter in a new light; and on May 22, 1863, the War Department established the Bureau of Colored Troops, another innovation of the Civil War in that it was an example of Federal volunteer formations without official ties to specific states (others being the various U.S. sharpshooter regiments and the invalid Veteran Reserve Corps). By the end of the war 100,000 African Americans had enrolled as U.S. Volunteers while many other blacks served in state units, elsewhere in the armed forces, and as laborers for the Union Army. About 180,000 African Americans served the Union cause over the course of the war, making them an irreplaceable source of Army manpower.

Fiasco at Fredericksburg

After Antietam both armies returned to face each other in Virginia, Lee situated near Culpeper and McClellan at Warrenton. But McClellan's slowness, his failure to accomplish more at Antietam, and perhaps his rather arrogant habit of offering gratuitous political advice to his superiors, coupled with the intense anti-McClellan views of the joint Congressional Committee on the Conduct of the War, convinced Lincoln that he could retain him in command no longer. On November 7 Lincoln replaced him with Burnside, who had won distinction in operations that gained control of ports on the North Carolina coast and who had led the IX Corps at Antietam. Burnside, acutely aware of his own limitations, accepted the post with reluctance.

Burnside decided to march rapidly to Fredericksburg and then to advance along the railroad line to Richmond before Lee could intercept him. (*See Map 28.*) Such a move by the army, now 120,000 strong, would cut Lee off from his main base. Burnside's advance elements reached the north bank of the Rappahannock on November 17, well ahead of Lee. But a series of minor failures delayed the completion of pontoon bridges, and Lee moved his army to high ground on the west side of the river before the Federal forces could cross. Lee's situation resembled McClellan's position at Malvern Hill that had proved the folly of frontal assaults against combined artillery and infantry strong points. But Burnside thought the sheer weight of numbers could smash through the Confederates.

To achieve greater ease of tactical control, Burnside had created three headquarters higher than corps—the Right, Center, and Left Grand Divisions under Maj. Gens. Edwin V. Sumner, Joseph Hooker, and William B. Franklin, respectively—with two corps plus cavalry assigned to each grand division. Burnside originally planned to make the main thrust by the Center and Left Grand Divisions against Jackson's positions on a long, low-wooded ridge southeast of the town. The Right Grand Division would cross three pontoon bridges at Fredericksburg and attack Marye's Heights, a steep eminence about one mile from the river where Longstreet's men were posted. On the morning of December 15, he weakened the attack on the left, feeling that under cover of 147 heavy siege and field guns on the heights on the Union side of the river much could be achieved by a better-balanced attack along the whole line.

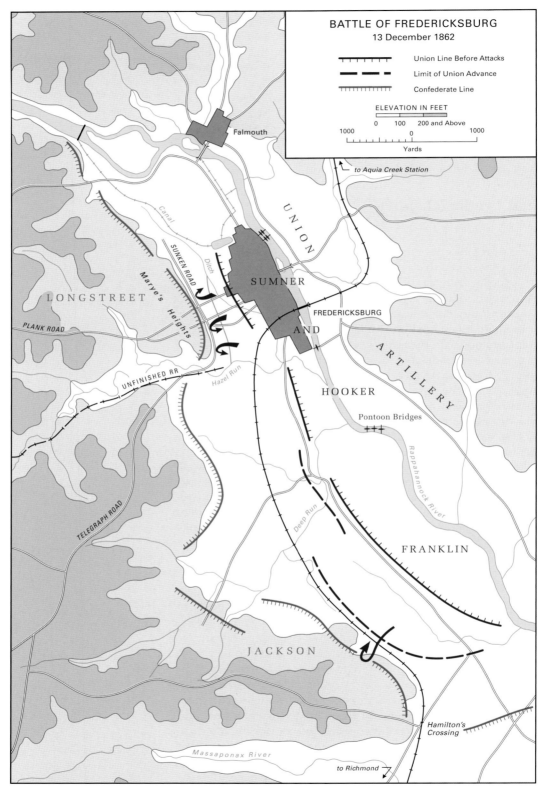

BATTLE OF FREDERICKSBURG
13 December 1862

Union Line Before Attacks
Limit of Union Advance
Confederate Line

ELEVATION IN FEET
0   100   200 and Above

1000   0   1000
Yards

to Aquia Creek Station

Falmouth

UNION

Canal

Ditch

SUMNER

LONGSTREET

Marye's Heights

SUNKEN ROAD

PLANK ROAD

AND

FREDERICKSBURG

ARTILLERY

HOOKER

UNFINISHED RR

Hazel Run

Pontoon Bridges

Rappahannock River

TELEGRAPH ROAD

Deep Run

FRANKLIN

JACKSON

Hamilton's
Crossing

Massaponax River

to Richmond

Map 28

SIDEBURNS

At the onset of the American Civil War, many considered Union Maj. Gen. Ambrose E. Burnside (1824–1881) a brilliant commander. He was relegated to a supporting role, however, after his costly failure to capture Fredericksburg in December 1862. He is best remembered for his peculiar facial hairstyle. Burnside let his hair connect to his moustache, while he kept his chin clean shaven. At the time, this style became known as burnsides. Later, while he served as a senator from Rhode Island, the syllables were reversed to create the now familiar term "sideburns."

Burnside's engineers had begun laying the bridges as early as December 11. But harassment from Confederate sharpshooters complicated the operation, and it was not until the next day that all the assault units were over the river. After an artillery duel on the morning of the thirteenth, the fog lifted to reveal dense Union columns moving forward to the attack. Part of the Left Grand Division, finding a weakness in Jackson's line, drove in to seize the ridge; but as Burnside had weakened this part of the assault, the Federals were not able to hold against Confederate counterattacks. On the right, the troops had to cross a mile of open ground to reach Marye's Heights, traverse a drainage canal, and face a fusillade of fire from the infamous sunken road and stone wall behind which Longstreet had placed four ranks of riflemen. In a series of assaults the Union soldiers pushed to the stone wall but no farther. As a demonstration of valor, the Union attacks all along the line were exemplary; as a demonstration of tactical skill, they were tragic. Lee, personally observing the failed attacks on the Confederate right wing, commented: "It is well that war is so terrible—we should grow too fond of it."

The Army of the Potomac lost 12,000 men at Fredericksburg, while the Army of Northern Virginia suffered only 5,300 casualties. Burnside planned to renew the attack on the following day. Jackson, whose enthusiasm in battle sometimes approached the point of frenzy, suggested that the Confederates strip off their clothes for better identification and strike the Army of the Potomac in a night attack. But Lee knew of Burnside's plans from a captured order and vetoed the scheme. When the Federal corps commanders talked Burnside out of renewing the attack, both armies settled into winter quarters facing each other across the Rappahannock. Fredericksburg, a disastrous defeat, was otherwise noteworthy for the U.S. Army in that the telegraph first saw extensive battlefield use, linking headquarters with forward batteries during the action—a forerunner of twentieth century battlefield communications.

Jackson, whose enthusiasm in battle sometimes approached the point of frenzy, suggested that the Confederates strip off their clothes for better identification and strike the Army of the Potomac in a night attack.

The War in the West: The Twin Rivers Campaign

Students of the Civil War often concentrate their study on the cockpit of the war in the east—Virginia. The rival capitals lay only a hundred miles apart, and the country between them was fought over for four years; and, arguably, the Eastern Theater had a more immediate effect on public opinion and morale in the much more populous east. But it was the Union armies west of the Appalachians that marched the greatest distances and struck some of the hardest blows against the Confederacy.

These Union forces in late 1861 were organized into two separate commands. Brig. Gen. Don Carlos Buell commanded 45,000 men from a headquarters at Louisville, Kentucky; while General Halleck with headquarters at St. Louis, Missouri, had 91,000 under his command. These troops were generally raw, undisciplined western volunteers. Logistical matters and training facilities were undeveloped, and as Halleck once wrote in disgust to his superior in Washington, "affairs here are in complete chaos."

Affairs were no better among the Confederate forces farther south. Facing Buell and Halleck were 43,000 scattered and ill-equipped Confederate troops under General Albert Sidney Johnston. Charged with defending a line that stretched for more than 500 miles from western Virginia to the border of Kansas, Johnston's forces mostly lay east of the Mississippi River. They occupied a system of forts and camps from Cumberland Gap in western Virginia through Bowling Green, Kentucky, to Columbus, Kentucky, on the Mississippi. Rivers and railroads provided Johnston with most of his interior lines of communications, since most of the roads were virtually impassable in winter. To protect a lateral railroad where it crossed two rivers in Tennessee and yet respect Kentucky's neutrality and to block the critical Tennessee and Cumberland Rivers, the Confederates had built Fort Henry on the Tennessee River and Fort Donelson on the Cumberland River just south of the boundary between the two states. This gave the Confederates an important strategic advantage. On the other hand, hampering the Confederate buildup were Southern governors whose states' rights doctrine led them to believe that defense of their respective states had higher priority than pushing forward the needed men and munitions to a Confederate commander, Johnston, at the front.

At the beginning of 1862, Halleck and Buell were supposed to be cooperating but had yet to do so effectively. On his own, Buell moved in mid-January to give token response to Lincoln's desire to help the Unionists in east Tennessee. One of his subordinates succeeded in breaching the Confederate defense line in eastern Kentucky in a local action near Mill Springs, but Buell failed to exploit the victory.

In Halleck's department, Brig. Gen. Ulysses S. Grant, at the time an inconspicuous district commander of volunteers at Cairo, Illinois, had meanwhile proposed a river expedition up the Tennessee to take Fort Henry. After some hesitancy and in spite of the absence of assurance of support from Buell, Halleck approved a plan for a joint Army-Navy expedition. On January 30, 1862, he directed 15,000 men under Grant, supported by armored gunboats and river craft of the U.S. Navy under a flag officer, Andrew H. Foote, to "take and hold Fort Henry." The actions of subordinate commanders were at last prodding the Union war machine to move.

Capture of Forts Henry and Donelson

Grant landed his troops below Fort Henry and together with Foote's naval force moved against the Confederate position on February 6. At the Federals' approach the Confederate commander sent most of his men to Fort Donelson. Muddy roads delayed the Union Army's advance, but Foote's seven gunboats plunged ahead and in a short firefight induced the defenders of Fort Henry to surrender. Indeed, the Confederates had lowered their colors before Grant's infantry could reach the action. The Tennessee River now lay open to Foote's gunboats all the way to northern Alabama.

General Grant was no rhetorician. Sparing with words, he never bombarded his troops with Napoleonic manifestos as McClellan did. After the capture of Fort Henry he simply telegraphed the somewhat surprised Halleck: "I shall take and destroy Fort Donelson on the 8th and return to Fort Henry." But inclement weather delayed the Federal movement until February 12. Then river craft carried some of the troops around to Fort Donelson. The rest of the troops moved overland under sunny skies and unseasonably mild temperatures. The spring-like weather induced the youthful soldiers to litter the roadside with overcoats, blankets, and tents.

Winter once more descended upon Grant's forces (soon to swell to nearly 27,000 men) as they invested Fort Donelson. Johnston, sure that the fall of this fort would jeopardize his entrenched camp at Bowling Green, hurried three generals and 12,000 reinforcements to Fort Donelson and then retired toward Nashville with 14,000 men. Even without reinforcements, Fort Donelson was a strong position. The main earthwork stood 100 feet above the river and with its outlying system of rifle pits embraced an area of 100 acres. The whole Confederate position occupied less than a square mile. Grant and Foote first attempted to reduce it by naval bombardment, which had succeeded at Fort Henry. But this time the Confederate defenders handled the gunboats so roughly that they withdrew. Grant then prepared for a long siege, although the bitter cold weather and lack of assault training among his troops caused him to have some reservations.

The Confederates, sensing they were caught in a trap, attempted a sortie on February 15 and swept one of Grant's divisions off the field. But divided Confederate command, not lack of determination or valor on the part of the fighting men, led to the ultimate defeat of the attack. The three Confederate commanders could not agree upon the next move, and at a critical moment Grant ordered counterattacks all along the line. By the end of the day Union troops had captured a portion of the Confederate outer works. Now surrounded by Union forces that outnumbered them almost two to one, the Confederate leaders decided they were in a hopeless situation. In a scene resembling something from a comic opera, Brig. Gen. John B. Floyd, who had been Buchanan's Secretary of War and feared execution as a traitor, passed the command to Brig. Gen. Gideon Pillow. Pillow passed the command immediately to Brig. Gen. Simon B. Buckner, who asked Grant, an old friend, for terms. Soon afterward Grant sent his famous message: "No terms except unconditional and immediate surrender can be accepted. I propose to move immediately upon your works." A legend and a nickname—Unconditional Surrender Grant—were born.

Some Confederates escaped with Floyd and Pillow, and Col. Nathan B. Forrest led his cavalry through frozen backwaters to safety. But the bulk of the garrison, "from 12,000 to 15,000 prisoners … also

"No terms except unconditional and immediate surrender can be accepted. I propose to move immediately upon your works."

20,000 stand of arms, 48 pieces of artillery, 17 heavy guns, from 2,000 to 4,000 horses, and large quantities of commissary stores," fell into Federal hands. It was a major Union victory.

Poor leadership, violation of the principle of unity of command, and overly strict adherence to position defense had cost the South the key to the gateway of the Confederacy in the west. The loss of the two forts dealt the Confederacy a blow from which it never fully recovered. Johnston had to abandon Kentucky and most of middle and west Tennessee. The vital industrial and transportation center of Nashville soon fell to Buell's advancing army. Foreign governments took special notice of the defeats. For the North, the victories were the first good news of the war. They set the strategic pattern for further advance into the Confederacy. In Grant the people had a new hero, and he received promotion to major general.

Confederate Counterattack at Shiloh

As department commander, Halleck naturally received much credit for these victories. President Lincoln decided to unify command of all the western armies, and on March 11 Halleck received the command. Halleck, nicknamed Old Brains, was well known as a master of the theory and literature of war. Lincoln's decision gave him jurisdiction over four armies: Buell's Army of the Ohio; Grant's Army of the Tennessee; Maj. Gen. Samuel R. Curtis' Army of the Southwest in Missouri and Arkansas; and Pope's Army of the Mississippi. While Pope, in cooperation with Foote's naval forces, successfully attacked New Madrid and Island No. 10 on the Mississippi River, Halleck decided to concentrate Grant's and Buell's armies and move against Johnston at Corinth in northern Mississippi. Grant and Buell were to meet at Shiloh (Pittsburg Landing) near Savannah on the Tennessee River. Well aware of the Federal movements, Johnston decided to attack Grant before Buell could join him. (*Map 29*) The Confederate army, 40,000 strong, marched out of Corinth on the afternoon of April 3. Muddy roads and faulty staff coordination made a shambles of Confederate march discipline. Mixed-up commands, artillery and wagons bogged down in the mud, and green troops who insisted upon shooting their rifles at every passing rabbit threatened to abort the whole expedition. Not until late in the afternoon of April 5 did Johnston's army complete the 22-mile march to its attack point. Then the Confederate leader postponed his attack until the next morning, and the delay proved costly.

Grant's forces were encamped in a rather loose battle line and apparently anticipated no attack. The position at Shiloh itself was not good, for the army was pocketed by the river at its back and a creek on each flank. Because the army was on an offensive mission, it had not entrenched. Grant has often been criticized for this omission, but entrenchment was not common at that stage of the war. However, the fact that the principle of security was almost completely disregarded is inescapable. Very little patrolling had been carried out, and the Federals were unaware that a Confederate army of 40,000 men was spending the night of April 5 just two miles away. The victories at Forts Henry and Donelson had apparently produced overconfidence in Grant's army, which like Johnston's was only partly trained. Even Grant reflected this

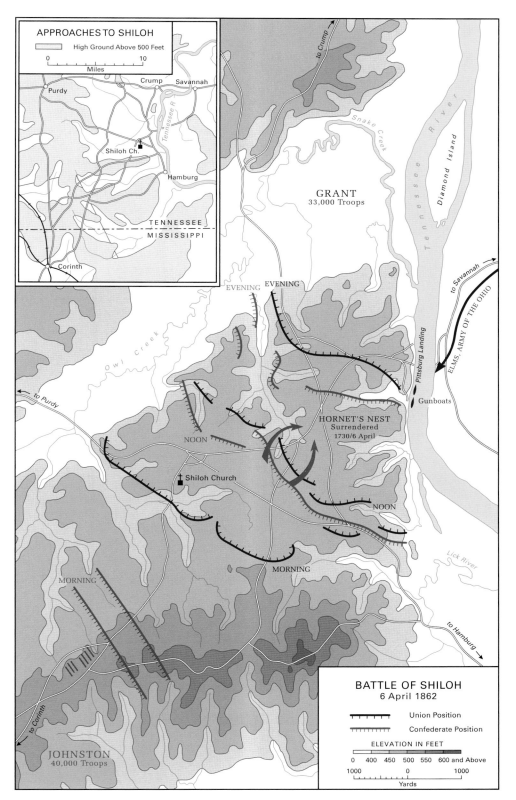

Purdy
Crump   Savannah
Tennessee R.
Shiloh Ch.
Hamburg

TENNESSEE
MISSISSIPPI

Corinth

GRANT
33,000 Troops

Snake Creek
Tennessee River
Diamond Island

to Crump

to Savannah
ELMS, ARMY OF THE OHIO

Pittsburg Landing
Gunboats

Owl Creek

to Purdy

EVENING   EVENING

NOON

HORNET'S NEST
Surrendered
1730/6 April

Shiloh Church

NOON

MORNING

Lick River

MORNING

to Hamburg

to Corinth

JOHNSTON
40,000 Troops

BATTLE OF SHILOH
6 April 1862

Union Position
Confederate Position

ELEVATION IN FEET

0   400 450 500 550 600 and Above

1000   0   1000
Yards

Map 29

feeling, for he had established his headquarters at Savannah, nine miles downstream.

Achieving near total surprise, Johnston's men burst out of the woods early on April 6, so early that Union soldiers turned out into their company streets from their tents to fight. Some fled to the safety of the landing, but most of the regiments fought stubbornly and yielded ground slowly. One particular knot of Federals rallied along an old sunken road, which the Confederates named the Hornet's Nest because of the stinging shot and shell they had to face there. Although this obstacle disrupted Johnston's timetable of attack, by afternoon the Confederates had attained local success elsewhere all along the line. At the same time the melee of battle badly disorganized the attackers. Johnston's attack formation had been awkward from the beginning. He had formed his three corps into one column with each corps deployed with divisions in line so that each corps stretched across the whole battlefront, one behind the other. Such a formation could be effectively controlled neither by army nor corps commanders.

Then, almost at the moment of victory, Johnston himself was mortally wounded while leading a local assault. General Beauregard, Johnston's successor, suspended the attack for the day and attempted to straighten out and reorganize his command. As the day ended, Grant's sixth division, which had lost its way while marching to the battlefield, reached Shiloh along with advance elements of Buell's army.

The next morning Grant counterattacked to regain the lost ground, and the Confederates withdrew to Corinth. There was no pursuit. Shiloh was the bloodiest battle fought in North America up to that time. Of 63,000 Federals, 13,000 were casualties. The Confederates lost 11,000. Fortunate indeed for the Federals had been Lincoln's decision to unify the command under Halleck; this act had guaranteed Buell's presence and prevented Johnston from defeating the Union armies separately. Grant came in for much denunciation for being surprised, but President Lincoln loyally sustained him. "I can't spare this man; he fights."

Halleck was a master of military maxims, but he had failed to concentrate all his forces immediately for a final defeat of Beauregard. As it was, Pope and Foote took Island No. 10 in April, opening the Mississippi as far as Memphis. Halleck, taking personal command of Grant's and Buell's forces, then ponderously advanced toward Corinth. Remembering Shiloh, he proceeded cautiously, and it was May 30 before he reached his objective. Beauregard had already evacuated the town. Meanwhile, Capt. David G. Farragut with a naval force and Maj. Gen. Benjamin F. Butler's land units cracked the gulf coast fortifications of the Mississippi and captured New Orleans. By mid-1862, only strongholds at Vicksburg and Port Hudson on the Mississippi blocked complete Federal control of that vital river.

Perryville to Stones River

Despite these early setbacks the Confederate armies in the west were still full of fight. As Federal forces advanced deeper into the Confederacy, it became increasingly difficult for them to protect the long lines of river, rail, and road supply and communications. Guerrilla and cavalry operations by colorful Confederate "wizards of the saddle" like John Hunt Morgan, Joseph Wheeler, and Colonel Forrest followed Forrest's adage of "Get 'em skeered, and then keep the skeer on 'em." Such tactics completely disrupted the timetable of Federal offensives.

By summer and fall rejuvenated Confederate forces under General Bragg, Lt. Gen. Edmund Kirby Smith, and Maj. Gen. Earl Van Dorn were ready to seize the initiative. Never again was the South so close to victory, nor did it ever again hold the initiative in every theater of the war.

The overall Confederate strategy called for a three-pronged advance from the Mississippi River all the way to Virginia. Twin columns under Bragg and Smith were to bear the brunt of the western offensive by advancing from Chattanooga into east Tennessee, then northward into Kentucky. They were to be supported by Van Dorn, who would move north from Mississippi with the intention of driving Grant's forces out of west Tennessee. The western columns of the Confederacy were then to unite somewhere in Kentucky.

At the same time these movements were to be coordinated with the planned invasion of Maryland, east of the Appalachians, by General Lee's Army of Northern Virginia. Much depended upon speed, good coordination of effort and communications, and the result of the attempts to woo Kentucky and Maryland into the arms of the Confederacy. Victory could stimulate Northern peace advocates, such as the Southern sympathizers known as Copperheads, to lobby for a peace treaty. Furthermore, a successful invasion might induce Great Britain and France to recognize the Confederacy and to intervene forcibly to break the blockade. This last hope was a feeble one. Emperor Napoleon III was interested primarily in advancing his Mexican schemes; he considered both recognition and intervention but would not move without British support. Britain, which pursued the policy of recognizing de facto governments, would undoubtedly have recognized the Confederacy eventually had it won the war. The British government briefly flirted with the idea of recognition and might have done so if the Confederates had put together a string of victories, but throughout the war Britain adhered to a general policy of neutrality and respect for the Union blockade.

At first, things went well for the Confederates in the west. Bragg caught Buell off guard and without fighting a battle forced the Federal evacuation of northern Alabama and central Tennessee. But when Bragg entered Kentucky, he became enmeshed in the politics of "government making" in an effort to set up a state regime that would bind Kentucky to the Confederacy. Also, the Confederate invasion was not achieving the expected decisive results, since few Kentuckians joined Bragg's forces and an attempt at conscription in east Tennessee failed completely. Without popular support, the invading Confederate forces faced eventual failure.

Buell finally caught up with Bragg at Perryville, Kentucky, on October 7. Finding the Confederates in some strength, Buell began concentrating his own scattered units. The next morning, fighting began around Perryville over possession of drinking water. Brig. Gen. Philip H. Sheridan's division forced the Confederates away from one creek and dug in. The battle as a whole turned out to be a rather confused affair, as Buell sought to concentrate units arriving from several different directions on the battlefield itself. Early in the afternoon Maj. Gen. Alexander M. McCook's Union corps arrived and began forming a line of battle. At that moment Maj. Gen. Leonidas Polk's Confederate corps attacked and drove McCook back about a mile, but Sheridan's troops held their ground. Finally a Union counterattack pushed the Confederates out of the town of Perryville. Buell himself remained at headquarters, only two-and-a-half miles from the field, completely unaware of the extent of the engagement until it was nearly over. The rolling terrain had caused an "acoustic shadow," whereby the sounds of the conflict were completely inaudible to the Federal commander. While the battle ended in a tactical stalemate, Bragg suffered such severe casualties that he was forced to retreat. Coupled with Van Dorn's failure to bypass Federal defenses at Corinth and carry out his part of the strategic plan, this setback forced the Confederates to abandon any idea of bringing Kentucky into the Confederacy.

By Christmas Bragg was back in middle Tennessee, battered but still anxious to recoup his losses by recapturing Nashville. Buell, having been dilatory in pursuing Bragg after Perryville, had been replaced in command of the Army of the Ohio (now restyled the Army of the Cumberland) by Maj. Gen. William S. Rosecrans. In spite of urgent and even threatening letters from the War Department, the new commander would not move against Bragg until he had collected abundant supplies at Nashville. Then he would be independent of the railroad line from Nashville to Louisville, a line of communications continually cut by Confederate cavalry.

On December 26 Rosecrans finally marched south from Nashville. Poorly screened by Union cavalry, his three columns in turn knew little about Confederate concentrations near Murfreesboro, thirty miles southeast of the Tennessee capital. Here, Bragg had taken a strong position astride Stones River on the direct route to Chattanooga and proposed to fight it out. Rosecrans moved into line opposite Bragg on the evening of December 30. Both army commanders proceeded to develop identical battle plans—each designed to envelop the opponent's right flank. Bragg's objective was to drive Rosecrans off his communications line with Nashville and pin him against the river. Rosecrans' plan had the same objective in reverse, that of pinning the Confederates against the stream. Victory would probably belong to the commander who struck first and hard.

HARDEE'S TACTICS

Before William J. Hardee (1815–1873) published *Rifle and Infantry Tactics* drill manual in 1855, the Army used Winfield Scott's system based on eighteenth-century French experience and training. When 1840s-era longer rifles dictated changes in infantry tactics, then–Secretary of War Jefferson Davis selected Hardee as a brevet lieutenant colonel to design the changes. Published in June 1855, *Tactics* created a lighter, faster infantry but failed to solve the problem of accurate rifle fire from great distances. After Hardee joined the Confederate Army in 1861, he revised his manual; the South used it almost exclusively during the Civil War.

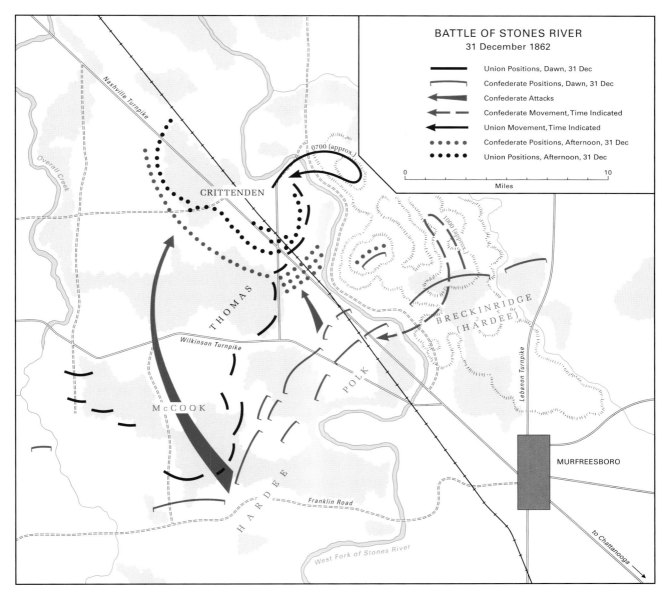

Map 30

Insufficient Federal security, as well as Rosecrans' failure to ensure that the pivotal units in his attack plan were also properly posted to thwart Confederate counterattacks, resulted in Confederate seizure of the initiative as the battle of Stones River opened on December 31. (*Map 30*) At dawn Maj. Gen. William J. Hardee's corps with large cavalry support began the drive on the Federal right. Undeceived by their opponent's device of extra campfires to feign a longer battle line, Confederate attacking columns simply pushed farther around the Union flank and promptly rolled the defenders back. Applying the principles of mass and surprise to achieve rapid success, Bragg's battle plan forced Rosecrans to modify his own. The Union leader pulled back his left flank division, which had jumped off to attack Maj. Gen. John C. Breckinridge's Confederate units north of Stones River. While Sheridan's division, as at Perryville, provided stubborn resistance to General Polk's corps in the center, Hardee's units continued their drive and by noon saw the Union battle line bent back against the Nashville pike. Meanwhile, the Confederate cavalry had wrought havoc among Rosecrans' rear area elements. As was typical of many Civil War battles, the attacking columns of Polk and Hardee became badly intermingled. Their men began to tire, and by afternoon repeated Confederate assaults against the constricted Union line along the Nashville pike had bogged down.

That night Rosecrans held a council of war. Some of the subordinate commanders wanted to retreat. Rosecrans and two of his corps commanders, Maj. Gen. Thomas L. Crittenden and Maj. Gen. George H. Thomas, vetoed the scheme. Brigades were then returned to their proper divisions, stragglers rounded up, and various other adjustments made in the Federal position. New Year's Day, 1863, dawned quietly, and little action occurred that day.

The sunrise of January 2 revealed Rosecrans still in position. Bragg directed Breckinridge to attack the Union left wing, once more thrown across Stones River on the north. But massed Union artillery shattered the assaults, and counterattacking Federals drove Breckinridge's men back to their line of departure. The armies remained stationary on January 3, but Bragg finally withdrew from the battlefield that evening, permitting victory to slip from his grasp. Tactically a draw, Stones River so badly mangled the Army of the Cumberland that it would be immobilized for six months. Yet, more than most other battles of the war, Stones River was a conflict between the wills of the opposing army leaders. Rosecrans, supported by Thomas and others, would not admit himself beaten and in the end won a victory of sorts.

The great Confederate counteroffensives of 1862 had failed in the west, yet Chattanooga, the key to east Tennessee and Georgia, remained in Southern hands. Farther west, Federal forces had penetrated only slightly into northern Mississippi. The war was simply on dead center in the west at the end of the year.

The War West of the Mississippi

If the major fighting of the Civil War occurred in the "older" populated sections of the United States, the youthful area of the American frontier across the Mississippi saw its share of action also. Missouri and Kansas, deeply involved in the political issues that precipitated the conflict, and even the distant New Mexico Territory, were all touched by military operations.

The Southwest was a particularly rich plum, for as one Confederate commander observed, "The vast mineral resources of Arizona, in addition to its affording an outlet to the Pacific, makes its acquisition a matter of some importance to our Govt." Also, it was assumed that Indians and the Mormons in Utah would readily accept allegiance to almost any government other than that in Washington. The Far West was seen as an area of great opportunity for the Confederates.

It was with these motives in mind that early in 1862 Confederate forces moved up the Rio Grande valley and proceeded to establish that part of New Mexico Territory north of the 34th Parallel as the Confederate Territory of Arizona. Under Brig. Gen. Henry H. Sibley, inventor of a famous tent bearing his name, the Confederates successfully swept all the way to Santa Fe, capital of New Mexico, bypassing several Union garrisons on the way. But Sibley was dangerously overextended; and Federal troops reinforced by Colorado volunteers surprised the advancing Confederates in Apache Canyon on March 26 and 28 as the Confederates sought to capture the largest Union garrison in the territory at Fort Union.

One of the bypassed Federal columns under Col. Edward R. S. Canby from Fort Craig meanwhile joined the Fort Union troops against the Confederates. Sibley, unable to capture the Union posts, unable to resupply his forces, and learning of yet a third Federal column converging on him from California, began a determined retreat down the Rio Grande valley. By May he was back in Texas and the Confederate invasion of New Mexico had ended. The fighting, on a small scale by eastern standards, provided valuable training for Federal troops involved later in Indian Wars in this area. Indeed, while the Confederate dream of a new territory and an outlet to the Pacific was shattered by 1862, Indian leaders in the mountain territories saw an opportunity to reconquer lost land while the white men were otherwise preoccupied. In 1863 and 1864 both Union and Confederate troops in the Southwest were kept busy fighting hostile tribes.

In Missouri and Arkansas, fighting had erupted on a large scale by the early spring of 1862. Federal authorities had retained a precarious hold over Missouri when General Curtis with 11,000 men chased disorganized Confederates back into Arkansas. But, under General Van Dorn and Maj. Gen. Sterling Price, the Confederates regrouped and embarked upon a bold counteroffensive that ended only at Pea Ridge on March 7 and 8. Here, Van Dorn executed a double envelopment as half his army stole behind Pea Ridge, marched around three-fourths of Curtis' force, and struck Curtis' left rear near Elkhorn Tavern while the other half attacked his right rear. But in so doing, the Confederates uncovered their own line of communications; and Curtis' troops turned around and fought off the attacks from the rear. After initial success, Van Dorn and Price were unable to continue the contest and withdrew. For three more years guerrilla warfare would ravage Missouri, but the Union grip on the state was secure.

The year 1862, which began with impressive Union victories in the west, ended in bitter frustration in the east. Ten full-scale and costly battles had been fought, but no decisive victory had yet been scored by the forces of the Union. The Federals had broken the great Confederate counteroffensives in the fall, only to see their hopes fade with the advent of winter. Apparently the Union war machine had lost its earlier momentum and only decisive victories could regain the initiative.

DISCUSSION QUESTIONS

1. How and why did Union war aims and policies change over the course of the war?

2. Which theater of war was the most decisive in 1862, and why?

3. What are the benefits and problems of achieving unity of command? Could the Union have accomplished the goal of unity of command effectively? Why didn't it?

4. Why should the Peninsula Campaign have worked? What caused it to fail, and how did this failure impact on Union war aims?

5. "War is too important to leave to the generals." To what degree does this apply to the Civil War in 1862?

6. It has been said that many of the political generals appointed by Lincoln delayed Union victory through sheer incompetence. Attack or defend this observation, citing examples.

RECOMMENDED READINGS

Catton, Bruce. *Glory Road*. New York: Anchor Books, 1990.

————. *Mr. Lincoln's Army*. New York: Anchor Books, 1990.

Connelly, Thomas L. *Army of the Heartland: The Army of Tennessee, 1861–1862*. Baton Rouge: Louisiana State University Press, 2001.

Freeman, Douglas Southall. *Lee's Lieutenants: A Study in Command*, 3 vols. New York: Scribner Classics, 1997, vol. 1, chs. 10–43; vol. 2.

Hennessy, John J. *Return to Bull Run: The Battle and Campaign of Second Manassas*. Norman: University of Oklahoma Press, 1999.

Sears, Stephen W. *To the Gates of Richmond: The Peninsula Campaign*. New York: Ticknor & Fields, 1992.

Sword, Wiley. *Shiloh: Bloody April*. New York: William Morrow, 1974.

Tanner, Robert G. *Stonewall in the Valley: Thomas J. "Stonewall" Jackson's Shenandoah Valley Campaign, Spring 1862*, rev. ed. Mechanicsville, Pa.: Stackpole Books, 1996.

Williams, Kenneth P. *Lincoln Finds a General: A Military Study of the Civil War*, 5 vols. New York: Macmillan, 1949–1959, vol. 1, chs. 4–13; vol. 2, chs. 14–16; vol. 3, chs. 5–15; vol. 4, chs. 10–11.

Williams, T. Harry. *Lincoln and His Generals*. New York: Gramercy Books, 2000, chs. 4–8.

Other Readings

Cooling, Benjamin F. *Forts Henry and Donelson: The Key to the Confederate Heartland*. Knoxville: University of Tennessee Press, 1987.

Cozens, Peter. *No Better Place To Die: The Battle of Stones River*. Urbana: University of Illinois Press, 1990.

Dowdy, Clifford. *The Seven Days: The Emergence of Lee*. New York: Little, Brown, 1964.

Esposito, Vincent J., ed. *The West Point Atlas of American Wars*, 2 vols. New York: Holt, Rinehart, and Winston, 1978, vol. 1, Maps 25–83.

Glatthaar, Joseph T. *Forged in Battle: The Civil War Alliance of Black Soldiers and White Officers.* Baton Rouge: Louisiana State University Press, 2000.

Jones, Virgil C. *The Civil War at Sea,* 3 vols. New York: Holt, Rinehart, and Winston, 1960, vol. 1, chs. 25–28; vol. 2, chs. 1–16.

Luvaas, Jay, and Harold W. Nelson, eds. *Guide to the Battle of Antietam: The Maryland Campaign in 1862.* Lawrence: University Press of Kansas, 1996.

Sears, Stephen. *Landscape Turned Red: The Battle of Antietam.* Norwalk, Conn.: Easton Press, 1988.

Shea, William L., and Earl J. Hess. *Pea Ridge: Civil War Campaign in the West.* Chapel Hill: University of North Carolina Press, 1992.

Vandiver, Frank E. *Rebel Brass: The Confederate Command System.* Baton Rouge: Louisiana State University Press, 1993.

11

THE CIVIL WAR, 1863

At the beginning of 1863 the Confederacy seemed to have a fair chance of ultimate success on the battlefield. But during this year three great campaigns would shape the outcome of the war in favor of the North. One would see the final solution to the control of the Mississippi River. A second, concurrent with the first, would break the back of any Confederate hopes for success by invasion of the North and recognition abroad. The third, slow and uncertain in its first phases, would result eventually in Union control of the strategic gateway to the South Atlantic region of the Confederacy—the last great stronghold of secession and the area in which the aims of military operations were as much focused on destroying the economic infrastructure of the South as defeating main-force rebel units.

The East: Hooker Crosses the Rappahannock

The course of the war in the east in 1863 was dramatic and in many ways decisive. After the battle of Fredericksburg in December 1862, Maj. Gen. Ambrose E. Burnside's Army of the Potomac went into winter quarters on the north bank of the Rappahannock, while the main body of General Robert E. Lee's Army of Northern Virginia held Fredericksburg and guarded the railway line to Richmond. During January of the new year, Burnside's subordinates intrigued against him and went out of channels to present their grievances to Congress and President Abraham Lincoln. When Burnside heard of this development, he asked that either he or most of the subordinate general officers be removed. The President, not pleased with either Burnside's string of failures or his ultimatum, accepted the first alternative and on January 25, 1863, replaced Burnside with Maj. Gen. Joseph Hooker. The new commander had won the sobriquet Fighting Joe from overly enthusiastic journalists because of his reputation as a hard-fighting division and corps commander. He was highly favored in Washington, but in appointing him the President wrote a fatherly letter in which he warned the general against rashness and

Joseph L. Hooker
Matthew Brady, n.d.

overambition, reproached him for plotting against Burnside, and concluded by asking for victories.

Under Hooker's able administration, discipline and training improved. Morale, which had fallen after the Fredericksburg debacle, rose as Hooker regularized the furlough system and improved the flow of rations and other supplies to his front-line troops. Abolishing Burnside's grand divisions, Hooker returned to the previous corps organization of seven corps, each numbering about 15,000 men. One of Hooker's most effective innovations was the introduction of corps badges to provide a sense of identity in a unit and improve esprit de corps. He also took a long step toward improving the army's cavalry arm, which up to this time had been assigned many diverse duties and was split up into small detachments. Hooker regarded cavalry as a combat arm of full stature, and he concentrated his units into a cavalry corps of three divisions under Brig. Gen. George Stoneman. On the other hand, Hooker made a costly mistake in decentralizing tactical and administrative control of his artillery to his corps commanders. This may have improved tactical usage of artillery, but it prevented the focusing of massive amounts of artillery on a single front. As a result the artillery, in which the Union had a distinct advantage in numbers, would not be properly massed in the coming action at Chancellorsville and thus was not as effective as it could have been.

Hooker had no intention of repeating Burnside's tragic frontal assault at Fredericksburg. With a strength approaching 134,000 men, Hooker planned a bold double envelopment that would place strong Union forces on each of Lee's flanks. (*Map 31*) He hoped to take advantage of his superior numbers to outmaneuver Lee. He ordered three of his infantry corps to move secretly west up the Rappahannock and Rapidan and to ford the streams to outflank Lee to the north. Meanwhile, two more corps, having conspicuously remained opposite Fredericksburg, were to strike across the old battlefield there to tie down Lee's forces. Two more corps were held in reserve. The cavalry corps, less one division that was to screen the move upriver, was to raid far behind Lee's rear to divert him.

Hooker's plan was superb, his execution faulty. The three corps moved quickly up the river and by the end of April had crossed and advanced to the principal road junction of Chancellorsville. They were now in the so-called Wilderness, a low, flat, confusing area of scrub timber and narrow dirt roads in which movement and visibility were extremely limited. Maj. Gen. John Sedgwick crossed the Rappahannock at Fredericksburg on the twenty-ninth, and the two remaining corps moved to within supporting distance of Hooker at Chancellorsville. So far everything had gone according to plan, except that Stoneman's diversion had failed to bother Lee. One of Brig. Gen. J. E. B. Stuart's brigades kept Stoneman under surveillance while the main body of cavalry shadowed Hooker so effectively that the Southern commander knew every move the Union Army made. By the morning of April 30, Lee was aware of what was afoot and knew that he was threatened by double envelopment. Early on May 1, Hooker was sending his columns east, toward the back door to Fredericksburg. A less bold and resolute man than Lee would have retreated south at once and with such ample justification that only the captious would have found fault. But the

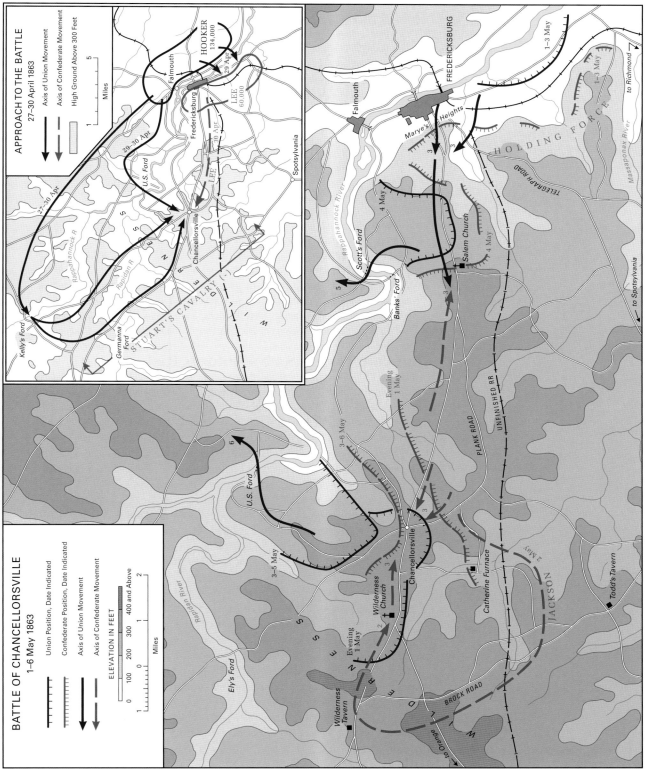

BATTLE OF CHANCELLORSVILLE
1–6 May 1863

▬▬▬▬ Union Position, Date Indicated

▬▬▬▬ Confederate Position, Date Indicated

➡ Axis of Union Movement

⇢ Axis of Confederate Movement

ELEVATION IN FEET

0   100   200   300   400 and Above

0   1   2
Miles

APPROACH TO THE BATTLE
27–30 April 1863

➡ Axis of Union Movement

⇢ Axis of Confederate Movement

▨ High Ground Above 300 Feet

0   1   5
Miles

HOOKER
134,000

LEE
60,000

Falmouth

Fredericksburg

U.S. Ford

Kelly's Ford

Germanna Ford

Rappahannock R.

Rapidan R.

Chancellorsville

Spotsylvania

STUART'S CAVALRY

27–30 Apr

29–30 Apr

29 Apr

30 Apr

FREDERICKSBURG

Falmouth

Marye's Heights

HOLDING FORCE

Rappahannock River

Massaponax River

TELEGRAPH ROAD

to Richmond

to Spotsylvania

Scott's Ford

Banks' Ford

Salem Church

1–3 May

1–3 May

3–3

3–3

4 May

4 May

4 May

5

Evening
1 May

3–6 May

PLANK ROAD

UNFINISHED RR

U.S. Ford

Rapidan River

Ely's Ford

3–5 May

Chancellorsville

Wilderness Church

Catherine Furnace

JACKSON

2 May

Todd's Tavern

BROCK ROAD

Wilderness Tavern

Evening
1 May

to Orange

6

Map 31

GENERAL ORDERS 100

General Orders 100, Instructions for the Government of the Armies of the United States in the Field, dated April 24, 1863, was drafted by professor Francis Lieber, a German immigrant who had sons fighting on both sides of the Civil War. The orders established guidelines for the conduct of war, particularly with regard to the treatment of enemy soldiers, prisoners, and occupied civilian populations. The orders attempted to strike a balance between humanitarian impulses and the brutal necessities of war. They were widely copied by European armies and provided a framework upon which subsequent international law would be based.

Southern general, his army numbering only 60,000, decided to take a bold risk. Using the principles of the offensive, maneuver, economy of force, and surprise to compensate for his inferior numbers, he decided to attack an enemy almost twice his size. Instead of retreating, he left a small part of his army to hold the heights at Fredericksburg and started west for Chancellorsville with the main body. Lee's superb intelligence and reconnaissance, based largely on his expert cavalry force, provided him with accurate and timely intelligence so Hooker's every move was known to him while his own were hidden from Hooker.

Chancellorsville: Lee's Boldest Risk

It seemed as if at this point in the battle Hooker simply lost his courage. Since he did not know exactly where Lee was, he began taking counsel of his fears and failed to follow his own plan. Over the vehement protests of his corps commanders, he ordered the troops back into defensive positions around Chancellorsville, surrendering the initiative to Lee. The Federals established a line in the forest, felled trees for an abatis, and constructed earth-and-log breastworks. Their position faced generally east and south, anchored on the Rappahannock on the east; but in the west along the Orange turnpike, it was weak, unsupported, and hanging in the air. Lee brought his main body up and on May 1 made contact with Hooker's strong left. At the same time, Stuart's cavalry discovered Hooker's vulnerable right flank and promptly reported the intelligence to Lee. Conferring that night with Lt. Gen. Thomas "Stonewall" Jackson, Lee made a truly daring decision. Facing an army much greater than his own, having already divided his forces by leaving some units back at Fredericksburg, he decided to divide his forces again to further envelop the envelopers. Accordingly, Lee committed 17,000 men against Hooker's left to hold it in place while Jackson with 26,000 men made a wide, fifteen-mile swing to get beyond Hooker's right flank. Lee's decision was technically a violation of the principles of mass and concentration; but the principles are guides, not laws. A bold commander can knowingly undertake a higher measure of calculated risk if the potential reward is high enough. And Lee was probably the boldest risk taker of the war. In addition, while Lee's two forces were separated, their common objective was the Army of the Potomac and their ultimate routes converged on a common center.

Jackson's force, in a ten-mile-long column, moved out before day-break on May 2, marching southwest first then swinging northwest to get into position. The Federals noted that something was happening off to the south but were unable to penetrate the defensive screen; Hooker soon began to think that Lee was actually retreating. In the late afternoon Jackson turned onto the Orange turnpike beyond Wilderness Tavern. This move put him west of Hooker's right flank; since the woods thinned out a little at this point, it was possible to form a line of battle. Because time was running short and the hour was late, Jackson deployed in column of divisions, each division formed with brigades abreast, the same kind of confusing formation General Albert S. Johnston had used at Shiloh. Shortly after 5:00 P.M. Jackson's leading division, shrieking the "rebel yell" and driving startled rabbits and deer before it, came charging out of the woods, rolling up the different brigades of Maj. Gen. Oliver O. Howard's XI Corps. Despite a few heroic attempts to stand in the face of the rebel onslaught, the Union troops retreated in disarray. Jackson pressed forward, but fresh Union troops, the disorganization of his own men, and oncoming darkness stymied the attack. While searching for a road that would permit him to cut off Hooker from United States Ford across the Rappahannock, Jackson fell victim to friendly fire. The Confederate leader was wounded and died eight days later. During the night of May 2, Stuart, Jackson's temporary successor as corps commander, re-formed his lines. Against Stuart's right Hooker launched local counterattacks that at first gained some success, but the next morning he withdrew his whole line. Once more Hooker yielded the initiative at a moment when he had a strong force between Lee's two divided and weaker forces.

Stuart renewed the attack during the morning as Hooker pulled his line back. To complicate matters further, Hooker was knocked unconscious when a shell struck the pillar of the Chancellor house against which he was leaning. Until the end of the battle he was dazed and incapable of

THE DEATH OF STONEWALL JACKSON

Soon after dark on the second day of fighting at Chancellorsville, a bullet fired by his own troops struck down one of the South's most celebrated soldiers, the corps commander Thomas Jackson (1824–1863). Confederate soldiers in the part of the battle line where Jackson fell were understandably nervous, for a band of 200 federal troops had just been discovered and taken prisoner in the woods behind the Confederate front line. Not long after, some Confederates caught sight of a lone Union officer between the two armies, and a few shots fired at him grew into a general fusillade along a brigade-wide front. A little while later, on a path through another part of the woods, Jackson received the wounds that contributed to his death from pneumonia a week later. The shots that felled him may not have "doomed the Confederacy," as one historian has put it, but it was certainly the most famous friendly fire incident in American history.

exercising effective command, but he did not relinquish it nor would the army's medical director declare him unfit. Union artillery, centrally located but not centrally controlled, might have proven decisive at this point of the battle; but its fires were not coordinated. Meanwhile Sedgwick, who shortly after Jackson's attack had received orders to proceed through Fredericksburg to Chancellorsville, had assaulted Marye's Heights. He carried it about noon on May 3, but the next day Lee once more divided his command, leaving Stuart with 25,000 to guard Hooker, and moved himself with 21,000 to thwart Sedgwick. In a sharp action at Salem Church, Lee forced the Federals off the road and northward over the Rappahannock at Banks' Ford. Lee made ready for a full-scale assault against the Army of the Potomac, now huddled with its back against the river on May 6; but Hooker ordered retirement to the north bank before the attack. Confederate losses were 13,000, Federal losses 17,000. But Lee lost a great deal with the death of Stonewall Jackson. Actually, Lee's brilliant and daring maneuvers had defeated only one man—Hooker—and in no other action of the war did moral superiority of one general over the other stand out so clearly as a decisive factor in battle. Chancellorsville exemplified Napoleon's maxim: "The General is the head, the whole of the army." When the general was offensively minded and not averse to calculated risks, the result was dramatic. Chancellorsville remains an example of what a bold commander can accomplish against a larger, but poorly coordinated, enemy. Using trusted corps commanders, operating along interior lines, and carefully orchestrating a maneuver led Lee to what many consider his boldest victory.

Lee was so successful in part because Hooker made so many mistakes. Hooker was in many ways a talented tactical commander with a good reputation. But in spite of Lincoln's injunction, "This time, put in all your men," he allowed nearly one-third of his army to stand idle during the heaviest fighting. Here again was a general who could effectively lead a body of troops under his own eyes but could not use maps, reports, and messages to evaluate and control situations that were beyond his range of vision. Hooker, not the Army of the Potomac, lost the battle of Chancellorsville. Poor coordination, poor intelligence, irresolute decisions, and timid reactions to setbacks led to Hookers' being completely "out-generaled." Yet for the victors, Chancellorsville was in many ways a hollow triumph. It was dazzling, a set piece for the instruction of students of the military art ever since, but it had been inconclusive, winning glory and little more. It left government and army on both sides with precisely the problems they had faced before the campaign began. However, Lee had triumphed once again as he drove the Union forces back onto the defensive. His logistical lines were secure, and Richmond remained unthreatened. Now it was time again for him to take the war into the North.

Here again was a general who could effectively lead a body of troops under his own eyes but could not use maps, reports, and messages to evaluate and control situations that were beyond his range of vision.

Lee's Second Invasion of the North

By 1863 the war had entered what Maj. Gen. William T. Sherman later called its professional phase. The core of troops was well trained, although a constant flow of new replacements required constant "seasoning"; and large numbers had ample combat experience. Officers had generally mastered their jobs and were deploying their forces fairly skillfully in accordance with the day's tactical principles. Furthermore, the increased range and accuracy of weapons, together with the nature of the terrain, had induced some alterations in tactics—more skirmishers and increasing distance between soldiers as they sought to avoid the worst effects of the hail of rifled musket fire—alterations that were embodied in a revised infantry manual published in 1863. Thus, by the third year of the war, battles had begun to take on certain definite characteristics. The battle of Gettysburg in early July is a case in point.

Gettysburg was, first of all, a generally unplanned battle—neither side knew that their forces would be brought together at that obscure crossroads for the greatest land battle on the North American continent. It stands out in American myth as one of the most dramatic battles with individual heroism and extraordinary valor on both sides as victory or defeat seemed separated by only a hair's breadth. The three-day battle began as a meeting engagement, followed by each side's attempting to bring a preponderance of troops onto the field as the battle raged. Some 43,500 Americans were casualties of this great battle, and Lincoln's address over the cemetery of the dead was to be enshrined as a masterpiece of American historic prose. Gettysburg has become the most famous of the battles of that cruel war.

After the great victory at Chancellorsville in May, the Confederate cause in the Eastern Theater had looked exceptionally bright. If 60,000 men could beat 134,000, then the Confederacy's inferiority in manpower was surely offset by superior generalship and skill at arms. Vicksburg was not yet under siege, although Maj. Gen. Ulysses S. Grant had ferried his army over to the east bank of the Mississippi. If Confederate President Jefferson Davis and General Lee were overly optimistic, they could hardly be blamed. Both felt it important to take the battle into the enemy's territory to relieve the threat against Richmond, gather subsistence for the troops from the rich Northern farmland, and perhaps, just perhaps, garner another astounding victory that might capture Washington itself or force the Union to sue for peace. It was a gamble, of course, but Lee was a gambler and Davis only slightly less so. Lee made ready to move into Pennsylvania. By this time the Union objectives in the east were clearly defined: to continue operations against Confederate seaports—an attempt to seize Fort Sumter on April 7 had failed—and to destroy Lee's army. President Lincoln's orders made clear that the destruction of the Army of Northern Virginia was the major objective of the Army of the Potomac. The capture of Richmond was to be only incidental.

On June 30, 1863, the Army of the Potomac numbered 115,256 officers and enlisted men with 362 guns. It consisted of 51 infantry brigades organized into 19 divisions, which in turn formed 7 infantry corps. The cavalry corps had 3 divisions. The field artillery, 67 batteries, was assigned by brigades to the corps, except for army reserve artillery, restoring much of the power of the chief of artillery and redressing the problem of decentralized misuse of artillery noted at Chancellorsville. The Army of Northern Virginia, having numbered 76,224 men and 272 guns in late May, now was organized into 3 infantry corps, each led by a lieutenant general and larger than its Union counterpart. The death of Jackson had forced this change, with Richard S. Ewell and Ambrose P. Hill joining James Longstreet as lieutenant generals and commanders of the reorganized corps. Stuart's cavalry retained its role, directly answering to Lee. In each corps were 3 divisions, and most divisions had 4 brigades. Of the 15 field artillery battalions of 4 batteries each, 5 battalions were attached to each corps under command of the corps' artillery chiefs, leaving no artillery in army reserve.

A Battle Flag for the Army of Northern Virginia, ca. 1863

JAMES LONGSTREET (1821–1904)

Known as Old Pete and Lee's War Horse, Longstreet became one of the Civil War's most controversial figures. Hard hitting in the attack, he nevertheless sensed the power of the tactical defense in an age of rifled weapons and field fortifications and preferred to fight from the defensive. His performance at Gettysburg drew fire from postwar critics who believed that, when Lee rejected his repeated advice to outflank the strong Federal position, Longstreet sulked and thereby cost the South the battle. Yet Lee never uttered direct criticism of Longstreet, who stood by him to the end at Appomattox. He was one of the most valued and trusted lieutenants to General Lee.

In early June Lee began moving his units away from Fredericksburg. In his advance he used the Shenandoah and Cumberland Valleys, for by holding the east-west mountain passes he could readily cover his approach route and lines of communications. Hooker got wind of the move; he noted the weakening of the Fredericksburg defenses, and on June 9 his cavalry, commanded by Brig. Gen. Alfred Pleasonton, surprised Stuart at Brandy Station, Virginia. Here on an open plain was fought one of the few mounted, saber-swinging, cut-and-thrust cavalry combats of the Civil War. Up to now the Confederate cavalry had been superior; but at Brandy Station, the Union horsemen "came of age," and Stuart was lucky to hold his position.

When the Federals learned that Confederate infantrymen were west of the Blue Ridge and heading north, Hooker started to move to protect Washington and Baltimore. Earlier Lincoln had vetoed Hooker's proposal to seize Richmond while Lee went north. As the Army of Northern Virginia moved through the valleys and deployed into Pennsylvania behind cavalry screens, the Army of the Potomac moved north on a broad front, crossing the Potomac on June 25 and 26. Lee dispersed his forces to gain speed of movement and gather as much in the way of supplies as possible. He had extended his infantry columns from McConnellsburg and Chambersburg on the west to Carlisle in the north and York on the east.

After Brandy Station and some sharp clashes in the mountain passes, Stuart set forth on another dramatic ride around the Union Army. Granted a maximum degree of discretion by Lee, Stuart operated largely on his own initiative but forgot that his primary role was to serve as Lee's eyes and ears. He failed to send back messages on the movements of the Union Army and did not adequately screen Confederate movements from Union cavalry. The results were disastrous. It was only on the afternoon of July 2, with his troopers so weary they were almost falling from their saddles, that Stuart rejoined Lee in the vicinity of Gettysburg, too late to have an important influence on the battle. His absence had deprived Lee of prompt, accurate information about the Army of the Potomac. When Lee learned from one of Longstreet's spies on June 28 that Hooker's men were north of the Potomac, he ordered his widespread and vulnerable units to concentrate at once near Cashtown.

After Chancellorsville, Lincoln, though advised to drop Hooker, had kept him in command of the Army of the Potomac on the theory that he would not throw away a gun because it has misfired once. But Hooker soon became embroiled with Maj. Gen. Henry W. Halleck over whether or not he had the authority to move troops out of Harpers Ferry to reinforce his army and, in a moment of pique, requested his own relief. Lincoln, losing all confidence in Hooker's judgment, promptly took him up on his offer. Hooker was replaced by one of his corps commanders, Maj. Gen. George G. Meade, who was awakened unexpectedly before dawn on June 28 to receive word of his promotion. He immediately faced the challenge of assuming command of an Army that had only limited time to find, fix, and defeat a dangerous foe. Meade, who was to command the Army of the Potomac for the rest of the war, started north on a broad front at once but within two days began planning to fight a defensive action in Maryland and issued orders to that effect. However, not all his commanders received the order, and events overruled him.

Gettysburg

During the afternoon of June 30 outposts of both armies clashed north and west of the quiet little Pennsylvania market town of Gettysburg. The terrain in the area included rolling hills and broad, shallow valleys. Gettysburg was the junction of twelve roads that led to Harrisburg, Philadelphia, Baltimore, Washington, and the mountain passes to the west that Lee controlled. As initial elements of both forces collided, the local commanders sent reports and recommendations to their superiors, who relayed them upward; both armies, still widely dispersed, started moving toward Gettysburg. (*See Map 32.*)

On July 1 Union cavalrymen under the command of Brig. Gen. John Buford, Jr., fought a dismounted delaying action against infantry troops of General Hill's Third Corps northwest of town. By this stage of the war cavalrymen, armed with saber, pistol, and breechloading

Part of the Gettysburg Battlefield, ca. 1863.
Matthew Brady, a photographer who organized and led a significant
effort to chronicle the Civil War in photographs, stands in the center.

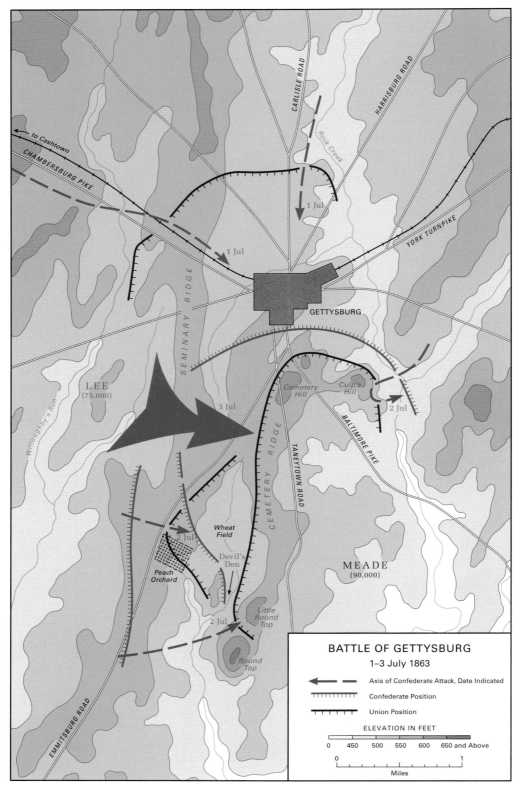

to Cashtown

CHAMBERSBURG PIKE

CARLISLE ROAD

HARRISBURG ROAD

Rock Creek

1 Jul

1 Jul

YORK TURNPIKE

SEMINARY RIDGE

GETTYSBURG

LEE
(75,000)

Willoughby's Run

3 Jul

Cemetery
Hill

Culp's
Hill

2 Jul

CEMETERY RIDGE

TANEYTOWN ROAD

BALTIMORE PIKE

Wheat
Field

2 Jul

Peach
Orchard

Devil's
Den

MEADE
(90,000)

2 Jul

Little
Round
Top

Round
Top

EMMITSBURG ROAD

BATTLE OF GETTYSBURG
1–3 July 1863

Axis of Confederate Attack, Date Indicated

Confederate Position

Union Position

ELEVATION IN FEET

| 0 | 450 | 500 | 550 | 600 | 650 and Above |

0   1

Miles

Map 32

carbine, were often deployed as mounted infantrymen who rode to battle but fought on foot. The range and accuracy of the infantry's rifled muskets made it next to impossible for mounted men to attack foot soldiers in position, but in this instance the infantry was attacking dismounted troopers in defensive positions. With their superior speed, mobility, and firepower, cavalrymen, as witnessed in the Gettysburg campaign, were especially useful for screening and reconnaissance but also for advance guard actions in which they seized or held important hills, river crossings, and road junctions pending the arrival of infantry. During the morning hours of July 1, this was the role Union horsemen played on the ridges north and west of Gettysburg. Buford, with a keen eye for terrain and confidence in his troops, identified the key terrain of Cemetery Hill and held the enemy in place until the arrival of Maj. Gen. John F. Reynolds' I Corps at ten o'clock in the morning and Howard's XI Corps by noon.

By midday on the first, two corps of the Army of the Potomac were locked in battle with Hill's Confederate Corps, with elements of Ewell's Corps moving up to support it. The latter, advancing from the north and northeast, broke the stretched lines of the XI Corps and drove the Federals back through Gettysburg in confusion. The Union infantry rallied behind artillery positioned on Cemetery Hill south of the town. Lee, who reached the field about 2:00 P.M., ordered Ewell at about 4:30 or 5:00 to take Cemetery Hill, "if he found it practicable." However, before preparations were complete for an attack, it began to get dark and Ewell failed to press his advantage. By nightfall the Confederates settled into positions extending in a great curve from northeast of Culp's Hill, westward through Gettysburg, thence south on Seminary Ridge. During the night the Federals, enjoying interior lines, moved troops in strength onto the key points of Culp's Hill, Cemetery Hill, and Cemetery Ridge, forming a great inverted "fishhook."

Meade arrived on the battlefield at midnight and, despite the confusion inherent in arriving in the midst of operations, quickly had a grasp of the battle. He decided to fight on that ground and not retreat. Accordingly, he put his forces in movement for a major defensive battle and completed his dispositions by the morning of July 2. The Union line was strong except in two places. In the confusion of battle, Little Round Top was unoccupied except for a series of small signal detachments. And the commander of the III Corps, Maj. Gen. Daniel E. Sickles, on his own responsibility moved his line forward from the south end of Cemetery Ridge to higher ground near the Peach Orchard; his corps lay in an exposed salient. He believed he was moving forward onto higher and more easily defensible ground, but he completely failed to coordinate his action. By early afternoon, five corps were arrayed along the Union battle line with one in reserve and one more still marching to reach Gettysburg.

On the Confederate side, Lee still retained the power of choice. He could continue the attack, despite the unfavorable ground and the fact that not all his troops were yet in place. He could play it safe and wait, bring up the rest of Longstreet's corps, or even try to get the Union Army to attack him in his own strong position on Seminary Ridge. Or he could break contact and retreat, hoping to bring the Union Army out of its positions and maneuver against it as it attempted to pursue

Little Round Top Signal Flag

JOSHUA L. CHAMBERLAIN (1828–1914)

A former Bowdoin College professor, Colonel Chamberlain had led the 20th Maine for only a month when they met destiny at Gettysburg. Late in the afternoon of July 2, 1863, the 20th Maine repulsed three Confederate assaults against the extreme Union left among the boulders and trees along the southern slopes of Little Round Top. Again, enemy infantry climbed the hill. Low on ammunition with no help available and retreat inadmissible, a wounded Chamberlain ordered a bayonet charge. Those Confederates not killed or captured fled in panic; and Little Round Top, key to the Union line, was secured. Chamberlain received the Medal of Honor.

him. However, Lee was not in the mood to retreat or passively defend; he wanted to attack despite his disadvantages.

Lee was faced with the usual dilemma of generals on the attack during the Civil War. Every commander wanted to combine frontal assaults with envelopments and flanking movements, but the difficulty of timing and coordinating the movements of such large, often not fully trained, bodies of men in broken terrain made intricate maneuvers difficult. The action on the second day at Gettysburg graphically illustrates the problem. Lee wanted to bring up Longstreet's corps to strike at the Federal left while Hill and Ewell attacked to their fronts. However, coordination broke down. Longstreet's men were forced to march almost in front of Union positions to reach their attack positions and had to countermarch on a number of occasions to avoid being observed. The attack did not start until almost four in the afternoon. As they moved forward, they struck strong Union positions at a jumbled pile of rocks, south of the Peach Orchard and forward of Little Round Top, nicknamed the Devil's Den. The smoke of battle was thick over the fields south of Gettysburg, and the cries of the wounded mingled with the crash of musketry. The whole sector had become a chaos of tangled battle lines as units overlapped each other.

As the battle was raging to the east of Little Round Top, Brig. Gen. Gouverneur Warren discovered that no infantry held this critical position. Through General Meade he passed a request to the commander of the V Corps, Maj. Gen. George Sykes, to send two brigades and some artillery to the hill. They arrived just in time. The Confederates moved through the Devil's Den and launched a furious assault against Little Round Top, now defended by Col. Strong Vincent's brigade composed of regiments from Maine, New York, Pennsylvania, and Michigan. The Union soldiers threw assault after assault back. Particularly hard hit was the 20th Maine, commanded by Col. Joshua Chamberlain. The Confederates attacked time and time again, but were each time driven back. Finally, running short on ammunition, Colonel Chamberlain ordered a desperate bayonet charge that broke the rebel attackers' spirit. The position at Little Round Top was safe.

With Little Round Top secured by the Union, Longstreet threw a second division against Sickles' troops in the Peach Orchard and Wheatfield; this cracked the Federal line, and the Confederate troops drove as far as Cemetery Ridge before Meade's reserves halted their advance. Lee attempted to coordinate his units so that they would attack progressively from right to left, and one of Hill's divisions assaulted Cemetery Ridge in piecemeal fashion but was driven off. In the north, Ewell attacked about 8:00 P.M. and captured some abandoned trenches near Culp's Hill, but Federals posted behind stone walls proved too strong. As the day ended the Federals held all their main positions. The Confederates had fought hard and with great bravery, but the Union Army, operating in interior lines, had been able to move troops in a timely fashion to all threatened spots in the line and had stubbornly defended against the Confederate assaults.

Meade, after requesting the opinions of his corps commanders in a council of war, decided to defend, rather than attack, on July 3. Lee planned to launch a full-scale, coordinated attack along the line with all the forces he could muster. The main attack, however, was to be a massive frontal assault by nine brigades from three divisions of Longstreet's and Hill's corps against the Union center, which was held by Maj. Gen. Winfield Scott Hancock's II Corps. The assault was to be preceded by a massive artillery barrage.

The infantry's main fire support during the war was provided by direct-firing field artillery. Rifled guns of relatively long range were available and could have provided indirect fires, but the soldiers on both sides preferred the 12-lb. smoothbore cannon, especially the popular Napoleon. Rifled cannon were harder to clean; their fuses were not always as effective; their greater range could not always be effectively used because development of a good indirect fire control system would have to await the invention of the field telephone and the radio; and the rifled guns had to be rebored once the rifling wore down. Both types of cannon were among the artillery of the two armies at Gettysburg.

About 1:00 P.M. on July 3, Confederate gunners opened fire from 140 pieces along Seminary Ridge in the greatest artillery bombardment witnessed on the American continent up to that time. For perhaps two hours the barrage continued, destroying Union artillery and caissons in the center of the line. The Union infantry was able to shelter behind a stone wall that ran in front of its position and was relatively unharmed.

"PICKETT'S" CHARGE

"For every Southern boy fourteen years old," William Faulkner wrote, "not once but whenever he wants it, there is the instant when it's still not yet two o'clock on that July afternoon in 1863." It was then, on the third day of the battle of Gettysburg, that the Confederates launched an assault by more than 10,000 infantry, intended to break the Union line on Cemetery Ridge. A low rise divided the approach to the Union lines, so that neither Pickett's Virginian Division nor the predominantly North Carolinian Division to its left could see, much less support, the other during most of the advance. Under heavy artillery fire all the way, the attack failed. Union forces held their ground, and Lee's army began its retreat to Virginia the next day. Recriminations continued for decades afterward, with North Carolinians blaming Virginians for the failure and Virginians blaming General Longstreet, a Georgian. Asked in later years why the charge had failed, Pickett himself is supposed to have answered, "Well, I always thought the Yankees had something to do with it."

Rudolph Ellis of Philadelphia as Officer of the Day, *Jefferson Chalfont, n.d.*

The Union artillery, while taking a beating, was not knocked out; artillery reinforcements were quickly rushed to the threatened center. Union guns did slow their rate of firing, in part to conserve ammunition, and the silence seemed to be a signal that the Confederates should begin their attack.

Under the overall tactical command of General Longstreet, around 11,000 men emerged from the woods on Seminary Ridge, dressed their three lines as if on parade, and began the mile-long, twenty-minute march toward Cemetery Ridge. Although known popularly as Pickett's Charge after Maj. Gen. George E. Pickett, over half the soldiers belonged to units other than Pickett's division. Brig. Gen. James J. Pettigrew, in charge of Maj. Gen. Henry Heth's division of four brigades, led another main element. Two brigades from Maj. Gen. William D. Pender's division, commanded by Maj. Gen. Isaac R. Trimble, joined them. In essence there were two poorly coordinated assaults on the Union Center with Trimble and Pettigrew on the Confederate left and Pickett's three brigades on the right.

The assault force, forty-seven regiments altogether, moved at a walk until it neared the Union lines then broke into a run as it neared the summit of the ridge. Union artillery on the south end of the ridge opened fire and enfiladed the gray ranks. Despite heavy casualties the

Confederates kept their formation until they came within rifle and canister range of the II Corps; by then the lines and units were intermingled. Remnants of Pickett's three brigades actually reached and crossed the stone wall defended by Brig. Gen. John Gibbon's 2d Division of the II Corps, only to be quickly cut down or captured. Pettigrew's men were hit in the front and flank by deadly rifle fire and canister and fell short of breaching the Union lines north of a sharp turn in the stone wall called the Angle. Trimble's men tried to support Pettigrew's attack but were broken by Union fire and could go no farther. The survivors of all three divisions withdrew to Seminary Ridge, and the field fell quiet.

Both Union and Confederate forces were too exhausted for further attacks. Both sides had fought hard and with great valor. Among 90,000 effective Union troops and 75,000 Confederates, there were more than 51,000 casualties. The Army of the Potomac lost 3,155 killed, 14,529 wounded, and 5,365 captured or missing. Of the Army of Northern Virginia, 3,903 were killed, 18,735 wounded, and 5,425 missing or captured. If Chancellorsville was arguably Lee's finest battle, Gettysburg was clearly his worst; yet the reversal did not unnerve him or reduce his effectiveness as a commander. The invasion had patently failed, and on July 4 he began to retreat toward the Potomac. As that river was flooded, it was several days before he was able to cross. Mr. Lincoln, naturally pleased over Meade's defensive victory and elated over Grant's capture of Vicksburg, thought the war could end in 1863 if Meade launched a resolute pursuit and destroyed Lee's army on the north bank of the Potomac. But Meade's own army was too mangled; and the Union commander moved cautiously, permitting Lee to return safely to Virginia on July 13.

Gettysburg was the last important action in the Eastern Theater in 1863. Lee and Meade maneuvered against each other in Virginia, but there was no more significant fighting in the East. There were stirring events in the Western Theater, however.

The West: Confusion over Clearing the Mississippi

In the west, the major challenge facing the Union armies was the capture of Vicksburg and the seizure of control of the Mississippi River. Initially, however, the Federals faced the same problems of divided command that had plagued armies in the east. General Grant, with over 60,000 men, remained in western Tennessee guarding communication lines. Brig. Gen. Don Carlos Buell's army of 56,000, after containing Bragg's invasion of Kentucky, had been taken over by Maj. Gen. William S. Rosecrans, whose hard-won victory at Murfreesboro at the end of 1862 had nevertheless immobilized the Army of the Cumberland for nearly half a year. To the south, Union forces under the command of Maj. Gen. Nathaniel P. Banks controlled New Orleans as part of the Department of the Gulf. Coordinating the movement of all these forces would prove a true leadership challenge.

Late in 1862 President Lincoln and Secretary of War Edwin M. Stanton worked out their own plans to accomplish the fall of Vicksburg, however without coordinating that plan effectively with their senior military commanders. They wrote somewhat vague orders for a simultaneous advance north from New Orleans and south from

Tennessee. General Banks was to command the move northward from New Orleans, and command of the southbound expedition was to go to Maj. Gen. John A. McClernand. Both were relatively untried as Army commanders. They were also volunteer officers and politicians who often dabbled in intrigue to gain favors. Further, McClernand was to operate within Grant's department but independently of him, often a recipe for trouble. When General Halleck found out about the Lincoln-Stanton plan, he persuaded the President to put Grant in command of the southbound expedition and to make McClernand one of his subordinates.

Grant's Campaign against Vicksburg

General Grant first tried a combined land and water expedition against Vicksburg in December 1862–January 1863. He sent General Sherman downriver from Memphis, but the Confederates under Maj. Gen. Earl Van Dorn and Brig. Gen. Nathan B. Forrest raided and cut his 200-mile-long line of communications. Sherman himself bogged down before Vicksburg; Grant, perhaps also wishing to keep close rein on McClernand, who ranked Sherman, then determined on a river expedition that he would lead in person. Late in January Grant arrived near Vicksburg with upwards of 45,000 men organized into three corps: the XIII Corps under McClernand, the XV Corps under Sherman, and the XVII Corps under Maj. Gen. James B. McPherson. During the ensuing campaign Grant received two more corps as reinforcements to bring his total strength to 75,000 men.

Vicksburg had almost a perfect location for defense. (*Map 33*) At that point on the river, bluffs rose as high as 250 feet above the water and extended for about 100 miles from north to south. North of Vicksburg lay the Yazoo River and its delta, a gloomy stretch of watery, swampy bottom land extending 175 miles from north to south, 60 miles from east to west. The ground immediately south of Vicksburg was almost as swampy and impassable. The Confederates had fortified the bluffs from Haynes' Bluff on the Yazoo, 10 miles above Vicksburg, to Grand Gulf at the mouth of the Big Black River 40 miles below. Vicksburg could not be assaulted from the river, and sailing past it was extremely hazardous. The river formed a great "U" there, and Vicksburg's guns threatened any craft that tried to run by. For the Union troops to attack

GRANT AND HEADQUARTERS

Grant prospered because he could learn the complexities of command away from Washington and the glare of newspaper publicity. He made mistakes and learned from them. Because of the scarcity of trained officers, his staff initially consisted of civilians in uniform; and he formed the habit of writing his own orders. They were clear, succinct, unambiguous—like the man himself. He cultivated a climate at his headquarters that allowed free-wheeling discussion of the difficulties and possibilities facing his forces, what one historian has labeled "an open headquarters." Junior officers could express their opinions, and Grant could pick and choose among them.

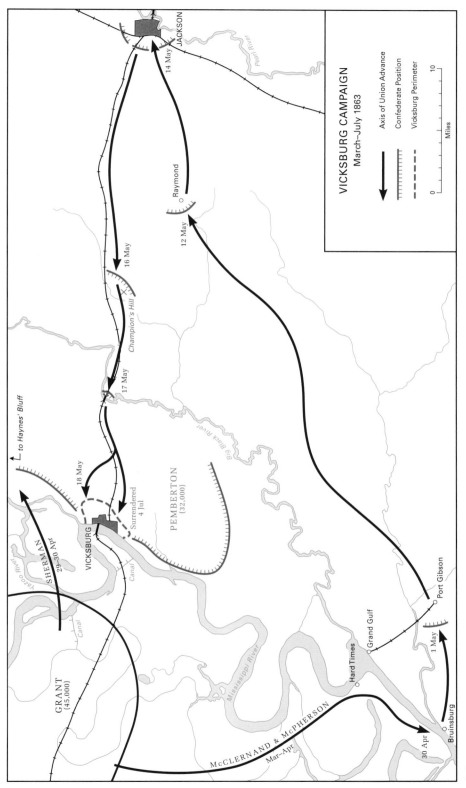

VICKSBURG CAMPAIGN
March–July 1863

Axis of Union Advance
Confederate Position
Vicksburg Perimeter

0   5   10
Miles

JACKSON
14 May

Pearl River

Raymond
12 May

16 May
Champion's Hill

17 May

Big Black River

to Haynes' Bluff

18 May

Surrendered
4 Jul

PEMBERTON
(32,000)

SHERMAN
29–30 Apr

Yazoo River

VICKSBURG
Canal

Canal

GRANT
(45,000)

Mississippi River

McCLERNAND & McPHERSON
Mar–Apr

Hard Times

Grand Gulf

1 May

Port Gibson

30 Apr
Bruinsburg

Map 33

successfully, they would have to get to the high, dry ground east of town. This would put them in Confederate territory between two enemy forces. Lt. Gen. John C. Pemberton commanded some 30,000 men in Vicksburg, while the Confederate area commander, General Joseph E. Johnston (now recovered from his wound at Fair Oaks), concentrated the other scattered Confederate forces in Mississippi at Jackson, the state capital, 40 miles east of Vicksburg.

During late winter and early spring, with the rains falling, the streams high, and the roads at their wettest and muddiest, overland movement was impossible. Primarily to placate discontented politicians and a critical press, Grant made four attempts to reach high ground east of Vicksburg. All four were unsuccessful, foiled either by Confederate resistance or by natural obstacles. One of the more spectacular efforts was digging canals. These projects had as their objective the clearing of an approach by which troops could sail to a point near the high ground without being fired on by Vicksburg's guns. All failed. That Grant kept on trying in the face of such discouragement is a tribute to his dogged persistence, and that Lincoln supported him is a tribute to his confidence in the general. The trouble was that Grant had been on the river for two months, and by early spring Vicksburg was no nearer falling than when he came.

On April 4 in a letter to Halleck, Grant divulged his latest plan to capture Vicksburg. Working closely with the local naval commander, Rear Adm. David D. Porter, Grant evolved a stroke of great boldness. He decided to use part of his force above Vicksburg to divert the Confederates. The main body would march southward on the west side of the Mississippi, cross to the east bank below the city, and, with only five days' rations, strike inland to live off a hostile country without a line of supply or retreat. As he told Sherman, the Union troops would carry "what rations of hard bread, coffee, and salt we can and make the country furnish the balance." Porter's gunboats and other craft, which up to now were on the river north of Vicksburg, were to run past the batteries during darkness and then ferry the troops over the river. Sherman thought the campaign too risky, but the events of the next two months were to prove him wrong.

While Sherman demonstrated near Vicksburg in March, McClernand's and McPherson's corps started their advance south. The rains let up in April, the waters receded slightly, and overland movement became somewhat easier. On the night of April 16 Porter led his river fleet past Vicksburg, whose guns, once the move was discovered, lit up the black night with an eerie bombardment. All but one transport made it safely; and starting on April 30, Porter's craft ferried the troops eastward over the river at Bruinsburg below Grand Gulf. The final march against Vicksburg was ready to begin.

At this time the Confederates had more troops in the vicinity than Grant had but never could make proper use of them. Grant's swift move had bewildered Pemberton. Then too, just before marching downstream, Grant had ordered a brigade of cavalry to come down from the Tennessee border, riding between the parallel north-south railroad lines of the Mississippi Central and Mobile and Ohio. Led by Col. Benjamin H. Grierson, this force sliced the length of the state, cutting railroads, fighting detachments of Confederate cavalry, and finally reaching Union lines at Baton Rouge, Louisiana. Most important, for the few days that counted most, it drew Pemberton's attention away from Grant and kept the Confederate general from discerning the Union's objectives.

Once more, divided counsel hampered the coordination of Confederate strategy. Davis had sent Johnston west in December 1862 to take overall command of the theater, an imposing task, for Pemberton's army in Mississippi and Bragg's in Tennessee were widely separated. Things were further confused by Davis' directive to Pemberton to hold Vicksburg at all costs while Johnston recognized the potential trap and ordered him to move directly against Grant. In such a situation Pemberton could do little that was right. He tried to defend too great an area; he had not concentrated but dispersed his forces at Vicksburg, the Big Black River, and along the railroad line to Jackson, where Johnston was gathering more troops. As is often the case, whoever tries to defend everything often ends up losing everything.

Grant took Port Gibson on May 1, and Sherman's corps rejoined the main force. Now the Union commander decided that he must defeat Johnston before turning on Vicksburg. He moved northeastward and fought his way into Raymond on May 12, a move that put him squarely between Johnston and Pemberton and in a position to cut the Confederate line of communications. The next day Sherman and McPherson marched against the city of Jackson with McClernand following in reserve ready to hold off Pemberton if he attacked. The leading corps took Jackson on May 14 and drove its garrison eastward. While Sherman occupied the state capital to fend off Johnston, the other two corps turned west against Pemberton and Vicksburg. Pemberton tried too late to catch Grant in open country. He suffered severe defeats at Champion's Hill (May 16) and Big Black River Bridge (May 17) and was shut up in Vicksburg. In eighteen days Grant's army had marched 200 miles, had won four victories, and had finally secured the high ground along the Yazoo River that had been the goal of all the winter's fruitless campaigning. In this lightning operation, Grant had proven himself a master of maneuver warfare and a bold risk-taker.

Grant assaulted the Vicksburg lines on May 15 and 22, but as Sherman noted of the attacks: "The heads of columns have been swept away as chaff from the hand on a windy day." The only recourse now was a siege. Grant settled down and removed McClernand from command after the attack of May 22, during which the corps commander sent a misleading report, then later slighted the efforts of the other corps and publicly criticized the army commander. Grant replaced him with Maj. Gen. Edward O. C. Ord and ordered the army to dig trenches around the city and place powerful batteries of artillery to command the enemy positions.

The rest was now a matter of time, as Sherman easily kept Johnston away and the Federals advanced their siege works toward the Confederate fortifications. Food became scarce, and the troops and civilians inside Vicksburg were soon reduced to eating mules and horses. Shells pounded the city, and the Federal lines were drawn so tight that one Confederate soldier admitted "a cat could not have crept out of Vicksburg without being discovered." The front lines were so close that the Federals threw primitive hand grenades into the Confederate works. By July 1 the Union troops had completed their approaches and were ready

> Food became scarce, and the troops and civilians inside Vicksburg were soon reduced to eating mules and horses.

for another assault. But Vicksburg was starving, and Pemberton asked for terms. Grant offered to parole all prisoners, and the city surrendered on Independence Day. Since Grant was out of telegraphic contact with Washington, the news reached the President via naval channels on July 7, the day before General Banks' 15,000-man army, having advanced upriver from New Orleans, captured Port Hudson. The Union now repossessed the whole river and had sliced the Confederacy in two. Once more Grant had removed an entire Confederate army—40,000 men—from the war, losing only one-tenth that number in the process.

Chickamauga Campaign

One week before the surrender of Vicksburg and the Union victory at Gettysburg, General Rosecrans moved out of Murfreesboro, Tennessee, and headed for Chattanooga, one of the most important cities in the south because of its location. (*Map 34*) It was a main junction on the rail line linking Richmond with Knoxville and Memphis. President Lincoln had long recognized the importance of railroads in this area. In 1862 he said, "To take and hold the railroad at or east of Cleveland [near Chattanooga], in East Tennessee, I think fully as important as the taking and holding of Richmond." Furthermore, at Chattanooga, the Tennessee River cuts through the parallel ridges of the Appalachian Mountains and forms a natural gateway to north or south. By holding the city, the Confederates could threaten Kentucky and prevent a Union penetration of the southeastern part of the Confederacy. If the Union armies pushed through Chattanooga, they would be in position to attack Atlanta, Savannah, or even the Carolinas and Richmond from the rear. As Lincoln told Rosecrans in 1863, "If we can hold Chattanooga and East Tennessee I think the rebellion must dwindle and die."

After the spring and summer campaigns in the east, the Davis government in Richmond approved a movement by two divisions of Longstreet's corps of Lee's army to the west to reinforce the hard-pressed Bragg. Longstreet's move, a 900-mile trip by rail involving 10,000–15,000 men and six batteries of artillery, began on September 9.

RAILROADS IN THE CIVIL WAR

During the decade before the Civil War U.S. railroads expanded from 9,000 miles of track to over 30,000, located disproportionately in the North; the Northern railroads were also generally better constructed, managed, and maintained. Superior rail communications gave the Union an enormous advantage in strategic mobility, largely negating the Confederacy's nominal possession of interior lines. Movement of supplies by rail was crucial for both armies, so that the securing or destruction of railways were important campaign objectives. In addition, substantial troop movements by rail were an important feature of Civil War operations, most notably the transfer of two Union corps totaling 25,000 men from Virginia to Tennessee in autumn 1863 to lift the siege of Chattanooga. Union forces advancing into Confederate territory were supported by the U.S. Military Railroad—by the end of the war, the largest railroad in the world—whose operations were overseen by the West Point–trained engineer Herman Haupt.

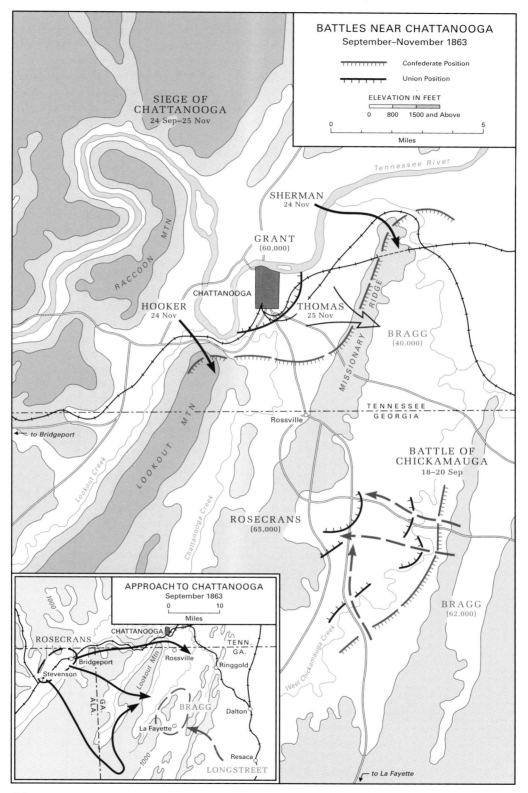

BATTLES NEAR CHATTANOOGA
September–November 1863

Confederate Position
Union Position

ELEVATION IN FEET
0   800   1500 and Above

0   5
Miles

SIEGE OF
CHATTANOOGA
24 Sep–25 Nov

Tennessee River

SHERMAN
24 Nov

GRANT
(60,000)

RACCOON MTN

CHATTANOOGA

HOOKER
24 Nov

THOMAS
25 Nov

MISSIONARY RIDGE

BRAGG
(40,000)

to Bridgeport

Rossville

TENNESSEE
GEORGIA

LOOKOUT MTN

Lookout Creek

Chattanooga Creek

BATTLE OF
CHICKAMAUGA
18–20 Sep

ROSECRANS
(65,000)

BRAGG
(62,000)

APPROACH TO CHATTANOOGA
September 1863

0   10
Miles

1000

ROSECRANS

CHATTANOOGA

TENN.
GA.

Bridgeport

Rossville

Ringgold

Stevenson

GA.
ALA.

Lookout Mtn

BRAGG

Dalton

La Fayette

1000

Resaca

LONGSTREET

West Chickamauga Creek

to La Fayette

Map 34

General Bragg

General Forrest

But a force under Burnside, who now commanded the Department of the Ohio, which was not part of Rosecrans' command, had penetrated the Cumberland Gap and had driven the Confederates from Knoxville. Longstreet had to go around by way of Augusta and Atlanta and did not reach Bragg until September 18. The rail network was rickety, and Longstreet's soldiers quipped that such poor rolling stock had never been intended to carry such good soldiers. Movement of Longstreet's troops from Virginia was nevertheless an outstanding logistical achievement for the Confederacy and a bold operational move.

Rosecrans meanwhile began planning how to use his numerical superiority (he had 65,000 available troops to Bragg's 46,250) to maneuver Bragg out of his positions in eastern Tennessee and move against Chattanooga. Faced with Confederates in strong positions around his base at Murfreesboro, Rosecrans decided to conduct a series of feints to mislead the enemy. Starting on June 24, he dispatched one division to the southwest of the city and a corps to the east to distract Bragg while moving the bulk of his army under corps commanders Maj. Gens. George H. Thomas and Alexander M. McCook to the southeast in a main attack on a critical mountain gap. Despite torrential rainfall and problems with muddy roads, the Union troops successfully seized Hoover's Gap, unhinging the Confederate defensive line. Forced to retreat, Bragg fell back on Tullahoma to defend his supply lines. However, after a few days of recovery it was apparent to him that Rosecrans intended to use his superior forces to continue trying to outflank his position. Rather than be trapped, Bragg retreated again and, abandoning eastern Tennessee, he moved back over the rain-swollen Tennessee River on July 6. He returned to Chattanooga and prepared to defend that key city. In a few weeks of rapid maneuvering, Rosecrans had driven Bragg's forces back to where they had started their offensive almost a year before.

After months of delay Rosecrans had accomplished the feat of completely outmaneuvering Bragg without a major battle. He next demonstrated across the river from Chattanooga as a diversion while actually sending the bulk of his army to cross the Tennessee River miles to the southwest. He planned to get in behind Bragg and bottle him up in Chattanooga. However, the Confederate general saw through the scheme and slipped away southward, abandoning the city while carefully planting rumors that his army was demoralized and in flight. Rosecrans then resolved to pursue, a decision that would have been wise if Bragg had been retreating in disorder.

There were few passes through the mountains and no good lateral roads. In full pursuit mode, Rosecrans dispersed his army in three columns over a forty-mile front to make use of the various passes. Watching Rosecrans carefully, Bragg stopped his retreat and concentrated his army about September 9 at La Fayette, Georgia, twenty miles south of Chattanooga. As his force was three times as large as any one of the Union columns, Bragg anticipated that he could hit each column in turn and defeat Rosecrans in detail. But his intelligence service failed him: he thought there were two, rather than three, Union columns and prepared plans accordingly. He first planned to strike what he thought was Rosecrans' right (actually Thomas' corps in the center) at McLemore's Cove on September 10. However, his subordinates moved slowly, and the attacks were made in desultory fashion. By the time Bragg's forces could converge, Thomas had pulled his troops back into safe positions. Bragg next planned to strike at Maj. Gen. Thomas L. Crittenden's corps on the Union left flank. Again, poor coordination prevented him from catching the enemy; Crittenden also pulled back behind the safety of Missionary Ridge. Thus, twice in three days Bragg missed a fine opportunity to inflict a serious reverse upon the Federals because of his subordinates' failure to carry out orders.

By September 13 Rosecrans was at last aware that Bragg was not retreating in disorder but was preparing to fight. The Union commander ordered an immediate concentration, but this would take several days and in the meantime his corps were vulnerable. Although Bragg was usually speedy in executing attacks, this time he delayed, awaiting the arrival of Longstreet's corps. He intended to attack the Union left in an attempt to push Rosecrans southward away from Chattanooga into a mountain cul-de-sac where the Federals could be destroyed.

By September 17 Bragg was positioned just east of Chickamauga Creek, a sluggish stream surrounded by dense woods. (*See Map 34.*) When Longstreet's three leading brigades arrived on September 18, Bragg decided to cross the Chickamauga and attack the Federal left. But Rosecran's forces there, with two corps almost fully concentrated, defended the fords so stoutly that only a few Confederate units got over the creek that day. During the night more Confederates slipped across, and by morning of the nineteenth about three-fourths of Bragg's army was over the creek and poised to attack.

By then, however, Rosecrans' third corps had arrived on the scene and Bragg faced a much stronger force than he had expected. The heavily wooded battlefield had few landmarks, and some units had difficulty maintaining direction. Bragg planned to attack all along the Union line, starting on its left and rippling down the line to the Union right in quick succession from roughly northeast down to the southwest. Over the course of the day, several of Bragg's toughest divisions (Maj. Gens. Alexander P. Stewart's, John Bell Hood's and Patrick R. Cleburne's) attacked and almost broke through the Union line on three separate occasions. Only the hasty movement of Union reserves stemmed the tide in each case.

The fighting was brutal and often hand-to-hand in the dense woods along the choked Chickamauga Creek. It was afterward called a soldier's battle, with little chance for grand strategy or operational deployments

THE NEW YORK DRAFT RIOTS

On July 13–17, 1863, several thousand rioters, mostly working-class Irish Catholics, smashed and burned government buildings and facilities belonging to the Republican Party to protest a newly implemented federal conscription system. They also attacked some well-to-do citizens on the street because they resented the $300 dollar commutation clause that allowed a wealthy man to hire a substitute to go in his place. Many rioters also vented their anger against blacks, killing at least a dozen, because they objected to fighting for the freedom of slaves who might then take their jobs by working for lower wages.

Union Officers on Missionary Ridge, *James Walker, 1864*

Grant at Chattanooga

Rosecrans' army, having started out offensively, was now shut up in Chattanooga as Bragg took up positions on Lookout Mountain and Missionary Ridge dominating the city. The Union commander accepted investment and thus surrendered his freedom of action. Burnside, at Knoxville, was too far away to render immediate aid. There were no strong Confederate units north of Chattanooga, but Rosecrans' line of communications was cut away. The Nashville and Chattanooga Railroad, instead of running directly into the city, reached the Tennessee River at Stevenson, crossed at Bridgeport southwest of Chattanooga, and ran through Confederate territory into town. River steamers could get to within only eight miles of Chattanooga; beyond, the Tennessee River was swift and narrow. Supplies therefore came over the mountains in wagons; but starting September 30, Confederate cavalry under Maj. Gen. Joseph Wheeler, one of Bragg's cavalry commanders, raided as far north as Murfreesboro. Though heavily and effectively opposed in his effort to tear up the railroad, he managed to destroy many precious Union supply wagons. With the mountain roads breaking down under the heavy traffic in wet weather, rations in Chattanooga ran short. Men went hungry, and horses and mules began to die of starvation. Rosecrans prepared to reopen his line of communications by means of an overland route to the west. But this route was dominated by Confederate troops on Raccoon and Lookout Mountains. Additional troops to clear these strong points were required if the Army of the Cumberland was to survive.

Washington finally awoke to the fact that an entire Union army was trapped in Chattanooga and in danger of capture. In a midnight council meeting on September 23, the President met with Secretary Stanton, General Halleck, and others to determine what could be done. As General Meade was not active in the east at that time, they decided to detach two corps, or about 20,000 men, from the Army of the Potomac and send them by rail to Tennessee under the command of General Hooker, who had been without active command since his relief in June. The selected forces included ten artillery batteries with over 3,000 mules and horses. The 1,157-mile journey involved four changes of trains, owing to differing gauges and lack of track connections, and eclipsed all other such troop movements by rail up to that time. The troops began to entrain at Manassas Junction and Bealton Station, Virginia, on September 25, and five days later the first trains arrived at Bridgeport, Alabama. Not all the troops made such good time: for the majority of the infantry the trip consumed about nine days. And movement of the artillery, horses, mules, baggage, and impedimenta was somewhat slower. Combined with a waterborne movement of 17,000 men under Sherman from Mississippi, the reinforcement of the besieged Rosecrans was a triumph of skill and planning.

Chickamauga had caused Stanton and his associates to lose confidence in Rosecrans. For some time Lincoln had been dubious about Rosecrans, who, he said, acted "like a duck hit on the head" after Chickamauga; but he did not immediately choose a successor. Finally, about mid-October, he decided to unify command in the west and to vest it in General Grant, who still commanded the Army of the Tennessee. In October Stanton met Grant in Louisville and gave him orders that allowed him some discretion in selecting subordinates. Grant was appointed commander of the Military Division of the Mississippi, which embraced the Departments and Armies of the Ohio, the Cumberland, and the Tennessee and included the vast area from the Alleghenies to the Mississippi River north of Banks' Department of the Gulf. Thomas replaced Rosecrans as Commander of the Army of the Cumberland, and Sherman was appointed to command Grant's old Army of the Tennessee.

Now that Hooker had arrived, the line of communications, or the "cracker line" to the troops, could be opened. Rosecrans had actually shaped the plan, and all he needed was combat troops to execute it. On October 26 Hooker crossed the Tennessee at Bridgeport and attacked eastward. Within two days he had taken the spurs of the mountains, other Union troops had captured two important river crossings, and the supply line was open once more. Men, equipment, and food moved via riverboat and wagon road, bypassing Confederate strong points, to reinforce the besieged Army of the Cumberland.

In early November Bragg weakened his besieging army by sending Longstreet's force against Burnside at Knoxville. This move reduced Confederate strength to about 40,000 about the same time Sherman arrived with two army corps from Memphis. The troops immediately at hand under Grant (Thomas' Army of the Cumberland, two corps of Sherman's Army of the Tennessee, and two corps under Hooker from the Army of the Potomac) now numbered about 60,000. Grant characteristically decided to resume the offensive with his entire force.

The Confederates had held their dominant position for so long that they seemed to look on all of the Federals in Chattanooga as their ultimate prisoners. One day in November Grant went out to inspect the Union lines and reached a point where Union and Confederate picket posts were not far apart. Not only did his own troops turn out the guard, but a smart set of Confederates came swarming out, formed a neat military rank, snapped to attention, and presented arms. Grant returned the salute and rode away. But plans were already afoot to divest the Confederates of some of their cockiness.

Grant planned to hit the ends of the Confederate line at once. Hooker would strike at Lookout Mountain; Sherman, moving his army upstream across the river from Chattanooga and crossing over by pontoons, would hit the northern end of Missionary Ridge. While they were breaking the Confederate flanks, Thomas' men could make limited, holding attacks on the center. The Army of the Cumberland's soldiers, already nursing a bruised ego for the rout at Chickamauga, realized that in the eyes of the commanding general they were second-class troops.

Hooker took Lookout Mountain on November 24 after a short struggle known as the Battle above the Clouds because of the height of the mountain and the mist that enshrouded it. On the same day Sherman crossed the Tennessee at the mouth of Chickamauga Creek and gained positions on the north end of Missionary Ridge. The next day his attacks bogged down as he attempted to drive south along the ridge. To help Sherman, Grant directed the Army of the Cumberland to take the rifle pits at the foot of the west slope of Missionary Ridge. These rifle pits were the first of three lines of Confederate trenches. Thomas' troops rushed forward and seized the pits. Then, having a score to settle with the Confederates positioned above them, the troops kept going up the hill despite attempts by their officers to stop them. Coming under fire from the pits above and in front of them, the Federals inexorably swept up the hill. One of the charging Union soldiers, Lt. Arthur MacArthur, father of Douglas MacArthur, was awarded the Medal of Honor for his heroism.

When Grant observed this movement, he muttered that someone was going to sweat for it if the charge ended in disaster. But Thomas' troops drove all the way to the top, some shouting "Chickamauga, Chickamauga"; in the afternoon Hooker swept the southern end of the ridge. The Federals then had the unusual experience of seeing a Confederate army disintegrate into precipitate retreat, throwing their blankets, knapsacks, and even weapons away as they ran. The surprised bluecoats beckoned to their comrades: "My God! Come and see them run!" Bragg personally mounted his horse and tried to stem the rout, but to no avail. Grant pursued Bragg's army the next day, but one Confederate division skillfully halted the pursuit while Bragg retired into Georgia to regroup.

The battles around Chattanooga and the subsequent campaign in eastern Tennessee ended in one of the most complete Union victories of the war. Bragg's army was defeated, men and materiel captured, and the Confederates driven south. The mountainous defense line that the Confederates had hoped to hold had been pierced; the rail center of Chattanooga was permanently in Union hands; and the rich, food-producing eastern Tennessee section was lost to the Confederacy. Relief had come at last for the Union sympathizers in eastern Tennessee. With

The Army of the Cumberland's soldiers, already nursing a bruised ego for the rout at Chickamauga, realized that in the eyes of the commanding general they were second-class troops.

Chattanooga secured as a base, the way was open for an invasion of the lower South.

Discussion Questions

1. What strategic challenges and choices did the North and South face in the opening days of 1863? What did each side choose to do with their opportunities and dangers?

2. Compare Hooker's plan to attack the Army of Northern Virginia with Rosecran's plan to seize Chattanooga. Why did one fail and the other succeed?

3. Compare Lee's second invasion of the North with his first. What are the similarities and differences in rationale, plans, and outcomes?

4. It is nearly midnight, July 1, 1863, at Gettysburg. Choose the role of Lee or Meade, devise a plan for the next day, and describe the steps you would need to follow to implement that plan.

5. What opportunities were available to Bragg after the battle of Chickamauga? What possibilities were left in November 1863? What would you have done?

6. Did the Confederacy stand any chance of independence by the end of 1863? To what degree would a negotiated settlement have been the best course of action for President Davis?

Recommended Readings

Carter, Samuel III. *The Final Fortress: The Campaign for Vicksburg, 1862–1863*. New York: St. Martin's Press, 1980, chs. 8–23.

Catton, Bruce. *Glory Road*. New York: Anchor Books, chs. 3–6.

Coddington, Edwin B. *The Gettysburg Campaign: A Study in Command*. Norwalk, Conn.: Easton Press, 1989.

Foote, Shelby. *The Civil War: A Narrative,* 3 vols. New York: Random House, 1963, vol. 2.

Freeman, Douglas Southall. *Lee's Lieutenants: A Study in Command,* 3 vols. New York: Scribner Classics, 1997, vol. 2, chs. 25–36; vol. 3, chs. 1–18.

Gallagher, Gary W., ed. *Fighting for the Confederacy: The Personal Recollections of General Edward Porter Alexander*. Chapel Hill: University of North Carolina Press, 1989.

Grant, Ulysses S. *Personal Memoirs of U. S. Grant*. New York: Penguin Books, 1999.

Sears, Stephen W. *Chancellorsville*. Boston: Houghton-Mifflin, 1996.

Weigley, Russell F. *A Great Civil War: A Military and Political History, 1861–1865*. Bloomington: Indiana University Press, 2000.

Williams, Kenneth P. *Lincoln Finds a General: A Military Study of the Civil War,* 5 vols. New York: Macmillan, 1949–1959, vol. 4, chs. 10–13; vol. 5.

Williams, T. Harry. *Lincoln and His Generals*. New York: Gramercy Books, 2000, chs. 9–12.

Other Readings

Coakley, Robert W. *The Role of Federal Military Forces in Domestic Disorders, 1789–1878*. Washington, D.C.: U.S. Army Center of Military History, 1989.

Editors of Military Affairs. *Military Analysis of the Civil War*. Milwood, N.Y.: KTO Press, 1977.

Esposito, Vincent J., ed. *The West Point Atlas of the Civil War*. New York: Holt, Rinehart, and Winston, 1978, vol. 1, maps 84–116.

Jones, Virgil C. *The Civil War at Sea,* 3 vols. New York: Holt, Rinehart, and Winston, 1960–1962, vol. 2, chs. 17–24; vol. 3, chs. 1–7.

Nelson, Harold W., and Jay Luvaas, eds. *The U.S. Army War College Guide to the Battle of Gettysburg*. Carlisle, Pa.: South Mountain Press, 1986.

Spruill, Matt, ed. *Guide to the Battle of Chickamauga*. Lawrence: University of Kansas Press, 1993.

Tucker, Glenn. *Chickamauga: Bloody Battle in the West*. Dayton: Morningside, 1975.

Wiley, Bell. *The Life of Billy Yank: The Common Soldier of the Union*. Baton Rouge: Louisiana State University Press, 1978.

———. *The Life of Johnny Reb: The Common Soldier of the Confederacy*. Baton Rouge: Louisiana State University Press, 1978.

12

THE CIVIL WAR, 1864–1865

From Bull Run to Chattanooga, the Union armies had fought their battles without benefit of either a grand strategy or a supreme field commander. Even after the great victories of 1863, the situation in 1864 reflected this lack of unity of command. During the final year of the war the people of the North grew restless; and as the election of 1864 approached, many of them advocated a policy of making peace with the Confederacy. President Abraham Lincoln never wavered. Committed to the policy of destroying the armed power of the Confederacy, he sought a general who could pull together all the threads of an emerging strategy and then concentrate the Union armies and their supporting naval power against the secessionists. After Vicksburg in July 1863, Lincoln leaned more and more toward Maj. Gen. Ulysses S. Grant as the man whose strategic thinking and resolution could lead the Union armies to final victory.

Unity of Command

Acting largely as his own General in Chief, although Maj. Gen. Henry W. Halleck had been given that title after George B. McClellan's removal in early 1862, Mr. Lincoln had watched the Confederates fight from one victory to another inside their cockpit of northern Virginia. In the Western Theater, Union armies, often operating independently of one another, had scored great victories at key terrain points. But their hold on the communications base at Nashville was always in jeopardy as long as the elusive armies of the Confederacy could escape to fight another day at another key point. The twin, uncoordinated victories at Gettysburg and Vicksburg, 900 miles apart, only pointed out the North's need for an overall strategic plan and a general who could carry it out.

Having cleared the Mississippi River, Grant wrote to Halleck and the President in the late summer of 1863 about the opportunities now open to his army. Grant first called for the consolidation of the autonomous western departments and the coordination of their individual

President Lincoln

armies. After this great step, he proposed to isolate the area west of the line Chattanooga-Atlanta-Montgomery-Mobile. Within this region, Grant urged a "massive rear attack" that would take Union armies in the Gulf Department under Maj. Gen. Nathaniel P. Banks and Grant's Army of the Tennessee to Mobile and up the Alabama River to Montgomery. The U.S. Navy would play a major role in this attack. Simultaneously, Maj. Gen. William S. Rosecrans was to advance overland through Chattanooga to Atlanta. All military resources within this isolated area would be destroyed.

Lincoln vetoed Grant's plan in part by deferring the Mobile-Montgomery phase. The President favored a demonstration by Banks up the Red River to Shreveport to show the American flag to the French occupying Mexico. Napoleon III had sent French soldiers to that country to install Maximilian, archduke of Austria, as emperor, taking advantage of the U.S. preoccupation with the Civil War. This was a clear violation of the Monroe Doctrine, but Lincoln could do little more than protest and demonstrate at the time. Banks' Department of the Gulf was left out of the consolidation of the other western commands under Grant in October 1863.

Grant's plan was further stymied after the Union defeat at Chickamauga and the subsequent need to break the siege at Chattanooga. After his own victory at Chattanooga in November, however, Grant wasted few hours in writing the President what he thought the next strategic moves should be. As a possible winter attack, Grant revived the touchy Mobile campaign while the Chattanooga victors were gathering strength for a spring offensive to Atlanta. Grant reasoned that Lee would vacate Virginia and shift strength toward Atlanta. For the Mobile-Montgomery plan, Grant asked for Banks' resources in the Gulf Department. Lincoln again balked because the Texas seacoast would be abandoned. Grant's rebuttal explained that Napoleon III would really be impressed with a large Army-Navy operation against Mobile Bay. The Red River campaign, Grant believed, would not provide as dramatic a demonstration. The President told Grant again that he had to heed the demands of Union diplomacy, but at the same time he encouraged Grant to enlarge his strategic proposals to include estimates for a grand Federal offensive for the coming spring of 1864.

Grant's plan of January 1864 projected a four-pronged continental attack. In concert, the four armies were to move on Atlanta, on Mobile (after Banks took Shreveport), on General Robert E. Lee's communications by a campaign across the middle of North Carolina on the axis New Bern–Neuse River–Goldsboro–Raleigh–Greensboro, and on Lee's Army of Northern Virginia in the hope of defeating it in an open battle. Lincoln opposed the North Carolina phase, fearing that Grant's diversion of 60,000 effective bayonets from formations covering Washington was too dangerous. Lincoln knew that Lee's eyes were always fixed on the vast amount of supplies in the depots around the Washington area.

Though Lincoln scuttled some of Grant's professional schemes, he never lost his esteem for Grant's enthusiasm and intelligence. In February 1864 Congress revived Winfield Scott's old rank of lieutenant general; and Grant was promoted on March 9, making him senior to all Union officers. Lincoln relieved Halleck as General in Chief and ordered Grant to Washington to assume Halleck's post; Halleck remained as Lincoln's military adviser and Chief of Staff, but his position was decidedly inferior to Grant's. During March the President, the new General in Chief, and Secretary of War Edwin M. Stanton ironed out command arrangements that had plagued every President since the War of 1812. Lincoln and Stanton relinquished powerful command, staff, and communications tools to Grant. Stanton, greatly impressed with Grant's public acclaim, cautioned his General Staff Bureau chiefs to heed Grant's needs and timetables.

General in Chief Grant reported directly to the President and the Secretary of War, keeping them informed about the broad aspects of his strategic plans and telling them in advance of his armies' needs. However, Grant removed himself from the politics of Washington and established his headquarters in northern Virginia with the Army of the Potomac. Though he planned to go quickly to trouble spots, Grant elected to accompany the Army of the Potomac under Maj. Gen. George G. Meade to assess Lee's moves and their effects on the other columns of the Union Army. By rail or steamboat, Grant was never far from Lincoln, and in turn the President visited Grant frequently. To tie his far-flung commands together, Grant employed a vast telegraph system.

In a continental theater of war larger than Napoleon's at its zenith, Grant's job, administratively, eventually embraced four military divisions, totaling seventeen subcommands wherein 500,000 combat soldiers would be employed. At Washington, Halleck operated a war room for Grant. Halleck eased his heavy administrative burden of studying the several Army commanders' detailed field directives by preparing brief digests, thus saving the General in Chief many hours of reading detailed reports. Halleck also kept Grant informed about supply levels at base depots and advance dumps in Nashville, St. Louis, City Point, Washington, Philadelphia, Louisville, and New York City. Under Stanton, Quartermaster General Montgomery C. Meigs, the most informed logistician and supply manager of his day, dispatched men and munitions to Grant's subcommands according to a strategic timetable. As the spring offensive progressed, Stanton, Halleck, and Meigs gave Grant a rear-area team that grasped the delicate balance between theater objectives and the logistical support required to achieve them.

Grant spent the month of April on the Rapidan front developing his final strategic plan for ending the war. In essence, he recapped all his views on the advantages to be gained from his victories in the Western Theater. He added some thoughts about moving several Federal armies, aided by naval power when necessary, toward a common center in a vast, concentrated effort. He planned to stop the Confederates from using their interior lines. He intended to maneuver Lee away from the Rapidan Wilderness and defeat the Army of Northern Virginia in open terrain by a decisive battle. Another Union force collected from the Atlantic seaport towns of the Deep South was to cut the James–Appomattox River line to sever Lee's rail and road links with the other parts of the Confederacy. Simultaneously, Maj. Gen. William T. Sherman's group of armies would execute a wide wheeling movement through the South to complete the envelopment of the whole country east of the Mississippi. Banks was still scheduled to make the attack through Mobile. Sherman's and Banks' assaults were meant to fix the

Kepie, or Forage Cap, Belonging to General Grant

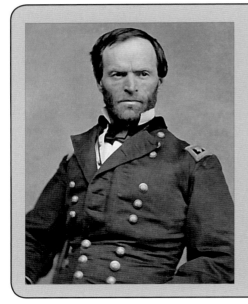

SHERMAN

"War is cruelty, and you cannot refine it," wrote William T. Sherman (1820–1891) to the mayor of Atlanta as he ordered all civilians out of the city before occupying it. Sherman prosecuted the war zealously. His troops began the year 1864 by tearing up 205 miles of railroad line in the state of Mississippi ("the most complete destruction of railroads ever beheld," Sherman reported) and ended it with the famous March to the Sea from Atlanta to Savannah. Sherman was popular with the troops, partly because he was far more successful than most Union generals and partly because his nervous temperament inclined him to stop and chat with anyone along the route of march, whether teamster, enlisted man, or officer. His letters and memoranda, both during the Civil War and after (he served as Commanding General of the Army from 1869 to 1883), show exemplary concern for the well-being of his soldiers.

rebels on the periphery while Grant struck at the center, or, as Lincoln described the plan, "Those not skinning can hold a leg."

By mid-April 1864 Grant had issued specific orders to each commander of the four Federal armies that were to execute the grand strategy. In round numbers the Union armies were sending 300,000 combat troops against 150,000 Confederates defending the invasion paths. Meade's Army of the Potomac and Maj. Gen. Ambrose E. Burnside's independent IX Corps, a combined force of 120,000 men, constituted the major attack column under Grant's overall direction. The enemy had 63,000 troops facing Grant along the Rapidan. Two subsidiary thrusts were to support Meade's efforts. Commanding a force of 33,000 men, Maj. Gen. Benjamin F. Butler with his Army of the James was to skirt the south bank of the James, menace Richmond, take it if possible, and destroy the railroads below Petersburg. Acting as a right guard in the Shenandoah Valley, Maj. Gen. Franz Sigel's 23,000 Federals were to advance on Lee's rail hub at Lynchburg, Virginia. With the northern Virginia triangle under attack, in the continental center of the line, Sherman's 100,000 men were to march on Atlanta, annihilate General Joseph E. Johnston's 65,000 soldiers, and devastate the resources of central Georgia. On the continental right of the line, Banks was to disengage as soon as possible along the Red River and with Rear Adm. David C. Farragut's blockading squadron in the Gulf of Mexico make a limited amphibious landing against Mobile. The day for advance would be announced early in May.

In rising from regimental command to General in Chief, Grant had learned much from experience; if he sometimes made mistakes, he rarely repeated them. Not a profound student of the literature of warfare, he had become by the eve of his grand campaign one of those rare leaders who combine the talents of the strategist, tactician, and logistician and who marry those talents to the principle of the offensive. His operations, especially those around Vicksburg, were models of the execution of the principles of war. He was calm in crisis; reversals and disappointments did not unhinge his cool judgment. He had what some have called "three o'clock in the morning" courage, keeping his composure even in those moments in the middle of the night when fears could often overpower lesser commanders. Grant also had mastered the dry-as-dust details of the logistical system and used common sense in deciding when to use the horse-drawn wagon, the railroad, or the steamboat in his strategic moves. Above all, Grant understood and applied the principle of modern war that the destruction of the enemy's economic resources—his ability to sustain his forces—is as necessary as the annihilation of his armies.

Lee Cornered at Richmond

On the morning of May 4, 1864, Meade and Sherman moved out to execute Grant's grand strategy. The combat strength of the Army of the Potomac, slimmed down from seven unwieldy corps, consisted of three infantry corps of 25,000 rifles each and a cavalry corps. Commanding the 12,000-man cavalry corps was Maj. Gen. Philip H. Sheridan, an energetic leader whom Grant brought east on Halleck's recommendation. Meade had dispersed his cavalry, using troopers as messengers, pickets, and train guards; but young Sheridan, after considerable argument, eventually succeeded in concentrating all of his sabers as a separate combat arm. Grant reorganized Burnside's IX Corps of 20,000 infantrymen, held it as a strategic reserve for a time, and then assigned the IX Corps to Meade's army. Lee's army, now 70,000 strong, was also organized into a cavalry and three infantry corps.

Grant's Council of War near Massaponax Church in Virginia, May 21, 1864. General Grant is standing behind the bench, looking over General Meade's shoulder at a map.

Grant and Lee were at the height of their careers, and this was their first contest of wills. Having the initiative, Grant crossed the Rapidan and decided to go by Lee's right, rather than his left. (*Map 35*) First, Grant wanted to rid himself of his reliance on the insecure Alexandria and Orange Railroads for supplies. Second, he wanted to end the Army of the Potomac's dependence on a train of 4,000 wagons (the Army's mobility was hobbled by having to care for 60,000 animals). Finally, Grant wanted to use the advantages of Virginia's tidewater rivers and base his depots on the Chesapeake Bay. He was willing to accept the risk inherent in moving obliquely across Lee's front in northern Virginia. He also hoped to find a weakness to his front that would allow him to slip around Lee's flank and get between him and Richmond.

With little room for maneuver, Grant was forced to advance through the Wilderness, where Hooker had come to grief the year before. As the army column halted near Chancellorsville to allow the wagon trains to pass the Rapidan, on May 5 Lee struck at Meade's right flank. Grant and Meade swung their corps into line and hit back. The fighting in the Battle of the Wilderness, consisting of assault, defense, and counterattack, was close and desperate in tangled woods and thickets. Artillery could not be brought to bear. The dry woods caught fire, and some of the wounded died miserably in the flame and smoke. On May 6 Lee attacked again. Lt. Gen. James Longstreet's I Corps, arriving late in battle but as always in perfect march order, drove the Federals back. Longstreet himself received a severe neck wound, inflicted in error by his own men, which took him out of action until October 1864. Lee, at a decisive moment in the battle, his fighting blood aroused to a white heat, moved forward personally and looked as if he wanted to lead an assault in person; but men of the Texas brigade with whom Lee was riding persuaded the Southern leader to go to the rear and direct the battle as their army commander. On May 7 neither side renewed the fight. The indecisive battle cost the Union nearly 17,000 casualties and the South some 10,000.

Now came the critical test of Grant's execution of strategy. He had been worsted, though not really beaten, by Lee, a greater antagonist than General Braxton Bragg, General Albert S. Johnston, or Lt. Gen. John C. Pemberton. After an encounter with Lee, each of the former Army of the Potomac commanders, McClellan, Burnside, and Hooker, had retired north of the Rappahannock River and postponed any further clashes with that great tactician. But Grant was of a different breed. He calmly ordered his lead corps to move south toward Spotsylvania as rapidly as possible to get around Lee's flank and interpose the Army of the Potomac between Lee and Richmond, hoping to achieve by mobility what he had not been able to do with battle.

Lee detected Grant's march and, using roads generally parallel to Grant's, also raced toward the key road junction at Spotsylvania. Maj. Gen. J. E. B. Stuart's cavalry harassed and slowed Grant; Lee arrived first and quickly built strong earth-and-log trenches over commanding ground that covered the roads leading to Richmond. In this crossroads race, Sheridan's cavalry would have been useful; but Meade had dissipated the cavalry corps' strength by deploying two divisions of horse to guard his already well-protected trains. Sheridan and Meade argued once again over the use of cavalry, and the General in Chief

Lee, . . . his fighting blood aroused to a white heat, moved forward personally and looked as if he wanted to lead an assault in person.

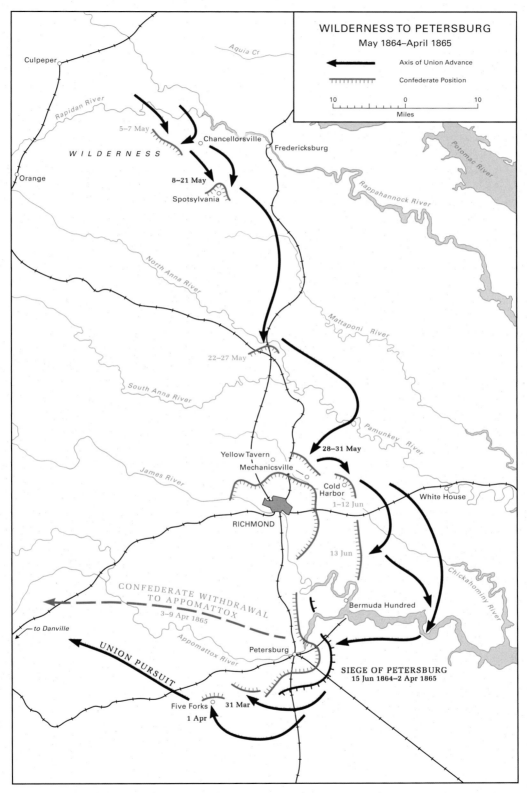

WILDERNESS TO PETERSBURG
May 1864–April 1865

← Axis of Union Advance

⊥⊥⊥⊥⊥ Confederate Position

10   0   10
Miles

Culper

Aquia Cr

Rapidan River

5–7 May

WILDERNESS

Chancellorsville

Fredericksburg

Rappahannock River

Potomac River

Orange

8–21 May

Spotsylvania

North Anna River

Mattaponi River

22–27 May

South Anna River

Pamunkey River

Yellow Tavern

Mechanicsville

28–31 May

James River

Cold Harbor

White House

1–12 Jun

RICHMOND

13 Jun

Chickahominy River

CONFEDERATE WITHDRAWAL
TO APPOMATTOX
3–9 Apr 1865

Bermuda Hundred

← to Danville

Appomattox River

Petersburg

UNION PURSUIT

SIEGE OF PETERSBURG
15 Jun 1864–2 Apr 1865

Five Forks

31 Mar

1 Apr

Map 35

COLD HARBOR

After several days of inconclusive sparring at North Anna, General Grant maneuvered his men southward in yet another attempt to outflank General Lee's Army of Northern Virginia. On May 31, 1864, General Sheridan's cavalry seized a vital crossroads near Cold Harbor. By gaining possession of Cold Harbor itself, Grant would be able to maneuver his army between Lee and the Confederate capital of Richmond. Late on June 1, the Union VI and XVIII Corps launched an assault that met with partial success. A follow-on Federal assault was delayed twenty-four hours as Grant waited for the II Corps to arrive. At dawn on June 3, the II, VI, and XVIII Corps attacked and were repulsed after briefly penetrating the enemy defensive line. Union casualties exceeded 7,000, while Confederate losses were 1,500. Cold Harbor pointed out once again the folly of frontal assaults against fortified positions.

backed Sheridan, allowing him to concentrate his cavalry arm. Grant gave Sheridan a free hand to stop Stuart's raids. Leading his corps south on May 9 in a long ride toward Richmond, its objective a decisive charge against Stuart, Sheridan did the job. He fought a running series of engagements that culminated in a victory at Yellow Tavern, just six miles north of Richmond, on May 11; the gallant Stuart was mortally wounded. The South was already short of horses and mules, and Sheridan's raid ended forever the offensive power of Lee's mounted arm. Lee, in addition, had lost another irreplaceable commander.

For four days beginning May 9 Meade struck in force at Lee's positions around Spotsylvania Court House but was beaten back each time. Twice the Federals broke through the trenches and divided Lee's army, but in each case the attackers became disorganized. Supporting infantry did not or could not close in, and Confederate counterattacks were delivered with such ferocity that the breakthroughs could be neither exploited nor held. On the morning of the eleventh, Grant wrote Halleck: "I propose to fight it out on this line if it takes all summer." He seemed as good as his word when the next day Grant launched an attack with twenty-four brigades under Maj. Gen. Winfield Scott Hancock, II Corps commander, against a narrow segment of the Confederate trench line. The attack, in an area known as the Bloody Angle or the Mule Shoe, broke the position wide open; and Union troops captured an entire Confederate division and two Confederate generals. Lee, however, recovered his equilibrium and reestablished his defensive line. On May 20, having decided the entrenchments were too strong to capture, Grant side-slipped south again, still trying to envelop Lee's right flank. His persistence led one Confederate to say of Grant, "we have met a man this time, who either does not know when he is whipped or who cares not if he loses his whole Army."

With smaller numbers, Lee skillfully avoided Grant's trap and refused to leave entrenched positions to be destroyed in open battle. Lee retired to the North Anna River and dug in. Grant did not attack the position directly but severed Confederate rail lines to the north and west of Lee before moving southeast again. Grant continued to move to his left in a daring and difficult tactical maneuver. Butler had meanwhile advanced up the peninsula toward Richmond, but General

P. G. T. Beauregard outmaneuvered him in May and bottled up Butler's men at Bermuda Hundred between the James and Appomattox Rivers. Eventually Butler and Banks, who did not take Mobile, were removed from command for their failure to carry out their assignments in the grand strategy.

Lee easily made his way into the Richmond defenses with his right flank on the Chickahominy and his center at Cold Harbor, the site of the Gaines' Mill action in 1862. The front extended for eight miles. A number of attacks on June 1 and 2 ended in Union repulses. However, on June 3 Grant thought he detected a weakness in the Confederate position and assaulted Lee's center at Cold Harbor. Though bravely executed, the attack was badly planned. The Confederates repulsed it with gory efficiency. In only a few short hours, Grant lost over 7,000 Union casualties; he later regretted that he had ever made the attempt. Cold Harbor climaxed a month of heavy fighting in which Grant's forces had 55,000 casualties against 32,000 for Lee. However, Grant was able to make good his losses within days of the battle, whereas Lee had no way to replace his.

After Cold Harbor, Grant executed a brilliant maneuver in the face of the enemy. He assembled all his corps on the north bank of the deep, wide James by June 14 and, stealing a march on Lee, sent them rapidly across a 2,100-foot pontoon bridge to the south bank. Once across, Grant began a move on lightly defended Petersburg. However, the maneuver came to nothing due to General Beauregard's stubborn defense of Confederate positions around Petersburg and General Butler's failure to prosecute a prompt supporting attack. The frustrated attacks slowed Grant enough to allow Lee to rush back and secure this vital city. Establishing a new and modern base depot at nearby City Point, complete with a rail line linking the depot with the front lines, Grant on June 18 undertook siege operations at Petersburg below Richmond, an effort that continued into the next year.

After forty-four days of continuous maneuver and fighting, Grant had finally fixed Lee in a condition of position warfare. This was now a war of trenches and sieges, conducted ironically enough by two masters of mobile warfare. Such warfare favored the side with the greater numbers and best logistics: the Union. Mortars were used extensively, and heavy siege guns were brought up on railway cars. Grant still sought to get around Lee's right and hold against Lee's left to prevent

THE CRATER

To breach the Confederate trenches at Petersburg, Union troops tunneled forward and placed a mine containing four tons of black powder under the opposite lines. An all-black infantry division trained for the assault; but the Army of the Potomac's General Meade, worried about political consequences if the black troops took heavy casualties, substituted an untrained white division the day before the mine was to blow. The first attack on July 30, 1864, went awry, and the black division had to enter the battle anyway; but by that time the Confederate defenders had recovered from initial shock and held their position around the thirty-foot-deep crater. Total Union casualties for the day were 3,798, nearly one-fifth of those engaged, for no gain.

him from shortening his line and achieving a higher degree of concentration. When Lee moved his lines to counter Grant, the two commanders were in effect maneuvering their fortifications to try and gain an advantage. However, Lee had earlier declared that he had to keep Grant from getting to the James River and fixing him in position. "If he gets there," he stated, "it will become a siege, and then it will be a mere question of time." Grant was now on the James, and the siege was firmly in place.

To help break the deadlock, Lee decided to ease the pressure with one of his perennial raids up the Shenandoah Valley toward Washington. In early July Confederate Maj. Gen. Jubal A. Early's corps advanced against Maj. Gen. David Hunter, who had replaced Sigel. Hunter, upon receiving confused orders from Halleck, retired north down the valley. When he reached the Potomac, he turned west into the safety of the Appalachians and uncovered Washington. Early saw his chance and drove through Maryland. Delayed by a Union force on July 9 near Frederick, he reached the northern outskirts of Washington on July 11 and skirmished briskly in the vicinity of Fort Stevens. President Lincoln and Quartermaster General Meigs were interested spectators. At City Point, Grant had calmly received the news of Early's raid. Using his interior waterway, he embarked the men of his VI Corps for the capital, where they landed on the eleventh. When Early realized he was engaging troops from the Army of the Potomac, he managed to escape the next day.

Grant decided that Early had eluded the Union's superior forces because they had not been under a single commander. He abolished four separate departments and formed them into one that embraced Washington, western Maryland, and the Shenandoah Valley. In August Sheridan was put in command with orders to follow Early to the death. Sheridan spent the remainder of the year in the valley, employing and coordinating his infantry, cavalry, and artillery in a manner that has won the admiration of military students ever since. He met and defeated Early at Winchester and Fisher's Hill in September and shattered him at Cedar Creek in October. To stop further raids and prevent Lee from feeding his army on the crops of that fertile region, Sheridan devastated the Shenandoah Valley.

Sherman's Great Wheel to the East

On March 17, 1864, Grant had met with Sherman at Nashville and told him his role in the grand strategy. Sherman, like Grant, held two commands. As Division of the Mississippi Commander, he was responsible for the operation and defense of a vast logistical system that reached from a communications zone at St. Louis, Louisville, and Cincinnati to center on a large base depot at Nashville. Strategically, Nashville on the Cumberland River rivaled Washington, D.C., in importance. A ninety-mile military railroad, built and operated by Union troops, gave Nashville access to steamboats plying the Tennessee River. Connected with Louisville by rail, Nashville became one vast storehouse and corral. If the city were destroyed, the Federal forces would have to fall back to the Ohio River line. Wearing his other hat, Sherman was a field commander with three armies under his direction.

With the promise of the return of his two crack divisions from the Red River expedition by May 1864 and with a splendid administrative system working behind him, Sherman was ready to leave Chattanooga in the direction of Atlanta. (*See Map 36.*) His mission was to destroy Johnston's armies and capture Atlanta, after Richmond the most important industrial center in the Confederacy. With 254 guns, Sherman matched his three small armies, and a separate cavalry command—a total force of more than 100,000 men—against Johnston's Army of Tennessee and Polk's Army of Mississippi, including Maj. Gen. Joseph Wheeler's cavalry, 65,000 men.

Sheridan's Ride
Buchanan T. Reed, n.d.

Sherman moved out on May 4, 1864, the same day the Army of the Potomac crossed the Rapidan. Johnston, realizing how seriously he was outnumbered, decided to go on the defensive, preserve his forces intact, hold Atlanta, and delay Sherman as long as possible. There was always the hope that the North would grow weary of the costly struggle and that some advocate of peaceful settlement might defeat President Lincoln in the election of 1864. From May 4 through mid-July the two forces maneuvered against each other. There were daily fights but few large-scale actions. As Sherman pushed south, Johnston would take up a strong position and force Sherman to halt, deploy, and reconnoiter. Sherman would then outflank Johnston, who in turn would retire to a new line and start the process all over again. On June 27 Sherman, unable to maneuver because the roads were muddy and seriously concerned by the unrest in his armies brought about by constant and apparently fruitless marching, decided to assault Johnston at Kenesaw Mountain. This attack against prepared positions, like the costly failure at Cold Harbor, was beaten back at the cost of 3,000 Union casualties. Sherman returned to maneuver and slowly but surely forced Johnston back to positions in front of Atlanta.

Johnston had done his part well. He had accomplished his missions and had so slowed Sherman that Sherman covered only 100 miles in seventy-four days. Johnston, his forces intact, was holding strong positions in front of Atlanta, his main base; but by this time President Jefferson Davis had grown impatient with Johnston and his tactics of cautious delay. In July he replaced him with Lt. Gen. John B. Hood, a much more impetuous commander.

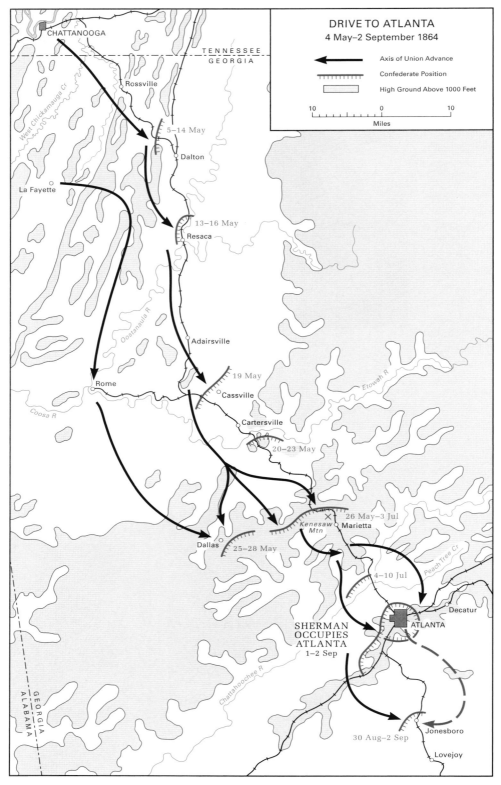

DRIVE TO ATLANTA
4 May–2 September 1864

Axis of Union Advance

Confederate Position

High Ground Above 1000 Feet

10   0   10
Miles

CHATTANOOGA

TENNESSEE
GEORGIA

Rossville

West Chickamauga Cr

5–14 May

Dalton

La Fayette

13–16 May

Resaca

Oostanaula R

Adairsville

Rome

19 May

Cassville

Etowah R

Coosa R

Cartersville

20–23 May

Kenesaw Mtn

26 May–3 Jul

Marietta

Dallas

25–28 May

4–10 Jul

Peach Tree Cr

Decatur

SHERMAN
OCCUPIES
ATLANTA
1–2 Sep

ATLANTA

Chattahoochee R

GEORGIA
ALABAMA

30 Aug–2 Sep

Jonesboro

Lovejoy

Map 36

On July 20, while Sherman was executing a wide turning movement around the northeast side of Atlanta, Hood left his fortifications and attacked at Peach Tree Creek. When Sherman beat him off, Hood pulled back into the city. While Sherman made ready to invest, Hood attacked again and failed again. Sherman then tried cavalry raids to cut the railroads, just as Johnston had during the advance from Chattanooga, but Sherman's raids had as little success as Johnston's. Sherman then began extending fortifications on August 31. Hood, who had dissipated his striking power in his assaults, gave up and retired to northwest Alabama. Sherman marched into Atlanta on the first two days of September, depriving the South of one of its key cities and railroad junctions. Sherman hoped that if Mobile could be taken, a shorter line for his supplies by way of Montgomery, Alabama, or still better by the lower Chattahoochee to Columbus, Georgia, would open. Tightening the noose still further, Admiral Farragut had entered Mobile Bay on August 5, 1864, with four Monitors and fourteen other ships but had no troops to take Mobile itself. Nevertheless, the capture of the harbor left the South with only one major port: Wilmington, North Carolina.

The fall of Atlanta gave President Lincoln's campaign for reelection in 1864 a tremendous boost. In addition, the psychological lift given the Union by Admiral Farragut's personal heroism in the battle of Mobile Bay greatly added to Lincoln's prestige.

Atlanta was only a halfway point in Sherman's vast wheel from the Western Theater toward the rear of Lee's Army of Northern Virginia. Abandoning the idea of catching up with Hood, Sherman by telegraph outlined his next strategic move to Lincoln and Grant in early September 1864. Sherman's two proposals proved him an able strategist as well as a consummately bold and aggressive commander. To defend Nashville, he suggested that he send two corps, 30,000 men, back to Maj. Gen. George H. Thomas. That commander would raise and train more men and be in position to hold Tennessee if Hood came north. To carry the offensive against the economic heart of the Confederacy, Sherman recommended that he himself take four corps (62,000 men), cut his own communications, live off the country, and march to the seacoast through Georgia, devastating and laying waste all farms, railways, and storehouses in his path. Whether he arrived at Pensacola, Charleston, or Savannah, Sherman reasoned he could hold a port, make

ATLANTA TO THE SEA AND INTO THE CAROLINAS

General Sherman led an army of 62,000 men on a massive raid through Georgia and South Carolina in late 1864 and early 1865. More than 90 percent of his enlisted force were combat veterans committed to victory, even if it meant war against noncombatants. Avoiding long, vulnerable logistics lines, Sherman's troops moved fast by living off the land. Destroying Southern morale and crops shortened the war. At times cutting a 250-mile-wide path, the Union army decimated parts of Georgia and then created even more havoc in South Carolina, the heart of secession. It was an epic march that helped to break the back of the rebellion.

contact with the U.S. Navy, and be refitted by Stanton and Meigs. Meigs promised to do the logistical job; and Lincoln and Grant, though their reaction to the plan was less than enthusiastic, accepted it in a show of confidence in Sherman.

Before marching out of Atlanta, Sherman's engineers put the torch to selected buildings and destroyed all railroads in the vicinity. On November 12, moving away from the Nashville depots toward Savannah, the Division of the Mississippi troops broke telegraphic contact with Grant. They had twenty days' emergency rations in their wagons but planned to replenish them by living off the country. Operating on a sixty-mile-wide front unimpeded by any Confederate force, Sherman's army systematically burned or destroyed what it did not need. The march became something of a rowdy excursion, but the destruction of private homes and towns has perhaps been exaggerated by popular myth. Sherman concentrated on destroying Confederate warehouses, depots, railroad lines, and other elements that assisted the Confederate war effort. His thrust deep into the Confederacy also liberated thousands of slaves, many of whom followed the Army in its march to the sea. Sherman's campaign, like Sheridan's in the Shenandoah, anticipated the economic warfare and strategic aerial bombardments of the twentieth century.

On December 10 Sherman, having broken the classic pattern by moving away from his logistical base, arrived in front of Savannah. Confederate forces evacuated the seaport on December 21, and Sherman offered it to the nation as a Christmas present. Awaiting him offshore was Meigs' floating seatrain, which enabled him to execute the last phase of Grant's strategy: a thrust north toward the line of the James River.

Thomas Protects the Nashville Base

Sherman, as the Western Theater commander, did not learn of Nashville's fate until he reached Savannah. He had planned Nashville's defense well enough by sending his IV and XXII Corps under Maj. Gen. John M. Schofield to screen Hood's northward move from Florence, Alabama. Schofield was to allow Thomas some time to assemble 50,000 men and strengthen Nashville. The aggressive Hood with his 30,000 men had lost a golden opportunity to trap Schofield at Spring Hill, Tennessee, on November 29, 1864. Unopposed, the Union troops made a night march across Hood's front to escape capture. Bitterly disappointed, Hood overtook Schofield the next day at Franklin.

At this point Hood could have upset Grant's timetable. Booty at Nashville might carry Hood to the Ohio or allow him to concentrate with Lee before Richmond. But Franklin turned into one of the Confederacy's most tragic battles. It commenced about 3:30 P.M. on November 30 and ended at dusk as Hood threw 18,000 of his veterans against a solidly entrenched force of Federals. Like Pickett's Charge at Gettysburg, Hood's frontal assault gained nothing. He lost over 6,000 men, about 15 percent of his total Army, including thirteen general officers. At nightfall Schofield brought his troops in behind Thomas' defenses at Nashville.

Hood was in a precarious position. He had been far weaker than Thomas to begin with; the battle of Franklin had further depleted

Reveille on a Winter Morning, *Henry Bacon, ca. 1868*

his army; and, even worse, his men had lost confidence in their commander. The Federals in Nashville were securely emplaced in a fortified
city that they had been occupying for three years. Hood could do little
more than encamp on high ground a few miles south of Nashville and
wait. He could not storm the city; his force was too small to lay siege;
to sidestep and go north was an open invitation to Thomas to attack
his flank and rear; and to retreat meant disintegration of his army. He
could only watch Thomas' moves.

Thomas, the Rock of Chickamauga, belonged to the "last boot-
lace" school of soldiering; he wanted every detail of supplies in place
before beginning any offensive operation. In comparison with Grant
and Sherman, he was slow; but he was also thorough. He had gathered and trained men and horses and was prepared to attack Hood
on December 10, but an ice storm the day before made movement
impossible. Grant and his superiors in Washington fretted at the delay,
and the General in Chief actually started west to remove Thomas. But
on December 15 Thomas struck like a sledgehammer in an attack that
militarily students have regarded as virtually faultless.

Thomas' tactical plan was a masterly, coordinated attack. His heavily weighted main effort drove against Hood's left flank while a secondary attack aimed simultaneously at Hood's right. Thomas provided an
adequate reserve and used cavalry to screen his flank and extend the

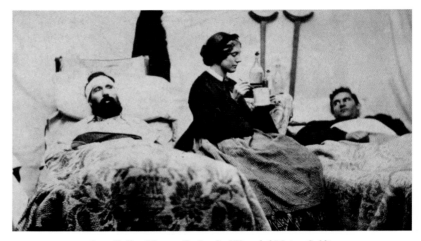

Anne Bell, a Nurse, Caring for Wounded Union Soldiers

envelopment of the enemy left. Hood, on the other hand, was over-extended; and his thin line was concave to the enemy, denying him the advantage of interior lines. Hood's reserve was inadequate, and his cavalry was absent on a minor mission.

The two-day battle proceeded according to Thomas' plan as the Federals fixed Hood's right while slashing savagely around the Confederate left flank. They broke Hood's first line on December 15, forcing the Southerners to retire to a new line two miles to the rear. The Federals repeated their maneuver on the sixteenth, and by nightfall the three-sided battle had disintegrated into a rout of Hood's army. Broken and defeated, it streamed southward, protected from hotly pursuing Union cavalry only by the intrepid rear-guard action of Maj. Gen. Nathan B. Forrest's horsemen. The shattered Army of Tennessee reached Tupelo, Mississippi, on January 10, 1865, but no longer existed as an effective fighting force. Hood was relieved of command, and his scattered units were assigned to other areas of combat. The decisive battle of Nashville had eliminated one of the two great armies of the Confederacy from a shrinking chessboard.

Lee's Last 100 Days

President Lincoln was delighted with Savannah as a Christmas present: In his congratulatory letter to Sherman and Grant, the Commander in Chief said that he would leave the final phases of the war to his two leading professional soldiers. Accordingly, from City Point, on December 27, 1864, Grant directed Sherman to march overland toward Richmond. At 3:00 P.M. on December 31, Sherman agreed to execute this last phase of Grant's continental sweep. In the final 100 days of the war, the two generals would clearly demonstrate the art of making the principles of warfare come alive and would prove that each principle was something more than a platitude. The commanders had a common objective: Grant and Meade would continue to hammer Lee. Sherman was to execute a devastating invasion northward through the Carolinas toward a juncture with Meade's Army of the Potomac, then on the line of the James River. Their strategy was simple. It called for the massing of strength and exemplified an economy of force. It would place Lee in an untenable position, cutting him off from all other Confederate commanders and trapping him between two Union armies. Surprise would be achieved by reuniting all of Sherman's original corps when Schofield, moving from central Tennessee by rail, river, and ocean transport, arrived at the Carolina capes. Solidly based on a centralized logistical system with protected Atlantic supply ships at their side, Grant and Sherman were ready to end Lee's stay in Richmond.

Robert E. Lee, the master tactician, divining his end, wrote to Davis that the Confederates would have to concentrate their forces for a last-ditch stand. In February 1865 the Confederate Congress conferred supreme command of all Confederate armies on Lee, an empty honor. Lee could no longer control events. Sherman moved through Columbia, South Carolina, in a destructive campaign much harsher than that visited on Georgia. Even the Union troops felt that South Carolina had started the war and should be punished for it. In February, Sherman took Wilmington, North Carolina, the Confederacy's last available port, and then pushed on. Johnston, newly reappointed to a command, had the mission of stopping Sherman's forces but could not. He interposed his small army of about 21,000 effectives in the path of two of Sherman's corps at Bentonville, North Carolina, on March 19. His initial attack gained some ground, but by the next day more of Sherman's forces were on the scene and Johnston had to continue his retreat. There would be no further major attempts to stop Sherman.

At Richmond and Petersburg toward the end of March, Grant renewed his efforts along a 38-mile front to get at Lee's right (west) flank. By now Sheridan's cavalry and the VI Corps had returned from the Shenandoah Valley, and the total force immediately under Grant numbered 101,000 infantry, 14,700 cavalry, and 9,000 artillery. Lee had 46,000 infantry, 6,000 cavalry, and 5,000 artillery.

On March 29 Grant began his move to the left. Sheridan and the cavalry pushed out ahead by way of Dinwiddie Court House in order to strike at Burke's Station, the intersection of the Southside and Danville Railroads, while Grant's main body moved to envelop Lee's right. But Lee, alerted to the threat, moved west. Lt. Gen. Ambrose P. Hill, who never stood on the defense if there was a chance to attack, took his corps out of its trenches and assaulted the Union left in the swampy forests around White Oak Road. He pushed Maj. Gen. Gouveneur K. Warren's V Corps back at first, but Warren counterattacked and by March 31 had driven Hill back to his trenches. On that day Sheridan advanced toward Five Forks, a road junction southwest of Petersburg, and there encountered a strong Confederate force—cavalry plus two infantry divisions under Maj. Gen. George E. Pickett—which Lee had dispatched to forestall Sheridan. Pickett attacked and drove Sheridan back to Dinwiddie Court House, but there Sheridan dug in and halted him. Pickett then entrenched at Five Forks instead of pulling back to make contact with Hill, whose failure to destroy Warren had left a gap between him and Pickett, with Warren's corps in between. Sheridan, still formally the commander of the Army of the Shenandoah, had authority from Grant to take control of any nearby infantry corps of the Army of the Potomac. He wanted Warren to fall upon Pickett's

ULYSSES S. GRANT (1822–1885)

Born Hiram Ulysses Grant and nicknamed Sam Grant during his early military experience in Mexico after graduation from West Point in 1843, Ulysses S. Grant bounced back from setbacks all of his life. His heavy drinking prompted his resignation from the Army in 1854 to avoid court-martial. He failed in a number of civilian jobs and was able to regain a commission in 1861 as a colonel of a volunteer regiment from Illinois only with the help of a local Congressman. He suffered military reversals at Belmont, Missouri, in 1861 and was caught by surprise at Shiloh the following year. Yet he also gained fame for his capture of Forts Henry and Donelson and his great victories at Vicksburg, Chattanooga, and over Robert E. Lee in a masterful campaign that in effect won the war. His memoirs, which he wrote as he lay dying to provide money for his nearly destitute family, are a masterpiece and show him as a caring, thoughtful, and simple man who was also a determined military commander. He is one of America's greatest generals.

exposed rear and destroy him, but Warren moved too slowly and Pickett consolidated his position. On April 1 Sheridan attacked again but failed to destroy Pickett because Warren had moved his corps too slowly and put most of it in the wrong place. Late in the afternoon, however, the Union attack struck Pickett's position in full force on both flanks. His position outflanked, Pickett ordered a retreat, but not quickly enough to avoid losing almost half his force of 10,000 as prisoners.

Grant renewed his attack against Lee's right on April 2. The assault broke the Confederate line and forced it back northward. The Federals took the line of the Southside Railroad, and the Confederates withdrew toward Petersburg. Lee then pulled Longstreet's corps away from the shambles of Richmond to hold the line, and in this day's action General Hill was killed. With his forces stretched thin, Lee had to abandon Richmond and the Petersburg fortifications. He struck out and raced west toward the Danville Railroad, hoping to get to Lynchburg or Danville, break loose, and eventually join forces with Johnston. But Grant had Lee in the open at last. He pursued relentlessly and speedily, with troops behind (east of) Lee and south of him on his left flank, while Sheridan dashed ahead with the cavalry to head Lee off. A running fight ensued from April 2 through 6. Lt. Gen. Richard S. Ewell's corps was surrounded and captured at Sayler's Creek. Lee's rations ran out; his men began deserting and straggling. Finally, Sheridan galloped his men to Appomattox Court House, squarely athwart Lee's line of retreat.

Lee resolved that he could accomplish nothing more by fighting. He met Grant at the McLean House in Appomattox on April 9, 1865. The handsome, well-tailored Lee, the very epitome of Southern chivalry, asked Grant for terms. Reserving all political questions for his own decision, Lincoln had authorized Grant to treat only on purely military matters. Grant, though less impressive in his bearing than Lee, was equally chivalrous. He accepted Lee's surrender, allowed 28,356 paroled

ROBERT E. LEE (1807–1870)

Four years after refusing the field command of the Union Army because he could not draw his sword against his native state of Virginia, Lee surrendered at Appomattox and, ironically, began his ascent to the status of perhaps the most admired figure in American military history. A modest, Christian gentleman, he was also a combative, bold, and skillful Napoleonic tactician who repeatedly turned back larger Federal forces in their efforts to capture the Confederate capital, Richmond. To Southerners, and indeed many Northerners, he remains the legendary symbol of the "Lost Cause," defeated in the end only by superior numbers and resources.

Confederates to keep their horses and mules, furnished rations to the Army of Northern Virginia, and forbade the soldiers of the Army of the Potomac to cheer or fire salutes to celebrate the victory over their old antagonists. Johnston surrendered to Sherman on April 26. The last major trans-Mississippi force gave up the struggle on May 26, and the grim fighting was over.

Dimensions of the War

Viewing the war in its broadest context, a historian could fairly conclude that a determined general of the North had bested a legendary general of the South, probably the most brilliant tactician on either side, because the Union could bring to bear a decisive superiority in economic resources and manpower. Lee's mastery of the art of warfare staved off defeat for four long years, but the outcome was never really in doubt. Grant and Lincoln held too many high cards; and during the last year of the war, the relations between the Union's Commander in Chief and his General in Chief set an unexcelled example of civil-military coordination. This coordination was essential to prosecuting a multitheater war characterized by the slow, yet steady expansion of the area brought back under Federal control over the course of four years of struggle. (*See Map 37.*)

In this costly war, the Union Army lost 138,154 men killed in battle. This figure seems large, but it is only slightly more than half the number (221,374) who died of other causes, principally disease, bringing the total Union dead to 359,528. Men wounded in action numbered 280,040. Figures for the Confederacy are incomplete, but at least 94,000 were killed in battle, 70,000 died of other causes, and an estimated 30,000 died in Northern prisons.

With the advent of conscription, mass armies, and long casualty lists, the individual soldier seemed destined to lose his identity and dignity. These were the days before regulation serial numbers and dog tags (although some soldiers made individual tags from coins or scraps of paper). But by the third year of the war various innovations had been introduced to enhance the soldier's lot. Union forces were wearing corps

ANDERSONVILLE AND ELMIRA PRISON CAMPS

Andersonville Prison in southern Georgia and Elmira Prison in south-central New York State became notorious during the final year of the Civil War for their deplorable living conditions and the high mortality rate of their inmates. Both camps suffered from severe overcrowding, rampant disease, and a lack of building supplies and food, the result mostly of wartime shortages and mismanagement rather than of deliberate malice (although in Andersonville there was evidence of the latter). Of the 45,613 Union prisoners held at Andersonville nearly 13,000 died; while at Elmira, nearly 3,000 of the 12,000 Confederates kept there perished. For his role the warden at Andersonville, Capt. Henry Wirz, was hanged in November 1865.

badges that heightened unit identification, esprit de corps, and pride in organization. The year 1863 saw the first award of the highest U.S. decoration, the Medal of Honor. Congress had authorized it on July 12, 1862, and in 1863 Secretary Stanton gave the first medals to Pvt. Jacob Parrott and five other soldiers. They had demonstrated extraordinary valor in a daring raid behind the Confederate lines near Chattanooga. The Medal of Honor remains the highest honor the United States can bestow on any individual in the armed services.

Throughout the western world, the nineteenth century, with its many humanitarian movements, evidenced a general improvement in the treatment of the individual soldier; and the U.S. soldier was no exception. The more severe forms of corporal punishment were abolished in the U.S. Army in 1861. Although Civil War medical science was primitive in comparison with that of today, an effort was made to extend medical services in the Army beyond the mere treatment of battle wounds. As an auxiliary to the regular medical service, the volunteer U.S. Sanitary Commission fitted out hospital ships and hospital units; provided male and, for the first time in the U.S. Army, female nurses; and furnished clothing and foods fancier than the regular rations. Similarly, the U.S. Christian Commission augmented the efforts of the regimental chaplains and even provided, besides songbooks and Bibles, some coffee bars and reading rooms.

The Civil War forced changes in the traditional policies governing the burial of soldiers. On July 17, 1862, Congress authorized the President to establish national cemeteries "for the soldiers who shall die in the service of the country." While little was done during the war to implement this Congressional action, several battlefield cemeteries (Antietam, Gettysburg, Chattanooga, Stones River, and Knoxville) were set up "as a final resting place for those who here gave their lives" in lieu of some nameless corner of a forgotten field.

The great conflict had also forced changes in ideas about the obligation of citizens to perform military service. Attrition in manpower had forced both South and North to turn to conscription to keep their armies up to effective strength. The Confederate government had enacted a draft law as early as April 1862. Late in that year Union governors were no longer able to raise enough troops for the Federal armies; and on March 3, 1863, Congress passed the Enrollment Act, an outright assertion of national conscription by the central government.

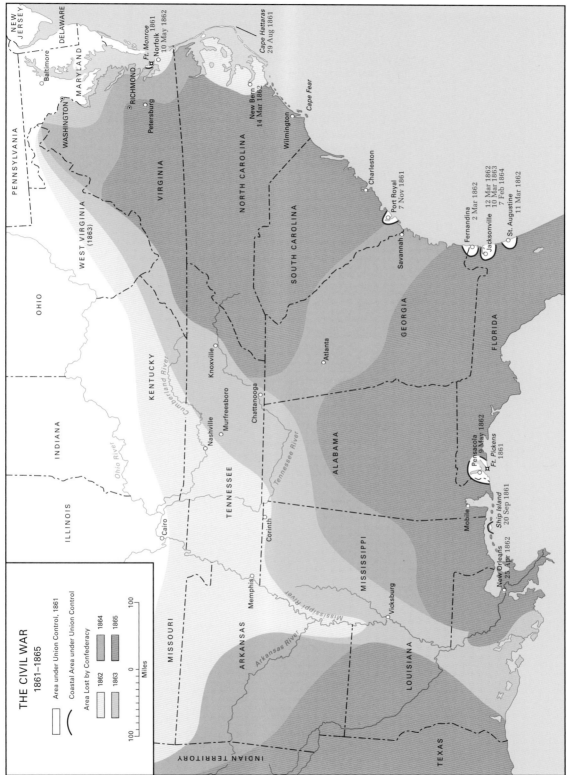

THE CIVIL WAR
1861–1865

Area under Union Control, 1861

Coastal Area under Union Control

Area Lost by Confederacy

1862 1864
1863 1865

Miles
100   0   100

NEW JERSEY

DELAWARE

Baltimore

MARYLAND

WASHINGTON

PENNSYLVANIA

OHIO

INDIANA

ILLINOIS

WEST VIRGINIA (1863)

Ft. Monroe 1861
Norfolk 10 May 1862

RICHMOND
Petersburg

VIRGINIA

Cape Hatteras 29 Aug 1861

NORTH CAROLINA

New Bern 14 Mar 1862

Wilmington

Cape Fear

Charleston

SOUTH CAROLINA

Port Royal 7 Nov 1861

Savannah

GEORGIA

Fernandina 2 Mar 1862
Jacksonville 12 Mar 1862 10 Mar 1863 7 Feb 1864
St. Augustine 11 Mar 1862

FLORIDA

KENTUCKY

Cumberland River

Ohio River

Knoxville

Nashville
Murfreesboro

Chattanooga

TENNESSEE

Tennessee River

Atlanta

ALABAMA

Pensacola 9 May 1862
Ft. Pickens 1861

Cairo

Corinth

Mobile

Ship Island 20 Sep 1861

Memphis

MISSISSIPPI

Vicksburg

Mississippi River

New Orleans 25 Apr 1862

MISSOURI

ARKANSAS

Arkansas River

LOUISIANA

INDIAN TERRITORY

TEXAS

Map 37

This law made able-bodied males between twenty and forty-five years of age liable for national military service. The Enrollment Act was not popular, as bloody draft riots in New York demonstrated after Gettysburg. Both the Confederate and the U.S. laws were undemocratic: they did not apply equally to all individuals. They provided for exemptions that allowed many to escape military service entirely. Comparatively few men were ever drafted into the Federal service, but by stimulating men to volunteer the Enrollment Act had its desired effect.

The principal importance of the Enrollment Act of 1863, however, does not lie in the effect it had on manpower procurement for the Civil War. This measure established firmly the principle that every citizen is obligated to defend the nation and that the Federal government can impose that obligation directly on the citizen without the mediation of the states. In addition, the act recognized that the previous system of total reliance on militia and volunteers would not suffice in a modern, total war.

As the western world's largest and longest conflict of the nineteenth century except the Napoleonic wars, the American Civil War has been argued about and analyzed since the fighting stopped. It continues to excite the imagination because it was full of paradox. Old-fashioned in that infantry attacked in the open in dense formations, it also foreshadowed modern total war. Though not all the ingredients were new, railroads, telegraph communications, steamships, balloons, armor plate, rifled weapons, wire entanglements, the submarine, large-scale photography, and torpedoes—all products of the burgeoning industrial revolution—gave new and awesome dimensions to armed conflict. It was also America's deadliest war and greatest national struggle to define what we were as a nation. The final determination was clear. America could not have endured "half-slave and half-free." With the curse of slavery lifted and the long struggle of many of our nation's newest citizens for their full civil rights just under way, the American Army turned to other unpleasant tasks: the occupation of the defeated Southern states and the long campaign to "settle" the Indian problem on the frontier.

DISCUSSION QUESTIONS

1. By 1864, what strategic options remained for the Confederacy?

2. Compare Grant's 1864 campaign with Scott's Anaconda Plan of 1861. What are the similarities and differences?

3. Was Sherman's and Sheridan's destruction of crops, warehouses and factories necessary? Why or why not? What was an alternative Union strategy to compel Southern submission?

4. To what degree did the very principle the Confederates claimed they were fighting for ("states rights") undermine their war effort?

5. Grant and Lee can be considered two of the greatest generals in American history. What were their strengths and weaknesses?

6. Thesis: The American Civil War was the first modern war. Why is this true? Why is this false?

Recommended Readings

Castel, Albert. *Decision in the West: The Atlanta Campaign of 1864*. Lawrence: University of Kansas Press, 1992.

Catton, Bruce. *A Stillness at Appomattox*. Austin, Tex.: Holt, Rinehart and Winston, 2000.

Cooling, B. Franklin. *Jubal Early's Raid on Washington, 1864*. Baltimore: Nautical and Aviation Publishing, 1989.

Glatthaar, Joseph T. *The March to the Sea and Beyond: Sherman's Troops in the Savannah and Carolinas Campaigns*. New York: New York University Press, 1985.

Grimsley, Mark. *And Keep Moving On: The Virginia Campaign, May–June 1864*. Lincoln: University of Nebraska Press, 2002.

McPherson, James M. *The Battle Cry of Freedom*. New York: Oxford University Press, 2003.

Scott, Robert G. *Into the Wilderness with the Army of the Potomac,* rev. ed. Bloomington: Indiana University Press, 1992.

Sommers, Richard J. *Richmond Redeemed: The Siege at Petersburg*. Garden City, N.Y.: Doubleday and Company, 1981.

Other Readings

Beringer, Richard E., et al. *Why the South Lost the Civil War*. Athens: University of Georgia Press, 1986.

Donald, David H., et al. *Why the North Won the Civil War*. New York: Simon and Schuster, 1996.

Hagerman, Edward. *The American Civil War and the Origins of Modern Warfare: Ideas, Organization and Field Command*. Bloomington: Indiana University Press, 1988.

Jones, Archer. *Civil War Command and Strategy: The Process of Victory and Defeat*. New York: Free Press, 1992.

Linderman, Gerald E. *Embattled Courage: The Experience of Combat in the American Civil War*. New York: Free Press, 1987.

Tidwell, William A. *April '65: Confeoderate Covert Action in the American Civil War*. Kent, Ohio: Kent State University Press, 1995.

13

DARKNESS AND LIGHT
THE INTERWAR YEARS
1865–1898

With the end of the Civil War, the great volunteer army enlisted for that struggle was quickly demobilized and the U.S. Army became once again a small regular organization. During the ensuing period the Army faced a variety of problems, some old and some new. These included, besides demobilization, occupation duty in the South, a French threat in Mexico, domestic disturbances, Indian troubles, and, within the Army itself, the old awkward relationship between the line and the staff departments. Despite a relative isolation from civilian society during the period 1865–1898, the Army developed professionally, experimented with new equipment of various kinds, and took halting steps toward utilizing the period's new technology in weapons. In a period of professional introspection and physical isolation, the Army still contributed to the nation's civil progress.

Demobilization, Reorganization, and the French Threat in Mexico

The military might of the Union was put on display late in May 1865, when Meade's and Sherman's armies participated in a grand review in Washington with Sherman's army alone taking six and one-half hours to pass the reviewing stand on Pennsylvania Avenue. It was a spectacle well calculated to impress on Confederate and foreign leaders alike that only a strong government could field such a powerful force. But even as these troops were preparing for their victory march, the War Department sent Sheridan to command an aggregate force of 80,000 men in the territory west of the Mississippi and south of the Arkansas, of which he put 52,000 in Texas. There Sheridan's men put muscle behind previous diplomatic protests against the presence of French troops in Mexico. The French had entered that country several years earlier ostensibly to collect debts, but since 1864 had maintained their puppet Maximilian on a Mexican throne in the face of opposition from Mexican patriot forces under Benito Juarez. While the American Civil War lasted, the United States had been unable to do more than protest this situation, for even diplomacy if too vigorous might have pushed France into an alliance with the South. Now stronger measures seemed necessary.

The military might in being in May 1865 was ephemeral, for the volunteers wanted to go home and Congress wanted to decrease the size of the Army. Because of the needs of occupation in the South and the French threat in Mexico, demobilization was spread over a period of eighteen months instead of the three in which it could have been accomplished. Nevertheless, it was rapid. On May 1, 1865, there were 1,034,064 volunteers in the Army, but by the middle of November, over 800,000 of them had been paid, mustered out, and transported to their home states by the Quartermaster Corps. A year later there were only 11,043 volunteers left in the service, most of whom were U.S. Colored Troops. These were almost all mustered out by late October 1867.

Lt. Gen. Ulysses S. Grant, the General in Chief, wanted to increase the Regular Army, kept small during the Civil War, to 80,000 men, but neither Secretary of War Edwin M. Stanton nor Congress would agree. Congress, on July 28, 1866, voted an establishment of 54,302 officers and enlisted men. Actual strength reached about 57,000 on September 30, 1867, a peak until 1898. In 1869 Congress cut the number of infantry regiments to 25 and the authorized strength to 45,000. In 1876 the regimental tables of organization were reduced to limit the total authorized force to 27,442, an authorization that remained virtually stationary until the Spanish-American War. A significant effect of the Civil War on the new organization of the Army was a provision in the 1866 act for four African American infantry regiments, reduced to two in 1869, and two African American cavalry regiments, though most of their officers would be white. In 1877 Henry O. Flipper of Thomasville, Georgia, became the first African American graduate of West Point and was assigned to one of these regiments, the 10th Cavalry. The infantry regiments were the 24th and 25th Infantries, and the other Cavalry regiment was the 9th Cavalry. During the long campaigns in the West these four regiments gained a certain measure of fame as tough and disciplined units.

Henry O. Flipper

Demobilization was not so rapid that Napoleon III was unaware of the strength of U.S. forces. In the spring of 1867 he finally withdrew his troops from Mexico and left Maximilian to die before a juarista firing squad. While there were other factors that help explain the French emperor's action and historians are not agreed on his motives, he could not have ignored the determination to enforce the Monroe Doctrine embodied in Sheridan's show of force, especially since Maj. Gen. John M. Schofield was then on a special mission in France to make this point clear.

Reconstruction

The Civil War settled once and for all the questions of slavery and of state sovereignty, but after Appomattox the problems of recon-

THE ARMY AND THE FREEDMEN'S BUREAU

Congress established the Bureau of Refugees, Freedmen, and Abandoned Lands in March 1865 to handle problems that had already arisen in Union-occupied parts of the South and were sure to persist after the Confederate surrender—especially that of convincing white southerners that slavery was in fact abolished. The Freedmen's Bureau, as it soon became known, was an agency within the Department of War but not a part of the U.S. Army, although its administrators and field agents were commissioned officers of the volunteers and the regulars. Across the rural South, Freedmen's Bureau agents spent most of their working hours adjudicating differences between landless black farmers and white landowners. The bureau also ran schools funded largely by private benevolent organizations and helped veterans of the U.S. Colored Troops file claims for bounties and pensions. Unfortunately, readmission of seceded states seemed more important to the nation than securing the rights of former slaves, and the Freedmen's Bureau never realized its full potential.

struction remained and with them the Army's involvement in Southern affairs. The nation had to be put back together, and the peace had to be won or the sacrifices of a terrible war would have been in vain. The Army had a principal role in reconstruction from the very beginning. As the Union armies advanced in the South, the civil government collapsed, except in Sherman's military district, and the Army found itself acting in place of the civil government by extending the function of its provost marshals from policing troops to policing and in effect governing the occupied areas. The duties of these provost marshals ranged from establishing garbage regulations to trying to determine the loyalty of Southern citizens. Near the end of the war, Congress created the Bureau of Refugees, Freedmen, and Abandoned Lands—the Freedmen's Bureau—and put it under the Army. Its primary purpose was to protect and help the former slaves. In late 1865 most of the governmental functions of the provost marshals were transferred to this bureau headed by Maj. Gen. Oliver O. Howard, a Civil War corps commander and a professional officer with antislavery convictions of long standing. As early as 1862 President Abraham Lincoln had appointed military governors, civilians functioning with military support, in Tennessee, Louisiana, and North Carolina.

After Lincoln's death, President Andrew Johnson went ahead with his own reconstruction plans. He declared the Civil War formally at an end in April 1866, liberally pardoned most former Confederates upon their taking a loyalty oath, and then permitted them to reestablish civil government. The leniency of this program, some historians now maintain, led the Army, under Grant, with Stanton in the War Department, to look to Congress rather than to the President, the Commander in Chief, for aid in protecting the Union forces in the South from harassment. Congress at the same time was in fundamental disagreement with the President's course. It therefore asserted its supremacy in a series of legislative acts, undoing all that President Johnson had done and placing the South under military control.

Congress set forth its basic plan in the Command of the Army Act (actually a part of the Army Appropriations Act of 1867) and the

Tenure of Office and the First Reconstruction Acts of March 1867. The first of these provided that all presidential orders to the Army should be issued through the General in Chief, whose headquarters would be in Washington and who could be removed only with Senate approval. Similarly, the Tenure of Office Act denied the President authority to remove Cabinet officers without approval of the Senate. The first of these acts sought to make Grant rather than the President supreme over the Army, while the Tenure of Office Act sought to keep Stanton in the War Department and the next year provided the principal basis for the impeachment of President Johnson when he suspended the Secretary from office without the Senate's consent.

The First Reconstruction Act divided the South into five military districts. The commanders of these districts were major generals who reported directly to Washington. This was an interesting command relationship, for it was customary to divide the country into geographical commands called divisions whose subordinate parts were called departments. In March 1867, however, there were only two divisions, the Missouri and the Pacific, with the rest of the country divided into the five military districts of the South and into departments that like the five districts reported directly to Washington. As time went by, the Army created additional geographical divisions; and in 1870 a Division of the South, comprising three territorial departments, administered military affairs in what had been the five reconstruction districts. There is a difference of opinion as to how much the First Reconstruction Act removed control of the reconstruction forces from President Johnson, although Grant advised Maj. Gen. Philip H. Sheridan, one of the district commanders, that these commanders, rather than the Executive in Washington, were the sole interpreters of the act. In July 1867 Congress incorporated this interpretation in the Third Reconstruction Act, which declared that "no district commander … shall be bound in his action by any opinion of any civil officer of the United States." As a consequence of the First and Third Reconstruction Acts, some historians regard the reconstruction forces as virtually a separate army under congressional control, thus distinguishing them from the forces in the territorial divisions and departments that remained clearly under the President.

Under the Reconstruction Acts the district commanders had to cope with such matters as horse stealing, moonshining, rioting, civil court proceedings, regulating commercial law, public education, fraud, removing public officials, registering voters, holding elections, and the approving of new state constitutions by registered voters. This occupation duty absorbed somewhat more than one-third of the Army's strength in 1867. As the Southern states were restored to the Union under the reconstruction governments, military rule came to an end and civil authorities assumed full control of state offices. This process was largely completed in 1870.

With the end of congressional reconstruction, the Army's direct supervision of civil affairs in the South came to an end and the number of troops on occupation duty, which already had fallen off markedly, was reduced further. Now its mission was to preserve the new state governments by continuing its protection of the African Americans and their white allies upon whom the governments rested, policing elections, helping to apprehend criminals, and keeping the peace in conflicts between rival state officials. The Ku Klux Klan, a postwar organization that had a considerable membership by 1870–1871, became an object of special concern to the Army, as it did to Congress, because of the Klan's terrorist tactics employed in an attempt to wrest the South from African American–Radical Republican control. Consequently, one of the most important Army functions in this period was support of federal marshals in an effort to suppress the Klan. This became an Army responsibility despite the restoration of state militia forces under the reconstruction governments as a means of relieving some of the burden on the regular troops, which were spread thin. Since many of these new militia forces consisted of African Americans, they were not very effective against white terrorists, who directed some of their acts against the militiamen themselves. These militia forces mainly performed general police duty and watched over elections and voting. Eventually, because of the opposition of white Southerners to African Americans in uniform, the African American militia forces were disbanded.

In April 1877, as a result of the compromise by which Rutherford B. Hayes became President after the disputed election of 1876, the last of the troops on reconstruction duty in the South were transferred to other duty and the federal military occupation of the South came to an end. The Army's role in the South in the years 1865–1877 was without precedent in the United States.

Domestic Disturbances

Aside from the Indian Wars and Sheridan's show of force on the Mexican border, the Army engaged in no conventional military operations of any consequence until the Spanish-American War, that is, for a period of over thirty years. There were, however, a number of domestic disturbances and incidents in which armed forces were used, not only in the South during the reconstruction period but elsewhere as well. Indeed, by 1878, when Congress forbade the use of federal troops without authorization by either "the Constitution or … Congress," there had been scores and perhaps hundreds of instances of their use by federal marshals in breaking strikes, enforcing local laws, collecting revenues, and arresting offenders.

In the summer of 1877 the Hayes administration used troops in the wave of railway strikes that marked the country's first great national labor dispute. These strikes spread to a dozen or more states and led to a number of requests for federal help. Thereupon, the Hayes administration pursued a policy of moving troops only to protect federal property or upon the request of a governor or federal judge. The Army stripped every post in Maj. Gen. Winfield Scott Hancock's Military Division of the Atlantic of its available men and also obtained troops from other posts. President Hayes also used some marines. During the strikes the President had his own source of information in Signal Corps observer-sergeants who reported to Washington at intervals concerning conditions as they saw them at their local weather stations.

Under the circumstances of their use, federal troops came into only limited contact with mobs during the 1877 strikes. They nevertheless contributed greatly to the restoration of order, as Hancock reported, "by their presence alone." The positive results were not due to the size of

> Since many of these new militia forces consisted of African Americans, they were not very effective against white terrorists, who directed some of their acts against the militiamen themselves.

the forces, for with only about 24,000 troops in the entire Army in 1877 only a small detachment could be used at any one place. But these regular troops were well disciplined; taking their cue from the President himself, they acted with considerable restraint in putting down the strikes, neither losing a single soldier nor causing the death of many civilians.

Although the Army became involved in other strike duty in the succeeding years of the century, the best-known instance was in the Pullman, or railway, strike of 1894 that, though centered in Chicago, also affected other parts of the country. President Grover Cleveland's order to hastily send troops to Chicago against the wishes of Governor John P. Altgeld provided that they should execute the orders and processes of federal courts, prevent obstructions to the movement of the mails, and generally enforce U.S. laws. In fact, they put down the strike. Other governors also protested the use of federal troops in their states. Maj. Gen. Nelson A. Miles, who commanded the 2,000 federal troops in Chicago (and who had advised against using them in the strike), did not use his men effectively, perhaps at first because he broke them up into small detachments in support of policemen and marshals at scattered points. New orders, however, required him to concentrate his forces and authorized him to fire upon rioters after a proper warning. A small company of regular troops under his command did fire upon a mob in Hammond, Indiana, on July 8, 1894, when they were about to be overwhelmed by many times their own number. At least one rioter was killed and a dozen or more wounded in this action.

The violence was actually much less in 1894 than in 1877; but with only about 28,000 officers and enlisted men in the Army, Schofield, the Commanding General, reported that while his troops performed their duty "promptly and effectively," the situation taxed them "nearly to the limit." He might have added that at least in California both sailors and marines were used. The U.S. Supreme Court unanimously sustained President Cleveland's actions in Chicago during the 1894 strike, with the result that a legal precedent was set for using federal troops within a state without its consent.

The National Guard Movement

Despite the use of regular troops in notable instances, the organized militia under state control saw more strike duty than did the regulars in the years after the Civil War. The volunteer militia organizations that had existed since the colonial period became in effect the only real militia in existence in those years. The events of the seventies in particular led many to fear another insurrection, and as a result Congress introduced legislation to improve and to provide better arms for the organized militia. In 1879, in support of this effort, the National Guard Association came into being in St. Louis; between 1881 and 1892 every state revised its military code to provide for an organized militia. Most states, following the lead of New York, called their militia the National Guard. As such, it was by 1898 the principal reserve standing behind the Regular Army but remaining a state military force.

There was a certain martial enthusiasm in the 1870s and 1880s, despite the general antimilitarism of the period, which swelled the ranks of the Guard. Also, the Guard attracted some persons because it was

The volunteer militia organizations that had existed since the colonial period became in effect the only real militia in existence in those years.

a fraternal group that appealed to the manly virtues of physical fitness, duty, and discipline; it attracted many because it was a kind of social club whose members enjoyed a local prestige. Although organized by states, the Guard had roots in the new nationalism of the period, as may be seen in its very name. Despite this new interest in the Guard, and although the War Department supported the Guard's proposal for a new militia act, apathy, states' rights, and antimilitarism prevented Congress from enacting the desired legislation. Through the efforts of the National Guard Association, the Guard nevertheless succeeded in securing an act in 1887 that doubled the $200,000 annual federal grant for firearms that the militia had enjoyed since 1808.

Isolation and Professional Development

The industrial unrest of the 1870s and later was a manifestation of the growing industrialization and urbanization of the nation in the last decades of the nineteenth century; but while labor organizations grew as never before, they were of relatively little influence until much later. Meanwhile, perhaps partly as a reaction to the terrible experiences of the Civil War, the ideals and philosophy of what modern historian Samuel P. Huntington calls business pacifism became dominant. Among other things, business pacifism rejected things military as outmoded in an industrial world designed to produce and sell goods; and it made an impression upon both intellectuals and the popular mind. It manifested itself as either indifference or outright hostility to the Regular Army, affected military appropriations, and philosophically separated the Army from the people. In the late 1860s and the 1870s, as Army appropriations fell off (and in 1877 were not even made until November), the Army became isolated from the society at large. It became isolated not only socially, but physically as well, for much of the Army was on lonely duty in the West. Those years, according to Army historian William A. Ganoe, were "The Army's Dark Ages." They caused the Army and the Navy to look inward and to develop a truly military viewpoint that differed fundamentally from business pacifism and civilian liberal thought in general.

> Business pacifism . . . manifested itself as either indifference or outright hostility to the Regular Army, affected military appropriations, and philosophically separated the Army from the people.

Paradoxically, in Huntington's words, the post–Civil War years were actually "the most fertile, creative, and formative in the history of the American armed forces." It took such a period of peace to develop the professionalism that would find employment in the world wars of the next century. In the Army, this professionalism took shape largely under the impetus of two men, General William T. Sherman and Col. Emory Upton, with the help of other reformers of lesser rank. Their contemporary, Rear Adm. Stephen B. Luce, was similarly the architect of a new professionalism in the U.S. Navy.

Sherman's fame of course rests upon his record in the Civil War, but he was also the Commanding General of the Army for almost fifteen years from 1869, when he succeeded Grant, to 1883, when Sheridan succeeded him—a record second only to that of Winfield Scott. Unlike Grant and two of the other five Commanding Generals before him, Sherman remained out of politics and thus began the tradition of political neutrality, which would be adhered to long after his time, although not religiously. In this and other ways he oriented the thought

EMORY UPTON (1839–1881)

Emory Upton, West Point Class of 1861, emerged from the Civil War with a reputation for tactical innovation that he cemented with the 1867 publication of A New System of Infantry Tactics. Adopted by the Army, Upton's system recognized the impact of breechloading rifles and other new technologies. He promoted reforms based on the Prussian military system and ideas such as the compulsory retirement of officers, advanced military schools, and examination for promotion. Secretary of War Elihu Root would arrange for the publication of The Military Policy of the United States, Upton's unfinished manifesto, as the basis for his own reform agenda. Upton sowed the seeds for a federal reserve force and an expansible army built upon a professional core. Some later interpreters would skew his work to fit their own purposes. Some of these interpretations would exacerbate the natural tensions between that professional core and the volunteer, citizen-soldiers who must under wartime circumstances provide the bulk of the manpower for the Army.

of the professional soldier. As Commanding General he became the architect for a system of postgraduate schools beyond the Military Academy through which an officer could learn the skills of his own branch of the service and finally the principles of higher command.

Emory Upton, a protégé of Sherman's, was the most influential of the younger officers who worked to reform the Army. He graduated from West Point in 1861 and was brevetted a major general during the Civil War. After the war he prepared a new system of infantry tactics; served as commandant of cadets at the Military Academy, 1870–1875; went on a mission to study the armies of Asia and Europe, which left him especially impressed by the German military system; and then became superintendent of theoretical instruction in the Artillery School at Fort Monroe. His best-known writings, *The Armies of Asia and Europe* (1878) and *The Military Policy of the United States* (1904), argued for numerous reforms. The second of these two books was unfinished at the time of his death by suicide in 1881 but was put in order by an associate and, circulating in the Army, became influential long before its publication. It presented a case for a strong regular military force based upon U.S. experience and subsequently provided the Regular Army with intellectual ammunition for shooting down the arguments of militia advocates for whom John A. Logan provided a text in his posthumously published *Volunteer Soldier of America* (1887). In Upton's view, a wartime army should consist entirely of regular formations, which meant that all volunteers should serve under regular officers. Upton borrowed this plan for an expansible Regular Army from John C. Calhoun. Without giving due weight to the strength of tradition, he wanted the United

States to abandon its traditional dual military system and replace it with a thoroughgoing professional army on the German model.

The Military Academy at West Point was at the base of the pyramidal structure of the Army educational system. Unfortunately, much of the vitality went out of the instruction at West Point after 1871 with the departure of Dennis Hart Mahan, the intellectual godfather of the postwar reformers. Although the War Department removed West Point from control of the Corps of Engineers in 1866, the Academy continued to provide heavily mathematical training and to turn out military technicians but at the same time lost its former eminence as an engineering school. As time went by, the technical content of the curriculum in both the Military Academy and the Naval Academy was reduced; but by 1900 the effort to combine basic military and liberal arts subjects set both institutions off from other collegiate institutions and from the mainstream of education in the United States.

The period of reduced emphasis on technical instruction at the Military Academy saw the rise of the special postgraduate technical schools that Sherman favored. When the Engineers lost their responsibility for West Point in 1866, a group of engineer officers founded the Essayons Club, which became the Engineer School of Application in 1885. In 1868 Grant revived Calhoun's Artillery School at Fort Monroe, Virginia, which had been closed since 1860. Also in 1868 a signal school of instruction opened at Fort Greble, D.C., and in 1869 moved to Fort Whipple (later Fort Myer), Virginia, where it continued until 1885. In 1881 Sherman founded the School of Application for Infantry and Cavalry at Fort Leavenworth, Kansas. Although at its beginning this school was little different from any of the other branch schools, it eventually fulfilled Sherman's hopes and evolved, with much of the credit due to Col. Arthur L. Wagner, into the General Service and Staff College. The Medical Department under Surgeon General George Miller Sternberg founded the Army Medical School in 1893.

Included in the act of 1866 that fixed the organization of the postwar Army was a provision authorizing the President to detail as many as twenty officers to teach military science in schools of higher learning. This supplemented the part of the Morrill Act of 1862 that had provided for military instruction in land-grant colleges. By 1893 the number of instructors had increased to one hundred. In this program can be seen the beginnings of the Reserve Officer Training Corps, although it would not be organized as such for many years.

Another significant aspect of the developing military professionalism of the years following the Civil War was the founding of professional associations and journals. Notable among them were the U.S. Naval Institute, founded in 1873, whose *Proceedings* would become well known; the Military Service Institution of the United States, whose *Journal* would become a casualty of World War I; the United States Cavalry Association, which published the *Cavalry Journal*; and the Association of Military Surgeons, which published *The Military Surgeon*. In 1892 the Artillery School at Fort Monroe founded *The Journal of the United States Artillery*; and in 1893 a group of officers at Fort Leavenworth founded the Infantry Society, which became the U.S. Infantry Association the following year and later published the *Infantry Journal*. Earlier, in 1879, *United Service* began publication as a journal of naval and military affairs.

FORT LEAVENWORTH AND THE WEST

The site of Fort Leavenworth, Kansas, on a bluff on the west bank of the Missouri River, is testimony to the independent judgment that army officers often had to exercise in 1827, the year of the fort's founding. Under orders to find a suitable site on the east bank of the river, Col. Henry Leavenworth was unsatisfied with the terrain. He continued upstream until he came to a likely place on the west bank. Twenty years later national expansion put Fort Leavenworth in the middle of the United States, and by 1882 it had become the logical spot for a school to further the education of cavalry and infantry lieutenants. The School of Application, as it was called, provided junior officers from the Army's scattered, often tiny garrisons with an education fit for the age of steam and electricity, of breechloading weapons and the new smokeless powder. Its successor, the Command and General Staff College, is still there. Fort Leavenworth is the oldest continually occupied Army post west of the Mississippi River.

Still earlier, in 1863, the *Army and Navy Journal*, as it came to be called, began a long run. It was not a professional journal like the others, but along with its social and other items about service personnel it carried articles, correspondence, and news of interest to military people that helped bind its readers together in a common professional fraternity.

Before the Civil War the Army had no professional personnel system in the modern sense. Traditionally, most officers came into the service from the Military Academy at the lowest rank and received promotions on the basis of seniority. The war, however, at least made the need for a retirement system evident; and in 1861 Congress provided for compulsory retirement for incapacity. In 1862 and 1870 it provided that after thirty years' service an officer might retire either voluntarily or compulsorily at the President's discretion. Finally, in 1882 legislation made retirement compulsory at age sixty-four, which prompted the retirements of Sherman, Maj. Gen. Montgomery C. Meigs, and Surgeon General Joseph K. Barnes. Beginning in 1890, promotions for all officers below the rank of major were by examination, thus insuring a minimum level of professional competence. In the mid-nineties, the Army instituted systematic character and efficiency reports for all officers.

Line and Staff

There was no end, during the years between the Civil War and the turn of the century, to the old controversy between the line of the Army and the staff departments. The controversy had its roots in a legally divided responsibility and received nourishment from a conception of war as a science and as the natural purpose of the military. Although Congress made Grant a full general in 1866, and although Sherman and Sheridan both held that rank after him, neither these officers (except Grant during postwar reconstruction) nor their successors were able to avoid the basic organizational frustrations of the office of Commanding General. The problems were inevitable because, as Army regulations put it as late as 1895, the military establishment in the territorial commands was under the Commanding General for matters of discipline and military control, while the Army's fiscal affairs were conducted by the Secretary of War through the staff departments. At the same time, no statutory definition of the functions of the Commanding General existed except to a limited extent late in the century in the matter of research and development. In practice this situation also diluted the Commanding General's control of the territorial departments, since obviously the distribution and diversion of logistical support for these departments by the staff heads and the Secretary of War would affect troop operations.

Basic to the controversy was an assertion of the primacy of the line over the staff departments, for which there was a theoretical foundation in the developing conception of war as a science and the practice of that science as the sole purpose of military forces. Since the Army existed only to fight, it followed that its organization, training, and every activity should be directed to the single end of efficiency in combat. Therefore, the staff departments, representing a technical-expertise approach to war, existed only to serve the purposes of the line, which represented professionalism. From that proposition it followed that the line, in the person of the Commanding General, should control the staff. It also followed that the Army should not become involved, as it did, in such activities as the advancement of science or exploration.

"The regular Army now is a very curious compound," Sherman observed in 1874 in hearings on a bill to reduce the Army. As the Commanding General, he had "no authority, control or influence over anything but the cavalry, artillery, and infantry, and such staff officers as are assigned by their respective chiefs, approved by the Secretary of War, and attached to these various bodies for actual service." To him the three services that he named were "the Army of the United States," while the rest simply went "to make up the military peace establishment." If the Army had to be pruned, he advised pruning the branches of this peace establishment, not the active regiments. To a question about who commanded the engineer battalion, he replied "God only knows, for I do not." In his opinion the Ordnance Department was "the softest place in the Army." Sons and nephews wanted to go into it, he declared, "especially young men with influential congressional friends." As for the 450 men of the "signal detachment," Sherman regarded them as "no more soldiers than the men at the Smithsonian Institution. They are making scientific observations of the weather, of great interest to navigators and the country at large. But what does a soldier care about the weather? Whether good or bad, he must take it as it comes."

Sherman's view was that of the Army command and of the line, but it did not prevail. In 1894 the situation in which heads of the staff departments spent their entire careers with their specialty and became technical rather than military experts was modified by the requirement that thereafter appointments to the staff departments should be from the line of the Army. However, this left the basic command problem still unresolved.

Technical Development

The record of the Army's technical development in the years down to the end of the century was not one of marked and continuous progress in every field, for it was hampered by military conservatism, insufficient funds, and the nation's slowness in adapting inventive genius to the art of war. Yet there was considerable progress. In transportation, with the extension of the trans-Mississippi railroads, it became possible to move whole wagon trains by lashing the wagons to flatcars and transporting the mules in closed cars. In ordnance there was progress, however slow; and there were notable beginnings, some of them of vast potential, in signal communications.

The Army was about as slow in adopting new weapons as it was in solving the problem of command that had plagued it for so long. Although Henry and Spencer breechloading repeating rifles with rim-fire cartridges were used during the Civil War, the typical Civil War infantry shoulder arm was a muzzleloading rifled musket. In the years immediately following the war, the Ordnance Department, faced with a shortage of funds, converted thousands of the Civil War muzzleloaders into breechloaders. Desiring a better weapon, however, the Army convened a board in 1872 to examine and test existing weapons. After the board had examined over a hundred weapons, the Army adopted the single-shot Model 1873 Springfield breechloader. This fired a center-fire, .45-caliber cartridge, the caliber that the Ordnance Department selected as most desirable for all rifles, carbines, and pistols. The 1889 model of this gun, which embodied its final modifications, was the last of the Army's single-shot, large-caliber, black-powder rifles and the principal shoulder arm of the National Guard as late as 1898.

The Springfield remained in service even after the adoption of newer weapons and despite the trend toward smokeless powder and repeating arms abroad. U.S. manufacturers were slow to develop the new powder, which had several clear advantages. It burned progressively, gradually increasing the velocity of the bullet as it traveled through the barrel. In addition, its increasing pressures permitted a refinement in the rifling that gave a greater spin to the bullet and produced a higher velocity and a flatter trajectory.

When smokeless powder became available in the United States, a board in 1890 recommended the adoption of the Danish .30-caliber, bolt-action Krag-Jörgensen rifle, which fired smokeless cartridges and had a box magazine holding five cartridges. The Army adopted the Krag, as it came to be known, in 1892; but Congress delayed production at the Springfield Armory for two years, until tests of fourteen American models failed to find a superior weapon. By 1897 the Krag had been issued throughout the Regular Army. When its manufacture was discontinued in 1904, the original 1892 model had been modified twice, in 1896 and 1898.

Of the several types of the early machine gun available during the Civil War, the most successful was the Gatling gun, which the Army did not adopt until 1866 when the war was over. Even the advocates of this gun failed to recognize its usefulness as an infantry weapon but instead looked upon it as either auxiliary to artillery or as a useful weapon for defending bridges or other fixed sites.

In artillery as in shoulder arms American technical genius lagged behind that in Europe, where breechloading artillery using smokeless powder became common in the late nineteenth century. Other European improvements were explosive shells and recoil-absorbing

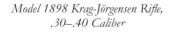

Model 1898 Krag-Jörgensen Rifle, .30–.40 Caliber

devices, which permitted refiring without re-aiming after every shot and opened the way to sophisticated sighting mechanisms and highly accurate indirect fire. Also, in the year before the Spanish-American War the French invented their famous 75-mm. gun. The U.S. Army nevertheless adopted some good rifled breechloaders, with the 3.2-inch rifle as the standard light field piece. These new guns replaced the old smoothbores, and steel replaced iron in their construction; but they still used black powder. The Army also had begun to experiment with steel carriages, pneumatic or hydraulic brakes, and mechanisms for elevating, traversing, and sighting artillery pieces.

The progress in artillery and armor plate was at least partly the result of the work of several boards. The first of these was the joint Army-Navy Gun Foundry Board provided by the Naval Appropriations Act of 1883. Its purpose was to consider the problem of how American industry could produce both armor plate and armor-piercing guns, upon which a modern navy depended, that would be comparable to the products of European industry. After touring European armament factories, the board recommended that the government award generous contracts to U.S. companies to stimulate their development of steels and forgings and that the government itself assemble the new materials into weapons at both the Naval Gun Factory and Army arsenals.

The new interest in the Navy in those years resulted in a need to examine coastal fortifications, which would have to be improved if new ships were not to be tied down to defense of the principal harbors. As a consequence the Endicott Board was set up in 1885 to plan for restoration of the coastal fortifications. Neither the world situation nor the existing naval technology justified the estimated cost of implementing the board's recommendations, but in 1888 Congress voted an initial appropriation and established a permanent body, the Board of Ordnance and Fortification, to supervise programs concerned with preparing coastal fortifications. This board was significant as the first War Department–wide agency for supporting research and development and as an attempt to place the important staff departments partly under the control of the Commanding General. Moreover, its failure served to point out the defects in the War Department's organization. The board remained in existence until 1920, but in 1890 and 1891 engineer expenditures and in 1892 ordnance expenditures were removed from the board's supervision. The actual work on the fortifications that followed was never completed, but during the nineties the Army abandoned the old forts around the principal harbors in favor of earthworks, armor-plated concrete pits, and great 10- and 12-inch disappearing rifles.

During the years after the Civil War there were several significant developments in signal communications under the Signal Corps, known as the Signal Service for many years. In 1867 the War Department restored electric field telegraphy to the Signal Corps, which had lost responsibility for it about three years earlier; and the corps quickly developed a new flying or field telegraph train, using batteries, sounders, and insulated wire. Then after constructing a telegraph line along the east coast in 1873 as an aid to the Life-Saving Service, the Signal Corps built long telegraph lines in both the Southwest and Northwest to provide communication between isolated military posts. These also provided facilities for transmitting weather reports. By 1881 these lines extended for slightly more than 5,000 miles.

In the late seventies, within a year or two of Alexander Graham Bell's patenting of the telephone, the Army was using it experimentally at Fort Whipple and between that post and Signal Corps offices in Washington. By 1889 a field-telephone kit, combining the Bell telephone, a Morse key, and a battery, had been developed but was believed too expensive for manufacture and issue at that time. About three years later, of ninety-nine garrisoned posts, fifty-nine had telephone equipment, some belonging to the Signal Corps and some rented from the Bell Telephone Company. About the same time the Army began using the telephone, it also became interested in the heliograph (mirrors reflecting sunlight to transmit Morse code) and found it to be particularly useful in the Southwest. There were also experiments as early as 1878 with homing pigeons.

Perhaps most significant of all the Signal Corps experimentation and developments of the period was the reintroduction of balloons into the Army in the early nineties for the first time since the Civil War. In 1893 the Signal Corps exhibited a military balloon at the World's Columbian Exposition in Chicago, and in 1896 it organized a model balloon train at Fort Logan, Colorado. Here were the beginnings that would lead to the development of Army aviation.

The backwardness of the United States in military technology in the 1890s, despite some important developments, would be misleading unless one looked beyond the specific military facts to examine the nation's industrial base. The United States was already an industrial giant. In 1890, only twenty-nine years after the beginning of the Civil War, the United States pulled ahead of Great Britain in the production of both pig iron and steel and thus became the world's leading producer. Moreover, in the decade of the nineties, the United States also surpassed Great Britain in coal production. In total manufactures, the nation's share jumped from less than 20 percent of the world volume in 1880 to more than 35 percent in 1913. With such an industrial base and potential, the Army of the nineties had no real need for concern.

Civil Accomplishment

The U.S. Army performed a variety of highly useful civil functions in the interwar years, despite the new professionalism that decried such activities as contrary to the natural purpose of an army. Upon the United States' purchase of Alaska from Russia in 1867 the Army assumed responsibility for Alaskan affairs except in matters concerning customs, commerce, and navigation, which became a responsibility of the Treasury Department. This situation continued until June 1877, when the Army withdrew from Alaska (partly because of the cost of maintaining a garrison in so remote a place) and left the Treasury Department in charge. For the next twenty years the Army's principal role in Alaska was in support of various explorations conducted by Army personnel, which had begun at least as early as 1869 when Capt. Charles W. Raymond of the Army Engineers explored the Yukon. Thereafter there were other explorations in the Yukon, the region of the Copper and Tanana Rivers, and to Point Barrow by variously 1st Lt.

The U.S. Army performed a variety of highly useful civil functions in the interwar years, despite the new professionalism that decried such activities as contrary to the natural purpose of an army.

Members of the Greely Expedition. Lieutenant Greely is in the front row, fourth from the left.

Frederick Schwatka of the 3d Cavalry, 2d Lt. William R. Abercrombie of the 2d Infantry, 2d Lt. Henry T. Allen of the 2d Cavalry, and 1st Lt. Patrick Henry Ray of the Signal Corps.

Ray's expedition to Point Barrow, 1881–1883, was successful in carrying out various meteorological and other observations. It returned safely, but the companion Lady Franklin Bay expedition to Ellesmere Island, 1881–1884, under 1st Lt. Adolphus W. Greely of the Signal Corps, was not nearly so fortunate. Although the Greely expedition reached a point farther north than any prior expedition and carried out its scientific observations, all but seven members of the party died before rescue (and one person died afterward) through failure of pre-arranged plans for receiving supplies. The Greely expedition grew out of the plans of Signal Corps 1st Lt. Henry W. Howgate for an Arctic colony at Lady Franklin Bay and out of the proposals of the International Polar Conference in Hamburg in 1879 for a chain of meteorological stations about the North Pole. The Ray expedition stemmed from the Hamburg Conference.

After the Civil War, the rivers and harbors work of the Corps of Engineers increased considerably, contributing substantially to development of the nation's water resources. Other notable contributions of the Engineers included their construction of public buildings, including supervision of the final work on the Washington Monument and on the State, War, and Navy Building, together with Brig. Gen. Thomas L. Casey's planning and supervision from 1888 to 1895 of the construction of what is now the main building of the Library of Congress. Beginning in 1878, the Engineers provided an officer to serve by presidential appointment as one of the three governing commissioners of the District of Columbia.

Of the four great surveys undertaken in the United States prior to establishment of the Geological Survey in the Interior Department in 1879, the Corps of Engineers had responsibility for two: the King Survey, 1867–1872, which made a geological exploration of the 40th Parallel, and the Wheeler Survey, 1871–1879, the geographical survey west of the 100th Meridian. The latter was more of a military survey in the tradition of the old Corps of Topographical Engineers than was the former, essentially a civilian undertaking. Both of these surveys nevertheless collected specimens of great use to scientists in the fields of botany, zoology, paleontology, and related disciplines.

Although the Navy was largely responsible for interoceanic canal surveys in the post–Civil War years, the first U.S. Isthmian Canal Commission, appointed by President Grant in 1872, had Brig. Gen. Andrew A. Humphreys, Chief of Engineers, as one of its three members. In 1874 Maj. Walter McFarland, Corps of Engineers, went out with naval assistance to examine the Nicaragua and Atrato-Napipi canal routes; and in 1897 Col. Peter C. Hains of the Engineers was one of the members President William McKinley appointed to the Nicaragua Canal Commission.

In the years from 1870 to 1891 the War Department organized and operated under the Signal Corps the nation's first modern weather service using both leased telegraph lines and, after they were built, the Army's own military lines for reporting simultaneous observations to Washington. Under Brig Gen. Albert J. Myer, the Chief Signal Officer, the service gained international renown; but partly because of the hostility of the War Department and the Army to the essentially civil character of the weather service and to its cost, Congress in 1890 directed transfer of the service to the Department of Agriculture, where it became the Weather Bureau in 1891. This loss of the weather service marked a general decline in the role of the military services in the cause of science. Although the Signal Corps retained responsibility for military meteorology, the Army had little need of it until World War I.

Of all the Army's civil contributions, those of its Medical Department, with immeasurable implications for the entire society, may well have been the most important. Indeed, medical research in the Army, in which a few outstanding men were predominant, did not reflect the decline in research that affected the other military branches of the period. One of the most notable of the Army's medical contributions was the Army Medical Library, or the Surgeon General's Library, which, though founded in 1836, did not come into its own until after 1868, when Assistant Surgeon John S. Billings began to make it into one of the world's great medical libraries. Similarly, in the same period, Billings developed the Army Medical Museum, which had been founded during the Civil War, into what would become in fact a national institute of pathology.

George Sternberg, who became the Surgeon General in 1893, was the leading pioneer in bacteriology in the United States and a worthy contemporary of Louis Pasteur and Robert Koch. Sternberg's official duties provided some opportunity for his studies, although he performed most of his research independently, some of it in the Johns Hopkins Hospital in Baltimore under the auspices of the American Public Health Association. He was appreciated by all except the more conservative of his colleagues who resisted the germ theory to about the same degree as physicians in private practice.

This loss of the weather service marked a general decline in the role of the military services in the cause of science.

The more than three decades from the end of the Civil War to the Spanish-American War took the Army through a period of isolation and penury in which it engaged in no large war but in which it had opportunity for introspection. It took advantage of this opportunity and in professional ways that would mean much to its future success moved from darkness and near despair into the light of a new military day. Yet throughout this period, the Army was engaged in a more active mission that for many allowed little time for retrospection or leisure, a mission that shaped Army traditions and myths for years to come. The Army had a war to fight before it would see accomplished at least some of the reforms toward which the new military professionalism looked—a long war in the American West against the Indians, or Native Americans.

Discussion Questions

1. What was the role of the U.S. Army in the occupation of the Southern states after the Civil War? Why was this such an unpopular mission?

2. What role should the U.S. Army have in domestic disturbances such as riots, large-scale strikes, etc.? What more recent uses of the Army in domestic interventions can you think of?

3. What is the difference between the militia and the National Guard?

4. What does the phrase "military professionalism" mean to you? Is the purpose of military education the learning of technical skills, the inculcation of a professional ethos or culture, or something else completely?

5. The argument of "line versus staff" is no longer as contentious as it once was. However, are there still differences between officers who are technical experts and those who are more generalists? If so, why is this a problem?

6. To what extent should the Army be involved in essentially non-military missions such as exploration, weather forecasting, or other "civilian" occupations?

Recommended Readings

Abrahamson, James L. *America Arms for a New Century: The Making of a Great Military Power*. New York: Free Press, 1981.

Ambrose, Stephen. *Upton and the Army*. Baton Rouge: Louisiana State University Press, 1993.

Coakley, Robert W. *The Role of Federal Military Forces in Domestic Disorders, 1789–1878*. Washington, D.C.: U.S. Army Center of Military History, 1988.

Cooper, Jerry M. *The Army and Civil Disorder: Federal Military Intervention in Labor Disputes, 1877–1900*. Westport, Conn.: Greenwood Press, 1980.

———. *The Rise of the National Guard: The Evolution of the American Militia, 1865–1920*. Lincoln: University of Nebraska Press, 1997.

Coffman, Edward M. *The Old Army: A Portrait of the American Army in Peacetime, 1784–1898*. New York: Oxford University Press, 1986.

Huntington, Samuel P. *The Soldier and the State: The Theory and Politics of Civil-Military Relations*. Cambridge: Harvard University Press, 1957.

Leckie, William H. *The Buffalo Soldiers: A Narrative of the Negro Cavalry in the West,* rev. ed. Norman: University of Oklahoma Press, 2003.

Risch, Erna. *Quartermaster Support of the Army: A History of the Corps, 1775–1939*. Washington, D.C.: U.S. Army Center of Military History, 1989.

Other Readings

Armstrong, David A. *Bullets and Bureaucrats: The Machine Gun and the United States Army, 1861–1916*. Westport, Conn.: Greenwood Press, 1982.

Bruce, Robert V. *1877: Year of Violence*. Indianapolis: Bobbs-Merrill, 1959.

Caswell, John E. *Arctic Frontiers: United States Explorations in the Far North*. Norman: University of Oklahoma Press, 1956.

Dawson, Joseph G. III. *Army Generals and Reconstruction: Louisiana, 1862–1877*. Baton Rouge: Louisiana State University Press, 1982.

Hill, Jim D. *The Minute Man in Peace and War: A History of the National Guard*. Harrisburg, Pa.: Stackpole Co., 1964.

Hume, Edgar E. *Victories of Army Medicine: Scientific Accomplishments of the Medical Department of the United States Army*. Philadelphia: Lippincott, 1943.

Jamieson, Perry D. *Crossing the Deadly Ground: United States Army Tactics, 1865–1899*. Tuscaloosa: University of Alabama Press, 1994.

Nenninger, Timothy K. *The Leavenworth Schools and the Old Army: Education, Professionalism and the Officer Corps of the United States Army, 1881–1918*. Westport, Conn.: Greenwood Press, 1978.

Thomas, Benjamin P., and Harold M. Hyman. *Stanton: The Life and Times of Lincoln's Secretary of War*. Westport, Conn.: Greenwood Press, 1980.

14

WINNING THE WEST
THE ARMY IN THE INDIAN WARS
1865–1890

Perhaps because of a tendency to view the record of a military establishment in terms of conflict, the U.S. Army's operational experience in the quarter century following the Civil War has come to be known collectively as the Indian Wars, although those inhabitants of America described by the catchall name of Indian did not have anything like a monolithic culture or society. Previous struggles with various Indian tribes, dating back to colonial times, had generally been limited as to scope and opponent (the Pequot war in New England that virtually exterminated that tribe being one of the more notable exceptions) and took place in a period when the Indian could withdraw or be pushed into vast reaches of uninhabited and as yet unwanted territory to the west. By 1865 this safety valve was fast disappearing; routes of travel and pockets of settlement had multiplied across the western two-thirds of the nation, and as the Civil War closed Americans in greater numbers and with greater energy than before resumed the quest for land, gold, commerce, and adventure that had been largely interrupted by the war.

The showdown between the older Americans and the new, between two ways of life that were basically incompatible, was at hand. The besieged Indian, with an alien civilization pressing in and a main source of livelihood, the buffalo, threatened with extinction, was faced with a fundamental choice: surrender or fight. Many chose to fight, and over the course of twenty-five years the struggle ranged over the plains, mountains, and deserts of the American West, a small-scale war characterized by skirmishes, pursuits, massacres, raids, expeditions, battles, and campaigns of varying size and intensity. Given a central role in dealing with the Indian, the Army made a major contribution to continental consolidation and in the process shaped itself as a culture and as an institution in many ways.

The Setting and the Challenge

After Appomattox the Army had to muster out over a million volunteers and reconstitute a regular establishment that had languished during the Civil War when bounties and short enlistments made service in the volunteers more profitable. There were operational commitments to sustain during and after the transition, some an outgrowth of the war just ended and others the product of internal and external situations that could not be ignored. Whereas the prewar Army of the 1850s was essentially a frontier Army, the postwar Army became something more. To defense of the frontier were added military occupation of the southern states, neutralization of the Mexican border during Napoleon's colonial enterprise under Maximilian, elimination of a Fenian (Irish Brotherhood) threat to Canada in the Northeast, dispersion of white marauders in the border states, and a growing mission of coastal defense. But the mission of pacifying the frontier consumed much of the interest and attention of large numbers of Army officers and men in the years between the Civil War and the Spanish-American War.

Life in the Frontier Army

One of the determining factors about life in the U.S. Army on the frontiers of America was the small size of the force engaged in operations in relative isolation from the country and from the rest of the Army. The Army was scattered throughout hundreds of small forts, posts, outposts, and stations throughout the American West, often with little more than a company of cavalry or infantry in each post. This isolation bred, on one hand, a strong sense of camaraderie, of bonding, within the Army in a way that only shared suffering can do. The officers and men often felt part of an extended family that had to look inward for strength as it relied on its own customs, rituals, and sense of honor separate from that distant civilian world or even from the very different military society "back East." This sense of unity, of "splendid isolation," kept the Army as an institution together during the harsh missions of western frontier duty but at the same time led far too often to professional and personal stagnation. Promotion was slow, and chances for glory were few given the dangers and hardships of small-unit actions against an elusive foe.

The isolation also bred a certain measure of reliance upon each other, as officers and soldiers developed various customs and rituals to bring structure to their lives. The formal rituals of a frontier post—life regulated by bugle calls, formal parades, Saturday night dances for the officers, distinctive uniforms, and unit nicknames—were attempts to deal with the tensions and pressures of a harsh life for a soldier and his family with low pay and little prestige. While perhaps glamorous in retrospect, or when seen through the eye of Hollywood movies, such small communities also had their share of drunkenness, petty squabbles, corruption, arguments over rank and quarters, and other seemingly minor disputes so well known by any who have experienced life in small-town America. It was a life at once dangerous and monotonous,

Artillery Helmet of the Late Nineteenth Century

comradely and isolated, professionally rewarding and stultifying. With low pay, poor quarters, an indifferent public, and a skilled foe that was at once feared, hated, and admired, the officers and men of the frontier Army seemed caught in a never-ending struggle with an elusive enemy and their environment. One historian summarized the Army post during this period on the frontier this way: "If one description could alone fit all frontier posts, it would be a monotonous routine relaxed only slightly by the color of periodic ceremony." This shared culture created many of the institutional myths and customs that continue to influence the Army's image of itself to this day.

The manpower strains of all the various missions after the Civil War plus manning all the frontier posts and stations badly strained the resources of a shrinking Regular Army. As the post–Civil War Army took shape, its strength began a decade of decline, dropping from an 1867 level of 57,000 to half that in 1876, then leveling off at an average of 26,000 for the remaining years up to the War with Spain. Effective strength always lay somewhere below authorized strength, seriously impaired by high rates of sickness and desertion, for example. Because the Army's military responsibilities were of continental proportions, involving sweeping distances, limited resources, and far-flung operations, an administrative structure was required for command and control. The Army was, therefore, organized on a territorial basis, with geographical segments variously designated as divisions, departments, and districts. There were frequent modifications of organization, rearrangements of boundaries, and transfers of troops and posts to meet changing conditions. (*See Map 38.*)

Development of a basic defense system in the trans-Mississippi West had followed the course of empire. Territorial acquisition and exploration succeeded by emigration and settlement brought the settlers increasingly into collision with the Indians and progressively raised the need for military posts along the transcontinental trails and in settled areas.

The annexation of Texas in 1845, the settlement of the Oregon boundary dispute in 1846, and the successful conclusion of the Mexican War with the cession to the United States in 1848 of vast areas of land all had drawn the outlines of the major task facing the Army in the West in the middle of the nineteenth century. During the period between the Mexican and Civil Wars, the Army had established a reasonably comprehensive system of forts to protect the arteries of travel and areas of settlement across the frontier. At the same time the Army had launched operations against Indian tribes that represented actual or potential threats to movement and settlement.

Militarily successful in some cases, these operations nevertheless hardened Indian opposition, prompted wider provocations on both sides, and led to the delineation of an Indian barrier to westward expansion extending down the Great Plains from the Canadian to the Mexican border. Brig. Gen. William S. Harney, for example, responded to the Sioux massacre of Lt. John L. Grattan's detachment with a punishing attack on elements of that tribe on the Blue Water in Nebraska in 1855. Farther south, Col. Edwin V. Sumner hit the Cheyennes on the Solomon Fork in Kansas in 1857 and Bvt. Maj. Earl Van Dorn fought the Comanches in two successful battles, at Rush Spring in future Oklahoma and Crooked Creek in Kansas in 1858 and 1859, respectively.

The Army on the Great Plains found itself in direct contact with a highly mobile and warlike culture that was not easily subdued.

In the Southwest, between the wars, Army units pursued Apaches and Utes in New Mexico Territory, clashing with the Apaches at Cieneguilla and Rio Caliente in 1854 and the Utes at Poncha Pass in 1855. There were various expeditions against branches of the elusive Apaches that involved hard campaigning but few conclusive engagements such as the one at Rio Gila in 1857. It was in this region in 1861 that Lt. George N. Bascom moved against Chief Cochise, precipitating events that opened a quarter century of hostilities with the Chiricahua Apaches.

In the Northwest, where numerous small tribes existed, there were occasional hostilities between the late 1840s and the middle 1860s. Their general character was similar to operations elsewhere: settler intrusion, Indian reaction, and U.S. Army or local militia counteraction with superior force. The more important events involved the Rogue River Indians in Oregon between 1851 and 1856 and the Yakima, Walla Walla, Cayuse, and other tribes on both sides of the Cascade Mountains in Washington in the latter half of the 1850s. The Army, often at odds with civil authority and public opinion in the area, found it necessary on occasion to protect Indians from settlers as well as the other way around.

The Regular Army's frontier mission was interrupted by the onset of the Civil War, and the task of dealing with the Indians was transferred to the volunteers. Although the Indians demonstrated an awareness of what was going on and took some satisfaction from the fact that their enemies were fighting each other, there is little evidence that they took advantage of the transition period between removal of the regulars and deployment of the volunteers. The so-called Great Sioux Uprising in Minnesota in 1862 that produced active campaigning in the Upper Missouri River region in 1863 and 1864 was spontaneous, and other clashes around the West were the result not of the withdrawal of the Regular Army from the West but of the play of more fundamental and established forces. The volunteer units were in many instances commanded by men of a very different stamp than were Regular Army units. In one instance, a Colorado volunteer cavalry unit, commanded by a volunteer colonel named John M. Chivington, attacked and massacred several hundred peaceful Cheyenne Indians at Sand Creek, Colorado, in 1864 in one the worst atrocities of the western wars. There were dangers in relying on volunteer units in this essential peacekeeping role. In any case, by 1865 overall Army strength in the frontier departments was about double what it had been in 1861. The volunteers kept pace with a continuing and gradually enlarging westward movement by further developing the system of forts their predecessors had begun.

The regional defense systems established in the West in the 1850s and 1860s provided a framework for the deployment of the Army as it returned from the Civil War to its frontier responsibilities. In the late summer of 1866 the general command and administrative structure for frontier defense comprised the Division of the Missouri, containing the Departments of Arkansas, Missouri, Dakota, and the Platte; the Division of the Pacific, consisting of the Departments of California and the Columbia; and the independent Department of the Gulf, whose area included Texas.

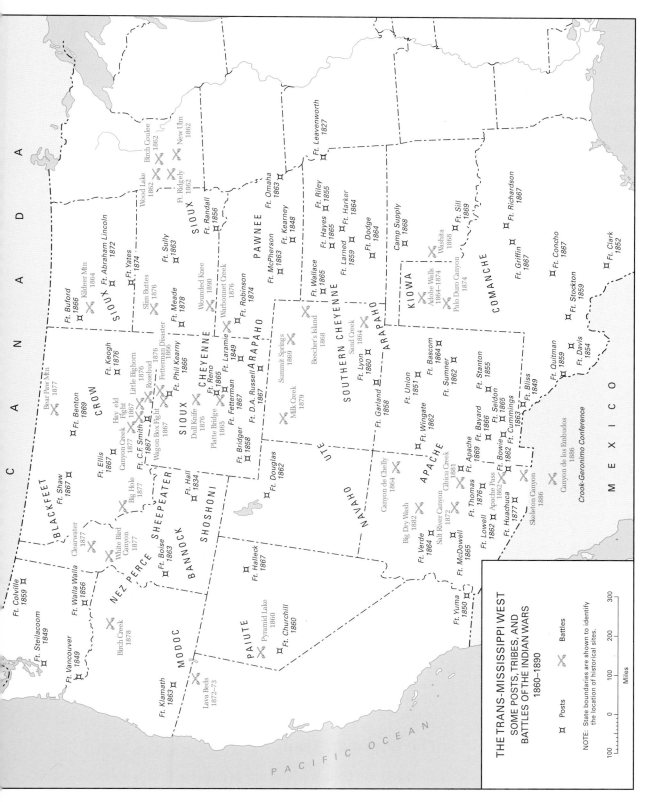

THE TRANS-MISSISSIPPI WEST

SOME POSTS, TRIBES, AND
BATTLES OF THE INDIAN WARS
1860–1890

⚓ Posts   ⚔ Battles

NOTE: State boundaries are shown to identify
the location of historical sites.

Miles
100   0   100   200   300

Map 38

However, by 1870 the Division of the Pacific included the Departments of the Columbia, California, and Arizona and the Department of the Missouri covered the Departments of the Dakota, the Platte, and the Missouri; the Department of Texas was included in the Division of the South.

The Army's challenge in the West was one of environment as well as adversary, and in the summer of 1866 General Grant sent a number of senior-officer inspectors across the country to observe and report on conditions. The theater of war was uninhabited or only sparsely settled, and its great distances and extreme variations of climate and geography accentuated manpower limitations, logistical and communications problems, and the difficulties of movement. The extension of the rail system only gradually eased the situation. Above all, the mounted tribes of the Plains were a different breed from the Indians the Army had dealt with previously in the forested areas of the East. Despite the fact that the Army had fought Indians in the West in the period after the Mexican War, much of the direct experience of its officers and men had been lost during the Civil War years. Until frontier proficiency could be reestablished the Army would depend on the somewhat intangible body of knowledge that marks any institution, fortified by the seasoning of the Civil War.

Of the officers who moved to the forefront of the Army in the Indian Wars, few had frontier and Indian experience. At the top levels at the outset, Grant had had only a taste of the loneliness of the frontier outpost as a captain. William T. Sherman had served in California during the 1850s but had not been involved in fighting. Philip H. Sheridan had served about five years in the Northwest as a junior officer, but neither Nelson A. Miles nor Oliver O. Howard had known frontier service of any kind. Wesley Merritt, George A. Custer, and Ranald S. Mackenzie all had graduated from West Point into the Civil War; and John Gibbon had only minor involvement in the Seminole War and some garrison duty in the West. Alfred Sully, also a veteran of the Seminole War and an active campaigner against the Sioux during Civil War years, fell into obscurity, while Philip St. George Cooke was overtaken by age and Edward R. S. Canby's experience was lost prematurely through his death at Indian hands. Christopher Augur, Alfred H. Terry, and George Crook were among the few upper-level Army leaders of the Indian Wars that had pre–Civil War frontier experience.

Thus, to a large degree the officers of the Indian Wars were products of the Civil War. Many brought outstanding records to the frontier, but this was a new conflict against an unorthodox enemy. Those who approached their new opponent with respect and learned his ways became the best Indian-fighters and in some cases the most helpful in promoting a solution to the Indian problem. Some who had little respect for the "savages" and placed too much store in Civil War methods and achievements paid the penalty on the battlefield. Capt. William J. Fetterman would be one of the first to fall as the final chapter of the Indian Wars opened in 1866.

The Bozeman Trail

While the Civil War was still in progress, gold was discovered in Montana and fortune seekers flocked to the area. Lines of communica-

> The theater of war was uninhabited or only sparsely settled, and its great distances and extreme variations of climate and geography accentuated manpower limitations, logistical and communications problems, and the difficulties of movement.

tions to the fields around Virginia City lay along circuitous routes, and pressure mounted for more direct access. The Army explored the possibilities and adopted a route, pioneered by John Bozeman, extending from Fort Laramie on the North Platte River and Oregon Trail, northwestward along the eastern base and around the northern shoulder of the Big Horn Mountains. Unfortunately, the trail cut through hunting grounds that a treaty in 1865 had reserved for the Sioux, Northern Cheyennes, and Arapahos.

The Indians resisted white incursions, and Maj. Gen. Patrick E. Connor's Powder River Expedition failed to stop their depredations. In 1866 the government, under public pressure and attracted to the gold resources as a means of relieving the financial strains of the Civil War, opened new negotiations but with indifferent results. A few friendly chiefs signed a new agreement at Fort Laramie, but others led by Red Cloud of the Sioux stalked out defiantly when Col. Henry B. Carrington marched in with a battalion of the 18th Infantry on his way to establish posts along the Bozeman Trail even before agreement with the Indians had been reached.

Although motivated by a sense of justice, treaty-making with the Indians more often than not constituted an exercise in futility for both parties. On the Indian side the tribes were loosely knit societies of individualists living a nomadic existence under leaders whose control and influence fluctuated with the fortunes of war. A treaty was no more binding than the degree of power, authority, and allegiance a leader might muster at any given time, Washington's understanding to the contrary. On the U.S. side, although the authority of negotiating officials was unquestioned, the power to enforce treaty provisions on highly independent settlers was another matter, and as breach after breach provoked the Indian to action, the Army was invariably called in to protect the offending citizens and punish the Indians, almost regardless of which group was at fault.

Colonel Carrington's battalion of 700 men departed Fort Laramie in June 1866 for the Big Horn country. Despite Red Cloud's threat to oppose the move, several families, including the commanding officer's, accompanied the force. At Fort Reno on the Powder River, some miles beyond the end of the telegraph, Carrington with a regular company relieved two companies of the 5th U.S. Volunteers, former Confederate prisoners who became so-called galvanized Yankees when they agreed

GALVANIZED YANKEES

During the last year of the Civil War, Plains Indian warfare reached a crescendo as more and more white travelers passed through the tribes' hunting territory. To keep the routes open, the Union Army recruited six regiments of Confederate prisoners of war out of the prison camps in the North. Those who signed up were mostly landless "poor whites" and immigrants who had been drafted into the Confederate Army and were disillusioned with the Southern cause. Swapping Confederate gray for Union blue, these "Galvanized Yankees" (so nicknamed after the process to cover metal with a rust-resistant zinc coating) garrisoned forts on major transportation routes until the Regular Army arrived to take their place in 1866.

attempt to confine them to specific geographical limits; it fell to the Army to force compliance. In his area, General Sheridan now planned to hit the Indians in their permanent winter camps.

While a winter campaign presented serious logistical problems, it offered opportunities for decisive results. If the Indians' shelter, food, and livestock could be destroyed or captured, not only the warriors but their women and children were at the mercy of the Army and the elements, and there was little left but surrender. These tactics, amounting to the total destruction of the Indian culture, raised certain moral questions for many officers and men that were never satisfactorily resolved.

Sheridan devised a plan whereby 3 columns would converge on the Indian wintering grounds just east of the Texas Panhandle: 1 from Fort Lyon in Colorado, 1 from Fort Bascom in New Mexico, and 1 from Camp Supply in the Indian Territory later to be called Oklahoma. The 7th Cavalry under Lt. Col. George A. Custer fought the major engagement of the campaign. Custer found the Indians on the Washita River and struck Black Kettle's Cheyenne village with eleven companies and from four directions at dawn on November 29, 1868, as the regimental band played "Gerry Owen," still the 7th Cavalry's regimental song. A fierce fight developed, which the Indians continued from surrounding terrain. By midmorning Custer learned that this was only one of many villages of Cheyennes, Arapahos, Kiowas, and Comanches extending for miles along the Washita. Facing such odds, Custer hastened to destroy the village and its supplies and, notably, about 875 ponies and horses; used an offensive maneuver to deceive the enemy; and under cover of darkness withdrew from the field, taking 53 women and children as prisoners. The 7th Cavalry lost 21 officers and men killed and 13 wounded in the Battle of the Washita; the Indians lost perhaps 50 killed and as many wounded. This battle was yet another instance of hitting the Indians in the winter months when the destruction of their villages and stored food killed or weakened more than did the initial military attack.

The Kiowas and Comanches did not lightly relinquish their hunting grounds and forsake their way of life. Some lived restlessly on a reservation in Indian Territory around Fort Sill; others held out. Sherman, now Commanding General of the U.S. Army; Sheridan, commanding the Division of the Missouri; and their field commanders would have to undertake several more major campaigns before these tribes were forced to accept reservation life. In 1871 reservation Kiowas raided into Texas, killing some teamsters of a government wagon train. General Sherman, visiting at Fort Sill, had the responsible leaders (Satanta, Satank, and Big Tree) arrested in a dramatic confrontation on the post between armed Indians and soldiers in which only Sherman's coolness prevented an explosion. Satank was later killed while attempting escape, and Satanta and Big Tree were tried and imprisoned for two years. Again in custody in 1876, Satanta took his own life.

There were other incidents on the Southern Plains before the Indians there were subjugated. An Army campaign in 1874–1875, known as the Red River War, involved about 3,000 troops and was launched in five columns, one under the command of Col. Nelson A. Miles and another under Col. Ranald S. Mackenzie, from bases in Texas, New Mexico, and Indian Territory against the Texas Panhandle refuge of

CUSTER

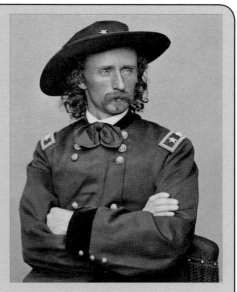

George A. Custer (1839–1876) graduated from West Point in 1861. A charismatic leader who won renown for his bold cavalry charges, he was commanding a brigade of cavalry two years later and a division within three. In 1866 the end of the Civil War and the reorganization of the Regular Army reduced Custer to lieutenant colonel and second in command of a regiment. He "found some difficulty in adapting himself to his altered position," wrote his commanding general, sponsor, and champion, Philip Sheridan, when Custer's indiscipline and erratic behavior resulted in a court-martial and a year's suspension without pay. As Custer led his regiment toward the Little Bighorn, no one is certain what his real hopes and ambitions were; but it is clear that his goal, as ever, was personal glory. Unfortunately, he and most of his command were killed to gain that fame.

General Custer during His Civil War Heydey

the Plains tribes. On September 24 Colonel Mackenzie and the 4th Cavalry found the winter camps of the Comanches, Kiowas, Cheyennes, and Arapahos in the deep Palo Duro Canyon on the Staked Plains. Mackenzie's surprise attack separated the Indians from their horses and belongings, which were destroyed. The campaign continued all winter and into the following spring, with many Indians finally surrendering in desperation and being placed on the reservation.

The Northwest

Not all the Indian Wars were fought with Plains tribes. The Army engaged in wars with several Pacific slope tribes in the 1870s, and the operations were widely scattered over the mountainous northwestern quarter of the trans-Mississippi West.

The Modoc War of 1872–1873 began when the Modocs, who had been placed on a reservation in southern Oregon with the more numerous and traditionally unfriendly Klamaths, returned without permission to their home in the Lost River country on the California border. When the Army attempted in November of 1872 to take them back to the reservation, fighting broke out and the Indians retreated into a natural fortress, the Lava Beds at the southern end of Tule Lake. Over the course of six months there were four engagements in which regular and volunteer troops with superior strength and weapons incurred heavier losses than did their opponents. The extended efforts of a peace commission made little headway and ended in tragedy when two of the members, Brig. Gen. Edward R. S. Canby and the Reverend Eleaser Thomas, both unarmed, were shot while in conference with the Indians. The Modocs finally surrendered; and four of their leaders, including Canby's murderer, Captain Jack, were hanged.

The practice of uprooting the Indians from their homeland was also the cause of the Nez Perce War in 1877. The Nez Perce had been friendly to the settlers from the days of their contact with Lewis and Clark. Although they had ceded some of their lands to the newcomers, they refused to give up the Wallowa Valley in northeastern Oregon. Encroachment increased, stiffening the lines of political pressure back to Washington and leading inevitably to decisions favorable to the settlers and mandating the removal of the Nez Perce to the Lapwai Reservation across the Snake River in Idaho. Some elements of the tribe complied; but Chief Joseph and his people did not, and the Army was ordered to move them. A series of irresponsible actions by both sides led to hostilities.

In a remarkable campaign that demonstrated the unique capabilities of guerrilla forces and the difficulties that formal military units have in dealing with them, the Nez Perce led the Army on a 1,300-mile chase over the Continental Divide punctuated by a number of sharp engagements. The Indians used the terrain to great advantage, fighting when circumstances favored them, side-stepping around opposing forces or breaking contact when the situation dictated it. They lived off the land, while the Army was tied to supply trains that were vulnerable to Indian attack. But their women and children often hindered the Indians' freedom of movement, and eventually Army superiority in strength and weapons began to tell. Indian rifles were no match for howitzers and Gatling guns, and Indian mobility could not outstrip the Army's use of the telegraph to alert additional forces along the Nez Perce line of flight. The battles of White Bird Canyon, Clearwater, Big Hole, Canyon Creek, and Bear Paw Mountain involved hundreds of troops and

Thornburgh's Battle *(against the Ute Indians), Frank Tenney Johnson, 1965*

GENERAL CROOK (1828–1890)

Graduating thirty-eighth in a class of forty-three at West Point, George Crook would be the lowest ranking cadet ever to attain the rank of major general in the Regular Army. Laconic and reserved, Crook reveled in field duty. Wounded while fighting Indians in 1857, he carried the arrowhead to his grave. During the Civil War he rose to command a corps. Afterward he returned to the frontier, where he would remain for the rest of his career. A keen student of Indian life and culture, he died while still on active duty after thirty-eight years of military service.

numerous units under Maj. Gen. Oliver O. Howard, Col. John Gibbon, Maj. Samuel D. Sturgis, and Lt. Gen. Nelson A. Miles. There were heavy casualties on both sides before Chief Joseph surrendered. Joseph concluded the peace talks with one of the most memorable speeches in western history. "Hear me, my Chiefs," one army observer remembered Joseph saying, "I am tired. My heart is sick and sad. From where the sun now stands I will fight no more forever."

In 1878 and 1879 Army forces took the field against various bands of Indians in mountain areas of the Northwest. Operations against the Bannocks, Sheepeaters, and Utes were relatively minor. The Bannock War was caused by settler intrusion on the Camas Prairie in Idaho, where camas roots were a prime source of food for the Indians. The Sheepeater War, also centered in Idaho, broke out when the Indians were charged with several murders they probably did not commit. The Ute War in northwestern Colorado grew out of the misguided methods and impractical idealism of Indian Agent Nathan C. Meeker. Regardless of what caused them, these wars meant hard campaigning and casualties for the Army and the Indians.

The Southwest

The Apaches were among the Army's toughest opponents in the Indian Wars. The zone of operations embraced the territories of Arizona and New Mexico, western Texas, and Mexico's northern provinces. Despite the fact that hostile Apaches were relatively few in number and the theater was essentially secondary, they tied down sizable forces over a long period of time.

Post–Civil War Apache troubles extended from the late 1860s, when the Army campaigned against Cochise, through the seventies and eighties, when Victorio and Geronimo came to the fore. On the Army side the important factor was the assignment of Bvt. Maj. Gen. George Crook to the Southwest, where he served two tours between 1871 and 1886. Crook was an able administrator as well as an outstanding soldier and proved to be a relentless opponent of the Indian on the battlefield and a steadfast friend off it. As commander of the Department of Arizona he organized at key locations a number of mobile striking forces under experienced frontier officers and launched them in a concerted campaign supported by mule pack trains. Acting under an 1866 congressional act that authorized the Army to enlist up to a thousand Indian scouts (they came from

Tracking Victorio, *Don Stivers, 1988*

traditionally friendly tribes like the Crow and Pawnee or from friendly elements of warring tribes), Crook also employed Apache scouts. Converging columns and persistent pursuit brought results, and he left Arizona in relative quiet when he went to the Department of the Platte in 1875.

The quiet in the Southwest did not last long. Largely at the instigation of politicians, merchants, contractors, and other self-serving whites, several bands of mutually uncongenial Apaches were transferred from desirable areas to the unhealthy San Carlos Reservation in the Arizona lowlands. As a result, much of what Crook had accomplished was undone as disgruntled Apaches again turned to raiding and killing. In the summer of 1881, for example, an Apache medicine man stirred the Indians to heights of religious fervor that led to a sharp clash on Cibicu Creek with troops commanded by Col. Eugene A. Carr, one of the Army's most experienced Indian-fighters. The action was highlighted by perhaps the most notable instance of disaffection when the Indian scouts with the command turned on the regulars.

Throughout the Indian Wars there was constant friction between the War and the Interior Departments over the conduct of Indian affairs. A committee of the Continental Congress had first exercised this responsibility. In 1789 it was transferred to the Secretary of War, and in 1824 a Bureau of Indian Affairs was created in the War Department. When the Department of the Interior was established in 1849, the Indian Bureau was transferred to that agency. Thus administration of Indian affairs was handled by one department while enforcement lay with another. General Crook explained to a congressional committee in 1879: "As it is now you have a divided responsibility. It is like having two captains on the same ship."

Crook returned to Arizona in 1882 to restore the Apaches' confidence in the white administration, move the Apaches along the paths of civilization, and spar constantly with the Indian Bureau. On the military side, he took the field against dwindling numbers of hostiles, cooperating with Mexican officials and authorized to cross the international boundary in pursuit of the renegades. Crook met with Geronimo in the Sierra Madre Mountains in March of 1886 and negotiated a surrender that brought in all but Geronimo and a few followers who backed out at the last moment. When Washington failed to back the field commander in the conditions on which he had negotiated the surrender, Crook asked to be relieved. Miles replaced him, and Lt. Charles B. Gatewood entered Geronimo's mountain fastness to arrange a surrender and bring the Apache campaigns to a close.

The Northern Plains

All the elements of the clash of cultures and civilizations were present in the events leading to the final subjugation of the Indians. The mounted tribes of the Great Plains were astride the main corridors of westward expansion, and this was the area of decision. The treaty of 1868 had set aside the Great Sioux Reservation in South Dakota; and the Army had abandoned the Bozeman Trail, leaving the Powder River region as Indian country. The Sioux, the Northern Cheyenne, and their allies were thus north of the main transcontinental artery along the Platte. Although the arrangement worked for several years, it was doomed by the seemingly irresistible march of settlers. The Sioux rejected white overtures for a right-of-way for the Northern Pacific Railroad; when surveyors went ahead anyway they ran into Indian resistance, which led to the dispatch in 1873 of a large military expedition under Col. David S. Stanley up the Yellowstone Valley. The next year General Sheridan sent Custer and the 7th Cavalry on a reconnaissance through the Black Hills, within the Sioux Reservation. When geologists with the expedition found gold, the word spread rapidly and prospectors filtered into the area despite the Army's best efforts to keep them out. Another treaty was broken, and band by band angry reservation Indians slipped away to join nontreaty recalcitrants in the unceded Powder River region of Wyoming and Montana.

In December 1875 the Indian Bureau notified the Sioux and Northern Cheyennes that they had to return to the reservation by the end of the following month. Since the Indians were in winter quarters in remote areas and would have had little chance against the elements, they did not obey. As the deadline passed, the Commissioner of Indian Affairs appealed to the Army to force compliance. Sheridan, mindful of his success with converging columns against the Southern Plains tribes, determined upon a similar winter campaign in the north.

Two columns were planned: one under Crook from Fort Fetterman and the other under Brig. Gen. Alfred H. Terry from Fort Abraham Lincoln in the Dakota Territory. In March 1876 Crook's force, directly commanded by Col. Joseph J. Reynolds, launched its foray on schedule

Geronimo (left center) *at Meeting with General Crook*
(second from right, seated) *in 1886*

but returned within a month. Reynolds had entered the valley of the Powder and surprised a Cheyenne-Sioux camp but failed to press an initial advantage and withdrew without punishing the Indians. Terry's column never left its fort. The abortive campaign was not renewed until the spring, when Sheridan pressed his subordinates into renewing their attacks, this time with three columns under Crook, Gibbon, and Terry directed against the Powder River area.

General Terry marched west from Fort Abraham Lincoln in Dakota Territory in May, his principal element the 7th Cavalry under Custer. Colonel Gibbon had earlier moved east from Fort Ellis in western Montana with a mixed force of infantry and cavalry, while General Crook moved north from Fort Fetterman on the North Platte in Wyoming at the end of May with a force heavily weighted in cavalry. Crook made the first contact. The Sioux and Northern Cheyennes learned of his approach along Rosebud Creek, and 1,500 warriors moved to meet him. Crook had fifteen companies of cavalry and five of infantry, 1,000 men, plus another 300 friendly Indians and civilians. The two forces met on roughly equal terms on the seventeenth in heavy fighting. Tactically, neither side carried the field conclusively enough to claim a victory. Strategically, Crook's withdrawal to a supply base to the south gave the Battle of the Rosebud the complexion of a defeat for the Army, especially in view of developments on the Little Bighorn River fifty miles northwest, which his continued advance might have influenced decisively.

While Crook was moving north to his collision on the Rosebud, Terry and Gibbon, marching from east and west, had joined forces on the Yellowstone River at its confluence with the Powder, where a supply base serviced by river steamer was established. Terry sent out the 7th Cavalry to scout for Indian sign, and Maj. Marcus A. Reno with six companies (the cavalry company was not called a troop until 1883) reconnoitered up the Powder, across the Tongue River, and into the valley of the Rosebud. Here on June 17 Reno found a fresh trail leading west out of the valley and across the Wolf Mountains in the direction of the Little Bighorn. He was unaware, and was thus unable to inform his superiors, that Crook was also in the Rosebud valley and had been engaged and blocked by a large force of Indians not far upstream on this very same day.

Terry held a council of war aboard the steamer Far West to outline his plan. Custer's 7th Cavalry would move south up the Rosebud, cross the Wolf Mountains, and enter the Little Bighorn valley from the south. Gibbon, joined by Terry, would ascend the Bighorn River and its tributary, the Little Bighorn, from the north, trapping the Indians between the two forces.

As it happened, Custer moved at least a day early for the cooperative action envisioned in Terry's plan. On June 25, 1876, the 7th Cavalry crossed the Wolf Mountains and moved into the valley of the Little Bighorn. (*See Map 39.*) Custer was confident of his capability to handle whatever he ran up against, convinced that the Indians would follow their usual practice of scattering before a show of force and completely unaware that he was descending upon one of the largest concentrations of Indians ever assembled on the Plains. Perhaps as many as 6,000–7,000 Sioux and Northern Cheyennes, with as many as 2,000 warriors under such leaders as Crazy Horse, Sitting Bull, Gall, Crow King, Lame Deer, Hump, and Two Moon, would confront Custer in the Battle of the Little Bighorn.

Around noon of this Sunday in June, Custer sent Capt. Frederick W. Benteen with three companies to scout to the left of the command, not an unusual move for a force still attempting to fix the location of an elusive enemy and expecting him to slip away on contact. It is also possible that Custer, knowing the value of the principle of surprise, hoped to catch the foe unawares. About 2:30 p.m., still two miles short of the river when the upper end of an Indian village came into view, Custer advanced three more companies under Major Reno with instructions to cross the river and charge the Indian camp. With five companies Custer moved off to the right, still screened by a fold of ground from observing the extent of his opposition, perhaps with the thought of hitting the Indians from the flank—of letting Reno hold the enemy by the nose while he, Custer, kicked him in the seat of the pants. As Custer progressed, he rushed Sgt. Daniel Kanipe to the rear to hurry the pack train and its one-company escort forward and shortly afterward dispatched Trumpeter John Martin with a last message to Benteen that a "big village" lay ahead and to "be quick—bring packs."

Sitting Bull

INDIAN SCOUTS

When engaged in Indian campaigns, the U.S. Army often employed scouts as guides, trackers, and diplomats. American commanders realized that the most effective scouts were Indians recruited from each tribe's traditional enemies. For example, Cheyenne warriors were often employed in campaigns against the Sioux. Indian scouts gained the confidence and respect of Army leaders who quickly learned to follow their advice. George Custer, however, ignored warnings from his Arickara and Crow scouts not to advance against the Indian villages on the Little Big Horn and as a result lost 267 men in battle. The insignia of the Indian Scouts, crossed arrows, was later adopted as the special insignia of the First Special Service Force, a commando unit, in World War II and as the branch insignia of U.S. Army Special Forces.

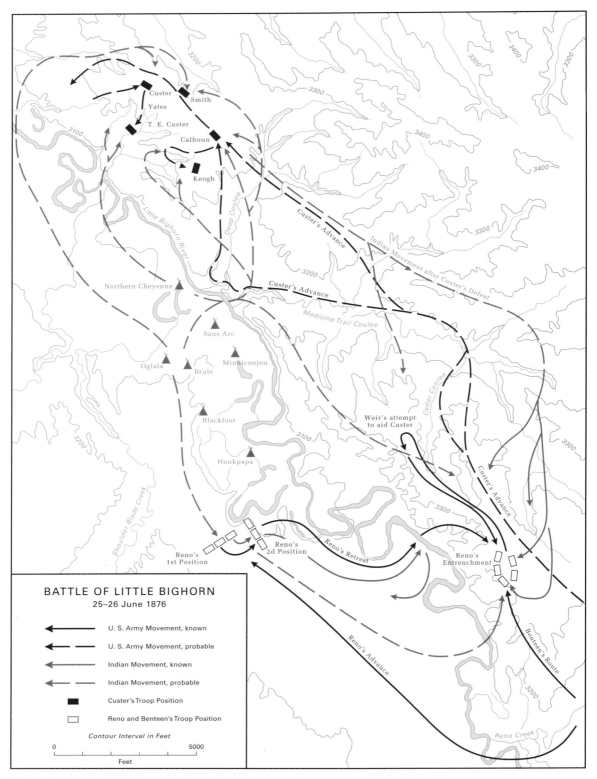

BATTLE OF LITTLE BIGHORN
25–26 June 1876

← ▬▬▬	U. S. Army Movement, known
← ▬ ▬ ▬	U. S. Army Movement, probable
← ▬▬▬	Indian Movement, known
← ▬ ▬ ▬	Indian Movement, probable
■	Custer's Troop Position
☐	Reno and Benteen's Troop Position

Contour Interval in Feet

0   5000

Feet

Map 39

The main phase of the Battle of the Little Bighorn lasted about two hours. Reno, charging down the river with three companies and some Arickara scouts, ran into hordes of Indians, not retreating, but advancing, perhaps mindful of their creditable performance against Crook the week before and certainly motivated by a desire to protect their women and children and cover a withdrawal of the villages. Far outnumbered, suffering heavy casualties, and in danger of being overrun, Reno withdrew to the bluffs across the river and dug in.

Custer and his five companies, about 230 strong, moved briskly along the bluffs above the river until, some four miles away, beyond supporting distance and out of sight of the rest of the command, they were brought to bay and overwhelmed by an Indian force that heavily outnumbered them. When the last man had fallen and the dead had been plundered, the Indians turned their attention to Reno once again. Due to the absence of any military survivors, the exact conduct of Custer's "last stand" will probably never be known.

While the Indians had been chiefly absorbed on the Custer section of the field, Benteen's battalion and the pack train and its escorting company had moved up and gone into a defensive perimeter with Reno's force. An attempt to move in force in Custer's direction, despite a complete lack of knowledge of his location and situation, failed; the Reno defensive position was reoccupied and remained under attack until dark of the twenty-fifth and on through daylight hours of the twenty-sixth. The siege was finally lifted with the arrival of the Terry-Gibbon column on June 27.

The Custer disaster shocked the nation and was the climax of the Indian Wars. The Army poured troops into the Upper Plains; and the Indians scattered, some, like Sitting Bull's band, to Canada. But gradually, under Army pressure or seeing the futility of further resistance, the Indians surrendered and returned to the reservation. Thus their greatest single victory over the U.S. Army sowed the seeds of the Indians' ultimate defeat as the United States brought to bear its overwhelming power to settle the issue once and for all.

The last feeble gasp of the Indian Wars occurred in 1890 and grew out of the fervor of the Ghost Dance religion. The Sioux were particularly susceptible to the emotional excitement and the call of the old way of life represented in these ceremonies, and their wild involvement frightened the agent on the Sioux Reservation into calling for military protection. The Army responded by a series of military actions known as the Pine Ridge Campaign. One part of that campaign

Nebraska—Crazy Horse and his band of Oglala on their way from Camp Sheridan to surrender to General Crook at Red Cloud Agency, May 6, *from engraving by Berghavy / sketch by Hottes; June 1877*

PINE RIDGE

The Pine Ridge Reservation in South Dakota was the site of the last military conflict between the U.S. Army and American Indians. The reservation became the focal point of the Ghost Dance religion founded by the Paiute shaman Wovoka in 1890. Wovoka taught that a Messiah was coming to liberate the Indians and return their world to a time before whites had arrived. The Bureau of Indian Affairs banned the Ghost Dance and requested that the Army disperse its converts. This resulted in an extensive military campaign from November 17, 1890, to January 21, 1891, with multiple converging columns conducting operations in the states of Nebraska and North and South Dakota. Over 5,500 soldiers were involved in these operations to disarm and control Indians, which resulted in numerous armed engagements and dozens killed or wounded. The most controversial and costly battle of the campaign, for both sides, was the Battle of Wounded Knee on December 29, 1890; but the battle cannot be understood outside of the wider context of the campaign.

had the 7th Cavalry, now commanded by Col. James W. Forsyth, move to Wounded Knee Creek on the Pine Ridge Agency, where on December 29 the regiment attempted to disarm Big Foot's band. An Indian's rifle was discharged into the air as two soldiers disarmed him, precipitating a battle in which more than 150 Indians, including women and children, were killed and a third as many wounded, while 25 soldiers were killed and another 37 wounded.

The Battle of Wounded Knee was the last Indian engagement to fall in the category of warfare; later incidents were more in the realm of civil disturbance. The nineteenth century was drawing to a close, and the frontier was rapidly disappearing. Territories were being replaced by states, and new settlers, towns, government, and law were spreading across the land. The buffalo were gone, and the Indians were confined to reservations to depend on the government for subsistence. An expanded rail system was available to move troops quickly to trouble spots, and the Army could now concentrate its forces at the larger and more permanent posts and relinquish numerous smaller installations that had outgrown their usefulness. By 1895 the Army was deployed more or less equally around the country on the basis of regional rather than operational considerations.

In the quarter century of the Indian Wars the Army met the Indian in over a thousand actions, large and small, all across the American West. It fought these wars with peacetime strength and on a peacetime budget, while at the same time it helped shape Indian policy and was centrally involved in numerous other activities that were part and parcel of westward expansion and of the nation's attainment of its "manifest destiny." Along the way it developed a military culture of self-sufficiency, of experienced small-unit leaders and professionals serving together as part of a brotherhood of arms. Operations against the Indians seasoned the Army and forged a core of experienced leaders who would serve the republic well as it moved onto the world scene at the turn of the century.

DISCUSSION QUESTIONS

1. How did the Army have to change its organization and tactics to fight the Indian Wars as opposed to how it fought the Civil War?

2. Compare the Seminole Indian Wars with the Indian Wars on the Great Plains. What were the similarities and differences?

3. Which of the Indian-fighters was most successful in his campaigns, and why? Of the two approaches used—harsh destruction of villages and foodstuffs or winning of "hearts and minds" through assimilation and gentle treatment—which seemed to work best?

4. Why did hundreds of Indians join the Army as Indian Scouts—some earning the Medal of Honor for bravery against other Indians?

5. How would you have settled the "Indian question" during the 1860s and 1870s? What means would have been available to you as an Army officer to change what happened to the Indians, and how would you use those means?

6. What was Fetterman's big mistake? Custer's?

RECOMMENDED READINGS

Hutton, Paul A. *Phil Sheridan and His Army*. Norman: University of Oklahoma Press, 1999.

Larson, Robert W. *Red Cloud: Warrior-Statesman of the Lakota Sioux*. Norman: University of Oklahoma Press, 1997.

Leckie, William H. *The Buffalo Soldiers: A Narrative of the Negro Cavalry in the West*. Norman: University of Oklahoma Press, 1967.

McDermott, John D. *A Guide to the Indian Wars of the West*. Lincoln: University of Nebraska Press, 1998.

Rickey, Don. *Forty Miles a Day on Beans and Hay: The Enlisted Soldier Fighting the Indian Wars*. Norman: University of Oklahoma Press, 1963.

Sklenar, Larry. *To Hell with Honor: Custer and the Little Bighorn*. Norman: University of Oklahoma Press, 2000.

Tate, Michael L. *The Frontier Army in the Settlement of the West*. Norman: University of Oklahoma Press, 1999.

Utley, Robert M. *Cavalier in Buckskin: George Armstrong Custer and the Western Military Frontier*. Norman: University of Oklahoma Press, 2001.

———. *Frontier Regulars: The United States Army and the Indian, 1866–1891*. Lincoln: University of Nebraska Press, 1984.

Wooster, Robert. *The Military and United States Indian Policy, 1865–1903*. Lincoln: University of Nebraska Press, 1995.

Other Readings

Athearn, Robert G. *Forts of the Upper Missouri*. Englewood Cliffs, N.J.: Prentice-Hall, 1967.

Dunlay, Thomas W. *Wolves for the Blue Soldiers: Indian Scouts and Auxiliaries with the United States Army, 1860–1890*. Lincoln: University of Nebraska Press, 1982.

Hampton, Bruce. *Children of Grace: The Nez Perce War of 1877*. Lincoln: University of Nebraska Press, 2002.

Prucha, Francis P. *The Great Father: The United States Government and the American Indians.* Lincoln: University of Nebraska Press, 1995.

Reardon, Carol. *Soldiers and Scholars: The U.S. Army and the Uses of Military History, 1865–1920.* Lawrence: University Press of Kansas, 1990.

Smith, Thomas T. *The U.S. Army and the Texas Frontier Economy, 1845–1900.* College Station: Texas A&M University Press, 1999.

Utley, Robert M. *The Lance and the Shield: The Life and Times of Sitting Bull.* New York: Ballantine Books, 1994.

15

EMERGENCE TO WORLD POWER 1898–1902

In the latter part of the nineteenth century the United States, hitherto largely provincial in thought and policy, began to emerge as a new world power. Beginning in the late 1880s more and more Americans displayed a willingness to support imperialistic ventures abroad, justifying this break with traditional policy on strategic, economic, religious, and emotional grounds. Much of the energy that had been channeled earlier into the internal development of the country, especially into westward expansion along the frontier (which, according to the Census Bureau, ceased to exist as of 1890), was now diverted to enterprises beyond the continental United States. It was only a matter of time before both the Army and the Navy were called upon to support America's new interests overseas.

A New Manifest Destiny

This new manifest destiny first took the form of vigorous efforts to expand American trade and naval interests overseas, especially in the Pacific and Caribbean. Thus, in the Pacific, the United States took steps to acquire facilities to sustain a growing steam-propelled fleet. In 1878 the United States obtained the right to develop a coaling station in Samoa and in 1889, to make this concession more secure, recognized the independence of the islands in a tripartite pact with Great Britain and Germany. In 1893, when the native government in Hawaii threatened to withdraw concessions, including a site for a naval station at Pearl Harbor, American residents tried unsuccessfully to secure annexation of the islands by the United States. Development of a more favorable climate of opinion in the United States in the closing years of the century opened the way for the annexation of Hawaii in 1898 and Eastern Samoa (Tutuila) in 1899.

In the same period the Navy endeavored with little success to secure coaling stations in the Caribbean and Americans watched with interest the abortive efforts of private firms to build an isthmian canal in Panama. American businessmen promoted establishment of better trade relations with Latin American countries, laying the groundwork for the future Pan American Union. And recurrent diplomatic crises, such as the one with Chile in 1891–1892 that arose from a mob attack on American sailors in Valparaiso and the one with Great Britain over the Venezuelan–British Guiana boundary in 1895, drew further attention to the southern continent.

Trouble in Cuba

While economic and strategic motives contributed significantly to the new manifest destiny, it was concern for the oppressed peoples of Cuba that ultimately launched the United States on an imperialistic course at the turn of the century. Cuba's proximity to the United States and strategic location had long attracted the interest of American expansionists. Yet they were a small minority, and only when the Cubans rebelled against the repressive colonial policies of Spain did the general public turn its attention to the Caribbean island. This was true in 1868, when the Cubans initiated a decade-long rebellion, and again in 1895, when they rose up once more against continuing repression by the mother country. Many Americans soon favored some kind of intervention, but President Grover Cleveland was determined that the United States should adhere to a policy of strict neutrality. Events in Cuba increasingly made this difficult.

When after almost a year of costly fighting the Spanish had failed to suppress the rebellion, they turned to harsher measures. A new Captain-General in Cuba, Valeriano Weyler, attempted to isolate the rebels from the population by herding women, children, and old people from the countryside into detention camps and garrisoned towns. This poorly executed reconcentrado policy led to the death of thousands of civilians from disease and starvation. Weyler's methods gave newspapers in the United States an opportunity to make sensationalistic attacks on Spanish policies. They portrayed the war in Cuba as a struggle between the "butcher" Weyler and high-minded patriots struggling bravely for freedom from Old World authoritarianism.

Despite mounting public pressure, Cleveland's successor as President, William McKinley, also tried to avoid war with Spain. He might

Wreck of the Maine, *1898*

have succeeded had the American battleship *Maine* not been sunk on February 15, 1898, in Havana harbor as a result of a mysterious explosion with a loss of 260 lives. The vessel was in port ostensibly on a courtesy call but actually to provide protection for American citizens in Cuba. A naval investigating commission appointed by the President announced on March 25 that the *Maine* had gone down as a result of an external explosion, a conclusion that even today is in doubt. To most Americans, however, the report indicated Spanish treachery. After diplomatic efforts failed to defuse the crisis, Congress on April 19 authorized the use of force to secure Cuba's independence. Six days later, on April 25, Congress issued a formal declaration of war. So began the conflict that McKinley and Cleveland had tried to avoid, a war for which the country was ill prepared.

Mobilizing for War

The extent of unpreparedness for overseas combat varied considerably in the two military services. In the decade preceding the war, the Navy, thanks to the efforts of career officers such as Rear Adm. Stephen B. Luce, Capt. Alfred T. Mahan, and Benjamin Tracy, Secretary of the Navy in Harrison's administration, as well as to the willingness of Congress to appropriate the necessary funds, had carried out an extensive construction and modernization program. The historical writings of Alfred T. Mahan were particularly influential in establishing the framework of a global, blue-water fleet focused on the dominance of the Navy, the establishment of refueling bases, and the aggressive protection of commerce. During the same period, the Naval War College at Newport, Rhode Island (established in 1885 through the efforts of Admiral Luce), had provided the Navy with a strong corps of professional officers trained in the higher levels of warfare and strategy, including the far-ranging doctrines of Mahan.

The Army was not so fortunate. During the quarter of a century preceding 1898, the Army averaged only about 26,000 officers and men, most of whom were scattered widely across the country in company- and battalion-size organizations. Consequently, the Army rarely had had an opportunity for training and experience in the operation of units larger than a regiment. Moreover, the service lacked a mobilization plan, a well-knit higher staff, and experience in carrying on joint operations with the Navy. The National Guard was equally ill prepared. Though the Guard counted over 100,000 members, most units were poorly trained and inadequately equipped. Thus, while most regulars were armed with Krag-Jorgensen rifles firing smokeless powder cartridges, most guardsmen were still equipped with Springfield rifles that could fire only black powder ammunition.

The utility of the Guard was further compromised by question as to whether it was legal for Guard units to serve abroad. Consequently, as in the Civil War, the national government on April 22 called upon the states to raise 125,000 volunteers for federal service. Guardsmen were encouraged to enlist, and in some cases entire regiments of militia volunteered for federal service, thereby permitting the units to remain intact. In most cases, however, guardsmen enrolled as individuals and took their places alongside men devoid of any military background in

> The Army rarely had had an opportunity for training and experience in the operation of units larger than a regiment.

entirely new organizations. War fever soon led Congress to increase the size of the volunteer force by an additional 75,000 and to create some special forces, including 10,000 enlisted men "possessing immunity from diseases incident to tropical climates," the so-called Immunes. It also authorized more than doubling the size of the Regular Army to nearly 65,000. By war's end in August 1898, the regular forces numbered 59,000 and the volunteers 216,000, a total of 275,000. Regardless of whether these men were regulars or volunteers, the vast majority of them had had little or no military experience prior to the war.

Mobilizing, equipping, and supplying the burgeoning wartime Army placed a severe burden on the War Department. With neither a military planning staff nor in peacetime the funds necessary to plan for war, the department was ill prepared for any kind of major mobilization. Further complicating matters were basic disagreements concerning the strategy to be followed and the way mobilization should be conducted.

To the extent the United States had a strategy for the conduct of the war against Spain, it consisted of maintaining a naval blockade of Cuba while Cuban insurgent forces carried on a harassing campaign against Spanish troops on the island. Supporters of this policy (Captain Mahan was among its more articulate advocates) believed that it would lead eventually to the surrender of the Spanish forces and the liberation of Cuba. No direct clash between American and Spanish troops was visualized; American land forces would simply occupy Cuba as soon as the Spanish departed.

More or less in conformity with this strategy, Maj. Gen. Nelson Miles, Commanding General of the Army, proposed to assemble, train, and equip a small force of about 80,000 using the Regular Army as a nucleus. There would be ample time to prepare this force, since Miles deemed it unwise to land any troops in Cuba before the end of the unhealthy rainy season in October. The first step was to concentrate the entire Regular Army at Chickamauga Park, Georgia, where it could receive much-needed instruction in combined-arms operations.

So deliberate and cautious a plan, however, was by mid-April 1898 not in harmony with the increasing public demand for immediate action against the Spanish. With an ear to this demand, Secretary of War Russell M. Alger ignored General Miles' advice. He ordered the regular infantry regiments to go to New Orleans, Tampa, and Mobile, where they would be ready for an immediate descent on Cuba. (*Map 40*) (Later

"EMBALMED BEEF"

In December 1898 Nelson A. Miles, the Commanding General of the Army, made a sensational public charge that refrigerated beef supplied to the Army during the Spanish-American War had been "embalmed" with harmful preservative chemicals. Miles also criticized canned boiled beef that the troops universally reviled for its poor quality, tastelessness, and often nauseatingly spoiled condition. Official inquiries found no evidence of harmful chemicals in either type of beef but concluded that use of the easily spoiled canned beef in the tropics was a serious mistake. Despite these findings, the myth of embalmed beef persisted in the public imagination.

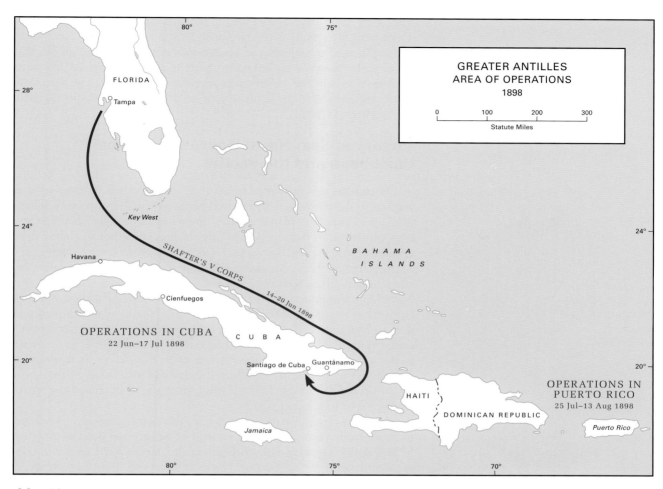

Map 40

some infantry troops did go to Chickamauga Park, where they trained with the regular cavalry and artillery concentrated there.)

The decision to mobilize large volunteer forces compounded the problems of equipping, training, and supplying the Army. In the spring and summer of 1898, thousands of enthusiastic but inexperienced volunteers poured into newly established camps. A taste of military life soon curbed the enthusiasm of most of them, for in the camps they found chronic shortages of the most essential equipment. Even such basic items as underwear, socks, and shoes were lacking. A steady diet of badly prepared food, unbelievably poor sanitary conditions, and inadequate medical facilities complemented the equipment shortages. Red tape and poor management in the War Department's supply bureaus (the Ordnance Department possibly excepted) delayed correction of some of the worst deficiencies, while the shortage of capable volunteer officers further limited the quality of training received in the camps.

Confusion and inefficiency likewise characterized the War Department's conduct of operations. Since Congress had provided no machinery in the department for the peacetime coordination of foreign policy with the country's military posture, the nation went to war without any kind of overall plan of operations or even adequate intelligence about the enemy. Given time, the Army might have devised adequate operational plans; but public opinion, political pressures, and the trend of events demanded the launching of an immediate expedition against the Spanish in Cuba.

Victory at Sea: Naval Operations in the Caribbean and the Pacific

A Pennsylvania artilleryman would wear a khaki cotton field coat such as this.

Fortunately, it turned out that the really decisive fighting of the war fell to the much better prepared Navy, although last-minute alterations in its strategic plan seriously threatened to reduce its effectiveness. Shortly after the war began, rumors circulated that an enemy fleet under Admiral Pascual Cervera y Topete was approaching the east coast of the United States. An alarmed public demanded that measures be taken to defend the Atlantic seaboard. In deference to this demand, the Navy Department in late April 1898 withheld some of its best fighting ships from Rear Adm. William T. Sampson's North Atlantic Squadron, sent to blockade Cuba. These ships, formed into a "flying squadron" under Commodore Winfield S. Schley, set up a watch for Cervera. This move was in conflict with the provisions in the Navy's strategic plan that, based upon Mahan's doctrines, called for maintaining Sampson's squadron at full strength in the Caribbean, ready to intercept any Spanish fleet sent to relieve Cuba.

In the western Pacific, meanwhile, the Navy was able to adhere to its strategic plan—the latest version of which had been completed in June 1897. Developed by officers at the Naval War College in collaboration with the Office of Naval Intelligence, the plan provided for an attack on the Philippines, leading to the destruction of Spanish warships there, the capture of Manila, and a blockade of the principal Philippine ports. The basic objectives of the plan were to weaken Spain by cutting off revenues from the Philippines and to place the United States in the position of having something to offer the Spanish as an inducement to make peace after Cuba had been freed.

The Navy began to actively prepare for war in January 1898, and in late February Theodore Roosevelt, as Acting Secretary of the Navy (Secretary John D. Long was ailing), cabled orders to American naval commanders, instructing them to get their squadrons in readiness for action. Commodore George Dewey of the Asiatic Squadron responded by assembling his ships at Hong Kong, where they could take on coal and supplies preparatory to an attack on the Philippines. Thus, on April 24, when McKinley finally ordered the Asiatic Squadron to initiate hostilities, Dewey was ready. He sailed into Manila Bay on the night of April 30 and the following morning located Spain's weak and dilapidated naval squadron at Cavite. In a few hours and without loss of a single American life, he sank or disabled the entire Spanish force. In the days immediately following, he also silenced the land batteries defending Manila harbor; but the city itself continued to resist. With barely enough men to maintain his own squadron, Dewey requested the dispatch of land forces from the United States to help take Manila.

EMILIO AGUINALDO (1869–1964)

Despite modest military abilities, Emilio Aguinaldo embodied the Philippines' struggle for independence; and his capture, while not ending the rebellion, certainly helped weaken it. After taking an oath of allegiance to the United States, Aguinaldo spent the next thirty years as a farmer. When Japan invaded the Philippines in 1941, he participated in the Japanese puppet government. Charged as a collaborator after the war, he was soon pardoned. Having lived through three colonial administrations, he finally witnessed the birth of a free and independent Philippines in July 1946. He died in 1964 at the age of 95.

While Dewey blockaded Manila and awaited reinforcements, the Filipinos rose up in revolt against their Spanish overlords. The Philippines had rebelled against Spain in 1896, a conflict that had ended only in December 1897 with a pact that had included the exile of the insurgent leadership to Hong Kong. Spain, however, did not fully live up to its part of the pact; and upon the outbreak of war between the United States and Spain in April 1898, pro-independence Filipinos once again took up arms against the Spanish. Seeking to capitalize on this development, Dewey arranged for Emilio Aguinaldo, the leader of 1897 insurgent government, to return to the Philippines in May. Aguinaldo immediately sought to reassert control over the revolutionary movement, forming an army and declaring the islands independent. By the time American ground troops began to arrive at the end of June, Filipino revolutionaries already controlled the majority of the archipelago, as the Spanish Army had withdrawn to Manila and a few other key cities. The Americans thus joined the Filipinos in besieging Manila.

Operations in the Caribbean

As in the Pacific, naval developments would determine when and where the Army undertook operations in the Caribbean. During the early part of May 1898, the whereabouts of the Spanish Fleet under Admiral Cervera remained a mystery. Lacking this information, the Army could not precisely fix the point where it would launch an attack. Nevertheless, the War Department pushed preparations at Tampa, Florida, for an expedition under General Miles to be put ashore somewhere near Havana. But persistent rumors of the approach of the Spanish Fleet to Cuban waters delayed this expedition while the Navy searched further for Cervera. News at last reached Washington near the end of May that the Spanish admiral had skillfully evaded the American naval blockade and on the nineteenth had slipped into the bay at Santiago de Cuba. (*See Map 40.*)

The Navy, at first not at all certain that it was actually Cervera's fleet in Santiago, sent Admiral Sampson to inspect the harbor. As soon as the American naval commander had ascertained that the four cruisers and several smaller war vessels were indeed Spanish, he bombarded the forts at the entrance to Santiago Bay. Unable to silence them, Sampson decided against trying to run the heavily mined harbor entrance. Instead, he sent Lt. (Junior Grade) Richmond P. Hobson to bottle up

Embarking for Cuba, *Charles Johnson Post, 1930*

the enemy fleet by sinking the collier Merrimac athwart the channel. When this bold project failed, Sampson requested army forces to seize the Spanish batteries, at the same time dispatching marines ashore to secure a site for a naval base east of Santiago. In the first land skirmish of the Cuban campaign, the marines quickly overcame enemy resistance and established the base at Guantánamo Bay.

Upon receipt of Sampson's request for land forces, the War Department, already under strong public pressure to get the Army into action, ordered Maj. Gen. William R. Shafter to embark with the V Corps from Tampa as soon as possible to conduct operations against Santiago in cooperation with the Navy. This corps was the only one of the eight that the War Department had organized for the war that was anywhere near ready to fight. Composed chiefly of regular Army units, it had been assembling at Tampa for weeks when the order came on May 31 for its embarkation; it would require another two weeks to get the corps and its equipment on board and ready to sail for Cuba.

Many factors contributed to the slow pace of preparation. There was no overall plan and no special staff to direct the organization of the expeditionary force. Moreover, Tampa was a poor choice for marshaling a major military expedition. Selected because of its proximity to Cuba, Tampa had only one pier for loading ships and a single-track railroad connecting with mainline routes from the north. It could not, therefore, readily accommodate the flood of men and materiel pressing in upon it. So great was the congestion that freight cars were backed up on sidings as far away as Columbia, South Carolina, waiting to gain access to the port. When a freight car finally did reach the port area, there were no wagons to unload it and no bill of lading to indicate what was in it. When it came to loading the ships, of which there were not enough to carry the entire corps, supplies and equipment were put on board with little regard for unloading priorities in the combat zone should the enemy resist the landings.

In spite of the muddle at Tampa, by June 14 nearly 17,000 men were ready to sail. On board were 18 regular and 2 volunteer infantry regiments; 10 regular and 2 volunteer cavalry squadrons serving dismounted; 1 mounted cavalry squadron; 6 artillery batteries; and a Gatling gun company. The expedition comprised a major part of the Regular Army, including all of the regular African American combat regiments. Departing Tampa on the morning of the fourteenth, the V Corps joined its naval convoy the next day off the Florida Keys and by June 20 had reached the vicinity of Santiago.

While the troops on board endured tropical heat, unsanitary conditions, and cold, unpalatable rations, Shafter and Sampson conferred on how to proceed against Santiago. Sampson wanted the Army to storm the fort on the east side of the bay entrance and drive the Spanish from their guns. Then his fleet could clear away the mines and enter Santiago Bay to fight Cervera's squadron. Lacking heavy artillery, Shafter was not sure his troops could take the fort, which crowned a steep hill. He decided instead to follow the suggestion of General Calixto Garcia, the local insurgent leader, and land his forces at Daiquiri, east of Santiago Bay. (*See Map 41.*)

On June 22, after heavy shelling of the landing areas, the V Corps disembarked amid circumstances almost as confused and hectic as those at Tampa. Captains of many of the chartered merchant ships refused to bring their vessels close to shore. Their reluctance slowed the landing of troops and equipment already handicapped by a shortage of lighters. Horses, simply dropped overboard to get ashore on their own, swam out to sea in some instances and were lost. An alert enemy defense might well have taken advantage of the chaotic conditions to oppose the landings effectively. But the Spanish, though they had more than 200,000 troops in Cuba—36,000 of them in Santiago Province—did nothing to prevent Shafter's men from getting ashore. Some 6,000 landed on June 22 and most of the remaining 11,000 on the two days following. In addition, 4,000 to 5,000 insurgents under General Garcia supplemented the American force.

Battle of Santiago

Once ashore, elements of the V Corps moved westward toward the heights of San Juan, a series of ridges immediately east of Santiago, where well-entrenched enemy troops guarded the land approaches to the city. On June 23, Brig. Gen. Henry W. Lawton, commanding the vanguard, advanced along the coast from Daiquirí to Siboney, which then became the main base of operations. The next day, Brig. Gen. Joseph Wheeler, the Confederate Army veteran, pushed inland along the road to Santiago with dismounted cavalry to seize Las Guásimas after a brief skirmish with rear guard elements of a retiring Spanish force. This move brought American units within five miles of the San Juan Heights, where they paused for a few days while General Shafter assembled the rest of his divisions and brought up supplies. Even in this short time, Shafter could observe the debilitating effects of tropical climate and disease on his men. He was aware, too, that the hurricane season was approaching. Consequently, he decided to launch an immediate attack on the defenses of Santiago.

Shafter's plan was simple: a frontal attack on the San Juan Heights. For this purpose, he deployed Brig. Gen. Jacob F. Kent's infantry division on the left and Wheeler's dismounted cavalry on the right, the entire force with supporting elements comprising 8,000 troops. But before he made the main advance on the heights, Lawton's infantry division with a supporting battery of artillery, more than 6,500 men, was to move two miles north to seize the fortified village of El Caney, cutting off Santiago's water supply and, if necessary, intercepting rumored Spanish reinforcements. This action completed—Shafter thought it would take about two hours—Lawton was to turn southwestward and form on the right flank of Wheeler's division for the main assault. A brigade that had just landed at Siboney was to advance in the meantime along the coast in a feint.

The attack, which moved out at dawn on July 1, soon became badly disorganized because of poor coordination, difficult terrain, and tropical heat. The corpulent Shafter, virtually prostrated by the heat, had to leave the direction of the battle to others. At a stream crossing on the crowded main trail to San Juan Heights, enemy gunners scored heavily when a towed Signal Corps balloon pinpointed the front of the advancing line of troops. Lawton's division, delayed in its seizure of El Caney by a stubborn enemy defense, misplaced artillery, and the necessity of withdrawing a volunteer unit armed only with telltale black powder, did not rejoin the main force until after the assault had ended. Despite these unexpected setbacks, Kent's and Wheeler's divisions at midday launched

THE ROUGH RIDERS

Colonel Roosevelt in Rough Rider Uniform, ca. 1898

The 1st U.S. Volunteer Cavalry, initially commanded by Col. Leonard Wood, was popularly known as the Rough Riders. It was composed of western volunteers, cowboys, and woodsmen and raised in large measure by the forceful personality of its second in command, the future President Theodore Roosevelt. During the Spanish-American War, the unit charged detached Spanish works on Kettle Hill in front of Santiago, Cuba, on July 1, 1898, along with other elements of the Cavalry Division, V Corps. Roosevelt led the Rough Riders from the front, revolver in hand. Concurrently the 1st Division attacked the main Spanish position on San Juan Ridge. By the time the Americans reached the Spanish lines, the defenders had fled. Newspaper accounts magnified the Rough Riders' role in the victory but not their bravery and daring.

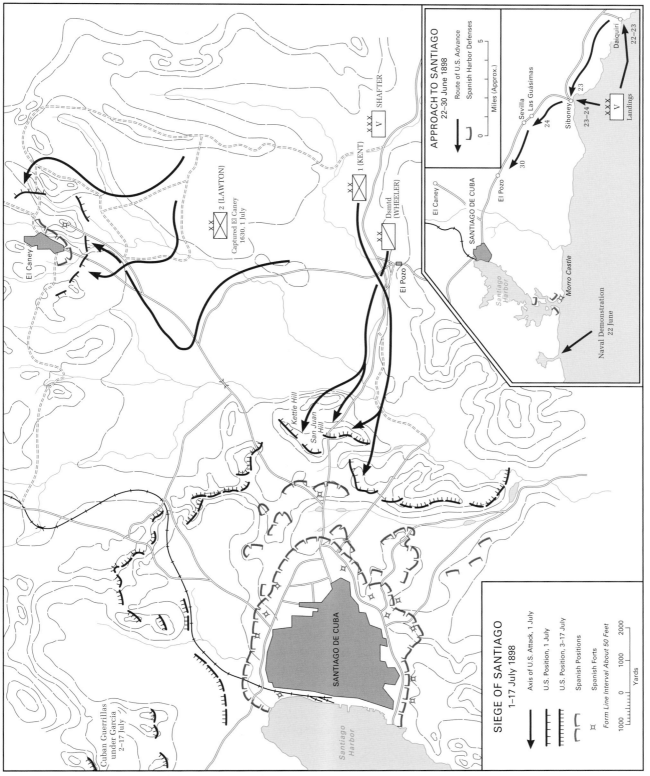

APPROACH TO SANTIAGO
22–30 June 1898

Route of U.S. Advance
Spanish Harbor Defenses

Miles (Approx.)
0   5

Daiquiri
22–23
Landings
XXX V
23–24
Siboney
23
24
Las Guásimas
Sevilla
30
El Pozo
El Caney
SANTIAGO DE CUBA
Santiago Harbor
Morro Castle
Naval Demonstration
22 June

El Caney

Captured El Caney
1630, 1 July

2 (LAWTON)

XXX V
SHAFTER

1 (KENT)

Dsmtd
(WHEELER)

El Pozo

Kettle Hill
San Juan Hill

Cuban Guerrillas
under García
2–17 July

SANTIAGO DE CUBA

Santiago Harbor

SIEGE OF SANTIAGO
1–17 July 1898

Axis of U.S. Attack, 1 July
U.S. Position, 1 July
U.S. Position, 3–17 July
Spanish Positions
Spanish Forts
Form Line Interval About 50 Feet

Yards
1000   1000   2000

Map 41

a strong frontal attack on the Spanish forward defensive positions. Cavalry units of Wheeler's division, including the 9th Cavalry and part of the 10th, both African American regiments, and the 1st U.S. Volunteer Cavalry (the "Rough Riders"), now commanded by newly commissioned Lt. Col. Theodore Roosevelt, seized Kettle Hill, separate from the central heights. Then Kent's infantry regiments, supported by Gatling guns, stormed up San Juan Hill in the main ridge line, driving the Spanish from blockhouse and trench defenses and compelling them to retire to a strongly fortified inner line. Thus the day ended with the Americans' having achieved most of their initial objectives. The cost was high: nearly 1,700 casualties sustained since the start of operations against Santiago.

Concerned with the increasing sickness that was thinning the ranks of the V Corps and faced by a well-organized Spanish second line of defense, General Shafter cabled Secretary Alger on July 3 that he was considering withdrawing about five miles to higher ground between the San Juan River and Siboney. The shift would place his troops in a position where they would be less exposed to enemy fire and easier to supply. Alger replied that "the effect upon the country would be much better" if Shafter continued to hold his advanced position.

San Juan Hill, July 10, 1898, *Charles Johnson Post, 1930*

The V Corps commander then sought to get the Navy to enter Santiago Bay and attack the city. But neither the Navy Department nor President McKinley was willing to sanction this move. Just when the whole matter threatened to become an embarrassing public debate between the two services, the Spanish resolved the issue.

By early July serious shortages of food and ammunition had convinced the Spanish that Santiago must soon fall. While Cervera considered flight from the port hopeless, he had no recourse but to attempt it. Officials in both Havana and Madrid had ordered him, for reasons of honor, to escape when Santiago appeared about to surrender. Finally, on the morning of July 3, while Sampson and Shafter conferred ashore, Cervera made his dash for the open sea, hoping to reach the port of Cienfuegos on the south coast of Cuba. As soon as the Spanish Fleet appeared, Sampson's squadron, temporarily under the command of Commodore Schley, gave chase and in less than two hours destroyed Cervera's force; four cruisers were crippled and run ashore, one destroyer was beached, and another was sunk.

A few days later General Shafter persuaded the Spanish leaders in Santiago that they had no choice except to surrender. On July 16 they signed the unconditional terms demanded by the McKinley administration, which provided for the surrender of 11,500 troops in the city and 12,000 others in the vicinity of Santiago. The formal surrender ceremony took place on the following day.

During preparations for the Santiago campaign, General Miles personally had been overseeing the organization of a second expedition to seize Puerto Rico. On July 21 he sailed from Guantánamo with more than 3,000 troops. His original strategy was to land at Cape Fajardo in the northeast part of the island, where he could establish a base of operations for a subsequent advance west to the capital, San Juan. For reasons not entirely clear, but probably because of a desire not to have to cooperate with the Navy in the attack on San Juan, Miles, while still at sea, changed his plans and on July 25 landed forces at Guanica on the southeastern coast. Meeting virtually no opposition, the Americans shortly occupied the port of Ponce. In early August, after the arrival of more than 10,000 additional troops from the United States, General Miles, using Ponce as a base of operations, launched a four-column drive toward San Juan. There was little bloodshed—casualties for the campaign totaled fewer than fifty—and, in fact, most Puerto Ricans welcomed the American troops. The campaign ended on August 13 when word reached the island that Spain had signed a peace protocol the previous day.

Back in Cuba, conditions for the Army were much less pleasant. The spread of malaria, typhoid, and yellow fever among Shafter's troops at Santiago threatened to have far deadlier consequences than had the actual fighting. Concern over this problem led a number of Shafter's senior officers to draft a joint letter proposing immediate evacuation of the Army from Cuba. Addressed to the Commanding General, this round robin letter came to the attention of the press before it reached Shafter. Hence, Washington officials read it in the newspapers before learning of its content from the general himself. Naturally the whole episode, coming at the time when peace negotiations were beginning, caused a sensation. Although acutely embarrassing for the Army and General Shafter, the incident did have the salutary effect of hastening measures to evacuate thousands of troops to Montauk Point, Long Island, where the Army Medical Department already had taken steps to establish a quarantine camp. There, those who had contracted tropical infections received the necessary treatment. The Army's nearly disastrous experience with the debilitating effects of disease and climate in Cuba did, however, spur the Medical Corps to determine the causes of yellow fever, inaugurating a long-term program of research and study into what henceforth would be a permanent concern of the Army, the maintenance of the health and effectiveness of American troops in a tropical environment.

The Fall of Manila

In another tropical setting halfway around the world from Cuba, the final military episode of the war took place. On June 30 the first

> The spread of malaria, typhoid, and yellow fever among troops at Santiago threatened to have far deadlier consequences than had the actual fighting.

contingent of American ground troops disembarked in the Philippines. By the end of July 1898, 13,000 volunteer and 2,000 regular troops, constituting the VIII Corps under Maj. Gen. Wesley Merritt, had reached the islands. These troops had embarked from west coast ports (chiefly San Francisco) with a minimum of the confusion and difficulty that had characterized the launching of the Cuban expedition. In spite of the long voyage across the Pacific, they were in good condition and ready to start operations against the 13,000 Spaniards trapped inside Manila. Between the Americans and the Spanish lay Aguinaldo's revolutionary army, also numbering around 13,000 men.

Although the Americans and the Filipinos shared a common interest in defeating Spain, relations between the allies deteriorated steadily during the summer. The most important reason was a fundamental difference in objectives. The goal of the insurgents was immediate independence for the Philippines. After some hesitation, the McKinley administration began to express the view that the United States ought to retain the islands for itself. Thus, by late summer the two allies eyed each other warily.

The Spanish commander in Manila realized his situation was hopeless but believed he must put up at least token resistance, not only for honor's sake, but also to avoid a court-martial back home. He greatly feared that a rebel assault might lead to a massacre of the garrison. The Americans shared the Spaniard's desire to keep the insurgents out of Manila, not only for humanitarian reasons but also to deny the independence movement the political legitimacy it would garner by occupying the capital city, a prize the Americans wanted for themselves. After persuading the Filipinos to give them a small portion of the front lines, Dewey struck a secret deal with the Spanish governor in which the Spanish agreed to make only minimal resistance to an American assault if the Americans in turn promised to keep the Filipino army out of the city. On August 13, after a short but not entirely bloodless battle, Merritt's soldiers occupied central Manila, shutting out their chagrined allies. Operations at Manila cost the Americans a total of 17 killed and 105 wounded.

Formal surrender ceremonies came the following day—actually two days after the government in Madrid had signed a protocol suspending hostilities. News of the protocol had not yet reached Manila because a cable Dewey had cut when he first entered Manila Bay still had not been repaired.

After negotiations in Paris in the fall of 1898, the United States and Spain signed a peace treaty on December 10. By its terms Spain gave up sovereignty over Cuba, which became an independent state, ceded Puerto Rico and Guam to the United States, and accepted $20 million in payment for the Philippines. Thus fatefully did the Americans commit the nation to a new role as a colonial power in the Far East, with momentous future consequences that few at the time could anticipate.

The Philippine-American War, 1899–1902

News of the Treaty of Paris brought no comfort to Filipino nationalists. Since the fall of Manila an uneasy truce had existed between the

Filipino army that continued to surround Manila and the Americans inside the city. After consolidating his hold over much of the archipelago, Aguinaldo established a republic with a capital at Malolos, northeast of Manila, and made preparations to resist the United States should it attempt to assert its claims of sovereignty over the islands. As the soldiers of both sides waited anxiously to see if the U.S. Congress would ratify the Treaty of Paris, relations between the erstwhile allies deteriorated and scuffles became common. It was only a matter of time before full-scale violence erupted.

That moment came on the night of February 4, 1899, when Filipino and American patrols traded shots near a disputed village in the neutral zone that separated the two armies. The firing quickly spread along the entire front line; and at dawn Maj. Gen. Elwell S. Otis, who had replaced General Merritt, launched an offensive to drive the Filipinos off the high ground that overlooked the northern portion of the American lines. Though no one knows to this day who fired the first shot, the war was on. Meanwhile, back in Washington, a deeply divided Senate narrowly ratified the Treaty of Paris on February 6. Having formally purchased the Philippines from Spain, the United States declared its newfound possession to be in a state of insurrection. Thomas B. Reed, the Speaker of the House of Representatives, remarked ruefully, "We have bought ten million Malays at $2.00 a head unpicked, and nobody knows what it will cost to pick them."

In February 1899 Aguinaldo's Army of Liberation of the Philippines had arrayed up to 40,000 men around Manila with additional detachments of militia distributed throughout the archipelago. Organized as

General Otis' Staff and Assistants in Their Quarters in Manila, 1899

a conventional military force, the Army of Liberation lacked training, discipline, and equipment. Worst of all, it was plagued with incompetent and inexperienced leaders. Otis, by contrast, had fewer than 20,000 men available in Manila, the vast majority of whom were state volunteers who expected to be discharged now that the war with Spain had ended. Nevertheless, the volunteers fought well: by late February they had driven the Filipino army from Manila and crushed a revolt within the city itself. By the end of March the VIII Corps had captured the capital of the Philippine Republic at Malolos, twenty-five miles northeast of Manila and inflicted a series of sharp defeats on Filipino forces. Aguinaldo's army would never recover from the losses it suffered during the first weeks of the war in terms of men, materiel, and morale. Nevertheless, it stubbornly remained in the field, retiring to the north in front of the advancing Americans while additional detachments continued to threaten Manila from the south, compelling Otis to launch several expeditions into southern Luzon to stabilize his southern flank.

The summer of 1899 brought a hiatus to the campaign. The small size of Otis' army became increasingly felt the farther he pushed from Manila, while disease and fatigue reduced some regiments by 60 percent. The onset of the monsoon season further complicated the situation, as did the political need to send the state volunteers home. Congress had attempted to meet the military needs of the new war in March when it authorized the enrollment of a temporary force of 35,000 volunteers for Philippines service. Unlike the volunteers of 1898, who had been organized by the states under officers appointed by state governors, the men of 1899 were organized directly by the federal government as U.S. Volunteers, with a term of service set to expire at the end of June 1901. By September 1899 the new U.S. Volunteer regiments, together with additional units of regulars, had begun to arrive in the Philippines; but their arrival merely offset the departure of the state volunteers, thus leaving the VIII Corps with an effective force of just under 27,000 men.

Otis nevertheless was determined to press ahead with a major offensive north of Manila, an offensive that he hoped would destroy the Army of Liberation once and for all. In early October he launched a three-pronged attack. Moving up on the right, General Lawton captured San Isidro and approached San Fabian on the Lingayen Gulf in an attempt to prevent the insurgent army from retreating into the mountains. Maj. Gen. Arthur MacArthur of Civil War fame, in the center, pushed up the central Luzon plain, seized Tarlac, and then moved on to Dagupan. Meanwhile, Brig. Gen. Loyd Wheaton, on the left, went by ship from Manila to San Fabian, moving inland to defeat the insurgents at San Jacinto before linking up with MacArthur at Dagupan. The operation succeeded in destroying part of Aguinaldo's army and dispersing the remainder, but it did not end the war. Aguinaldo escaped into the mountains of northern Luzon, and in November 1899 he ordered the remnants of his army to shift from conventional to guerrilla warfare.

The change of tactics was well considered. The Philippine Islands were a labyrinth of rice paddies, mountains, and jungles pierced only by rough trails and a few primitive roads. In this arena, Filipino guerrillas enjoyed numerous advantages over the Americans, not the least of which were their familiarity with the terrain and people and their acclimation to the region's enervating tropical climate. Aguinaldo, realizing that he lacked the resources to conduct a coordinated, conventional defense, organized his forces into a number of highly autonomous regional commands, each of which included a core of full-time "regular" soldiers backed by part-time militiamen. Together, these forces waged a war of ambushes, raids, and surprise attacks designed to keep the Americans off balance. Although some guerrillas wore uniforms, many did not; and even those who freely did changed into civilian clothes and hid their weapons to disguise their true identity from American patrols. This "chameleon act," whereby the guerrillas transformed themselves into obsequious "amigos" in the blink of an eye, made them difficult to counter, especially given the Army's lack of familiarity with Filipino language and customs.

Complementing the guerrillas in the field was a clandestine civil-military organization that acted as a shadow government in the villages, enforcing insurgent edicts, raising recruits, collecting supplies and "taxes," and gathering intelligence on American activities. Since many of the leaders of the resistance were from the middle and upper classes, they were able to exploit the oligarchic nature of Philippine society and the system of patron-client relationships upon which it was based to further the movement's influence over the people. Using a mixture of genuine nationalism, paternalism, propaganda, and terror (including the assassination of pro-American Filipinos), the leaders of the resistance maintained their control over the population despite their inability to defeat the U.S. Army in the field.

In fact, military victory was never the aim of Filipino leaders after 1899. Instead, they sought to undermine America's will to continue the struggle by harassing U.S. military forces. The Filipinos were well aware that many Americans opposed the government's venture in imperialism, and they consciously played to this audience. Realizing that 1900 was an election year in the United States, they sought to stir up as much trouble as they could in the hope that a disenchanted electorate would replace McKinley with the avowed anti-imperialist, William Jennings Bryan, in the presidential election.

Otis responded to the changed circumstances of the war by dividing the VIII Corps into several geographical commands, each of which was responsible for the pacification of a particular region of the Philippines. Regiments assigned to these districts were further broken down and dispersed among hundreds of small posts, most of which were located in or near towns. The posts served three purposes: they helped protect the population from guerrilla intimidation; they interfered with the ability of the population to provide food and recruits to the guerrillas; and they served as launching pads for innumerable small-unit patrols and raids into the bush in search of the guerrillas and their bases. The dispersion caused many difficulties in terms of logistics, morale, and command and control, while the effects of disease and fatigue threatened to undermine the effectiveness of many small garrisons. Nevertheless, the aggressive posture adopted by the Americans kept the guerrillas dispersed and on the run, thereby undermining both their ability and their will to continue the war.

Tactically the Army performed well during the guerrilla phase of the Philippine War. Guerrilla ambushes, while frustrating and difficult to prevent, were rarely devastating and could be countered by sound tactics and proper security measures. Meanwhile, the Americans attempted to take the war to the enemy, sending small columns to search for and destroy his camps and supply bases while other units made night raids on villages to round up suspected insurgent leaders. The clandestine nature of the enemy's organization frequently frustrated these operations, but over time the Americans gradually eroded the insurgents' capability to resist. Of particular assistance in spreading control and separating the guerrillas from the ordinary citizens was the growing number of Filipinos who agreed to take up arms in American service—over 15,000 by war's end in such organizations as the Philippine Constabulary, the Philippine Scouts, and various other police and paramilitary organizations.

Bullets were not America's only answer to Filipino resistance, however, for Otis was not just the commander of American military forces in the Philippines but the military governor as well. Following McKinley's instructions to "win the confidence, respect, and admiration of the inhabitants of the Philippines," both Otis and General MacArthur who succeeded him in May 1900 worked to restore the norms of civil society. They built schools and roads, refurbished markets, and introduced improved systems of health and sanitation. They offered amnesty to guerrillas willing to turn themselves in and rewards to those who handed over their weapons as well. They restored government services, at first using American officers as governing officials but gradually transferring political control to Filipinos, beginning in the towns and villages. They were aided in their work by a body of American civilian commissioners led by William H. Taft that became the legislature for the Philippines in the fall of 1900. Although soldiers and civilians sometimes clashed over their respective authority and the speed at which the transition from military to civilian rule should take place, both worked toward the mutual goal of restoring law, order, and administration to the Philippines.

By the end of the first full year of guerrilla warfare, the Americans had clearly gained the upper hand. Hounded by American forces (which had reached an all time high of 70,000 men) dispirited by McKinley's reelection, and tempted by American promises of future peace and prosperity, one Filipino leader after another laid down his arms and returned to civil life. For those who refused to come in from the bush, MacArthur stepped up the pressure, permitting the use of imprisonment, deportation, execution, and the confiscation and/or destruction of property to punish guerrillas and their supporters to a greater degree than had been permitted heretofore. MacArthur and Taft complemented this firmer wielding of the sword by a greater extension of the olive branch, creating in December 1900 the Federalist Party, a Filipino political organization that supported American rule in return for the establishment of representative government and increased local autonomy. The party proved an effective tool in competing with resistance leaders for the allegiance of the Filipino people. Then, in March 1901, a small band of American soldiers and Filipino auxiliaries led by Brig. Gen. Frederick Funston dealt the resistance a further demoralizing blow when they succeeded in capturing Aguinaldo through a ruse. By July 1901 sufficient progress had been made to permit the establish-

FREDERICK FUNSTON (1865–1917)

A born adventurer who lacked formal military training, Frederick Funston fought alongside Cuban revolutionaries before receiving a volunteer commission in 1898. Sent to the Philippines, he fought with distinction but was denied a commission in the Regular Army. He was about to muster out in early 1901 when he learned of the location of Aguinaldo's headquarters. Throwing caution to the wind, he penetrated Aguinaldo's headquarters by pretending to be a prisoner, then turned the tables and seized Aguinaldo. The exploit won Funston a commission as a brigadier general in the Regular Army.

ment of full civilian rule in many parts of the Philippines under Taft, who became Governor-General of the Philippines.

Despite this progress, another full year of war remained. The most serious fighting occurred in southern Luzon and on the island of Samar, where the resistance movement remained strong. The burden for these last campaigns fell upon the regulars as the U.S. Volunteers of 1899 mustered out of service in the summer of 1901. Hardest hit was the 9th Infantry, which lost nearly an entire company to a guerrilla surprise attack in the village of Balangiga, Samar, in September 1901. The Army responded to this continued resistance with increasingly stringent methods, including the destruction of buildings and crops and the imposition of population concentration measures not unlike the notorious reconcentrado methods that had proven so distasteful to the American public prior to the outbreak of the Spanish-American War. Some officers, frustrated by the enemy's elusiveness, even resorted to torture to gain information. These sterner measures, coupled with the continued promise of equitable treatment and representative government, ultimately broke the back of the resistance movement. The last major revolutionary commanders surrendered in the spring of 1902; and on July 4 the United States officially proclaimed the insurrection to be over. In actuality, some sections of the Philippines continued to be troubled by violence, banditry, and rebellion for several more years, particularly in the Moslem areas that had never been fully pacified by Spain. But American rule was never seriously challenged again.

In his official report upon the end of the war, Secretary of War Elihu Root concluded, "it is evident that the insurrection has been brought to an end both by making a war distressing and hopeless on the one hand and by making peace attractive." Ultimately, the United States employed a carrot-and-stick policy to both entice and cower the Filipino population into submission. Force broke the back of the resistance; positive measures undermined it and helped reconcile the nationalists to their defeat. Neither would have been as effective without the other, but finding the right mix of benevolence and coercion had been difficult.

Ultimately, over 126,000 regular and volunteer soldiers served in the Philippines between 1899 and 1902. Of these, 1,000 died in battle or of wounds received in battle, 3,000 more died of disease and other causes, and nearly another 3,000 were wounded. The price of empire was not inconsiderable.

The Boxer Uprising

One important argument advanced for retaining the Philippines was that they would serve as a convenient way station on the way to China. The dominant problem in China at the end of the nineteenth century was its threatened partition by the Great Powers, who sought to carve up the weak Manchu Empire into a number of colonies, protectorates, and "spheres of influence." The United States had no territorial ambitions in China and opposed partition, largely because it feared losing access to China's lucrative commercial markets. Consequently, in September 1899 the United States announced its preference for what it termed an Open Door policy in China in which everyone would enjoy equal access to trading rights.

Years of foreign exploitation, however, had fueled anti-foreign and anti-Christian sentiment in China that was about to erupt into violence. In early 1900 a secret society dedicated to purging China of foreign influences, known to westerners as the Boxer movement, began killing foreigners and Chinese Christians. The Dowager Empress sympathized with the Boxers, and consequently the government did little to stop them. The wave of violence climaxed in June when a large force of Boxers entered Peking. Fearing for their lives, most foreigners as well as many Chinese converts fled to the foreign legations quarter in Peking, defended by a composite force of 600 legation guards and civilians. There, they were besieged by thousands of Boxers.

Although the McKinley administration disliked the idea of becoming involved in foreign alliances, it agreed to join with the other powers (Britain, France, Germany, Russia, Austria-Hungary, Italy, and Japan) to rescue their beleaguered nationals. About 100 U.S. marines joined a 2,100-man international force under British Admiral Sir Edward

Typical Officer's Sleeping Quarters in China, ca. 1900

"I'LL TRY, SIR!"

Company E, 14th Infantry, part of the allied relief expedition to Peking, held a position directly opposite the thirty-foot-high city walls on August 14, 1900. The unit had no ladders or ropes, but the company commander believed it possible to scale the wall using hand holds. He called for volunteers. A young soldier, Musician Calvin P. Titus, said, "I'll try, sir!" Titus, although under fire, made it to the top; the remainder of his company soon followed. It was a critical action toward allowing the allies to force their way into the city and relieve the besieged legations.

Seymour in an attempt to relieve the foreign quarter in Peking. Vastly outnumbered, the relief column failed to reach the imperial capital. Meanwhile, on June 17 coalition warships bombarded the Taku forts guarding Tientsin, the port city nearest to Peking. Regarding both the Seymour expedition and the assault on the Taku forts as hostile acts, the Chinese government declared war on the coalition nations and added its own troops to those besieging the foreign legations. Meanwhile, coalition forces besieged Tientsin, which finally fell to assault on July 13–14—an assault that cost the 9th Infantry eighty-eight casualties when coalition commanders committed the regiment to an ill-considered attack over marshy ground that stalled under heavy fire.

Tientsin's fall opened the way to Peking, and during the following weeks additional coalition troops arrived to create a second relief expedition, this time numbering 19,000 men. The American contribution to this second force, officially titled the China Relief Expedition, consisted of 2,500 soldiers and marines under Maj. Gen. Adna R. Chaffee. On August 4 the multinational force set out for Peking, seventy miles away, in temperatures that exceeded 100 degrees. Since the coalition lacked an overall leader, decisions were made by majority vote in a council of the various national commanders. Coordination between the various contingents was difficult at best and contributed to a friendly fire incident in which Russian artillery mistakenly opened fire on American infantry. Such shortcomings notwithstanding, the expedition succeeded in defeating the Chinese in several sharp engagements and arrived outside of Peking in mid-August.

A final council of war assigned each national contingent a gate to attack along the city's outer walls but agreed to postpone the assault when the Russian commander stated that his troops needed time to recuperate from the grueling march from Tientsin. The agreement was short lived, however, for on the evening of August 13 the Russians stole a march on the rest of the allies and attacked Peking on their own at the gate originally assigned to the Americans. News of the Russian action led first the Japanese and then the American and British contingents to make a mad dash for the city. There, on the morning of the fourteenth, they found the Russians pinned down at the Tung Pien gate unable to make further headway. Soldiers of the 14th Infantry scaled the city's outer wall and cleared the gate, relieving the trapped Russians and opening the way for additional soldiers to pour into the city. Meanwhile, the British penetrated the outer wall at another point and

ARMY WAR COLLEGE

When Secretary of War Elihu Root took office in 1899, the Army lacked a senior service school. The officer corps of what had been scant years before a frontier Army required educational preparation for modern war. Recognizing this need, which his military advisers confirmed, Root in November 1901 directed

that a War College be established. In February 1903 President Theodore Roosevelt and Secretary Root spoke at the laying of the cornerstone for the Army War College building, designed by the prominent architectural firm of McKim, Mead, and White, at Washington Barracks (now Fort McNair), D.C.

Army War College's Roosevelt Hall, Fort McNair

relieved the legation quarter. The following day, Capt. Henry J. Reilly's Light Battery F of the U.S. 5th Artillery shattered the gates of the city's inner wall with several well-placed salvos, opening the way for the allied troops to occupy the central Imperial City.

The capture of Peking and the relief of the legation quarter did not end operations in China. The coalition organized a military government in which each nationality was given a section of Peking to govern, while expeditions combed the countryside to root out the last vestiges of Boxer resistance. The American contingent participated in only a few of these expeditions, partly because the United States was anxious to transfer troops back to the ongoing war in the Philippines and partly because it believed that the expeditions, often brutally conducted, did more harm than good. In a few months all resistance had ended, but prolonged negotiations delayed the final signing of the Boxer Peace Protocol until September 1901. Under its terms the Chinese government agreed to pay the coalition members $333 million and to give them exclusive control over the legation quarter with the further right to place troops along the Peking-Tientsin-Shanhaikwan railway to ensure open communications between the capital and the sea.

After the conclusion of peace, the American contingent left China except for a detachment from the 9th Infantry that remained in Peking as a legation guard until 1905 when marines resumed this duty. The Boxer Peace Protocol had long-term implications for the Army, however, for in 1912 the United States decided to invoke its right to station troops along the Peking-Tientsin-Shanhaikwan railway when revolution threatened China's internal stability. Thus began the 15th Infantry's long sojourn in China, duty that would last until 1938 when the United States, fearful of becoming embroiled in Japan's escalating aggression against China, withdrew the garrison after a 26-year stay.

All totaled, some 5,000 soldiers participated in the China Relief Expedition of 1900–1901. Of these, about 250 were killed, wounded, or died of disease. The participation of the United States in the expedition marked the first time since the American Revolution that the country had joined with other powers in a military operation. The nation's first foray into coalition warfare had not been easy, marred as it was by poor planning, miscommunication, and national jealousies. Suspicious of the motivations of some of its "allies" and desirous of maintaining its freedom of action, the United States refused to put its troops under the command of foreign generals during the conflict. Nevertheless, the intervention in China represented one more instance of America's changing role in world affairs. Although many Americans still believed that the nation could adhere to its historic principles of isolationism, America's growing economic and political interests abroad demanded otherwise. The dawn of the twentieth century had heralded the first stirrings of the United States as a world power; and as events in Cuba, China, and the Philippines had demonstrated, changes would be needed in many long-established institutions and policies to meet the requirements posed by the nation's growing role in world affairs.

DISCUSSION QUESTIONS

1. How did political considerations influence the planning and execution of military operations in Cuba, the Philippines, and China? Do similar considerations influence military operations today?

2. How well prepared was the United States to project power beyond its borders in 1898?

3. What challenges did the U.S. Army face in waging expeditionary warfare at the turn of the century? Do these same challenges remain today?

4. Should the United States have intervened in Cuba at all? Explain your answer.

5. How did the Army overcome guerrilla warfare in the Philippines?

6. What lessons can be derived by studying multinational operations during the Boxer Rebellion?

RECOMMENDED READINGS

Birtle, Andrew J. U.S. *Army Counterinsurgency and Contingency Operations Doctrine, 1860–1941*. Washington, D.C.: U.S. Army Center of Military History, 2001.

Cosmas, Graham A. *An Army for Empire: The U.S. Army in the Spanish-American War*. College Station: Texas A&M University Press, 1998.

Gates, John M. *Schoolbooks and Krags: The U.S. Army in the Philippines, 1898–1902*. Westport, Conn.: Greenwood Press, 1973.

Linn, Brian M. *The Philippine War, 1899–1902*. Lawrence: University Press of Kansas, 2000.

Purcell, Victor. *The Boxer Uprising: A Background Study*. Hamden, Conn.: Archon Books, 1974, especially ch. 12.

Risch, Erna. *Quartermaster Support of the Army: A History of the Corps, 1775–1939.* Washington, D.C.: U.S. Army Center of Military History, 1989, ch. 12.

Tan, Chester C. *The Boxer Catastrophe.* New York: Octagon Books, 1967.

Trask, David F. *The War With Spain in 1898.* Lincoln: University of Nebraska Press, 1996.

Other Readings

Alger, Russell A. *The Spanish-American War.* New York: Harper, 1901.

Cosmas, Graham A. "San Juan Hill and El Caney, 1–2 July 1898," in *America's First Battles,* ed. Charles E. Heller and William A. Stofft. Lawrence: University Press of Kansas, 1986.

May, Glenn A. *Battle for Batangas: A Philippine Province at War.* New Haven, Conn.: Yale University Press, 1991.

Sexton, William T. *Soldiers in the Sun: An Adventure in Imperialism.* Freeport, N.Y.: Books for Libraries Press, 1971.

16

TRANSITION, CHANGE, AND THE ROAD TO WAR, 1902–1917

For the United States the opening years of the twentieth century were a time of transition and change. At home it was a period of social change, often designated the Progressive Era, when political leaders such as President Theodore Roosevelt undertook to solve the economic and social problems arising out of the rapid growth of large-scale industry in the late nineteenth century. Increasing public awareness of these problems as a result of the writings of the "Muckrakers" and social reformers provided popular support for efforts to solve them by legislative and administrative measures. In foreign affairs it was a period when the country had to begin adjusting its institutions and policies to the requirements of its new status as a world power with imperial responsibilities. In spite of a tendency after the end of the War with Spain to follow traditional patterns and go back to essentially isolationist policies, the nation's new responsibility for overseas possessions, its expanding commercial interests abroad, and the continued unrest in the Caribbean made a reversion to insularity increasingly unfeasible.

The changing conditions at home and abroad inevitably affected the nation's military establishment. During the decade and a half between the War with Spain and American involvement in World War I, both the Army and the Navy would undergo important reforms in organization and direction. Although the United States did not participate in any major conflict during these years, both services were frequently called upon to assist with administration of newly acquired possessions overseas. Both aided with protection of investments abroad threatened by native insurrections, revolutions, and other internal disturbances. And both contributed in other ways to upholding the vital interests of the nation in an era of greatly increased competition for commercial advantage and colonial empire. Much of the experience gained in the decades of the Indian Wars was used to great advantage in the essentially constabulary duties required to police an empire, but much needed to be done to modernize the military and prepare it for its new role in world affairs.

Modernizing the Armed Forces

The intensification of international rivalries led most of the Great Powers to seek additional protection and advantage in diplomatic alliances and alignments. By the early years of the twentieth century the increasingly complex network of agreements had resulted in a new and precarious balance of power in world affairs. This balance was constantly in danger of being upset, particularly because of an unprecedented arms race characterized by rapid enlargement of armies and navies and development of far more deadly weapons and tactics. While the United States remained aloof from such "entangling alliances," it nevertheless continued to modernize and strengthen its own armed forces, giving primary attention to the Navy—the first line of defense.

The Navy's highly successful performance in the Spanish-American War increased the willingness of Congress and the American public to support its program of expansion and modernization. For at least a decade after the war Theodore Roosevelt, Senator Henry Cabot Lodge of Massachusetts, and other leaders who favored a "Big Navy" policy with the goal of an American fleet second only to that of Great Britain had little difficulty securing the necessary legislation and funds for the Navy's expansion program.

For the Navy another most important result of the War with Spain was the decision to retain possessions in the Caribbean and the western Pacific. In the Caribbean, the Navy acquired more bases for its operations such as that at Guantanamo Bay in Cuba. The value of these bases soon became apparent as the United States found itself intervening more frequently in the countries of that region to protect its expanding investments and trade. In the long run, however, acquisition of the Philippines and Guam was even more significant, for it committed the United States to defense of territory thousands of miles from the home base. American naval strength in the Pacific had to be increased immediately to ensure maintenance of a secure line of communications for the land forces that had to be kept in the Philippines. One way to accomplish this increase, with an eye to economy of force, was to build a canal across the Isthmus of Panama to allow Navy ships to move more rapidly from the Atlantic to the Pacific as circumstances demanded. Another was to acquire more bases in the Pacific west of Hawaii, which was annexed in 1898. Japan's spectacular naval victories in the war with Russia and Roosevelt's dispatch of an American fleet on a round-the-world cruise from December 1907 to February 1909 drew public attention to the problem. But most Americans failed to perceive Japan's growing threat to U.S. possessions in the western Pacific, and the line of communications to the Philippines remained incomplete and highly vulnerable.

The Navy worked hard to expand the fleet and incorporate the latest technological developments in ship design and weapons. The modernization program that had begun in the 1880s and had much to do with the Navy's effectiveness in the Spanish-American War continued

By the early years of the twentieth century the increasingly complex network of agreements had resulted in a new and precarious balance of power in world affairs.

in the early 1900s. Construction of new ships, stimulated by the war and Roosevelt's active support, continued at a rapid rate after 1898 until the Taft administration and at a somewhat slower pace thereafter. By 1917 the United States had a Navy unmatched by any of the Great Powers except Great Britain and Germany.

The Army, aware of the serious deficiencies revealed in the War with Spain and of the rapid technological changes taking place in the methods of warfare, also undertook to modernize its weapons and equipment. Development of high-velocity, low-trajectory, clip-loading rifles capable of delivering a high rate of sustained fire had already made obsolete the Krag-Jörgensen rifle, which the Army had adopted in 1892. In 1903 the Regular Army began equipping its units with the improved bolt-action, magazine-type Springfield rifle, which incorporated the latest changes in weapons technology. The campaigns of 1898 also had shown that the standard rod bayonet was too flimsy; starting in 1905, the Army replaced it with a sturdy knife bayonet. The 1906 addition of a greater propellant charge in ammunition for the Springfield provided even higher muzzle velocity and deeper penetration of the bullet. Combat at close quarters against the fierce charges of the Moros in the Philippines demonstrated the need for a hand weapon less cumbersome and having greater impact than the .38-caliber revolver. The Army found the answer in the recently developed .45-caliber Colt automatic pistol, adopted in 1911, that was to remain a mainstay of the Army for most of the rest of the century.

Far more significant in revolutionizing the nature of twentieth century warfare than these improved hand weapons was the rapid-firing machine gun. The manually operated machine gun—the Gatling gun—which the Army had adopted in 1866, was employed successfully in the Indian Wars and the Spanish-American War. American inventors,

THE COLT .45

In 1892 the Army began to replace the .45-caliber, single-action revolvers it had used since 1873 with a more modern .38-caliber, double-action weapon. During the Philippine campaigns, a series of bloody encounters with highly motivated Moro tribesmen in the close country of Mindanao showed that the lighter weapon's stopping power was insufficient. A series of tests using commercially available ammunition against live and cadaver animals by the Ordnance Department in 1904 led to a specification for a .45-caliber pistol firing a 230-grain bullet at 800 feet per second. Manufacturers submitted nine pistols (six semiautomatic models, two conventional double-action revolvers, and the unique Webley-Fosbery automatic revolver) for ordnance testing in early 1907. A redesigned version of the winning pistol, John M. Browning's Colt Model 1906 semiautomatic, was adopted in 1911 and served with only minor modifications as the Army's main handgun until 1985.

Pistol, Caliber .45, M1911. Browning's self-loading pistol had a detachable seven-round magazine.

including Hiram Maxim, John Browning, and Isaac N. Lewis, the last an officer in the Army's coast artillery, took a leading part in developing automatic machine guns in the years between the Civil War and World War I. Weapons based on their designs were adopted by many of the armies of the world. But not until fighting began in World War I would it be generally realized what an important role the machine gun was to have in modern tactics. Thus, in the years between 1898 and 1916, Congress appropriated only an average of $150,000 annually for procurement of machine guns, barely enough to provide four weapons for each regular regiment and a few for the National Guard. Finally in 1916 Congress voted $12 million for machine-gun procurement, but the War Department held up its expenditure until 1917 while a board tried to decide which type of weapon was best suited to the needs of the Army.

Development of American artillery and artillery ammunition also lagged behind that of west European armies. The Army did adopt in 1902 a new basic field weapon, the three-inch gun with an advanced recoil mechanism. Also, to replace the black powder that had been the subject of such widespread criticism during the War with Spain, both the Army and the Navy took steps to increase the domestic output of smokeless powder. By 1903 production was sufficient to supply most American artillery for the small Regular Army.

Experience gained in the Spanish-American War also brought some significant changes in the Army's coastal defense program. The hurriedly improvised measures taken during the war to protect Atlantic ports from possible attack by the Spanish Fleet emphasized the need for modern seacoast defenses. Under the strategic concepts in vogue, construction and manning of these defenses were primarily Army responsibilities since in wartime the naval fleet had to be kept intact, ready to seek out and destroy the enemy's fleet. On the basis of recommendations by the Endicott Board, the Army already had begun an ambitious coastal defense construction program in the early 1890s. In 1905 a new board headed by Secretary of War William Howard Taft made important revisions in this program with the goal of incorporating the latest techniques and devices. Added to the coastal defense arsenal were fixed, floating, and mobile torpedoes and submarine mines. At the same time the Army's Ordnance Department tested new and more powerful rifled artillery for installation in the coastal defense fortifications in keeping with the trend toward larger and larger guns to meet the challenge of naval weapons of ever-increasing size.

Of the many new inventions that came into widespread use in the early twentieth century in response to the productive capacity of the new industrial age, none was to have greater influence on military strategy, tactics, and organization than the internal combustion engine. It made possible the motor vehicle, which, like the railroad in the previous century, brought a revolution in military transportation, and the airplane and tank, both of which would figure importantly in World War I. The humble internal combustion engine was not as exciting or as dramatic a development as the machine gun or a new type of howitzer, but its long-term impact changed the face of warfare and made possible the huge mechanized formations that were to dominate war in the latter half of the twentieth century.

ELIHU ROOT

"I took the United States for my client," said seasoned New York attorney Elihu Root (1845–1937) of his accession as Secretary of War in 1899. Having been denied enlistment in the Union Army because of poor health, he was not a veteran. Yet despite his initial unfamiliarity with military affairs, Secretary Root initiated some of the most significant Army reforms of the twentieth century. He subsequently served as Secretary of State and U.S. Senator. For his War Department role in administering Cuba, Puerto Rico, and the Philippines acquired in the Spanish-American War, and his work as Secretary of State on U.S. relations with Japan and Latin America, he received the Nobel Peace Prize for 1912.

Elihu Root,
Secretary of War, 1899–1904
Raimundo de Madrazo, 1907

Reorganization of the Army
Establishment of the General Staff

After the Spanish-American War the Army also underwent important organizational and administrative changes aimed in part at overcoming some of the more glaring defects revealed during the war. Although the nation had won the war with comparative ease, many Americans realized that the victory was attributable more to the incompetence of the enemy than to any special qualities displayed by the Army. In fact, as a postwar investigating commission appointed by President William McKinley and headed by Maj. Gen. Granville M. Dodge brought out, there was serious need for reform in the administration and direction of the Army's high command and for elimination of widespread inefficiency in the operations of the War Department.

No one appreciated the need for reform more than Elihu Root, a New York lawyer whom McKinley appointed Secretary of War in 1899. The President had selected Root primarily because he seemed well qualified to solve the legal problems that would arise in the Army's administration of recently acquired overseas possessions. But Root quickly realized that if the Army was to be capable of carrying out its new responsibilities as an important part of the defense establishment of a world power, it had to undergo fundamental changes in organization, administration, and training. Root, as a former corporation lawyer, tended to see the Army's problems as similar to those faced by business executives. "The men who have combined various corporations … in what we call trusts," he told Congress, "have reduced the cost of production and have increased their efficiency by doing the very same thing we propose you shall do now, and it does seem a pity that the Government of the United States should be the only great industrial establishment that cannot profit by the lessons which the world of industry and of commerce has learned to such good effect."

Beginning in 1899, Root outlined in a series of masterful reports his proposals for fundamental reform of Army institutions and concepts to achieve that "efficiency" of organization and function required of armies in the modern world. He based his proposals partly upon recommendations made by his military advisers (among the most trusted were Adjutant General Maj. Gen. Henry C. Corbin, and Lt. Col. William H. Carter) and partly upon the views expressed by officers who had studied and written about the problem in the post–Civil War years. Root arranged for publication of Col. Emory Upton's *The Military Policy of the United States* (1904), an unfinished manuscript that advocated a strong, expansible Regular Army as the keystone of an effective military establishment. Concluding that after all the true object of any army must be "to provide for war," Root took prompt steps to reshape the American Army into an instrument of national power capable of coping with the requirements of modern warfare. This objective could be attained, he hoped, by integrating the bureaus of the War Department, the scattered elements of the Regular Army, and the militia and volunteers.

Root perceived as the chief weakness in the organization of the Army the long-standing division of authority, dating back to the early nineteenth century, between the Commanding General of the Army and the Secretary of War. The Commanding General exercised discipline and control over the troops in the field; while the Secretary, through the military bureau chiefs, had responsibility for administration and fiscal matters. Root proposed to eliminate this division of authority between the Secretary of War and the Commanding General and to reduce the independence of the bureau chiefs. The solution, he suggested, was to replace the Commanding General of the Army with a Chief of Staff, who would be the responsible adviser and executive agent of the President through the Secretary of War. Under Root's proposal, formulation of broad American policies would continue under civilian control.

A lack of any long-range planning by the Army had been another obvious deficiency in the War with Spain, and Root proposed to overcome this by the creation of a new General Staff, a group of selected officers who would be free to devote their full time to preparing military plans. Planning in past national emergencies, he pointed out, nearly always had been inadequate because it had to be done hastily by officers already overburdened with other duties. Pending congressional action on his proposals, Root in 1901 appointed an ad hoc War College Board to act as an embryonic General Staff. In early 1903, in spite of some die-hard opposition, Congress adopted the Secretary of War's recommendations for both a General Staff and a Chief of Staff but rejected his request that certain of the bureaus be consolidated.

By this legislation Congress provided the essential framework for more efficient administration of the Army. Yet legislation could not change overnight the long-held traditions, habits, and views of most Army officers or of some congressmen and the American public. Secretary Root realized that effective operation of the new system would require an extended program of reeducation. This need for reeducation was one important reason for the establishment of the Army War College in November 1903. Its students, already experienced officers, would receive education in problems of the War Department and of high command in the field. As it turned out, they actually devoted much of their time to war planning, becoming in effect the part of the General Staff that performed this function.

In the first years after its establishment the General Staff achieved relatively little in the way of genuine staff planning and policy making. While staff personnel did carry out such appropriate tasks as issuing in 1905 the first Field Service Regulations for government and organization of troops in the field, drawing up the plan for an expeditionary force sent to Cuba in 1906, and supervising the Army's expanding school system, far too much of their time was devoted to day-to-day routine administrative matters.

The General Staff did make some progress in overcoming its early weaknesses. Through experience, officers assigned to the staff gradually gained awareness of its real purpose and powers. In 1910, when Maj. Gen. Leonard Wood became Chief of Staff, he reorganized the General Staff, eliminating many of its time-consuming procedures and directing more of its energies to planning. With the backing of Secretary of War Henry L. Stimson (1911–1913), Wood dealt a decisive blow to that element in the Army itself that opposed the General Staff. In a notable controversy, he and Stimson forced the retirement in 1912 of the leader of this opposition, Maj. Gen. Fred C. Ainsworth, The Adjutant General.

The temporary closing of most Army schools during the Spanish-American War and the need to coordinate the Army's educational system with the Root proposals for creating a War College and General Staff had provided an opportunity for a general reorganization of the whole system, with the overall objective of raising the standards of professional training of officers. In 1901 the War Department directed that the schools of instruction for officers thereafter should be the Military Academy at West Point; a school at each post of elementary instruction in theory and practice; the five service schools (the Artillery School, Engineer School of Application, School of Submarine Defense [mines and torpedoes], School of Application for Cavalry and Field Artillery, and Army Medical School); a General Staff and Service College at Fort Leavenworth; and a War College. The purpose of the school at Leavenworth henceforth was to train officers in the employment of combined arms and prepare them for staff and command positions in large units. To meet the requirements for specialized training as a result of new developments in weapons and equipment, the Army expanded its service school system, adding the Signal School in 1905, the Field Artillery School in 1911, and the School of Musketry in 1913.

Creation of the General Staff unquestionably was the most important organizational reform in the Army during this period, but there were also a number of other changes in the branches and special staff designed to keep the Army abreast of new ideas and requirements. The Medical Department, for example, established Medical, Hospital, Army Nurse, Dental, and Medical Reserve Corps. In 1907 Congress approved the division of the artillery into the Coast Artillery Corps and the Field Artillery and in 1912 enacted legislation consolidating the Subsistence and Pay Departments with the Quartermaster to create the Quartermaster Corps, a reform Secretary Root had recommended earlier. The act of 1912 also established an enlisted Quartermaster service corps, marking the beginning of the practice of using service troops instead of civilians and combat soldier details.

In the new field of military aviation, the Army failed to keep pace with early twentieth century developments. Contributing to this delay

THE ARMY AND THE WRIGHT BROTHERS

On July 30, 1909, a frail biplane sporting a 24-horsepower engine took off from the parade ground at Fort Myer, Virginia. Orville Wright was at the controls with Lt. Benjamin D. Foulois aboard as a passenger-observer. This was the third and final test to see if the flyer, as Orville and his brother Wilbur referred to their machine, satisfied the War Department's specifications for a military "aeroplane." In slightly more than twenty-eight minutes they returned, having traveled an average speed of 42.583 miles per hour over a measured course. The U.S. Army Signal Corps purchased the world's first military aircraft for $30,000.

Wright Bros. Experimental Military Aircraft, *Imra Maduro Peixotto, 1909*

were the reluctance of Congress to appropriate funds and resistance within the military bureaucracy to the diversion of already limited resources to a method of warfare as yet unproved. The Army did not entirely neglect the new field—it had used balloons for observation in both the Civil and Spanish-American Wars and, beginning in 1898, the War Department subsidized for several years Samuel P. Langley's experiments with power-propelled, heavier-than-air flying machines. In 1908, after some hesitation, the War Department made funds available to the Aeronautical Division of the Signal Corps (established a year earlier) for the purchase and testing of Wilbur and Orville Wright's airplane. Although the Army accepted this airplane in 1909, another two years passed before Congress appropriated a relatively modest sum ($125,000) for aeronautical purposes. Between 1908 and 1913, it is estimated that the United States spent only $430,000 on military and naval aviation, whereas in the same period France and Germany each expended $22 million; Russia, $12 million; and Belgium, $2 million. Not until 1914 did Congress authorize establishment of a full-fledged Aviation Section in the Signal Corps. The few military airplanes available for service on the Mexican border in 1916 soon broke down, and the United States entered World War I far behind the other belligerents in aviation equipment, organization, and doctrine.

Reorganization of the Army
The Regular Army and the Militia

In the years after the Spanish-American War nearly a third of the Regular Army troops, on the average, served overseas. Most were in the Philippines suppressing the insurrection and, when that conflict officially ended in mid-1902, stamping out scattered resistance and organizing and training a native force known as the Philippine Scouts. Other regulars were garrisoned in Alaska, Hawaii, China, and elsewhere. To carry out its responsibilities abroad and to maintain an adequate defense at home, the Regular Army from 1902 to 1911 had an average of 75,000 officers and men, far below the 100,000 that Congress had authorized in 1902 to fill thirty infantry and fifteen cavalry regiments supported by a corps of artillery. To make up for this deficiency in size of the regular forces and at the same time to remedy some of the defects revealed in the mobilization for the War with Spain, the planners in the War Department recommended a reorganization of the volunteer forces.

Secretary Root took the lead in presenting to Congress in 1901 a program for reform of the National Guard. In response to his recommendations, Congress in 1903 passed the Dick Act, which thoroughly revised the obsolete Militia Act of 1792. It separated the militia into two classes—the Organized Militia, to be known as the National Guard, and the Reserve Militia—and provided that over a five-year period the Guard's organization and equipment would be patterned after that of the Regular Army. To help accomplish these changes in the Guard, the Dick Act made federal funds available; prescribed drill at least twice a month, supplemented with short annual training periods; permitted detailing of regular officers to Guard units; and directed the holding of joint maneuvers each year. The new measure failed, however, to significantly modify the longstanding provisions that severely restricted federal power to call up Guard units and control Guard personnel, which limited its effectiveness. Subsequent legislation in 1908 and 1914 reduced these restrictions to some extent, giving the President the right to prescribe the length of federal service and with the advice and consent of the Senate to appoint all officers of the Guard while the Guard was in federal service.

PHILIPPINE SCOUTS

A number of locally recruited scout companies were formed during the Philippine Insurrection (1899–1902) even before the 1901 law that formally authorized their creation as part of the U.S. Army. Filipinos served as enlisted personnel and NCOs in Philippine Scout units that by 1922 included infantry, cavalry, and field artillery regiments under an officer corps that remained primarily American even after Filipinos became eligible for commissioning through the U.S. Military Academy in 1914. Trained and equipped as Regular Army units, they mounted a valiant defense against the Japanese during World War II. Reconstituted as the New Scouts by the U.S. Armed Forces Voluntary Recruitment Act of 1945, the force continued to protect American and Filipino interests until its official dissolution in 1950.

The military legislation passed in 1908 contained one additional provision that was to have far-reaching consequences. On April 23, 1908, the creation of the Medical Reserve Corps authorized the placement of several hundred medical personnel on a federal reserve status to be called to active duty if needed to augment the regular medical doctors. This was the small and humble beginning of the U.S. Army Reserve that in the future would train, commission, mobilize, and retain hundreds of thousands of officers. This legislation established the third component of the U.S. Army in addition to the Regular Army and the National Guard. The U.S. Army Reserve was to be a federal reserve, not belonging to the states, which would help provide the basis for the actual implementation of the expansible army theory.

The Creation of Larger Units

Although the largest permanent unit of the Regular Army in peacetime continued to be the regiment, experience in the Spanish-American War, observation of new developments abroad, and lessons learned in annual maneuvers all testified to the need for larger, more self-sufficient units composed of the combined arms. Beginning in 1905, the *Field Service Regulations* laid down a blueprint for the organization of divisions in wartime, and in 1910 the General Staff drew up a plan for three permanent infantry divisions to be composed of designated Regular Army and National Guard regiments. Because of trouble along the Mexican border in the spring of 1911, the plan was not implemented. Instead, the Army organized a provisional maneuver division and ordered its component units, consisting of three brigades of nearly 13,000 officers and men, to concentrate at San Antonio, Texas. The division's presence there, it was hoped, would end the border disturbances.

The effort only proved how unready the Army was to mobilize quickly for any kind of national emergency. Assembly of the division required several months. The War Department had to collect Regular Army troops from widely scattered points in the continental United States and denude every post, depot, and arsenal to scrape up the necessary equipment. Even so, when the maneuver division finally completed its concentration in August 1911, it was far from fully operational: none of its regiments were up to strength or adequately armed and equipped. Fortunately, the efficiency of the division was not put to any battle test; and within a short time it was broken up and its component units returned to their home stations. Because those members of Congress who had Army installations in their own districts insisted on retaining them, the War Department was prevented from relocating units so that there would be greater concentrations of troops in a few places. The only immediate result of the Army's attempt to gain experience in the handling of large units was an effort to organize on paper the scattered posts of the Army so their garrisons, which averaged 700 troops each, could join one of three divisions. But these abortive attempts to mobilize larger units were not entirely without value. In 1913, when the Army again had to strengthen the forces along the Mexican border, a division assembled in Texas in less than a week, ready for movement to any point where it might be needed.

Caribbean Problems and Projects

The close of the War with Spain brought no satisfactory solution for the Cuban problem. As a result of years of misrule and fighting, conditions on the island were deplorable when the war ended. Under provisions of the Teller amendment, the United States was pledged to turn over the rule of Cuba to its people. American forces, however, stayed on to assist the Cubans in achieving at least a modicum of economic and political stability. The first step was to set up a provisional government, headed in the beginning by Maj. Gen. John R. Brooke and later by General Wood. This government promptly undertook a program of rehabilitation and reform. An outstanding achievement was eliminating yellow fever, which had decimated Army troops during the war. Research and experiments carried out by the Army Medical Department culminated in the discovery that a specific type of mosquito transmitted the dread disease. When a concerted effort was generated to control the places where that mosquito bred, the disease was dramatically reduced and the overall improvement in troop health in the tropics was significant.

When order had been restored in Cuba, a constituent assembly met. Under the chairmanship of General Wood, it drew up an organic law for the island patterned after the American Constitution. At the insistence of the United States, this law included several clauses known as the Platt amendment, which also appeared in the subsequent treaty concluded in 1903 by the two countries. The amendment limited the amount of debt Cuba could contract, granted the United States naval bases at Guantanamo and Bahia Honda, and gave the United States the right to intervene to preserve "Cuban independence" and maintain a government "adequate to the protection of life, property and individual liberty." In 1902, after a general election and the inauguration of the republic's first president, the Americans ended their occupation. But events soon demonstrated that the period of tutelage in self-government had been too short. In late 1906, when the Cuban government proved unable to cope with a new rebellion, the United States intervened to maintain law and order. On the advice of Secretary Taft, President Roosevelt dispatched more than 5,000 troops to Havana, the so-called Army of Cuban Pacification that remained in Cuba until early 1909. Again in 1912 and 1917, the United States found it necessary to intervene but each time withdrew its occupying forces as soon as order was restored. Not until 1934 did the United States, consistent with its new Good Neighbor Policy, give up the right of intervention embodied in the Platt amendment.

The emergence of the United States as a world power with a primary concern for developments in the Caribbean Sea increased the long-time American interest in an isthmian canal. Discovery of gold in California in 1848 and the rapid growth of the West Coast states had underlined the importance of developing a shorter sea route from Atlantic ports to the Pacific. The strategic need for a canal was dramatized for the American people during the Spanish-American War by the 66-day voyage of the battleship *Oregon* from Puget Sound around Cape Horn to Santiago, where it joined the American Fleet barely in time to participate in the destruction of Admiral Pascual Cervera y Topete's ships.

A few months after the end of the War with Spain, McKinley told Congress that a canal under American control was "now more than ever indispensable." By the Hay-Pauncefote Treaty of 1901, the United States secured abrogation of the terms of the Clayton-Bulwer Treaty of 1850 that required the United States to share equally with Great Britain in construction and operation of any future isthmian canal. Finally, in 1903, the long-standing question of where to build the canal (Nicaragua or Panama) was resolved in favor of Panama. An uprising in Panama against the government of Colombia provided President Roosevelt with an opportunity to send American naval units to support the rebels, assuring establishment of an independent republic. The new republic readily agreed to permit the United States to acquire control of a ten-mile strip across the isthmus, to purchase the property formerly belonging to the French syndicate that had attempted to construct a canal in the 1880s, and to build, maintain, and operate an interoceanic canal. Congress promptly appropriated the necessary funds for work to begin, and the Isthmian Canal Commission set about investigating the problem of who should construct the canal.

When the commission advised the President that overseeing the construction of so vast a project was beyond the capabilities of any private concern, Roosevelt decided to turn the job over to the Army. He reorganized the commission, assigning to it new members—the majority were Army officers—and in 1907 appointed Col. George W. Goethals as its chairman and chief engineer. In this capacity, Goethals, a graduate of the Military Academy who had served in the Corps of Engineers since 1882, had virtually sole responsibility for administration of the canal project. Displaying great organizational ability, he overcame many serious difficulties, including problems of engineering, employee grievances, housing, and sanitation, to complete the canal by 1914. Goethals owed a part of his success to the support he received from the Army's Medical Department. Under the leadership of Col. William C. Gorgas,

Construction of Locks for the Panama Canal, April 5, 1913

THE ARMY, MALARIA, AND THE PANAMA CANAL

William C. Gorgas (1854–1920) headed the Medical Department's tropical disease program in Panama. It was one of the world's great plague regions for yellow fever and malaria; twenty years earlier those diseases had wrecked a French company's attempt to construct an interoceanic canal. Gorgas concluded that malaria posed the greatest danger in Panama. Upon arrival he launched an intensive study of the life cycle of the carrier, the mosquito. His efforts at mosquito abatement eradicated yellow fever but could only contain malaria. Still the death rate plummeted, removing the medical barrier to the successful completion of the Panama Canal.

who earlier had played an important role in administering the sanitation program in Cuba, the Army carried through measures to control malaria and virtually wipe out yellow fever, ultimately converting the Canal Zone into a healthy and attractive place to live and work.

The completed Panama Canal stood as a magnificent engineering achievement and an outstanding example of the Army's fulfillment of a peacetime mission, but its opening and operation under American administration were also highly significant from the point of view of military strategy. For the Navy, the Canal achieved economy of force by eliminating the necessity for maintaining large fleets in both the Atlantic and Pacific. For the Army, it created a new strategic point in the continental defense system that had to be strongly protected by the most modern fortifications manned by a large and well-trained garrison.

The Army on the Mexican Border

Early in the twentieth century the Army found itself frequently involved in hemispheric problems, not only with the countries of the Caribbean region, but also with the United States' southern neighbor, Mexico. That nation, after a long era of relative political stability, entered a period of revolutionary turmoil. Beginning in 1911, internal conflicts in the northern part of the country led to recurrent incidents along the Mexican border, posing a serious threat to peace. President William Howard Taft first ordered strengthening of the border patrols and then, in the summer of 1911, concentration of the maneuver division at San Antonio. After a period of quiet, General Victoriano Huerta in 1913 deposed and replaced President Francisco Madero. The assassination of Madero shortly thereafter led to full-scale civil war between Huerta's forces and those of General Venustiano Carranza, leader of the so-called Constitutionalists, and Emiliano Zapata, chief of the radicals. Woodrow Wilson, who had succeeded Taft as President, disapproved of the manner in which Huerta had come to power. In a significant shift from traditional American policy, the President decided not to recognize Huerta on the grounds that his assumption of power did not meet the test of "constitutional legitimacy." At the same time, Wilson imposed an arms embargo on both sides in the civil war. But in early 1914, when Huerta's forces halted the Constitutionalists, Wilson endeavored to help Carranza by lifting the embargo.

PANCHO VILLA

Pancho Villa (1878–1923) was an inspired leader of cavalry in the early years of the Mexican Revolution. Beginning in 1914, however, he lost a series of battles to President Carranza's well-trained forces. Villa raided Columbus, New Mexico, in 1916, hoping to provoke American intervention and use Mexican national feeling to depose Carranza. Villa's intimate knowledge of the terrain and his widespread popular support in northern Mexico allowed him to escape the grasp of General Pershing's Punitive Expedition, but Carranza was much too wily to side with the Americans. Pershing thus lost militarily, while Villa lost politically.

Resentment over Wilson's action contributed to the arrest in February of American sailors by followers of Huerta in the port of Tampico. Although the sailors were soon released with an expression of regret from Huerta, Rear Adm. Henry T. Mayo, commanding the American Fleet in the area, demanded a public apology. Huerta refused. Feeling that intervention was unavoidable and seeing an opportunity to deprive Huerta of important ports, President Wilson supported Admiral Mayo and proposed to occupy Tampico, seize Vera Cruz, and blockade both ports. When a German steamer carrying a cargo of ammunition arrived unexpectedly at Vera Cruz in late April, the United States put ashore a contingent of marines and sailors to occupy the port and prevent the unloading of the ship. Naval gunfire checked a Mexican counterattack and by the end of the month an American force of nearly 8,000 (about half marines and half Army troops) under the command of Maj. Gen. Frederick Funston occupied the city. For a time war with Mexico seemed inevitable, but both Wilson and Huerta accepted mediation and the Mexican leader agreed to resign. Carranza had barely had time to assume office when his erstwhile ally, Francisco "Pancho" Villa, rebelled and proceeded to gain control over most of northern Mexico.

Despite the precariousness of Carranza's hold on Mexico, President Wilson decided to recognize his government. It was now Villa's turn to show resentment. He instigated a series of border incidents that culminated in a surprise attack by 500 to 1,000 of his men against Columbus, New Mexico, on March 9, 1916. Villa's troops killed a substantial number of American soldiers and civilians and destroyed considerable property before units of the 13th Cavalry drove them off. The following day President Wilson ordered Brig. Gen. John J. Pershing into Mexico to assist the Mexican government in capturing Villa.

On March 15 the advance elements of this punitive expedition entered Mexico in "hot pursuit." For the next several months Pershing's troops chased Villa through unfriendly territory for hundreds of miles, never quite catching up with him but managing to disperse most of his followers. Although Carranza's troops also failed to capture Villa, Carranza soon showed that he had no desire to have the United States do the job for him. He protested the continued presence of American troops in Mexico and insisted upon their withdrawal. Carranza's unfriendly attitude, plus orders from the War Department forbidding attacks on Mexicans who were not followers of Villa, made it difficult for Pershing to deal effectively with other hostile Mexicans who blocked his path without running the risk of precipitating war. Some clashes with Mexican government troops actually occurred. The most important took place in June at Carrizal, where scores were killed or wounded. This action once again created a critical situation and led President Wilson to call 75,000 National Guardsmen into federal service to help police the border.

Aware that the majority of Americans favored a peaceful solution, Wilson persuaded Carranza to resume diplomatic negotiations. The two leaders agreed in late July to submit the disputes arising out of the punitive expedition to a joint commission for settlement. Some time later the commission ruled that the American unit commander in the Carrizal affair was at fault. Although the commission broke up in January 1917 without reaching agreement on a plan for evacuating Pershing's troops, relations between the United States and Germany had reached so critical a stage that Wilson had no alternative but to order withdrawal of the punitive expedition.

Pershing failed to capture Villa, but the activities of the American troops in Mexico and along the border were not entirely wasted. Dispersal of Villa's band put an end to serious border incidents. More important from a military point of view was the intensive training in the field received by both Regular Army and National Guard troops who served on the border and in Mexico. Also, the partial mobilization drew more attention to the still-unsolved problem of developing a satisfactory system for maintaining in peacetime the nucleus of those trained forces that would supplement the Regular Army in national emergencies. Fortunately, many defects in the military establishment, especially in the National Guard, came to light in time to be corrected before the Army plunged into the war already under way in Europe.

JOHN J. PERSHING (1860–1948)

Pershing was often referred to as Black Jack Pershing, though the nickname's origins are in doubt. His leadership of the 10th Cavalry Buffalo Soldiers, a colored unit, may have led to the harsh epithet; though he had previously taught at a school for African Americans near his hometown of Laclede, Missouri, which also could have been the nickname's genesis. His pacification successes in the Philippines from 1901–1903 led to his direct promotion by President Theodore Roosevelt from captain to brigadier general and his appointment as Governor of Mindanao, where he served from 1906 to 1913. He did not get along well with everyone, though; his battles with Chief of the War Department General Staff Peyton C. March over who was in control of the Army during World War I would lead to factions within the Army. His promotion after World War I to the unique rank of General of the Armies would cap an unusual career.

John Joseph Pershing
Richard Leopold Seyffert, 1975

America could not ignore the huge conflict raging in Europe. At various times it seemed as if the country was going to be dragged into the war, only to retreat from the precipice each time. When the Germans sank the U.S. merchant ship *Gulflight* on May 1, 1915 and then the British liner *Lusitania* a week later with the loss of 128 American lives, American public opinion finally began to recognize that the United States might have to become involved. Voices calling for more preparedness began to seem more sensible.

Among the voices were those of former Secretary of War Elihu Root, ex-President Theodore Roosevelt, and former Secretary of War Henry L. Stimson. Another was that of General Wood, whose term as the Army's Chief of Staff had expired just over a year after President Wilson and his peace-oriented administration had come to office. Following a practice he had introduced while Chief of Staff of conducting summer camps where college students paying their own way could receive military training, Wood lent his support to a similar four-week camp for business and professional men at Plattsburg Barracks, New York. Known as the Plattsburg idea, its success justified opening other camps, assuring a relatively small but influential cadre possessing basic military skills and imbued with enthusiasm for preparedness.

Yet these were voices of a heavily industrialized and articulate east. Few like them were to be heard from the rural south, the west, or a strongly isolationist midwest where heavy settlements of German-Americans (called by some, derisively, hyphenated Americans) detected in the talk of preparedness a heavy leaning toward the nation's historic Anglo-Saxon ties. There was in the country a strong tide of outright pacifism, which possessed an eloquent spokesman in Wilson's Secretary of State, William Jennings Bryan.

The depth of Bryan's convictions became apparent in the government's reaction to the sinking of the *Lusitania*. Although Bryan agreed with the President's first diplomatic protest over the sinking, he dissented when the President, dissatisfied with the German reply and determined to insist on the right of neutrals to engage in commerce on the high seas, insisted on a second and stronger note. The Secretary resigned.

Although sinkings by submarine continued through the summer of 1915, Wilson's persistent protest at last produced an apparent diplomatic victory when in September the Germans promised that passenger liners would be sunk only after warning and with proper safeguards for passengers' lives. Decelerating their campaign, the Germans actually acted less in response to American protests than to a realization that they lacked enough submarines to achieve substantive victory by that means that would outweigh the diplomatic cost.

American commerce with Europe meanwhile continued, particularly in munitions; but because of the British blockade almost all was with the allied nations. The British intercepted ships carrying foodstuffs to Germany and held them until their cargoes rotted. Just after mid-1915 they put even cotton on a long list of contraband and blacklisted any U.S. firm suspected of trading with the Central Powers. These were deliberate and painful affronts, but so profitable was the munitions trade that only the southern states, hurt by the loss of markets for cotton, raised loud protest. In October 1915 President Wilson repealed a ban earlier imposed on loans to belligerents, thereby further stimulating trade with the Allies.

While Americans as a whole remained opposed to entering the war, their sympathy for the allied cause grew. A combination of allied propaganda and German ineptitude was largely responsible. The propagandists were careful to ensure that nobody forgot the German violation of Belgian neutrality, the ordeal of "Little Belgium." Stories of babies mutilated and women violated by German soldiers were rampant. The French executed nine women as spies during the war; but it was the death of a British nurse, Edith Cavell, at the hands of the Germans that the world heard about and remembered. Clumsy German efforts at propaganda in the United States backfired when two military attachés assigned to posts in America were discovered financing espionage and sabotage. The Germans did their cause no further good in October 1916 when one of their submarines surfaced in Newport Harbor, sent an officer ashore to deliver a letter for the German ambassador, then submerged and sank nine allied ships close off the New England coast.

Continuing to champion neutrality and seeking—however unsuccessfully—to persuade the belligerents to establish international rules of submarine warfare, President Wilson was personally becoming more aware of the necessity for military preparedness. Near the end of a nationwide speaking tour in February 1916, he not only called for creation of "the greatest navy in the world" but also urged widespread military training for civilians, lest some day the nation be faced with "putting raw levies of inexperienced men onto the modern field of battle." Still upholding the cause of freedom of the seas, he refused to go along with congressmen who sought to forbid Americans to travel on armed merchant ships.

Wilson nevertheless continued to demonstrate a fervent hope for neutrality. A submarine attack in March on the French steamer *Sussex* with Americans aboard convinced the President's adviser, Edward M. "Colonel" House, and his new Secretary of State, Robert Lansing, that the nation should sever diplomatic relations with Germany. A fiery speech of self-justification by the German chancellor in the Reichstag and a cynical reply to an American note of protest did nothing to discourage that course. Wilson went only so far as to dispatch what amounted to an ultimatum, demanding that the Germans cease the submarine war against passenger and merchant vessels or face severance of relations with the United States.

While questioning the American failure to deal as sternly with the British blockade and rejecting the charge of unrestricted submarine warfare, Germany again agreed to conform to American demands for prior warning and for protecting the lives of passengers. Wilson in turn saw that unless something could be done about the British blockade the German vow probably would be short lived. When a protest to the British availed nothing, the President offered the services of the United States to negotiate a peace. That brought little positive response from either side.

The National Defense Act of 1916

Some of the President's growing inclination toward the cause of preparedness could be traced to increasing concern on the part of members of his administration, most notably the Secretary of War, Lindley M. Garrison. As an annex to the Secretary's annual report in September

1915, Garrison had submitted a study prepared by the General Staff entitled, "A Proper Military Policy for the United States." Like proposals for reform advanced earlier by Stimson and Wood, the new study turned away from the Uptonian idea of an expansible Regular Army, which Root had favored, to the more traditional American concept of a citizen army as the keystone of an adequate defense force. Garrison proposed more than doubling the Regular Army, increasing federal support for the National Guard, and creating a new 400,000-man volunteer force to be called the Continental Army, a trained reserve under federal control as opposed to the state control of the Guard.

Although Wilson refused to accept more than a small increase in the Regular Army, he approved the concept of a Continental Army. Garrison's proposal drew support in the Senate, but not enough to overcome adamant opposition in the House of Representatives from strong supporters of the National Guard. Influential congressmen countered with a bill requiring increased federal responsibility for the Guard, acceptance of federal standards, and agreement by the Guard to respond to a presidential call to service. Under pressure from these congressmen, Wilson switched his support to the congressional plan. This, among other issues, prompted Garrison to resign.

There the matter might have bogged down had not Pancho Villa shot up Columbus, New Mexico. Facing pressing requirements for the National Guard on the Mexican border, the two halls of Congress at last compromised, incorporating the concept of the citizen army as the foundation of the American military establishment but not in the form of a Continental Army. They sought instead to make the National Guard the nucleus of the citizen force.

Passed in May and signed into law the next month, the bill was known as the National Defense Act of 1916. It provided for an army in no way comparable to those of the European combatants and produced cries of outrage from those still subscribing to the Uptonian doctrine. It also contained a severe restriction inserted by opponents of a strong General Staff, sharply limiting the number of officers who could be detailed to serve on the staff at the same time in or near Washington. The bill represented nevertheless the most comprehensive military legislation yet enacted by the U.S. Congress. The National Defense Act of 1916 authorized an increase in the peacetime strength of the Regular Army over a period of five years to 175,000 men and a wartime strength of close to 300,000. Bolstered by federal funds and federal-stipulated organization and standards of training, the National Guard was to be increased more than fourfold to a strength of over 400,000 and obligated to respond to the call of the President. The act also established both an Officers' and an Enlisted Reserve Corps and a Volunteer Army to be raised only in time of war. This provision expanded the Medical Reserve Corps, established in 1908, into a full-spectrum federal reserve force that would mobilize and train over 89,476 officers during World War I. To accomplish this, the act created a new Reserve Officer Training Corps (ROTC) program to establish training centers for officers at colleges and universities.

Going beyond the heretofore-recognized province of military legislation, the National Defense Act of 1916 also granted power to the President to place orders for defense materials and to force industry to comply. The act further directed the Secretary of War to conduct a survey of all arms and munitions industries. A few months later the Congress demonstrated even greater interest in the industrial aspects of defense by creating the civilian Council of National Defense made up of leaders of industry and labor, supported by an advisory commission composed of the secretaries of the principal government departments, and charged with the mission of studying economic mobilization. The administration furthered the preparedness program by creating the U.S. Shipping Board to regulate sea transport while developing a naval auxiliary fleet and a merchant marine.

An End to Neutrality

As a new year of war opened, German leaders decided that they had lost so many men at Verdun and on the Somme that they would have to assume the defensive on the Western Front; their only hope of quick victory lay with the submarines, of which they now had close to 200. By operating an unrestricted campaign against all shipping, whatever the nationality, in waters off the British Isles and France, the Germans believed they could defeat the Allies within six months. While they recognized the strong risk of bringing the United States into the war by this tactic, they believed they could starve the Allies into submission before the Americans could raise, train, and deploy an Army. They were nearly right.

The German ambassador in Washington continued to encourage Wilson to pursue his campaign for peace even as the Germans made their U-boats ready. On January 31, 1917, Germany informed the U.S. government and other neutrals that beginning the next day U-boats would sink all vessels, neutral and allied alike, without warning.

While the world waited for the American reaction, President Wilson searched for some alternative to war. Three days later, still groping desperately for a path to peace, he went before the Congress not to ask a declaration of war but to announce a break in diplomatic relations. This step, Wilson hoped, would be enough to turn the Germans from their new course.

Wilson could not know it at the time, but an intelligence intercept already had placed in British hands a German telegram that when released would remove any doubt as to German intentions toward the United States. This message was sent in January from the German Foreign Secretary, Arthur Zimmermann, to the German ambassador to Mexico, proposing that in the event of war with the United States, Germany and Mexico would conclude an alliance with the adherence of Japan. In exchange for Mexico's taking up arms against the United States, Germany would provide generous financial assistance. Victory achieved, Mexico was to regain her lost territories of Texas, New Mexico, and Arizona.

Cognizant of the impact the message was bound to have on the United States, the British were nevertheless slow to release it; they had to devise a method to assure the Americans of its authenticity while concealing from the Germans that they had broken the German diplomatic code. On February 23, just over a month after intercepting the telegram, the British turned over a copy to the American ambassador in London.

> In exchange for Mexico's taking up arms against the United States, Germany would provide generous financial assistance. Victory achieved, Mexico was to regain her lost territories of Texas, New Mexico, and Arizona.

When President Wilson received the news, he was angered but still unprepared to accept it as cause for war. In releasing the message to the press, he had in mind not inciting the nation to war but instead moving Congress to pass a bill authorizing the arming of American merchant ships, most of which were standing idle in American ports because of the submarine menace. As with the break in diplomatic relations, this, the President hoped, would so impress the Germans that they would abandon their unrestricted submarine campaign.

Congress and most of the nation were shocked by revelation of the Zimmermann message; but with their hopes for neutrality shattered, pacifists and pro-Germans countered with a roar of disbelief that the message was authentic. Zimmermann himself silenced them when in Berlin he admitted to having sent the telegram.

In the next few weeks four more American ships fell victim to German U-boats. Fifteen Americans died. At last convinced that the step was inevitable, the President went before Congress late on April 2 to ask for a declaration of war. Four days later, on April 6, 1917, the United States declared war on Germany: a war for which the U.S. Army was far from being prepared.

The Army Transformed

The years 1902 to 1917 saw the United States entering fully upon the world stage, and that entrance mandated that the Army change itself accordingly. The Army was forced to shed most of its Indian-fighting past and transform itself into an Army for an empire. As an imperial police force it pacified the Philippines, occupied Cuba and Puerto Rico, and participated in the international intervention force into China during the Boxer Rebellion. At the same time, it continued to fulfill its obligations as a homeland security force as it conducted operations along the southern border of the United States and into Mexico itself. The Army had by necessity become a much more capable force than ever before, equipped for overseas expeditions and for the essentially constabulary duties of America's new empire.

Although the Army was forced to make numerous practical changes to cope with the new challenges of America's becoming a world power, it also underwent a series of intellectual changes that established a framework for even greater changes to come. At the heart of these changes were the reforms undertaken by Secretary of War Root during his years in office (1899–1904). These Root reforms (changing the command structure of the Army with the establishment of the office of Chief of Staff with a General Staff and breaking the power of the bureau chiefs; the creation of the National Guard with training, organization, and equipment in line with the Regular Army; and the reorganization of the Army school system including the establishment of the Army War College in 1903) were essential in increasing the professionalism of the Army and forcing it to look outward to the new challenges to come.

Thanks to the reforms of the early twentieth century, for the first time the Army would have some of the basic intellectual and procedural tools in hand to prepare and conduct contingency plans for a wide variety of operations. It would have a corps of regular officers and men supported by a National Guard available for federal service on relatively short notice. When the National Defense Act enhanced the reforms in 1916, the result was little short of revolutionary. The Root reforms laid the basis for transforming the Army into a modern, albeit still modestly sized military force suitable for the new missions that had to be performed.

Yet events outside the United States were moving quicker than any peacetime reform packages could hope to contain. The United States' involvement in the war in Europe would shortly mandate the whole-sale remaking of its Army yet again. This massive conflict that began in 1914 in Europe was to change all of America's assumptions when it came to armies and international commitments. The war was terrifying to behold, with million-man armies locked in deadly combat in trenches that scarred hundreds of miles of the landscape of northern France. Deadly armies of conscripts equipped with machine guns, vast arrays of artillery, airplanes, and tanks showed to any intelligent observer how ill prepared the American Army would be for the challenges of modern warfare. A new, and severe, test for American arms was on the horizon.

DISCUSSION QUESTIONS

1. What lessons do you believe the U.S. Army should have been able to use from its Indian-fighting days in the new situation of policing an empire?

2. Why was the Army so slow to adopt new technology even in the face of dramatic changes in the scope and scale of European warfare?

3. Of what value were the Root reforms? Why did a civilian Secretary of War have to implement these reforms rather than the senior Army uniformed leadership?

4. What was the "Plattsburg idea," and how influential do you think it was?

5. Was the United States justified in intervening in Mexican affairs in 1916? What were some of the unintended consequences for the U.S. Army as a result of this expedition?

6. Should America have entered World War I? How could it have been avoided?

RECOMMENDED READINGS

Abrahamson, James L. *America Arms for a New Century: The Making of a Great Military Power.* New York: Free Press, 1981.

Ball, Harry P. *Of Responsible Command: A History of the U.S. Army War College.* Carlisle Barracks, Pa.: Alumni Association of the U.S. Army War College, 1983, chs. 1–7.

Challener, Richard D. *Admirals, Generals, and American Foreign Policy, 1898–1914.* Princeton: Princeton University Press, 1973.

Finnegan, John R. *Against the Specter of a Dragon: The Campaign for American Military Preparedness, 1914–1917.* Westport, Conn.: Greenwood Press, 1974.

Hewes, James E., Jr. *From Root to McNamara: Army Organization and Administration, 1900–1963.* Washington, D.C.: U.S. Army Center of Military History, 1983.

Lane, Jack C. *Armed Progressive: A Study of the Military and Public Career of Leonard Wood.* San Rafael, Calif.: Presidio Press, 1978.

Leopold, Richard W. *Elihu Root and the Conservative Tradition.* Boston: Little, Brown, 1954.

Morison, Elting E. *Turmoil and Tradition: A Study of the Life and Times of Henry L. Stimson.* Boston: Houghton Mifflin, 1960, chs. 9–15.

Nenninger, Timothy K. "The Army Enters the Twentieth Century, 1904–1917," in *Against All Enemies: Interpretations of American Military History from Colonial Times to the Present,* ed. Kenneth J. Hagen and William R. Roberts. Westport, Conn.: Greenwood Press, 1986.

———. *The Leavenworth Schools and the Old Army: Education, Professionalism, and the Officer Corps of the United States Army, 1881–1918.* Westport, Conn.: Greenwood Press, 1978.

Smythe, David. *Guerrilla Warrior: The Early Life of John J. Pershing.* New York: Scribner's, 1973.

Other Readings

Armstrong, David A. *Bullets and Bureaucrats: The Machine Gun and the U.S. Army, 1861–1916.* Westport, Conn.: Greenwood Press, 1982.

Beale, Howard K. *Theodore Roosevelt and the Rise of America to World Power.* Baltimore: Johns Hopkins University Press, 1984.

Clendenen, Clarence C. *Blood on the Border: The United States Army and the Mexican Irregulars.* New York: Macmillan, 1969.

Detrick, Martha. *The National Guard in Politics.* Cambridge: Harvard University Press, 1965.

Deutrich, Mabel E. *Struggle for Supremacy: The Career of General Fred C. Ainsworth.* Washington, D.C.: Public Affairs Press, 1962.

Langley, Lester D. *The Banana Wars: United States Intervention in the Caribbean, 1898–1934.* Wilmington, Del.: SR Books, 2002.

Linn, Brian. *Guardians of Empire: The U.S. Army and the Pacific, 1902–1940.* Chapel Hill: University of North Carolina Press, 1997.

McCullough, David. *The Path Between the Seas: The Creation of the Panama Canal, 1870–1914.* New York: Simon & Schuster, 1977.

Millett, Allan R. *The Politics of Intervention: The Military Occupation of Cuba, 1906–1909.* Columbus: Ohio State University Press, 1968.

Reardon, Carol. *Soldiers and Scholars: The U.S. Army and the Uses of History, 1865–1920.* Lawrence: University Press of Kansas, 1990.

Skowronek, Stephen. *Building a New American State: The Expansion of National Administrative Capacities, 1877–1920.* Cambridge: Cambridge University Press, 1982, chs. 1, 2, 4, 7, Epilogue.

EPILOGUE
THE AMERICAN ARMY
1775–1917

The evolution of the U.S. Army, from its humble origins in the colonial militia through its official creation during the Revolution and the massive bloodletting of the Civil War to the first tentative steps on the path to empire, was slow and uncertain. Throughout this long evolution, American citizens wavered between the ideals of a "nation in arms," of a citizen militia, and the stability of a well-trained, professional standing army. Safe behind its ocean barriers and supported by the intellectual ideals of its enlightenment-trained founders, America resisted the creation of a large standing military force as both unnecessary and dangerous to its liberty.

Yet, at the same time, few could doubt that a standing army often came in handy. How else was the frail new nation, huddled along the eastern seaboard of a massive continent, to cope with the continuing mission of Indian-fighting and frontier-policing for most of its formative years? At the same time, only an obtuse observer of the world stage could believe that the dynamic empires of Europe would not at some point in time turn their attentions again to the new republic. It was thus essential for a prudent nation to maintain a small, solid core of professional soldiers for an expansible force to preserve the security of the nation in any future conflict.

Building on the colonial tradition of defending the expanding settlements from Indians, the American Army could not ignore its vital role as a force in being even if it conflicted with the philosophy of the founding fathers. Necessity required such a force; but inclination continued to keep it small, except during the years of crisis of the Revolution (1775–1783) and the Civil War (1861–1865). Even in those instances, and especially in the latter case, much of the fighting was done by volunteer formations that were disbanded at the end of the war; the Regular Army grew only slightly during America's first century, even during the horror of the Civil War.

A powerful, continuous dichotomy existed between the forces that wanted to rely primarily on a militia and those who saw the necessity for a strong standing army. Most of the American people maintained—and despite the evidence of their own experience continue to maintain—that as members of a democracy they were basically peaceful in nature. Americans imaged themselves as an unmilitary people, content to go about their business of trade or farming with little notice given to the outside world and committed to the principles of peace. Though much taken with their self-image, Americans were in many ways very warlike. As a nation they constantly fought against Native American tribes and soon moved like a torrent into the west, sweeping away the indigenous people and conquering the Mexican lands between the coasts.

This expansionism, whatever the rationale or justification, was essentially a warlike act by a dynamic, restless, and violent people. Granted, most of the "conquest" was accomplished as much by waves of immigrants as by arms. There was only a small standing army to serve as initial scouts, military spearhead, and police force; but that small army was a critical factor in the expansion. Not content with merely conquering the continent, in the space of a few years America expanded outward into the Caribbean region and across the Pacific to Hawaii and the Philippines. At the same time Americans seemed content to follow George Washington's words of advice to "steer clear of permanent alliances" and stand "against the insidious wiles of foreign influence." Thus Americans convinced themselves that as a people apart they would not need a large standing Army despite their many aggressive tendencies. The oceans and a small Navy would protect them from others while they consolidated their hold on the middle portion of the continent.

Yet both ideals, opposing a large standing army and staying out of foreign quarrels, were to be difficult to sustain in the twentieth century and beyond. Unbeknownst to Americans, the country was on the verge of an almost unrelenting series of wars and conflicts on the world stage that would demand new ideas and a new Army at each turn. The Army and its institutions would be forced to change, react, and change again in ways as yet unforeseen. If the previous centuries were any indication, the Army and the American people would remain flexible enough to change and grow accordingly to respond to each new challenge ahead.

An essential part of the Army's ability to change and adapt was the slow, but far from steady, growth of professionalism within the Army: a sense that serving in the Army was a unique calling with special standards. The essence of a profession, as opposed to merely a vocation, is that a profession establishes standards of performance of a complex set of duties and responsibilities, often binds its practitioners to those standards with some form of oath or charge, and then internally creates a system of discipline to enforce those standards. Thus members of a profession, with their own unique bodies of wisdom, training, and beliefs, tend to believe that they stand apart from the rest of society. Historically the ministry, medicine, law, teaching, and the military have been viewed in western societies as professions; although over the years the term professional has been more and more widely used for a variety of trades and jobs.

If the U.S. Army is a profession, and it seems to fit the definition, how then did the Army become that way? How did soldiers and officers begin to see themselves as professionals rather than just citizens temporarily serving in the military? What unique standards or duties did the Army adopt as part of this trend, and how did it enforce those standards? These are critical questions, especially given America's current reliance on a professional military to perform myriad duties throughout the world. It can certainly be said that the seeds for today's professional Army were sowed in the eighteenth and nineteenth centuries.

The growth of professionalism in the U.S. Army probably occurred more quickly in the officer corps than in the enlisted ranks. In part this was due to the American military's European heritage: the officers often were members of the upper classes who brought their distinct sense of identity and apartness with them. This "class consciousness" of the officer corps changed, albeit slowly, over time due to the inherently democratic instincts of Americans who looked with deep suspicion on any manifestation of a "superior" class based on inherited wealth or social position. The officer corps, recruited increasingly from the middle class with the path open to all through the portals of the Military Academy at West Point, became based on merit rather than social class.

Nevertheless, officers retained a sense of belonging to a unique "calling" with the unifying precepts of duty, honor, and country forming the standards that bound them to their profession and to each other. This sense of uniqueness spread throughout the Army as noncommissioned officers and soldiers began to identify more and more with their comrades in the Army rather than with civilians. Their service alone set them apart from most Americans. Uniforms, ceremonies, drill, rank, discipline, and other elements reinforced this sense of being different. This sense of apartness and uniqueness was probably a good thing. Without such a distinct corporate identity, the Army may not have been able to sustain itself during the years of isolation and trial on America's frontiers.

Along with a sense of apartness, it was equally essential for the Army to establish standards of training and duty performance that would formally teach new members exactly what was expected of them. Initially, this would involve training all recruits in their units rather than any in standardized schools. Only officers were exposed to some measure of standardized training (here again, West Point led the way); but after the initial schooling that led to a commission, officers also were expected to learn on the job. Only after the Civil War did the Army begin to establish schools of application for the combat arms, and only after the start of the twentieth century did it create the Army War College for education in strategic thinking and higher levels of the management of war policy.

As the American Army faced test after test along the frontier, it increasingly developed standards not just of duty performance (what soldiers or officers need to do as the technical components of their craft) but also of conduct: how soldiers, officers, and noncommissioned officers are to behave toward each other. From a relative isolation from American society grew a sense of being a self-sufficient social entity as well as a unique vocation with arduous tasks not borne or perhaps even understood by the rest of society. From this apartness grew customs, traditions, and behaviors every bit as important in forming a sense of professionalism as any listing of tasks or training in necessary technical skills. As the Army grew such a sense of corporate identity, it developed the belief that only other members of the society understood the special pressures of the military and only other members could discipline wayward soldiers or officers.

By the early days of the twentieth century, the U.S. Army can be said to have evolved into an organization with all the aspects of a profession: a unique set of skills, formal initiation and indoctrination, training, rituals, standards of conduct, and the means to enforce that conduct. Though small, especially by European standards, the U.S. Army on the eve of "The Great War" was a tried and tested organization with a strong sense of professional identity and deep roots and traditions based on years of service to the nation. Building upon the past and only reluctantly drawn into the future, the U.S. Army stood on the threshold of world conflict, not entirely understanding the challenges ahead but nonetheless fully committed to respond to the needs of the nation wherever those needs led.

INDEX